Falklands Facts and Fallacies

The Falkland Islands in History and International Law

A refutation of Marcelo Kohen and Facundo Rodríguez,
*Las Malvinas entre el Derecho y la Historia/
The Malvinas/Falklands between History and Law*

Graham Pascoe

Second edition, revised and updated

2022

Grosvenor House
Publishing Limited

All rights reserved
Copyright © Graham Pascoe and Peter Pepper, 2022

First published in Great Britain in 2020 by Graham Pascoe

This second edition published by Grosvenor House Publishing in 2022

The right of Graham Pascoe to be identified as the author of this
work has been asserted in accordance with Section 78
of the Copyright, Designs and Patents Act 1988

The book cover is copyright to Graham Pascoe
The moral right of the author has been asserted.

This book is published by
Grosvenor House Publishing Ltd
Link House
140 The Broadway, Tolworth, Surrey, KT6 7HT.
www.grosvenorhousepublishing.co.uk

This book is sold subject to the conditions that it shall not, by way of
trade or otherwise, be lent, resold, hired out or otherwise circulated
without the author's or publisher's prior consent in any form of binding or cover
other than that in which it is published and without a similar condition
including this condition being imposed on the subsequent purchaser.

A CIP record for this book
is available from the British Library

ISBN 978-1-80381-088-1
eBook ISBN 978-1-80381-090-4

The illustration on the front cover shows the remains of the dock and warehouse built by the British soon after 1771 at Port Egmont in the Falklands, where Commodore John Byron claimed the islands for Britain in January 1765. Spain attacked the British settlement here in 1770, unleashing the First Falklands Crisis, the first of three major international crises over the islands (all described in this book).

Contents

Chapter		Page
	Introduction: Why we wrote this book	9
1	**Discovery; later sightings; treaties; the Nootka Sound Convention**	**12**
	1.1 Papal bulls	12
	1.2 The discovery of the Falkland Islands	13
	1.3 Early maps; the Portuguese connection	15
	1.4 Later maps; later sightings	21
	1.5 The treaties that were not broken	24
	1.6 Britain's abandoned plan to survey the Falklands in 1749-50	25
	1.7 The misrepresented treaty: the Nootka Sound Convention limits Spanish sovereignty	26
	1.8 Conclusion	30
2	**The first inhabitants; the First Falklands Crisis, 1767-1771**	**31**
	2.1 The first inhabitants, 1764	31
	2.2 The First Falklands Crisis, 1767-71: Part I (Spain versus France)	31
	2.3 The First Falklands Crisis, 1767-71: end of Part I; Parts II and III; the Anglo-Spanish agreement, 22 January 1771	33
	2.4 The "chearful" British at Port Egmont; the miserable Spaniards at Puerto Soledad	43
	2.5 Britain closes down Port Egmont, but reserves the right to return	45
	2.6 New industries for the Falklands – sealing and whaling; Port Egmont destroyed	45
	2.7 Spain's sovereignty in the islands to 1811 and its limitations	46
3	***Uti possidetis* – did Argentina inherit the Falklands from Spain?**	**49**
4	**The years 1811-25**	**54**
	4.1 An insignificant act	54
	4.2 The Spanish withdrawal from the Falklands, 13 February 1811	54
	4.3 Non-displays of Argentine sovereignty in the Falklands, 1811-1820	54
	4.4 An irrelevant letter, 1816	56
	4.5 The wreck of the *Isabella*; Captain Barnard marooned in the Falklands, 1813-14	57
	4.6 David Jewett; Argentina's supposed "official taking of possession of the islands in 1820"	58
	4.7 David Jewett: the myths	71
	4.8 The years 1821-1824; Spain protests to the United States, 1822	75
	4.9 Louis Vernet; the 1824 expedition	76
	4.10 The years 1824-5; the United Provinces do not include the Falklands in their territory	85
	4.11 Spain protests to Britain, 1825	86
	4.12 The Treaty of Amity, 1825	87
	4.13 The year 1825: no Argentine presence in the Falklands; the *Beaufoy* in the islands	87
	4.14 Conclusion	88
5	**Louis Vernet's five years in the Falklands, 1826-31**	**89**
	5.1 Louis Vernet's five years in the Falklands: some basic facts	89
	5.2 Louis Vernet's five years in the Falklands: Phase I, 1826-8	91
	5.3 Britain not informed about Vernet's concession, 1826	91
	5.4 Louis Vernet's five years in the Falklands; Phase I (continued), to 1828	92
	5.5 Louis Vernet's five years in the Falklands: Phase II, 1828-9	96
	5.6 Vernet's 1828 concession declared invalid by the Argentine government, 1882	96
	5.7 Britain again not informed of Vernet's concession, 1828; he preferred British sovereignty	97
	5.8 Emilio Vernet's diary; a British flag hoisted in the Falklands, 25 May 1828	99
	5.9 Vernet buys horses and black slaves for the Falklands	100
	5.10 Vernet's Spanish map	101
	5.11 Lavalle's coup; HMS *Tribune*; Antonio Rivero; Vernet appointed CPM; his circular	102
	5.12 Mathew Brisbane's rescue of the castaways from the *Hope*	104

5.13	Incorrect account by Kohen and Rodríguez of Brisbane's rescue of the men of the *Hope*	105
5.14	Vernet's offer to Woodbine Parish; private versus public functions	106
5.15	The presidio; the *Tiburtina* wrecked; Parish informs London of Vernet's concessions	107
5.16	Louis Vernet's five years in the Falklands: Phase III, 1829-1831	108
5.17	Britain protests against the comandancia decree, 19 November 1829	109
5.18	So-called acts exercising a public function and/or Argentine sovereignty	109
5.19	The "Águila" myth	110
5.20	The money myth – Vernet's truck system	114
5.21	Conclusion	117

6 The Second Falklands Crisis, 1831-1833 — **118**

6.1	Vernet's "Advertisement", 1831	118
6.2	Emilio Vernet's movements; more people for Port Louis	120
6.3	The Second Falklands Crisis, Part I: Vernet seizes three American ships	122
6.4	Britain's warning to Vernet not to molest British ships	124
6.5	Vernet's illegal contract with Captains Congar and Davison	125
6.6	The United States Supreme Court rules that Vernet's seizures were illegal	125
6.7	The *Superior* sails; Vernet's contract with the *Belleville* men	126
6.8	Vernet's land-contract with William Langdon; Vernet's English map	127
6.9	Vernet leaves the Falklands; he appoints William Smyley	128
6.10	The United States reacts to Vernet's seizures of American ships	129
6.11	Louis Vernet's misunderstanding of the *Lexington*'s purpose	132
6.12	The Second Falklands Crisis, Part II: the *Lexington* raid	132
6.13	Captain Congar returns to New York	137
6.14	Britain reacts to reports of American activity in the Falklands	137
6.15	Impasse in Buenos Aires – Francis Baylies breaks off US-Argentine diplomatic relations	138
6.16	Argentina sends a ship and a commandant	140
6.17	Britain protests against the appointment of Mestivier	141
6.18	Commandant Mestivier arrives; the *Clio* and the *Tyne* set off for the Falklands	141
6.19	Mestivier murdered; the Argentine garrison goes on the rampage	143
6.20	Pinedo carries on harassing American ships; Joseph Trott's revenge	145
6.21	The murderers caught; the garrison prepares to leave; Argentina reneges on its debts	146
6.22	The Second Falklands Crisis, Part III: the *Clio* arrives; Pinedo returns to Port Louis	147
6.23	The Second Falklands Crisis, Part III (con.): no Part IV (no second *Lexington* raid)	150
6.24	The Second Falklands Crisis, Part III (con.): those expelled and those not expelled	151
6.25	The Expulsion Myth	156
6.26	Kohen and Rodríguez confuse two *Rapids*	158
6.27	Britain in the 1830s was anti-colonialist	158
6.28	HMS *Tyne* arrives and leaves again	159
6.29	Argentine protests begin, 1833 – and end, 1849; silent vs. overt acquiescence	159
6.30	The *Clio* reaches port; 4 versions of Onslow's report; trials of Pinedo and the mutineers	160
6.31	The year of limbo; Charles Darwin's first visit, 1833; the "1833 Port Louis Log"	161
6.32	The Port Louis murders, 26 August 1833	163
6.33	The Rivero Myth	165
6.34	The inhabitants struggle to survive, August 1833-January 1834; several captured	167
6.35	Henry Smith arrives	168
6.36	Charles Darwin's second visit, 1834; the murderers' odyssey	169
6.37	Why was Rivero not put on trial? Kohen's and Rodríguez's false assumption	170
6.38	The British government considers withdrawing the British presence	173
6.39	The US Supreme Court rules, 1839: Vernet's seizures of ships were illegal in US law	174
6.40	Conclusion	175

7 The years 1840-1850; the end of Argentina's title — 176

7.1 Population developments; lands granted to both British and non-British inhabitants — 176
7.2 The establishment of the colony; the first Governor — 177
7.3 Sir William Molesworth's suggestion, I, 25 July 1848 – not repeated in 1849 — 179
7.4 The Anglo-French intervention around the River Plate — 180
7.5 Peace negotiations; Henry Southern arrives, October 1848 — 181
7.6 Sir William Molesworth's suggestion, II, 26 June 1849: no mention of the Falklands — 183
7.7 The Chelsea pensioners; Henry Southern notes Argentine acquiescence — 184
7.8 Palmerston's Commons statement, 27 July 1849: Argentina's acquiescence — 186
7.9 No protest from Buenos Aires; the Moreno-Palmerston exchange — 187
7.10 Press reports of the Convention of Peace — 189
7.11 The Convention of Peace: what it says – and what Kohen and Rodríguez suppress — 189
7.12 The Convention of Peace: what it does not say – and what Kohen and Rodríguez distort — 195
7.13 The so-called "Arana-Southern treaty" was a peace treaty — 199
7.14 What Kohen and Rodríguez did not know: Southern quashes Rosas's attempt to raise the Falklands question — 200
7.15 Argentine protests, 1833-1849; Argentina's symbolic last protest, 27 December 1849 — 201
7.16 Critical date, 15 May 1850: the Convention of Peace is ratified; end of the Argentine title — 203
7.17 Later opinions of the Convention of Peace — 206
7.18 The Le Prédour treaties, 1850 — 210
7.19 No Argentine protests after the Convention of Peace — 210
7.20 Conclusion — 211

8 The years 1850-1890 — 212

8.1 The fall of the Rosas dictatorship, 1852; Argentina breaks apart — 212
8.2 The Falklands not mentioned in debates on drafting the 1854 Buenos Aires constitution — 213
8.3 The *Germantown* incident, 1854 — 214
8.4 Non-evidence of Argentina's lack of acquiescence — 215
8.5 The Falklands not mentioned in debates on drafting the Argentine constitution, 1860 — 216
8.6 Argentina becomes reunited, but does not resume protesting — 217
8.7 Argentina's acquiescence in Britain's possession of the Falklands — 217
8.8 Acquisitive prescription; protests — 218
8.9 Court cases, I: the Beagle Channel case, 1977 — 219
8.10 Court cases, II: the *Libya/Chad* case at the International Court of Justice, 1994 — 221
8.11 *Nullum tempus*: the legitimist view of sovereignty; eternal titles; limits of prescription — 221
8.12 "Historical ties": is Argentina's claim to title or to historical title? — 225
8.13 "Background sovereignty": historical ties vs legal ties of territorial sovereignty — 226
8.14 Effective territorial possession — 227
8.15 Foreign consulates imply recognition — 228
8.16 Argentina protests against the presence of a Uruguayan consulate in Stanley, 1952 — 230
8.17 The significance of the visit of the Spanish expedition, 1863 — 231
8.18 Acts by Argentina that showed acquiescence in Britain's possession of the Falklands — 233
8.19 Another Falklands family – the Goss family — 235
8.20 British acts of sovereignty (« effectivités ») in the Falklands in the 1850s, 60s and 70s — 237
8.21 International recognition: the UPU; a new Falklands industry; no Argentine protests — 239
8.22 Maps; the 1882 Latzina map; Argentina's inconsistency, I — 239
8.23 The Affair of the Map: Phase I, 1884-5; Britain protests — 245

	8.24	Estoppel	250
	8.25	Arthur Barkly in the Falklands, March-December 1886	252
	8.26	The Affair of the Map: Phase II, 1887-8; Argentina's last protest	253
	8.27	The foundation of the *Falkland Islands Magazine*, 1889	255
	8.28	More Argentine maps and books fail to claim the Falkland Islands	256
	8.29	The Heligoland Connection; Classic Imperialism, 1890: land before people	258
	8.30	Conclusion	262
9	**The years 1890-1955**		**263**
	9.1	Argentina's inconsistency, II: British arbitration over Argentina's territory, I, 1899-1902	263
	9.2	Feeble examples from Kohen and Rodríguez	265
	9.3	No mention of the Falklands in the Argentine Messages to Congress	265
	9.4	More feeble examples from Kohen and Rodríguez	267
	9.5	Two faulty books: Groussac 1910 and Goebel 1927	268
	9.6	South Georgia and the Falkland Islands Dependencies	269
	9.7	Conclusion	275
10	**The people; self-determination; the Falklands at the United Nations**		**277**
	10.1	The people, I	277
	10.2	Louis Vernet's problems; the Lavalleja connection	281
	10.3	Vernet eventually claims, and receives, compensation from Britain	284
	10.4	The people, II	285
	10.5	Plebiscites; referendums	286
	10.6	The Falklands referendum, March 2013	289
	10.7	The Falklands at the UN, I	290
	10.8	The resolution Argentina misuses – UN Resolution 1514 (XV), 14 December 1960	291
	10.9	The resolution Argentina never mentions – UN Resolution 1541 (XV), 15 December 1960	295
	10.10	The territoriality of self-determination	298
	10.11	Argentina's worries; the C24	299
	10.12	The Falklands at the UN, II: Britain's and Argentina's statements, 8 September 1964	301
	10.13	Amateur Argentine invasions of the Falklands: Miguel Fitzgerald, 8 September 1964	302
	10.14	The Falklands at the UN, III: José María Ruda's erroneous speech, 9 September 1964	303
	10.15	UN Resolution 2065 (XX), 16 December 1965; Bonifacio del Carril's specious theory	309
	10.16	Interests versus wishes: UN Resolution 2065 misused by Argentina	313
	10.17	The UN International Covenant on Civil and Political Rights (ICCPR), 16 December 1966: all peoples of Non-Self-Governing Territories have the right to self-determination	313
	10.18	UN Resolution 2625 strengthens Resolutions 1514 and 1541; ignored by Argentina	314
	10.19	The 1960s and 70s; more amateur invasions, 1966 and 1968; Argentina treats UN Resolution 2065 as void, February 1976	315
	10.20	Kohen's and Rodríguez's misunderstanding of the Falklands constitution	318
	10.21	Court cases, III: the *Western Sahara* case at the International Court of Justice, 1975	318
	10.22	Argentina's inconsistency, III: British arbitration over Argentina's territory, II, 1964-6	320
	10.23	Another Resolution "emptied" by Argentina: UN Resolution 31/49, 1 December 1976	320
	10.24	The Third Falklands Crisis – the unmentioned war, 1982; the Falklands at the UN, 1982, 1986, 1987 and later	321
	10.25	Transitory disposition – Argentina's claim enshrined (but destroyed), August 1994	330
	10.26	Argentina's failed attempt to move the goalposts at the UN, 2008	332
	10.27	Ban Ki-moon affirms the universality of self-determination, 2016	333
	10.28	Self-determination: the Chagos connection	333
	10.29	Territorial integrity, I: the Kuwait connection	339
	10.30	Court cases, IV: Territorial integrity, II: the Kosovo case at the International Court of Justice, 2010	340
	10.31	Conclusion: the Falklands are not Argentine territory	342
11	**Summary of conclusions**		**343**
	Glossary of terms, abbreviations and conventions		**352**
	Select Bibliography		**355**

Falklands Facts and Fallacies

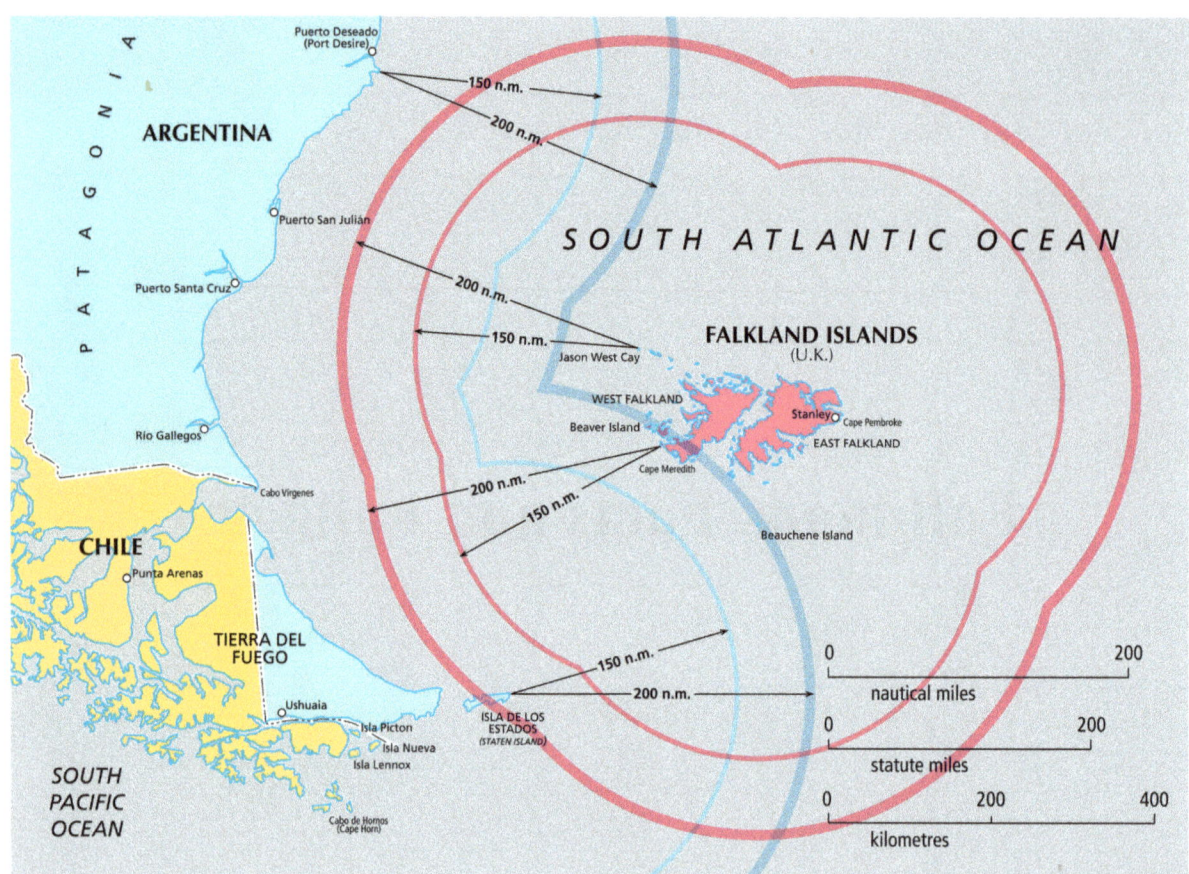

Map 1: Position. The pink lines indicate circles of 150 and 200 nautical miles radius drawn from the extreme points on the Falklands coasts; the pale blue lines indicate circles of 150 and 200 nautical miles radius drawn from the extreme points on the coast of Argentina. The map is entirely unofficial and the lines indicate only distance, not zones claimed by any of the countries involved. Both maps: Craig Asquith.

Map 2: Size. The Falklands superimposed on southern Britain at the same scale, with Stanley on the same latitude in the northern hemisphere as it actually is in the southern hemisphere: 51°42′ South, marked here in red. The red latitude is correct for both Britain and Stanley, but those in black refer only to Britain.

Introduction
Why we wrote this book

In common with many other places,
the Falkland Islands have suffered at the hands of the historian.[1]

The proper role for historians… is to challenge and even explode national myths.[2]

Everyone is entitled to their own opinions but not to their own facts.[3]

In December 2007 the Argentine Embassy in London organised a seminar entitled "Argentine Rights and Sovereignty" at the London School of Economics (LSE), chaired by Professor George Philip, at which the Argentine claim to the Falkland Islands was publicly presented in Britain for the first time. The statements made at that seminar by the Argentine participants contained some serious historical errors, as did the accompanying official pamphlets published by the Argentine government. We therefore held a seminar at the LSE in May 2008, also chaired by Professor Philip, in which we refuted those errors, and we put a 40-page paper online entitled *Getting it right: the real history of the Falklands/ Malvinas*, with its Spanish translation *Más Allá de la Historia Oficial: La Verdadera Historia de las Falklands/ Malvinas* ["Beyond the Official History: the True History of the Falklands/ Malvinas"]. In that paper we published historical materials that demonstrated the falsehood of many Argentine statements both at the seminar and in the official pamphlets.

The day after our presentation we gave a copy of our paper to the Argentine embassy in London, and later, in Buenos Aires, we gave copies to both Liliana del Castillo of the "Observatorio Malvinas" (an arm of the Argentine government), and to the late Arnoldo Canclini, a distinguished Argentine historian, President of the "Instituto de Las Malvinas"; Peter Pepper briefly discussed it with Liliana del Castillo, and Arnoldo Canclini went through it with other members of the Malvinas Institute and also discussed it in detail with Peter in two meetings. Thus the Argentine government and the major institution centrally concerned with the Argentine claim to the Falklands were fully informed of our findings. They made no criticisms of our work, then or later.

In May 2012 we put another paper online, of 10 pages, entitled *False Falklands History at the United Nations: How Argentina misled the UN in 1964 – and still does*, followed in September 2012 by its Spanish translation, *Historia falsa sobre las Falklands/Malvinas ante la Organización de las Naciones Unidas: Cómo la Argentina engañó a la ONU en 1964 – y sigue haciéndolo*. This second paper was devoted to an analysis of the speech delivered at the UN in New York by the Argentine representative José María Ruda on 9 September 1964, which marked the beginning of a new stridency in Argentina's presentation of its claim (see section 10.14 below). We refuted the multitude of errors and fallacies in that speech, which have nevertheless been constantly repeated by Argentine writers and governments. By 2012 *Getting it right* had got out of date (for example, the Falklands Councillors illustrated were no longer in office, and the islands' constitution had changed), so in mid-2012 we took the Spanish version down from the Internet, and in mid-2013 the English version too.

We were therefore surprised and flattered when in March 2016 Professor Marcelo Kohen, a leading Argentine international lawyer, professor of international law at the University of Geneva, published together with Facundo Rodríguez, an Argentine lawyer specialising in international law, a 300-page book in Buenos Aires attacking us personally, entitled *Las Malvinas entre el derecho y la historia: Refutación del folleto británico "Más allá de la historia oficial. La verdadera historia de las Falklands/Malvinas"* ["The Malvinas between law and history: Refutation of the British pamphlet 'Beyond the official history. The True History of the Falklands/Malvinas' "]. They mention us by name over 120 times in the course of their attempt to refute what we say, and in addition say over 100 times "the British pamphlet".

However, their book is nothing like a refutation of our work, and it is not "true history" at all –

---

[1] From an anonymous article, "Graves at Port Egmont and other matters", in the *Falkland Islands Magazine and Church Paper*, No. VI, Vol. XXXIII, Stanley October 1921, p. 9. For the *Falkland Islands Magazine*, see section 8.27.
[2] Margaret MacMillan, *The Uses and Abuses of History*, Toronto 2008, p. 39.
[3] Attributed to US Senator Daniel Patrick Moynihan (1927-2003).

it is riddled with historical errors, fallacies, omissions, and legal distortions. Its portrayal of the history and legal status of the Falklands is so far from the truth that we felt we could not allow it to stand unrefuted, so we have written this book to set the record straight. We have also taken the opportunity to print some highly significant documents which have never been published before, plus others which were published long ago but have become unjustly forgotten. Much of this book is therefore pioneer history writing, quite apart from being a refutation of the false account by Kohen and Rodríguez.

Their distortions begin right at the beginning: they write as if *Getting it right* and *False Falklands History* were two versions of the same paper – over 100 times they refer to "the British pamphlet", as if there were only one. They also suppress the different purposes of the two papers: *Getting it right* refuted the errors at the Argentine presentation in December 2007, while *False Falklands History* did the same for José María Ruda's speech in 1964. We took down *False Falklands History* from the Internet, in both English and Spanish, in 2016, and we intend to replace it with a much more detailed account. Some of the errors we refuted in both papers were the same of course, since Argentina has continued to present a false version of the history and legal status of the Falklands, but our papers were quite different in focus and in scope (*Getting it right* was four times as long as *False Falklands History*). And neither of them was a "British pamphlet" in the sense of having anything to do with the British government, the Falkland Islands government, or any official authority. We are two amateur historians, no more and no less. To clarify our respective roles: the work on this book was done jointly, and we are here defending ourselves jointly, as "Pascoe and Pepper", against the attacks by Kohen and Rodríguez, so naturally the text uses "we", "us" and "our", but the work has not been evenly apportioned between us – the lion's share of the background research was done by Peter, with contributions from Graham, while the actual text was written by Graham, which is why Graham appears as sole author on the front cover.

On 2 May 2017 Kohen and Rodríguez placed an English translation of their book online, *The Malvinas/Falklands between History and Law:*[1] *Refutation of the British Pamphlet "Getting it Right: The Real History of the Falklands Malvinas"*. That translation also appeared as a print-on-demand book in July 2017, and all quotes we give here are taken from it, but we give page-numbers only of the paper Spanish edition, since the online and print-on-demand English versions have differing page numbers (with typically 163 and 234 pages) and both may of course be altered. All our internal cross-references within this book are to our own sections, not to pages; all page-numbers in source-references refer to other works including that by Kohen and Rodríguez.

The two authors aim to "refute" our research findings and to "prove" that the Falklands rightfully belong to Argentina, but they fail in that aim, since they base their contentions on a false version of Falklands history. The history of the Falklands has hitherto been extremely poorly understood. All previous authors – whether British, American or Argentinian – have with few exceptions (e.g. Ernesto Fitte) simply rehashed the descriptions in earlier books, ignoring the vast mass of original documentation on the islands' history held in the Argentine national archives in Buenos Aires (Archivo Nacional de la Nación, AGN), as also in London in the Public Record Office (The National Archives), and in Stanley and some other places. Those authors ultimately based their work on a mere handful of original accounts, some of which were wrong to start with, such as Louis Vernet's seriously erroneous account of David Jewett's visit to the islands in 1820, which has been slavishly followed by many authors who have then copied inaccurately from each other (sections 4.6, 4.7).

It is important to get the history right, since history is the only basis for the Argentine claim to the Falklands – Argentina has no political claim (the Falkland Islanders are not clamouring to join Argentina) nor any kind of geographical claim (section 10.1). And history is the raw material of justice – no correct judgement can be based on false history. We have spent more decades than we care to remember researching into the history of the Falklands, piecing together the story of what really happened – all historians have to be detectives, after all, just as all detectives have to be historians. We therefore feel well placed to recount the real history of the islands.

---

[1] Their Spanish title runs "entre el derecho y la historia" ["between law and history"], but the English translation reverses the order: "between History and Law"]. We feel history comes first, hence the subtitle of this book.

We have been working on two books: first, *The Falklands Saga*, which now runs to some 2,800 pages and over two million words, containing not only the islands' history in great detail, but also the texts of hundreds of original documents, many of them in full, in English and also (if different) in their original language, Spanish, French, German, Latin or Dutch; and secondly *A New History of the Falkland Islands*, a one-volume digest of the larger book. A fuller account of the history and legal status of the Falklands will be found in those works – when we find time to finish them…

We have done a great deal more research in the 12 years since we wrote *Getting it right* in 2008; we have found much documentation that was unknown to us then, so we have revised and/or extended our view of certain parts of the story. If that constitutes "shifting our ground", then so be it; we would be stupid if, faced with new evidence, we did not alter our view to match the facts. So here we supply much extra detail and some additional arguments, in order to demonstrate the untruth of what Kohen and Rodríguez assert. Our book is therefore over three times as long as theirs – 267,000 words as against their 80,000 – but we make no apology for that, nor for mentioning some things in several places; one of our aims has been to supply a convenient source for checking the facts, and that is easier to do if we offer more than one chance to find them.

The history of the Falklands, if correctly told, demonstrates that they are not part of Argentina and that Argentina has no title to them; they are a separate country with its own history and its own people. Rightful title to the islands is held by Britain; the islands' inhabitants are the holders of territorial sovereignty and possess the full right of external self-determination; they are thus not in a colonial situation. At present they freely choose to remain in partnership with Britain. For a summary of our conclusions see chapter 11.

Finally, we wish to emphasise again that this book is not an official publication; like our two online papers, it is merely the work of two interested amateurs. We have not been commissioned to write it, and we speak for no one – neither for the Falkland Islanders, nor for the Falkland Islands government, nor for the British government. We have received no financial support from any of them or from any other source. Our views and findings do not coincide precisely with any official standpoint, but we have considered the available evidence in detail for a very long time, and we believe that our conclusions reflect the verdict of history and of international law.

Graham Pascoe
Peter Pepper

Note on the second edition

This second edition has been thoroughly revised and updated; it contains a number of corrections, additions and improvements, including all the corrections issued on a separate Errata sheet in June 2020, which have now been integrated into the text. Historical research is an ongoing process, so (unsurprisingly) a couple of aspects of the story have emerged in greater clarity since the first edition of this book appeared in March 2020. The two most noteworthy changes are first, the account of the maps by Thomas Bowen and Thomas Brown (p. 270), which was just in time to be included on the separate Errata sheet, and secondly, more importantly from the historical point of view, the account of Berkeley Sound on 27 October 1820 (pp. 62 and 73). The Sound was perhaps not quite empty when Jewett arrived; there may have been two ships there, though it seems more likely that they left the Sound before Jewett's arrival. They were the Stonington sealers *Emeline* and *Catharina* – not any of the ones often erroneously stated to have been there. The account here has been amended to accommodate all the changes made. The section numbers, and therefore all internal cross-references, remain unchanged.

In all cases of difference between the first and second editions, this second edition naturally corrects and supersedes the first edition.

Graham Pascoe
Peter Pepper
June 2022

CHAPTER ONE: Discovery; later sightings; treaties

In our point-by-point rebuttal of the work by Kohen and Rodríguez,[1] we shall broadly keep to their chapter divisions and refute their assertions in the order in which they occur in their book.

1.1 Papal bulls

As regards the possession of the Falklands, we said in our 2008 paper, *Getting it right*, (pp. 3-4):

Following Columbus's "discovery" of the New World in 1492, Pope Alexander VI issued a series of Bulls (official papal pronouncements, named after their lead seal or "bulla") granting all the new lands to Spain. Alexander VI was a Spaniard from Valencia, Rodrigo Borja, probably the most corrupt and immoral pope in history,[2] and he was keen to please King Ferdinand of Spain.

By the Bull *Inter Caetera* in 1493, Pope Alexander VI "gave" to Spain the whole of America, both north and south – including the whole of what is now the United States and Canada. This "grant" was immediately disputed by Portugal. In 1494, in order to settle the dispute, Spain and Portugal signed a pact known as the "Treaty" of Tordesillas. This gave Portugal a large portion of the papal grant and divided up the whole of the undiscovered non-Christian world between Spain and Portugal. The dividing line at about 47° W thus gave Brazil to Portugal, but the rest of North and South America "remained" Spanish.

In their chapter 1 (pages 25-48) Kohen and Rodríguez criticise us for not mentioning the Bulls *Dudum si quidem* and *Ea quae*, so we would like to remedy that omission by mentioning that there were in fact five relevant papal Bulls, two entitled *Inter Caetera*, of 3 and 4 May 1493, the second of which laid down a boundary line between Spanish and Portuguese claims, 100 leagues (about 300 miles) west of the Cape Verde Islands, thus awarding the whole of the Americas to Spain, north and south, except for the extreme tip of Brazil; the third Bull, *Eximiae devotionis*, also of 4 May, merely confirmed Spain's rights and still awarded Brazil to Spain, and the fourth, *Dudum siquidem* of 26 September 1493, went yet further, giving Spain unlimited rights to all such new lands. The fifth Bull, *Ea quae pro bono pacis*, issued by Pope Julius II on 24 January 1506, confirmed the arrangements made by Spain and Portugal in their Treaty of Tordesillas.

In *Getting it right* we pointed out that the papal Bulls broke the basic legal principle *nemo dat quod non habet* ["no one gives what he does not possess"] – the Pope did not possess those lands, so he was not entitled to "award" them to anyone – and that the Bulls were not accepted by the kings of England or France. Kohen and Rodríguez assert that at the time those kings were Catholic and recognised the authority of the Pope over princes, and they assert that papal Bulls were an accepted part of European public law. However, as the Swiss historian Jörg Fisch points out:[3]

The Pope was not recognized as the temporal head of Christianity in the late Middle Ages and could not therefore create international law binding all states without their consent.

That was demonstrated by Spain and Portugal when they signed the Treaty of Tordesillas – it breached the papal Bulls by moving the Pope's boundary line without his consent 270 leagues further west, to 370 leagues west of the Cape Verdes, "assigning" all lands west of the line to Spain, those to the east of it to Portugal. As Fisch says:[4]

During the next centuries relations between Spain and Portugal were based on the treaty of Tordesillas; the bulls were legally irrelevant. If the papal bulls were not considered as valid between the two Iberian powers it is difficult to maintain that they were good titles against other states…

From the point of view of any third country the Treaty of Tordesillas was *res inter alios acta* ["a matter arranged between others"], so it was not binding on any other countries. In other words, neither the papal Bulls nor the Treaty of Tordesillas had the slightest validity as regards the possession of the Falkland Islands.

---

[1] See Introduction for details. Quotes here from the English version, but page nos. refer to the paper Spanish version.
[2] [2008 footnote:] Alexander VI, known as the "Borgia Pope", was famous for his orgies; his four known illegitimate children included the murderer Cesare Borgia and the notorious Lucrezia Borgia, widely regarded as a poisoner.
[3] Jörg Fisch, "The Falkland Islands in the European Treaty System 1493-1833", in *German Yearbook of International Law / Jahrbuch für Internationales Recht*, Berlin, vol. 26, 1983, p. 108.
[4] Fisch 1983, pp. 108-109.

1.2 The discovery of the Falkland Islands

Kohen and Rodríguez then (p. 28) move on to consider the discovery of the islands. They head their next section: "Pascoe and Pepper acknowledge that England did not discover the Falklands/Malvinas", which is perfectly true – we said in *Getting it right* (pp. 4-5):

> Though definite proof is lacking, there is evidence that the islands were first discovered by an unrecorded Portuguese expedition before Magellan set sail. The evidence is found in two early maps, one made by the Portuguese cartographer Pedro Reinel in about 1522 – the very first map to show the Falklands – the other a French copy of a Portuguese map bought in Lisbon by André Thevet (1516-1592), a Franciscan friar and prolific writer on many subjects; this copy is now in the manuscript of a large unpublished work by Thevet in the Bibliothèque Nationale de France in Paris. These two maps of Portuguese origin suggest that it was Portuguese navigators who first saw and mapped the Falklands.

Kohen and Rodríguez base their account on what they call "One reference on the subject, which the authors of the British pamphlet clearly reviewed and used but fail to mention", namely the richly illustrated book *Las Islas Malvinas* by the Argentine diplomat Vicente Guillermo Arnaud (Buenos Aires 2000).[1] They are right again there – we know it well, but did not mention it in our paper because its account of the discovery of the Falklands is incorrect. We analyse it in our forthcoming *Falklands Saga*, but we have room here only for a brief account of its many failings.

In their account of the discovery of the islands, Kohen and Rodríguez partly follow Arnaud, but they have noticed that he fudges the issue – he says the islands were discovered and then "rediscovered" (below). Unlike Arnaud, they plump for a single discovery, by Amerigo Vespucci (a Florentine who worked for both Spain and Portugal; America is named after him), sailing on Spanish service, on 7 April 1502 (17 April by the Gregorian calendar). They say (following Arnaud, p. 171) that that is shown by the "Soderini Letter" dated 7 September 1504,[2] and they quote part of it. They say not a word (and nor does Arnaud) about its highly dubious nature – M. F. Force suggested in 1879 that it is a forgery;[3] George Tyler Northup, who translated and edited it in 1916,[4] doubted its authenticity;[5] Alberto Magnaghi argued in 1926 that it is a forgery,[6] and in 2006 the British historian Felipe Fernández-Armesto finally confirmed that it is indeed a forgery – he says: "The *Soderini Letter* is the work that would mark Vespucci, if he really wrote it, as a fool or a knave, or both"; he calls it "a fake" and "a publisher's confection", and concludes that it was cobbled together by other writers whom he refers to as "the compilers" or "the editors".[7]

By contrast, there exist two letters which are widely regarded as genuine, in which Vespucci recounts his discoveries in letters to his patron, Lorenzo di Pierfrancesco de' Medici. In those letters he describes two voyages to South America, in 1499-1500 and 1501-2; on the second voyage he spent March to early May 1502 sailing up the Brazilian coast, and crossed the equator in mid-ocean around 27 May.[8] He went nowhere near the Falklands.

Arnaud, Kohen and Rodríguez seem unaware that the Soderini Letter is known to be a forgery, and they apparently do not know it exists in three partly contradictory versions, all extremely badly written, known as P and M (both in bad Italian), and H (in bad Latin). They quote a passage from

---

[1] Kohen and Rodríguez 2015, p. 32, referring to Vicente Guillermo Arnaud, *Las Islas Malvinas: Descubrimiento, primeros mapas y ocupación, Siglo XVI* ["The Malvinas Islands: Discovery, first maps and occupation, 16th Century"], Buenos Aires 2000.

[2] This is a text entitled *Lettera di Amerigo Vespucci delle isole nuovamente trovate in quattro suoi viaggi* ["Letter of Amerigo Vespucci concerning the isles newly discovered on his four voyages"], purporting to be a letter by Vespucci to Piero Soderini (ruler of Florence 1502-12).

[3] Quoted in Frederick J. Pohl, *Amerigo Vespucci: Pilot Major*, New York 1944, p. 158.

[4] George Tyler Northup, *Amerigo Vespucci: Letter to Piero Soderini, Gonfaloniere* (*Vespucci Reprints, Texts and Studies*: *The Soderini Letter in Translation*): facsimile, with translation and notes in separate vol., Princeton 1916.

[5] Northup 1916, pp. 29-30.

[6] Alberto Magnaghi, *Amerigo Vespucci; studio critico*, Rome 1926.

[7] Felipe Fernández-Armesto (who is of Spanish origin but was born and brought up in Britain), *Amerigo: The Man Who Gave his Name to America*, New York and London 2006, pp. 126, 134, 186, 190; his sketch-map (p. xi) omits southern Patagonia, Tierra del Fuego and the Falklands, and does not imply that Vespucci even reached the River Plate.

[8] Pohl 1944, pp. 123-125, and map, p. 124; Fernández-Armesto considers these letters probably authentic (2006, pp. 114-120), but unlike Pohl, he does not believe they are in Vespucci's own hand.

Arnaud in which he quotes the Argentine historian Enrique de Gandía, who quotes part of the Soderini letter, not in the original, but in a bad Spanish translation of Northup's English translation, published in Buenos Aires in 1951.[1] De Gandía claims that the letter shows that Vespucci discovered the Malvinas on 7 April 1502[2] in a tempest, when he skirted some new land, a bare coast without any harbours. Kohen and Rodríguez quote de Gandía – their defective English translation reads: "It lasted for five days so terrible storm, where we had to navigate entirely a bare poles, entering into the sea two hundred and fifty leagues" [*sic*];[3] they then add in their own words: "As De Gandía shows us, if one places oneself before a map at the latitude of 52° south and moves out from the coast along that parallel for 250 leagues, one will certainly encounter the Malvinas."

However, that demonstration is impossible – 250 leagues are about 750 miles, and the Falklands are only some 300 miles from the Patagonian coast along the 52nd parallel. In any case, the "250-league" passage only occurs in texts M and H; there is no such passage in text P.[4] And it is only the bad Spanish translation (quoted by de Gandía, Arnaud, and Kohen and Rodríguez) that says the ships sailed for 250 leagues along the 52nd parallel; the original texts say they reached the 52nd parallel, but then a tempest began from the south-west and they ran before it for four days before skirting the new land – they had been sailing hard for four days to the north-east *away* from the 52nd parallel before they saw the new land. They then turned for Portugal; the tempest increased and they ran before it towards the Equator for five days, and (only in texts M and H) for 250 leagues – the new land was not at the *end* of the 250 leagues but *before* it. And the whole thing is a forgery anyway; in April 1502 Vespucci was sailing up the Brazilian coast. In short, the idea that the Falkland Islands were discovered by Amerigo Vespucci is a myth based on a forgery which is worthless as evidence and does not even suggest that the land mentioned was on the 52nd parallel.

Vicente Arnaud was faced with a problem: he wished to credit the round-the-world expedition of Ferdinand Magellan with the discovery of the Falklands (following Laguarda Trías, see section 1.3), but he was unwilling to drop Vespucci – both were sailing on Spanish service, and like other Argentine authors he was keen to credit Spain with the discovery. So he falls between two stools – in his final summary, after crediting Vespucci with the discovery of the islands on 7 April 1502, he states: "the Malvinas Islands were rediscovered in 1520 by ships of the Spanish expedition of Ferdinand Magellan…".[5] Kohen and Rodríguez drop that piece of fudge and attribute the discovery solely to Amerigo Vespucci. In so doing, they depart both from Arnaud and from the line taken by recent Argentine governments, which have done the opposite, dropping Vespucci and ascribing the discovery solely to Magellan.[6] As we shall see, none of those accounts is correct.

---

[1] Arnaud 2000, pp. 149 (4 lines) and 171 (14 lines), quoting Enrique de Gandía, "Claudio Alejandro Ptolomeo, Colón y la exploración de la India Americana", in *Investigaciones y Ensayas*, no. 13, Buenos Aires, July-December 1972, p. 74-75. The same translation, by Ana María R. de Aznar, Buenos Aires 1951, is also quoted in Alfredo Bruno Bologna, *Los derechos de la república Argentina sobre las islas Malvinas…*, Buenos Aires 1988, p. 24.

[2] Only the M and P texts give 7 April; text H has 2 April (Northup 1916, translation vol., notes p. 63).

[3] This is the peculiar text of the online and print-on-demand English versions of Kohen and Rodríguez 2015; it is p. 32 in the printed Spanish version, which quotes de Gandía 1972, p. 74-75, correctly, from Arnaud 2000, p. 171.

[4] The P text is illustrated in Northup 1916, facsimile vol., pp. 28-29; the "250-league" passages from texts M and H are quoted in Northup 1916, translation vol., notes p. 63. Our translation will appear in *The Falklands Saga*.

[5] Arnaud 2000, p. 235.

[6] The following official Argentine government pamphlets, all published in Buenos Aires, state that the Falklands were discovered in 1520 by Magellan's expedition (all are anonymous but give the government department responsible, here in square brackets): (1) [Observatorio Malvinas], *Islas Malvinas*, March 2007 (and in English: *Islas Malvinas, Georgias del Sur y Sandwich del Sur / Malvinas, South Georgia and South Sandwich Islands*, December 2007); (2) [foreign ministry], *Argentine Republic / The Question of the Malvinas Islands / A story of colonialism. A United Nations cause*, September 2012; (3) [foreign ministry], *Islas Malvinas. Argentina, sus derechos, y el diálogo necesario / Malvinas Islands. Argentina, its rights and the need for dialogue*, February 2013; (4) [education ministry], *Malvinas para todos: Memoria, soberanía y democracia, Un material para compartir en la escuela, en la familia, en el barrio, en las redes sociales* ["Malvinas for all: Memory, sovereignty and democracy, Material to be shared in school, in the family, in the neighbourhood, on social networks"], April 2014; (5) [Malvinas secretariat], *Soberanía Argentina en Malvinas a 50 años del "Alegato Ruda" / Argentine Sovereignty over Malvinas 50 years after the Ruda Statement*, September 2014; (6) [foreign ministry], *La Cuestión Malvinas: A 50 años de la resolución 2065 (XX) de las Naciones Unidas*, June 2015.

1.3 Early maps; the Portuguese connection

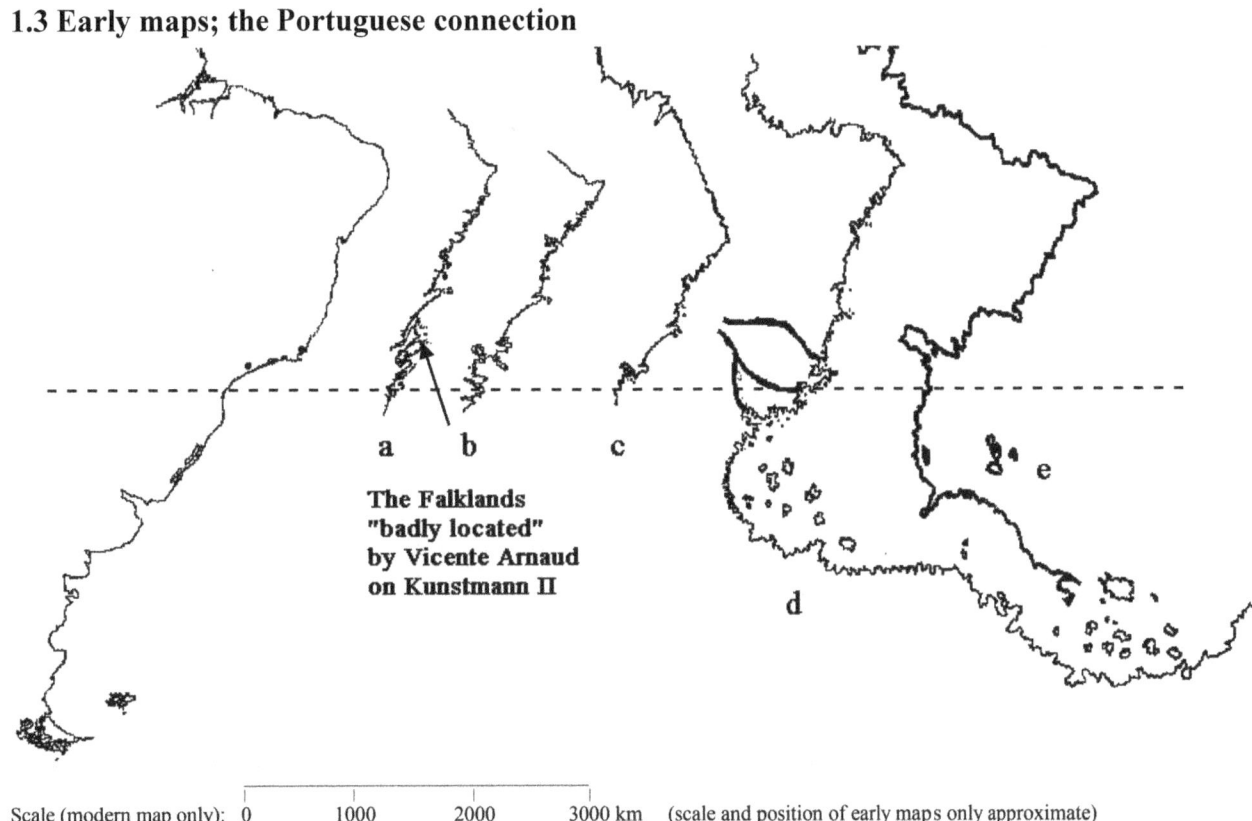

1.3a Nothing below Cananor: The real coastline of South America (left) and Arnaud's first five early maps: (a) "Kunstmann II" 1502-6; (b) Maiollo 1504; (c) Caverio 1505; (d) Piri Reis 1513; and (e) Lopo Homem 1519; the dashed line marks the position of "Cananor" (or equivalent). On all of them the factual coastline ends there, 1,500 kilometres north of the River Plate; everything further south on maps d and e is imaginary (they both run much further south-east than shown here). The large 3-mouthed river on the Piri Reis map is fictitious, and the islands on Kunstmann II which Arnaud identifies as the Falklands are near São Paulo.

Kohen and Rodríguez maintain (again following Vicente Arnaud) that the Falklands are shown on five early maps dated between 1502 and 1519, which they list (p. 30), but it is important to clear up that error. Arnaud devotes over 80 pages of his book to those five maps: (a) the map of around 1502-6 known as "Kunstmann II", (b) the Maiollo planisphere of 1504, (c) the Caverio portolan map of 1505, (d) the Piri Reis map of 1513, and (e) the Lopo Homem map of 1519[1] (see fig. 1.3a).

Arnaud's account proves nothing except his inability to understand early maps. He identifies some tiny blobs on the coast of Kunstmann II as the Falklands, though he does concede that they are "mal ubicadas" ["badly located"], which is certainly true, given that they are misplaced by some 2,500 kilometres (if a map misplaced London by 2,500 kilometres, it might appear in the Sahara desert). He was clearly unaware of the "latitude-distortion" on all maps of the western hemisphere made before around 1524 – they all show South America too big and much too far south. This latitude-distortion is discussed in an analysis of the Piri Reis map by Gregory McIntosh,[2] who also illustrates three more maps with a Brazilian coastline similar to that on Arnaud's first five.[3] Arnaud also failed to recognise the significance of the place-names, which fix the latitude: they all show the Brazilian coast down to "Cananor" (spelt variously), the place near modern São Paulo where Vespucci calculated that the Tordesillas dividing-line crossed the coast – but no further.

In figure 1.3a the real South American coastline is placed beside the coastline on Arnaud's first five maps at roughly the same scale, located according to "Cananor". South of that, the factual part of all those maps ends, 2,500 kilometres north of the Falklands – the coastline either ends in mid-

---

[1] Arnaud 2000, pp. 66-145, 181-183, 235.
[2] Gregory C. McIntosh, *The Piri Reis Map of 1513*, Athens (Georgia) and London 2000.
[3] They are the King-Hamy map of *c.* 1502-04, the "Kunstmann III" map of *c.* 1502-08, and the Francisco Rodrigues map of 1511-13 (McIntosh 2000, p. 39). None goes further south than "Cananor".

parchment as in maps (a), (b) and (c), or else, as in (d) and (e), makes a fictitious connection with the mythical Southern Continent postulated to exist by the first-century Greek geographer Ptolemy. None of them goes as far south as the River Plate, let alone the Falklands.

But Arnaud also discusses and illustrates two early maps which do show the Falklands – the two we mentioned in *Getting it right*: **(1)** the "Pedro Reinel map" of around 1522-4,[1] an updated version of a map drawn around 1519 by the Portuguese mapmaker Pedro Reinel, who worked in Seville in 1519 on the preparations for the expedition of Ferdinand Magellan of 1519-22 (the first to sail round the world), and **(2)** the "Thevet map" of 1586, a French copy of an earlier Portuguese map:

(1) The Pedro Reinel map (illustrated in Kohen and Rodríguez, p. 29, from Arnaud's folded colour plate) is in the Topkapı Sarayı Müzesi, İstanbul, Turkey; it is labelled in Portuguese, with some place-names in northern Brazil not found on any other map. It is the earliest map to show the Falklands, and is among the very first western-hemisphere maps without latitude-distortion. The land is truncated below 55° South; it does not show the Magellan Strait, and it shows only the north coast of the Falklands. The French cartographic historian Marcel Destombes says that the attribution of this map to Pedro Reinel "makes it very probable that this was the original document prepared for Magellan's expedition under the direction of Ruy Faleiro", and he concludes that the map predated Magellan's expedition but was "updated" afterwards: "I believe it to be a copy, made by Pedro Reinel himself between 1522 and 1524, of a previous map, also drawn by him in 1519".[2]

When the Portuguese captured Magellan's flagship *Trinidad* at Ternate in the Moluccas on 21 October 1522 after Magellan's death, they seized the papers of the expedition's cartographer Andrés de San Martín, who had already died. Among them were "two planispheres belonging to Magellan and made by Pedro Reinel".[3] Thus it seems likely that Magellan carried the original version of this map with him; it apparently records an otherwise unknown Portuguese expedition before Magellan's much more famous one; the earlier expedition visited northern Brazil and also found the Falklands, and must have returned home before mid-1519 in time for their discoveries to be passed to Magellan. So they were his trailblazers – they returned with no Pacific passage to show for their efforts, but they knew how far south there was no way through. It was their good work that allowed Magellan to make the really vital discovery – the Strait that now bears his name. Thanks to the trailblazers, he knew how far south he had to sail. Since no account of that earlier expedition survives, the names of those real discoverers of the Falklands are lost. That is sad indeed.

(2) The Thevet map (our figs. 1.3b and 1.3c, below, taken direct from the original) is labelled « *Les Isles de Sanson ou des Geantz* » ["The Islands of Sanson or of the Giants"], and is the earliest map to show the Falklands in detail (though most of it is wildly inaccurate). It was first published in 1982 by Roger Hervé;[4] he sent a copy of his book to the Uruguayan historian Rolando Laguarda Trías, who in 1983 published a monograph on the map[5] maintaining that it shows that the Falklands were discovered in July 1520 by the crew of the *San Antonio*, one of Magellan's ships, which deserted him in the Strait and returned to Spain. Of Thevet's long text, Laguarda Trías had only a fragment printed by Hervé to go on, but he adds the conjecture that it was the cartographer Andrés de San Martín who drew the original map on which Thevet's map is based. Laguarda Trías accepts the suggestion made in 1945 by Enrique Ruiz Guiñazú that the name "Islas de Sanson" was proposed by the French chaplain Bernard Calmette on 28 July 1520, the feast of the obscure Breton

---

[1] It was described in two articles by Marcel Destombes : « L'Hémisphère austral en 1524: une carte de Pedro Reinel à Istanbul », in *Comptes rendus du Congrès International de Géographie*, Amsterdam 1938, vol. II, pp. 175-185, and *id.*, "The Chart of Magellan", in *Imago Mundi* vol. XII, 1955, pp. 479-187; Destombes makes it clear that the name "Chart of Magellan" means "chart made *for* Magellan", not "chart made *by* Magellan". Both articles reproduced in facsimile in Günter Schilder et al., *Marcel Destombes (1905-1983)*, Utrecht and Paris 1987.
[2] Destombes 1955, pp. 71, 72, 79.
[3] Destombes 1955, p. 66, note 2.
[4] Roger Hervé, *Découverte Fortuite de l'Australie et de la Nouvelle-Zélande par des Navigateurs Portugais et Espagnols entre 1521 et 1528*, Paris 1982. English translation by John Dunmore, *Chance Discovery of Australia and New Zealand by Portuguese and Spanish Navigators between 1521 and 1528* (Palmerston North, New Zealand, 1983).
[5] Rolando A. Laguarda Trías, *Nave Española descubre las Islas Malvinas en 1520* ["Spanish ship discovers the Malvinas Islands in 1520"], Montevideo, Uruguay, 1983.

saint St Sanson.¹ He believes such a good map can only have been made by a good cartographer like Andrés de San Martín, so he cannot accept that the map was made after the *San Antonio* deserted Magellan, since by then neither Calmette nor San Martín was still aboard – Calmette's fate is obscure, while San Martín sailed on in the *Victoria* and was killed on the island of Cebú on 1 May 1521.² Kohen and Rodríguez assert on p. 31 that San Martín "seems to have travelled to Spain on the ship 'San Antonio' (under the command of the pilot Alvaro de Mesquita)", but the sources disprove that.

Arnaud says (wrongly) that the Thevet map is "irrefutable documentary proof" that Magellan's expedition discovered the Falklands,³ but Kohen and Rodríguez only partly follow that theory. They illustrate Thevet's map (their p. 31, photographed from Arnaud 2000), but they do not accept that the islands were discovered by the *San Antonio*; they attribute the discovery to Vespucci, but state that the crew of the *San Antonio* were the first to set foot on the islands and that Andrés de San Martín made the map which was later copied for André Thevet. So Kohen and Rodríguez disagree with Rolando Laguarda Trías, with Vicente Arnaud, and with Argentine governments, and have their own theory about the discovery of the islands and the making of Thevet's map.

We have seen that Vespucci did not discover the Falklands, but did Magellan's expedition discover them and make the map on which Thevet's map is based? The documentation shows that they did not. The expedition's records show that Magellan's whole fleet, including the *San Antonio*, spent from 31 March to 24 August 1520 refitting at San Julián on the Patagonian coast, and the time they spent there is well documented – a mutiny was put down, the *San Antonio* was refitted and the *Santiago* was wrecked exploring the coast, though her crew were rescued. The explorers then had a famous encounter with some local inhabitants of remarkable size, one of whom was captured on board Magellan's ship. This incident soon gave rise to the belief that the area was populated by giants, called by Magellan "Pathagoni",⁴ who gave their name to the region whether they existed or not. The expedition's records mention no visit to any islands,⁵ but Laguarda Trías contends that during those five months the *San Antonio* discovered the Falklands and that they were mapped by Andrés de San Martín, who established their latitudes by estimation.⁶ He says the *San Antonio* left San Julián on 23 July and reached the Falklands on 28 July, the day of St Sanson, after whom he believes Calmette named the islands. In fact Calmette may have been ashore under arrest at the time, but Laguarda Trías says he must have been aboard, since only he could have suggested the name of a saint that would have been unknown to the Portuguese or Spaniards.⁷ That sounds like circular reasoning to start with, and there is another basic defect in the theory: early maps never call the islands "Islas de San Sanson", but only "Islas de Sanson" – there is always a "San" missing. This casts doubt on the idea from the outset.

And the theory also has a serious practical weakness. It would mean that just when the fleet was about to sail on south, the crew of the *San Antonio* must have slipped away secretly without telling Magellan and sailed out into the Atlantic for *over 500 kilometres*, following a very precise course east-southeast from San Julián – a little further north or south and they would have found only empty Atlantic. The theory requires them to have found the Falklands and to have made a complete survey, i.e. the basis for Thevet's map. They would have had to sail right round the unknown and dangerous coasts of the islands (about *another 1,000 kilometres*), in winter with short hours of daylight and stormy weather, or they would not have known they had found islands instead of the fabled "Southern Continent". They would have had to look into several inlets including Salvador

---

¹ Laguarda Trías 1983, p. 54; Enrique Ruiz Guiñazú, *Proas de España en el Mar Magellanico* ["Spanish prows in the Magellanic Sea"], Buenos Aires 1945, p. 88.
² F.H.H. Guillemard, *The Life of Ferdinand Magellan...*, London 1890, pp. 264-266; Arnaud 2000, p. 192.
³ Arnaud 2000, p. 193.
⁴ "Patagón" is sometimes said to be the Spanish or Portuguese for "big feet" or "large paws", but neither language has such a word; the Argentine historian María Rosa Lida de Malkiel suggested in 1952 that it came from the name of a giant in "Primaleón", a heroic romance published in Salamanca in 1512 (Laguarda Trías 1983, pp. 48-49).
⁵ Guillemard 1890, pp. 162, 186.
⁶ Laguarda Trías 1983, p. 28.
⁷ Laguarda Trías 1983, p. 53.

Water and Falkland Sound, both clearly depicted on the map; they would then have had to sail <u>over 500 kilometres</u> back to San Julián, and they would have had to find it without mishap on the tricky Patagonian coast. They would have been away for a month, and would have sailed 2,000 kilometres in winter weather, but they would have had no time for refitting or reprovisioning since the *San Antonio* left San Julián with the fleet on 24 August 1520.[1] Their absence would have had to remain unrecorded by the expedition's chroniclers,[2] and Andrés de San Martín would have had to move back to the *Victoria* – the *San Antonio* deserted Magellan and returned to Spain, but San Martín sailed on in the *Victoria* into the Pacific, where he was killed in May 1521. And the *San Antonio*'s crew would have had to organise a perfect conspiracy of silence, since the accounts they gave after their return to Seville mention no such trip, before or after deserting Magellan.

We find this scenario so absurd as to be unworthy of serious consideration. The theory that the original for the Thevet map was made by Andrés de San Martín in July 1520 aboard the *San Antonio* fails to pass the simple test of feasibility. The same goes for Laguarda Trías's conclusion:[3]

… the present critical study… demonstrates in an indisputable way the priority of Spanish sovereignty…; all of that confirms that it is to Argentina, the legitimate heiress to the territorial rights of Spain in this part of America, that belongs in fact and by right, without any kind of doubts or any sort of restrictions, the absolute and indisputable sovereignty over the Sansón-Malvinas islands.

That is twaddle. Mere discovery has never conferred possession of anything.

The truth is simpler: Marcel Destombes says that when Thevet was writing his *Grand Insulaire* (in 1586-7), he took the latitudes and longitudes of all the Atlantic islands he describes from the map by Gerardus Mercator printed in Duisburg in 1569.[4] It shows the Falklands as four tiny blobs rather too far north, which explains why Thevet's latitudes are too far north (most early maps place the islands, if shown at all, too far south). In short, Andrés de San Martín had nothing to do with Thevet's Falklands map.

Thus there is no evidence to link the map with the *San Antonio*, but there is much negative evidence against it. In their accounts the crew of the *San Antonio* mentioned no visit to any islands on their outward or return journey; they said they returned up the coast, and on their way home they were short of provisions, which would have ruled out any exploring. Thevet's old Portuguese captain referred to "ships" (below), whereas the *San Antonio* would have been alone, and the form of the islands' name on early maps does not suggest they were named after St Sanson.

So, to set the record straight: neither Vespucci nor Magellan discovered the Falklands. The likelihood is that they were discovered by an otherwise unrecorded Portuguese expedition before Magellan set sail. There is naturally no negative evidence, whereas there is some positive evidence in the form of Pedro Reinel's and André Thevet's maps, with their clear "Portuguese connection".

The Thevet map is therefore of great interest. In the caption to their illustration of it, Kohen and Rodríguez say (again following Vicente Arnaud) it was made "By Captain Pilot Andrés de San Martín in 1520" – here they are simply repeating the false assertion which has become standard in Argentine works including pamphlets published by the Argentine government. None of the authors of those works did any detailed research on the map, or consulted the authoritative works (such as those by Destombes and Karrow) that we mention here in our footnotes. Thus the myth has become established in Argentina that the map dates from 1520 and that it is by Andrés de San Martín. Neither of those things is true.

---

[1] Date of 24 August 1520 given in Guillemard 1890, p, 186; other accounts give different dates.
[2] Journals of the voyage were written by Antonio Pigafetta and Francisco Albo (from Brazil to the Strait only), and Maximilian of Transylvania interviewed the surviving crew of the *Victoria* after their return to Spain and wrote the first published account. None of those authors mentions the *San Antonio* leaving San Julián independently, nor any islands anywhere near the Falklands.
[3] Laguarda Trías 1983, p. 57.
[4] Destombes 1972, p. 128; facsimile Utrecht and Paris 1987, p. 408. The relevant portion of Mercator's 1569 map is finely reproduced in Marcel Watelet, ed., *Gérard Mercator, Cosmographe*, Antwerp 1994, p. 197; Watelet's caption: « *Atlas de la mappemonde de 1569, planche no 29-30: Amérique du Sud. Rotterdam, Maritiem Museum Prins Hendrik, Atlas 91* ». It shows a group of small islands in much the same position as given by the coordinates on Thevet's map.

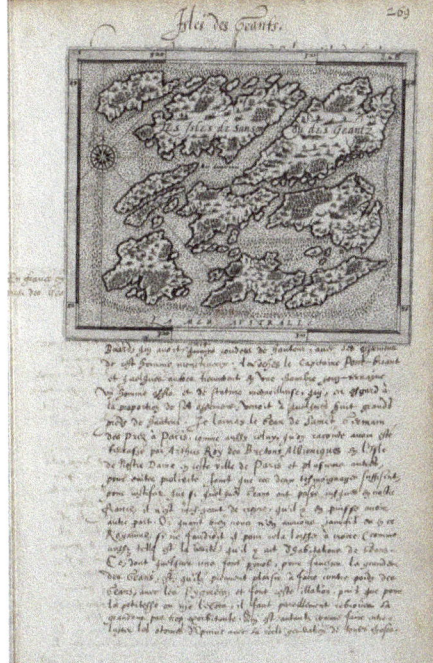 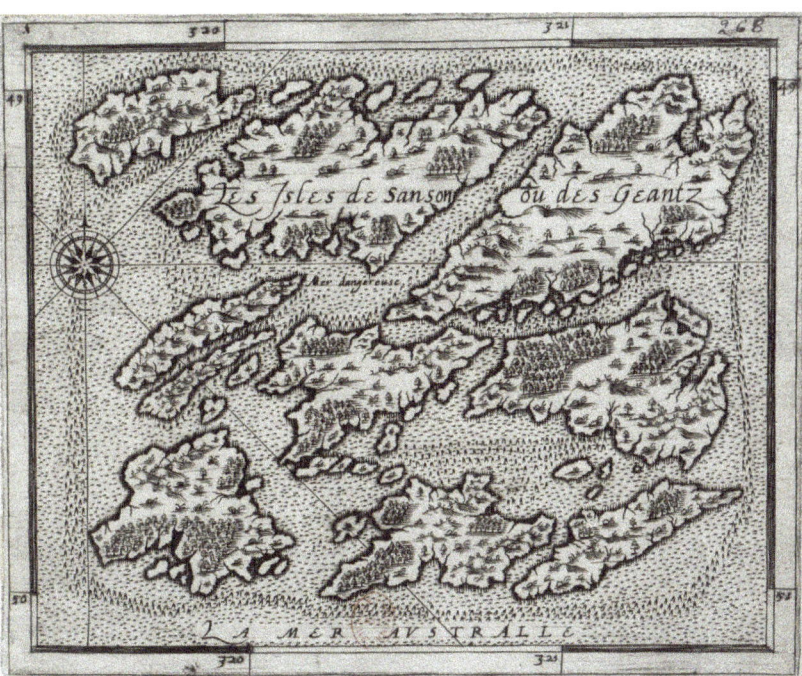

1.3b The Thevet map in André Thevet's *Grand Insulaire* (1586-7): it is pasted (crookedly) by its left-hand edge on to fol. 269, so that it can be turned like a page to reveal the top of the text on fol. 269 *recto*, and it has an oblong hole cut in the paper at left to reveal the marginal comment « En France on a veu des Geans » ["In France Giants have been seen"]. (BN Ms. fr. 15 452, fols. 268 and 269)

1.3c The Thevet map: "The Islands of Sanson or of the Giants", engraved by Thomas de Leu, *c.* 1586, here about half size (the original is 14.6 cms high by 17.9 cms wide to the outermost lines of the frame). The little pointed marks like sharks' fins all round the coasts indicate navigational dangers; it is the only map still in the *Grand Insulaire* on which the marks go all the way round the islands, and it is the only one with its own individual folio number, 268. The latitudes and longitudes show the islands in roughly the right place for the Falklands and at roughly the right size. (BN Ms. fr. 15 452, fol. 268)

The Thevet map is in fact an engraving made around 1586, most probably by the Fleming Thomas de Leu (1560-1612); it is in the first of two large manuscript volumes in the Bibliothèque Nationale in Paris entitled *Grand Insulaire*,[1] dating to 1586-7, by the eccentric Franciscan friar André Thevet (1516-92).[2] In the text of the *Grand Insulaire* Thevet says he obtained a map of the islands from an old Portuguese captain in Lisbon; that map is lost but was the basis for the map in his book. Since Roger Hervé first published the Thevet map in 1982 it has been illustrated in several Argentine works, but always separately, divorced from its context; as far as we know it has never been illustrated before in colour, nor as it actually appears in the manuscript (as in our fig. 1.3b).

The written text of the manuscript describes islands all over the world, in 263 sections, one for each island; Robert Karrow postulates that there were originally 263 maps,[3] one in each section. Only 84 maps now remain *in situ* in the two volumes, but a total of 142 survive.[4] The Falklands map is the only one that has its own folio number, 268; all the others merely bear the number of the adjacent page. The text of the manuscript has never been printed; internal evidence shows that it

---

[1] André Thevet, *Le Grand Insulaire et Pilotage d'André Theuet, Angoumoisin, Cosmographe du Roy. Dans lequel sont contenus plusieurs plants* [sic] *d'isles habitées, et deshabitées, et description d'icelles* (undated, but datable to 1586-7), in the Bibliothèque Nationale de France, Paris (BN), Ms. fr. 15 452 (vol. I) and 15 453 (vol. II); the Falklands map is in vol. I, fol. 268. Part of the manuscript is accessible online under http://gallica.bnf.fr/ark:/12148/btv1b9065908x/ f307. image, but at the time of writing it does not (or not yet) include the section on the Falklands. The full relevant text in French and English will appear in *The Falklands Saga*.

[2] Biography by Frank Lestringant, *André Thevet: Cosmographe des derniers Valois*, Geneva 1991; see also Marcel Destombes, « André Thevet (1504-1592) et sa contribution à la cartographie et à l'océanographie », in *Proceedings of the Royal Society of Edinburgh 1972*, pp. 123, 128; facsimile Utrecht and Paris 1987, pp. 401, 408.

[3] Robert W. Karrow Jr., *Mapmakers of the Sixteenth Century and their Maps*, Chicago 1993. In Karrow's list of mapmakers, André Thevet (in Latin Andreas Thevetus) is no. 77 (pp. 529-546). Karrow lists the maps from the *Grand Insulaire* on pp. 536-545; the map of « Les Isles de Sanson ou des Geantz » is his no. 77/148 (p. 539).

[4] Karrow 1993, p. 536 ; Destombes 1972, p. 130 (1987 reprint: p. 410). Lestringant gives bibliographical details and lists some detached maps from the *Grand Insulaire* recently found (1991, pp. 386-391).

dates from 1586-7 and is partly based on the maps, so the maps were made around 1586. The maps are proof prints from engraved copper blocks, all in the same style – the appearance of the Falklands map does not derive from the makers of the original map on which it is based (which may have been very different) but from the later engraver Thomas de Leu, whose style is very distinctive. Like most other maps in the *Grand Insulaire*, the Falklands map bears two latitudes and two longitudes, which give an indication of geographical position and of scale. The latitudes, 49° and 50°, place the islands a couple of degrees too far north, while the longitudes, 320° and 321° (in the Ptolemaic tradition of calculating longitude eastwards round the world from the Canary Islands), place them a few degrees too far east. The coordinates are not quite accurate, but are as good as could be expected from the 16th century. They show islands that extend roughly 100 kilometres from north to south and roughly 200 kilometres from east to west – they are large islands, not mere specks. The map depicts islands recognisable as the Falklands, and the coordinates identify the islands unambiguously: they are the Falklands.

The text accompanying the map, headed « Isles des Geants » ["Islands of the Giants"],[1] is typical of Thevet's rambling, chaotic style and his mixture of fact and fantasy. He begins by saying that those who believe that all giants had been killed by the Flood are wrong; there were remains or portraits of giants in France, and if there had been giants in France, it was reasonable to believe that there were some elsewhere, for example on the islands he is about to describe. He says: "the name of Sansom or of the Giants has been given them because just as that Israelite did many things far removed from the ordinary power of men, he has also been said to be among those who were accompanied by supernatural strength like that of our Giants", and then goes on:[2]

In… the twenty-first book of my **Cosmography**[3] I only spoke of one of these Islands, which is called by its inhabitants **Perhamboup** and by those of the mainland **Pacahocaf**, which is distant from the continent some eight or ten leagues. There are very many others, in which these little fellows of eight or nine feet in height have set up their hovels. The first who set foot in these Islands were some Portuguese, who were accompanying **Ferdinand Magellan** in his voyage;[4] they wishing to obtain supplies of fresh water, found themselves disappointed in their intentions, chiefly because they could not land on these Islands owing to the approaches, which are very dangerous; for in order to land on them, approaching the land which lies at the North-east, the coast full of surf-beaten rocks and sandbanks with very few deep parts, they brought their ships no closer than a cannon-shot, to guard themselves from the dangers, and sent in two little vessels and some sailors to reconnoitre these **Giants' Islands**. Of this I am assured by an old Portuguese Captain, a good Pilot, whom I found in the city of Lisbon in Portugal, who said he had at that time visited these Islands, the plan of which I had from him, together with several others of this coast…

Thevet then describes how the Portuguese met the local giants: "they all at once saw swarming up a great multitude of clothed persons, by whom they were quite frightened, not being able to imagine what people they might be…". The giants' appearance was terrifying – they had "the coarse bloated faces of people who wanted only to bite [*sic!*], at which they [i.e. the Portuguese] retraced their route, since they feared that those great bodies would swallow them up in one gulp…". But after exchanging gifts, the giants and the Portuguese made friends, and:

Towards four o'clock in the evening the **Portuguese**, after infinite caresses and marks of gratitude… took their leave of those fine little chaps, and since then these Islands have been called Isles of Giants on account of the monstrous size of the inhabitants of the same…

Thevet then describes the frightening voices of the giants and their habits: they build no houses, but live in "tents" of hides; they wear animal skins and plait their hair. He concludes his account:

---

[1] Thevet writes the name five times, in four different ways: in the text heading and fol. 270 *recto* « Isles des Geants »; in the running text « Sansom » and « **Isles Geantées** » (both fol. 269 *recto*), and on the map « *Les Isles de Sanson ou des Geantz* ».

[2] BN Ms. fr. 15 452, fol. 269 *verso* – 271 *recto* (extracts); capitalisation as in the original; the words here printed in bold type are written somewhat larger and more clearly in the MS. These extracts are the first ever printed, apart from a 7-line fragment in Hervé 1982 (p. 42, fn. 85), translated into Spanish (inaccurately) in Laguarda Trías 1983, pp. 24-25.

[3] André Thevet, *La Cosmographie universelle d'André Thevet, cosmographe du roy*, Paris 1575.

[4] Some explorers "upgraded" their expeditions by falsely claiming that they were part of Magellan's expedition – details of such "upgraded" expeditions in Hervé 1982, p. 56 (Dunmore 1983, p. 49).

[fol. 271 *recto*] ... And since in my Cosmography and in my book Of Famous Men[1] I have long enough examined the rest of what might be appropriate touching the customs of these Insular Giants, I will conclude this discourse, and upon finishing this description I will present the elevation of these Islands... You see them surrounded on all sides with belts of terrors and sandbanks. Nevertheless in the interior the land promises very good fertility to those who would settle there and till the soil a little...

We feel it would be going too far to dismiss everything Thevet says as pure fantasy. We are not prepared to believe the Portuguese met any giants in the Falklands (Thevet put giants in his descriptions of several places), but the map's geographical details are very broadly correct, and Thevet visited Portugal and spoke Portuguese,[2] so the map's "Portuguese connection" is credible.

So until the contrary is demonstrated, we shall assume that the discoverers of the Falklands were the crews of at least two Portuguese ships, who were exploring the South Atlantic at the latest around 1518-19 and found the islands by chance – one might speculate that they were looking for the "Southern Continent", which was thought to be vast and rich.[3] Those crews were the first people to see the islands and the first to set foot on them; they met no giants (the islands were uninhabited), but they clearly had plenty of time for exploring. They sailed right round the islands and at least part of the way down Falkland Sound, and looked into Salvador Water in the north-east of East Falkland – the north-east is the most accurate part of the map, which is intriguing given that Pedro Reinel's map shows the north coast of the Falklands and the old captain told Thevet that the Portuguese arrived "approaching the land which lies at the North-east". That suggests that the Reinel and Thevet maps have more than a general "Portuguese connection"; it suggests that the originals on which they are based (which no longer survive) may even have been made by the same expedition. The old captain said he was aboard one of the Portuguese ships, and like other explorers at that time he seemingly "upgraded" his expedition by saying it was part of Magellan's much more famous expedition, which it had actually preceded. That seems the most reasonable theory about the discovery of the Falkland Islands.

1.4 Later maps; later sightings

Once the islands had been found, they began to appear on some 16th and 17th-century Spanish and Portuguese maps, as tiny blobs too far south and too near the coast, though even as late as the 1690s many maps did not mark them at all. Several authors have claimed that some early maps label the islands "Yslas de Sanson y de Patos" ["Islands of Sanson and of Ducks"] (e.g. Hervé 1982, p. 41), or "Islas de los Patos y de Sansón" ["Islands of the Ducks and of Sansón"] (e.g. Arnaud 2000, p. 237), but those readings are incorrect – those authors misread the labels on two maps made in 1527 and 1529 by the Portuguese mapmaker Diogo Ribeiro.[4] Each actually has two separate labels: one label is next to a small island near the coast (on the 1527 map "y: de los patos" and on the 1529 map "y.ª de los patos"), while another label is next to the Falklands (1527: "y · de s· son"; 1529: "yªs desanson"). Only the second label refers to the Falklands, and its first word is not "y" (Spanish for "and"); it is short for "yslas" ["islands"]. So the Falklands are not named "yslas de los patos y de sanson" – their earliest name was only "Yslas de Sanson" (variously spelt).

Kohen and Rodríguez assert (p. 34) that the name is Spanish; they give it on their page 32 as

---

[1] André Thevet, *Les vrais pourtraits et vies des hommes illustres*, Paris 1584. Both book titles normal size here.
[2] For Thevet's visits to Portugal see Jean Baudry, *Documents inédits sur André Thevet...*, Paris 1982, p. 5, and Roger Schlesinger, ed., *Selections from André Thevet's "Les vrais pourtraits..."*, Urbana 1993, pp. 2-5.
[3] The real Antarctica was not discovered till the 19th century, and turned out to be disappointingly small and cold.
[4] Reproduced in Johann Georg Kohl, *Die beiden ältesten General-Karten von Amerika...* ["The two oldest general maps of America..."], Weimar 1860. The originals (now in the Herzogin Anna Amalia Bibliothek, Weimar), are now very worn; we have checked Kohl's versions against digital scans of the originals, and are grateful to Annett Carius-Kiehne for providing the scans. In *Cartografía Magallánica 1523-1945*, Punta Arenas (Chile) 1999, p. 6, Mateo Martinic prints the two Weimar maps from Kohl but identifies that of 1529 as Vatican 1529 and the one of 1527 as Weimar 1529, and labels them "K. Kretschmer 1892" (i.e. Konrad Kretschmer, *Die historischen Karten zur Entdeckung Amerikas* ["The historical maps on the discovery of America"], Frankfurt am Main 1892; new ed. by Günter Braun and Albrecht von Gleich, Hamburg 1991). Martinic's article "The 'S. Anton or Sanson' Islands, first cartographic mention of the Falkland Islands in the 16th century", in the *Falkland Islands Journal* (*FIJ*) vol. 8 (1), 2002, p. 27, includes a map credited to "Vatican Apostolic Library", but it is from Kretschmer 1892, plate XV (merely redrawn from Kohl).

"Ysla de Sansón y de Patos" ["Island of Sansón and of Ducks"],[1] and on p. 34 as "Sansón o de los Patos" ["Sansón or of the Ducks"], but we have found no map or author that gives the name in those forms, and its origin is unclear anyway. "Islas de Sanson" may be a Spanish misunderstanding of a Portuguese name, "Ilhas d'Asenção" ["Ascension Islands"] – a map by Francisco Rodrigues of about 1511-13 labels a mid-Atlantic island "Ilha dacemçam", and one by Sebastião Lopes of about 1581 places the label "I. daçemçam" beside the Falklands.[2] Or else, as André Thevet says (see section 1.3), there may be a connection with the biblical Samson. But in the last analysis it is impossible to say where the name came from; in the absence of written accounts, all the confident theories so far offered are doomed to remain mere speculative conjectures.

As Kohen and Rodríguez say, we do not accept that the Falklands were discovered by John Davis in 1592, as used to be claimed in British books. That is clearly impossible – the islands are shown on the Reinel and Thevet maps originating before 1520, and it seems possible that a Spanish ship spent several months in the islands in 1540, though we no longer think it as likely as we did when we wrote *Getting it right* in 2008 (p. 5). She was one of four ships sent out by the bishop of Plasencia, Gutierre de Vargas Carvajal, organised by Francisco Camargo and led by Francisco de la Ribera. Her name is unknown since the surviving accounts of her voyage are all fragmentary. One account survives in two partial copies, one contemporary, the other of about 1570, and a second is in the archives of the Spanish defence ministry in Madrid, and was recently placed online.[3] The first account was printed by Luis Torres de Mendoza in 1866,[4] and was reprinted and analysed in a Chilean naval magazine in 1879,[5] which concluded that the ship visited the Isla de los Estados and islands in the Magellan Strait. Julius Goebel analysed it in 1927;[6] he gave the ship the Latin name *Incognita* ["Unknown"], and concluded that she had been in the Falklands. However, in 1928 Héctor Ratto published an analysis supporting the 1879 Chilean article and denying that Goebel was right.[7] In 1967 the first account was analysed by the Argentine vice admiral Ernesto Basílico,[8] who argued that the ship was in the Falklands, mostly in Queen Charlotte Bay on West Falkland. However, the second account, from the Spanish defence ministry, supports the view that the ship remained around the Strait of Magellan and did not visit the Falklands. At any rate, even if the ship was in the Falklands, no Spaniards saw the islands for over 200 years after December 1540.[9]

As we said in *Getting it right* (p. 5), John Davis's sighting of the islands in 1592 was the first to be printed – in 1600 the geographical writer Richard Hakluyt published a brief account of it by a

---

[1] Kohen and Rodríguez, pp. 31-32, supported by reference to Arnaud 2000, p. 191, who quotes the *Islario General* by Alonso de Santa Cruz, written in 1541 and known as the *Islario de Santa Cruz*. It was edited, with a German translation, by Franz von Wieser in *Die Karten von Amerika in dem Islario General des Alonso de Santa Cruz, Cosmógrafo des Kaisers Karl V.* ["The Maps of America in the Islario General of Alonso de Santa Cruz, Cosmographer to [Holy Roman] Emperor Charles V"], Innsbruck 1908. The relevant passage runs: "… And from there they took their course onwards for the coast, having reached and discovered some islands which were eighteen leagues to the east of the port of Saint Julian, to which they gave the name of Yslas de Sanson y de Patos ["Islands of Sanson and of Ducks"]…" (von Wieser 1908, p. 58, translation by Graham Pascoe). However, the *Islario* is famously badly written; it was combined from several written accounts now lost, and is not a reliable source; the islands are much more than 18 leagues from the coast, and on its plate XV they are only labelled "y^{a}s de sanson"; there is no "patos" label.

[2] Examples in McIntosh 2000, p. 30 and Martinic 1999, p. 27; "em" and "am" indicate the Portuguese nasal vowels.

[3] A copy dated 5 January 1795, of a letter dating from 1541 from Christoval Rayzer to Lazaro Aleman reporting the arrival at San Tomé of one of Camargo's ships, online under http:// bibliotecavirtualdefensa.es/ BVMDefensa/i18n/ consulta/resultados_ocr.cmd?buscar_cabecera=Search+for&id=2936&tipoResultados=BIB& posicion=1&forma=ficha (accessible only after payment). We are grateful to Roger Lorton for drawing our attention to this document.

[4] Luis Torres de Mendoza, *Colección de documentos relativos al descubrimiento, conquista y organización...* ["Collection of documents concerning the discovery, conquest and organisation..."] vol. V, Madrid 1866 (bibliography in Basílico 1967, p. 193).

[5] [Anon.], *Anuario Hidrográfico de la Marina de Chile*, vol. 5, 1879.

[6] Julius Goebel, *The Struggle for the Falkland Islands*, New Haven (Connecticut), pp. 16-31.

[7] *Bordejeando. Descubrimientos, Exploraciones y Levantamientos Marítimos Patagónicos*, by "H. Doserres" (pen-name of Héctor R. Ratto), Buenos Aires 1928, p. 168.

[8] Ernesto Basílico, *La Armada del Obispo de Plasencia y el Descubrimiento de las Malvinas* ["The Fleet of the Bishop of Plasencia and the Discovery of the Malvinas"], Buenos Aires 1967.

[9] Rear Admiral Laurio H. Destéfani, *Las Malvinas en la Época Hispana (1600-1811)*, Buenos Aires 1981, p. 67.

member of Davis's crew, John Jane, a "a man of good obseruation", as Hakluyt calls him.[1] After Davis the next expedition to see the Falklands was that of Sir Richard Hawkins (1560?-1622), who sailed past the islands in the *Daintie* on 2 February 1594, but whose account was not published till 1622.[2] We did not mention him in *Getting it right*, since he was only one of many explorers who sailed past the islands without stopping. Several authors have doubted that he saw the Falklands,[3] among whom are Kohen and Rodríguez, who quote (p. 30) part of what they call his "fantastic" description, including his comments that he was in around 48° south latitude and that he saw many fires. They say that since the islands were uninhabited, the fires he saw make it "simply impossible" that he saw the Falklands. But they suppress much of his account, which tells a different story – he says that the western part of the land:[4]

... riseth in three mounts, or round hillockes... This we call poynt Tremountaine. Some twelve or foureteene leagues from this poynt to the east-wardes... lyeth a low flat iland of some two leagues long; we named it Fayre Iland... Some three or four leagues easterly from this iland, is a goodly opening, as of a great river, or an arme of the sea... And eight or tenne leagues from this opening, some three leagues from the shore, lyeth a bigge rocke, which at the first wee had thought to be a shippe under all her sayles; but after, as we came neere, it discovered it selfe to be a rocke, which we called *Condite-head*; for... it is like to the condite heads about the cittie of London.[5] All this coast... lyeth next of any thing east and by north, and west and by south. The land, for that it was discovered in the raigne of Queene Elizabeth... in a perpetuall memory of her chastitie, and remembrance of my endeavours, I gave it the name of "HAWKINS maiden-land".

In that passage Hawkins mentions several identifiable features – he describes the steep Jason Islands ("poynt Tremountaine"), what was perhaps Sedge Island ("Fayre Island"), the opening into Byron Sound ("a goodly opening"), and the Eddystone Rock ("Condite-head").

The fires he saw were clearly peat set on fire by lightning, a well-known occasional occurrence in the Falklands. Once alight, the peat may burn for weeks or even months in ever-widening irregular broken circles, resulting in a number of separate fires dotted about over a large area, which might easily be taken for the camp fires of local inhabitants – several islands in the Falklands are called "Burnt Island", since their peat cover had burnt at some time. Hawkins says they sailed along "well neere threescore leagues of the coast" (almost 180 miles, fairly close to the correct figure of around 150 miles), and that the coast lay more or less east-west. There is nowhere comparable on the Patagonian coast, and those details leave little room for doubt that he saw the Falklands – far from being "fantastic", the description is instantly recognisable. Violet Boyson points out that later navigators certainly believed he had seen the Falklands; she mentions a chart of around 1720 which marks them "Hawkins's Maidenland",[6] and the name is also used on the influential chart by John Hawkesworth of 1773 (which she does not mention).

Authors who doubt that Hawkins saw the Falklands, including Kohen and Rodríguez, assume that his latitude of 48° was right and his description wrong, but it was the other way round – most of his *Observations* were written up from memory later, when he remembered the islands but not the latitude. In that, he was not alone – in 1684 William Ambrose Cowley gave 47° 40´, and in 1722 Jacob Roggeveen gave 45°-49°, though both clearly describe sailing past the Falklands (which lie around 51-52° South; see Map 2 in the Introduction).[7] So although navigators vividly remembered

---

[1] John Jane's account is in Richard Hakluyt's *Principal Navigations...*, London 1600, vol. III, p. 846.
[2] *The Observations of Sir Richard Havvkins K^{nt}, in his Voiage into the South Sea. Anno Domini, 1593*, London 1622, reprinted and ed. by C.R. Drinkwater Bethune, London 1847 (henceforth "Hawkins 1622/1847").
[3] They include Drinkwater Bethune, in Hawkins 1622/1847, p. 108, fn.; Commander B.M. Chambers, in *The Geographical Journal*, vol. xvii no. 4, April 1901, pp. 414-423; Paul Groussac, *Les Iles Malouines: nouvel exposé d'un vieux litige* ["The Malouine Islands: a new account of an old legal dispute"], Buenos Aires 1910, pp. 75-81, Spanish translation *Las Islas Malvinas por Paul Groussac...*, Buenos Aires 1936, pp. 82-89; and Goebel 1927, pp. 35-42.
[4] Hawkins 1622/1847, pp. 106-108; capitals and italics in original.
[5] The "Condite heads" (i.e. conduit heads) in London were the small wellhouses in such places as Cheapside, where people could draw piped water brought into the City from outside.
[6] Violet Boyson, in *The Falkland Islands*, Oxford 1924, pp. 23-24. Kohen and Rodríguez did not know she was a woman – they refer (p. 173) to "El autor británico V. F. Boyson"!
[7] Cowley's journal is in the British Library, MS Sloane 54, *The Voyage of William Ambrosia Cowley, Marriner...* (1683-6); it was published in garbled form in William Hacke, ed., *A Collection of Original Voyages...*, London 1699;

what they saw, they sometimes got their latitudes wrong.

In *Getting it right* (p. 5) we discussed the Falklands' "rival names":

> The islands derive their English name from Falkland Sound, the name given to the waterway between the two main islands by Captain John Strong, who spent several days in the islands in January 1690 in his ship *Welfare*.[1] The name "Falkland Islands"... was first used in the journal of Woodes Rogers in December 1708, and was first published in 1712 in his account[2] ... The French Geographer Royal, Guillaume Delisle,... on two maps of 1720 and 1722... called them "Les Iles Malouines", after the port of St Malo in Brittany, home port of the French ships which had visited the Falklands. The Spaniards never had a name of their own for the Islands, but from the mid-1760s they adopted the French name "Iles Malouines", adapting it into "Islas Maluinas". Around 1805 they began to spell it "Malvinas", though as late as 1811 they still sometimes spelt it "Maluinas". "Malvinas" is now the Spanish name for the islands; in its current form it is a century later than the English name.

Kohen and Rodríguez summarise our account of the rival names, and point out that the question of which name was earlier is irrelevant to the question of sovereignty. They are right there of course, but their comment reveals their single-minded concentration on the question of sovereignty, which we do not mention in this context; our concern was simply to put the historical record straight in view of contentions by various authors, including internet bloggers, who wrongly maintain that the original name for the islands was « Iles Malouines ».

1.5 The treaties that were not broken

Under the heading "Bilateral treaties prove that Britain recognised Spanish sovereignty over the region of the Falklands/Malvinas", Kohen and Rodríguez again reveal (pp. 35-48) their narrow, simplistic, "legitimist" view of sovereignty, i.e. a view that regards sovereignty as an abstract quality that simply exists, independent of any practical considerations such as active presence, acquiescence, passage of time, or acceptance by other countries. They refer to the Treaties of Madrid of 1670 and Utrecht of 1713, which we briefly mentioned in *Getting it right* (pp. 5-6); we said that both treaties referred to territories "possessed" by Spain, and that Spain did not possess the Falklands in 1670 or in 1713. Kohen and Rodríguez quote passages from those treaties, asserting that Britain recognised Spanish sovereignty in Spanish South America, but that is untrue – Britain's behaviour always showed that Britain never accepted any such claim by Spain.

Those treaties do not ban Britain from navigating in the South Atlantic – Britain always claimed and maintained that right. We mentioned in *Getting it right* (p. 6) that Britain occupied the South Atlantic island of St Helena in 1659; Kohen and Rodríguez say (p. 37) that that proves nothing, since the island had been in the Portuguese sphere under the Treaty of Tordesillas and Spain had never claimed it. But their mention of the Treaty of Tordesillas is a red herring – no country except Spain and Portugal saw the South Atlantic as divided into a Spanish and a Portuguese sphere, and Spain never mentioned Tordesillas in any dealings with other countries. Throughout the 17th and 18th centuries British ships sailed to India and Asia both round the Cape of Good Hope and round Cape Horn; for Britain the freedom of navigation was paramount and was always maintained. Britain never accepted Spanish sovereignty in the South Atlantic, and that was made abundantly clear by the British government during the First Falklands Crisis of 1770-71 (chapter 2).

It is interesting to note that Louis-Antoine de Bougainville (see section 2.1) denied that the Treaties of Madrid of 1670 and Utrecht of 1713 gave Spain any title to the Falklands – in a note to the duc de Choiseul on 5 September 1765 he pointed out that the Treaty of Madrid makes no mention of the actual limits of Spanish possessions, and that in Article 8 of the Treaty of Utrecht the queen of Great Britain [Anne] promised to assist the Spaniards to recover the former limits of their possessions in America on the same footing as in the time of "Charles II" (when of course the

---

Roggeveen's log was published in *De Reis van M[ijnhee]r. Jacob Roggeveen ter Ontdekking van het Zuidland (1721-1722)* ["The Voyage of Mijnheer Jacob Roggeveen for the Discovery of the South Land (1721-1722)"], ed. F. E. Baron Mulert, 's Gravenhage 1911; English translation by Andrew Sharp: *The Journal of Jacob Roggeveen*, Oxford 1970.

[1] [2008 footnote:] He named the Sound after Viscount Falkland, who was one of the owners of the *Welfare* and was later First Lord of the Admiralty (1693-94). Strong's unpublished log is in the British Library, Sloane MS 3295.

[2] [2008 footnote:] Woodes Rogers, *A Cruising Voyage round the World...*, London 1712, pp. 103-106.

islands were not possessed by Spain).[1] Kohen and Rodríguez say (p. 36) that the 1670 Treaty contained a "prohibition of navigating to or trading with Spanish territories in America. It is evident that it was impossible to for Britain [*sic*] to acquire sovereignty over areas to which they could not even go." But as we said in *Getting it right*, the treaty "nowhere mentions any British acceptance of Spanish sovereignty", and Jörg Fisch confirms that interpretation – he says that the Treaty was:[2]

a mutual recognition of the respective possessions in America and of the exclusive right to trade with them. The exact extent of these possessions, however, remained undefined, which meant that no further restriction as to the access to the American coasts and to the navigation in the seas around America could be inferred.

As regards the Treaty of Utrecht of 1713, Kohen and Rodríguez say (p. 39) that we are wrong in *Getting it right* in saying that it referred to territories "possessed" by Spain – but then they go on to say that it guaranteed "the integrity of all the possessions of the Spanish Crown". We fail to see the difference. They say that the only limits of Spanish possessions were those laid down by the Treaty of Tordesillas, but that is nonsense – that treaty regulated only the mutual relations of Spain and Portugal and left all other countries unaffected. No international treaties defined the precise extent of Spain's or Britain's possessions, which allowed Britain and Spain to follow their own differing views of the meaning of possession. Britain's "*de-facto*-ist" view of possession was finally – reluctantly – accepted by Spain in the Nootka Sound Convention of 1790 (section 1.7).

1.6 Britain's abandoned plan to survey the Falklands in 1749-50

Kohen and Rodríguez then consider (pp. 40-41) Britain's dropping of a plan to send an expedition to survey and perhaps occupy the Falklands in 1749 (which we did not mention in *Getting it right*). They say that the British government informed the Spanish government of the plan, and infer that Britain therefore did not consider itself sovereign in the islands and recognised Spanish sovereignty. That is all untrue.

In fact the British government did not recognise Spanish sovereignty, nor accept any Spanish right to limit Britain's freedom to explore anywhere in the world including the South Atlantic. The plan to send an expedition to the islands was itself proof of that, as Jean-Etienne Martin-Allanic makes clear – he refers to "the constancy of the British in regarding the Malouine Islands as theirs and in intending to occupy them despite Spain's protests."[3]

What happened was highly significant for the later history of the islands. Captain George Anson had recommended them as a place of supply for British expeditions, in his best-selling account of his round-the-world voyage of 1740-44 published in 1748;[4] thereupon, in early 1749, the British Admiralty began to consider sending an expedition to set up an establishment in the Falklands and/or the non-existent "Pepys Island",[5] but the proposals were leaked to French agents and to the

---

[1] Martin-Allanic 1964, pp. 251-253 (bibliography in chapter 2); "Charles II" might refer to Carlos II of Spain (reigned 1665-1700) or Charles II of Britain (reigned 1660-1685).

[2] Fisch 1983, p. 115.

[3] Martin-Allanic 1964, p. 85.

[4] [Richard Walter, but often referred to as if by Anson], *A Voyage round the World...*, 5th ed., London 1749, Book I, chapter IX, pp. 90-92. Kohen and Rodríguez refer erroneously (p. 40) to the "British Admiral Anson's attempt to conduct an expedition to the Falkland/Malvinas islands in 1749"; there was no such attempt, but only some internal British government plans to send an expedition as Anson recommended. Kohen's and Rodríguez's footnote, p. 41, referring to Goebel 1927, "p. 225" (quoting instructions by the Duke of Bedford to Benjamin Keene, British ambassador in Madrid, to inform the Spanish government that no settlement was intended, nor any offence to Spain) refers to the Spanish translation of Goebel, *La Pugna por las Islas Malvinas*, Buenos Aires 1983; in Goebel's English original it is pp. 197-198. Letters written in 1749 by and to the Duke of Bedford on a proposed British expedition to the Falklands are printed in English in Ricardo Caillet-Bois (ed.), *Colección de Documentos relativos a la Historia de las Islas Malvinas*, Buenos Aires 1957, vol. I, pp. 16-23; Bedford pointed out that Britain reserved its right to send out ships to explore any part of the world, and Spain's fears that the plan might harm Spain's rights were unjustified.

[5] "Pepys Island" was named by William Hacke in *A Collection of Original Voyages...*, London 1699 (his garbled edition of Ambrose Cowley's journal, BL MS Sloane 54), pp. 5-6. Cowley himself does not use the name, and was clearly describing the Falklands; it was Hacke who placed islands in two places and invented the name "Pepys Island", after Samuel Pepys (1633-1703), clerk and secretary to the Admiralty, 1660-89. Kohen and Rodríguez misspell the island "Peppys" (pp. 40, 50, 51), apparently unaware that the name is pronounced /piːps/, i.e. "Peeps". Pepys's private

Spanish ambassador in London, the Irishman Richard Wall; the French government warned Spain in June and November 1749, and Wall was twice ordered by the Spanish government to protest vigorously against such a design by Britain. In addition, the veteran Malouin explorer Jean-Baptiste Bénard de La Harpe (1683-1765) heard about the British plan from his contacts in Saint-Malo, and on 7 December 1749 he passed the information to the French government. He had been inspired with the idea of a French settlement in the Falklands ever since he sailed past the islands on 14 October 1705 aboard the *Saint-Charles-Borromée*, one of many French ships from Saint-Malo that had sailed to the Pacific around that time and had encountered the Falklands.[1] Following Bénard de La Harpe's warning, the French government on 8 January 1750 ordered the French ambassador in Madrid, the comte de Vaulgrenant, to warn Spain a third time of Britain's plan, and Spain protested to Britain yet again. The British government did not want to antagonise Spain and was hoping for the renewal of the *asiento* (the right to take slaves from Africa to Spanish America) in the peace settlement after the War of the Austrian Succession, so for those practical, commercial reasons Britain shelved the venture – but only for a while.[2] There was no recognition of Spanish sovereignty by Britain. At that time Spain knew neither the position of the Falklands nor whether there was only one island or several.[3] In short, Britain did not initially inform Spain of the plan; Spain found out as the result of leaks in Britain and from warnings by France.

The significance of the dropping of the British plan lies in the fact that France warned Spain three times about it. That gave Spanish ministers their most powerful argument in forcing France to leave the islands in the 1760s (section 2.2) – having warned Spain about Britain's plan to send an expedition to the islands, France could hardly go ahead and do exactly the same.

1.7 The misrepresented treaty: the Nootka Sound Convention limits Spanish sovereignty

Departing somewhat from chronological order, Kohen and Rodríguez then consider (pp. 42-48) the Nootka Sound Convention of 28 October 1790, known in Spanish as "El Tratado de San Lorenzo del Escorial", since it was signed at the palace of that name near Madrid.[4] It ended a dispute between Britain and Spain in 1789-90 over an inlet called Nootka Sound on what is now Vancouver Island on the west coast of Canada (which Spain claimed as Spanish territory). It almost led to war; Britain rapidly mobilised and obtained support from Prussia and the Netherlands, but Spain's former ally France was collapsing as the Revolution took hold, so Spain backed down and made extensive concessions to Britain in order to preserve peace. As N.A.M. Rodger says in his

---

diary, 1660-69, is the most famous diary in English (ed. by Robert Latham and William Matthews, *The Diary of Samuel Pepys*, 11 vols., London 1970-83, of which see 1st ed. vol. 11, p. 344, last line).

[1] Those voyages led the French royal geographer Guillaume Delisle to coin the name « Iles Malouines » ["The Saint-Malo Islands"] on two maps of 1720 and 1724; the Spaniards Hispanicised it to "Maluinas", and from around 1800 to "Malvinas". For the *Saint-Charles-Borromée* see M. E. W. Dahlgren, « Voyages Français à Destination de la Mer du Sud Avant Bougainville (1695-1749) », in *Nouvelles Archives des Missions Scientifiques et Littéraires...*, vol. XIV, Paris 1907, pp. 455-456. See also Martin-Allanic 1964, pp. 110-117.

[2] Martin-Allanic 1964, pp. 84-85, 117.

[3] Martin-Allanic 1964, pp.176, 290-291.

[4] The most detailed account of the Nootka Sound Convention is in William Ray Manning, "The Nootka Sound Controversy", in *Annual Report of the American Historical Association for the Year 1904*, Washington DC 1905. Until the 20th century the terms "convention" and "treaty" were synonymous. The original text of the Convention was of course in French; the official British copy is in PRO 93-99-4A. The full text is reproduced from *BFSP* in Raphael Perl, *The Falkland Islands Dispute in International Law and Politics*, London / Rome / New York 1983, pp. 145-150, and in facsimile from Perl in Rudolf Dolzer, *The Territorial Status of the Falkland Islands (Malvinas)...*, New York/ London/ Rome 1993, pp. 246-251; almost full text in a slightly different English translation in Manning 1905, pp. 455-456. In view of the importance of the Nootka Sound Convention in settling a major territorial dispute, we find it odd that in the 483-page work by Marcelo Kohen and Mamadou Hébié (eds.), *Research Handbook on Territorial Disputes in International Law*, Cheltenham (UK) and Northampton (USA) 2018, it is virtually unmentioned; it is mentioned only incidentally on p. 52 in a chapter by Mamadou Hébié on the acquisition of original titles of territorial sovereignty, in a sentence that reads: "Thus, Spain relied upon other colonial powers' acquiescence in the Nootka Sound dispute with Russia" [*sic*!]. A footnote refers to a letter of 4 June 1790 from the king of Spain to the ambassadors of other powers, so we presume that the letter demands the acquiescence of e.g. Russia in Spain's view of the dispute. However, Hébié fails to say so, and in any case his reference to "the Nootka Sound dispute with Russia" is nonsensical.

authoritative naval history of Britain:[1]

... by the height of the crisis in the spring of 1790 a formidable fleet was already assembled... the weakness of France, now in political turmoil, left Spain unsupported. By July, when Howe's fleet at Spithead numbered forty-three sail of the line, Spain was forced to give ground, and in October she conceded most of Britain's claims.

Rodger calls the Convention a "stinging humiliation of the Bourbon powers" (i.e. Spain and France) and quotes a British official, Undersecretary J. B. Burges, who said "we are vastly pleased".

The Nootka Sound Convention cemented the diplomatic victory of a powerful Britain over a weak and friendless Spain, and for the first time opened large parts of the Spanish colonial empire to British trade and even settlement, which Spain had hitherto prohibited. Accordingly, the Convention was enthusiastically welcomed in Britain but fiercely condemned in Spain; in Britain it was approved by a large majority in both houses of Parliament and was welcomed by the British government and the Mayor and Common Council of the City of London,[2] and the British negotiator Alleyne Fitzherbert was rewarded by being ennobled under the title of Baron St Helens.[3] By contrast, the harsh criticism in Spain contributed to the overthrow of the Spanish negotiator Count (conde) de Floridablanca, who was dismissed in February 1792.[4]

But to read some accounts of the Nootka Sound Convention, including that by Kohen and Rodríguez, one might be forgiven for imagining that the opposite had happened – that Britain had accepted a treaty that reduced Britain's rights in South America and even banned Britain from the Falklands.[5] That is a total distortion of the facts, which can be traced back to the misrepresentation of the Convention by Julius Goebel in 1927;[6] his flawed accounts of several parts of Falklands history have been influential because there was no other published account.

Goebel even gets the date of the signing of the Convention wrong, giving it as 25 October 1790 (1927, p. 427); it was actually 28 October, as the text of the Convention itself states twice. His misunderstanding (or misrepresentation) of the Convention is remarkable – Article 6 permits Britain to form "Establishments" (which could of course include permanent settlements) on "the Eastern and Western Coasts of South America and the islands adjacent" except south of parts of the coast and of the islands already occupied by Spain;[7] Goebel quotes Article 6 in full (p. 428), yet he still goes on to state (p. 429) that "The British right to colonize was recognized only as far as the northwest coast of North America was concerned". That is not what the Convention says.

---

[1] N. A. M. Rodger, *The Command of the Ocean: A Naval History of Britain, 1649-1815*, London 2004, pp. 364-365. "Sail of the line" means battleships; Admiral Richard Howe, later 1st Earl Howe, KG (1726-99), was in 1790 the commander-in-chief of the Royal Navy; Spithead is the fleet anchorage north-east of the Isle of Wight.

[2] Manning 1905, pp. 460-461.

[3] He is commemorated in the general area of Nootka Sound by Mount St Helens (in Washington State, USA), which was sighted on 19 May 1792 by Commander George Vancouver, RN, surveying the north-west coast of North America in HMS *Discovery*; he named it to honour Fitzherbert for strengthening Britain's interests in the Americas.

[4] Manning 1905, p. 459; in a footnote p. 462, Manning mentions documents in the Archivo Histórico Nacional, Madrid, dated 1790 to 1797, complaining at "the injustice of England in demanding such extravagant terms".

[5] Asserted or implied in e.g. Enrique Ferrer Vieyra, *Las Islas Malvinas y el Derecho Internacional* ["The Malvinas Islands and International Law"], Buenos Aires 1984, pp. 65, 137; Freedman 2005/2007, vol. I, p. 6; Juan José Cresto, *Historia de las Islas Malvinas...* ["History of the Malvinas Islands..."], Buenos Aires 2011, p. 209, and in [Anon.], *Malvinas en la historia: Una perspectiva suramericana*, Lanús, Buenos Aires, 2011, p. 101.

[6] Julius Goebel, *The Struggle for the Falkland Islands: A study in legal and diplomatic history*, New Haven (Connecticut) 1927 (with 14 illustrations); the 2nd ed., Port Washington (N.Y.) 1971, is a facsimile reprint of the 1927 ed. with all illustrations; the 3rd ed., New Haven and London 1982, is also a facsimile reprint of the 1927 ed., but text only, no illustrations, with a preface (dated May 1982) and an introduction (dated July 1968) by Professor J. C. J. Metford. For Goebel see section 9.5.

[7] Article 6 reads (translation here by Graham Pascoe): "Art 6: It is further agreed with respect to the Eastern and Western Coasts of South America, and to the Islands adjacent, that the respective Subjects shall in future form no Establishment on the Parts of those Coasts situated to the South of the Parts of the same Coasts and of the Islands adjacent already occupied by Spain. Provided that the said respective Subjects shall retain the Liberty to land on the Coasts and Islands so situated for the Purposes of their Fishery, and of building Huts there and other temporary works serving only for those Purposes". Original French text in PRO 93-99-4A, fol. 3 *recto-verso*. "Huts" in the Falklands were always of stone of course, so they were never "temporary" – the remains of several of them still can still be seen.

Another of Goebel's distortions is that he says (p. 429): "There was a definite pledge by both parties not to establish new colonies in the South Pacific and South Atlantic" – in fact the Convention does not prohibit colonies throughout the South Pacific or South Atlantic, but only to the south of places already occupied by Spain. Goebel asserts (p. 431) that Britain agreed "not to establish colonies to the south of regions *already occupied* by the Spanish" [Goebel's italics], but again that is not what the text says – it does not refer to "regions" but only to "the Parts of these same Coasts" (« les Parties de ces mêmes Côtes ») already occupied by Spain – the Spanish settlements only counted in themselves, not as commanding a whole region.

The truth is that the Nootka Sound Convention did not *reduce* Britain's rights in the Americas; it greatly *extended* them at the expense of Spain – that was why the British welcomed it and the Spaniards condemned it. As William Manning explained in 1905:[1]

The immediate result for England was that she obtained free access to an extended coast... It was the first express renunciation of Spain's ancient claim to exclusive sovereignty over the American shores of the Pacific Ocean and the South Seas. It marks the beginning of the collapse of the Spanish colonial system.

The Swiss historian Jörg Fisch agrees with Manning; he heads his section on the Convention "The Opening of the South Sea 1790", and shows that the rights given to British subjects were extensive with only minor limitations.[2] Articles 3 and 6 permitted them to practise "fishery" (mainly the killing of seals, but also of fish and whales, plus activities on land such as constructing stone storehouses, forges, shelters, etc., and hunting birds for food) on all the coasts of Spanish South America, including the Falklands of course, and also allowed them to form "Establishments" (which could include permanent settlements) on the parts of those coasts "not already occupied" by Spain. Article 4 prohibited British subjects from landing, "fishing" and forming "Establishments" in places less than 10 leagues (30 miles or 50 kilometres) from the parts of the coasts "already occupied" by Spain; most of the Falklands is more than 50 kilometres from the only Spanish settlement, Puerto Soledad (Port Louis), so this ended Spanish opposition to British activities in the islands except in the north-eastern part. Jörg Fisch says the purpose of Article 6 was to confirm a "mutual abandonment of attempts to gain control over the Strait of Magellan and Cape Horn" – that was why it permitted Britain to set up "Establishments" everywhere except south of the parts of the coasts and islands already occupied by Spain. It thus opened up all of the Falklands north of the latitude of Puerto Soledad to British settlement, including a large area around Port Egmont and West Point Island, where British ships had been active for a quarter of a century.

There was also a secret article, which we mentioned in *Getting it right* (p. 8); it permitted Britain to make an "Establishment" south of places occupied by Spain, if "the Subjects of any other Power" did so; it did not require any further Spanish consent, so this became part of Britain's general rights in the Falklands accepted by Spain. As soon as Louis Vernet purported to sell land to the south of Port Louis in 1831 (section 6.8), the secret article came into force and authorised Britain to set up an establishment in the Falklands at any time after 1831. Kohen and Rodriguez assert (p. 46) that since Argentina had "succeeded to Spain's rights, there was no settlement established by 'subjects of other powers', but only a continuation of Spain's rights", but if Argentina were a successor state, as Kohen and Rodriguez claim, it inherited Spain's obligations as well as rights, so Vernet's sale of land for settlement south of Port Louis violated Britain's rights under Article 6 of the Convention. Or, if Argentina was not a successor state to Spain, Vernet was a "subject of another power" and by selling land to the south of Port Louis he activated the secret article in the Convention.

The Nootka Sound Convention presupposed that the most southerly Spanish settlement on any coast would be permanent. But Port Louis ceased to exist as a Spanish outpost in 1811, when its garrison and prisoners were withdrawn and it became uninhabited. From that moment Spain ceased to be capable of enforcing any regulations in the islands. That strengthened Britain's claim to sovereignty – Spain had withdrawn, but British sealing vessels were still active.

---

[1] Manning 1905, pp. 461-462.
[2] Fisch 1983, pp. 120-123.

Kohen and Rodríguez follow Goebel in wrongly asserting that the Convention banned Britain from the Falklands. They quote (p. 43) his statement that "*The terms of the sixth article by inference forbade any landing at the Falklands as they were a place already occupied by Spain*" (Goebel p. 431; his italics); they too quote the whole of Article 6, and like Goebel they misrepresent it: they say (p. 44) that it "not only reaffirms the prohibition of navigation and fishing, but also the prohibition of establishing settlements on the coasts and islands already occupied by Spain" – by saying "the coasts" they omit the vital restriction to "*parts* of the same coasts", and though they also quote (p. 43) Article 4, with its permission to Britain to navigate and "fish" everywhere except within 10 leagues of parts of the coasts already occupied by Spain, they fail to draw the correct conclusion: that the coast consisted of occupied and unoccupied parts, and Britain had extensive freedom to operate in the unoccupied parts.

They mention (pp. 46-48) three British authors who come to the same conclusion as Goebel: Gaston de Bernhardt and John Field (officials at the British Foreign Office) and Professor Malcolm Deas (a British historian specialising in Latin America).[1] Kohen and Rodríguez quote from all three, without noting that none of them explains why the Convention was welcomed in Britain but condemned in Spain, and that none of them notes that it changed the behaviour of the Spaniards in the islands (section 2.7). Gaston de Bernhardt's memorandum on the Falklands is an extremely superficial piece of work; he deals only with the *correspondence* connected with the islands, so his account jumps from 1849 to 1884, as he found no official correspondence between Britain and Argentina in those years. In fact those years were a vital period in the history of the Falklands, but de Bernhardt did not consider any of the many other aspects which are vital to an understanding of the case. He does not mention the Convention of Peace (a watershed in the Falklands dispute which cancelled what preceded it, see section 7.11), nor the cessation of the annual protests in the Messages to the Buenos Aires Legislature after 1849, nor statements by Argentine leaders that confirmed the dropping of Argentina's Falklands claim, nor foreign recognition of British sovereignty in the islands. In 1928 Field slavishly repeated – largely *verbatim* and without comment – most of what de Bernhardt had written in 1910, so he provides no additional support. De Bernhardt's shoddy work, repeated by Field, seriously misled the Foreign Office as to the real legal situation of the Falklands, and thus contributed to the weakness of Britain's negotiating stance in the 1960s and 70s. And Deas added nothing of significance to what the other two had written; all those three writers' accounts of the islands' legal situation are defective.

As Manning, Fisch and Rodger all confirm, the Nootka Sound Convention was in fact a great triumph for Britain. Before 1790, Spain had asserted total "blanket" sovereignty over all of Spanish South America whether there was any local Spanish presence or not – Spain had viewed its territories in the Americas as a single unit, the whole of which counted as occupied by Spain although vast areas had no physical Spanish presence, and Spain prohibited all other countries from trading with Spanish possessions. But from 1790 Spain was forced for the first time to accept that there was a difference between territories physically occupied and territories not occupied – as Jörg Fisch puts it (his pp. 122-123), from then on Spain accepted that Spanish South America consisted of "a patchwork of occupied and unoccupied parts".

The fundamental change brought about by the Convention was that it forced Spain to accept *measured dimensions* to the extent of her sovereignty. Spain now accepted that as against Britain (though not other countries), Spanish rights in the Falklands were divided into what we here call

---

[1] Those sources are: **(1)** Gaston de Bernhardt, "Memorandum respecting the Falkland Islands", 7 December 1910, doc. 9755 in the *Foreign Office Confidential Print* (*FOCP*), London 1910; reprinted as doc. 259 in *British Documents on Foreign Affairs* (*BDFA*), ed. George Philip, Part I, vol. 1, Bethesda (Maryland, USA) 1991, pp. 358-406; Spanish translation in Enrique Ferrer Vieyra, *Segunda Cronología Legal Anotada sobre las Islas Malvinas (Falkland Islands)* ["Second Annotated Legal Chronology on the Islas Malvinas (Falkland Islands)"], Córdoba (Argentina) 1993, pp. 377-411; **(2)** John W. Field, *Memorandum respecting the Falkland Islands and Dependencies*, 29 February, 1928, in PRO FO 371-12735, fol. 157ff; another copy in PRO FO 371-24168, fol. 268ff (both paginated pp. 1-40); Spanish translation in Ferrer Vieyra 1993, pp. 429-480, and **(3)** Malcolm Deas, "Notes on the issue of Falkland Islands sovereignty for House of Commons, Committee on Foreign Affairs", in House of Commons, Foreign Affairs Committee, Minutes of Evidence, 17/1/83, pp. 127-137; Spanish translation in Ferrer Vieyra 1993, pp. 596-601.

three "zones":

Zone (1), within a circle of 10 leagues radius (30 miles or 50 kilometres) around the actual Spanish presence at Puerto Soledad (around 20% of the islands' land area): exclusive Spanish rights; Britain had no right of exploitation or settlement;

Zone (2), everywhere in the islands outside zone 1 (around 80% of the islands' land area): Britain had the right of exploitation ("fishing", i.e. mainly sealing);

Zone (3), everywhere that was in zone 2 and was also north of the latitude of Puerto Soledad (around 20% of the islands' land area): Britain had the right of settlement as well as "fishing".

In short, from then on the Falklands were no longer a single unit – Spain's rights in one part of the islands did not confer rights in the rest, so Britain was entitled to treat parts of the islands (and of course vast areas of the mainland coasts of South America) as *res nullius* for both exploitation and colonisation. Goebel's statement that the Falklands *"were a place already occupied by Spain"* is false because after 1790 they no longer counted as a single place; they had been divided up by the Nootka Sound Convention into three zones with different distributions of Spanish and British rights. So Goebel is also wrong in saying (p. 466): "The Spanish right to the Falklands became absolute at this moment, if, indeed, it had not been before." In fact, far from banning Britain from the Falklands, the Convention expressly gave Britain the right to exploit about 80% of the islands' land area (our zone 2), and also to establish settlements in about 20% of the land area (zone 3).

So Kohen and Rodríguez are wrong in stating (pp. 100 and 101) that there were no *terrae nullius* ["no man's lands"] in Latin America after the South American countries began to achieve independence[1] – from 1790 there were territories that Britain (though not other countries) could treat as *terrae nullius*. What counted was actual local occupation of specific areas, not a mere claim.

Thus after 1790 Spain no longer claimed exclusive sovereignty in the Falklands, while Britain's rights continued, tacitly accepted by Spain under the Anglo-Spanish agreement of 1771 (see section 2.3), in which both countries had reserved their positions, and now strengthened by the Nootka Sound Convention. Kohen and Rodríguez correctly say (p. 117) that "exclusivity" is one of the elements that characterise territorial sovereignty, but they fail to point out that Spain lost that exclusivity, first by tacitly tolerating Britain's claim in 1771 and then from 1790 onwards by limiting her own rights.

The change was reflected in Spain's behaviour in the islands – from 1790 onwards the Spanish commandants were under orders to permit activity by British citizens, but not by those of other nationalities (section 2.7). Thus by the 1820s, when Argentina first became involved in the Falklands, Britain already possessed extensive and long-standing prior rights in the islands. Argentina could not inherit more rights than Spain had possessed, so it was not possible for Argentina to inherit total unrestricted sovereignty over the islands without Britain's consent.

1.8 Conclusion

To sum up: Kohen and Rodríguez are wrong in ascribing the discovery of the Falklands to Amerigo Vespucci in 1502 and the making of the original for Thevet's map to Andrés de San Martín on Magellan's expedition in 1520. In fact the islands were probably discovered at the latest around 1518-19 by an unrecorded Portuguese expedition that preceded Magellan.

They are also wrong in denying that Sir Richard Hawkins saw the Falklands in 1594 – his account makes it clear beyond doubt that he sailed past the islands.

They err in maintaining that the treaties of Madrid of 1670 and Utrecht of 1713 show that Britain accepted Spain's sovereignty in the Falklands, and they misinterpret the Nootka Sound Convention of 1790, which in fact greatly extended Britain's rights in the islands and deprived Spain of the unrestricted 100% sovereignty she claimed.

---

[1] Kohen and Rodríguez may be following Arnaud 2000, p. 241; he quotes César Díaz Cisneros, who says in "La soberanía de la República Argentina en las Malvinas ante el Derecho Internacional", in *Soberanía argentina en el Archipiélago de las Malvinas y en la Antártida*, La Plata 1951, p. 385, that there is "a principle or rule derived from the Bull of 1493 and the Treaty of Tordesillas: in America there was no territory that was *res nullius*, nor could the existence of it be imagined". That is incorrect.

CHAPTER TWO: the first inhabitants; the First Falklands Crisis, 1767-1771

In their chapter 2 (pp. 49-97), Kohen and Rodríguez consider three aspects of Falklands history: (1) the first settlements; (2) the Anglo-Spanish agreement of 1771; and (3) the Spanish withdrawal in 1811. We shall now briefly examine those aspects and correct their assertions.

2.1 The first inhabitants, 1764

The first settlement in the Falkland Islands was founded by a young French aristocrat, Louis-Antoine de Bougainville (1729-1811), who had served with distinction in the Seven Years' War (1756-63), in which France had lost her last Canadian territories to Britain. Bougainville had been an eyewitness of the fall of Quebec to the British in 1759 and was keen to make up for France's losses. He resolved to found a French colony in the Malouine Islands,[1] and was supported by Louis XV's mistress Madame de Pompadour and the influential duc de Choiseul.[2] He had two ships built in Saint-Malo: the frigate *Aigle* and the corvette *le Sphinx*, and recruited two families of French-Canadians as inhabitants; 17 crewmen from the ships also agreed to live in the islands.

They set sail on 8 September 1763,[3] the first expedition in history that set out to go to the Falkland Islands – all previous ones had merely come across them on the way to somewhere else. On 3 February 1764 they sailed into what is now Berkeley Sound[4] in north-eastern East Falkland, and during the next few weeks, at a place Bougainville named « Port Louis », beside a rounded inlet later known in English as the "basin" off the north shore of the Sound, they constructed the first buildings in the islands, including a cross-shaped stone house for the governor with an octagonal central room (chapter 5, figs. 5.4b, 5.4c). He took possession of the islands for France, and sailed on 8 April, leaving a French community of 28 people in their new home, including four women and three small children. Some of them were from « Acadie » (Nova Scotia, Canada), which France had lost to Britain. He left cattle and horses on East Falkland, which thrived and ran wild; the beef and hides from the cattle later became a major economic resource, though no wild cattle now remain.

2.2 The First Falklands Crisis, 1767-71: Part I (Spain versus France)

Bougainville's activities started what we call the First Falklands Crisis, the first of three major international crises over the islands – the others were the Second Falklands Crisis, 1831-3 (chapter 6) and the Third Falklands Crisis, 1982 (the Falklands War, section 10.24). The First Falklands Crisis had three episodes, which we call Part I (Spain versus France); Part II (Spain versus Britain); and Part III (Britain versus France, a brief encounter at Port Louis in December 1766).

Bougainville ran up against an insurmountable problem: Spain operated a policy of *mare clausum* ["closed sea"], attempting to completely exclude all other countries from trading with the Spanish South American empire. That policy lasted until the Nootka Sound Convention forced Spain to back down in 1790 (section 1.7). By contrast, Britain maintained a policy of *mare apertum* ["open sea"], in which the seas and trade were open to all. The two policies were mutually incompatible, so there was bound to be a clash.

On 21 June 1764, four days before Bougainville arrived back in France, a British expedition set sail on a round-the-world voyage that was to include a visit to the Falklands. It was commanded by Captain the Honourable John Byron (1723-86), grandfather of the sixth Lord Byron, the poet (1788-1824), and comprised the 24-gun *Dolphin* and the 16-gun *Tamar*. The purpose of the voyage was first, to survey the (non-existent) Pepys Island (section 1.6) and "His Majesty's Islands called

---

[1] The history of Bougainville's Falklands venture is recounted in very great detail in Jean-Étienne Martin-Allanic, *Bougainville navigateur et les découvertes de son temps* ["Bougainville as navigator and the discoveries of his time"], 2 vols., Paris 1964. It is by far the most detailed published work on any aspect of the history of the Falklands, but it has until recently been sadly disregarded. Pages 1-814 are in vol. I, 815-1600 in vol. II, so volume numbers are superfluous. Pages 1-600 and 920-1250 are mainly about the Falklands; the rest is about Bougainville's circumnavigation and his later life. Kohen and Rodríguez list it in their bibliography and mention it in two brief footnotes, but otherwise ignore it.
[2] Etienne-François, comte de Stainville, duc [Duke] de Choiseul (1719-85), Secretary of State for the Marine and Colonies 13 October 1761 to 10 April 1766, foreign minister 10 April 1766 to 24 December 1770.
[3] Antoine-Joseph Pernetty, *Histoire d'un Voyage aux Isles Malouines...*, Paris 1770, vol. I, p. 77; Martin-Allanic 1964, p. 118. Kohen and Rodríguez (p. 50) wrongly give 15 September for the date of Bougainville's setting sail.
[4] Pronounced in the Falklands "Barkly", not "Burkly" (Jane Cameron, pers. comm.).

Falkland's Islands", then to explore the Atlantic eastwards from the Falklands, and finally to promote British trade, especially in the Pacific; in particular it was to search for a "north-west passage" from the Pacific to the North Atlantic.[1] All that was bound to annoy Spain, so the British government tried to prevent news of the expedition from leaking out and forcing its abandonment, as had happened in 1750 – they hoped to present Spain with a *fait accompli* that would enable Britain to retain a foothold in the South Atlantic. So the expedition was kept secret, and the Admiralty confiscated all logbooks – there are 17 logs from the voyage in the Public Record Office (PRO) in London.[2] Kohen and Rodríguez (pp. 58-59) imply that the secrecy indicated that Britain recognised that the islands were under Spanish sovereignty, but the truth is the opposite: the expedition was undertaken in direct opposition to Spanish claims to possess the islands.

Bougainville arrived back in France on 25 June 1764, and three days later reported to Louis XV, recommending that Spain be given an assurance that the new colony represented no threat to her commerce. Though France and Spain were allied under the Bourbon "Family Compact" of 15 August 1761, they were rivals in various areas including the Americas. For the delicate task of approaching Spain Choiseul chose Augustin de Béliardi, who was regarded as an expert on all things Spanish. Béliardi said the Spaniards did not regard the French as brothers or even friends – they hated all foreigners, especially the French, and he thought it would prove impossible to get Spain to accept a French presence in the islands.[3]

His hard-nosed prediction was spot-on – the Spaniards were already moving to put an end to the venture. On 3 September 1764 the marqués de Grimaldi (1720?-1789), foreign minister to Carlos III, wrote to the Spanish ambassador to France, the conde [Count] de Fuentes, saying that if France persisted, Spain had only to remind the French king that in 1750 Britain had agreed to drop a plan to survey and perhaps occupy the islands (and thus infringe Spain's claimed rights), after protests from Spain following French warnings. Having warned Spain that Britain was about to infringe Spain's rights, Spain's ally France could hardly set out to infringe them in the same way. That proved to be the clinching argument that put an end to the French venture in the Falklands.

Unaware of the threat to his enterprise, Bougainville set sail on 6 October 1764 for his second visit to the Malouine Islands in the *Aigle*, along with 116 people including 53 settlers. But while he was away, Choiseul agreed to hand the islands over to Spain. He had lost his temper in a meeting on 13 December with the Spanish chargé d'affaires, Fernando de Magallón. Magallón had asked about the Malouine Islands, and Choiseul had shouted at him, saying the islands were French, that their name proved it, since it was derived from Saint-Malo, and that France could use them as a base to oppose the English. Magallón calmly repeated Spain's strongest argument: that in 1750 Britain had dropped a plan to send two frigates to the islands when Spain protested after French warnings. The next day, ashamed by his outburst, Choiseul went to the Spanish embassy to make amends. He said that the main aim of both France and Spain was to prevent the English from occupying the islands; if Spain would not allow France to occupy them, he was prepared to withdraw the people Bougainville had left there, and Spain should form a strong establishment to forestall the English.

That was it. He had made an offer he could not go back on, and Spain was not going to let him forget it. From that moment, the Malouine Islands were lost to France.

In January 1765 John Byron reached the Falklands, where at Saunders Island, north of West Falkland, he found an excellent anchorage and named it Port Egmont after the Earl of Egmont, First Lord of the Admiralty. On 21 January 1765 he took possession of the islands for Britain.[4] He introduced many place-names including Port Egmont, Berkeley Sound, Cape Tamar, the Eddystone Rock, Cape Dolphin and Cape Carysfort, which are still used today, over a quarter of a millennium later. However, he left no British presence and sailed on 27 January. And he disobeyed his instructions – he neither explored the South Atlantic nor searched for a north-west passage, but set

---

[1] Byron's secret orders are printed in full in Robert E. Gallagher (ed.), *Byron's Journal of his Circumnavigation 1764-1766*, London 1964.

[2] The 17 logs are in the PRO, bound (with others) in 5 vols., with signatures Adm 51 and Adm 55.

[3] Martin-Allanic 1964, pp. 164-173.

[4] The date of 21 January is confirmed by the many logs of the expedition; the incorrect date of 23 January on a plaque erected at Port Egmont itself in the 1990s is derived from a garbled pirated log, the only one to be published.

off across the Pacific, apparently hoping to find the fabulously rich Isles of Solomon. In the event he missed all major islands including Australia and Tahiti, and returned to Britain in May 1766 after the fastest circumnavigation up to that time. One of the crewmen of the *Dolphin*, Erasmus Gower, visited Port Egmont again in 1770, and witnessed a serious international incident (section 2.3).

Bougainville reached Port Louis on 5 January 1765, and after delivering supplies and settlers to the settlement, he sailed again on 27 April, leaving 75 people at the colony. He wrote in his journal "I leave 3 women pregnant. The Country is good for Propagation…".[1] He felt optimistic at the progress of his colony, but it was all in vain – Béliardi was about to leave for Madrid to hand the islands to Spain. Back in France, Bougainville was received by Choiseul on 25 August 1765 and recounted his expedition. Then Choiseul told him. The settlement in the Malouine Islands was to be handed over to Spain. Kohen and Rodríguez imply (p. 52) that Bougainville merely accepted without comment the instruction by Choiseul to go to Madrid to arrange the handover, but that is wide of the mark – Bougainville was stunned, and at once began to fight back. On 26 August he wrote a memorandum to Choiseul, in which he said:[2]

Spain has no right to advance any pretensions to that establishment. It is an accepted principle that new territories belong to their first occupant… Even accepting that the whole of South America belongs to Spain, what rights can she have to an island situated 80 leagues from the extremity of that continent…?

On 5 September he gave Choiseul another memorandum saying he regarded "the cession of those islands to Spain" as highly damaging to the interests of France – his use of the word "cession" shows he saw the islands as rightfully French, not Spanish. Nevertheless, he said that if the islands were to be ceded to Spain, "for reasons which it is not the province of an individual to discuss", there should be some recompense from Spain: either another suitable territory, or advantages for French trade. In the event there was neither.

Meanwhile, on 26 September 1765 the British Admiralty ordered Captain John McBride to sail to the Falklands and form a British settlement. He set off on 8 October with the frigate *Jason*, the sloop *Carcass* and the storeship *Experiment*, and reached Port Egmont on 8 January 1766.

2.3 The First Falklands Crisis, 1767-71: end of Part I; Parts II and III; the Anglo-Spanish agreement, 22 January 1771

On 21 October 1766 the Spanish government began Part II of the First Falklands Crisis by starting a dispute over the islands with Britain: Prince Masserano, the Spanish ambassador in London, protested sharply at the British expeditions to the islands, declaring that the king of Great Britain had "aimed a mortal blow" at the rights of the king of Spain and at his crown.[3] That dispute took a long time to mature, but it brought Spain and Britain to the brink of war.

McBride spent almost a year in the islands before looking for the French settlement at Port Louis, then he looked for a few days, found it on 4 December 1766, and ordered the French to leave – the British government held the islands to be British, believing they had been discovered by John Davis in 1592. They were wrong in that, but at the time neither France nor Spain knew any better. That was the brief Part III of the First Falklands Crisis; it had no repercussions since McBride had no orders to actually expel the French, and he dropped a bombshell which ended any resistance they might have offered – he told them that France had agreed to withdraw from the islands in favour of Spain. He also told them where Port Egmont was – the French had never found it, and the Spaniards did not find it till Mario Plata in the *San Felipe* found it on 17 December 1769 (below).[4]

McBride sailed for Britain on 19 January 1767, leaving a British garrison of about 90 men in the islands. He thus consolidated the claim raised by Byron in 1765, and he left his mark on the Falklands in several ways: he had stone buildings including houses, a wharf, walled gardens and storehouses built at Port Egmont, the ruins of which can still be seen; he landed pigs on several

---

[1] Details from the partial copy of Bougainville's journal of the voyage, in the Bibliothèque Nationale, Paris, BN 9407, fols. 47 *verso* – 48 *recto*; account here mainly from Martin-Allanic 1964, pp. 215, 238-239, 243-273, 421.
[2] Martin-Allanic 1964, p. 248.
[3] Martin-Allanic 1964, pp. 922-925.
[4] Martin-Allanic 1964, pp. 519, 1015.

islands, which multiplied and became an important source of food for later visitors (though no wild pigs now remain); and he made the best maps of the islands up to that time. He used Byron's place-names and also introduced many names which are still used, including the Jason Islands and Carcass Island (after his two ships), Cape Percival, Cape Orford, Cape Meredith and Fox Bay. In 1773 John Hawkesworth published a 1-sheet chart based on McBride's maps, which was used by the Spaniards as well as the British.[1]

Kohen and Rodríguez make great play (p. 53-60) of the fact that the British establishment at Port Egmont was set up secretly – it certainly was, but their implication is that Britain accepted that the islands were under Spanish sovereignty. In fact the reverse was true; by setting up an establishment in the South Atlantic, Britain demonstrated that it did *not* accept that Spain (or France) had exclusive rights in the area – the secrecy was in order to set up a *fait accompli* that Spain would have to accept. Britain was of course well aware that Spain *claimed* the whole of southern South America and the seas around it, but for Britain a mere claim without any physical possession was weaker than the British claim by discovery. So the British government saw itself as fully justified in occupying the islands and in ordering the French and Spaniards to leave. Neither then nor later did Britain ever recognise Spanish sovereignty.

Spain, with its rigid "exclusionist" policy, would not permit any activity by any other power within what it regarded as exclusively Spanish territory, and so, to Bougainville's great sorrow, the French settlement was handed over to Spain in April 1767 – on 1 April the French flag flew for the last time over Port Louis; it was hauled down at sunset and on 2 April the Spanish flag was raised,[2] thus ending Part I of the First Falklands Crisis.

Kohen and Rodríguez assert several times (pp. 49, 52, 54, 56, 58) that France recognised Spain's sovereignty under the principle of *uti possidetis* (for which see chapter 3), but that is going too far. They quote Bougainville's formal statement of 4 October 1766 acknowledging receipt of the sum of 618,108 *livres*, 13 *sous* and 11 *deniers*, in the French currency of the day, the *livre tournois*, paid to him by Spain in compensation for his private expenses,[3] and accepting that the French establishment was "illegitimate" and that the islands belonged to the Spanish king, but they do not mention that Bougainville also made it clear that he was acting in submission to the orders of the king of France (implying that he would not have done so if he had had the choice). He also emphasised that the handover to Spain was voluntary; Kohen and Rodríguez draw attention to that statement (p. 55), but they fail to realise its importance. The fact that Louis XV and Bougainville were making a *voluntary* handover of their assets in the islands (such as cannons and ships) implies that they did not see the handover as compulsory. They were making a goodwill gesture to Spain, a political gesture, not a gesture imposed by law. In all the documentation of the handover there was no mention of any cession of the islands themselves to Spain, which allowed both parties to maintain their opposing views in private. Bougainville believed to the end of his life that the islands were – and remained – rightfully French, since France had occupied them first and Spain had not

---

[1] McBride's original survey maps made in 1766 are in the United Kingdom Hydrographic Office (UKHO) in Taunton, shelf 34f, numbered C75, C77, C78, C79 34f, C81 34f and C82; the 1-sheet chart is in John Hawkesworth, *Account of the Voyages...*, London 1773, vol. I, opp. p. 41. The Spanish Malaspina expedition of 1789-94, which visited the Falklands in 1789 and 1794, used Hawkesworth's chart made from McBride's maps – Malaspina says "In general... we found captain McBride's chart very accurate", while a chart he had obtained in Montevideo was "most inaccurate" (Andrew David *et al.*, eds., *The Malaspina Expedition 1789-1794*, vol. I, London 2001, p. 98).

[2] Martin-Allanic 1964, pp. 534-535. Exactly 215 years later to the day, on 2 April 1982, the flag of another Spanish-speaking country was hoisted in the islands.

[3] Kohen and Rodríguez 2015, p. 54; full text in Martin-Allanic 1964, pp. 377-378. The French currency at the time, the *livre tournois*, was divided into 20 *sous* each of 12 *deniers*, like the pound sterling of 20 shillings each of 12 pence (in Latin *solidi* and *denarii*) but at this period the *livre* was worth only about 10d or 11d sterling (less than a shilling, or about 22-24 *livres* to the pound). So Bougainville received about £27,000 in money of the day. Some authors (though not Kohen and Rodríguez) assert wrongly that Spain purchased the islands from France, e.g. J.C.J. Metford, "Falklands or Malvinas? The Background to the Dispute" (introduction, dated July 1968, to the 3rd ed. of Goebel 1927, New Haven and London 1982, p. xv); Douglas Kinney, *National Interest/National Honor...*, New York 1989, p. 298; Sir Lawrence Freedman, *The Official History of the Falklands Campaign*, Abingdon 2005/2007, vol. I, p. 4; Rodolfo H. Terragno, *Historia y Futuro de las Malvinas*, Buenos Aires 2006, pp. 300-304 and 307-308; and Jamie Trinidad, *Self-Determination in Disputed Colonial Territories*, Cambridge 2018, p. 136.

purchased them, while Spain continued to believe that they had always been Spanish and had never been legally possessed by France in the first place.

It is thus absurd to maintain, as do Manuel Pedro Peña and Juan Angél Peña in two recent works,[1] that Spain inherited France's title to the islands. They maintain that the title of France, as the first occupier, was "perfect", and that it was inherited by Spain when Spain took the islands over in 1767, including France's "precedence of possession", thus "backdating" Spain's title to 1764.[2] Much the same is briefly asserted by Kohen and Rodríguez, who say (on their p. 21) that Argentina's claim to the islands is based, among other things, on "Spain's continuation of France's right of first occupant (1764)", and they then proceed to extend that mere "continuation" of Spain's rights to "the right of first occupancy" (their p. 25). However, that is an untenable assertion: Spain always denied that France had possessed any title at all, so Peña and Peña, and Kohen and Rodríguez, are retrospectively granting to Spain something whose existence Spain energetically denied. Spain regarded the French as trespassers on Spanish territory; one cannot obtain a title to one's own territory from a trespasser.

After the takeover of the French settlement by Spain there remained two establishments in the Falklands: British at Port Egmont and Spanish at Port Louis. In August 1767 Port Louis was christened Puerto Soledad or "Port Solitude" by Francisco Bucareli y Ursúa, Governor of Buenos Aires, when Bougainville dined with him and described the islands.[3] Spain knew about the British presence in the islands, and on 25 February 1768, in accordance with Spain's exclusionist policy, King Carlos III signed an order commanding Governor Bucareli and Felipe Ruiz Puente, the first Spanish governor of the islands, to find the British establishment and expel it by force.

We shall refer to that order as "the Expulsion Order". Neither Carlos III nor any of his ministers seem to have had the slightest qualms about issuing it, and were horrified when the hapless Bucareli carried it out – it brought Spain and Britain to the brink of war and committed Spain to telling a direct lie (that there had been no such order and Bucareli had been exceeding his instructions). At Puerto Soledad Ruiz Puente received the Expulsion Order around 20 September 1768, but Spanish dilatoriness meant that he took over a year to take any action. Meanwhile, on 15 October 1768, a squadron of four frigates commanded by Captain Juan Ignacio de Madariaga left Cadiz to put the Expulsion Order into effect. They arrived in Montevideo on 3 January 1769, and nine months later Bucareli ordered Madariaga to prepare an expedition to expel the British from the Maluinas. Madariaga put Fernando de Rubalcava in command of a small squadron consisting of a frigate and two small ships, and he set off in January 1770 to fulfil the Expulsion Order.[4]

In the Falklands the British and Spaniards had already found each other. On 28 November 1769 the new British commander at Port Egmont, Captain Anthony Hunt, in Byron's former ship *Tamar*, encountered the schooner *San Felipe* (formerly Bougainville's *La Croisade*), commanded by Ángel de Santos, who had been sent by Governor Ruiz Puente to look for the British. Hunt and Santos had a tense meeting aboard the *Tamar*, in what is now White Rock Bay at the north end of West Falkland. Santos was irritated that the English captain did not introduce himself, but perhaps he failed to recognise a monosyllabic "Hunt" as an introduction – to Spanish ears "Hunt" sounds like a mere grunt or cough. Each of them firmly informed the other that the islands belonged to his respective king;[5] Santos then reported back to Ruiz Puente, who sent him back under the command of Lieutenant Mario Plata, who carried letters for Hunt. Plata and Hunt duly exchanged letters, each maintaining that the islands belonged to his king, then they parted again, and Plata set off to look

---

[1] Manuel Pedro Peña and Juan Angél Peña, *Falklands or Malvinas: Myths & Facts*, Sevilla 2018, an adapted English version of Manuel P[edro] Peña, *Malvinas: Mito & Realidad: Desde los primeros avistamientos, hasta la consolidación de los derechos* ["Malvinas: Myth & Reality; From the first sightings, to the consolidation of rights"], Buenos Aires April 2016.
[2] Peña and Peña (Spanish) 2016, pp. 376-378; (English) 2018, pp. 302-303.
[3] Martin-Allanic 1964, pp. 574-576; the original name was usually "Puerto Soledad", i.e. without "de la", and the name was not changed in April 1767 as Kohen and Rodríguez assert (p. 57) but in August. It is sometimes stated that the place was named after an image of the Virgin Mary in the chapel there, but it was the other way round – the image was taken there in January 1768 and named "Nuestra Señora de la Soledad" after the place.
[4] Martin-Allanic 1964, pp. 1004, 1019-1021.
[5] Martin-Allanic 1964, p. 1011.

for Port Egmont. And on 17 December he found it; Hunt was already back there, and invited Plata and Santos to spend the night aboard the *Tamar*. During dinner the Spanish and British again exchanged letters and protests, each ordering the others to leave the islands,[1] though the atmosphere was cordial – they were all simply seamen doing their duty, in a remote and inhospitable part of the world. The Spaniards returned to Puerto Soledad, and at Port Egmont the British waited.

On 25 January 1770 the 14-gun sloop *Swift* arrived, commanded by Captain George Farmer, who on 3 February took over the settlement at Port Egmont from Anthony Hunt, though Hunt remained in charge. On 18 February Rubalcava found Port Egmont, and there followed another tense exchange of letters, Hunt and Rubalcava each ordering the other to depart from the islands, which were the exclusive possession of his respective king. The Spanish ships then sailed back to Puerto Soledad, and Ruiz Puente sent two ships to Buenos Aires asking for orders – and reinforcements.[2] Hunt left on 7 March in the *Tamar* and sailed straight to Plymouth to inform the British government of what had happened in the Falklands.[3]

On the same day, Farmer left in the *Swift* to explore the Patagonian coast – and disaster struck. On 13 March the ship was wrecked at Port Desire (now Puerto Deseado); three of her crew of 91 were drowned, and the surviving 88 men were in desperate straits as they had saved almost nothing but their boats. The survivors' sufferings in the weeks after the shipwreck were vividly described in an eyewitness account by one of her crew, Lieutenant Erasmus Gower, published thirty years later in 1801, by which time he was Admiral Sir Erasmus Gower.[4] Farmer sent their largest boat with 7 men to get help from Port Egmont, which they reached safely after crossing some 370 miles (600 kilometres) of stormy ocean. There was nothing for it: the only remaining ship, the 14-gun sloop *Favourite*, sailed and rescued the castaways, and brought them back to Port Egmont on 16 April.

In Buenos Aires Bucareli now gave Madariaga a powerful squadron of five frigates, and at long last the expedition set sail on 11 May 1770 to expel the British. Bucareli sent despatches to the Spanish government stating that in obedience to the order of 25 February 1768 he had sent an expedition to the Maluinas to expel the British. His despatches arrived at Cadiz in August 1770, and gave the Spanish government a nasty shock.[5]

On 2 June 1770 Anthony Hunt arrived in Britain with the ominous news that Spanish ships had visited Port Egmont in December 1769 and February 1770 and had ordered the British to leave.[6]

Madariaga's squadron reached Port Egmont on 6 June,[7] and George Farmer knew his hour had come. He ordered the *Favourite* to be hauled close to the shore, and for four days there ensued an angry exchange of letters, each side ordering the other to leave the islands. The British were play-acting of course – they knew they were beaten. In fact the Spaniards said they had arrived in such strength in order to enable a capitulation with honour, and it was arranged that both sides would make a show of violence and fire without harming anyone, whereupon the British would capitulate to overwhelming force having saved their honour.[8] So, on 10 June 1770, Colonel Antonio Gutiérrez landed his infantry and artillery and drew them up ready to attack, while the British landed two six-pounder guns, ten swivel guns and small arms. Gower says the Spaniards fired several shots over the blockhouse and the British fired a few over the ships,[9] which satisfied honour on both sides, and the British then surrendered. The Spaniards and British treated each other with courtesy and all arrangements went smoothly. Several accounts state that the *Favourite*'s rudder was removed for 20

---

[1] Texts in Manuel Hidalgo Nieto, *La Cuestión de las Malvinas*, Madrid 1947, p. 624.
[2] Martin-Allanic 1964, pp. 1020-1022.
[3] Andrew David, "Anthony Hunt and his encounters with Spanish vessels when stationed in the Falklands, in HMS *Tamar*, 1768-70", in *FIJ* vol. 8 (4), 2005, p. 99 (but note that the prefix "HMS" for Royal Navy ships was not used before about 1789-90).
[4] Sir Erasmus Gower, *An account of the loss of His Majesty's sloop Swift...*, London 1803; extracts in *FIJ* 1970, pp. 24-29. He had been a crewman of Byron's *Dolphin* in 1765 (section 2.2).
[5] Martin-Allanic 1964, pp. 1022-1024.
[6] David 2005, pp. 99; 100, fn. 10. Note that on p. 99 David misdates Hunt's arrival in Plymouth as 3 May.
[7] Account here from Martin-Allanic 1964, pp. 1034-1038 and fns. 88 and 91, p. 1053; letters (in Spanish) in Hidalgo Nieto 1947, pp. 660-662, 665-671; summary in Goebel 1927, fns. 18 & 19, p. 276. Details corrected from Gower 1801.
[8] Terms of the agreement between Farmer, Maltby and Madariaga in Hidalgo Nieto 1947, pp. 667-671.
[9] Gower 1801, p. 42; Goebel states that the Spaniards fired at the blockhouse (1927, p. 277), but Gower disproves that.

days to prevent her from escaping, which was seen as an insult in Britain,[1] but Gower shows that the indignation over the "disgrace" was overdone – he says the rudder was in need of repair and would have been sent ashore anyway, and the repairs only took three or four days, after which the rudder was brought back to the *Favourite* by a Spanish launch.[2]

On 22 June Madariaga sailed back round to Puerto Soledad and on 30 June left for Spain; Gower says the British were told on 13 July that they could leave, and duly sailed on the 14th (or 15th; he gives two different dates).[3] The *Favourite* made all sail for England with the whole British garrison from Port Egmont aboard plus her own crew and the crew of the *Swift* – Gower says the ship was "crouded".

The die had been cast and Britain had been expelled from the Falklands, but the extreme slowness of communications caused a delayed-action effect: the sinister visit of Spanish ships to Port Egmont in February was unknown in Europe till Hunt arrived in June (at much the same time as the British were actually being expelled); the sending of Bucareli's expedition in May to dislodge the British was not known in Europe till August, and news of the actual expulsion of the British in June only became known when the *Favourite* arrived in September.

In August 1770 Bucareli's despatches arrived at Cadiz informing the Spanish government that he had sent an expedition to expel the British from the Maluinas. The letters caused immediate consternation in Madrid, as the realisation sank in that there was real danger of war. Aghast, foreign minister Grimaldi instructed Fuentes, the Spanish ambassador to France, to tell the French king and government that the conversations between the British and Spanish commanders at Port Egmont had not been as civil as at first supposed, which had led Bucareli to send an expedition. That was a lie, of course; Bucareli had sent his expedition as a direct response to the Expulsion Order from Madrid. In the end Grimaldi managed to avoid war, though at the expense of ceasing to deny Britain's rights in the Falklands, and also at the risk of Spain's being exposed as lying, since he stuck to the untrue story that Bucareli had reacted to provocation by Hunt instead of orders from Madrid. But the gamble paid off – the Expulsion Order remained secret, and Britain never found out the real reason why Bucareli sent Madariaga to Port Egmont.[4]

For five months, from August 1770 to January 1771, tense negotiations took place in London between Britain and Spain, partly with French mediation, while all three countries mobilised their fleets and there was a real danger of a major war over the Falklands. Spain fought long and hard to get Britain to accept three points: (a) that the insult had been mutual (that the insult to Britain, the expulsion, had been caused by Hunt's insulting behaviour towards Rubalcava at Port Egmont); (b) that the British establishment had been illegal since Spain had prior rights in the islands; and (c) that Britain would abandon the islands. In the end Spain was forced to give way on all three counts, and to accept that only the Spanish expedition had been at fault; to refrain from asserting prior Spanish rights; and to be satisfied with mere verbal assurances that Britain was not attached to the islands.

In a vain attempt to shut the stable door after the horse had bolted, the Spanish navy minister, Julián de Arriaga, sent a despatch to Bucareli on 25 August 1770, stressing that the orders of 25 February 1768 were not to be applied in the Maluinas but only to other places on the Pacific or Atlantic coasts of South America – the Maluinas were different from any other part of Spain's dominions.[5] That admission was naturally not passed on to Britain, but it was too late anyway.

In London on 5 September, the Spanish ambassador Prince Masserano told Lord Weymouth (Secretary of State for the Southern Department and hence responsible for relations with France and Spain)[6] that the governor of Buenos Aires, Bucareli, had taken it upon himself to expel the British

---

[1] Martin-Allanic 1964, p. 1037 and fn. 96, p. 1053; Philpott 1997 (see section 2.4), p. 9, quoting Captain Farmer to Philip Stephens, 22 September 1770, in PRO Adm 1/1900/20.
[2] Gower 1801, pp. 43-44.
[3] Gower 1801, pp. 44 ("14th") and 48 ("15th").
[4] Account in this and the following paragraphs mainly from Martin-Allanic 1964, p. 1003, 1007-1008, 1027-1028.
[5] Martin-Allanic 1964, pp. 1007-1008.
[6] Thomas Thynne, 3rd Viscount Weymouth (1734-1796), Viceroy of Ireland 1765, Secretary of State for the Northern Department 1768, for the Southern 1770; resigned December 1770; created 1st Marquess of Bath 1789 (Martin-Allanic 1964, p. 1009, fn. 15). Under the reform of British administration on 27 March 1782, the Northern and Southern

from Port Egmont by force, "entirely without express instructions from the king" – a straight lie. Weymouth said the use of force made it difficult to avoid unpleasant consequences, but the fact that Bucareli had acted without orders suggested a solution: was Masserano authorised to disavow Bucareli's action? Masserano was naturally unable to answer.

That same day, as Masserano was lying to Weymouth in London, Madariaga reached Cadiz bringing confirmation that the British had indeed been expelled from the Falkland Islands.[1]

In London on 9 September 1770 the British Cabinet decided on Britain's reaction, and Lord Weymouth informed Masserano that Britain expected satisfaction on two preliminary points:[2]

(1) The disavowal of the conduct of Governor Bucareli of Buenos Aires; and
(2) The reestablishment of the British at Port Egmont.

Once Spain had conceded those points, a discussion of principles could follow:

(3) Negotiations on the question of the rights claimed by each crown in the islands.

In fact the question of "rights" (i.e. sovereignty), which Spain was keen to settle, was never discussed at all and the final agreement left the matter open.

On 22 September 1770 the *Favourite* arrived in Britain bringing the news that the British had been expelled from Port Egmont.[3] Now the cat was well and truly out of the bag, and the talks in London took place against a background of steadily increasing tension and the mobilisation of the fleets of Britain, Spain and France. Various solutions were suggested by Spain and France, and put to Britain, and vice versa; the diplomatic despatches were carried back and forth between Madrid, Paris and London by government couriers galloping heroically on horseback, or bucketing along in fast postchaises, the length and breadth of western Europe as winter closed down. They generally took about 5-8 days between Madrid and Paris, and 4-5 days between Paris and London.

Point (2), the reestablishment of the British at Port Egmont, was quickly agreed, but point (1), the disavowal of Bucareli's conduct, proved more difficult, since Spain was keen not to admit having been in the wrong and wanted to put the blame on Bucareli. But in telling Britain that Bucareli had acted without orders, Spain ran up against a problem: the British government demanded that Spain disavow Bucareli's action. That would have been no problem if he had indeed been exceeding his instructions; he would have been punished and Spain would have declared that his actions had not been ordered by his government. But they *had* been ordered by his government; in claiming the opposite, the Spaniards were simply lying.

Point (3), the discussion of "rights", i.e. sovereignty, proved equally difficult. Spain wanted Britain to accept that Spain had "prior rights of sovereignty" over the islands, and on 3 December 1770 the duc de Choiseul, who played a leading role in the negotiations, presented a draft that made that point clear (we call it "C.3" for "Choiseul's point 3"):[4]

(C.3) [Full text:] The said declaration of Prince Masserano is an authentic proof of the regret of the King, his master, at a matter which might have troubled the good understanding between the two Crowns, but cannot prejudice the prior rights of His Catholic Majesty to the islands called Malouines and by the English Falkland, rights founded upon the antiquity and primacy of discovery, upon possession and upon treaties, which rights His Catholic Majesty declares that the reestablishment consented to by him, of the port called Egmont, cannot diminish.

Departments became the Foreign Office and the Home Office respectively, with new areas of responsibility.

[1] Martin-Allanic 1964, pp. 1037-1038. Goebel misdates Madariaga's arrival as 11 August (1927, p. 282); Martin-Allanic notes (fn. 34, p. 1009) that Goebel took the erroneous date from his source, Danvila y Collado, *Reinado de Carlos III*, 1829, p. 122.

[2] Martin-Allanic 1964, p. 1028. The numbers (1), (2), (C.3), etc., are our own (not in any of the sources).

[3] Martin-Allanic 1964, fn. 108, p. 1053.

[4] This is the full text of (C.3); original in Martin-Allanic 1964, p. 1115: « Ladite déclaration du prince de Masseran est une preuve authentique du chagrin du Roi, son maître, sur un fait qui aurait pu troubler la bonne intelligence entre les deux Couronnes, mais ne peut pas préjudicier aux droits antérieurs de S.M. Catholique, sur les îles appelées Malouines et par les Anglais Falkland, droits fondés sur l'ancienneté et la primauté de la découverte, sur possession et sur les traités, auxquels droits S.M. Catholique déclare que le rétablissement consenti de sa part, au port dit Egmont, ne pourra donner atteinte. » "His Catholic Majesty" was the king of Spain.

But Britain flatly refused to accept that wording, and the final definitive version of the agreement made no mention of any prior rights of Spain. Louis XV was keen above all to avoid war – the French treasury was empty, there was unrest in parts of the country, and Britain's position was hardening. So he decided on a political solution and dropped his support for Choiseul's hard line. On Christmas Eve 1770 he dismissed Choiseul and banished him to his country estate, opening the way for a watered-down version of the agreement, which was accepted by Carlos III.

The final version had two parts: a declaration by Spain and its acceptance by Britain (sometimes called the "counter-declaration"). Its wording was very different from all previous proposals. The Spanish declaration contained the following points (here condensed and with "F" for "Final"):

(F.1) The Spanish king disavows the expedition that expelled the British from Port Egmont;
(F.2) Port Egmont to be restored to the state it was in on 10 June 1770;
(F.3) Spain declares that this agreement in no way affects the question of the prior rights of sovereignty over the islands.

Both sides agreed to drop Bucareli and Hunt from point (F.1), since Spain still refused to disavow Bucareli, and British ministers could not have appeared before Parliament with a disavowal of Hunt, but Spain agreed to say "disavowed" rather than the milder "disapproved". Point (F.2) had already been agreed on, and under point (F.3) Britain accepted a Spanish declaration that contained no explicit reference to *Spain's* rights but merely stated that the question of "prior rights" (whatever they may have been) remained open. The rights of both countries remained undefined.

Once the final text had been drawn up (in faulty French), the Anglo-Spanish agreement was signed in London on 22 January 1771 by Lord Rochford (Weymouth's successor as Secretary of State for the Southern Department) and Spanish ambassador Prince Masserano.[1] War between Britain and Spain had been averted, but that was not the end of the controversy. The agreement has two omissions which have been discussed *ad nauseam* for over two centuries: it does not mention the abandonment of the islands, and it contains no specific reservation of Spanish rights.

As regards the first omission, there were rumours both in Madrid and London that Britain had made a "secret promise" (or "tacit convention") to abandon the Falklands without insisting that Spain abandon them too, thus implicitly accepting Spain's right to the islands, which British ministers had always firmly denied. There were several oral "off-the-record" comments by British ministers that Britain had no interest in the Falklands and would not remain there indefinitely, but they were far from a full-fledged "secret promise". In 1833 the British Foreign Secretary Lord Palmerston asked the King's Advocate, Sir Herbert Jenner, to search the Foreign Office files for any reference to a secret promise, and informed the Argentine ambassador in London, Manuel Moreno, that no such thing had been found.[2] Many treaties have had secret clauses or articles which later became public, but that has not happened with the Anglo-Spanish agreement of 1771.

Like some other authors,[3] Kohen and Rodríguez assert there was a secret promise, and devote several pages to it (pp. 67-73), even mentioning (p. 67, referring to *Getting it right*, p. 8) Sir Herbert Jenner's statement that he had found no evidence of it, but they also give several contemporary quotations by people not involved in the negotiations, implying that there had been a secret promise. In fact the existence of such a promise was explicitly denied by Lord Rochford himself, in a despatch to Colonel John Blaquiere, secretary to the British embassy in Paris, on 6 December 1771: "with regard to the Promise alledged, I think it proper to assure you, that neither Myself nor any other of His Majesty's Ministers to my knowledge ever made any such",[4] and on 19 November

---

[1] The text is printed in the original (faulty) French in Georg Friedrich von Martens (Georges Frédéric de Martens), *Recueil de Traités…*, 2nd ed. Gottingue [Göttingen, Germany], vol. II, 1817, pp. 1-2; also reproduced in Paul Groussac, *Les Iles Malouines…*, Buenos Aires 1910, p. 123 and fn.; Spanish translation: *Las Islas Malvinas por Paul Groussac…*, Buenos Aires 1936, pp. 134-135. Full text (in corrected French!) in *British and Foreign State Papers* (*BFSP*) *1833-1834*, London 1847, pp. 1387-1388; facsimile of *BFSP* in Perl 1983, pp. 326-327; English translation in Charles Jenkinson [First Earl of Liverpool], *A Collection of all the Treaties…*, London 1785, vol. iii, pp. 234-236.
[2] Letter from Jenner to Lord Palmerston, 30 November 1833, PRO CO 78/1, fols. 285 *recto* to 287 *recto*.
[3] E.g. Goebel 1927, pp. 316-363, and Ricardo Zorraquín Becú in his full-length book, *Inglaterra prometió abandonar las Malvinas* ["England promised to abandon the Malvinas"], Buenos Aires June 1982.
[4] Rochford to Blaquiere, later 1st Baron de Blaquiere KCB, PC (1732-1812), in PRO SP 78-283, fol. 280 *verso*.

1773 Rochford wrote to Blaquiere's successor, Colonel Horace St Paul: "The Assertion that there was a tacit Convention is absolutely false, I frequently dared the Spanish Ambassador, when he was here, to declare if any One had ever given him any such Promise, and to do him Justice, he constantly declared, that no such promise had in any shape whatever been made him...".[1]

The existence of a secret promise has also been definitively disproved by Jean-Etienne Martin-Allanic. His researches in French, Spanish and British archives revealed many *rumours* of a secret promise, but no evidence of a promise as such. If a secret promise had existed in a tangible form such as a written document, it would have been present not only in British archives but in Spanish and French ones too, but he found none, and he quotes documents that imply there was no such thing.[2] He gives much evidence for the Spaniards' lack of trust in anything the British said; the Spaniards' exasperation suggests that they would not have believed a secret promise even if there had been one.[3] And Masserano's remark to Lord Rochford on 22 April 1771 (three months after the agreement was signed), that the king of Spain would prefer a promise from the mouth of the British sovereign to any written agreement,[4] strongly suggests that there had been no such promise. In short, the secret promise is a myth. There was no secret promise by Britain to leave the Falklands, but only oral hints that Britain would some day leave the islands – with the right to return.

The second omission is the fact that point (F.3) of the Spanish declaration does not mention Spain's prior right of sovereignty; it simply states that the restoration to Britain of Port Egmont:[5]

... cannot nor ought any wise to affect the question of the prior right of sovereignty of the Malouine islands, otherwise called Falkland's Islands.

Unlike Choiseul's point (C.3) of 3 December 1770 (above), it does not mention *Spain's* prior rights of sovereignty – in signing the agreement Britain neither recognised any prior rights of Spain, nor surrendered any British rights; both countries' rights were restored to their state as before 10 June 1770, and the question of prior right of sovereignty – whatever it may have been – was left open. It is thus incorrect to refer to a Spanish "reservation of right"; there was no such thing.

Nevertheless, some authors have wrongly asserted that Spain made a reservation of her rights.[6] We call that assertion the "Spanish Rights Myth". Those authors included the mysterious polemicist "Junius", whose letters attacking the government, the king and the corruption of public life had been appearing in the *Public Advertiser* since January 1769.[7] Junius devoted his letter no. XLII of 30 January 1771 to the agreement on the Falkland Islands – he hit on the truth in saying of the expulsion of the British "the whole plan seems to have been formed and executed in consequence of deliberate orders, and a regular instruction from the Spanish court", but he was wide of the mark in saying: "the Spaniard... says, *I give you back possession, but I adhere to my claim of prior right*"[8] – he failed to notice that the agreement made no mention of prior Spanish rights. Other pamphleteers made the same mistake, so the government looked for someone to defend the agreement.

They found Dr Samuel Johnson (1709-84), the major British literary figure of the late 18th century: essayist, dramatist, wit, conversationalist, editor of Shakespeare, author of the *Dictionary of the English Language* (1755) and *Lives of the Poets* (10 vols.), and subject of James Boswell's

---

[1] Rochford to St Paul (1729-1812), in PRO SP 78-290, fol. 86 *recto-verso*.
[2] E.g. Martin-Allanic 1964, pp. 1208, 1210, 1217, 1225, 1227-8.
[3] E.g. Martin-Allanic 1964, p. 1232.
[4] This remark is noted by Goebel (1927, p. 404), but he does not draw the obvious conclusion from it.
[5] Quote here from Jenkinson 1785, vol. iii, p. 235; it does not read "ought in any wise". We are puzzled that Kohen and Rodríguez maintain (p. 64) that in *Getting it right* we accuse Argentina of using "a wrong translation of the Masserano declaration" – in fact we said (p. 7) "Argentina has constantly repeated a false version of this declaration", i.e. that Argentina has repeated a false account of what the declaration contained.
[6] E.g. Groussac 1910: French p. 126, Spanish translation 1936, p. 137; Goebel 1927, pp. 317-318, 362, 363; Dolzer 1993, pp. 46-47; German version Heidelberg 1986, p. 35; Peter Beck, *The Falkland Islands as an International Problem*, London 1988, p. 64, quoting Enrique Ferrer Vieyra, *An Annotated Legal Chronology of the Malvinas (Falkland) Islands Controversy*, Córdoba 1985, pp. 35-36; Freedman 2005/2007, vol. I, p. 5.
[7] The author of the *Letters of Junius* has never been identified. In *Junius: A Bibliography of the Letters of Junius...*, Fairview (New Jersey) and London 1986, Francesco Cordasco catalogues 693 items, and on p. 221 lists 58 people who have been suggested as having been "Junius".
[8] Extracts from *The Letters of Junius*, Routledge ed., London 1875, pp. 252-256; italics in original.

Life of Samuel Johnson (1791). In March 1771 there duly appeared in London an anonymous 75-page pamphlet costing 1s. 6d., which supported the government as robustly as the pamphleteers had attacked it.[1] Its author was soon known to be Johnson, and his forthright style and measured Latinate cadences are much in evidence. He is the voice of reason, urging moderation and emphasising the advantages of the agreement for Britain. He calmly points out that sovereignty was subject to practical limitations:[2]

If sovereignty implies undisputed right, scarce any prince is a sovereign through his whole dominions; if sovereignty consists in this, that no superiour is acknowledged, our King reigns at Port Egmont, with sovereign authority.

To all those who (like Junius) had jumped to the conclusion that Spain had made a reservation of Spanish rights, Johnson soberly points out that the question of "right" (sovereignty) was "a right of which no formal resignation was ever required" (Spain had never asked Britain to surrender her claim to sovereignty) and it had not been discussed at all during the negotiations but had been left for resolution at some future date.[3]

Thus Kohen and Rodríguez misunderstand the position. They say (p. 65):

Pascoe and Pepper highlight a proposal made during the negotiations to explicitly recognise Spanish sovereignty, which was not accepted by the British government… However, the fact that no explicit recognition of Spanish sovereignty was given in the declaration did not mean that Spain had abandoned its position and implicitly accepted that of the other party. In the final text, only one party formulated a reservation of sovereignty: Spain. The other failed to do so… What sovereignty could this possibly be but Spain's?

There are three misunderstandings there. First, they imply (pp. 65, 196) that we said in *Getting it right* that the dropping of "the explicit formula recognising Spanish sovereignty" (i.e. point C.3) meant that Spain accepted the British position. In fact we said (p. 7):

… the question of the prior right of sovereignty was left as it had been before the dispute – **both** countries' rights were left untouched, Britain's as well as Spain's.

We did not imply that Spain accepted Britain's position; we simply pointed out that the formula in the final agreement was neutral – each country reserved its position against the other.

Secondly, Kohen and Rodríguez repeat the Spanish Rights Myth (i.e. that Spain "formulated a reservation of sovereignty"). In fact Britain refused to permit it: at a meeting on 20 December 1770 with French chargé d'affaires Jacques Batailhé de Francès (who acted as intermediary between Britain and Spain), the British Prime Minister Lord North[4] insisted that any agreement must be neutral in effect; Britain had neither contested nor accepted Spain's rights, so Britain could only accept such a declaration if the reparation of the injury committed on 10 June left all previous rights unaltered and restored the previous *status quo* without any reciprocal gains or losses of title.[5]

And thirdly, the Argentine authors are also wrong in implying that by "sovereignty" both sides accepted that only Spain's sovereignty was meant. All British ministers including Lord North made it clear that Britain did not recognise any sovereignty by Spain in the islands, nor did they explicitly deny it – they always left the question of sovereignty open. They accepted that it might be discussed and resolved at some future date, but during the negotiations it was not on the table at all. In other

---

[1] [Anon., but known to be by Samuel Johnson], *Thoughts on the Late Transactions Respecting Falkland's Islands*, London 1771. Spanish translation, *Pensamientos acerca de las últimas negociaciones relativas a las Islas Malvinas y otros escritos* (eds. Pablo Massa and Federico Lafuente), Buenos Aires 2003.
[2] Johnson 1771, pp. 36-37.
[3] Johnson 1771, p. 37: "When the possession is conceded, where is the evil that the right, which that concession supposes to be merely hypothetical, is referred to the Greek Calends for a future disquisition?", i.e.: "Once possession has been granted, what can be wrong in referring the right of sovereignty, which that granting makes merely theoretical, to an indefinite future for discussion?" (Not one of Johnson's best sentences).
[4] Frederick North, later 2nd Earl of Guilford (1732-92), Prime Minister 28 January 1770 to 22 March 1782; till 1790 he sat in the House of Commons (for Banbury) since his father, Francis North, 1st Earl of Guilford (1704–1790), was still alive; Lord North was a "courtesy title" he bore until his succession to the peerage in 1790.
[5] Martin-Allanic 1964, pp. 1179-1181.

words, the two sides tacitly "agreed to disagree" – each side reserved its position and tolerated the other's claim to be the exclusive possessor of the islands, as the price for avoiding war.

Kohen and Rodríguez (p. 66) criticise us for saying that Dr Johnson confirmed that both countries reserved their rights, and for not giving any quote to prove it. So here is one – Johnson makes it clear that the agreement did not assert Spain's prior rights but left all questions of right exactly as they had been before the dispute, so that Grimaldi could say:[1]

We have already… granted you the whole effect of right, and have not denied you the name. We have not said that the right was ours before this concession, but only that what right we had, is not by this concession vacated.

Thus Johnson underlines that the agreement left all rights in the islands unchanged. Kohen and Rodríguez misquote him by adding a phrase in square brackets, making him refer to "This reserve [of Spanish sovereignty]…". Johnson did not in fact refer to a reserve of Spanish sovereignty – that is a misrepresentation of the Anglo-Spanish agreement of 1771.

The Argentine authors' implication that only Spanish sovereignty can have been meant, and that Britain therefore accepted Spanish sovereignty, is disproved by an episode they do not mention, which we call "Rochford's bombshell". Rochford dropped his bombshell after the signing of the agreement, during the discussions on the arrangements for handing back Port Egmont to Britain: the Spanish side initially insisted that a British expedition should be sent to Puerto Soledad to receive Port Egmont from the Spanish governor, but the British Cabinet suspected it was a ruse intended to force Britain to recognise Spanish sovereignty in the islands. Britain therefore suggested that the British expedition should go to Port Egmont or Buenos Aires, but the Spanish side refused point-blank, so Lord Rochford dropped his bombshell: on 28 February 1771 he told Francès that he was drawing up orders to Captain John Stott, who was to receive Port Egmont back from Spain. And since the Anglo-Spanish agreement laid down that Port Egmont was to be returned exactly as before, those orders would be the same as those to former British commanders at Port Egmont – Stott was to be ordered to go to Puerto Soledad and expel the Spaniards, since the Falkland Islands were solely British territory, where the Spaniards were present illegally. Francès was horrified, as was the Spanish government – Britain was apparently preparing to go to war over the Falklands after all. Thereupon Spain backed down and allowed Stott to go to Port Egmont. He sailed on 9 April 1771 in the frigate *Juno*, and at Port Egmont on 16 September he received the British establishment back from the Spaniards.[2]

So honour was saved, and both countries reserved their positions over the Falkland Islands –each side maintained its exclusive claim to sovereignty; Britain in no way recognised Spanish sovereignty, either then or later. Indeed, in 1888 Dr Francisco Latzina, director of the Argentine national statistical office and hence a high-ranking Argentine government official who was entitled to write authoritatively about Argentina's territory, published a 750-page work in Spanish on the geography of Argentina, in which he said in his chronological table:[3]

1771 I 22 Spain implicitly recognises the right of the English to the Malvinas.

That is perhaps going a little far; Spain agreed to tolerate Britain's rights in the islands without formally recognising them, and by the same token Britain tolerated Spain's rights without formally recognising them, but it was nevertheless noteworthy that in 1888 such an important Argentine official accepted Britain's rights in the Falklands so clearly (see also section 8.28).

In short, the Anglo-Spanish agreement of 1771 was a triumph for Britain. Spain was forced to give way on all three points: (1) to disavow Bucareli's expedition and refrain from all criticism of Hunt; (2) to return Port Egmont to Britain exactly as it was before 10 June 1770, and (3) to refrain from asserting that Spain had prior rights in the islands. Thus ended the First Falklands Crisis.

---

[1] Johnson 1771, p. 38.
[2] Martin-Allanic 1964, pp. 1221-1226; 1242-1245; Stott's report to the Admiralty, 9 December 1771; text in *BFSP 1833-1834* (vol. XXII), printed London 1847, pp. 1391-1392, facsimile reprint of *BFSP* text in Perl 1983, pp. 330-331.
[3] F[rancisco] Latzina, *Geografía de la República Argentina*, Buenos Aires 1888, p. 665.

2.4 The "chearful" British at Port Egmont; the miserable Spaniards at Puerto Soledad

2.4a The dock and remains of a warehouse at Port Egmont, built soon after 1771. (Photo Peter Pepper)

After the return of the British there were once again two establishments in the Falklands, British at Port Egmont and Spanish at Puerto Soledad. At Port Egmont the British built more stone buildings, the ruins of which can still be seen, including a large warehouse and a dock (fig. 2.4a).[1] Judging by the entertaining memoir of life at Port Egmont by Bernard Penrose,[2] who lived there from 1772 to 1774, the two garrisons had no contact whatever with each other. Penrose describes how "chearful" the British were, and says "the glory of our colony was the gardens… we were plentifully supplied with potatoes, cabbages, broccoli, carrots, turnips, borecole [i.e. kale], spinnage, parsley, lettuce, English cellery, mustard, cresses, and some few, but very fine cauliflowers," though "beets and radishes quite baffled our utmost art."

The contrast with life at Puerto Soledad was striking. The Spaniards were uniformly miserable, and on several occasions suffered from scurvy as a result of their lack of fresh food. The history of Puerto Soledad was recounted (sketchily and uncritically) by Gómez Langenheim in 1939[3] and by Destéfani in 1981,[4] and was first analysed in detail by Wayne Bernhardson in 1989;[5] *DFB* gives biographies of its governors, while its contacts with the outside world were chronicled by Ernesto Fitte.[6] The British and French were happy and optimistic, but the Spaniards hated the islands, and Bernhardson comments: "the Spanish colonial era produced an abundance of documentation revealing that the Malvinas were a hardship post, detested by their occupants."[7] After Puerto

---

[1] The remains at Port Egmont are described in Robert Philpott, "An archaeological survey of Port Egmont, the first British settlement in the Falkland Islands", in *Post-Medieval Archaeology*, vol. 30 (for 1996), London 1997.
[2] Bernard Penrose, *An Account of the Last Expedition to Port Egmont…*, London 1775.
[3] Antonio Gómez Langenheim, *Elementos para la Historia de nuestras Islas Malvinas*, ["Materials for the History of our Malvinas Islands"] 2 vols., Buenos Aires 1939; it is full of historical errors (see sections 5.1, 5.3, 5.8, 5.19).
[4] Laurio H. Destéfani, *Las Malvinas en la época hispana (1600-1811)* ["The Malvinas in the Spanish period (1600-1811)"], Buenos Aires 1981. There was of course no Spanish presence in the islands before 1767.
[5] Wayne Bernhardson, *Land and Life in the Falkland Islands*, unpublished doctoral thesis, Berkeley 1989 (copy in JCNA). We are grateful to him for providing us with a copy; as it is unpublished we give his full sources.
[6] Ernesto J. Fitte, "Cronología Marítima de las Islas Malvinas", in *Investigaciones y Ensayos* vol. 4, Buenos Aires January-June 1968, pp. 153-189.
[7] Bernhardson 1989, pp. 146-147.

Soledad became a "presidio" (a frontier garrison and penal settlement) in 1769, there were many soldiers and convicts, so the presence of women was soon prohibited.

Kohen and Rodríguez say (p. 81) that Puerto Soledad was inhabited by "a military detachment, prisoners, settlers and Catholic priests," but there were in fact no settlers. They say that "the British sources" are wrong in implying that the Spanish establishment was a prison, but that was its major function, apart from being a "tripwire" presence to enable a Spanish response to any threat in the area (though it did not fulfil that function very well). The first group of 20 prisoners arrived at Puerto Soledad in December 1769; most of them were soldiers convicted of serious offences such as murder, armed assault, desertion, robbery, contraband and theft, who were sent to serve sentences ranging from six years to life imprisonment. They included Spaniards from Spain, "criollos" (people of Spanish descent born in South America), South American Indians, and one black.[1] In late 1771 some of them took part in a mutiny led by the infantry lieutenant Nicolás de Arteta, who with five soldiers and nine prisoners rebelled against authority. It seems they intended to escape to Port Egmont – if they had got there, they might have caused another international incident, but they failed and were sent to Montevideo for trial.[2] The presence of the prisoners at Puerto Soledad was a constant security risk. A soldier was killed by a prisoner in 1792;[3] in 1795, of the 27 prisoners, no fewer than 11 had been involved in acts that led to violent death; several had been convicted of armed assault and robbery, though others were military deserters.[4] In another incident on 1 March 1800, a ship's boy of the *Atrevida*, Juan Bonet, stabbed Manuel Acosta to death during an argument; this did not involve a prisoner, but was indicative of the state of discipline at the time.[5]

Kohen and Rodríguez comment (p. 85) that as far as sovereignty was concerned, it was immaterial whether the Spaniards were happy or not – that is true of course, but our brief remarks in *Getting it right* (p. 7) were intended as an antidote to the uniformly positive account by Gómez Langenheim, who praises the "good regime of government and the excellent administration prevailing at that time."[6] That is nonsense – Puerto Soledad was shockingly badly run, life there was lonely and miserable, and Spanish officials were often in despair.

During the term of office of Francisco Gil y Lemos as governor at Puerto Soledad (1774-7) the islands were demoted from a "gobernación" to a "comandancia", and their commander became a "comandante" with limited responsibilities rather than a "gobernador" with general powers.[7] Overall authority was initially exercised by the Viceroy of Peru, himself subservient to Madrid, but on 1 August 1776 Carlos III signed a "cédula real" [royal warrant] setting up the Viceroyalty of the River Plate, with its seat of government at Buenos Aires. It covered not only what is now Argentina but the whole of Paraguay and Uruguay, parts of Bolivia and the whole of southern Chile – modern Argentina covers only part of the territory of the Viceroyalty of La Plata, which lessens the force of Argentina's claim to have inherited the Falklands from Spain (chapter 3).[8]

Kohen and Rodríguez misleadingly say three times (pp. 79, 80, 194) that Spain appointed 32 governors of the islands, and that in 1790 (p. 43) Spain appointed its 13th governor, but they seem unaware that in 1783, owing to the hardship of the post and the never-ending complaints of its commandants, a rota system began, under which each commandant served one or more tours of duty: six served two tours and three served three. There were 32 tours of duty, but not 32 governors

---

[1] Bernhardson 1989, p. 126 & fn. 85 p. 156, from a letter by Diego de Andecochea to Ruiz Puente, 19 December 1769, in AGN IX, 16-9-2.

[2] Bernhardson 1989, pp. 125-6 & fn. 83 p. 156, from a letter by Ruiz Puente to Juan José de Vértiz, 28 December 1771, in AGN IX, 16-9-3.

[3] Bernhardson 1989, pp. 136-137, no source given.

[4] Bernhardson 1989, p. 137 & fn. 117 p. 159; Josef de Aldana y Ortega's report, 10 June 1795, AGN IX, 16-9-10.

[5] Destéfani 1981, pp. 298-299.

[6] Gómez Langenheim 1939, vol. I, p. 203.

[7] María Laura San Martino de Dromi, *Gobierno y administración de las Islas Malvinas (1776-1833)*, Buenos Aires 1996, pp. 13-16; Iago Gil Aguado, "Francisco Gil y Lemos, gobernador de las islas Malvinas (1774-1777)", in *Espacio, Tiempo y Forma*, vol. 25, Buenos Aires 2012 (we are grateful to Roger Lorton for drawing our attention to this article).

[8] Maps of all Spanish South American Viceroyalties around 1800 are given in Cathryn L. Lombardi, John V. Lombardi and K. Lynn Stoner, *Latin American History: a Teaching Atlas*, Madison (Wisconsin) 1983, p. 32.

– only 20 individuals served. The man Kohen and Rodríguez call the "13th governor", Capitán de fragata Ramón de Clairac y Villalonga, was actually the 9th individual commandant; he served the 13th tour of duty (from 16 May 1789 to 30 June 1790), but it was his third tour.[1]

2.5 Britain closes down Port Egmont, but reserves the right to return

In late 1773 or early 1774 the British government decided to withdraw the garrison from Port Egmont; the decision was announced to Parliament by Lord North in early February 1774, and was passed on by the Earl of Rochford to the British ambassador Lord Grantham in Madrid, in a letter dated 11 February 1774 explaining that the evacuation was for reasons of economy: "the truth is, that it is neither more nor less than a small part of an economical Naval regulation."[2] A major part of the reason for that economy was of course the rising tension in the North American colonies – the "Boston Tea Party" had taken place on 16 December 1773. The expense of an outpost in the distant Falkland Islands began to seem unjustifiable; British sovereignty had been demonstrated, and Britain could return at any time, so the government sent an expedition to bring the garrison home. On 21 May 1774 they left the islands for Britain in the *Endeavour* (Captain James Cook's ship on his first circumnavigation), leaving a lead plaque on the door of the blockhouse stating that the territory was the property of King George III, thus stating Britain's *animus revertendi* ["mind to return"]. They anchored at Woolwich on 30 September.[3] Kohen and Rodríguez say (pp. 76-77) that Spain understood Britain to have "abandoned" Port Egmont, but although it may have suited the Spanish government to assume that, the position was actually different – in the British government's view the islands were British territory, so Britain had the right to return whenever it chose. Thus the Argentine authors are wrong to draw the conclusion that Britain's departure from Port Egmont confirmed that there had been a secret promise by Britain to abandon the islands.

2.6 New Falklands industries: sealing and whaling; Port Egmont destroyed

At Port Egmont there was a seamless transition from one phase in the history of the Falklands to the next – just before the British garrison left, three American whalers arrived, *Montague*, *Thomas* and *King George*, the precursors of hundreds of ships, American, British, and a few others, which exploited the islands' natural resources – "fishing" was becoming a major industry. The catching of fish was only a small part of it; "fishing" meant principally the killing of seals and whales for oil, and of seals for fur and skins. From the mid-18th to the mid-19th century this trade employed some 3,000 ships and 50,000 men worldwide.[4] At its height there were about a hundred ships active at the same time, mostly sealers plus a few whalers, and the Falklands were a major centre for both. Almost all the crews were American or British – they Anglicised the French name « Iles Malouines » as "The Maloons", and often called West Falkland "English Maloon", since the language spoken there was English; East Falkland was sometimes "Great Maloon", but more often "Spanish Maloon", after the Spanish garrison. Those crews often spent long periods ashore; at Port Egmont they stored supplies in the storehouses, grew vegetables in the gardens, and (until 1780) lived in the houses.

The Spaniards decided to put an end to these activities, and Kohen and Rodríguez mention (p. 77) the order sent from Madrid on 30 June 1777 by José de Gálvez, Minister for the "Indies" (i.e. South America) to burn and destroy the buildings at Port Egmont (Kohen and Rodríguez pp. 78, 224). The Argentine authors make a point of saying (p. 78) that the order was sent in a time of peace and was thus not a mere act of war (which would carry much less legal weight), but in fact it was not carried out until March 1780,[5] by which time Spain and Britain were indeed at war – Spain

---

[1] See list of Spanish commandants in David Tatham (ed.), *The Dictionary of Falklands Biography...* (*DFB*), Ledbury 2008, pp. 571-572.
[2] Rochford to Grantham 11 February 1774, text printed in *BFSP 1833-1834* (London 1847), p. 1393; facsimile of *BFSP 1833-1834* in Perl 1983, p. 332.
[3] Penrose 1775, pp. 67-81.
[4] A. G. E. Jones lists some of these ships (mainly the British ones), in *Ships employed in the South Seas Trade, 1775-1861*, Canberra (Australia), vol. I, 1986. His (confessedly incomplete) 45-page index lists some 1,800 ships.
[5] Description of destruction, with accompanying correspondence, in Hidalgo Nieto 1947, pp. 291-294.

declared war on Britain on 21 June 1779, intervening in the American War of Independence, which ended on 3 September 1783. Thus the buildings at Port Egmont were destroyed in wartime, which is unremarkable. Even after the destruction British and American sealers and whalers regularly used Port Egmont and even partly rebuilt it – the Spaniards were powerless to stop them.

2.7 Spain's sovereignty in the islands to 1811 and its limitations

The two Argentine authors say (p. 74) that there was never a single protest by Britain against the Spanish presence in the islands. That is true, but they fail to explain why. The reason was that Britain had tacitly agreed in 1771 to tolerate the Spanish presence and to refrain from going to war to put an end to it, though still holding the view that the islands were British territory and that the Spaniards were there illegally. In the same way, Spain had tacitly agreed in 1771 to tolerate the British presence and to refrain from going to war to end it, though still seeing the islands as Spanish territory and the British presence as illegal. Having agreed to tolerate the Spanish presence, it would have been illogical for Britain to protest against it.

As explained in section 2.3, after the 1771 agreement Britain and Spain *both* claimed 100% sovereignty over the Falklands and each held the other to be present illegally, but both had agreed to take no action in the matter. It was an anomalous situation – it was not normal for a country to tolerate another country's claim to what it saw as its own territory without going to war, but both sides had agreed that the game was not worth the candle and had put the issue "on ice".

According to Kohen and Rodríguez (p. 95), Spain's sovereignty in the islands till 1811 was "effective, exclusive, continuous, peaceful, public and in good faith", and they say (p. 81) that those who governed the islands:

… occupied themselves essentially in maintaining the Spanish presence… and in keeping a check on the activity of the other powers in the region. It was an official public presence, which no maritime power ignored nor could ignore… it applied its legislation in the whole of the archipelago and exercised the power of policing in and around the entirety of the islands.

That passage derives ultimately from Julius Goebel, who wrote in 1927:[1]

… the Spanish exercised the fullest sovereignty over the whole group of islands, not limiting their acts of government and control to the islands themselves, but extending their powers over the surrounding seas in an effort to prohibit or at least make more difficult fishing activities of other nations in the South Seas.

That is all nonsense; Spain exercised nothing like "the fullest sovereignty", and Spanish activity in the islands was minimal, as the detailed research by Wayne Bernhardson demonstrates – he says:[2]

Spain's lack of commitment to what was, to her, an environmentally marginal place occupied only to prevent other European powers from doing so meant dereliction and misery for those assigned there… Asserting its regional hegemony, Spain maintained a half-hearted occupation for nearly half a century, during which the Islands became a military hardship post and penal colony.

Spain's sovereignty in the Falklands was not "effective", "exclusive" or "continuous". It was not effective because before the advent of aircraft in the later 20th century any form of control, whether attempted by France, or Britain, or Spain, or by Louis Vernet, or the province of Buenos Aires, was tenuous and often non-existent. The islands have a total land area of 12,173 square kilometres (4,700 square miles) – larger than Jamaica (10,800 sq. km.) or Cyprus (9,200 sq. km.) – and there are 750 islands in the group, with complex indented coastlines and many dangerous rocks and reefs (see Maps 1 and 2 in the Introduction). The Spaniards were present only in the north-east corner around Puerto Soledad, and were absent from the rest. Kohen and Rodríguez say "Frequent journeys were made around the archipelago" by Spanish ships (p. 81), but in fact the Spaniards only sent a ship around the islands at irregular intervals, initially about once a year, but later less and less often. Many British and American sealers spent long periods around the western Falklands without ever encountering a Spaniard, and the British and Americans in the islands sometimes outnumbered

---

[1] Goebel 1927, p. 432.
[2] Bernhardson 1989, pp. 146-147, reparagraphed here.

the Spaniards. The Spaniards sometimes attempted to hinder them by destroying stocks of coal, hides, etc., but were powerless to stop them. Spain's sovereignty was never effective.

And after 1790 Spain's sovereignty was not exclusive either. Kohen and Rodríguez say (p. 117) that exclusivity is "one of the elements which characterise territorial sovereignty", and they presumably believe that Spain held exclusive sovereignty in the Falklands. On that point they make two incorrect assertions:

(a) They say (p. 42) that the Nootka Sound Convention of 1790 (for which see section 1.7) was "a key treaty for the recognition of Spanish sovereignty over the islands and Britain's obligation to respect it", and (p. 45) "Spain was the nation exercising sovereignty over the Falklands/Malvinas in 1790, and Great Britain undertook not to interfere with its possession", and:

(b) They say that "it was Spain which authorized British subjects to temporarily perform activities of a private nature in its possessions" (p. 44).

They are wrong on both counts, because:

(a) After 1790 Britain still retained its claim to the islands (tacitly accepted by Spain in 1771), and Spain also accepted that Spanish rights as against Britain had been greatly diminished by the Nootka Sound Convention – Spain accepted that British subjects were entitled to exploit about 80% of the land area of the islands, and to form permanent settlements ("establishments") in the north-western 20% (see our description of the "zones" of rights in section 1.7).

(b) There was no question of Spain's being entitled to "authorise" British activities. "Authorisation" presupposes that the "authoriser" has the right to deny authorisation, but if one is obliged to permit something, one cannot be said to be authorising it. Under the Nootka Sound Convention Spain had lost the right to prevent British commercial activities in most of the islands and to form settlements in part of them, so Spain had lost the right to authorise such activities – Britain could perform them without reference to Spain. Kohen and Rodríguez say (p. 87-8) that "The activities of private persons are not manifestations of sovereignty", which is true but irrelevant – the point is that from 1790 the activities of private British individuals constituted a *limitation of Spanish sovereignty* since Spain had lost the right to prevent them. Those individuals possessed rights in the islands which overrode Spain's claimed authority, so Spanish sovereignty was no longer exclusive.

Finally, Spain's sovereignty was not continuous. There were long periods when most of the islands never saw a single Spaniard, and the only effective authority was exercised by the British and American seamen who exploited the islands, who obeyed their own code of conduct. The Spaniards played no part in that.

In an attempt to demonstrate the power of the Spaniards over the British in the islands, Kohen and Rodríguez mention (p. 82) two occasions on which British ships were stopped and their crews arrested by Spanish officers. However, the first example dates from August 1790, before the Nootka Sound Convention, when Spain had not yet been forced to accept a limitation of Spanish sovereignty, and the second dates from February 1806, when Spain and Britain were yet again at war (between 1804 and 1808). The arrest of enemy citizens in war is unremarkable and does not demonstrate Spain's authority in any particular way, but in peacetime Britain's privileges under the Nootka Sound Convention limited Spain's rights.

The outbreak of the French revolutionary wars distracted Britain from benefiting from its new rights to exploit large areas of South America. Louis XVI was guillotined in Paris on 21 January 1793, and on 1 February France declared war on Britain. That soon swept most British merchant ships from the South Atlantic, since they were liable to be captured by French warships or privateers. For two decades virtually all the ships visiting the Falklands were American.

From 1790 the Spanish commandants in the Falklands made a clear distinction between British and American ships and men, as is shown by a report sent to the Spanish authorities in Buenos Aires by Comandante Pedro Pablo Sanguineto dated 8 October 1793,[1] recounting an inspection tour

---

[1] Report by Pedro Pablo Sanguineto, 8 October 1973, in AGN, VII, 2-3-4, fols. 109-112. Wayne Bernhardson also mentions (1989, p. 135 & note 112, p. 159) a report from Pedro Pablo Sanguineto in AGN VII, 2-3-4, likewise dated 8 October 1793, but Bernhardson gives it the title "Extracto del diario del Alférez de Navío don Juan Latre, 8 October 1793", which the report we quote here does not bear, and some of the details are different.

by the brig *San Julián de Gálvez*. The Spaniards had apparently been told by some "English" deserters that there were ships sealing in the islands which had together amassed up to 20,000 sealskins. There were three or four "large ships" wintering around San Carlos, with some 150 men, mostly "Americans and very few royalists" (i.e. British). The fact that hardly any of the men were British meant that the ships were fair game for the Spaniards to expel from the islands. The *Gálvez* was sent to check, and sailed on 2 August 1793 under Juan Latre. Once the *Gálvez* had found the ships, their captains were called aboard one by one, and were informed of the "most recent conventions made between Their Catholic and Britannic Majesties" (i.e. the Nootka Sound Convention). The *Gálvez*'s officers, on their return to Puerto Soledad, gave Sanguineto a list of 12 sealing ships that they had found (all American, two from Providence, Rhode Island, the rest from New York), largely concentrated around San Salvador and West Point Island (for which they used Spanish names), with crews totalling some 200 men, who had collected 800 or 900 sealskins and had built a stone smithy and planted gardens surrounded by walls. Each captain was informed that he was not allowed to remain any longer in the islands but was to depart at once. It is clear from Sanguineto's report that the Spaniards felt entitled to expel the ships because very few of their crewmen were British.

The different treatment accorded by the Spanish commandants to British and American seamen was known to Louis Vernet, who evidently found another report by Juan Latre which we have not located. Vernet wrote in his "Report" to Vicente Maza of 10 August 1832:[1]

On the 29th of July, 1793, the Governor Sanguineto learned that, in the Islands… were various foreign fishing Vessels; he… resolved that Lieut. Don Juan Latre, in the Brig *Galvez*, should… expel them. The *Galvez* sailed on the 11th of September, and found in the Isla Quemada[2] the American Brig *Nancy*, Captain Gardener, to whom he addressed the following Note:– "In consequence of the recent Treaties between the Spanish and British Governments, and of the orders I have received from the Commander and Governor of these Islands of Malvina, it is my duty to inform you that you have no right either to fish or to anchor in the neighborhood of Spanish Settlements; as solely the English Royalists are allowed to fish at 10 leagues from the said Establishments…"

Those instructions confirm that the Nootka Sound Convention had deprived Spain of an important part of her claimed sovereignty in the Falklands: the right to prevent activities by British subjects. Spain was obliged to permit their commercial activities, especially of course "fishing" (i.e. sealing) throughout the islands except in the north-eastern corner, and also to permit permanent settlement in the north-western fifth of the islands.

So any Spanish rights inherited by Argentina did not amount to full unrestricted sovereignty – and as Kohen and Rodríguez rightly say (p. 112), Argentina succeeded to Spain's rights *and obligations* under Article 4 of the Treaty of Recognition, Peace, and Friendship between Spain and Argentina of 21 September 1863,[3] in which Spain for the first time recognised the independence of the whole of Argentina. One of those obligations was to permit British activities in the Falklands. Argentina's inherited rights were limited in various ways, which will be examined in the next chapter.

---

[1] Louis Vernet's report to Maza of 10 August 1832, "Informe del Comandante Político y Militar de Malvinas", henceforth "(Vernet's) 'Report'," in *Colección de Documentos Oficiales…* ["Collection of Official Documents…"], Buenos Aires 1832, henceforth "*Colección* 1832" (full title in Bibliography). The *Colección* 1832 is also printed in *British and Foreign State Papers (BFSP) 1832-1833*, vol. XX, London 1836 (here "*BFSP 1832-1833*"), pp. 311-441. This quote is in Vernet's "Report", in *Colección* 1832, p. 92 (in Spanish); English text here from *BFSP 1832-1833*, vol. XX, London 1836, p. 415.
[2] "Burnt Island"; there were several so named, indicating that their peat cover had at some time been burnt.
[3] Full text, in English only, in *BFSP* vol. LIII, 1862-1863, pp. 306-311 (London 1868). The treaty was ratified by Argentina on 7 November 1863 and by Spain on 9 January 1864; ratifications were formally exchanged in Madrid on 20 June 1864 (William Columbus Davis, *The Last Conquistadores: the Spanish Intervention in Peru and Chile 1863-1866*, Athens, Georgia, 1950, p. 13, fn.). See also section 8.17.

CHAPTER THREE: *uti possidetis* – did Argentina inherit the Falklands from Spain?

In their chapter 3, Kohen and Rodríguez move on to consider Argentina's succession to Spain's rights in the Falklands. They begin by explaining the principle of *uti possidetis*, but they present the traditional Argentine view that upon achieving independence Argentina simply inherited the islands from Spain, and that was that, thanks to *uti possidetis*. That was far from being the case, so we shall begin with our own brief overview of the principle before considering the version asserted by Kohen and Rodríguez and its many weaknesses.

The doctrine or principle of *uti possidetis* originated in Roman law, as a prohibition issued by a praetor (a high-ranking Roman magistrate) in disputes over immovable property (houses, land, etc.). If the current possessor could demonstrate peaceful possession that had not been obtained by wrongful means, the Praetor awarded "title" (the legally indisputable right to the property) to him by proclaiming:

Uti eas aedes, quibus de agitur, nec vi nec clam, nec precario alter ab altero possidetis, quominus ita possideatis, vim fieri veto.[1]

Assuming that you took possession of the house in question from the other party neither by force, nor by stealth, nor on sufferance, I forbid the use of force to prevent you from possessing it in that way.[2]

The formula is sometimes summarised as *uti possidetis, ita possideatis*, literally "as you possess, so may you possess", meaning in effect "provided you possessed rightfully in the first place, your rightful possession shall continue"; the principle is known for short as *uti possidetis*, and is sometimes used to mean "the state of possession at a given time", as in "the *uti possidetis* of 1810".

This principle has often been applied to territory in questions of "state succession", i.e. the inheritance from one state to a successor state, typically from a colonial power to newly independent countries. In such cases it means that the successor states should retain such territory as was defined by the former colonial boundaries. It has been applied effectively in Africa, where almost all the colonial borders have remained the borders of the successor states even though they do not fit the ethnic divisions of the indigenous peoples.

The success of the principle in Africa contrasts sharply with its failure in Latin America. It was adopted by Latin American countries in Article VII of the Treaty of Confederation signed at the Congress of Lima on 8 February 1848, in a complex form which gave a certain importance to the boundaries of earlier Spanish regions but also allowed the new republics to appoint commissioners to determine boundaries; it thus served only as a general guideline and was never a rigid principle, contrary to what is sometimes stated. No date was given from which *uti possidetis* was to operate, and the date 1810 was mentioned only in connection with states that split up after 1810.[3]

Some authors assert that *uti possidetis* is a universal principle,[4] and Kohen and Rodríguez follow that line. They give examples of cases in which it has been applied by courts in international

---

[1] Latin text, with discussion, in John Bassett Moore, *Costa Rica-Panama Arbitration: Memorandum on Uti Possidetis*, Rosslyn, Virginia (USA) 1913, esp. pp. 5-8.

[2] This translation by Graham and Henni Pascoe; we have done our best, but it is impossible to render the Latin naturally into English (or any other language), and all previous attempts we have found are even less satisfactory than ours. *Possidetis* is present tense ("you possess"); we use a past tense ("took possession") since "possess from the other" is not good English, and what is relevant is the way possession began. The phrase *alter ab altero* ["the one from the other"] does not rule out acquisition from the other party's predecessors. *Precario* means "by entreaty" (i.e. by asking) or "on sufferance", implying that the original possessor gave no formal permission but has simply failed to object. Moore prints (1913, p. 6) two translations: (1) from Muirhead, *Historical Introduction to the Private Law of Rome*, [Edinburgh] 1899, p. 206: "As you possess the house in question, the one not having obtained it by force, clandestinely, or by permission from the other, I forbid force to be used to the end that you may not continue so to possess it", and (2) from Edward Poste, *Gaii Institutionum Iuris Civilis Commentarii Quattuor or Elements of Roman Law By Gaius*, [Oxford] 1871, p. 505: "Whichever party has possession of the house in question, without violence, clandestinity or permission in respect of the adversary, the violent disturbance of his possession I prohibit". Those translations keep the present tense of *possidetis* but run into other problems, and neither can be called felicitous.

[3] Extensive discussion in Moore 1913, esp. pp. 31-40, with full text of Article VII pp. 37-38. Moore's discussion shows that the use of *uti possidetis* for establishing Latin American boundaries did not begin until the 1840s.

[4] Stated e.g. in Vicente E. Berasategui, *Malvinas, Diplomacia y Conflicto Armado: Comentarios a la Historia Oficial Británica*, Buenos Aires June 2011, p. 34.

disputes, and assert (pp. 100, 101) that the operation of the principle meant that in the early 19th century, as Latin American countries began to gain independence, there were no *terrae nullius* ["no man's lands"] in Latin America. That is untrue; in 1770 Spain had accepted that the Falklands were different from other Spanish possessions, and from 1790 there were vast areas in mainland South America, and extensive areas in the Falklands, that Britain (but no other country) was entitled to regard as *terrae nullius* under the Nootka Sound Convention – what counted was *actual local occupation* by Spain, not a mere claim without real presence on the ground (section 1.7).

Nevertheless, *uti possidetis* is the ultimate basis of the "irredentist" Argentine claim to the Falklands, i.e. the claim that the Falklands are an "unredeemed" part of Argentina "occupied" by Britain (in reference to territory, an irredentist claim is therefore *ipso facto* a legitimist claim, see sections 4.8, 4.9, 4.11, 8.11). That has been the official position of Argentine governments since the 1940s, and has been stated repeatedly at the United Nations since the mid-1960s. However, it has many weaknesses, which arise from six basic problems:

1) The first is the **nature of possession**. There are two schools of thought on this point: some authorities only accept *uti possidetis de facto*, i.e. the rightful and actual occupation of a territory, while others also accept *uti possidetis juris* (or *uti possidetis de jure*), which accepts law alone, without actual occupation, as being a sufficient basis for possession.[1] Under the Nootka Sound Convention Spain had been forced to drop its earlier "absolutist" or "legitimist" position (that Spain held sovereignty in the whole of South America under *uti possidetis juris* without reference to actual occupation), and had been forced to accept Britain's "*de-facto*-ist" position, under which sovereignty was only held in (or near) places actually occupied. Revealingly, Kohen and Rodríguez refer only to *uti possidetis juris* (e.g. pp. 100, 101, 105) – they sometimes say *uti possidetis* for short, but they never mention *uti possidetis de facto*. Britain still sees sovereignty from the practical, "democratic" viewpoint of *de facto* authority; Argentina follows the old "legitimist" Spanish view.

2) The second problem is **encumbrance**: the continued existence of an earlier claim which "encumbers" a later claim, i.e. limits its force by diluting its exclusivity. In this case Spain's continuing claim weakened the force of Argentina's new claim from the outset. Some Argentine writers assert that Argentina inherited Spain's rights in the Falklands immediately upon the revolt of Buenos Aires from Spain on 25 May 1810,[2] but that is patently false – throughout 1810 and well into 1811 Spain still had a garrison at Puerto Soledad (Port Louis) and was thus still in *de facto* possession of at least that part of the islands. Moreover, on withdrawing in February 1811 Spain stated a clear intention to return, and as late as 1822 and 1825 asserted her claim to the whole of South America (thus including the Falklands) by protesting against the recognition of the United Provinces of the River Plate by the United States and Britain (sections 4.8, 4.11).[3] Those protests preserved Spain's rights at least for some time, during which Spain's continuing claim was an encumbrance on Argentina's claim. The United States chargé d'affaires in Buenos Aires, Francis Baylies, stated in his long letter to the Buenos Aires foreign minister Manuel Maza dated 10 July 1832: "If the rights of Spain are dormant, they are not extinct; and the Undersigned has little doubt of her ability to maintain her actual rights (if any) over the Falkland Islands…".[4]

---

[1] Mikulas Fabry, *Recognizing States: International Society & the Establishment of New States Since 1776*, Oxford 2010, pp. 66-70 and fns. 86 and 88 p. 77.

[2] Asserted in e.g. Mario D. Tesler, *Expedición de David Jewett a las Islas Malvinas 1820-1821*, Santa Fe 1968, pp. 148-151; in [Anon., published by the Argentine army], *Conflicto Malvinas*, Buenos Aires 1983, vol. II, p. 14; and in Enrique Bravo, *La guerra de las i* ["The war of the i's"], Buenos Aires 1999, p. 13.

[3] Protest by the Spanish Minister to the United States, Señor Anduaga, 9 March 1822, quoted in John Bassett Moore, *Digest of International Law*, Washington DC 1906, vol. I, pp. 86-87, and also in Julius Goebel, *The Recognition Policy of the United States*, New York 1915, pp. 136-137; and protest by the Spanish foreign minister Francisco de Zea Bermúdez to the British chargé d'affaires at Madrid, 21 January 1825, in Herbert Arthur Smith (ed.), *Great Britain and the Law of Nations*, Vol. I, London 1932, pp. 152-62. See also Fabry 2010, p. 61 and p. 74 note 54.

[4] Full text in *BFSP 1832-1833*, (London 1836), pp. 338-355; extracts in William R. Manning, *Diplomatic Correspondence of the United States: Inter-American Affairs 1831-1860*, vol. I: *Argentina, Documents 1-387*, Washington DC 1932, pp. 111-126; this quote in *BFSP* p. 348 and Manning p. 120. For Baylies see sections 5.14, 6.15.

3) The third problem is **restrictions**: by the Nootka Sound Convention Spain surrendered her earlier claim to absolute sovereignty over her South American territories, including the Falklands, and accepted that Britain had extensive rights in the islands. After 1790 Spain's rights in the Falklands were restricted, so any rights inherited from Spain were restricted in the same way, since Argentina cannot have inherited more than Spain possessed. Argentina inherited not only Spain's rights but Spain's obligations, including the obligation to accept British economic activity (mainly "fishing", i.e. sealing) and Britain's right to establish settlements in the islands (section 1.7). That could only have been changed by agreement with Britain.

4) The fourth problem is what we call **identity of heir** – the question as to what precise entity is to inherit a claim that has split up. If the *uti possidetis* of 1810 had been applied rigorously, there would now be five independent states in mainland Spanish-speaking America, whose borders would be those of the four Spanish Viceroyalties (New Spain, Peru, New Granada, and Río de la Plata) plus the Captaincy-General of Venezuela. But there are sixteen independent mainland states; with few exceptions, not a single land border between modern Spanish-speaking Latin American states corresponds to the borders of the former Viceroyalties, and there have been innumerable later changes and readjustments,[1] including two in 1899-1902 and 1964-6 in which the extent of Argentina's territory was fixed by Britain (sections 9.1, 10.22). Most of those many changes were breaches of *uti possidetis* – it would be hard to find any other principle that has been so extensively honoured in the breach rather than in the observance. If the Viceroyalty of La Plata had become independent as a single state and the Falklands were the only part detached from it, then that single state could raise a unitary claim to the islands, but that is not the case; the former Viceroyalty split up in a complex way, into several independent countries plus parts of others. Thus Spain's title to the Falklands (already less than perfect) was split between Bolivia, Paraguay, Uruguay, the United Provinces of the River Plate (which later became Argentina), and parts of Peru and Chile.

In legal terms it is therefore unclear whether Argentina was a "continuing state" that took over all Spain's rights, or simply one of several "successor states", in which case inheritance of Spain's rights would not have been automatic but would have been subject to agreement among the successors.[2] In some cases of territorial dissolution one continuing state is clearly dominant – on the breakup of the Soviet Union in 1991 Russia was so much larger than the other successor states that there was immediate international recognition that it had succeeded to the Soviet Union's rights (e.g. its United Nations seat), whereas on the breakup of Yugoslavia in the early 1990s Serbia was less than half the size of the former state and the other successor states refused to accept Serbia's automatic inheritance of Yugoslavia's rights. Modern Argentina does not correspond to the territory of the former Viceroyalty: it covers only part of the Viceroyalty's area; the Intendancy of Buenos Aires excluded much of what is now northern Argentina, and the present division of Patagonia between Argentina and Chile does not follow any Spanish division. Moreover, in the 1810s and 20s it was unclear which provinces were actually in the United Provinces of the River Plate and which were not. For a long time it was not clear whether they included Uruguay and Paraguay (section 8.1), so it was unclear whether they too inherited a share of Spain's rights in the Falklands (which were not exclusive anyway). Furthermore, it was (and remained) unclear whether Spain's rights in the islands were inherited by the United Provinces as a whole or solely by the province of Buenos Aires, which was "charged" with the foreign policy of all the provinces.

Kohen and Rodríguez (p. 108) mention that we treat the question of "identity of heir" in *Getting it right* (they say on our "p. 7"; it is actually on p. 4 in both languages), and they assert that "Pascoe and Pepper make an argument that is not advanced by any State". That is untrue; the problem of

---

[1] For South American border changes and disputes see Gordon Ireland, *Boundaries, Possessions, and Conflicts in South America*, Cambridge (Massachusetts), 1938, 334 pp; there have been many more boundary disputes since 1938. Several maps showing boundary changes in South America are printed in Cathryn L. Lombardi and John V. Lombardi, *Latin American History: A Teaching Atlas*, Madison (Wisconsin), 1983.

[2] For the necessity of agreement between successor states see Marcelo G. Kohen and Patrick Dumberry, *The Institute of International Law's Resolution on State Succession and State Responsibility: Introduction, Text and Commentaries*, Cambridge 2019, p. 53. This work considers only cases and situations arising after around 1900, and mentions neither the Falklands nor the Nootka Sound Convention.

"identity of heir" was recognised by US envoy Francis Baylies, who in his letter of 10 July 1832 pointed out to Manuel Maza the territorial limitations of Argentina's claim:[1]

The ancient Vice Royalty of the Rio de la Plata is now divided between several distinct Nations, having no dependency on each other... If, then, the sovereign rights of Spain to those Southern Islands, descended to the ancient Vice Royalty of the Rio de la Plata, by virtue of the Revolution – and if that Vice Royalty is now divided into several Sovereignties, independent of each other; to which one of these several Sovereignties shall these rights be assigned?

That objection shows that Argentina inherited only a portion of Spain's rights, not all of them.

5) The fifth problem is that of **applicability**: in the Americas *uti possidetis* was only agreed between the mainland Spanish-speaking countries, whereas in some parts of South America several other countries were involved: on the mainland, Britain in British Honduras (now Belize) and British Guiana (now Guyana), the Netherlands in Dutch Guiana (now Suriname) and France in French Guiana (still a French overseas territory today); and in the offshore islands Britain, Denmark, France, the Netherlands, and (in Cuba and Puerto Rico) Spain. Those countries were not party to any decision on *uti possidetis*, and the histories of those territories diverged from the mainstream of the Spanish colonial empire. As Paul Hensel *et al.* say:[2]

The Latin American application of *uti possidetis* was also limited in effect to the territories of former Spanish colonies, with no impact on borders with (contemporary or former) colonies of other foreign powers. [...] ... it seems clear that the intraregional provisions of *uti possidetis* were only intended to apply to relations between the former Spanish colonies of Central and South America.

The *de facto* British presence in the Falklands from January 1766, antedating that of Spain by over a year, plus a continuous British economic involvement in the islands from then onwards and the British rights of sovereignty tolerated by Spain under the 1771 agreement, plus those conferred on Britain under the Nootka Sound Convention, seriously dilute the applicability of *uti possidetis* to the Falklands. Even Spain accepted that the Falklands were different from other Spanish territories – the Spanish minister of state, the marqués de Grimaldi, told the French ambassador on 23 July 1770 that the Spaniards were milder towards the British than to the French because the rights of Spain to territories on this side of the Magellan Straits were not so securely established and were disputed by Britain, and on 25 August 1770 the Spanish navy minister de Arriaga told Francisco Bucareli, Governor of Buenos Aires, that the Maluinas were different from any other part of Spain's claimed dominions (section 2.3).[3] And after the Nootka Sound Convention in 1790 the Spanish commandants in the Falklands received orders to permit the "English Royalists" to exploit the islands, as Louis Vernet wrote in his "Report" in 1832 (section 2.7).

One might put it in a nutshell by saying that although the Falklands are in *South* America, they are not in *Latin* America, and are thus not covered by a principle that applied only to relations between Latin American successor states to Spain.

6) The sixth problem is the **critical date** from which the principle is to apply. The Spanish-speaking South American republics agreed in the 1840s that the territory of each republic should in principle correspond to the old Spanish territorial divisions, but the areas actually held by the emerging republics, from the dates of their declarations of independence onwards, varied widely as the fortunes of battle and politics ebbed and flowed; the choice of certain critical dates would extinguish some republics and double the size of others. Like some other Argentine authors, Kohen and Rodríguez say (p. 117) that 1810 should be taken as the critical date, but that is untenable. In the case of the Falklands there is a strong case for taking 1850 as the critical date (section 7.16).

---

[1] Baylies 10 July 1832, in *BFSP 1832-1833*, p. 349; Manning 1932, p. 121.
[2] Paul R. Hensel, Michael E. Allison and Ahmed Khanani, "Territorial Integrity Treaties, *Uti Possidetis*, and Armed Conflict over Territory", a paper presented at the 2006 Shambaugh Conference "Building Synergies: Institutions and Cooperation in World Politics", University of Iowa 13 October 2006, online under http://www.paulhensel.org/ Research/iow06.pdf, accessed 6 March 2011, pp. 14, 21.
[3] Martin-Allanic 1964, pp. 1000, 1007-1008.

All those six problems (**nature of possession, encumbrance, restrictions, identity of heir, applicability** and **critical date**) mean that Argentina did not inherit a perfect title to the Falklands. Thus it is untrue to say "Argentina inherited the Falklands from Spain". Argentina inherited Spain's *rights and obligations* in the Falklands, and Spain's rights amounted to less than 100% sovereignty, while Spain's obligations conferred extensive rights on Britain. Those rights could only have been changed with Britain's agreement, which was neither sought nor forthcoming. In short, Argentina acquired only **part of an encumbered and restricted title**, and the encumbrance and restrictions continued throughout Argentina's 8-year presence in the islands.

Kohen and Rodríguez misrepresent not only Argentina's position but the historical and legal facts. They say (pp. 21, 25):

(p. 21): Argentina's position has remained exactly the same since the time of independence... The islands are Argentine by virtue of its succession to Spain's rights, the concrete display of sovereignty by the new South American nation from the beginning of the process of independence in 1810 until 1833, year of the eviction by Britain, and the lack of Argentine consent to the British occupation since 1833. The succession to Spain's rights is justified by the recognition of Spanish sovereignty by the main European maritime powers, by Spain's continuation of France's right of first occupant (1764), and by its continuous exercise of sovereignty over the islands until 1811 – an exclusive exercise between 1774 and 1811. [...] (p. 25): the essence of the Spanish, and consequently Argentine, claim is based on other arguments,[1] such as: 1) recognition by maritime powers – including England – that the region, including the islands, belonged to Spain; 2) the right of first occupancy and 3) the continuous, public and peaceful exercise of sovereignty until 1811.

All that is untrue. Argentina's position has *not* remained exactly the same – Argentina dropped its claim to the islands completely in 1850, and abandoned it by showing overt acquiescence for decades in Britain's possession of the islands; from 1810 till 1829 there was *no* concrete display of Argentine sovereignty; Argentina's succession to Spain's rights was *encumbered* by Spain's continuing claim and *restricted* by the weaknesses we have indicated in this chapter; there was absolutely *no* "recognition of Spanish sovereignty by the main European maritime powers"; Britain's occupancy *antedated* Spain's, and Spain's "exercise of sovereignty" was severely *limited* by Britain's rights under the Nootka Sound Convention of 1790 (section 1.7). The evidence we present in this book refutes all the points made by Kohen and Rodríguez.

---

[1] I.e. other arguments than discovery, the papal Bulls and the Treaty of Tordesillas, mentioned earlier in the sentence.

CHAPTER FOUR: the years 1811-25

Kohen and Rodríguez misleadingly head their chapter IV "Argentine administration, 1810-1833" (pp. 113-187). In fact for most of that period there was no "Argentine administration" whatever and no Argentine presence in the Falklands, whereas Britain's rights were upheld by a constant British civilian presence in the form of sealers and whalers. As elsewhere much of what Kohen and Rodríguez say is untrue, while other things are true but irrelevant. They depart on occasion from strict chronological order; we follow only partly the order of their presentation.

4.1 An insignificant act

They begin by mentioning (p. 113) "The first Argentine administrative act concerning the Falklands/ Malvinas five days after the constitution of the First Patriotic Government in 1810" [i.e. on 30 May 1810]. This turns out to be an order issued by the new republican authorities in Buenos Aires, that the penultimate Spanish commandant, Gerardo Bordas, should be paid what was owed him. Kohen and Rodríguez say (p. 115)[1] that this first public act of the new government demonstrates the "governmental continuity" in respect of the Malvinas, and they add that it is little wonder that "Pascoe and Pepper do not even mention this public act, which is widely known".

Little wonder indeed – in the 40 pages of our paper *Getting it right* we did not have room to mention such an infinitesimally tiny event, which in any case had absolutely no effect on the Falklands since at that time, and for eight months afterwards, there was a Spanish commandant in the islands, Pablo Guillén Martínez, who had served from January 1810 and remained in office at Puerto Soledad until February 1811. Kohen and Rodríguez say (p. 117) that from 1810 the emerging South American nations no longer recognised Spanish sovereignty, and that therefore 1810 is the "critical date" for establishing the inheritance of Spanish territory by the new South American states. That is not true – for "critical date" see chapter 3 and section 7.16.

4.2 The Spanish withdrawal from the Falklands, 13 February 1811

As Kohen and Rodríguez say (p. 116), the Spanish governor in Montevideo issued orders on 8 January 1811 to withdraw the Spanish garrison from the Malvinas. Accordingly, Captain Manuel Moreno sailed to Puerto Soledad in the brig *Gálvez*, collected the garrison and prisoners, released the cattle and horses, and sailed again on 13 February 1811, leaving a lead plaque asserting that the island and all it contained was the property of the Spanish king, Fernando VII. The plaque was a statement of an *animus revertendi* ["a mind to return"], like the plaque left by the British at Port Egmont in 1774. Kohen and Rodríguez correctly say that there was no abandonment of sovereignty by Spain, though they do not mention the plaque. Such a plaque fulfils much the same function as an owner's name in a book, and in reference to territory it has the effect of maintaining the original owner's claim for a time, though there is no agreement as to how long that time may be.

4.3 Non-displays of Argentine sovereignty in the Falklands, 1811-1820

The Argentine authors then consider (pp. 117-137) the years 1811-1820, in which they maintain there were "displays of Argentine sovereignty and absence of any British claim". A closer examination reveals that there were in fact no "displays of Argentine sovereignty".

The first "display of Argentine sovereignty" they mention (p. 118) is nothing of the sort. It is merely a letter dated 2 March 1811 from Manuel Belgrano, an important figure in Argentina's independence struggle, in the newspaper *Correo de Comercio*, complaining of the "ingleses", who "constantly circulate" around the coasts of Patagonia and the Malvinas hunting whales (he does not mention seals), and adding that when asked by an officer of a Spanish frigate why they were in those seas, the crew of an "inglés" ship replied that those seas were open to all. That is all.

Kohen and Rodríguez comment that the "marinos ingleses" (their English translation reads "British sailors", but it should say "English", i.e. English-speaking)[2] never invoked any claimed

---

[1] As explained in the Introduction, we quote from the English translation of Kohen and Rodríguez, but we give page-numbers from the paper Spanish version of 2015.

[2] "Inglés" meant both British and Americans; the Spaniards did not distinguish consistently between them, just as the British and Americans often called all Spanish-speakers "Spaniards", whether they were from Spain or South America.

British sovereignty over Malvinas, but statistically speaking those "ingleses" were more likely to have been American than British, so they would hardly have mentioned British sovereignty. And whether they were American or British, their reply merely meant "We have a perfect right to be here". How that can be taken to be a "display of Argentine sovereignty" is beyond us.

The second "display of Argentine sovereignty" turns out to be equally devoid of substance. First mentioned very briefly by the Argentine historian Ricardo Caillet-Bois, it was a request by "Enrique" (Henry) Jones of the British-owned brig *El Rastrero*, addressed to the authorities in Buenos Aires on 30 January 1813, for permission to go to the Malvinas and southern coasts to hunt seals. Kohen and Rodríguez illustrate (p. 119) the register entry recording the request,[1] and assert that "This act unquestionably shows the perception a British subject had regarding the sovereignty of the United Provinces of the Rio de la Plata in the Falklands/Malvinas". They imply that in 1813 it was natural for a British subject wishing to exploit the Falklands to go to Buenos Aires to ask permission. That is nonsense – Captain Jones's request demonstrates nothing. He was Henry Libanus Jones (1787-1861), a Welshman, who had been resident in Buenos Aires since about 1810 and was to live in Argentina for the rest of his life, playing a significant role in the opening up of the Patagonian coast.[2] A request made in Buenos Aires by a resident of Buenos Aires is irrelevant and says nothing about the "perception" of British citizens. None of the hundreds of British captains based in Britain asked Spain or the Buenos Aires authorities for permission to hunt seals in the Falklands, either before or after Argentine independence, and Argentina never harassed British ships which put into Buenos Aires en route to or from the Falklands.

Kohen and Rodríguez then (pp. 119-120) attack us sharply for our "lack of seriousness" in our account of the years 1811-20 in *Getting it right*. They quote our comment (our p. 9) that:

After 1811, the Falklands had no resident population, though they were still visited by many British and American ships, whose crews sometimes spent long periods ashore in the islands, built stone houses and huts, and even grew vegetables. So the language spoken in and around the Falklands from 1811 onwards was English, as it had been since the 1770s except at Puerto Soledad.

The two Argentine authors say (p. 120) that "Making a point about the language spoken in a deserted territory is comical", especially "the suggestion that this could be of some relevance in regard to the question of sovereignty". In fact of course the Falklands were far from deserted; there were sometimes over a hundred British and American seamen in the islands, some of whom spent a year or even two years there. The remarks by Kohen and Rodríguez reveal their narrow-minded focus on sovereignty; we discussed sovereignty in *Getting it right* too of course, and rebutted the incorrect assertions of Argentine authors about it (though Kohen and Rodríguez nonetheless repeat those assertions), but there is more to our account than that. Every country has a cultural history as well as a legal history, and the Falklands are no exception. Unlike Kohen and Rodríguez, we – and many others – see the Falklands as a real country with its own fascinating and epic history, which differs dramatically from the cultural, political and legal history of Argentina.

In our forthcoming books, we describe in some detail the visits of English-speaking crews to the islands from the 1760s onwards, and the extent of their influence on the islands. They not only built stone houses, the ruins of some of which still stand; they landed pigs and rabbits, which became an important source of food – the pigs were the salvation of some American visitors in 1813-14 (section 4.5), as were the rabbits for some Argentine visitors in 1824 (section 4.9). The English-speaking crews also introduced many place-names that have been used in the islands for centuries – Byron and McBride gave some places their names a quarter of a millennium ago in the 1760s, and in the years 1811-20, for example, the visits of American sealers such as Edmund Fanning led to the

---

[1] They give the signature of the entry (AGN VII, 7-4-5), but their source was Ricardo R. Caillet-Bois in *Una Tierra Argentina: Las Islas Malvinas* ["An Argentine Land: The Malvinas Islands"], 3rd ed., Buenos Aires 1982, p. 180, note 6 (p. 178 in the 1st ed., Buenos Aires 1948, p. 180 in the 2nd ed., 1952, of which the 3rd ed. is a facsimile reprint). Caillet-Bois also gives the reference AGN, División Colonia, Sección Gobierno, Hacienda, S. V, C. X, A. 4, N° 6, which Kohen and Rodríguez also give, though they do not mention that he misread "Jones" as "Torres".

[2] Details from an article by David Williams, in the local paper *El Regional*, Gaiman, Chubut, Argentina, "Henry Libanus Jones: su Verdadero Origen..." ["Henry Libanus Jones, his True Origin..."], published in two parts in March and April 2003, available online under http://www.histarmar.com.ar/InfHistorica/Jones-1.htm.

place-names Fannings Head and the Volunteer Rocks.[1] And as regards sovereignty, the British crews were exercising Britain's rights under the 1771 agreement and the Nootka Sound Convention (sections 2.3, 1.7), and would have been entitled to set up permanent settlements in the north-west of the islands – some of their establishments were certainly semi-permanent, and some stone buildings such as forges, storehouses and dwellings were used for some years, if not continuously. A. G. E. Jones (1986) lists some 1,800 ships, mostly British ones, that visited the South Atlantic from the 1770s to the 1860s (section 2.6), including several (*Uxbridge*, *Adeona*, *Unicorn*) captained by the Scottish captain William Low, who from 1813 spent many years in the area and often visited the Falklands, in whose history he played a notable role (sections 6.1, 6.32).

Kohen and Rodríguez say none of that constitutes a British claim to sovereignty, and point out that the Argentine ships *Espíritu Santo* (as they spell the name), *San Juan Nepomuceno* and *25 de Mayo* went to the South Atlantic, and that the *Espíritu Santo* was in the Malvinas in 1819. Actually, the *Espirito Santo* (as her owners spelt her) had a mainly British crew, who on Christmas Day 1819 claimed the South Shetland Islands for Britain – they saw themselves as agents of British sovereignty, not Argentinian (section 4.6). In any case, if Argentine ships were a display of Argentine sovereignty, then the very much more numerous British ships were a much stronger display of British sovereignty.

4.4 An irrelevant letter, 1816

The next purported "display of Argentine sovereignty" is just as flimsy. Kohen and Rodríguez (pp. 120-121) head their brief account of it "General San Martín and the Falklands/Malvinas", referring to José Francisco de San Martín y Matorras (1778-1850), an Argentine general who liberated large parts of South America from Spanish rule, including Argentina, where he is a national hero. His connection with the Falklands is non-existent, but on 14 June 2012 the then president of Argentina, Cristina Fernández de Kirchner, attended the United Nations decolonisation committee, the "Committee of 24" or "C24", in New York (with a 90-strong Argentine delegation), and read out part of a letter by San Martín which she said was significant in showing that such an important person had mentioned the Malvinas Islands before 1833.[2]

Now there is nothing wrong in mentioning the Malvinas Islands (anyone is free to do so), but we are puzzled that Kohen and Rodríguez bother to mention this letter – they say it indicates that for "the officials who wrote the note" the Malvinas were part of Argentine territory. How that counts as a "display of Argentine sovereignty" is beyond our understanding, and in any case it turns out that the letter is irrelevant. It was written by San Martín on 14 August 1816, addressed to the deputy governor of the city of San Juan, but most of it is a quote from a letter from the (unnamed) minister of war dated 31 July 1816. The war minister (who was Antonio Berutti), quoted by San Martín, asks the deputy governor to release any soldiers held within his jurisdiction who had been sentenced to be punished in the presidios of Patagones, Malvinas, or others. That is all.

In other words, if there were any such soldiers, they were in San Juan, not in the Malvinas. Far from being a "display of Argentine sovereignty" it might equally indicate that the war minister and San Martín did *not* regard the islands as Argentine territory – they knew any such prisoners had not gone to the Malvinas despite having been sentenced to go there.

So the letter says nothing whatever about Argentine sovereignty over the Falklands, but Cristina de Kirchner's speech may have fixed the erroneous idea in some Argentinians' minds that Argentina was present in the islands in 1816. That false impression was reinforced by the then Argentine foreign minister Héctor Timerman, who mentioned the letter at the C24 on 20 June 2013. Despite its entire lack of relevance, the original letter was transferred in August 2014 from the archives of the Argentine foreign ministry to the Malvinas Museum in Buenos Aires, at a ceremony attended by the Argentine minister of culture, Teresa Parodi, who described it as "an essential document to build on our sovereignty" and added that this means "the Liberator was aware of our

---

[1] Edmund Fanning, *Voyages round the World...*, 1st ed. New York 1833; 2nd ed. New York 1838; new ed. Salem, Massachusetts, 1924; his ship was the *Volunteer*. In the Falklands Fannings Head always has an "s".
[2] Details from the website of the Presidencia de la Nación Argentina. For the C24 see section 10.11.

Malvinas Islands, even before they were usurped by the British in 1833". The director of the museum, Jorge Giles, then made the absurd claim that: "The letter is evidence that while becoming a free nation Argentina was exercising sovereignty over the Malvinas Islands."[1] That is twaddle of course, but it shows how "trifles light as air" are used by Argentine governments – and by Kohen and Rodríguez – to support the Argentine claim to the Falklands.

4.5 The wreck of the *Isabella*; Captain Barnard marooned in the Falklands, 1813-14

We are also puzzled by the importance Kohen and Rodríguez give to this episode, which they claim (p. 121) shows "that foreign sailors knew that sovereignty over the islands belonged to Spain or the new-born Argentina and the fact that their presence could be considered illegal". All that is nonsense – the episode in fact demonstrates that "foreign" seamen (i.e. foreign to modern Argentinians) did *not* know what was going on in the islands, and they cannot have known of any Argentine sovereignty since there was none.

The *Isabella* episode was an epic sequence of shipwreck and maroonings in the Falklands that lasted from February 1813 to November 1814, during the War of 1812 (1812-14) between Britain and the United States. It is an extraordinary story of bad luck, good luck, treachery, fortitude, and survival in the wilderness, which brought despair, great suffering and mortal danger to those involved. But no one died; all were rescued in the end, and one person even contrived to be born – Eliza Providence Durie, born on Eagle (now Speedwell) Island on 21 February 1813, the first British subject born in the Falkland Islands. The story has been told by David Miller,[2] by Captain Charles Barnard (the principal victim)[3] and by Lieutenant Richard Lundin,[4] and will be retold in detail in *The Falklands Saga*; we have room here for only a brief summary.

The American sealing captain Charles Barnard arrived in the Falklands on 7 September 1812 in his sealing vessel *Nanina*, and while he and his crew were in the western Falklands, the British brig *Isabella* was wrecked on 9 February 1813 on Eagle Island at the south end of Falkland Sound. All 54 people aboard survived and put up tents and huts on the island, and the ship's longboat, with six men aboard including Lundin, was sent to Buenos Aires to seek help. They set off on 22 February 1813 (the day after the birth of Eliza Durie), and after a gruelling 40-day voyage they reached Buenos Aires, where the resident British officer, Captain Peter Heywood of HMS *Nereus* (who had sailed with Captain William Bligh in HMAV *Bounty*[5]) sent the decrepit British Royal Navy brig HMS *Nancy* to the islands to rescue the *Isabella*'s castaways. Meanwhile Barnard had found them and offered to take them to Buenos Aires in the *Nanina*, but some of the British captured the *Nanina* (the two countries were at war) and sailed away in June 1813, marooning Barnard and four of his crew members, plus his dog Cent, in midwinter in the Falklands. They survived in great hardship for almost a year and a half, moving in their boat around the outer islands to the west of West Falkland, surviving mainly on meat from the wild pigs. The pigs were the descendants of those landed by Captain John McBride (section 2.3) and later visitors, and had thrived and become large and dangerous (but Cent proved an expert pig-catcher). Sadly, like the wild cattle and horses, the pigs were wiped out in the late 19th century.

For two months, October to December 1813, Barnard was marooned alone on New Island by the other four, though they eventually rejoined him and asked his forgiveness. The *Nancy* arrived in the islands in May 1813 and rescued the *Isabella*'s 55 castaways from Eagle Island, but failed to search properly for the five men, and the *Nanina* and the *Nancy* left without them. Eventually, after one year, five months and fifteen days alone in the bleak, uninhabited Falkland Islands, Barnard and

---

[1] Details and quotes from the "Mercopress" website, 18 August 2014.
[2] David Miller, *The Wreck of the Isabella*, Barnsley (Yorkshire), 1995.
[3] Charles Barnard, *A Narrative of the Sufferings and Adventures of Capt. Charles H. Barnard...*, New York 1829; new ed. by Bertha S. Dodge: *MAROONED: Being a Narrative of the Sufferings and Adventures...*, Middletown, Connecticut, 1979.
[4] [Anon.], "Narrative of a Voyage from new South Wales in 1812-1813", in *Lowe's Edinburgh Journal*, October 1846, pp. 281-314; internal evidence shows that it is by Lundin.
[5] "His Majesty's Armed Vessel"; the *Bounty* left Britain in 1787 and the prefix "HMS" ("His Majesty's Ship") was not used before 1789.

his four companions were rescued in November 1814 by two British brigs – the British commander-in-chief on the South American Station, Rear Admiral Manley Dixon, had instructed all British ships touching at the Falklands to look out for them, and his instructions bore fruit.

Kohen and Rodríguez print (p. 122) some quotes from Barnard (in Bertha Dodge's edition), in which he says he feared the people he saw on Eagle Island might be Spanish, and was relieved to see that one of them was a woman and that some of them were British Marines.[1] The two authors say (p. 123) that Barnard's remarks "prove" that "foreign" seamen considered the islands to belong to Spain and that they themselves were sealing illegally, but that is nonsense. British seamen and the British government held the islands to be British; Spain held them to be Spanish but accepted a restriction of Spanish sovereignty under the Nootka Sound Convention, which gave British seamen extensive rights to exploit almost the whole of the islands, plus the right of permanent settlement in the north-western part. And to Americans like Barnard, the islands were open to all, not a Spanish, Argentine or British possession – at that time the United States government held them to be part of the high seas and did not recognise any territorial sovereignty by any country.

The two Argentine authors mention (p. 123) the visit to Port Louis (Puerto Soledad) by Richard Lundin on 8 March 1813 on the epic voyage in the *Isabella*'s longboat to Buenos Aires to fetch help. Kohen and Rodríguez say that they "had the intention of heading to the Spanish settlement", but they did not actively look for the Spaniards. On Eagle Island before the longboat left, the senior officer, Captain Durie, wrote letters to Montevideo, to the British admiral commanding at Rio de Janeiro, and to "the Governor of the Falkland Islands", i.e. the Spanish governor (they did not know the Spaniards were long gone), but they took ten days to get up Falkland Sound, and as Lundin says, they "resolved to give up any further search after a settlement in these islands; but to proceed to Monte Video". In the event they found Puerto Soledad by chance – the boat hit a rock at the entrance to Salvador Water, and while four of her six-man crew[2] were making repairs, Lundin and an American seaman called Ford did some exploring. They found a track with marks of carriage wheels, and followed it till they saw houses in the distance; they avoided being attacked by the wild cattle, and eventually reached the former settlement. It was a ghost town partly in ruins; they cut some cabbages in the abandoned gardens, but were glad to leave again.

Kohen and Rodríguez say (pp. 124-5) that the British commanding officer in the River Plate (i.e. Heywood) would have had an excellent chance to assert British sovereignty in the Falklands, but limited himself to rescuing the castaways, not performing any act of sovereignty but ordering his "subordinate" (i.e. Lieutenant William D'Aranda of the *Nancy*) to return to the River Plate. To that, one can only say that if the territory was British, there was no need for an act of sovereignty. In short, the behaviour of British and American seamen was not a "display of Argentine sovereignty".

4.6 David Jewett; Argentina's supposed "official taking of possession of the islands in 1820"

Kohen and Rodríguez devote 13 pages (pp. 125-137) to what they call "The official taking of possession of the islands by Argentina in 1820". This refers to the visit of David Jewett to the Falklands in 1820-21, which has been described with extraordinary inaccuracy by many writers, American, British and Argentinian, including Kohen and Rodríguez themselves, and by Argentina at the United Nations. All those accounts suffer from their authors' ignorance of history: they rely on erroneous later accounts (including that by Louis Vernet; see section 4.7) instead of contemporary documents, and they are unaware of the important details in ships' logbooks. They also fail to realise how several distinct episodes were related. We have room only for an extremely brief account here, but it will show that Kohen and Rodríguez fail to understand what happened.

The story of the complex events in the Falklands in the year 1820 begins three years earlier: on 17 September 1817 the French 22-gun corvette *Uranie* of 350 tons, commanded by a 38-year-old nobleman, Louis-Claude de Saulces de Freycinet (1779-1842), left Toulon on a round-the-world exploring voyage. Almost a year later on 23 August 1818 the 266-ton American ship *General Knox*, commanded by William B. Orne, left her home port of Salem, Massachusetts, in company with the

---

[1] They quote (in Spanish) Barnard's remarks from Dodge 1979, pp. 53-54; the original is in Barnard 1829, pp. 18-19.
[2] Kohen and Rodríguez say the boat had 7 aboard, but Lundin himself says her crew were "six in all" (1846, p. 290).

40-ton shallop (small schooner) *Governor Brooks*, for a sealing voyage of almost three years.[1] Orne later acquired a second shallop, perhaps called *Penguin*. Unlike most sealing ships, which normally visited several sealing grounds, Orne's three vessels remained entirely in the Falklands, where they spent over two years from late 1818 to early 1821. The shallops moved around the islands as "tenders", their crews killing seals and taking the skins and oil to the *General Knox*, which remained at anchor at West Point Island. Various other visitors to the islands, some of whom later became famous, encountered or contacted Captain Orne and his vessels during that time.

In 1819 the British made an important discovery in the Antarctic Ocean south of the Falklands – the South Shetland Islands.[2] They were first seen on 19 February by William Smith, captain of the British brig *Williams*, who noted the vast numbers of seals in the area. On his return voyage he saw the islands again and on 16 October 1819 sent a boat ashore and claimed them for George III.[3]

The news of this new sealing ground spread fast – it meant a bonanza for sealing captains if they moved fast enough. There ensued a veritable run of ships to the South Shetlands, some of which called at the Falklands on the way, but it took them a long time to get there. In late 1819 news of the discovery reached Buenos Aires, where there was a growing and enterprising community of British merchants, some of whom chartered the brig *Espirito Santo* (mentioned by Kohen and Rodríguez, see section 4.3), with a mainly British crew and a British master (navigating officer), Joseph Herring, and sent her to the South Shetlands. The *Espirito Santo* was the first sealing ship to get there, and on Christmas Day 1819 some of her crew landed on Rugged Island, raised the Union Jack and claimed the islands for Britain (not knowing that they had already been claimed in October by Captain Smith of the *Williams*).[4] Another ship that reacted quickly to the news was the 131-ton brig *Hersilia* from Stonington, Connecticut. Her captain was James P. Sheffield, whose second mate was the 20-year-old Nathaniel Brown Palmer (1799-1877), later a noted Antarctic explorer. Sheffield put in at the Falklands and learnt of the South Shetlands from other sealers; he at once sailed there, collected 8,868 sealskins, and on 27 February 1820 confirmed the new discovery at Buenos Aires on his way home to Stonington.[5]

Many Stonington shipowners sprang into action, and fitted out nine ships to sail to the new sealing grounds,[6] including the *Free Gift* and Nathaniel Brown Palmer's first command, the *Hero*. The *Hero* was of only 44 tons, 47 feet long, but Palmer made some important discoveries in her, including part of the Antarctic Peninsula later known as Palmer Land.[7] The *Hero* sailed on 12 August 1820 in company with a larger ship, the *Express*; other Stonington ships that followed were the *Hersilia* (again), the *Clothier* (which was wrecked in the south), the *Emeline*, the *Catharina* and the *Spark*. From New York went the *Jane Maria, Aurora, Henry*, and *Charity*; Nantucket sent the *Huntress* (Captain Christopher Burdick), and several ships sailed from other American ports.

British ships also took part in the run: the *Hetty* of London, the Liverpool ship *George*, the *Hannah*, the *Lady Troubridge*, the *Anne*, and also the *Jane* of Leith in Scotland, a 160-ton American-built brig captured during the War of 1812. She was commanded by James Weddell (1787-1834), whose memoirs are an important source for the history of the Falklands in the 1820s.[8]

---

[1] Kenneth J. Bertrand, *Americans in Antarctica*, New York 1971, pp. 115-116. Orne collected 5,000 sealskins and 600 barrels of oil from the Falklands, and returned to Salem on 5 June 1821 (Bertrand 1971, p. 116).
[2] R.J. Campbell, *The Discovery of the South Shetland Islands, 1819-1820...*, London 2000, pp. 3-4, 46; Bertrand 1971, p. 42, and Alan Gurney, *Below the Convergence...*, London 1997, pp. 173-4, 191. The islands were also known as "New [South] Shetland", etc.
[3] Account in this paragraph mostly from Gurney 1997, pp. 152-157, and Campbell 2000, pp. 40-43, 201.
[4] Gurney 1997, p. 158; Campbell 2000, p. 187. Campbell prints (pp. 190-191) the full text of Herring's account dated 3 July 1820, from the *Imperial Magazine* for August 1820; he does not mention the Falklands.
[5] Fanning 1833, pp. 429-430; Weddell 1827, pp. 69-72; Bertrand 1971, pp. 43-58; Gurney 1997, pp. 159, 161, 174, 191; Campbell 2000, p. 187-188; Edouard Stackpole, *The Voyage of* The Huron *and* The Huntress..., Mystic (Connecticut), November 1955, pp. 10-13; John R. Spears, *Captain Nathaniel Brown Palmer...*, New York 1922, pp. 23-28.
[6] For the American sealers see Bertrand 1971, pp. 61, 123; Gurney 1997, pp. 174-177; Stackpole 1955, p. 15-17, 19.
[7] The voyage of the *Hero* is recounted in Bertrand 1971 and in Spears 1922.
[8] James Weddell, *A Voyage towards the South Pole...*, London 1825; 2nd extended ed. London 1827. Facsimile reprint of 1827 ed., with new introduction by Sir Vivian Fuchs, Newton Abbot 1970. Weddell is pronounced "Weddle".

His three voyages to the South Atlantic brought him fame as an explorer but no financial reward.¹

While all those ships, American and British, were busy preparing to go to the South Shetlands, the *Uranie* was on her way home from her round-the-world voyage, and was wrecked in Berkeley Sound in the Falklands on 14 February 1820. All the 120 people on board survived, and set up a large camp on the south shore of the Sound to await rescue. On 19 March one of William Orne's two shallops arrived, and Louis de Freycinet asked her captain to sail back to Orne at West Point Island requesting rescue. The master of the shallop took ten days to reach Port Egmont, where James Weddell was anchored in the *Jane*. The shallop sailed on to West Point Island, followed by the *Jane*; at West Point Island Weddell soon heard about the *Uranie* and realised the Americans were trying to keep the news of the wreck from him, to keep the salvage money for themselves. He requested a passage round to Port Louis in Orne's other shallop, the *Governor Brooks*; Orne himself joined him, and at Port Louis they met Freycinet. Orne's price for rescuing the castaways was too high, and in the end they were rescued by the American ship *Mercury*, in which the *Uranie*'s company left the islands on 27 April. Freycinet gave Weddell his longboat, which Weddell named *Rose* after Freycinet's wife and used as a tender.

Meanwhile, in mid-March 1820, a ship left Buenos Aires which eight months later was to play a much misunderstood role in the Falklands. She was the frigate *Heroína*, commanded by David Jewett (1772-1842), an American from New London, Connecticut,² who had been a US Navy captain and had sailed as a privateer in the War of 1812.³ The end of the Napoleonic Wars in 1815 had left him unemployed, and like many American and British seamen he went to South America, where the emerging independent republics were fighting against Spain. In Buenos Aires on 21 June 1815 he received a privateering commission issued by the United Provinces (the future Argentina), licensing him to attack all Spanish ships, with the proviso that Spanish property found under the flags of Britain or the United States was to be respected. During his voyage he captured at least five Spanish ships, and returned to Buenos Aires in 1817.⁴ On 15 January 1820 the Buenos Aires minister of war and marine, Matías de Irigoyen, gave him a privateering commission appointing him captain of the *Heroína*, with the rank of army colonel, and when he left on his next voyage in March 1820, he again sailed as a privateer licensed to capture Spanish ships.

Privateering was an internationally accepted way of waging war until it was abolished by the Paris Declaration Respecting Maritime Law of 16 April 1856. The term "privateer" referred to both ships and captains, so the *Heroína* was a privateer and Jewett himself was a privateer too. Privateers only existed in wartime, and had a purpose that was legal only in war: to aid a belligerent state's war effort by capturing enemy ships without cost to the state. Privateers were of course armed, but they were not warships. Warships were government ships, and their crews received wages from the state, which were disbursed when they were "paid off" at the end of each voyage. Privateers were privately owned ships, whose crews were paid by the ship's backers and/or owners, who bought the ship's supplies and fitted her out; they bore the risk but shared with the captain and crew the profits from any ships captured ("prizes"), which was the incentive for the operation and also helped the state to wage war. The state paid nothing; its role was only to provide the necessary legitimacy by issuing a privateering commission or licence.

The *Heroína* was owned by a Buenos Aires merchant of Irish origin, Patrick (Patricio) Lynch

---

¹ On his three voyages Weddell paid four visits to the Falklands, all in command of the *Jane*: (1) February-November 1820 (*Uranie*; Jewett); (2) October 1821 (with the *Beaufoy* under McLeod; met Charles Barnard); (3) May-October 1823 (with the *Beaufoy* under Brisbane), and (4) February-March 1824 (same voyage, still with the *Beaufoy* under Brisbane). He died in poverty, unmarried, in lodgings in London, on 9 September 1834 aged only 47. Biography in A.G.E. Jones, *Polar Portraits: Collected Papers*, Whitby 1992, pp. 375-381. See entry by Ann Savours in *DFB*.

² For Jewett's life see Frederic Clarke Jewett, *History and Genealogy of the Jewetts of America...*, New York 1908 (2 vols., 1197 pages), vol. I, pp. 197, 334; Mario Tesler, *Malvinas: Como EE. UU. provocó la usurpación inglesa* ["Malvinas: How the US provoked the English usurpation"], Buenos Aires 1979, pp. 37-41; José Antonio da Fonseca Figueira, *David Jewett...*, Buenos Aires 1985, and also our entry in *DFB*.

³ Da Fonseca Figueira 1985, pp. 20-21; 24-30; fn. 16, p. 32.

⁴ Da Fonseca Figueira 1985, p. 43, 44-47, 50-52, 58, 134, fn. 1. The Argentine naval historian Ánjel Justiniano Carranza (1834-99) refers to at least five Spanish ships that Jewett captured, in *Campañas Navales de la República Argentina*, vol. III, Buenos Aires 1916, p. 221; new ed. 1962 vol. II, p. 211.

and some American partners; they fitted the ship out but were unable to obtain the guns and ammunition, which the Buenos Aires government supplied at Lynch's request from the state arsenal.[1] The government gave Jewett a military rank since he was in the service of the state (if indirectly), and he was in charge of government property (guns and ammunition), but it was otherwise a typical privateering voyage in a private ship. Privateering was a hit-or-miss business – some privateer shipowners and crews made a great deal of money, while others ended up destitute.

There were strict rules governing privateering, and if a privateer breached the rules he was guilty of piracy. Thus every prize captured had to be presented to a prize court for judgement, and until the court ruled that the ship was "lawful prize" the cargo hatches had to be kept sealed. Every privateer captain had to carry a privateering commission issued by a national government, confirming that he was a privateer and authorising him to attack ships of that government's enemy – without that document, he would be a pirate. The United Provinces were at war with Spain but not with Portugal, and Jewett knew that.

The Buenos Aires government regarded him as a privateer and no more; his function was simply to capture Spanish ships. Jewett's commission (which survives) did not order him to claim the Falkland Islands or to go there at all.[2] Some Argentine authors assume there must have been orders to Jewett to claim the Falklands,[3] but that reveals their ignorance of what a privateer was. Jewett's only profit from the voyage would be from the prizes he took; there was no money to be made in the Falklands, and the islands were a vast distance from the most likely place to find Spanish ships (the North Atlantic), so any order to claim the Falklands would have amounted to sabotaging his privateering voyage. As it turned out, Jewett's expectations of rich pickings in the North Atlantic were dramatically disappointed, but neither he nor the government knew that beforehand. And even after the government knew he was in the Falklands, it issued no instructions to him or his successor William Mason that gave them any role in the islands (such as governor), nor even implied that they were on Argentine territory – Mason was simply ordered to continue the privateering voyage. In short, when Jewett set off he aimed only to capture Spanish ships.

His voyage was a disaster. Patricio Lynch and partners had done some shameless profiteering, and the ship and her stores were in a parlous state – the ship and the water-casks leaked, and many of her crew died of scurvy from the bad food. As a privateer hoping to capture Spanish ships, Jewett naturally headed for the North Atlantic, and after a delay caused by the need to take on water, they "proceeded towards the coast of Spain", as he put it in his "Letter 3" (for which see below), but they failed to find a single Spanish ship, in contrast to his previous voyage. Some officers tried to make Jewett give up and go to the United States, but he refused. On 28 July 1820, breaking the rules of privateering, he captured the 22-gun Portuguese merchantman *Carlota*; he put a prize crew aboard the ship and broke the rules again by taking her crew and passengers off and putting them aboard a ship bound for the Azores. He now had two well-armed vessels with which to capture Spanish ships. He turned south for Madeira and the Cape Verde Islands, heading for Brazil on the lookout for Spanish ships, but found none in the South Atlantic either. Some of his crew complained that they had not come to wage war on the Portuguese flag and began to plot against him, whereupon he had several men shot on deck for mutiny – Weddell says Jewett told him four men; the Portuguese prize-court report says six men. Then there was a mutiny among the prize crew in the *Carlota*, but Jewett foiled that too and sailed on.[4] What he intended to do with the *Carlota* in the end is unknown; he could not claim her as a prize since she was Portuguese, but at any rate he now had two well-armed vessels with which to capture Spanish ships.

But in capturing a neutral ship, Jewett left the path of legality and became a pirate. From then on, all his acts were illegal; it was not possible to commit piratical acts and remain a legal privateer. Pirates were subject to "universal jurisdiction" – they were *hostis humani generis* ["an enemy of the human race"], so that any court, in any country, was entitled to punish them and to confiscate their

---

[1] Request by Linch dated 9 September 1819, in Da Fonseca Figueira 1985, pp. 70-71.

[2] Jewett's commission is illustrated in Da Fonseca Figueira 1985, p. 74, and in Kohen and Rodríguez 2015, p. 126.

[3] E.g. Mario D. Tesler, *Expedición de David Jewett a las Islas Malvinas 1820-1821*, Santa Fe (Argentina) 1968, p. 142; Rodolfo Terragno, *Historia y futuro de las Malvinas*, Buenos Aires 2006, p. 247.

[4] Summary here from Jewett's "Letter 3", Weddell 1825, and the 1822 Portuguese prize-court report (below).

ship. That was why some of Jewett's crew mutinied against him – he had made them into pirates, and if caught they could be imprisoned anywhere or even hanged. That was not what they had signed up to. In the end the *Heroína* was condemned for piracy by a prize court in Portugal and her later captain William Mason and her crew were imprisoned at Lisbon for two years. The court ruled that Jewett too was a pirate, but could not imprison him since by then he was in Brazil.

By October 1820 the American and British sealing ships were reaching the South Atlantic in their race to the South Shetlands. The Stonington ships *Hero* and *Express* approached the Falklands through "tremendous heavy Gales", as Nathaniel Brown Palmer wrote in his log on 15 October,[1] and on 17 October "at 10 Anchored in Berkley sound / found there two shallops Belonging to Ship G. Knox...". There were no Stonington ships (to which he was supposed to act as a tender), so on 18 October he sailed out of Berkeley Sound and turned west for West Point Island. On 20 October, among the islands between Port Egmont and the Tamar Pass, Palmer met James Weddell in the *Jane*, who was moving east in company with the *Rose* and the *Eliza*. Palmer sailed on westwards and in the evening anchored beside William Orne's *General Knox* at West Point Island.

That day, 20 October 1820, in a storm in the South Atlantic to the north of the Falklands, the *Carlota* disappeared. She may have foundered in the storm, but it is at least conceivable that her crew (Jewett's prize crew, mostly American or British), who had already staged a mutiny against Jewett and been foiled, simply decided to abandon the voyage and make their own way in the world. Or they may have lost sight of the *Heroína* in the storm and made strenuous efforts to find her, but failed, whereupon they decided to abandon the voyage. It was fairly easy to disguise a ship, and they may have gone to some neutral port and sailed under a different name. There is no evidence for that, but nor is there for her sinking in the storm – she may have continued her career in another guise or not, but at that point she disappears from history.

At any rate Jewett now had only the *Heroína*; he had lost half his firepower, many of his crew were sick with scurvy and men were dying, so in desperation he decided to sail further south to the Falklands, where his crew could recover but could not desert him. And, as he thought, he would be able to lie in wait for Spanish ships without risking the dangers of the open sea.

Meanwhile, having found no Stonington ships at West Point Island, Palmer set off back east on 22 October looking for them. At Whale Bay he was joined by Weddell with the *Jane*, *Eliza* and *Rose*, and on 25 October they all sailed on eastwards, Weddell slowly following Palmer. On 26 October Palmer entered Berkeley Sound and anchored next to the Stonington schooner *Emeline*, and the next day he wrote in his log that he sailed west up Berkeley Sound, heading "for the Town to get some Birds" – the "Town" was Port Louis, though it consisted only of a few ruins. He found the Stonington brig *Catharina*, and after stocking up with "Birds" (no doubt mainly Upland Geese, very good eating), he set off to leave the islands. Near the mouth of the Sound some men from the *Catharina* boarded the *Hero*, saying one of their boats had capsized; two men had drowned and they were looking for the other two. Palmer helped them for a while, but without success, so he gave up.[2] Near Kidney Island he met up with the *Express*, and on the evening of 27 October 1820 the *Hero* and the *Express* turned south out of Berkeley Sound and left the Falklands for the South Shetlands, to assist the Stonington ships with their sealing.

And just as they left, David Jewett arrived from the north in the *Heroína* – he wrote in his "Letter 3" (below), "I entered the Bay of this port on the 27th (civil) day of October 1820 at the close of the same." He probably saw the *Hero* and the *Express*, but they were soon out of sight. It has been stated for 180 years by some writers (section 4.7) that the *Hero* was at Port Louis at the same time as Jewett, but the *Hero*'s logbook disproves that.

So many of Jewett's crewmen were sick or had died of scurvy that there were not enough fit men to take the ship to Port Louis, so he anchored "about ten miles from the antient town of

---

[1] Account here from Palmer's log in the Library of Congress, Washington DC, Manuscript Division, Marine Misc. Acc. 3680; we are grateful to Anne Thacher of the Stonington Historical Society for printouts of the relevant days. When around the Falklands Palmer used the conventional or "civil" day, not the "nautical day" which was 12 hours ahead.

[2] The *Catharina* had arrived on 25 October; she and the *Emeline* were looking for two other Stonington ships, *Clothier* and *Spark*, which which they left the islands on 25 November 1820 (Bertrand 1971, pp. 112-113). It therefore seems likely that they were no longer in the Sound when Jewett arrived, and neither he nor Weddell mentions any other ships.

Soledad" – the geography of Berkeley Sound is shown in fig. 4.6a. The accounts by Palmer, Jewett and Weddell all make it clear that when Jewett arrived, Berkeley Sound was deserted – he and his crew were on their own. His sick men remained aboard the *Heroína* while he worked for several days with his few fit men putting up tents of sails to get the sick men ashore as soon as possible.

4.6a Weddell's chart of Berkeley Sound, 1825: the rounded inlet at left below the title is the "basin" at Port Louis (for a modern plan see chapter 5, figs. 5.4b, 5.4c); the ruins of the settlement are not marked, but are here arrowed. The "French Wreck" at lower centre is the *Uranie*. Weddell misplaces the name "Hog Island" and puts it on Long Island; Hog Island is actually the roughly triangular island midway between Long Island and the northern shore. The name "Port Louis" is also misplaced: it was the settlement that was called Port Louis, not the western end of Berkeley Sound. Salvador Water (sometimes called Port Salvador) is off the picture several miles to the west. Jewett anchored somewhere at the far right. (Weddell 1825, opp. p. 97)

On 2 November a severe storm hit the islands; at West Point Island it struck Orne's *General Knox* and the *Huntress*, whose captain Christopher Burdick wrote in his log that at midday "it blew tremendous the sch[oone]r heeling well over…".[1] Weddell had now reached Salvador Water on the north coast of East Falkland, where he rode out the gale, and that day he had a visitor or visitors, who walked several miles from Port Louis over the low hills through the storm with a letter.

The letter was from David Jewett; Weddell printed it in his book five years later, and it has been much misrepresented in works on the Falklands. We call it "Letter 1"; Jewett's original does not survive, but Weddell copied it out in the manuscript of his book, in which it reads as follows:[2]

["**Letter 1**", as copied by Weddell in his own hand:] National Frigate Heroind at
 Port Soledad Nov"r 2"d 1820

Sir, / I have the honor to inform you of the circumstance of my arrival at this Port Commissioned by the Supreme Government of the United Provinces of South America to take possession of these Islands in the name of the Country to which they naturally appertain, In the performance of this duty it is my desire to act towards all friendly flags with the most distinguished Justice and politeness.[3]
A principal object is to prevent the wanton destruction of the sources of supply to those whose necessities compel, or invite them to visit the Islands, and to aid and assist such as require it, to obtain a supply with the least trouble and Expense. As your views do not enter into contravention or competition with these orders, and as I think mutual advantage may result from a personal interview, I invite you to pay me a visit on board my ship where I shall be happy to accomodate you during your pleasure. I would also beg you so far as comes within your sphere, to communicate this information to other British subjects, in this vicinity. I have the honor to be / Sir / Your mo: obed"t Hum: S"t / Sig"d Jewitt Colonel of the Marine of the United Provinces of South America and Commander of the Frigate Heroind.

Jewett's commission did not order him to go to the Falklands, and whatever he may have told Weddell or others, there is no evidence that he was commissioned to take possession of the

---
[1] Quoted from the *Huntress*'s log in Edouard A. Stackpole, *The Sea-Hunters*, New York 1953, p. 358.
[2] Scott Polar Research Institute (SPRI), Cambridge, Weddell Papers, MS 1521/2 (henceforth "Weddell MS"), pp. 96-97, here with Weddell's spelling and punctuation, relineated; printed slightly differently in Weddell 1825/1827, pp. 103-104; the misreadings "Heroind" and "Jewitt" derive from Jewett's handwriting.
[3] Jewett's commission ordered him to punish all excesses "committed in prejudice to the friendly or neutral flag" (stated in the report of the Portuguese Auditor General, 30 April 1822, below).

Falklands. The idea is illogical; he was a privateer looking for Spanish prizes, to help the United Provinces in the war with Spain while making a profit for Patricio Lynch and partners.

But so far he had drawn a complete blank – he had found no Spanish ships in the North Atlantic, so he had gone to the South Atlantic, now with two ships, and had sailed further and further south. But he found no Spanish ships in the South Atlantic either, and after the loss of the *Carlota* he was back to one ship. And his crew were falling sick and dying – he might not make it back to Buenos Aires, and if he did he would return with no prizes, a leaking ship and a dying crew. It was urgent to allow his crew to recover, so the Falklands were a good place to go – he could lie in wait for Spanish prizes instead of scouring the Atlantic. So he decided to go to the Falklands.

In other words, David Jewett was not *sent* to the Falklands at all. When he left Buenos Aires in March 1820 he expected to capture Spanish ships in the Atlantic, send them with prize crews to Buenos Aires, and then return to Buenos Aires himself. He never intended to go to the Falklands.

His reference in Letter 1 to "other British subjects" is significant – he knew the distant ship in Salvador Water was British, but did not know her name or the name of her captain. Salvador Water is visible from the gentle rise north-west of Port Louis, and the *Jane*'s British flag would have been visible through a telescope. It is also significant that the *Jane* was the only ship he contacted; if any ships had been in Berkeley Sound, his men would have had to go *past* them in their boat on their way to deliver Letter 1 to Weddell. There were clearly no ships nearer at hand. Weddell says that after receiving Jewett's letter he waited till the next morning (3 November) and then walked "7 or 8 miles" overland from Salvador to Berkeley Sound, where a boat took him to the *Heroína*. Neither Weddell nor Jewett mentions any other ships, and Weddell's account makes it clear that he boarded the *Heroína* alone. The conclusion is inescapable: there were no other ships, and Letter 1 was written to no one but Weddell himself – the idea that it was written to many captains[1] is a myth.

By then Jewett and his crew had spent a week halfway down Berkeley Sound. Weddell spent most of 3 November helping Jewett to move the *Heroína* to Port Louis, where Jewett and his few fit men landed the sick and housed them in tents made of sails, as he says in Letter 3, and Weddell says some of them were housed in the old bread-oven. Jewett invited Weddell to spend the night on board, and that evening he recounted the story of his voyage, with a detailed account of the sickness of his crew and his foiling of the mutiny, after which he "was under the distressing necessity of pronouncing sentence of death, on two officers and two Seamen", who were shot on deck. He told Weddell that of his original crew of 200, some 90 were either sick or had died, while "50 had been put on board a prize". But he did not tell Weddell that the prize was Portuguese, so Weddell never found out that he had committed piracy – that was something that was vital for Jewett to conceal. Weddell presumably walked back to the *Jane* on 4 November and then took the *Jane*, the *Rose* and the *Eliza* round to Port Louis.

And just at that juncture, a few ships taking part in the rush to the South Shetlands put in to Berkeley Sound – Weddell says "several vessels", so there were perhaps a handful or so. On 6 November some of their captains watched as Jewett held a ceremony of "taking possession" of the Falklands. Weddell's eyewitness account runs in his original manuscript:[2]

> In a few days he took formal possession of these Islands for the Patriot government of Buenos Ayres, read a declaration under their colours, planted on a port[3] in ruins, and fired a salute of 21 Guns. On this occasion the officers were all in full uniform, being exactly that of our navy, which but ill accorded with the delapidated state of his Ship, but he was wise enough to calculate upon the effect of such parade upon the minds of the masters of ships who were in the Islands,[4] and as he had laid claim to the wreck of the French Ship before mentioned, to the entire exclusion of several vessels which had arrived bound to New Shetland, an authoritative appearance he saw necessary. In fact he struck such a terror on the minds of some Ship masters, lest they

---

[1] Stated e.g. in Tesler 1979, p. 42, and in Mary Cawkell, *The History of the Falkland Islands*, Oswestry 2001, p. 43.
[2] Weddell MS pp. 104-105; the printed version (Weddell 1825/1827, pp. 111-112), omits the passages Weddell deleted.
[3] *Sic* also in 1825 and 1827 editions, p. 111. Weddell presumably means that the flag flew over the ruins of the port at Port Louis. Jewett's Letter 2, however, says "fort".
[4] Kohen and Rodríguez (p. 127, fn. 20) quote this part of Weddell's account (from the 1827 ed., p. 111) – but their quote ends with "in the Islands", thus omitting two important points: (a) Jewett's dispute with the other captains about access to the *Uranie*, and (b) Weddell's "several vessels", which makes it clear that only a few ships were involved.

should be taken or robbed, that one of them ~~foolishly~~ proposed taking up arms against him but on my pointing out to him how groundless were his fears, and introducing him to Captⁿ Jewitt, he confessed his mistake, and ~~rather expressed himself in language of adulation, which shewed him to be a man of little discernment, and less spirit~~. his fears subsided.

Weddell's account suggests that Jewitt had annoyed some captains by excluding them from the wreck of the *Uranie*. Wrecks were an important source of wood and iron for repairs, and no British or American crews accepted that Jewitt had any right to dictate to others – to the British the islands were British and they were on home ground, while to the Americans the islands were open to all. Fortunately for Jewitt, those present did not know that he had committed piracy, otherwise the call to take up arms against him might have been heeded.

Kohen and Rodríguez comment (p. 128) that Weddell had been a Royal Navy captain, and assert that with his knowledge and experience of the region, he could not be unaware of a British sovereignty claim over the islands, "if it existed", so that some reaction on his part should have been expected. But Weddell makes it clear that he was worried about what Jewitt might do:[1]

… I saw he was much in want of men, and conceived it possible that by my being unaccommodating he might entice my crew or perhaps force them into his service… I had only to trust to safety to a strict observance of neutrality, but the Ship remained in peace and I slept undisturbed.

It would have been silly of Weddell to provoke a confrontation with Jewitt by pointing out that the islands were British, so he maintained a "strict observance of neutrality". Kohen and Rodríguez (pp. 128, 129) criticise the fact that there was no reaction or resistance from Weddell or other British subjects; they point out in other contexts too (e.g. pp. 53, 60, 73, 74, 79) that Britain failed to protest when they say it should have protested, but their comments stand in sharp contrast to their airy dismissal (pp. 222-3) of Argentina's failure for over a third of the 19th century to protest against Britain's possession of the Falklands (sections 7.15, 7.19, 8.7, 8.8).

On 9 November 1820, a week after writing Letter 1 to Weddell, Jewitt wrote a letter to Captain William Orne of the *General Knox*, informing him that he had taken possession of the islands on 6 November. Orne himself evidently did not go to Port Louis (or there would have been no need for the letter), but one or both of his tenders presumably arrived there, so Jewitt wrote the letter to be taken to Orne at West Point Island. We call it "Letter 2"; the original does not survive, but Orne took it back to his home port of Salem, Massachusetts, where he arrived on 5 June 1821, and it was printed in the *Salem Gazette* on 8 June 1821, and again in the *Times* in London on 3 August.

Our figs. 4.6b and 4.6c illustrate the two printings. The *Times* misspelt Orne's name as "Orme", misdated the *Salem Gazette* announcement as 12 June (*recte* 8 June), and made two changes that misleadingly implied that the letter was sent to many people – at the bottom Orne was omitted as the addressee, and there were no square brackets round the word "CIRCULAR", implying that the letter itself bore the word. Kohen and Rodríguez falsify Letter 2 in five ways:

1) They illustrate only the *Times*'s version of it, obscuring the important extra details in the *Salem Gazette*.

2) They falsify it in their Spanish edition by "photoshopping" the *Times* masthead above it, as shown in our fig. 4.6d, suggesting that it was the top item on the editorial page. In fact the *Times* printed it among minor news items in column 5 on page 2 – immediately above it was actually an article about the Russian economy, as shown in fig. 4.6c.

3) In their running text in both Spanish (pp. 128-9) and English they print a mixture of the two versions, combining them in a way that is revealed by their footnote[2] – they took the first half from *BFSP* vol. XX, p. 422, which correctly quotes the first half of the *Salem Gazette* version but omits the last two paragraphs, so they added the second half from the *Times*, from "It is my desire" to the end. That explains why their versions both use the *Salem Gazette*'s "this present November" but the *Times*'s "I am, Sir, D. JEWETT…" (in Spanish without "I am, Sir"). They do not faithfully represent either of the two printed versions.

4) They illustrate (p. 130) the *Times* version including the reference to "Captain Orme" [*sic*], but in their

---

[1] Weddell MS, pp. 99, 104; printed editions 1825/1827, pp. 106, 111.
[2] Footnote 22 on p. 129 of Kohen and Rodríguez 2015 reads: "Partially in *BFSP*, 1832-1833, vol. XX, p. 422. Spanish version in Ferrer Vieyra, Enrique, *Segunda Cronología*…, op. cit., p. 26. Reproduced in newspapers mentioned infra."

running text, in both Spanish (pp. 128-9) and English versions, they suppress the addressee completely and add the assertion that "Colonel Jewett circulated the following note to the captains of the ships present in the region", for which there is no evidence whatever – Letter 2 was actually written to Captain Orne alone.

5) In their Spanish version only (p. 128) they introduce extra falsifications by quoting Letter 2 in Enrique Ferrer Vieyra's faulty Spanish translation of the *Times* version. That translation contains two blatant errors. First, it makes Jewett say that his possession ceremony was performed in the presence of "many" American and British citizens ("numerosos ciudadanos"), but in Letter 2 Jewett himself says "several" citizens, which suggests only a modest number. The second error is worse: the *Salem Gazette* shows the letter was written to William B. Orne, the addressee at the bottom (fig. 4.6b), and in it Jewett asks Orne "to communicate this intelligence to any other vessels of your nation". The *Times* made the "vessels" singular, which makes little difference, but Ferrer Vieyra makes the "nation" plural and says "los otros navíos de sus naciones" – "the other vessels of your nations"! That naturally gives the false impression that it was sent to many captains.

Kohen and Rodríguez had the text of the *Times* version but chose to print Ferrer Vieyra's faulty Spanish translation of it and also to assert in their own text that the letter was written to "the captains of the ships present". In fact Jewett's letters were each written to a single addressee – Letter 1 to Weddell, Letter 2 to Orne. The idea that they were written to many captains is a myth.

No more is known of Jewett's "possession-taking" than what Weddell says, but some authors have added speculative assumptions such as the idea that Jewett prohibited hunting, sealing, or whaling. As can be seen by his Letters 1 and 2, he did no such thing. Some have assumed that by "sources of supply" in Letter 1 Jewett meant the seals, cattle, geese, etc., and they imply that the visiting ships were "annihilating the marine fauna" which he wished to conserve.[1] But those fauna were abundant in 1820; "conservation" was not yet a concept, and Jewett had no means of hunting himself, nor of preventing other ships from hunting. As Weddell makes clear, one of Jewett's main concerns was to reserve supplies from wrecks for himself.

After writing Letter 2, Jewett remained at Port Louis in the *Heroína* for almost six months until April 1821; Weddell surmised that "his principal business was to refresh his crew", but that would have taken only a week or two. Jewett's motive was actually to capture Spanish ships as prizes, but not a single one appeared, and he made no move against any British or American ships – they were busy killing seals, but he was indifferent to the fate of the "marine fauna", and he did nothing to defend "territorial sovereignty", as da Fonseca Figueira asserts. In fact he and his crew did nothing constructive in the Falklands at all. That is confirmed by a letter to him dated 20 January 1821 from Laureano de Ansoátegui, the commander of the troops, who pointed out that the men had signed on for an eight-month cruise, with a further optional four months; the eight months had expired, so he asks what they could achieve in the remaining months, given the purpose of their contract:[2]

… its express purpose is to cruise for the remaining four months, not to vegetate in this Port as we are… suppose we were to cruise for the not fully three months remaining to complete the second term… what provisions and so on do we lack? … prolonging our stay in this place brings us no advantage at all…

That shows that Jewett and his crew did nothing in the Falklands except "vegetate". Jewett dismissed and arrested Ansoátegui for insubordination and had him confined ashore. But Jewett himself was frustrated too, as there was not a single ship he could capture – after the sealing ships had left for the South Shetlands, Berkeley Sound was usually empty.

That is, until the American schooner *Rampart* arrived in late January 1821, commanded by Captain Thomas Farrin, en route to Spain from Spanish-held Peru, with a cargo of cocoa, cotton, wool and cascarilla rind (a spice). The *Rampart* was the first remotely eligible ship that had turned up; she was American but at least she carried Spanish cargoes. By now Jewett was so desperate to give up his voyage and resign his position that he grasped at this straw: he seized the ship as a prize, thus committing piracy again, this time against the United States – he had been a pirate since capturing the *Carlota*, and continued that role in capturing the *Rampart*.

---

[1] E.g. Da Fonseca Figueira 1985, p. 97.
[2] Letter by Ansoátegui (1782-1847) aboard the *Heroína* at Puerto Soledad, 20 January 1821, in AGN X, 5-1-3. Kohen and Rodríguez do not mention this letter, but they mention (p. 131) an earlier letter by Ansoátegui in the same file, of 27 November 1820, merely to show that he addressed Jewett as "Commandant of this island" (which is irrelevant).

> **SALEM,**
> FRIDAY MORNING, JUNE 8, 1821.
>
> **FALKLAND ISLANDS.**
>
> Capt. Orne, who arrived here on Tuesday last from the Falkland Islands, has furnished us with the following act of sovereignty, for publication.
>
> [CIRCULAR.]
>
> *National Frigate Heroina,*
> *at Port Soledad, Nov. 9, 1820.*
>
> SIR, I have the honor to inform you of my arrival at this port, to take poffeffion of thefe Iflands, in the name of the Supreme Government of the United Provinces of South America.
>
> This ceremony was publicly performed on the fixth day of this prefent November, and the National Standard hoifted at the fort under a falute from this frigate, in the prefence of feveral citizens of the United States, and fubjects of Great Britain.
>
> It is my defire to act towards all friendly flags with the moft diftinguifhed juftice and hofpitality; and it will give me pleafure to aid and affift fuch as may require them, to obtain refrefhments, with as little trouble and expenfe as poffible.
>
> I have to beg of you to communicate this intelligence to any other veffels of your nation, whom it may concern.
>
> I am, Sir, your most obed't. humble servant,
> D. JEWETT,
> *Colonel of the Marine of the United Provinces of South America, Commander of the Frigate Heroina.*
>
> To Capt. Wm. B. Orne,
>   ship General Knox, of Salem.

4.6b Letter 2: *The Salem Gazette*, 8 June 1821.

4.6c Letter 2 repeated: *The Times*, London, 3 August 1821, p. 2, col. 5, as actually printed.

4.6d Letter 2 photoshopped: the *Times* masthead added by Kohen and Rodríguez (2015, p. 130).

In both cases not only the captures were piratical, but the treatment of the ships afterwards: Jewett removed the crew and passengers from the *Carlota*, and he failed to seal the *Rampart*'s cargo hatches pending judgement by a prize court, as required by privateering law – her cargo was sold in Buenos Aires without the necessary legal condemnation. Both those things were breaches of the law of privateering and made him a pirate, in addition to the illegal capture of both ships in the first place. Portugal and the United States were incensed, and his successor William Mason and the *Heroína* herself were condemned for piracy by the Portuguese prize court (below).

Aboard the *Heroína* at Port Louis on 1 February 1821, frustrated at the total lack of prizes and the behaviour of his crew, Jewett wrote a long letter in English to the Buenos Aires government resigning his command and asking to be relieved.[1] We call it "Letter 3"; he put it aboard the *Rampart* and sent her under a prize crew to Buenos Aires. In summary, it runs as follows: he begins by stating that this is "the first and only opportunity, to announce the painful history of events which have followed in distressing and rapid succession, from our leaving the waters of La Plata, up to the present moment"; then, slightly misquoting *Othello*, he says that in recounting the hardships of his voyage "I shall naught extenuate, nor aught set down in malice".[2] He says violent gales caused the ship to leak and spoilt their stores; their water-casks leaked; the morale of officers and men was bad, and some began to protest against the state of the ship and demand that they go to the United States, but he managed to quieten them and stave off a near-mutiny. On 27 July they saw a ship of war, and captured her the next day after a gun-battle, in which she fired "a full broadside of round grape and langrage[3] & musketry" but in the end surrendered. She was the 22-gun Portuguese ship *Carlota*, with a crew of 62, a full cargo and 14 passengers. He put a prize crew aboard and the two ships sailed on in company. On the night of 12-13 August he foiled a mutiny in the *Heroína* led by the ship's sailing master; from 28 August the crew began to fall ill and die in large numbers from scurvy, and he discovered another mutiny – some men were planning to seize the *Carlota*. He foiled this plot too, but in a storm on 20 October they lost sight of her. He made for the Falklands, and towards evening on 27 October 1820 the *Heroína* arrived in Berkeley Sound with most of her crew sick. He anchored ten miles from the "antient town of Soledad" [Port Louis], explored the shores in his boat, then moved the ship up to a better anchorage. Some men recovered on shore, though others died, and the survivors went aboard again on 12 December. On 20 January 1821 the commanding officer of the troops, Ansoátegui, tried to make him return to Buenos Aires, so Jewett had him confined ashore, offering him the option of taking passage in a British ship that was there. Finally, Jewett asks to be relieved of his command. So ends his Letter 3.

But in that letter he suppresses some very important details. He does not mention that he put the *Carlota*'s crew and passengers aboard another ship (another piratical action after the capture of the ship); he mentions the mutinies but does not say that he had some men shot, or that the *Carlota*'s Portuguese nationality was their motive. And he says not a word about "taking possession" of the Falklands! That last omission is highly significant – he had had no contact with Buenos Aires for almost a year, and when contact was finally made, he chose not to inform the government that he had laid claim to the Falklands. If he had been ordered to take possession of the Falklands he would scarcely have omitted to mention that he had done so.

The *Rampart* reached Buenos Aires on 17 February 1821, and on 27 February, in response to Jewett's request in Letter 3, the government appointed the British-born Colonel William Robert Mason to replace Jewett as captain of the *Heroína*. Kohen and Rodríguez imply (p. 136) that Buenos Aires knew about Jewett's "taking possession" of the islands, but the government's reaction strongly suggests that they knew nothing about it and did not see the islands as Argentine territory. They gave Mason no land-based role (such as governor), and in the orders given to Mason and the

---

[1] AGN, Marina Corsarios 1820-1831, X, 5-1-3, no doc. no.; signed 13-page letter in English in Jewett's hand. A contemporary translator made a faulty Spanish translation of it, likewise in AGN X, 5-1-3; the translator silently omitted some things that eluded him, e.g. the quote from *Othello* and the word "langrage". That translation was printed as a paraphrase (not the original text) in Carranza 1916, vol. III, pp. 169-177; new ed. 1962, vol. II, pp. 165-172; the actual text of the old Spanish translation was first printed *verbatim* (though with errors and omissions), in Mario D. Tesler, *Expedición de David Jewett a las Islas Malvinas 1820-1821*, Santa Fe (Argentina) 1968, pp. 128-139. Tesler misread a few words in the Spanish manuscript and was unable to read others – in four places he puts suspension points where he has left out a word, e.g.: "En este... y sin venir", where the original reads "En este momento y sin venir", and he twice puts "(sic.)" where he prints a nonsensical word having failed to read the original, e.g. "las pijios (sic.) de agua" where it reads "las Pipas de agua" (translating Jewett's "Water casks"). Tesler must have known of the English original in the same file in the AGN, but he does not mention it, so the Argentine authors who have reprinted his version (e.g. da Fonseca Figueira 1985, pp. 105-115, and Eduardo C[esar] Gerding, *La Saga de David Jewett*, Buenos Aires 2006, pp. 103-113) did not know Jewett wrote in English, nor that Tesler's Spanish version was faulty.
[2] Cf. *Othello* Act V, scene II, lines 345-346: "nothing extenuate, / Nor aught set down in malice".
[3] **Langrage**, also **langridge**: hollow iron cases filled with pieces of iron, an early form of shrapnel (*OED*).

new (unnamed) commander of the troops they said nothing that implied that they were on Argentine territory. Mason was merely appointed captain of the *Heroína* and was ordered to continue the privateering voyage and hence to leave the islands.[1] Mason reached Port Louis on 21 April in a Dutch ship; the next day he took command of the *Heroína*, and on 23 April Jewett left for Buenos Aires in the Dutch ship with some crew members of the *Heroína*.[2] Mason remained in the Falklands for 20 days after Jewett's departure, then sailed in the *Heroína* on 13 May 1821 leaving Port Louis deserted. So by June 1821, when the *Salem Gazette* printed Jewett's Letter 2, with its promise of "refreshments" and "most distinguished justice and hospitality", both Jewett and Mason were gone from the Falklands, and with them all presence from Buenos Aires.

The seizure of the *Rampart* drew an angry response from John Murray Forbes, the "Special Agent of the United States at Buenos Aires" – he was the nearest thing there was to a US ambassador, as the United States did not yet recognise the independence of the United Provinces. On 24 February 1821 Forbes wrote to the Governor of Buenos Aires, Martín Rodríguez, requesting that the unloading of the *Rampart* be suspended until her captain had been notified, and that the privateering regulations should be fully observed, but learnt on 26 February that the *Rampart*'s cargo was already being sold – his request had been ignored since he was not recognised as an ambassador. On 10 March 1821 Forbes wrote to US Secretary of State (foreign minister) John Quincy Adams (later US President, 1825-9), complaining that "every possible irregularity has been committed, the Crew has never been examined, the Hatches have never been sealed, the Cargo has been discharged without notification to the Captain…".[3]

Forbes also wrote on 14 September to Buenos Aires foreign minister Bernardo Rivadavia, complaining of the depredations of ships under various South American flags, and on 6 October the Buenos Aires government issued a decree asserting that privateering was a legitimate means of warfare, but also cancelling all existing commissions and tightening the rules for future privateering commissions.[4] In other words, Buenos Aires was abandoning the practice of privateering until further notice, but reserved the right to recommence it. So Forbes's protest against Jewett's capture of the *Rampart* had its desired effect, and Buenos Aires indirectly disavowed Jewett's action. That ended the dispute. Eleven years later in 1832 under similar circumstances there was to be no such disavowal, and Buenos Aires escalated the dispute so far as to cause a 12-year breach of diplomatic relations between the United States and Argentina (section 6.15).

Buenos Aires clearly remained ignorant of Jewett's making a claim to the Falklands until a report arrived in November 1821 from British sources: the Buenos Aires paper *El Argos* of Saturday 10 November 1821[5] printed a brief report from the Spanish newspaper *Redactor* of Cadiz, datelined "Gibraltar, August 1821", saying that "colonel *Jewett*" had taken possession of the "islas Falksand" [*sic*!]. Kohen and Rodríguez say (p. 129) that the "circular" was published in Spain in *El Redactor* and was reproduced in the *Argos* of Buenos Aires on 10 November, but that is untrue – our fig. 4.6c gives the full text from the *Argos* (we also reproduced it in full in *Getting it right*, p. 10). The Cadiz newspaper got its information from Gibraltar, no doubt from the *Gibraltar Chronicle* reporting from the *Times* of 3 August 1821, which had wrongly implied that Jewett's Letter 2 was a circular (fig. 4.6d).

---

[1] Two sets of orders, to Jewett and Mason 27 February 1821, and to the commander of the troops, 28 February 1821, in AGN X, 5-1-3, no doc. nos. (p. 1 of the former illustrated in Kohen and Rodríguez 2015, p. 137).

[2] Disgusted with his service for the United Provinces, and perhaps fearing exposure as a pirate, Jewett went to Brazil and joined the Imperial Brazilian navy, reaching the rank of vice-admiral. In 1827 he married Eliza McTiers; their only child, Augustine David Lawrence Jewett, was born on 12 January 1830. During the war between Brazil and the United Provinces (1826-8) the Brazilian navy blockaded Buenos Aires, and Jewett became an enemy of Argentina; during the Second Falklands Crisis (1831-3) he assisted the United States and helped Captain Silas Duncan of the USS *Lexington* by suggesting ways of annoying Argentina. Jewett retired in 1836 and died in Brazil on 26 July 1842; his wife died a few months later (F.C. Jewett 1908, p. 334; da Fonseca Figueira 1985, pp. 145-147, 175-179; Francis Baylies, letter to US Secretary of State Edward Livingston, 1 January 1833, in Manning 1932, p. 168).

[3] Details and quote in William R. Manning, ed., *Diplomatic Correspondence of the United States Concerning the Independence of the Latin-American Nations*, Washington DC 1925, vol. I, pp. 569-570, 583-584.

[4] Forbes to Rivadavia 14 September 1821, in Manning 1925, pp. 583-584; decree of 6 October 1821 pp. 590-591.

[5] Da Fonseca Figueira (1985, p. 96) wrongly gives the date of the *Argos* announcement as 10 December 1821.

> GIBRALTAR—Agosto de 1821—El coronel *Jewett* de la marina de las Provincias Unidas de Sur de America, y comandante de la fragata *Heroina*, en circular fecha 9. de noviembre de 1821 en el puerto de la Soledad, previene haber tomado el 6. posesion de las islas Falksand en nombre de dichas provincias. (Redactor de Cadiz.)

4.6e *El Argos de Buenos Aires*, **10 November 1821 (full text of announcement).**[1]

While in command of the *Heroína* William Mason captured two ships, the first a legitimate prize, the Spanish brig of war *Maipú*, which he sent to Buenos Aires under a prize crew,[2] but on 11 July he captured a Portuguese ship, the *Viscondesa do Rio Seco*[3] – that was piracy. The *Heroína* was already a pirate ship and Jewett was a pirate, but Mason himself was not a pirate until he captured a neutral ship. From then on, all his actions were illegal. The *Heroína* was leaking again, so in November 1821 he put in to Gibraltar, where he spent four months, but in March 1822 news of the *Heroína*'s capture of Portuguese ships reached Portugal, so a Portuguese frigate, the *Perla*, lay off Gibraltar waiting for the *Heroína* to come out. Mason made a dash for it on 19 March, but the *Perla* captured the *Heroína* off Morocco the next day and took her into Lisbon.[4] She was condemned as fair prize by the Lisbon prize court and sold, and in April 1822 the court convicted Mason of piracy. He and some of his men spent two years in a prison hulk at Lisbon, till they were released in 1824 by the intervention of the British Minister in Lisbon, Sir Edward Thornton.[5]

The report on Mason's trial in the prize court, by Auditor General of Marine Manuel José de Figueredo, dated 30 April 1822, stated regarding Jewett's capture of the *Carlota* in the *Heroína*:[6]

… this Corvette exercised the infamous traffic of piracy, plundering all vessels she could overhaul… the Heroine having fallen in… with the Portuguese ship Carlotta… she captured her after two hours' combat, transferring the Carlotta's crew to the Heroine… until they were put on board of a vessel bound to the Island of Florez…; and… part of the crew of the Heroine saying they had not come to make war against the Portuguese flag, the Commander of the Heroine David Jewett, classed this proceeding of his crew as a mutiny, and ordered two officers and four seamen to be shot… It is further shewn that during the time the Heroine was anchored in the Falkland or Malvina Islands… an American Schooner entered the harbour where she lay, when the Pirate immediately remitted her with her Cargo to Buenos Ayres…

The court asked Mason why the *Carlota* had been taken, but he refused to answer, saying it had been before he was in command. The court's final verdict on the *Heroína* was that:

… there is no doubt of her being a pirate and not a legal privateer…: because, all and every prize she took ought to have been competently tried and condemned, before any person should be suffered to touch any of the cargo… he confesses that the United Kingdoms of Portugal and Brazil are considered as friendly with Buenos-Ayres… The result of all this is, a convincing proof that the Commander, officers & crew of the Heroine were pirates that infested the high seas…

Thus the Portuguese prize court ruled that both Jewett and Mason had committed piracy, Jewett in capturing the Portuguese *Carlota* and the American *Rampart*, and Mason in seizing the Portuguese *Viscondesa do Rio Seco*. As well as the Portuguese and American nationality of three of the *Heroina*'s prizes, the fact that they and their cargo had not been declared lawful prize by a court also counted as piracy. Since piracy was subject to universal jurisdiction, any court in any country could have condemned Jewett, Mason and the ship. The Portuguese court therefore had jurisdiction

---

[1] "GIBRALTAR – August 1821 – Colonel *Jewett* of the navy of the United Provinces of South America, and commander of the frigate *Heroina*, in a circular dated 9 November 1821 in the port of la Soledad, warns that on the 6th he took possession of the Falksand islands [*sic*] in the name of the said provinces. (Redactor of Cadiz.)"
[2] Carranza vol. III, 1916, pp. 180-181; 1962 vol. II, p. 175.
[3] Details in a letter in English by Mason dated 10 September 1822, from the prison hulk "San Sebastian" (*São Sebastião*) at Lisbon, in AGN X, 5-1-3.
[4] Details from the report by *Perla*'s captain in Carranza vol. III, 1916, pp. 182-184 (1962 vol. II, pp. 177-178).
[5] Manning 1932, p. 174.
[6] Report printed in full in English translation in Manning 1932, fn. 1, pp. 169-171.

in the case and also ruled that Jewett's seizure of the *Rampart* was piracy, even though she was not Portuguese. Jewett escaped conviction and imprisonment only because he was not present in court – by 1822 he was in Brazil, where he became an inveterate enemy of Argentina.

Since by definition pirates operate outside the law, they cannot perform legitimate acts of territorial sovereignty. In international law Jewett's "act of possession" at Port Louis was invalid.

That, then, was the real story of David Jewett and his visit to the Falklands.

4.7 David Jewett: the myths

However, a whole structure of myths has arisen about Jewett's visit to the Falklands – myths which have been repeated for 180 years by successive authors, including Kohen and Rodríguez. Many myths were launched by Louis Vernet (for whom see section 4.9) in his "Report" of 10 August 1832 to the Buenos Aires acting foreign minister Manuel Vicente Maza. Most of its historical parts were written by the lawyer and politician Valentín Alsina,[1] who confused Jewett's actions with Vernet's own activities ten years later – and he misread Jewett's signature as "Daniel Jewitt", which was repeated in books for over a century. The account of Jewett reads in part:[2]

When Jewitt arrived at La Soledad, he found disseminated in the Islands, more than 50 Foreign Vessels. I will name some of them:— ENGLISH—Ship, *Indian*, Capt. Spiller, from Liverpool; Brig, *Jane*, Weddle, from Leith; do., *Hette*, Bond, from London; do., *George*, Richardson, from Liverpool; Cutter, *Eliza*, Powell, Liverpool; do., *Sprightly*, Frazier, from London. AMERICAN—Ships, *General Knox, Eucane, Newhaven*, and *Governor Hawkins*; Brigs, *Fanning* and *Harmony*; Schooners, *Wasp, Free Gift*, and *Hero*—from New York and Stonington… In the presence of these Vessels anchored in the port of La Soledad, Jewitt took possession, firing a salute of 21 guns, with the artillery which he landed. He treated them all with urbanity, and notified to them in writing the fact of the Republic having taken possession, and the prohibition to Fish on the Islands, or kill Cattle thereon, under the penalty of detention, and the remission of the Infringers to Buenos Ayres to be tried.

Most of that is untrue. Some of the listed ships were certainly not at Port Louis when Jewett was there; Jewett certainly did not land his artillery (he had only a few fit men); there is no evidence that he notified anyone except William Orne of his possession-taking; he mentioned no penalties or trials; and the only prohibition he made was to exclude other crews from exploiting the wreck of the *Uranie*. But Vernet's "Report" became widely known, since Maza had it printed in English and Spanish in the collection of documents presented to the Buenos Aires legislature on 18 September 1832 ("*Colección 1832*" / "*Papers Relative* 1832") as part of the Buenos Aires case in the dispute with the United States over the *Lexington* raid (section 6.12), and it was printed in English in London in 1836 in *BFSP*. Many writers have based their accounts of Jewett's visit on it (including Kohen and Rodríguez), and it has contributed to Argentina's presentations at the United Nations.

Unfortunately Vernet's "Report" is riddled with errors. In *The Falklands Saga* we shall examine the many myths derived from it, including erroneous accounts of Jewett's Falklands visit by 36 authors.[3] All of them apart from Louis Vernet himself rehash incorrect earlier accounts; most of them incorrectly assume that Jewett was specifically sent to the Falklands by the Buenos Aires government; they wrongly state that he found many ships at Port Louis when he arrived; some of

---

[1] Stated (without source) in Alfredo L. Palacios, *Las Islas Malvinas, Archipiélago Argentino*, Buenos Aires 1934, pp. 40-41; 2nd ed. 1946, p. 43, and also stated by Mario Tesler (pers. comm.).
[2] Vernet's "Report", in *BFSP 1832-1833*, pp. 418-419; Spanish in *Colección* 1832, fols. 49 *recto* to 50 *verso*; mentioned but not quoted in Kohen and Rodríguez 2015, p. 132. Full title of the "Report" and *Colección* 1832 in Bibliography.
[3] I.e. **1.** Louis Vernet (1832); **2.** Robert FitzRoy (1839); **3.** Paul Groussac (1910/1936).**4.** Violet Boyson (1924); **5.** Wilfred Down (1927); **6.** Julius Goebel (1927); **7.** Alfredo Palacios (1934/1946); **8.** Antonio Gómez Langenheim (1934, 1939); **9.** Ricardo R. Caillet-Bois (1948/1952/1982)**10.** José María Ruda (1964); **11.** José Luis Muñoz Azpiri (1966); **12.** Mario Tesler (1968, 1979); **13.** Laurio Destefani (1982)**14.** Hugo Gambini (1982); **15.** Andrew Graham-Yooll (1983); **16.** Ian Strange (1983); **17.** Adrián Hope (1983); **18.** Virginia Gamba (1984); **19.** Fritz and Olga Hoffmann (1984); **20.** José da Fonseca Figueira (1985); **21.** Enrique Ferrer Vieyra (1985, 1993); **22.** Peter Beck (1988); **23.** Barry Gough (1992); **24.** Rudolf Dolzer (1986/1993); **25.** Christian Maisch (2000); **26.** Mary Cawkell (2001); **27.** Eduardo Gerding (2003, 2006); **28.** Sir Lawrence Freedman (2005/2007); **29.** Rodolfo Terragno (2006); **30.** Gerald Roberts (2007); **31.** Lanús University (2011), **32.** Juan José Cresto (2011), **33.** Marcelo Kohen and Facundo Rodríguez (2015, 2017), **34.** Marc Shucksmith-Wesley (2018), **35.** Jorge González Bonorino (2018) and **36.** Fundación Malvinas (2020).

them list ships that can be shown not to have been there; and many authors follow Vernet in misrepresenting Jewett's Letters 1 and 2, which in fact make no prohibitions, do not mention sealing, fishing, whaling or hunting, do not threaten any punishments and were not sent to a number of captains[1] (see the texts in section 4.6). Here we have room only for a brief account.

The number of "more than 50 Foreign Vessels" is a wild exaggeration; our research suggests that in the 1820s there were often several ships in the Falklands at the same time, occasionally a dozen, but rarely more; there were never anywhere near fifty ships in the islands at the same time. The documentation shows that when Jewett arrived, Berkeley Sound was empty, and he never moved from Port Louis, so he found no ships "disseminated in the islands". Vernet and Alsina no doubt obtained their list of ships mostly from people who knew the South Atlantic well, quite possibly from Mathew Brisbane, who by the time of Vernet's "Report" had spent some ten years in the area, and in 1832, like Vernet, was in Buenos Aires. They may also have found newspaper reports of ships active in the South Atlantic, especially in the South Shetlands, but no record existed of which ships went to Port Louis in 1820 and which did not, so their list is pure guesswork.

Vernet and Alsina name 15 ships "anchored in the port of La Soledad"; Kohen and Rodríguez say (p. 133) "Vernet's report reproduces the list of ships and captains that attended the ceremony of taking of possession in 1820… there it is: the full list of ships and captains", but that list (above) includes ships which were certainly not present: the *General Knox* was at West Point Island almost 200 kilometres away to the west; the *Hero* had left the Falklands on 27 October just before Jewett arrived (section 4.6), and the *Free Gift* was already in the South Shetlands (940 kilometres away) when Palmer arrived there in the *Hero* on 11 November,[2] so she can hardly have been at Port Louis five days earlier. Weddell says that at the time of Jewett's ceremony "several vessels which had arrived bound to New Shetland" were present, but the *Indian* was clearly not among them – she was at Valparaíso on 28 November bound for New South Shetland,[3] so she cannot have been at the Falklands on 6 November – she would have had to sail from Port Louis round Cape Horn *past* the South Shetlands without doing any sealing, and up to Valparaíso, although she was bound to the South Shetlands. Not many captains were that slow to realise they had overshot the mark.

Two ships Vernet listed were in the Falklands at roughly the right time (though not necessarily on 6 November), but their surviving records do not mention Jewett. The *George* of Liverpool was in the Falklands in November 1820 on her way to the South Shetlands, and her captain sent a letter which was reported in *The Times* on 29 March 1821, and also appeared by sheer coincidence in the very issue of the *Salem Gazette* of 8 June 1821 that reported Jewett's presence in the Falklands. The *George*'s crew were on East Falkland at the same time as Jewett, and left on 25 November 1820,[4] but the letter does not mention Jewett's "taking possession". For her crew to see Jewett's ceremony, they would have had to be at Port Louis – from even as close as Johnson's Harbour, Port Louis is not visible. So the *George*'s crew were either not there, or were there but her captain thought nothing of it. Either way, the *George* cannot be counted as being present during Jewett's ceremony. The *Hetty* of London (Vernet's "*Hette*") spent two weeks at Port Louis, at the head of "Barclay's sound"; her crew spent some time ashore and managed to shoot a bull as well as pigs and geese, according to one of her crew, Thomas Smith, born in Kent, who later published a colourful autobiography in America, including a brief account of the ship's visit to the Falklands in 1820.[5] Smith makes no mention of any "possession-taking" ceremony or of any other ship – he gives no date for the visit, but it seems likely that the *Hetty* left the islands before Jewett arrived and should

---

[1] These and other false assumptions are made by e.g. Adrián F. J. Hope, "Sovereignty and Decolonization of the Malvinas (Falkland) Islands", in *Boston College International and Comparative Law Review*, vol. VI no. 2, Spring 1983, pp. 413-414; Virginia Gamba, *El Peón de la Reina* ["The Queen's Pawn"], Buenos Aires 1984, p. 39; Dolzer 1993, p. 59; Dolzer's German version 1986, p. 45; V[iolet] F[enton] Boyson, *The Falkland Islands*, Oxford 1924, pp. 219-220; Goebel 1927, p. 434; Cawkell 2001, p. 90; Freedman 2005/2007, vol. I, p. 7; Terragno 2006, pp. 235, 236; Cresto 2011, pp. 239-242; Kohen and Rodríguez 2015, pp. 125-136.
[2] Nathaniel Brown Palmer, in the *Hero*'s log for 11-12 November 1820, Library of Congress, Washington DC.
[3] A. G. E. Jones 1986, p. 58.
[4] Date of 25 November 1820 for the *George*'s leaving the islands given in Campbell 2000, p. 108, fn.
[5] Thomas W. Smith (1801?-?1845), *A Narrative of the Life, Travels and Sufferings of Thomas W. Smith…*, Boston (Massachusetts), 1844, pp. 157-158.

likewise be deleted from Vernet's list.

Three ships had been in the Sound just before Jewett's arrival. The *Catharina* had arrived on 25 October; she and the *Emeline* had been in company with two other Stonington ships, the *Clothier* and the *Spark*, and were looking for the latter two ships. So it seems highly likely that on failing to find them in the Sound, they both left again, just as Palmer had left West Point Island on 22 October on finding no Stonington ships, and as Palmer recorded, the *Hero* left just as Jewett arrived. So by the time Jewett arrived, the Sound was in all probability deserted.

Argentine authors attach far more importance to the Jewett episode than it deserves, including Kohen and Rodríguez, who call it "The official taking of possession of the islands by Argentina in 1820" (p. 125), but in fact not even the Buenos Aires government attached any importance to it at the time. The government knew from February 1821, when the *Rampart* arrived, that David Jewett was in the Falklands; they could have appointed him "Governor of the Malvinas", and they could have made William Mason his official replacement as governor, but they did not. There was not a word in the government's orders to Mason or to Ansoátegui's successor that suggested that in the Malvinas they would be on Argentine territory; they were ordered to continue the privateering cruise and thus to leave the islands. And though Buenos Aires knew nothing about Jewett's "possession-taking" when they appointed Mason (since Jewett kept it secret), they knew about it from 10 November 1821, the day of the announcement in *El Argos*. But they showed no reaction; they neither formally announced the possession of the islands nor set up any presence there. Kohen and Rodríguez say (p. 134) that the Jewett episode offers "one of the many examples of British inaction", but the total absence of any Argentine action is much more significant.

The worst error by Kohen and Rodríguez is their failure to distinguish between pirates and privateers – they say (pp. 130-31, 135, 136, 288) that Jewett was an Argentine state official, and maintain (pp. 130-31) that "The fact of having been a privateer does not diminish the official nature of his actions". In fact by the time he reached the Falklands he was no longer a privateer but a pirate pure and simple. There was a vital legal difference, which was known to all seamen and governments: privateers were officially licensed to capture only the ships of the enemy in war, whereas pirates captured ships of any country including their own, both in peace and war. Licensed privateers were accepted by all seafaring countries including Argentina, and operated legally under the authority of the government of a belligerent power, whereas pirates were everywhere criminals and outlaws. Since their acts were illegal everywhere, pirates were subject to "universal jurisdiction" – they could be taken to court and punished (often with death) in any country, whether or not they had attacked that country's vessels. From the moment a privateer made a capture not covered by his commission, he ceased to be a privateer and became a pirate – as the Portuguese prize court ruled in 1822 in reference to the *Heroína*, "there is no doubt of her being a pirate and not a legal privateer" (section 4.6). It was not possible to be a pirate and a privateer at the same time.

Kohen and Rodríguez suppress all that – they do not mention Jewett's capture of the *Carlota* or the resulting mutiny among his crew, they omit his capture of the *Rampart*, and they completely suppress the report of the Portuguese prize court which ruled that Jewett, Mason and the ship *Heroína* were piratical. That ruling is printed in Manning 1932, fn. 1, pp. 169-171; Kohen and Rodríguez make use of Manning 1932 elsewhere, listing it in their bibliography (p. 298), and mentioning it in footnotes on their pages 169 and 179, so they can hardly have been unaware of the prize-court report. They knew of the contents of Jewett's Letter 3, but criticise us for pointing out that he failed to mention his "possession-taking", and mention only (p. 135) that its purpose was to describe his difficulties and ask to be relieved from his command – they say:

The authors of the pamphlet evoke the fact that Jewett, in his note sent to the government in Buenos Aires, told of the desperate conditions of his crew, but failed to mention the taking of possession. This means absolutely nothing. The objective of his note was to request relief in the face of the gravity of their situation.

They twice refer to it as a "note", but they must have been aware of its length and content – it runs to 13 closely-written sides and 3,800 words, and as we relate above, Jewett gives a detailed account of the capture of the *Carlota*, which was what made him a pirate.

It is thus incorrect for Kohen and Rodríguez to say (p. 130) "Jewett did not act as 'a pirate'".

The truth is that he *did* act as a pirate – but they attack us for saying so:

If we are talking about pirates and privateers, as Pascoe and Pepper do in referring to Jewett, it may be worth recalling that John Strong, the supposed British "discoverer" of the Falklands/Malvinas, was one. If one follows the British pamphlet, there were "good" and "bad" privateers. If they were British, at the service of His Majesty, they had the capacity to establish sovereignty over territory; if they were mere citizens or at the service of other nations, they could not.

That is a serious distortion. In *Getting it right*, we do not say that Strong discovered the islands; we say they were probably discovered by the Portuguese in 1518-19, as we do in this book too (section 1.3). And we do not say that Strong made the first recorded landing on the islands, which some authors have wrongly claimed.

The legal positions of Jewett and Strong were entirely different: unlike Jewett, Strong remained a legal privateer, with letters of marque (a commission carried by a vessel intended for trading as well as privateering) issued on 26 July 1689 by the joint British sovereigns King William III and Queen Mary II, authorising him to attack French ships, since Britain and France were at war.[1] He committed no acts of piracy and thus remained a privateer legally entitled to attack French ships. Jewett did not remain a privateer but became a pirate the moment he captured a neutral ship.

Thus the account of David Jewett's visit to the Falklands by Kohen and Rodríguez is seriously erroneous. That also applies to their statement about us in their Introduction (p. 21), that "the authors of the British pamphlet... admit... that David Jewett, a representative of the government of Buenos Aires, took control of the islands in 1820". In fact we did not say he "took control of the islands" (which would have been absurd; he did no such thing); in *Getting it right* (pp. 9 and 10) we refer in quotes to his "claim" to the Falklands and his "taking possession" of the islands, making it clear that there was no genuine claim or possession-taking. Kohen and Rodríguez suppress and distort the evidence.

Even if Jewett had remained a legal, legitimate privateer, his raising of a claim by Argentina would not have affected the two much better prior claims by Britain and Spain – he would simply have added another claim to those already existing, and his claim would have been inferior to the others. But he was not a privateer but a pirate; since all acts by pirates were illegal, they naturally could not perform legitimate acts of territorial sovereignty. So Jewett, as a pirate, did not even raise a claim to the Falklands – he did nothing valid at all.

In short, there was no "official taking of possession" of the Falklands by Argentina in 1820; an invalid claim was made without the knowledge of the Buenos Aires government by a pirate who soon regretted the act and kept it secret.

To sum up: there is no evidence that David Jewett was ordered to go to the Falklands and much evidence to the contrary. As soon as he captured the Portuguese ship *Carlota* he ceased to be a legal privateer and became a pirate; from then on all his actions were illegal in international law. He only decided to go to the Falklands after he had drawn a blank in both North and South Atlantic and his crew were beginning to die; Berkeley Sound was empty when he arrived, and the only ship he could contact was the *Jane* in Salvador Water. A few ships passed through Port Louis soon afterwards on their way to the new sealing grounds in the South Shetlands, and some of their captains plus James Weddell saw him "take possession" of the islands before they left again. Jewett wanted to use the islands as a base for capturing Spanish ships, but none appeared, so he and his crew "vegetated" for six months. During that time he did not move from Port Louis; he did not exercise any kind of sovereignty (he did not "take control of the islands") and did nothing to interfere with the activities of British and American sealing ships (he says in Letter 3 that there was a British ship in Berkeley Sound in January 1821). He was again guilty of piracy in seizing the American ship *Rampart*, but in the end he gave up, and did not tell Buenos Aires of his "act of possession". Jewett and his successor William Mason were merely captains of the *Heroína*; they never held any official position in the Falklands. Both were pirates, but only Mason was convicted and imprisoned; Jewett escaped punishment by going to Brazil. Pirates naturally cannot perform legitimate acts of territorial

---

[1] The text of Strong's letters of marque is copied in his log, BL Sloane MS 3295, fol. 1 *recto*.

sovereignty, so there was no "official taking of possession" of the Falklands by Argentina in 1820.

4.8 The years 1821-1824; Spain protests to the United States, 1822

In their next section (pp. 137-170), Kohen and Rodríguez consider what they call "Argentine acts of sovereignty" up to the year 1829; we feel a division at 1826 would be more natural, so our next chapter starts at that point. They criticise us (p. 138) for saying in *Getting it right* (p. 11) that after the Spaniards left in 1811 the Falklands were *res nullius* ["no one's thing", i.e. belonging to no country], but they omit to mention that we give our source for that statement in a footnote on the same page: it is stated in the authoritative 10-volume work on the foreign relations of Argentina by Andrés Cisneros and Carlos Escudé, who say:[1]

... upon the Spanish withdrawal in 1811, the Malvinas Islands remained *de facto* without a possessor (and without a human population), and became *res nullius*.

So we are not alone in saying that the islands belonged to no country after 1811; that opinion was published in Buenos Aires by the semi-official Argentine Council on International Relations.

But having asserted that the idea that the islands were *terrae nullius* ["no one's lands"] is "legal nonsense", Kohen and Rodríguez then go on to say that if they were *terrae nullius*, the only effective presence in the 1820s was Argentinian, which is indeed nonsense – there was a continuous British and American presence throughout the decade, but often no Argentine presence at all.

Kohen and Rodríguez then introduce the standard (and incorrect) Argentine argument from *uti possidetis*, saying that it "has as one of its objectives that of preventing the Spanish territories from being considered *res nullius* as a result of the independence of the American nations". They also say (pp. 100 and 101) that there were no *terrae nullius* in South America. That is incorrect – as we explained in section 1.7, the Nootka Sound Convention of 1790 laid down that there were large areas that Britain (though not other countries) was entitled to regard as *terrae nullius*, where British ships seamlessly continued the exercise of extensive rights conceded by Spain to Britain; neither Spain nor Argentina could thus claim unlimited sovereignty over the Falklands. And after William Mason left Port Louis in May 1821 there was no Argentine presence whatever, but there were many British and American seamen, some of whom set up shore establishments including stone buildings, workshops and gardens, whose remains can still be seen.

One visitor was James Weddell, who paid his second visit to the islands on his second South Atlantic sealing voyage in the *Jane*, this time accompanied by the cutter *Beaufoy* commanded by Michael McLeod, a Scotsman.[2] At New Island in September 1821 Weddell met Charles Barnard, now commanding his own sealing brig *Charity*. Barnard told the story of his marooning in 1813-14, which Weddell recounted in his memoirs in 1825; Weddell's inaccurate account evidently so incensed Barnard that he wrote his own book to set the record straight.[3]

By the early 1820s the reactionary Spanish king Fernando VII was clearly losing the battle to recover South America for Spain. Most of it was now held by the "rebels", who proclaimed the independence of several new republics. US President James Monroe decided to regularise the new state of affairs, and in his State of the Union Address on 8 March 1822 he announced the US government's intention to accord diplomatic recognition to the new states. Spain refused to accept their independence, and the next day the Spanish Minister to the United States, Señor Anduaga, protested to US Secretary of State John Quincy Adams against the intended recognition,[4]

---

[1] Andrés Cisneros and Carlos Escudé (eds.), *Historia General de las Relaciones Exteriores de la República Argentina* ["General History of the Foreign Relations of the Republic of Argentina"], published by the "Consejo Argentino para las Relaciones Internacionales" ["Argentine Council on International Relations", CARI], Buenos Aires 1998, vol. I p. 176, footnote (10 printed vols., also in full on the Internet under http://www.argentina-rree.com/ historia.htm).
[2] Gurney 1997, pp. 191-193.
[3] Weddell 1825/1827, pp. 89-93; Charles Barnard, *A Narrative of the Sufferings...*, New York 1829, pp. 207-211; the whole of Barnard's criticism of Weddell is omitted from Bertha Dodge's edition of 1979 and appears only in Barnard's original edition of 1829; it will appear in full in *The Falklands Saga*.
[4] Quoted in John Bassett Moore, *Digest of International Law*, 7 vols., Washington DC 1906, vol. I, pp. 86-87, and also in Julius Goebel, *The Recognition Policy of the United States*, New York 1915, pp. 136-137.

… declaring that it can in no way now, or at any time, lessen or invalidate in the least the right of Spain to the said provinces, or to employ whatever means may be in her power to reunite them to the rest of her dominions.

It is widely accepted by writers on international law that official protests have the effect of keeping a claim alive, though without changing or strengthening it (section 6.29). Anduaga's letter was a valid protest asserting Spain's claim to her territories in South America (including the Falklands of course). That protest kept Spain's claim, such as it was, alive for some while longer. Kohen and Rodríguez clearly accept the significance of protests, since they note several times that there was no protest by Britain at some juncture or other (e.g. pp. 53, 60, 73, 74, 79, 133, 134).

Most of the ships visiting the Falklands were British or American, but there was an occasional French one – a French round-the-world expedition arrived in the corvette *la Coquille* on 20 November 1822; they pitched their tents among the ruins of Port Louis, and remained till 18 December. The expedition was led by Louis-Isidore Duperrey (1786-1865), who wrote a long account of it,[1] as did his naturalist, René Primevère Lesson (1794-1849).[2] They used only Bougainville's French names for places in the islands, as did Freycinet in 1820. Like the United States, France did not regard the islands as Argentine, British or Spanish territory, and the French involvement in the islands in the 1820s and 1830s worried the British government (section 6.14).

As announced by President Monroe, on 27 January 1823 the United States appointed a diplomatic representative to the United Provinces of the River Plate (part of which later became Argentina).[3] At that time the territory of the United Provinces included Uruguay, parts of today's Bolivia, Peru, and Chile, and on some maps even Paraguay, but not Patagonia or the Falklands. In recognising the United Provinces, the US did not accept that the Falkland Islands belonged to Buenos Aires – the US recognised no territorial sovereignty over the islands, and in any case diplomatic recognition does not imply recognition of any specific territory held by either side.

James Weddell left Britain on 13 September 1822 for his third South Atlantic sealing voyage, again in the *Jane* but with the *Beaufoy* now commanded by Mathew Brisbane, a Scot from Perth aged about 22.[4] Brisbane was a gifted seaman and a natural leader, and later played a vital role in the Falklands, where he was murdered by the villain Antonio Rivero in 1833 (section 6.32). Weddell and Brisbane spent from 11 May to 7 October 1823 in the Falklands, and became thoroughly familiar with the islands. They then sailed south to continue sealing in Antarctic waters.[5]

Britain was the second country after the United States to recognise the independence of the United Provinces of the River Plate: on 15 December 1823 a consul-general was appointed in the person of Woodbine Parish (1796-1882). Parish represented Britain in Buenos Aires from April 1824 to March 1832, and played a pioneer role in establishing relations between Britain and Argentina. Just before Parish took up his post, an enterprising individual in Buenos Aires had begun a decisive association with the Falkland Islands. His name was Louis Vernet.

4.9 Louis Vernet; the 1824 expedition

Louis Vernet (1791-1871) was born in Hamburg, but he was not German; his family were French Huguenots,[6] Protestants whose ancestors had fled from France after the compulsory

---

[1] Louis-Isidore Duperrey, *Voyage Autour du Monde…*, 11 vols., Paris 1826-30. See also John Dunmore, *Visions & Realities: France in the Pacific 1695-1995*, Waikanae, New Zealand, 1997, p. 159.

[2] René Primevère Lesson, *Voyage autour du monde…*, Paris 1838; illustration of the expedition's tents in the ruins of Port Louis opp. p. 50. See also entry on Lesson by Ann Savours in *DFB*.

[3] Moore 1906, vol. I, p. 90.

[4] Gurney 1997, pp. 198-199; Weddell 1825/1827, p. 1. Brisbane always signed his first name with one "t", which we follow here. Brief details of Brisbane's career in A.G.E Jones, "Captain Matthew Brisbane", in *Notes & Queries* 1971, reprinted (without footnotes) in *FIJ* 1975, pp. 1-4, and again with all 12 footnotes in A.G.E. Jones, *Polar Portraits: Collected Papers*, Whitby 1992, pp. 111-114. Jones dates Brisbane's birth to 1787-88 (as does Alan Gurney in his *DFB* entry), but that is clearly wrong; Jones was unaware of Brisbane's own statements of his age in 1832 and 1833, which confirm that he was born around 1800. Gómez Langenheim's account (1939, vol. I, pp. 284-287), is riddled with errors, e.g. in making Brisbane an officer of the ships *Adventure* and *Beagle*, "commanded by Fitz Roy and Wedell".

[5] Account in Weddell MS 1521/2 in the SPRI, Cambridge, pp. 68ff. (printed in Weddell 1825/1827, pp. 76-80).

[6] French « Huguenot », perhaps derived from the German „Eidgenossen" ("oath-comrades", i.e. "confederates").

imposition of Catholicism by Louis XIV in 1685. In English his surname is usually pronounced "Ver-*nay*", though spellings such as "Vernit" or "Vernette" in documents suggest that some people pronounced it differently at the time. He was one of the eight children (all boys) of Jaques Vernet,[1] and grew up speaking German and French, to which he added fluent English and Spanish while living for a time in the United States and Buenos Aires.[2] He was a cosmopolitan with no strong allegiance to any country; some Argentine authors call him "apátrida" ["stateless"], by which they imply "disloyal" or even "traitorous", in reference to his dealings with Britain and his repeatedly expressed preference for British sovereignty.[3] He spelt his first name Louis, Ludewig, Lewis or Luis according to the language he was writing, and for the islands whose history he influenced so decisively he used "Falklands" or "Malvinas" depending only on the language.

Around 1817 he went to Buenos Aires, where in 1819 he married María Sáez (1800-1858). He had been brought up as a Protestant, but he was not religious and went through a Roman Catholic wedding ceremony – at that time marriages between Protestants and Catholics were illegal in

4.9a Louis Vernet (1791-1871).
Portrait by Luisa Vernet Lavalle de Llovera, in the Museo Histórico Nacional, Buenos Aires (Objeto 5462).

Buenos Aires. He and María eventually had six children.[4] He ran a trading firm, which provided him with the capital to go into land ownership and cattle-ranching. After the province of Buenos Aires obtained independence from Spain in 1810, farming and settlement expanded southwards into territory occupied by Indian tribes. The ranching of the wild cattle on these lands for meat and hides was extremely profitable and permitted a select few to amass huge fortunes and to dominate the province for much of the 19th century. Vernet invested too, and the resulting wealth provided the financial basis for his involvement in the Falklands. His first venture was a failure; his second attempt was more successful, but it was not financially viable and ended in disaster. The full story of his epic struggle to set up a settlement in the Falkland Islands has never been told; we will provide a detailed account in *The Falklands Saga*, but we have room here only for a brief sketch.

---

[1] The spelling « Jaques » rather than the more common « Jacques » is used in all the relevant documents.
[2] Brief account of the Vernet family by Jürgen Sielemann in *Hamburgische Geschichts- und Heimatblätter* [roughly "Hamburg Historical and Local Studies"], vol. 11 (Hamburg 1987), p. 1.
[3] He is called "apátrida" e.g. by Diego Luis Molinari in *La Primera Unión del Sur...*, Buenos Aires, 1961, pp. 52 and 108; and by Mario Tesler in *El Gaucho Antonio Rivero...*, Buenos Aires 1971, p. 202.
[4] See entry on Vernet by Peter Pepper in *DFB*.

In 1819 he began to lend money to Jorge Pacheco (1761-1833), a military veteran who was owed around 65,000 pesos by the Buenos Aires government. By 1821 Vernet had lent Pacheco 2,000 pesos, and on 11 April 1821 he made an agreement with Pacheco to support him until the government paid him its debts, half of which would go to Vernet. Pacheco's wife Dionisia Obes was the sister of Cipriana Obes, wife of Bernardo Bonavía, who had served three tours of duty as Spanish commandant in the Falklands between 1802 and 1808. As we say in *Getting it right* (p. 11), it was no doubt through this connection that Pacheco and Vernet learnt about the wild cattle on East Falkland – they were always referred to as "wild cattle", but they were technically feral, i.e. descended from domestic animals (the cattle brought by Bougainville and the Spaniards). They had become huge, fierce and dangerous, and to kill them required expert gauchos (South-American-style cowboys). Pacheco and Vernet at once saw a source of profit in exporting their valuable hides.

Ricardo Caillet-Bois states that Cipriana Bonavía was also one of several people who in 1823 and 1824 asked the Buenos Aires government for a concession to exploit the wild cattle in Buenos Aires province or the Falklands;[1] Kohen and Rodríguez (p. 141) mention that statement, and add their typical comment: "These concessions leave no room for doubt as to the exercise of sovereignty over the Falklands/Malvinas by the government of Buenos Aires in 1823 and 1824." Their claim that Argentina "exercised" sovereignty is nonsense; there was absolutely no exercise of sovereignty by Argentina at that time. A mere affirmation of sovereignty is irrelevant – any country can affirm its sovereignty anywhere, but that does not make it valid. As everywhere they display the "tunnel vision" of Argentine authors, who assume that the position was 100% clear, i.e. that Argentina had 100% sovereignty. That is simply not true.

The real legal position was that the Falklands were subject to several overlapping claims; Argentina was only one of several countries with a stake in the islands, none of which amounted to full sovereignty – there existed no unambiguous title to the islands. Kohen and Rodríguez subscribe to the medieval "legitimist" view, which regards sovereignty as an abstract quality that simply exists, independently of any practical considerations such as active presence, or acceptance by other countries. That of course was Spain's view at the time too – Spain's protests in 1822 (section 4.8) and 1825 (4.11) show that in the 1820s Spain claimed full 100% sovereignty over all its South American territories, regardless of the fact that it had lost control of them and that the US and Britain recognised the independence of the new republics. The US and Britain held the "democratic", practical view of sovereignty (chapter 3).[2] The legitimist view suffers from a basic, fatal defect – if history teaches us anything, it is that *things change*; nothing is immutable, and later events or agreements can wipe out any earlier title or rights, however solid they may have seemed. That incontrovertible fact reveals the inapplicability of the legitimst view of sovereignty.

In short, as Cisneros and Escudé say (section 4.8), and as we say in *Getting it right* (p. 10), Argentina had no sovereignty in the Falklands before Louis Vernet established a permanent settlement in the islands in 1826. That settlement began an Argentine connection which might gradually have evolved into valid sovereignty (i.e. it might have matured into a full Argentine title to the islands) but he made a disastrous mistake which made that impossible (chapter 6). At least he preserved an extensive archive of documents, many of them in English, which are now in the Argentine national archives, the Archivo General de la Nación (AGN) in Buenos Aires.[3] He also wrote an account in English entitled "Memoirs on the Falkland Islands" (henceforth "Vernet's 'Memoirs' "),[4] which has never been printed. Vernet's papers include correspondence, maps, contracts, financial statements and other records; they have been completely ignored by British historians, while Argentine authors have suppressed or misrepresented some of them since they undermine Argentina's claim to the islands. We have studied them for several decades, and base

---

[1] Caillet-Bois 1948, p. 197; 1952/82, p. 199.
[2] For the two views of sovereignty see e.g. Fabry 2010, especially pp. 66-70 and p. 77 fns. 86 and 88. In respect of Britain (though not of other countries) Spain had of course lost her 100% sovereignty over large areas of South America through the Nootka Sound Convention, as explained in section 1.7.
[3] In references to documents at the AGN, the roman numeral is the "Sala" (room); the next is the "legajo" (file or batch of documents), and the third is the document number. Some documents are unnumbered (here: "no doc. no.").
[4] AGN VII, 141 (no doc. no.), a 90-page booklet in English in Vernet's hand, written after he left the islands.

most of our account on them.

In an attempt to recover the money Pacheco owed him, Vernet prompted Pacheco to apply to the Buenos Aires government for a concession to allow him to exploit the wild cattle on East Falkland (Isla Soledad in Spanish), a privilege known as "usufruct", meaning the right to exploit property without owning it.[1] Caillet-Bois says the idea came from Martín Rodríguez, governor of Buenos Aires,[2] and that Rodríguez offered it as compensation for the government's debts to Pacheco, but he gives no source for those assertions, which are very probably incorrect. First, nothing in the documentation suggests that the idea came from the government; it is much more likely that the idea came from Pacheco (who knew of the wild cattle) and Vernet, who was in the cattle-slaughtering business. Secondly, there was no connection between the government's debts to Pacheco and the concession in the Falklands. The government did not offer Pacheco a concession in the islands as an easy way of paying its debts to him – in fact they paid him in money: a document from 1835 shows that after Pacheco's death in January 1833, Vernet petitioned to be paid 31,666 pesos out of public funds, being half of the 63,333 pesos in public funds Pacheco had held.[3] Caillet-Bois also says misleadingly that the concession related to "the wild cattle existing in the Malvinas islands" – in fact there were no cattle on any island except East Falkland, and all the negotiations referred only to that one island, not to all the islands.[4] Kohen and Rodríguez (p. 140) repeat Caillet-Bois's errors almost word for word.

On 23 August 1823 Pacheco petitioned Buenos Aires for a usufruct concession – theoretically he would have done better to petition Britain or Spain, since at the time their rights in the Falklands were superior to those of Buenos Aires. The government's reaction was lukewarm, to say the least: on 28 August it gave Pacheco permission to go ahead, but reserved the right to do what it liked with the territory – its short and oddly muted reply ran as follows:[5]

It not being within the power of the government to concede an exclusive privilege, or any right of property in the lands referred to, but nevertheless desiring to reconcile the interests of the petitioner within the limits of the authority it exercises, it concedes to him the permission that he requests to go to the Island of Soledad, one of the Malvinas, to make use of it in the terms that he has proposed, but in the knowledge that such a concession can never deprive the State of its right to dispose of that territory of the world as it might consider to best serve the general interests of the province, which will be ascertained in the future in accordance with how the resources provide the means of establishing himself there effectively and permanently. Return to the petitioner this original document, which decree will serve as sufficient authority. / Rivadavia

That is the full text of the reply. Kohen and Rodríguez (p. 140) say the concession to Pacheco "is a classic example of an act that not only shows the intention to act as sovereign, but also the effective exercise of sovereignty", but they quote only part of the reply, from "it concedes to him...", thus suppressing the important first part. That first part strongly suggests that Buenos Aires did *not* see itself as exercising full sovereignty in the islands – why otherwise did the government say it did not have the power to "concede an exclusive privilege, or any right of property"? If the government saw the islands as being under its own sovereignty, it would clearly have those rights. And why did it refer to "the limits of the authority that it exercises"? If it had full sovereignty over the islands, there would not have been any limits to its authority. Perhaps Buenos Aires was aware of Britain's rights in the islands and was keeping a low profile. Be that as it may, Vernet and Pacheco set about

---

[1] Petition and grant in AGN VII, 127, doc. 22; copies in legajo 129, doc. 58. Printed in Spanish in Muñoz Azpiri 1966, vol. 2, pp. 51-53 (petition); 53-54 (grant); text of grant only (in Spanish, from Muñoz Azpiri) in Dolzer 1986, p. 185; grant only, likewise in Spanish, in Dolzer 1993, p. 253.
[2] Caillet-Bois 1948, p. 190; 1952/82, p. 192.
[3] Document in AGN X, 16-6-5 JUSTICIA, request dated 16 March 1835, with reply from a judge dated 2 July 1835 saying there was no objection to the payment to Vernet of the sum requested, half of the public funds held by Pacheco.
[4] The first cattle were put on West Falkland by the British in 1839; only East and West Falkland ever had them.
[5] Original of petition, with original of grant written in the margins, in AGN VII, 127, doc. 22; copies in AGN VII, 129, doc. 58. Printed in Spanish in Gómez Langenheim 1939, vol. I, p. 217, and in José Luis Muñoz Azpiri, *Historia Completa de las Malvinas*, Buenos Aires 1966, vol. II, pp. 51-53 (petition); 53-54 (grant); grant only (in Spanish) in Dolzer 1986, p. 185; grant only, in Spanish, in the English version 1993, p. 253. Kohen and Rodríguez say (p. 140) that the grant was signed by governor Martín Rodríguez and Bernardo Rivadavia, but it is in fact signed only by Rivadavia, plus a squiggle which may or may not be Rodríguez's signature (he signs many other documents "Rodriguez").

organising an expedition to kill the wild cattle on East Falkland and export their hides.

We refer to this first effort as "the 1824 expedition". It has been poorly understood by historians, partly because some important documents are in German, written in „Kurrentschrift", the German handwriting in use at that time, which even Germans today find hard to decipher. These documents have never been considered by historians before; the full texts in German and English will appear in *The Falklands Saga*. We quote some extracts in English below, which are the first ever printed. There are also two accounts of the 1824 expedition written in English by Louis Vernet, a brief one in his "Memoirs" and a much more detailed account in a letter in English to Samuel Fisher Lafone written in 1837, on which we base our account unless otherwise indicated.[1] Ricardo Caillet-Bois uses both those accounts, and he even quotes from the letter to Lafone, but he gives no sources and suppresses the fact that the originals are in English. The documents in Spanish, including the expedition's cash book, are legible and tell a fairly full story, but most historians (including Kohen and Rodríguez) have relied on the faulty account by Caillet-Bois. We mention some of his errors and omissions here, but have room only for a brief treatment.

The 1824 expedition began with reckless financial extravagance, which left Vernet with debts that burdened him for much of his life. Although he was the major investor in the expedition, he did not take part in it and remained in Argentina slaughtering cattle. On 29 August 1823 Pacheco signed a partnership with a young Englishman, Robert Schofield (1798-1825), who had settled in Buenos Aires with his wife Sarah and their children. Schofield undertook to pay Vernet and Pacheco 20 reales for each animal slaughtered in the Falklands (i.e. 2½ pesos; a real was an eighth of a peso),[2] and at once began to squander the partnership's money. He bought two ships: the cutter *Rafaela* (for 3,000 pesos), which they fitted out for sealing, and the American brig *Fenwick* (5,000 pesos); he chartered the British brig *Antelope* for 1,000 pesos a month, and hired the mainly English-speaking crews of all three ships.[3] Pacheco and Vernet hired a retired officer, Pablo Areguati, to lead the expedition, and since affairs in South America were chaotic, they addressed a second petition to the Buenos Aires government on 18 December asking for some cannons, for a grant of land on which to raise sheep, and for Areguati to be given the title of "Comandante" – they thought he could form a militia of "peones" (labourers or farmhands, usually called "gauchos" in English).[4] The reply came the same day, but the government made only the land grant, not the rest. The full text of the grant runs:[5]

Buenos Ayres 18 Dec.r 1823. / Government considering it a duty to protect commerce and to encourage every branch of industry in the Country has thought proper to grant to the petitioner the lands that he solicits, under the express condition to make manifest its measurements under fixed boundaries, in order to obtain the titles of property, Gov.t reserving to itself to take the necessary measures on this and the other points solicited by the petitioner =Rodriguez=

Yet again the government's reaction was half-hearted: they granted the land (on condition that a survey be made), but reserved the right to decide the other points. In other words, they pointedly refused to grant the request for Areguati to be given the title of "Comandante". The survey was never made, so the land grant never in fact became valid. It is understandable that the government granted no cannons – Buenos Aires needed every cannon it could get, given the chaos around the River Plate – but it would have cost nothing to give Areguati a title, and might have strengthened his authority over the men, yet the government gave him no title or rank. As before, the Buenos Aires government were keeping a low profile – here again one is entitled to speculate that they deliberately avoided doing anything that might offend Britain.

Kohen and Rodríguez are keen to give the impression that Areguati was given full authority by

---

[1] Keeping-copy of Vernet to Lafone in English, 9 April 1837, in AGN VII 130, unnumbered after doc. 146 (16 pp.); Vernet's less detailed account in his "Memoirs" is in AGN VII 141 (no doc. no.), pp. 41-44.
[2] Vernet mentions this agreement in his description of his assets, signed 1 January 1826, AGN VII 129, doc. 58.
[3] Details and charter documents in the expedition's financial accounts in AGN VII 129, doc. 56.
[4] Spanish original of petition in AGN VII, 127, doc. 23; copies of petition and grant in AGN VII, 129, doc. 50; English translations made by Vernet in April 1829 for Woodbine Parish are in PRO FO 6 499, fols. 11 *recto* to 12 *recto*.
[5] Vernet's translation made for Parish, in PRO FO 6 499, fol. 12 *recto*.

the Argentine government – they say (p. 144):

… the importance of Areguatí's appointment lies in the will of the government of Buenos Aires to establish an authority to reside on the islands and in the physical presence of Areguatí on the islands as commander for most of 1824.

In fact Areguati was only in the islands for four months (he left again on 7 June 1824), and his authority did not even extend to the members of his own expedition, still less to British sealers, who threatened to denounce them to the British government (below).

The two Argentine authors criticise us (pp. 144-5) for saying in *Getting it right* (p. 11) that Caillet-Bois "fudges the question of Areguati's appointment", but that is exactly what he does – he quotes the passage "Gov.t reserving to itself to take the necessary measures on this and the other points solicited by the petitioner", but makes no mention of its implication that Areguati was not appointed commandant. Oddly, Kohen and Rodríguez quote that passage too (p. 143, with a wrong source-reference to Caillet-Bois, see footnote),[1] but nevertheless go on to assert that Areguati was appointed commandant. That incorrect assertion, which is made by other authors too, derives from Louis Vernet's "Report" made in 1832 to Argentine foreign minister Vicente Maza[2] – for some 130 years it was the only printed source available, so later writers followed it and all its errors (for its faulty account of David Jewett see sections 4.6 and 4.7). In fact neither Pacheco nor Areguati was given any official position by Buenos Aires.

Kohen and Rodríguez say (p. 144) that the fact that the *Rafaela* was armed shows that "the Government of Buenos Aires took the necessary measures to exercise its authority over the Falklands/Malvinas". That is nonsense – as Caillet-Bois correctly says, she was bought by the expedition, so she was not a government ship but a private one. And at that time all ships, even small ones like the *Rafaela*, carried a few guns for defence, since there were many threats at sea.

The expedition's financial accounts give a clear picture of its proceedings. They hired three foremen ("capatazes"): Juan Ganto, Aniceto Oviedo and Estanislado Argüello, at 40 pesos a month, and 23 gauchos at 16 pesos a month; their wages started on 23 December 1823, and the first supplies were bought on 26 December.[3] The *Rafaela* (Captain James Hastie) sailed on 29 December 1823 and reached the Falklands, but she disappears from the records and was clearly lost with all hands – Kohen and Rodríguez suppress that, though Ricardo Caillet-Bois speculates that she was "wrecked on the treacherous rocks of the islands".[4] The *Fenwick*, Captain Samuel Adams, left Buenos Aires on 11 January 1824 with two dozen men led by Pablo Areguati;[5] they took horses with them, which were vital for catching the wild cattle, but almost all the horses died on the way. They reached Port Louis on 2 February, but without horses they could not catch the cattle. They were soon suffering horribly from hunger, as Areguati wrote to Pacheco on 12 February 1824:[6]

Dear Sir and friend: we arrived here on the 2nd of this month without any mishap but with only five thin horses, all injured from being in the Ship. With them we could not even examine the terrain. We walked on foot about five leagues, and encountered no Cows at all, but only groups of bulls, in fours and sixes… We

---

[1] Kohen and Rodríguez 2015, p. 143, with footnote 53 giving as source "Caillet-Bois, Ricardo, *op. cit.* p. 203". The correct reference is 1948 p. 194; 1952/82 p. 196. The Argentine historian Mario Tesler, in "Gobernadores Que Nunca Fueron" ["Governors Who Never Were"], in *Clarín*, Buenos Aires 6 June 1974, pp. 2-3, dismisses the idea that Areguati was appointed – he says "in reality it was only a request, since he did not get appointed" ("en realidad solo fue un pedido, pues no llegó a ser nombrado"). Areguati never gives himself any title in his letters.
[2] The assertion is in Vernet's "Report" 1832, in *BFSP 1832-1833*, p. 419; Spanish in *Colección* 1832, p. [95], and also, following Vernet's account, in e.g. Boyson 1924, pp. 91-92 and fn. p. 92; Goebel 1927, p. 434; Antonio Gómez Langenheim, *La tercera invasión inglesa* ["The third British invasion", i.e. after those of 1806 and 1807], Buenos Aires 1934, p. 67; and by the Argentine UN Representative, Dr. José María Ruda, in his speech to the UN Decolonisation Committee ("the C24"), 9 September 1964 (text in Perl 1983, p. 360), for which last see section 10.14.
[3] Cash book for 1824 expedition, in AGN VII, 127, doc. 33, papers marked A-G.
[4] Caillet-Bois 1948, p. 196; 1952/1982, p. 198. It is pure speculation on his part that she was wrecked in the Falklands; she may have capsized on the open sea, or caught fire, or been wrecked on the Patagonian coast, etc.; Captain Samuel Adams told Vernet only that the *Rafaela* was lost "At or near the Falklands" (Adams to Vernet, in AGN VII 127, doc. 33, A No. 4). The *Rafaela*'s sailing date, 29 December 1823, is in AGN III 15, Capitanía del Puerto 1823.
[5] Copy of letter in English to Messrs Jackson and Broadfoot, Buenos Aires 24 February 1824, in AGN VII 132, doc. 7.
[6] AGN VII, 129, doc. 51, in Spanish; 1st half quoted in Caillet-Bois 1948, pp. 194-5 (1952/1982, pp. 196-7).

are without meat, without ship's biscuits, and without gunpowder for hunting. We support ourselves on roasted rabbits, because there is no fat meat since we cannot go out to slaughter as there are no horses. I have resolved to tell you that we are perishing. We stay under boards[1] during the worst of the cold and snows at this time; we have no Boat to go to the Island to cut straw, as no one from the two Ships will give me one since they need them. The captain of the Brig who brought us has helped us as much as he could; he is entirely a man of goodwill, but the captain of the Schooner did not behave himself well…[2]

They were ignorant of the climate, the fierceness of the cattle, and the whereabouts of seals and pigs – all those things were known to British and American sealers, many of whom knew the islands well. In his petition of 23 August 1823, Pacheco had undertaken to restore the houses at Port Louis, but Areguati says the members of the expedition were sheltering "under boards", perhaps meaning "below decks", or under boards for repairing the houses and which had not been used because the workmen were on strike – Emilio Vernet says in his letter in German of 4 April (below) that the English workmen refused to work as they were not being fed.

Kohen and Rodríguez say (p. 144), following Caillet-Bois,[3] that Louis Vernet instructed his brother Emilio and Areguati that when they arrived in the islands, they were to call all those present before them and proclaim Areguati commandant of the islands – but that instruction was issued only by Vernet, one of the commercial investors in the scheme, not by the government. Kohen and Rodríguez point out that Vernet says in his 1832 "Report" to Argentine foreign minister Vicente Maza that Areguati was appointed commandant of the islands, but that was wishful thinking by Vernet, disproved by the documentation. Areguati's letter in Spanish of 12 February and Emilio Vernet's in German of 4 April are both clearly their first communication from the islands, and neither mentions any ceremony. It seems they did not perform one – and even if they did, the entire lack of record means that it is of zero validity.

Around 1 March 1824 the *Antelope* left Buenos Aires for Port Louis with Schofield's group. Vernet says in his "Memoirs" that Schofield was "indebted to us ten thousand Dollars" (i.e. Spanish silver dollars or pesos), and he had "taken to drinking very hard", so Louis's brother Emilio (Jean Émile, born 1800, the sixth of the eight Vernet brothers) went too, to keep an eye on things. There were in all about 26 Spanish-speakers who went to the islands, and the crews of the three ships amounted to around 30-40 men, almost all English-speaking. But the three ships were never in the islands together, and the crew of the *Rafaela*, a small ship with probably no more than about 10 crewmen, all perished together with their captain James Hastie.

Meanwhile James Weddell returned to the Falklands for his fourth visit (25 February to 19 March 1824),[4] after spending the first part of 1824 around Tierra del Fuego and Patagonia. He parted from Mathew Brisbane in the *Beaufoy* and on 2 March 1824 reached New Island in the *Jane*. On 12 March he moved to Port Egmont, where three days later two Spanish warships arrived, the 70-gun battleship *Asia* and the 20-gun brig *Achille*. Weddell told them the best place to anchor, but the Spaniards ignored his advice and the *Asia* dragged her anchors in a gale on 16 March and was driven two miles from the landing place. Weddell was invited to dine aboard the *Asia* on the 17th, but the gale prevented the *Asia*'s boats from returning to the ship, whereupon Weddell took pleasure in demonstrating that his boats could row against the wind, and was duly rowed aboard "with apparent ease". Weddell clearly enjoyed his visit to Port Egmont; at the same time Areguati and his miserable starving band from Buenos Aires were struggling to survive at Port Louis ninety miles to the east, but Weddell knew nothing of them and sailed for Britain on 19 March.[5]

The *Antelope* arrived at Port Louis on 26 March 1824 with Robert Schofield and his party, including Schofield's wife Sarah, their children, and Emilio Vernet, but again almost all their horses had died. By then both the *Rafaela* and the *Fenwick* had left; the *Rafaela* disappeared, but Areguati had sent the *Fenwick* to Rio Negro to get horses, and Captain Adams says the *Fenwick* went twice

---

[1] The original, "baxo de tablas" [*sic*], meaning "under boards", is somewhat vague.
[2] I.e. Captain Samuel Adams of the brig *Fenwick* and Captain James Hastie of the cutter *Rafaela*.
[3] Caillet-Bois 1948, pp. 196-7; 1952/82, pp. 197-8. Caillet-Bois gives no source; it is actually in AGN VII 129, doc. 58.
[4] Account in Weddell's MS 1521/2 in SPRI, Cambridge, pp. 200-204; printed in Weddell 1825/1827, pp. 211-214.
[5] Weddell MS p. 205 (1825/1827, p. 216). Weddell reached Britain on 2 July 1824 (1825/1827, pp. 222-226).

from Port Louis to Rio Negro and back, and took about 70 horses to the Falklands.[1]

So now only the gauchos and some crewmen from the *Fenwick* and the *Antelope*, plus the crew and passengers of the *Antelope*, were present at Port Louis – a couple of dozen Spanish-speakers and about as many English-speakers. There were tensions between the two groups, and Schofield began to behave oddly, no doubt under the influence of drink. On 4 April Emilio wrote a deeply worried letter to Louis in German (which the Vernet brothers sometimes used for secrecy), recounting the complete chaos he found at Port Louis and a potentially serious clash between the English and Spanish speakers. The letter reads in part:[2]

Dear Louis, / Malvinas 4 April 1824 / We arrived here safely on the 26th of last month, but unfortunately with only 6 horses, only 3 of which are in fairly good condition; the other 20 died on the way.

Your concern regarding Schofield has proved only too well-founded, for it is not merely that he acted like an unwise person; it is now becoming clear that he is a great swindler and an arch-rascal, to whom no agreement is too sacred to break… Areguati, who has been here for 2 months and only brought 4 horses in very miserable condition, with which he could not even catch the cattle needed to sustain the people, has lived here the whole time in the greatest embarrassment, since they had nothing but farina [Spanish "flour"] and salt meat to eat, and they thus looked forward with impatience to the Antelope. So you can imagine his astonishment on hearing that ~~he~~ Schofield brings nothing… the [[Eng]]lishmen… have done nothing the whole ((time here)), since he prov[ided]] them with neither wine nor bread nor anything else… We had a great deal of trouble even to get them to fit up a s[mall]] dwelling for Schofield and his family, but since he has deceived us again here, they are leaving the work half completed… Yesterday towards evening we saw in the far distance 2 sails, a brig and a cutter, which naturally caused great joy, since we thought it was the Fenwick and the Rafaela. Schofield… sent Baker to them very early in the morning, to order them, should it be the Fenwick, to throw the horses overboard[3] and go back again; since it now turns out that it was not she but a whaler, that had put in here for fresh provisions, the said Baker came ashore this afternoon with c^{irca} 20 men from that ship armed with rifles, sabres & pistols, in the hope that the Englishmen here would desert to their side and thus enable them to rob us of all our provisions. [But]… since the Englishmen are likewise bitter towards Schofield, and Areguati's people would have cut them down at the slightest signal, they pretended they had only come to buy some tobacco and fresh meat and then went straight back on [[b]]oard the Antelope… All the craftsmen had resolved to go back in the Antelope, however we have agreed with a mason, a carpenter and a smith to work here for us for 4 months…

Schofield's widow Sarah later wrote that Baker had paid Schofield 1,000 pesos as a down-payment on an estate in Argentina; it seems he felt Schofield had double-crossed him and not provided the estate, so he decided to force the abandonment of the enterprise by taking what he could.[4]

Emilio wrote again in German to Louis on 8 April recounting another incident, and hoping that some men could be sent from Buenos Aires to protect them from "pirates":[5]

Dear Louis, / After another discussion which I have had with Schofield, I really do not know what to think of him, so before you undertake anything against him I would like to sound him out thoroughly first. He… is able to say that he had no part in the incident here on the 4th… The Brig Adiona [*sic*] of Grenock (Scotland), which came in here a few days ago, has now to our misfortune also taken the best wood from the wrecked ship. He [the *Adeona*'s captain] now threatens to denounce us as pirates to the English Governm^{t}. We are constantly and principally, since it is now winter, threatened by pirates, so it would we think be very good to send about 6 or 8 men from B[ueno]^s A[ire]^s merely with the duty of keeping guard here but under

---

[1] AGN VII, 127, doc. 33, A No. 4: reply from Captain Samuel Adams to Vernet dated 15 June 1838. "Rio Negro" was the normal English name of Carmen de Patagones (founded as a mere frontier fort in 1779).
[2] Letter in German (with Spanish dateline) from „Emil" Vernet to Louis Vernet, 4 April 1824, in AGN VII 132, doc. 28; translation by Graham Pascoe. The original is very tattered, with some loss of text, shown as follows: [[…] = text missing at left; […]] = text missing at right; ((…)) = text on detached fragment of paper; grey highlight = reading presumed; […] = our addition to improve sense; … = an omission here by us. The handwriting, in „Kurrentschrift", is small and very difficult to read; we are grateful to Roman and Hermine Fink for assisting in the deciphering.
[3] Not to kill them but to deprive the expedition of them – they would have swum ashore and run away. Horses and cattle are still pushed off boats in the Falklands to this day to swim ashore. The landscape is now well fenced, so they remain where they are wanted; before fencing began in the 1850s they would have escaped.
[4] Sarah Schofield to the British vice-consul in Buenos Aires, 27 December 1832, PRO FO 6 499, fol. 200 *recto*.
[5] Letter in German (with Spanish dateline) from „Emil" Vernet to Louis Vernet, in AGN VII, 132, doc. 8; translation by Graham Pascoe, full text here; 3 German letters by Emilio will appear in German and English in *The Falklands Saga*.

Areguati's command. / your faithful brother / Emil Vernet

Kohen and Rodríguez say several times (e.g. pp. 53, 60, 73, 74, 79, 128, 129) that at some point or other there was no British reaction when (they say) there should have been, but here is a very clear British reaction: a threat by the captain of the *Adeona* to denounce the group from Buenos Aires to the British government as "pirates". The captain of the sealing brig *Adeona* (as correctly spelt) at this time was apparently Andrew Low, related to her later captain William Low. His threat to denounce the expedition to the British government shows that he regarded the islands as British property and saw Areguati and his men as intruders. No wonder Emilio asked for guards to protect the expedition. But he did not get them.

Kohen and Rodríguez say that it is irrelevant whether the 1824 expedition was a failure or not; that is true of course, but they talk of Areguati's "effective presence" in the islands (p. 144), which is absurd. He exercised no effective control – many of his men refused to obey his orders, and the captain of the *Adeona* was so far from accepting Areguati's authority that he threatened to denounce him and his men to Britain as pirates. The clash may have provided the motivation for the raising of the British flag by the Argentinians at Port Louis in 1828 (section 5.8).

In late April 1824 Schofield suddenly sailed in the *Antelope*, taking the stores and abandoning the expedition, which then collapsed. He took a dozen men but left Areguati and the rest behind. He went to the coast of Argentina where Louis Vernet was killing cattle; Vernet recorded bitterly that the men demanded their wages, which he himself paid. Caillet-Bois quotes Vernet (in Spanish) as saying that Schofield's departure from the islands "appeared to him as a dream of which he had but a faint recollection", but he gives no source for the quote – it actually occurs in English, in Vernet's letter of 1837 to Samuel Fisher Lafone, mentioned above.[1] Caillet-Bois concealed the source because it did not suit his purposes – Lafone's association with Vernet resulted indirectly in the arrival of the ancestors of some of today's Falkland Islanders, and the southern part of East Falkland is named Lafonia after him.

Captain Adams arrived back at Port Louis in the *Fenwick* in late May 1824 on his second trip from Patagonia with horses, only to find that the project had been abandoned, so he left again on 7 June taking Areguati and some others. He reached Buenos Aires on 2 July, and Areguati was soon busy paying off the employees: the capatazes Juan Gauto and Estanislado Argüello were paid off on 12 July, and 16 others soon afterwards. But Adams had left the third capataz, Aniceto Oviedo, and seven gauchos behind – not the first people marooned in the Falklands, nor the last. They were rescued six weeks later by Captain John Robinson of the British sealing vessel *Susannah Ann*, which sailed on 24 July with Oviedo and the seven gauchos, leaving Port Louis a ghost town again, and reached Buenos Aires on 12 August.[2] The eight men were paid off the next day.[3]

The 1824 expedition had been an utter failure; it had not exported a single cattle-hide; it had not made a survey of the island (required for the grant to be valid under the terms of the grant of 18 December 1823), and it had made a loss of 29,311 pesos and 3 reales.[4] That loss remained a millstone round Vernet's neck for the rest of his involvement with the Falklands.

Kohen and Rodríguez misdate the end of the expedition – they say (p. 144) that Areguati left the islands "before the end of the year" [i.e. 1824] and that he was "comandante" in the islands for "most of 1824"; they give as their source Caillet-Bois, p. 198 (i.e. in the 1952/82 edition), but that page in Caillet-Bois contains no such statement and no date for the end of the expedition. Caillet-Bois merely says that Schofield arrived back in Buenos Aires in August 1824, and that the eight men left behind reached Buenos Aires "some time later" ("algún tiempo más tarde"), without

---

[1] Vernet in English to Samuel Fisher Lafone 9 April 1837, AGN VII, 130, unnumbered after doc. 146; quoted in Spanish translation, without source, in Caillet-Bois 1948 p. 196 (fn.), 1952/82 p. 198 (fn.).
[2] Dates of sailing and arrival of the *Susannah Ann*, and name of her captain, in AGN III, Capitanía del Puerto, 17, page later numbered "12". The *Susannah Ann*, also spelt *Susan[na] Ann[e]*, etc., was a 79-ton smack; she left Gravesend on 11 September 1823 and returned there on 27 June 1825 (Jones 1986, pp. 76 & 80, and in *FIJ* 1992, pp. 44-45).
[3] Pay for Oviedo at 40 pesos a month and for the other 7 (unnamed) men at 17 pesos a month, from 23 December 1823 to 13 August 1824, in AGN VII 127, doc. 33, parts A N° 12, B N° 6.
[4] Details from expedition's cash book and final account, 20 August 1825, in AGN VII, 127, doc. 33, parts A and B; also stated by Caillet-Bois (1948 p. 196, 1952/82 p. 198).

saying when. But he does not mention that Areguati and others were taken back to Buenos Aires by the *Fenwick*; he does say eight men were left behind, but he does not say that they were rescued by the *Susannah Ann* – yet again he suppresses the English connection.

In short, Kohen and Rodríguez paint a false picture of the 1824 expedition. It actually lasted a mere five months (February to July 1824) and was a commercial venture without active involvement of the Argentine government. Far from "exercising sovereignty" in the islands, the Buenos Aires government expressly refrained from appointing Pablo Areguati as "Comandante", and even stated that it had no power to confer an exclusive privilege in the islands. There is no record of any proclamation of Areguati as commandant, and he did not even possess authority over his own men, let alone over British sealers in the islands. Quite correctly, Kohen and Rodríguez omit all mention of Areguati and of the 1824 expedition from their conclusion.

4.10 The years 1824-5; the United Provinces do not include the Falklands in their territory

Following the United States, Britain was now considering formalising commercial and political relations with the newly independent South American countries including the United Provinces of the River Plate (which became Argentina). Foreign Secretary George Canning instructed the British consul-general in Buenos Aires, Woodbine Parish, to find out all he could about the United Provinces with a view to signing a treaty of recognition and friendship, so Parish wrote to Bernardino Rivadavia, foreign minister of the Province of Buenos Aires, asking for information. Rivadavia passed the request to his secretary Ignacio Núñez, to whom Parish wrote on 12 May 1824 officially asking for a report "that should comprise all those points on which it may seem desirable that my Government... should be informed". Núñez had the report printed when he was in Europe a year later, in a book of over 300 pages, in London in Spanish and English, and in Paris in French.[1]

Kohen and Rodríguez (pp. 147-8) mention Parish's request to Rivadavia, and give the English title of what they call "Núñez's reply" ("La respuesta de Núñez") – but they fail to mention that it was a 300-page book! And they falsify its contents by saying that "No annex makes any reference to the territorial composition of the United Provinces (or of Buenos Aires, the province on which the Falklands/Malvinas depended)".

That is untrue: Núñez's book includes a section beginning on p. 182 entitled "Extent and Situation of the Parts of the Provinces", which says about the province of Buenos Aires:[2]

That part of the province, lying between the rivers Paraná and la Plata on the north and east, and the Salado on the south and west, forms a tract, the greater diameter of which... is between 33 and 33½ degrees of south latitude, to the mouth of the Salado..., which is in the 36th degree, may contain about 66 straight leagues, inclining from north-west to south-east, and cutting the meridians at an angle of about 50 degrees. The less diameter, in the middle, is 23 straight leagues, which give a surface of 1518 square leagues. Beyond that tract settlements have also been extended to 37 degrees south, following the sea coast...

Since the above description was given, however, the country of Buenos Ayres has been extended 50 leagues more to the south... The communication between Buenos Ayres and Patagonia is kept up at present by sea... but all the operations of the government are now tending to establish a direct communication between both these countries by land. The barbarians who interrupt the passage will be speedily subdued by force of arms; and under military protection towns will be formed, which will not only facilitate that plan of intercourse, but also cause Buenos Ayres to extend her territory more than 20,000 square leagues in the quarter of the south in the temperate zone, as far as 52 degrees of south latitude. An attempt has been made to purchase that territory from the Indians; and for that purpose, in April 1822, a Commissioner of the Government of Buenos Ayres held a Conference with the principal Caziques of these Indians...

Moreover, the book contains on p. 186 a table listing the latitudes and longitudes of 42 places in the province of Buenos Aires, and it describes the situation of the city and province of Buenos Aires, with its maritime and riverine borders and its bordering provinces. It then proceeds more briefly to

---

[1] Ignacio Núñez, *Noticias históricas, politicas, y estadísticas de las Provincias Unidas del Río de la Plata...*, London 1825; English translation: *An account, historical, political, and statistical, of the United Provinces of Rio de la Plata...*, London 1825; French translation: *Esquisses, historiques, politiques et statistiques de Buenos-Ayres, des autres Provinces Unies du Rio de la Plata...*, Paris 1826. Parish's request to Núñez is printed on pp. 1-2.

[2] Núñez 1825, English translation pp. 182-184.

describe the other provinces, with their borders and neighbours: Entre Ríos, Corrientes, Paraguay (at that time part of the United Provinces), Tucuman, Upper Peru, Cochabamba, Charcas and La Paz, intermixed with descriptions of major cities, and including large areas which later became parts of other countries and did not join Argentina. To say that the book contains no reference to the territorial composition of the United Provinces is untrue.

It is therefore significant that in their descriptions of themselves neither Buenos Aires nor any of the other provinces made a single mention of the Falkland Islands. That is especially remarkable in Núñez's report on Buenos Aires, which was responsible for the foreign relations of the United Provinces. Núñez describes the seal fishery, mentioning San Antonio and San José in Patagonia,[1] but says nothing about the Falklands, and in the passage quoted above, he says the subduing of the Indians "will… cause Buenos Ayres to extend her territory… as far as 52 degrees of south latitude". His reference to the purchasing of the territory from the Indians shows that he was thinking only of Patagonia, and his use of the future "will" shows that Buenos Aires had not yet, in 1825, extended its territory as far south as 52 degrees, and thus did not include the Falklands (which lie at that latitude, see Map 2 in our Introduction). Woodbine Parish wrote an 85-page report for Canning based on Núñez, in which he mentions Patagonia as part of the United Provinces: he says 24 representatives in the Congress of the United Provinces had been assigned to Buenos Aires, 24 to the rest of the country, and "one for the settlement on the coast of Patagonia," but he does not mention the Falklands.[2] The conclusion is clear: to both Núñez and Parish the Falkland Islands were not part of Argentina.

4.11 Spain protests to Britain, 1825

The pig-headed Spanish king Fernando VII got wind of Britain's intention to recognise the United Provinces; Spain insisted that South America was eternally Spanish, and strongly objected to Britain's recognition of any part of it as independent. On 21 January 1825 the Spanish foreign minister Francisco de Zea Bermúdez (1779-1850) made a formal protest to the British chargé d'affaires at Madrid, saying "rebellion does not constitute a right", and accusing Britain of "disowning the legitimate rights of the King of Spain".[3] That reflected Spain's medieval, legitimist, *de jure* view of sovereignty as an abstract quality divorced from any practical considerations, in contrast to the democratic *de facto* view held by Britain and the United States, which saw sovereignty as a right which had to be established by effective exercise of power and recognition by other countries in order to be valid. Nevertheless, Zea Bermúdez's letter was a valid diplomatic protest by Spain against Britain's recognition of the independence of what became Argentina. Protests are a universally recognised way of keeping claims alive (sections 7.15, 8.7, 8.8), and protests were used by Argentina for that purpose for 17 years from 1833 to 1849 against Britain's possession of the Falklands. Those Argentine protests upheld Argentina's claim to the islands (such as it was) till it was ended by treaty in 1850, and Spain's protests upheld Spain's rights (such as they were), at least for a while.

Kohen and Rodríguez maintain (p. 139) that "Spain had no specific claim over the Falklands/Malvinas; it merely asserted its sovereignty over the entire territory of the Viceroyalty of the Rio de la Plata as well as over the rest of the rebel colonial dependencies in America." True, but what is the point of saying that? The Falklands were part of that territory, so they were claimed by Spain like the rest; to say that Spain did not have a specific claim to the Falklands implies that to have a valid claim to any given territory, Spain would have had to list all her former territories individually – and they were of vast extent. That is an absurd implication. In 1825 Spain still claimed the Falklands, and maintained her rights there by protesting, thus "encumbering" Argentina's claim with a pre-existing Spanish claim (chapter 3). The Argentine claim to the islands was in any case purely unilateral and internal; neither Spain nor any other country accepted it at all.

---

[1] Núñez 1825, English translation pp. 216-220.
[2] Parish's report dated 25 June 1824, in PRO FO 6/4, fols. 3 *recto* to 46 *recto*.
[3] Zea Bermúdez to the British chargé d'affaires at Madrid, 21 January 1825, in Herbert Arthur Smith (ed.), *Great Britain and the Law of Nations,* Vol. I, London 1932, pp. 152-62; both quotes here from p. 154. See also Mikulas Fabry 2010, p. 61 and p. 74 note 54.

4.12 The Treaty of Amity, 1825

Britain ignored the Spanish protest and on 2 February 1825 concluded a "Treaty of Amity, Commerce and Navigation" with the United Provinces; it was signed for Britain by Woodbine Parish in Buenos Aires, and ratifications were exchanged in London on 12 May 1825.[1] It did not imply British recognition of any claim by Argentina to the Falklands – diplomatic recognition merely formalises the acceptance of the existence of a state and of its government's authority; it does not confirm the territories ruled by that government. Kohen and Rodríguez assert (p. 146) that diplomatic recognition "includes or implies respect for territorial integrity", but diplomatic recognition does not even confirm recognition of the extent of territory held *de facto*, let alone of *de jure* rights to territory, still less recognition of mere *claims* to territory that is not physically held.[2] That would be absurd, as diplomatic recognition is always mutual – if it included recognition of *claims* to territory, then Argentina would also have recognised Britain's claim to the Falklands.

Various authors draw attention to the lack of any British reservation of rights over the Falklands in the Treaty of Amity, implying that the treaty indicated British recognition of Argentine rights.[3] Kohen and Rodríguez say (p. 147) "Neither party made a reservation or observation of any kind in relation to the Falklands/Malvinas", but it is more to the point that Britain asked Argentina for descriptions of its territories and products, and Argentina produced a detailed account including the extent of its territories (section 4.10) without mentioning the Falklands. The United Provinces clearly did not include the Falkland Islands.

4.13 The year 1825: no Argentine presence in the Falklands; the *Beaufoy* in the islands

Kohen and Rodríguez obscure the fact that there was a complete interruption between the end of the 1824 expedition and the beginning of Louis Vernet's next Falklands venture in 1826. They mention (p. 141) the consular verification of Vernet's documents in 1826 for his second venture *before* they deal (pp. 142-4) with the supposed "appointment" of Pablo Areguati as commandant in 1823 and his (fictional) "effective presence" in the islands in 1824. We mentioned those untruths about Areguati in section 4.9, and we recount Vernet's second venture in our next chapter where it belongs. Kohen and Rodríguez say (p. 147): "Argentina was already exercising authority over the islands", but that is untrue; for almost two years from July 1824 to June 1826 there was no Argentine presence whatever in the Falklands – but plenty of British and American ships, upholding the customary rights they had acquired over the previous 60 years, and the British ships were continuing the exercise of special rights accepted under the Nootka Sound Convention by Spain, which had not given up its own rights in the islands.

One of those British ships was the cutter *Beaufoy*, which left London on 21 August 1824 on another sealing voyage under Mathew Brisbane, this time alone, and reached the Patagonian coast on 6 December 1824. The log of this journey is now at the Scott Polar Research Institute (SPRI) in Cambridge, and has never been printed.[4] For six weeks from January 1825 the *Beaufoy* worked with the London sealer *Susannah Ann* around Tierra del Fuego, then Brisbane set off for the Falklands. He anchored at New Island on 3 April 1825, and spent almost six months in the islands, which he got to know even more intimately. He went back to Tierra del Fuego on 27 September, and on 3 January 1826 set sail for home. The log breaks off on 20 February; Weddell says Brisbane arrived in the Downs (off Deal in Kent) on 29 March.[5]

---

[1] "Treaty of Amity, Commerce, and Navigation, between His Majesty and the United Provinces of Rio de la Plata.– Signed at Buenos Aires, February 2, 1825"; full text (English and Spanish) in *BFSP 1824-1825* [= vol. XII], London 1846, pp. 29-37, also (Spanish only) in *Argentina – Reino Unido*, Buenos Aires 2004, pp. 2-6.
[2] On this point see Manning 1925, vol. I, pp. 87-88; Fabry 2010, p. 66 and fn. 88 p. 77.
[3] Implied also in e.g. Ruda's speech to the C24, 9 September 1964 (Perl 1983, p. 360, and quoted in Beck 1988, p. 69); stated in Caputo's speech at the UN, 17 November 1987 (UN doc. A/42/PV.70; *MGSS* vol. VII part 1, pp. 297-298; see section 10.24); in Lawrence Freedman, *Britain & the Falklands War*, Oxford 1988, p. 19; and in Terragno 2006, p. 253.
[4] SPRI, Cambridge, Weddell Papers no. 1521/1, anonymous, unpaginated.
[5] Weddell 1825/1827, p. 324; A.G.E. Jones, quoting *Lloyds List* of 11 April 1826, gives 10 April 1826 for Brisbane's return to the Downs (Jones 1992, p. 112).

4.14 Conclusion

In their account of developments from 1810 to 1825, Kohen and Rodríguez have failed to show that Argentina exercised any sovereignty in the Falklands. They give a false picture of David Jewett's visit to the islands in 1820, of the 1824 expedition, of the description of the United Provinces by Ignacio Núñez and of the 1825 Treaty of Amity, while the letters of 1811 and 1816 are irrelevant. There was no official Argentine presence in the islands throughout that time (the 1824 expedition was a private venture, and Areguati held no official position), but there was an extensive British and American presence, which in the case of British ships was a continuation of longstanding British rights.

CHAPTER FIVE: Louis Vernet's five years in the Falklands, 1826-31

In an attempt to recover the investment he had lost in the 1824 expedition, Louis Vernet now mounted another cattle-killing expedition to the Falklands, and this time he handled things himself. This second venture lasted just over five years, and took place in three phases. What we call "Phase I" (1826-8) was a repeat of the 1824 expedition, a purely commercial cattle-slaughtering scheme with gauchos but no women, since there was no intention to found a settlement. In "Phase II" (1828-9), a second group of inhabitants arrived: the black slaves; and in "Phase III" (1829-31), two more groups arrived: the settlers (who were neither gauchos nor slaves), and the Charrúa Indians. The settlers, mainly from Germany and Britain, included women and children since his 1828 concession required him to found a settlement. From 1828 to 1831, Vernet theoretically held the "freehold" of East Falkland (granted by Buenos Aires but not recognised elsewhere, and retrospectively declared invalid by the Argentine government in 1882, section 5.6), and in 1829-31 he held an official position awarded by the Buenos Aires government, but not recognised elsewhere.

In the last analysis Vernet's settlement was not financially viable,[1] and after only five years he became so desperate for money that he made a disastrous mistake – he seized three American ships, hoping that they would be declared his property by the Buenos Aires prize court. The court did so, but the decision brought him no benefit – in seizing the ships he brought down the wrath of the United States on his head and on Argentina too, resulting in a twelve-year breach of diplomatic relations between the two countries and the end of his involvement in the Falklands.

Vernet's activities have been very poorly understood by historians – British historians have completely ignored Vernet's papers, while Argentine historians have misused them, so that there prevails in Argentina a false picture of the Argentine involvement in the islands. Kohen and Rodríguez therefore give a severely distorted account of these vital years and draw false conclusions. Here and in chapter 6 we point out where their account is erroneous, and give a brief account of the events that took place and of their legal consequences.

5.1 Louis Vernet's five years in the Falklands: some basic facts

In considering the period of Argentine involvement in the Falklands, certain basic facts should be borne in mind, so we begin with a brief summary. The length of time from 11 June 1826, when Louis Vernet landed on the southern shore of Berkeley Sound, to 7 November 1831, when he finally left the islands by his own decision, was less than 5½ years, and he was absent for about half that time. During those 5½ years there was a constant turnover of people at the settlement at Port Louis – of the 25 men who landed with Vernet in June 1826, exactly two were still there five years later in June 1831 (Juan Gregorio Sánchez and Dionisio Eredia); all the others had left and been replaced by roughly as many new men. Many people spent only a few months at the settlement before leaving again – they spent less time in the islands than many of the British and American sealers and whalers, who are usually regarded as temporary visitors.

Kohen and Rodríguez quote (p. 162) Ricardo Caillet-Bois's statement that "Vernet considered that around three hundred people inhabited the islands at some point",[2] but that is seriously misleading – it is worded so as to include the phrase "three hundred people inhabited the islands", but that was never the case. Even if there were 300 people who *ever lived in the islands at all* during those years (which was undoubtedly an exaggeration by Vernet), they were not all there at the same time; there was a constant coming and going. Vernet made no censuses – it would have been pointless, as the population constantly changed – but we have collated lists of people arriving and leaving, and the names of people mentioned in diaries and letters, which show that the maximum number of people present at Port Louis *at any one time* was around 128, for only two months from July to September 1831, but there were mostly under 100 people there.

The entire land-based population lived at Port Louis, but Kohen and Rodríguez refer (p. 152) to "the settlements existing during the Argentine administration", and actually mention (p. 162) "two small towns [*sic!!*], called Rosas and Dorrego". Here they have yet again been misled by the

---
[1] Some account of his complex financial arrangements is given in AGN VII 129, doc. 56.
[2] Caillet-Bois 1948, p. 209; 1952/82, p. 211.

rightwing nationalist Argentine historian Antonio Gómez Langenheim, whose work is riddled with gross errors and fabrications. He invented two non-existent settlements, calling them "Rosas" and "Dorrego". He first used those names in 1934; he used them again in 1939,[1] and they are shown on the map in vol. II of his 1939 book, placed where the real settlements of Goose Green and Johnson's Harbour are (both were founded much later). Both "Rosas" and "Dorrego" are fictitious; there were in fact no settlements in the islands in Vernet's time except Port Louis.

By August 1831 the population of Port Louis consisted of four distinct groups:

(a) The gauchos (known as "peones" in Spanish, i.e. "farmhands"), who were Spanish-speaking and mostly came from the River Plate region. They generally amounted to about two dozen men, who constantly left and were replaced. Vernet did not regard them as settlers or colonists; they were merely his employees.

(b) The black slaves. In September 1828 Vernet purchased 31 black people in Argentina and took them to the islands; for a while in 1828-9 they formed the majority of the population of Port Louis.[2] Most were adults, but some were children, with one girl aged only 5. The documentation of their lives is sadly very sparse, but some of them were "new" slaves taken from slave ships coming from Africa, while others seem to have spent some time in South America. They no doubt spoke one or more West African languages among themselves, plus a little Spanish in communicating with the South Americans. The blacks were theoretically "indentured labourers" who were to be released after a term of years, but they were not paid in money, they could not own land, they were not free to come and go as they pleased, and their original African names were never used – some men and boys were given a surname in Spanish, often a name of a month, such as "Marzo", "Abril", "Julio" or "Octubre", but most women and some men were given no surnames. They were slaves in all but name, and we shall refer to them as slaves, as did some people at the time.

(c) The "settlers" or "colonists". With few exceptions these did not come from South America; Vernet wanted settlers from Britain, Germany or Holland. He apparently got none from Holland (there is no record of any Dutch settlers), but there were some British settlers and briefly a group of Germans including several families, who did not stay long; by late 1831 there were only two single German men left.

(d) The Charrúa Indians, the last group to arrive: a group of 5 men apparently sent from Montevideo by Louis Vernet's brother Emilio in July 1831. They were among the last survivors of the Charrúa nation, who had lived in and around Uruguay for millennia but had been massacred by Uruguayan government forces. It seems Emilio Vernet had seen them as promising gauchos, but in the Falklands they were forbidden to ride horses and were confined to menial tasks – the white Spanish-speaking gauchos were seemingly prejudiced against them. The 5 Charrúas were the only men who stayed with the murderer Antonio Rivero after the gauchos Juan Brasido and José María Luna had escaped from him (for which Brasido was murdered).

Hardly had the population reached its maximum of around 128 in mid-July 1831 than it began to decrease again: on 25 September 1831 the British brigantine *Elbe* left with just over a dozen people: Captain Daniel Carew of the *Breakwater* and the remaining crewmen of the American ships Vernet had seized, plus the disgruntled British settler Joseph Addyman, his wife Jane and their children. All of them were incensed at Vernet's treatment of them, and left the islands in disgust. There remained roughly 114-115 people; on 7 November 1831 Louis Vernet left the islands in the American schooner *Harriet* with his wife and children and some of his white servants and black slaves, totalling 29 people including the ship's crew (over a quarter of the remaining land-based population; see section 6.9), leaving about 85, and the American warship *Lexington* took 47 or 48 people (over half the remainder) in January 1832, leaving some 38 people at Port Louis. Britain was not involved in any of those removals of people.

We will now tell the history of Vernet's settlement in more detail; an extensive account will appear in *The Falklands Saga*, including much documentation that has never been printed before.

---

[1] Antonio Gómez Langenheim, *La tercera invasión inglesa* ["The third British invasion"], Buenos Aires 1934, pp. 108-109, and *Elementos para la Historia de nuestras Islas Malvinas*, Buenos Aires 1939, vol. I, p. 259.

[2] Vernet told Woodbine Parish in a memorandum dated 20 April 1829 (PRO FO 6 499, fol. 13 *recto*) that there were at Port Louis at that time 10 white inhabitants from Buenos Aires, 10 seafaring men, mostly English and Americans, Vernet's brother and brother-in-law, 18 "Negroes" indentured for 10 years and 12 "Negro" girls – 52 people in all. So there were 30 blacks in a population of 52 (see also section 5.15).

5.2 Louis Vernet's five years in the Falklands: Phase I, 1826-8

Vernet began Phase I of his second venture by hiring gauchos: on 25 November 1825 an agreement was drawn up listing 28 men;[1] Vernet's brothers Emilio and Carlos were to go to the islands too, plus his wife's brother Loreto Sáez. On 31 December 1825 Vernet and a Frenchman, Aristide Sacristie, signed a contract with Jorge Pacheco, which gave Sacristie and Vernet the use of Pacheco's concession of 23 August 1823 (section 4.9) – this venture was initially carried on under that concession, which "gave" Vernet only the usufruct of East Falkland (the right to exploit it without any land holding). A contract dated 5 January 1826 shows that Sacristie (and associates) had 3,400 pesos' worth of shares, while Vernet and associates had 11,600 pesos' worth.[2]

Since they feared a war with Brazil, a bogus contract was also made out ceding the usufruct to two British merchants in Buenos Aires called Green and Hodgson. This contract was dated 10 October 1825, and was in English, designed to be shown to any Brazilian ship or invading force. The purpose of this subterfuge was to give the impression of British protection for Vernet's enterprise – Brazilian forces would not have interfered with British activities, whereas anything connected with Buenos Aires was fair game. A secret contract was drawn up dated 10 December 1825 reversing the bogus contract, so that Green and Hodgson had no genuine title.[3] It seems likely that another reason for involving Britain was to provide insurance against any repeat of the clash between the members of the 1824 expedition and Captain Low of the *Adeona* (section 4.9) – the crews of British or American sealing vessels would not accept the validity of the Vernet-Pacheco concession but would refrain from attacking an expedition that had British papers. On 3 January 1826 all those papers were countersigned by the British vice-consul in Buenos Aires, Richard Poussett, who merely confirmed the authenticity of the signatures, quite possibly without reading the documents – it was not necessary to know the content of documents in order to confirm that they were valid where issued. The consulates of many countries offered (and still offer today) an authentication service: the consular officials state officially that the signatures are authentic and that the documents are valid in the country of issue. Vernet seems to have assumed that in presenting his documents to the British consulate he was informing the British government of his activities and demonstrating that he was not concealing anything. But he was mistaken.

5.3 Britain not informed about Vernet's concession, 1826

Kohen and Rodríguez mention the consular authentication (p. 141), giving as their source Gómez Langenheim 1939, vol. I, pl. 216 – they silently correct Gómez Langenheim's incorrect date of "3 February 1826" to 3 January, but they repeat his misreading of the vice-consul's signature as "Ponfsett". They comment (p. 141-2) on the lack of any British reaction at this time, and imply that Britain was uncertain of its sovereignty:

If the islands were British, Great Britain's representative in Buenos Aires would have objected to such concessions being made by a foreign government. Not only was there no reaction, but the British consul certified the authenticity of the Argentine documents. Again, Britain kept silent, when in fact it should have reacted if it really considered itself to be the sovereign of the Falklands/Malvinas Islands.

However, the documentation shows that Poussett did not inform the British government of Vernet's concession: we have checked the entire correspondence from the British legation in Buenos Aires to London during the period in question,[4] and there is no mention of it. That meant that the British government remained in ignorance of Vernet's concession (and of his later concession of 1828 too, see section 5.7). Vernet seems to have presumed that his openness meant Britain would not object

---

[1] AGN VII, 129, doc. 57.
[2] Contract in AGN VII 129, doc. 56.
[3] Contracts in AGN VII 127, doc. 22, no separate doc. nos.
[4] The correspondence from the British Consulate-General in Buenos Aires to the British government is contained in the following files: PRO FO 6 10 (January to December 1825); FO 6 11 (January to December 1826); FO 6 20 (January to December 1827); PRO FO 6 24 (January to December 1828); and FO 6 28 (January to December 1829); we have checked these entire files, which contain no mention whatever of Vernet's usufruct concession of 1823, authenticated in January 1826 (section 4.9), or of his later concession of 5 January 1828, authenticated on 30 January 1828 (5.7).

to his activities, and that he therefore in effect had British permission to continue – in a later letter to Woodbine Parish he said "the British consulate's seal affixed to said grants, lulled me… into security".[1] In that, of course, he was wrong; Britain knew nothing.

5.4 Louis Vernet's five years in the Falklands; Phase I (continued), to 1828

Kohen and Rodríguez are not interested in the history of the Falkland Islands, and therefore say almost nothing about Louis Vernet's struggle to set up his venture in 1826. We see the history of the Falklands as epic and fascinating, and we feel his efforts were so heroic that they deserve at least a brief mention.[2] He bought the British brig *Alert* (Captain John Ure), but then war with Brazil broke out, and Buenos Aires was blockaded by the Brazilian navy (in which David Jewett held high rank). The *Alert* left Ensenada on 12 January 1826 with the gauchos hidden below decks, and as a British ship she was allowed to pass, but only in ballast; the vital horses were not allowed through. Vernet owned 200 horses on the San José peninsula, but was prevented from collecting them by the blockading Brazilian corvette *Maria da Gloria*. He sailed to Bahía Blanca, where he hoped to get horses from the Indians, and arrived there on 29 January 1826, but the ship was damaged by grounding several times in the bay, and could not reach the Indians' trading place until six weeks later on 6 March!

Trading began on 7 March, with the Indians and the crew of the *Alert* separated by a partition on deck. The Indians exchanged rugs, skins and birds' feathers for tobacco, spirits, bread, and flour. After a week of this, the Indians allowed five gauchos to set off to fetch horses from Rio Negro on the Patagonian coast. Vernet chose Manuel Coronel to lead them and gave him 100 gold doubloons to buy the horses, and the five men set off on 16 March. At the end of March they returned empty-handed, bringing an order from the local commandant not to trade with the Indians – that was a privilege of Rio Negro residents. Vernet sent them back to Rio Negro with an explanation of their mission. They returned on 4 May, and this time they brought supplies and horses, of which Vernet chose the 50 best. He sent the rest to the San José peninsula with 16 gauchos, one of whom was Juan (Jean) Simon,[3] who was of French origin and later became Vernet's capataz (head gaucho) in the Falklands, where he was murdered by Antonio Rivero in 1833. The *Alert* was loaded with 48 horses, and sailed on 13 May 1826 for the Falklands after over two months at Rio Negro.

They were off Berkeley Sound by the evening of 3 June, and that night they opened their last bale of hay for the horses. Captain Ure stood off the Sound waiting for daylight, but by morning the current had carried them further out, and they could not get back until dusk. Then a winter gale sprang up and drove the *Alert* out to sea yet again, and the following night ten horses died. They could not get back to the Falklands until 9 June. That day Vernet wrote a title in English on the cover of a simple notebook: "Arrivals and Sailings of Vessels touching at the East Falklands Begun the 9th June 1826", which we call the "Port Louis Shipping Record 1826-31", or "PLSR".[4] It is an important source for reconstructing the events of the following six years, though it records only ships visiting Port Louis, which were only a small minority of the ships around the islands.

By the evening of 9 June they were desperate. They ran into Kidney Island harbour, anchored, and a boat's crew was sent ashore "to cut some tussuck grass, which was a very great treat for our starving horses", as Vernet wrote in his "Memoirs". It was now the southern winter, and the landscape was covered with snow – most of the gauchos had never seen snow before and refused to go ashore. Vernet had not intended to land in midwinter, but the delays had forced it upon him. He had a daunting task: they had no shelter; his horses were starving; provisions were short, and his gauchos were mutinous. Then his luck changed. Two days later the sun came out and the snow

---

[1] Vernet to Parish 23 July 1834, PRO FO 6 501, fol. 148 *verso*.
[2] Account here based on Vernet's "Memoirs on the Falkland Islands", AGN VII, 141 (no doc. no.).
[3] Note in English, in AGN VII, 129, doc. 57: 85 pesos paid to Baltazar Espinosa, Juan Simon, Gregory Maseo.
[4] Notebook in AGN VII, 129, doc. 61, in English apart from a few proper nouns, running from June 1826 to January 1832 (henceforth "Port Louis Shipping Record" or "PLSR"). There were 9 ships that visited Port Louis in 1826; 22 in 1827; 11 in 1828; 16 in 1829; 23 in 1830; 26 in 1831, and 2 in January 1832. Some ships paid several visits; the 109 entries in 5½ years represent 61 individual ships, of which 26 were American, 22 British, 6 French, 4 from Buenos Aires, 2 from "Malvinas" and 1 Swedish.

melted fast, as it often does in the Falklands. The landscape became green and lush, and spirits rose. Some gauchos landed and 35 horses were swum ashore and put to feed among the high tussock grass by the beach. Most soon recovered, although three more died after being landed.

That day, Sunday 11 June 1826, was a significant date in the history of the Falklands. From that day to this, the islands have been inhabited – they have had a resident land-based population. Louis Vernet had begun the permanent settlement of the Falkland Islands.

It took them five days to struggle along the southern shore of Berkeley Sound and around its western end, the horses floundering and constantly sinking up to their bellies in the peat, men and horses sleeping in the open in the bitterly cold Falklands winter. At last, on 16 June 1826, they reached the ruins of the old settlement, which Vernet renamed Port Louis or Puerto Luis, adopting its old French name but also naming it after himself. In 1822 René Lesson had found Port Louis deserted (see section 4.8), but when Vernet and his party arrived, two British ships, the cutter *Sprightly* of London and the brigantine *Star* of Liverpool, were "lying very snugly alongside of each other in the inner harbour of Port Louis, in winter quarters", as Vernet wrote.[1]

Vernet's party soon had a stroke of luck and found 22 tame horses, apparently some of those taken to the islands during the 1824 expedition, with which they caught some cattle to provide fresh beef. The wild horses fled when approached, but some were caught and broken in during 1826.

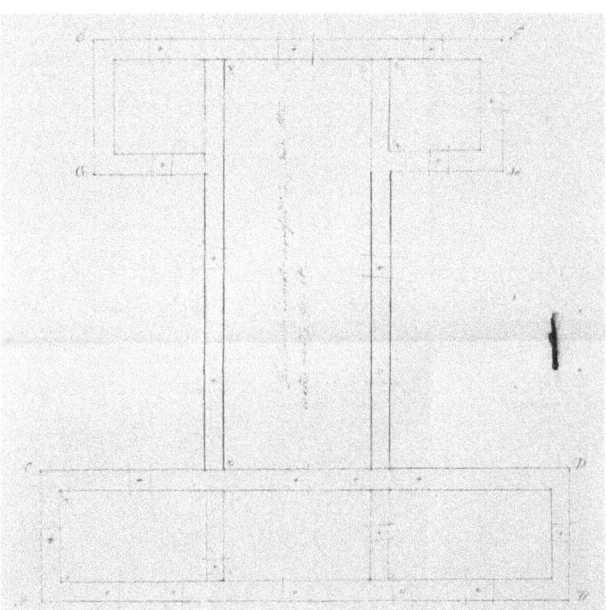

5.4a Louis Vernet's house at Port Louis, in PRO Adm 1/43, no doc. no., showing its state in late 1831. Vernet occupied only the southern block. Text in central part: "This part is not roofed in, but the walls ready for it."

The crews of the *Sprightly* and the *Star* helped to make Port Louis habitable and built several houses for Vernet and his men, using stone from the ruins of the former French and Spanish buildings.[2] The largest new building was Vernet's own house, which he called "the principal house", or in Spanish "la casa principal"; it was of one storey with a large roof garret, and was intended to be shaped like an H turned on its side (fig. 5.4a). The southern block was 80 feet east to west and 25 feet north to south (24.6 metres by 7.7 metres); the northern block was added later, 66 feet east to west and 20 feet north to south (20.3 metres by 6.2 metres). The "H" shape was never finished and the central part was still roofless in late 1831.

---

[1] Vernet's "Memoirs", p. 53. Caillet-Bois gives a totally misleading description of Vernet's first landing, by quoting René Lesson's remarks about the "silence of death" that reigned when Lesson himself visited Port Louis in 1822 (Lesson 1838, pp. 49-50; our section 4.8) – Caillet-Bois says (1948, p. 199; 1952/82, p. 201): "In front of the old Spanish settlement, Vernet disembarked: a silence of death reigned over the place…". Caillet-Bois's account is quoted by Juan José Cresto in *Historia de las Islas Malvinas…* ["History of the Malvinas Islands…"], Buenos Aires 2011, p. 266. In fact in 1826 Vernet did not land at Port Louis, and when he got there he did not find "a silence of death"; it is far more likely that there was some cheerful banter from the crews of the two British ships.

[2] Vernet's "Memoirs", p. 54; statement of account in AGN VII, 129, doc. 57.

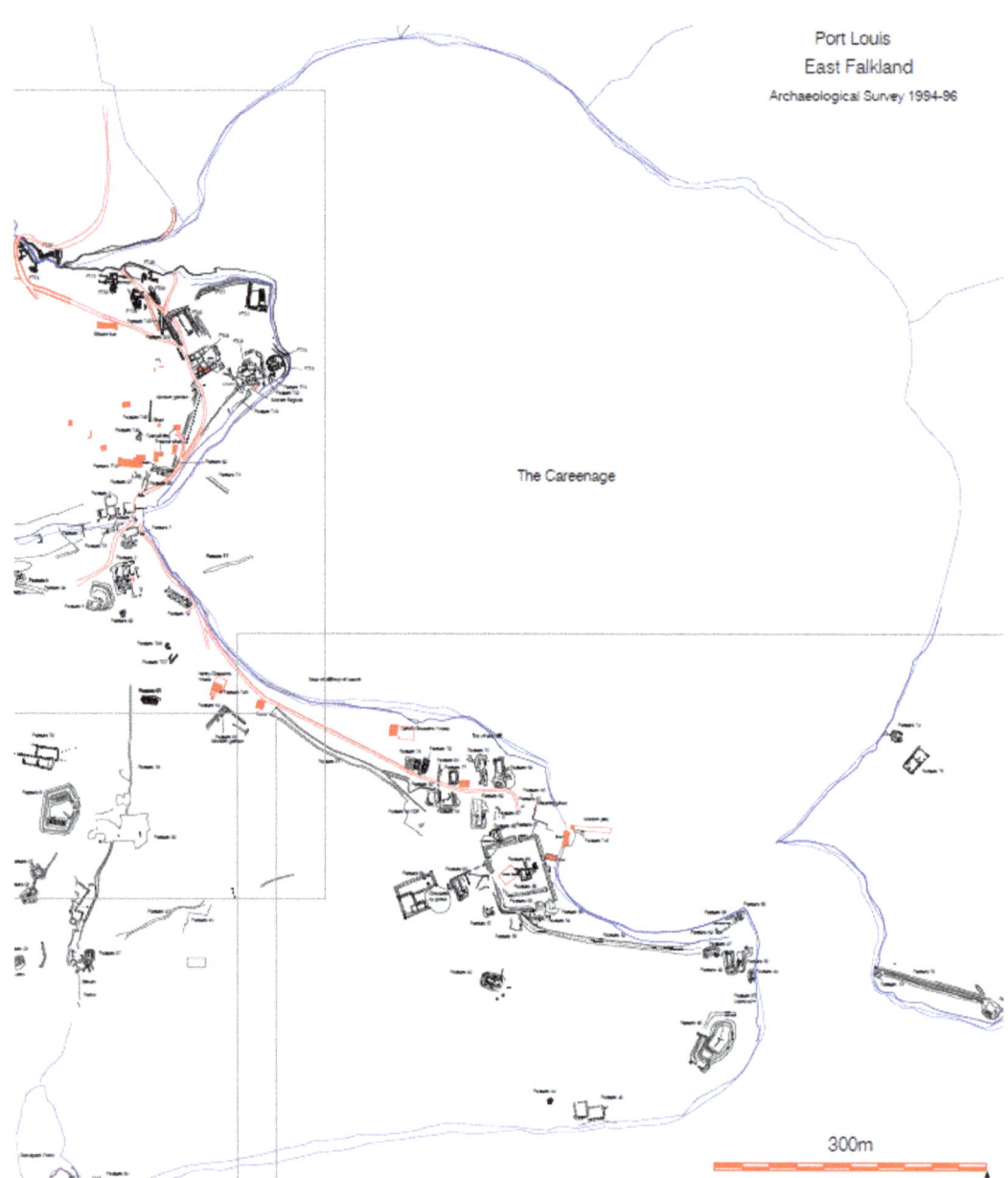

5.4b The inner basin at Port Louis ("The Careenage" is a later name), from Robert A. Philpott, *Port Louis. The first capital of the Falkland Islands…*, Stanley and Liverpool (forthcoming). Berkeley Sound is at bottom; the passage from the Sound into the basin at bottom right was known as "The Gut".

Louis Vernet lived in the house whenever he was in the islands; Emilio Vernet lived in it continuously from July 1826 to March 1831; the Argentine commandant Mestivier was murdered in the kitchen by Argentine soldiers in November 1832; Mathew Brisbane lived in the house from March 1833 and was murdered in the main room by Antonio Rivero in August 1833; the house was wrecked by Rivero and his group; the British resident naval officers made it habitable again and lived in it from 1834 to 1842, and Richard Moody, the first British Governor, lived in it from 1842 until he moved to Stanley on 15 July 1844. It is now known as Old Government House, and some of its walls still stand up to 2 metres high. Some Argentine authors, and the Argentine government at the United Nations, have wrongly identified a different building (the British barrack building of 1843) as Vernet's house (chapter 7, fig. 7.2a). The modern professional survey of Port Louis by Rob Philpott shows the layout of the existing buildings and remains (figs. 5.4b and 5.4c).[1]

---

[1] The remains of Vernet's house, and of all other early buildings at Port Louis, are described and illustrated in the detailed survey by Robert A. Philpott, *Port Louis. The first capital of the Falkland Islands…*, Stanley and Liverpool (forthcoming). We are grateful to Rob Philpott for providing us with a draft of this important work and permitting us to reproduce parts of one of his many illustrations in our figs. 5.4b and 5.4c.

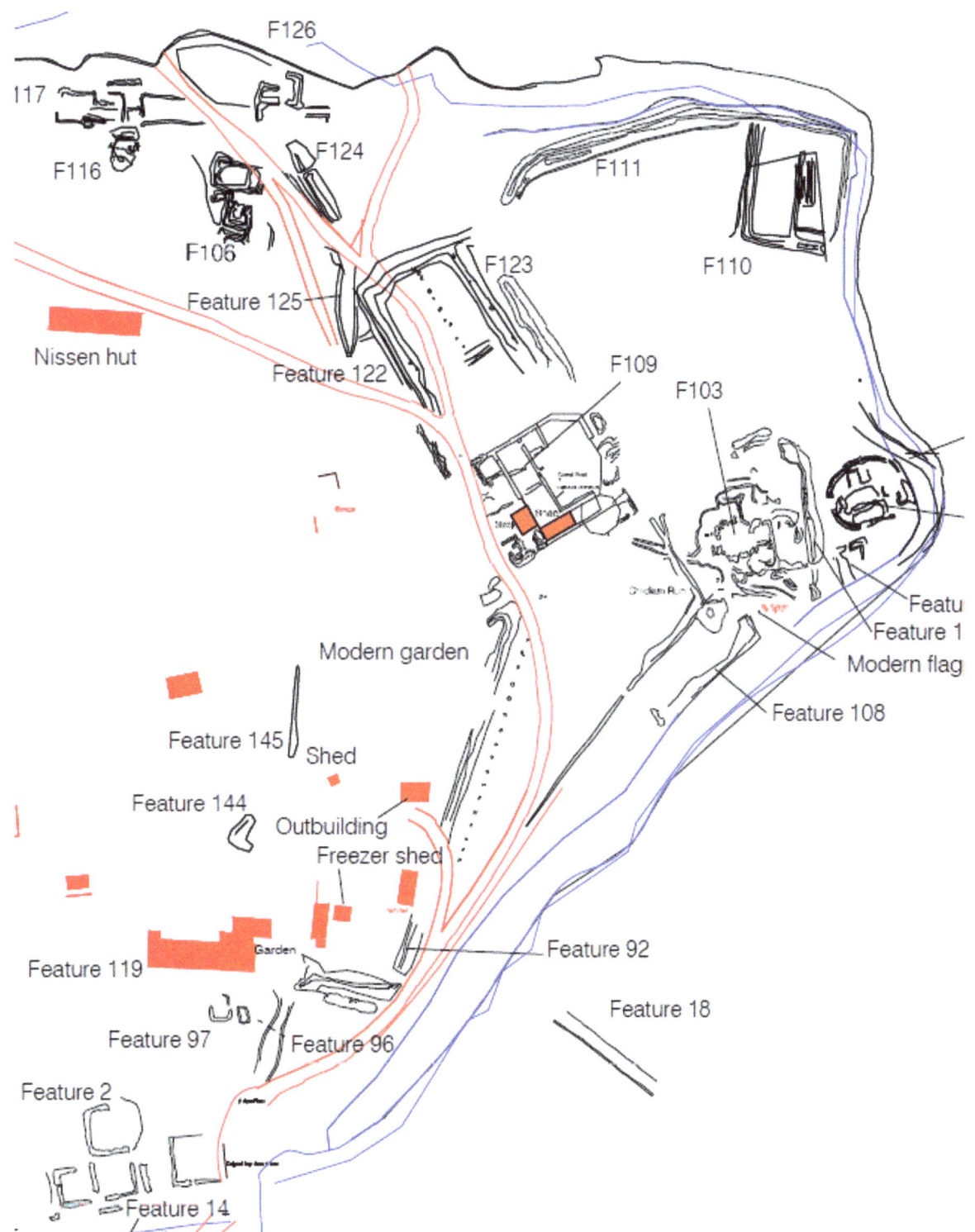

5.4c Detail of the northern part of Port Louis from fig. 5.4b, showing the present standing buildings (red) and ruins and foundations (black), the basin to the right. F109 (centre) is Vernet's house (later Mathew Brisbane's, Henry Smith's, and Richard Moody's); the southernmost red building (Feature 119) is the 1843 British barracks (chapter 7, fig. 7.2a); F103 is the remains of the French and Spanish governors' house.

On 9 September 1826 Vernet left on the first of several long absences, this time for over eight months. In the two years from his arrival he spent less than four months in the Falklands: three months from June to September 1826, and then less than three weeks in June 1827, after which he was away again till August 1828, leaving affairs at Port Louis to his brother Emilio (Jean Émile, b. 1800), who remained at Port Louis without interruption from June 1826 to March 1831.

Louis Vernet sailed in the *Alert* on 9 September for the San José peninsula to pick up the horses he had sent there, but contrary winds forced him to sail on to Montevideo. He arrived there on 26 September, but the *Alert* was condemned as unseaworthy; she was sold in October, but the proceeds barely covered the wages of the crew, who were paid off on 31 October. The insurance did not fully cover the value, so she was a major loss.[1] He chartered the British brig *Idris* and sailed to collect the horses and gauchos from the San José peninsula. But they had gone; the gauchos had used up their provisions and then left. So he sailed for the Falklands with supplies but without horses.

Before Vernet got back, the retired Royal Navy Lieutenant William Langdon (1790-1879), who played an indirect but important part in Falklands history, put into Port Louis in his ship *Hugh Crawford* on 22 May 1827 and left on 25 May (PLSR entry 20). He was surprised to find Vernet's settlement, where Emilio Vernet was in charge.[2] Six days after Langdon left, Vernet arrived in the *Idris*, but left again on 19 June for Montevideo with two gauchos, one of whom was Manuel Coronel, who did not wish to stay, though he returned to Port Louis in 1831 and stayed until his death in 1841, well into the British period, in which he became the capataz (head gaucho).

5.5 Louis Vernet's five years in the Falklands: Phase II, 1828-9

Louis Vernet was away again for 14 months from 19 June 1827 to 28 August 1828, making superhuman efforts to obtain the things most vital for his establishment: people, stores, finance, and above all horses. For a year after he left the islands in June 1827 the Brazilian navy blockaded the Buenos Aires coast, but he slipped through the blockade and on 5 January 1828 he petitioned Governor Manuel Dorrego[3] of Buenos Aires province to grant him "the Island of Soledad" [East Falkland]; "Statenland" [the Isla de los Estados]; the right of fishery throughout the Falklands and along the entire coast of the Republic; and freedom from taxes for 30 years. The same day, 5 January 1828, the government issued a decree granting most of what he requested.[4] Statenland and all of East Falkland were actually ceded to him, except the 30 square leagues granted to Pacheco and 10 square leagues on San Carlos Water, which the government reserved for itself, apparently as a site for a "presidio" or penal settlement, but Vernet was granted freedom from taxes for only 20 years, and he was given right of fishery only south of the Rio Negro. He was required to form a colony within three years, which put him under pressure to get things done. He was not interested in West Falkland since there were no cattle there, so he asked for, and was granted, only East Falkland – throughout the Vernet period the involvement from Buenos Aires was limited to East Falkland.

Unlike the earlier concession of 1823 (section 4.9), which had granted only the "usufruct" (the right to exploit the natural resources), this decree actually "ceded" the freehold of the island itself to Vernet, which led him to describe himself later as "Owner of the East Falkland Island"[5] or "sole proprietor with small exceptions of the whole East Falkland Island with all that it contained".[6]

Thus began Phase II of Vernet's second venture, with Vernet as "freeholder" of East Falkland aiming to set up a permanent settlement, but of course no other country recognised any rights of Buenos Aires to any part of the islands; to all other countries his concessions were null and void.

5.6 Vernet's 1828 concession declared invalid by the Argentine government, 1882

Vernet's 1828 concession was later ruled null and void in Argentina too. In 1882 the Argentine government declared in the Argentine Congress that the decree of 5 January 1828 was invalid since it had been issued only by the provincial government of Buenos Aires, not by the whole Congress of the Argentine Federation, which alone had the power to cede national territories. That was stated by the future Argentine foreign minister Francisco J. Ortiz in a debate during the session of 29 July 1882, which was discussing the attempt by the heirs of Louis Vernet (who had died in 1871) to

---

[1] Note referring to 10 January 1826, in Vernet's accounts, in AGN VII 130, doc. 2.
[2] Anonymous article "A Visit to the Falkland Islands" in *The United Service Journal...*, London 1832, Part III, p. 310.
[3] Manuel Dorrego (1787-1828), Governor of Buenos Aires Province 29 June to 20 September 1820 and from 17 August 1827 to 1 December 1828, when he was deposed by the coup led by Lavalle and shot on 13 December.
[4] Vernet's English translations of his petition and the government decree (signed by Buenos Aires foreign minister Juan Ramón Balcarce), as presented to Woodbine Parish in April 1829, are in PRO FO 6 499, fols. 6 *recto* to 8 *recto* (petition) and 8 *recto* to 10 *verso* (decree). Decree (but not petition) also printed as a fn. to Vernet's "Report" in *BFSP 1832-1833*, pp. 420-421, but neither is in the Spanish version of the "Report" in *Colección 1832*.
[5] Vernet's "Advertisement", March 1831, copy in PRO FO 6 499, fols. 152 *recto* to 155 *recto* (see section 6.1).
[6] Vernet's "Memoirs", pp. 64-65.

obtain compensation for his losses. Ortiz reported the decision of an official commission that had considered the question of compensation. He said:[1]

... the Executive Power [i.e. the government] of the Province of Buenos Aires... issued a decree giving to señor Don Luis Vernet as his property the Isla de la Soledad (which forms part of the Malvinas) and the Isla de los Estados, on condition, as the said decree indicates, that he was to establish colonies and maintain populations there for three years, at the end of which señor Vernet was to render account to the Government on the state of the colony, to decide on the matter.

The right on which señor Vernet [i.e. Louis Vernet's son] bases his request derives from that decree.

In the judgement of the Commission that decree gives him no right whatever...

From that cession arose a right without a justified reason, and which naturally had no legal force, since it had not been authorised by the General Congress of the Nation, which was the power that had to regulate grants of national territories.

In short, the Argentine government in 1882 regarded the central basis of Vernet's activities in the Falklands from 1828 as having been illegal. Kohen and Rodríguez (p. 163) criticise us for attempting in *Getting it right* to "minimise" the importance of Vernet's work as a proof of the exercise of Argentine sovereignty – but in 1882, in statements to Congress, the Argentine government itself retrospectively "minimised" his concession by declaring it invalid *ab initio*.

5.7 Britain again not informed of Vernet's concession, 1828; he preferred British sovereignty

That all lay in the future when on 30 January 1828 Vernet paid another visit to the British consulate in Buenos Aires to have his concession document authenticated, as he had done in 1826 (section 5.3). Such authentications were mere routine bureaucratic acts, so it was again done by the vice-consul, who was now Charles Griffiths. It seems likely that he did not actually read the document (which was not necessary for authenticating it), and like Vice-Consul Richard Poussett in 1826, Griffiths failed to inform London about it. Vernet clearly imagined Consul-General Woodbine Parish would be informed of his new concession, and to judge by a statement he made later, he also took that opportunity to say that he would be happy for the Falklands to come under British sovereignty – writing in the third person, he stated that:[2]

... to shew his good faith, he [Vernet] handed translations of these grants to the British Chargé d'Affaires for the information of the British Gov^t, and... represented to him that if the Islands should ever come under the british flag... he would in that case be most happy to render his best services towards the colonisation of them and the general Prosperity of the Islands as a british possession.

That was only one of various documents that make it very clear that Vernet preferred British sovereignty. Kohen and Rodríguez (p. 168) take us to task for mentioning Vernet's preference for British sovereignty in *Getting it right* (p. 15), and they refer to it as "the alleged preference of Vernet for British sovereignty", but in a curious case of self-refutation they then proceed to repeat several examples that we give – they quote (in Spanish) Woodbine Parish's statement in his report to the British government after meeting Vernet in April 1829, that:[3]

He would I believe be very happy if His Majesty's Government would take his Settlement under their protection...

Ricardo Caillet-Bois quotes that too, in Spanish translation, and says that Vernet was committing "an imprudence" based possibly on reservations by Parish and Vernet's own doubts as to Argentina's title to the islands.[4] Kohen and Rodríguez also repeat a quote from *Getting it right*, in which we mention that Vernet told William Langdon that he would be happy with British

---

[1] Text from the official record of proceedings in the Argentine Congress, *Diario de Sesiones*, Buenos Aires 29 July 1882, p. 311. Meetings on various dates are included under the date of 29 July, and the typesetting is careless – it transposes the "5" and the "8" in the date of Louis Vernet's grant, giving it as "8 January 1825" [*recte* 5 January 1828].

[2] Quote from AGN VII, 127, doc. 92, fol. 2 *recto* and *verso*, dating from 1835 at the earliest.

[3] Parish to Foreign Secretary Lord Aberdeen, 25 April 1829, in PRO FO 6 499, fol. 5 *recto* (see section 5.15).

[4] Caillet-Bois 1948, p. 303-304 (1952/1982, pp. 305-306).

sovereignty – Langdon wrote to the British government that:[1]

… from a conversation I had with M#r# Vernet upon the subject, I am authorized in saying no objection would be made to the occupation of it by the British Government, provided private property would not be interfered with.

Caillet-Bois quotes Vernet's statement as well, and he says yet again that Vernet was committing "an imprudence", which contributed to the decision by the "London Cabinet", i.e. the decision to reassert Britain's sovereignty in the islands.[2] That is actually not true – in fact, unfortunately for Vernet, Britain was simply not interested in occupying the islands at that time.

It is hard to see how, after repeating those quotes, Kohen and Rodríguez could still maintain that there was only an "alleged" preference by Vernet for British sovereignty. They say "the British arguments are not based on a note by Vernet or any other documented statement of his, but only on something that someone claimed Vernet said". They omit to mention that in *Getting it right* we also refer to two later cases in which Vernet himself made it clear that he would have been happy with British sovereignty, one in 1834[3] and a later one in 1858.[4] In addition, the undated quote above ("to shew his good faith…") is by Vernet himself, as is Vernet's "Advertisement" (section 6.1).

Griffiths duly authenticated the documents as requested.[5] Kohen and Rodríguez mention (p. 166) this consular authentication too, as they had earlier mentioned (p. 141) the authentication of Vernet's contract in 1826; they point out quite correctly that it was a typical example of consular "legalisation" of documents, and add that the documents referred to activities under the authority of the government of Buenos Aires. That, of course, is irrelevant; consular authentication only confirms that the documents were valid in the country of issue, and no other country accepted that Buenos Aires had any authority in the Falklands.

Kohen and Rodríguez take it for granted (as no doubt did Vernet himself) that Britain knew about Vernet's concessions but failed to protest. They say (p. 167):

If the islands belonged to His Britannic Majesty, the documents should have caught the attention of the British Consulate, particularly the authentication of the decree of January 5#th#, 1828. At the very least, as happened with the consular certification of the fictitious cession of the concessions to Pacheco in 1826, these certifications prove that Great Britain knew about the concession of terrains, fishing rights and franchises made by the Argentine government in 1823 and 1828 regarding the Falklands/Malvinas. The United Kingdom cannot validly invoke ignorance of these dispositions. In such circumstances, a reaction was required from the British government. But reaction came there none.

But Kohen and Rodríguez did not examine the consular correspondence, which tells a different story. We have examined the files of correspondence from the British consulate-general in Buenos Aires for the whole of the period 1825-8 in the Public Record Office (The National Archives) in London – and they contain no mention of Vernet's concessions, nor of their authentication. Neither in 1826 when Vernet went to the British consulate, nor in 1828,[6] did either of the vice-consuls, Poussett and Griffiths, mention any such thing to Parish or to London. They presumably saw the authentication of documents as a mere routine activity of no significance, and may not even have read Vernet's documents at all.

The case was different if a document involved expense for the British government, as did the agreement between Mathew Brisbane, Louis Vernet and Captain Oliver Keating in May 1829, which contained a contract authenticated by Griffiths, forwarded by Parish to London (section 5.12). Parish himself only found out about Vernet's 1828 concession in April 1829 (section 5.15),

---

[1] Letter from Lt William Langdon, 20 January 1832, to R.W.Hay, Permanent Under-Secretary at the Colonial Office, enclosing maps of the Falklands and his grant of "Section 3" by Vernet, in PRO FO 6 499, fols. 102 *recto* to 103 *recto*.
[2] Caillet-Bois 1948, p. 314 (1952/1982, p. 316).
[3] Vernet to Parish 23 July 1834, in PRO FO 6 501, fol. 147 *recto*.
[4] Vernet to Colonial Secretary Lord Stanley, 14 May 1858, printed in AGN VII, 134, doc. 45, p. 9.
[5] Louis Vernet's petition of 5 January 1828 and government grant of the same date, sealed and countersigned by Charles Griffiths, British Consulate, Buenos Aires, 30 January 1828, AGN VII, 129, doc. 63.
[6] PRO FO 6 24, January to December 1828, contains all the communications from the British consulate-general in Buenos Aires to London during that year. There is no mention of Vernet's concession or of its authentication.

and then informed the British government at once.

Vernet clearly imagined that he had shown the British government that he was not doing things behind Britain's back, but his actions were not reported to London and were thus in vain. He may simply have wanted documents to suggest to captains of visiting ships that he had British approval for his activities, to dissuade them from starting disputes such as the 1824 expedition had endured. But he was playing a double game.

So Kohen's and Rodriguez's assumption that London knew of Vernet's concession is wide of the mark. They even go so far as to say (p. 166) that the consular authorisation indicated British recognition of Argentine sovereignty. That is nonsense of course; it merely indicated that the documents were valid in Argentina, and in any case the British government could not protest against something of which it remained ignorant. They say much later in their book (p. 261) that "The British government did not consider that its silence over the Argentine concessions of 1823 and 1828 in the Falklands/Malvinas prevented it from reclaiming its sovereignty," and maintain that that constituted an "estoppel" which prevented it from later "reclaiming" sovereignty. Estoppel is a legal principle which prevents one party from going back on its earlier policy if another party would thereby suffer detriment, but it is clearly not involved here, since the British government was not pursuing any policy at all in failing to react to Vernet's concessions – it did not know about them, so there was no estoppel. By contrast, there was a clear case of estoppel in 1884 – see section 8.24.

5.8 Emilio Vernet's diary; a British flag hoisted in the Falklands, 25 May 1828

At Port Louis on 1 January 1828 Emilio Vernet began a brief diary,[1] which he kept up till 13 February 1831 when it breaks off at the bottom of a tattered and badly blotted page; it seems likely that he wrote more, but no more has survived. Like his elder brother Louis, he had grown up in Hamburg speaking French and German, and had learnt English in the United States and Spanish in Buenos Aires; his diary is in Spanish, though he always uses the English place-names for some places. Some 50 times he writes "Long Island" or "Longisland"; he writes "Johnson's Harbour" about 20 times; "Granthamsound" (6 times); Kidney Island (4); "Chois[s]eul Bay", now Choiseul Sound (3); Turf Island (5); Port Pleasant (once), and he invariably calls the Isla de los Estados by its English name "Statenland", some 15 times. The *lingua franca* at Port Louis was Spanish, but English was very much present in the background, in the place-names and in dealings with ships, whose crews were almost all English-speaking.

Emilio's diary records the comings and goings of ships at Port Louis and the work of the gauchos killing cattle and salting the hides for export. For its first two years the establishment was run much like Louis Vernet's cattle-killing activities in Patagonia – there were no women or children and the two dozen gauchos were merely Vernet's employees, who killed the cattle in return for pay. Emilio notes that on 24 May 1828 they put up two flagpoles, and he records the celebrations at Port Louis the next day, Argentine Independence Day, Sunday 25 May 1828:[2]

Good weather with some showers of hail and SW wind. At Sunrise we fired 3 guns and hoisted the English flag and that of Buenos Ayres, at midday we fired another 3 Guns and in the evening another 3. After a midday meal of meat in the skin and cakes which had been made for the occasion, we had target practice till sunset, when the people had a dance in the house of the Cooper which lasted until day.

The fact that the settlement hoisted a British flag has embarrassed more than one Argentine writer. Antonio Gómez Langenheim printed a few extracts from Emilio's diary in 1939, but attributed it wrongly to Louis Vernet and simply left out anything he did not like – he prints part of that entry but silently omits the British flag. His version reads "At sunrise we fired 3 guns and in the evening another 3."[3] That is yet another of his many manipulations of evidence.

Antonio Montarcé Lastra does not go quite as far as Gómez Langenheim in distorting the evidence: in the introduction to his edition of María Vernet's diary, he quotes that entry from

---
[1] Diary in AGN VII 141, no separate doc. no.; references here by date since several folios are bound in at the wrong place, others back to front (*verso* before *recto*).
[2] Emilio Vernet's diary, 25 May 1828; this is the whole of that day's entry.
[3] Gómez Langenheim 1939, vol. I, pp. 265-266.

Emilio's diary without omission and draws attention to the hoisting of the British flag, but he explains it by saying that the large proportion of Britons at the colony was leading to "gradual imperialist infiltration".[1] That is nonsense; there were no British people whatever at Port Louis at that time, nor any British ships (in fact there were no ships at all between the departure of the *Elisabeth* on 7 May and the arrival of the *Mercury* on 14 August), and the British government had no imperialist designs. Britain regarded the Falklands as British beyond question, but had no desire at the time to be involved in the expense of actually occupying them. Louis Vernet was not in the islands – as pointed out above, he was absent for 14 months from 19 June 1827 to 28 August 1828. And not a single ship is recorded in PLSR as coming from Buenos Aires to the islands in the entire year 1828, which might theoretically have brought the news of Vernet's concession of 5 January 1828. His success in obtaining a new concession was still unknown at Port Louis, so the flying of the British flag was not in celebration of any recently received good news.

Kohen and Rodriguez print (p. 150, fn.) Emilio's entry of 25 May 1828 in full, from Montarcé Lastra, and even mention that Gómez Langenheim omits the phrase about the hoisting of the British and Argentine flags, but they add, in an echo of Montarcé Lastra, that "No negative effect for the Argentine position can be attributed to the fact that the British flag was raised on 25 May. It was and is normal for foreigners to associate themselves with national festivals by raising their flags." That implies that there were British people present, which is not true; there was not a single British person there. The people in Vernet's 1826 expedition celebrated Argentine independence because they were Argentinians, but they were well aware that their activities were seen as illegal by British crews. British ships might turn up at any time, so they took a British flag to the islands and raised it to indicate goodwill towards Britain, to defuse in advance any possible clash like that with Captain Low of the *Adeona* during the 1824 expedition (section 4.9).

5.9 Vernet buys horses and black slaves for the Falklands

In early 1828 Vernet slipped through the Brazilian blockade to Montevideo, where he bought the large American vessel *Ospray* and her cargo of timber. He sailed to Rio Negro, which was no longer being blockaded as the war between Brazil and the United Provinces was coming to an end. But the *Ospray* grounded hard on the harbour bar and was severely damaged. The crew and passengers were saved, but the vessel and the cargo were lost. Both were insured, so the financial loss was "trifling", as Vernet put it, but the accident caused more delay and frustration.

He had planned to put a hundred horses aboard the *Ospray*, but there was no other vessel large enough at Rio Negro, so he chartered the *Combine*, Captain Gardner, of Salem, Massachusetts, which cost him 800 pesos a month, and bought a "polacra" (a small Mediterranean-style trading ship), which he calls *Tiburtina* in his "Memoirs",[2] though she was also called *Luisa*.

He took 65 horses aboard the *Combine*, and for the *Tiburtina* he purchased a human cargo: 19 black men and 12 black women. Six of them were children, bought at Rio Negro for 160 pesos each: a girl aged five, the others about 14, "indentured" for 10 or 13 years. Five of them had been taken from the slaving brig *Buen Jesus*, captured by the privateer *Presidente* in July 1828, and one was from the slaver *Goldfinch*,[3] but the origin of the 25 others is obscure. Some Argentine ships assisted Britain's suppression of the slave trade, but the fact that some "liberated" slaves were then sold in Argentina, as shown by Vernet's purchase, did not exactly contribute to ending it.

For Vernet the advantages of the blacks were obvious: they provided free labour and would

---

[1] Antonio Montarcé Lastra, *Redención de la Soberanía...* ["Redemption of Sovereignty..."], Buenos Aires 1946, p. 48.
[2] Vernet twice writes clearly "Tiburtina" in his "Memoirs" (AGN 141, no doc. no., pp. 67, 69); Caillet-Bois calls her "*Fiburtina*" (1948, p. 210; 1952/82, p. 212), apparently quoting from a 1933 Argentine translation of FitzRoy 1829.
[3] AGN VII, 132, docs. 64-69, each dated 15 July 1828, relating to 6 young blacks bought by Vernet for 160 pesos each, all taken from slavers by the privateer *Presidente* (5 from the *Buen Jesus* and 1 from the *Goldfinch*). The names were not of course their real names, but consisted of a Spanish first name, plus (for the boys) a month as a surname. They were: doc. 64: a girl of 5 years of age, "Benita" (indentured for 13 years); doc. 65: a boy of 14 years, "Valentin Abril" (for 10 years, from the slaver *Goldfinch*, presumably American); doc. 66: a girl of 14 years, "Julia" (for 10 years); doc. 67: a boy of 14 years, "Pablo Marzo" (for 10 years); doc. 68: a boy of 14 years, "Pedro Julio" (for 10 years); doc. 69: a boy of 14 years, "Vicente Mayo" (for 10 years).

cause no problems. There is no hint in the surviving documentation that they were treated badly, but of the 31 blacks Vernet bought in 1828, 4 are known to have died and 2 departed; there were 21 at Port Louis in mid-1831, so 4 are unaccounted for. If they too died in the islands, it would mean over a quarter of them died in three years, but the records are silent on the fate of the missing 4. Vernet took 4 black female slaves to Buenos Aires in the *Harriet* in November 1831, leaving 17 blacks at Port Louis. Of them, 14 went to Buenos Aires in the *Lexington* in January 1832, leaving only three: Gregoria Madrid, Carmelita, and the boy "Octubre" (who was drowned around March 1832).[1] Gregoria was aged about 16 when she arrived; she lived in the islands for 42 years and was the last survivor from Vernet's establishment – and the oldest-established resident of the islands – when she died in Stanley on 11 April 1871. In the Falklands these Africans lived further south than any other black people in the world, and played a notable part in the history of the islands. The fact that so little is known about them is a sad reflection on the times they lived in.

On 29 August 1828 Vernet reached Port Louis in the *Combine* after 14 months' absence. Yet again, many of the vital horses had died: only 37 were still alive out of the 65 taken aboard. On 2 September the *Tiburtina* arrived with the 31 blacks; Emilio Vernet records in his diary that most of the male blacks were landed on 4 September, but the 12 girls and women were left aboard for another 11 days and were landed on 15 September. All the blacks were theoretically "indentured labourers" bound for a term of years (up to 13 years, often 10 years), but they could not own land, were not free to come and go as they pleased, their original names were suppressed and they were not paid in money; they were slaves in all but name, and we refer to them as slaves. Most of them were taken from the islands to Buenos Aires by Henry Metcalf in the *Lexington* in January 1832, so their indentures presumably continued, but the indentures of the 3 who remained at Port Louis clearly lapsed since there was no one left to enforce the terms; they thus became "former slaves". The blacks were presumably not exactly enchanted by the cold, windy Falklands, but they put up with their lot, and Emilio records their dancing and singing (though perhaps they were remembering their lost homeland).

The *Combine* was then loaded up, three gauchos were put aboard, and she left on 15 September for Rio Negro carrying 700 "oxhides", 300 sealskins and 200 dozen rabbit skins, which realised enough profit to pay for her charter and some extras.[2]

5.10 Vernet's Spanish map

Kohen and Rodríguez mention and illustrate (pp. 152, 153) a map of East Falkland made by Louis Vernet around 1828. They say that Vernet's permission to exploit the terrestrial and maritime resources was not limited to East Falkland ("Isla Soledad" in Spanish) but was "conceived together with the Malvinas archipelago and other Argentine territories in the South". Actually, Vernet's land concession applied only to East Falkland and Isla de los Estados. Accordingly, this map shows only East Falkland; a sizeable corner of West Falkland should appear at top left, but is silently omitted. Apart from a few of the earlier English or French names, the map names the features in Spanish, so we call it Vernet's "Spanish map" (fig. 5.10a).[3] It is divided into sections numbered I to XI, coloured different shades in watercolours, representing concessions Vernet planned to sell to prospective settlers; the uninhabitable hills are shaded in black. The area around San Carlos Water has no number but is labelled "Del Estado" ["Of the State"] – it was reserved to the state of Buenos Aires under Vernet's 1828 concession (sections 5.5, 5.6), presumably as a site for a "presidio".

---

[1] "Octubre" was missing from the settlement for 14 months, and part of his body was found on 16 May 1833 in Berkeley Sound (entry in the "1833 Port Louis Log"; see section 6.31). Since there were two women called Gregoria, one was given the surname "Madrid", the other was apparently given no second name.

[2] Vernet's "Memoirs", p. 67. "Oxhides" were hides of wild (feral) cattle; there were no actual oxen (castrated bulls).

[3] Manuscript map of East Falkland, in AGN VII 134, doc. 20. The map was reproduced (from a pen-and-ink tracing of it) in Gómez Langenheim 1939, vol. I (endpapers), and also, from a black-and-white photo of the original, in Caillet-Bois 1948 opp. p. 208, and 1952 opp. p. 192; not in the 3rd ed. 1982.

5.10a Vernet's Spanish map (AGN VII, 134, doc. 20), labelled mostly in Spanish (also reproduced in Gómez Langenheim 1939, Caillet-Bois 1948 and 1952/1982, and Kohen and Rodríguez 2015). It shows only East Falkland, silently omitting part of West Falkland, which should appear at top left.

Kohen and Rodríguez, and other Argentine authors, suppress the fact that Vernet later made another map labelled in English, which we call his "English map". They cannot have missed it, since it is in the same folder as the Spanish map in the AGN, but they chose not to mention it since it provided clear evidence of Vernet's dealings with the British (see chapter 6, fig. 6.8a).

5.11 Lavalle's coup; HMS *Tribune*; Antonio Rivero; Vernet appointed CPM; his circular

On 16 November 1828 Vernet left Port Louis in the *Tiburtina* for Argentina with a cargo of salt beef, hides and tallow. The war against Brazil and the blockade of the coast had ended on 28 August – the government of Buenos Aires province under Governor Manuel Dorrego had signed a peace treaty with Brazil, in which Buenos Aires accepted the independence of Uruguay. Vernet reached Buenos Aires on 31 December 1828 to find there had been a military coup and civil war had broken out – Dorrego had been shot on 13 December without trial, and the *de facto* "governor" of Buenos Aires province was now General Juan Lavalle. Lavalle had led the Argentine forces in Uruguay and rejected the peace settlement with Brazil; he was a "Unitarian", who thought Argentina should be a unitary state including Uruguay. Lavalle's opponents were the "Federalists", who fought to make Argentina a federal state, also including Uruguay; among their leaders was Juan Manuel Ortiz de Rosas, who later dominated Argentina and played a vital part in the history of the Falklands.

In March 1829 Port Louis was visited by the largest ship to call there during Vernet's tenure: the 42-gun British frigate HMS *Tribune* spent 13 to 18 March 1829 in Berkeley Sound (PLSR entry 48). Emilio Vernet records in his diary that he spent a night aboard the ship on 15 March, and on 18 March bought shoes, socks and tobacco from her purser. The *Tribune* had been sent by the commander-in-chief on the Royal Navy's South American station, Rear Admiral Sir Thomas Otway, to the Falklands and the coast of Patagonia to "show the flag" and check for any pirates or captured prizes. Captain Wilson of the *Tribune* reported to Otway that he found all in order in Berkeley Sound, and there were "some settlers from Buenos Ayres (about 50 men women and children)" present.[1] The South Atlantic and the Cape Horn route were important for trade; Britain was concerned to ensure that no "nest of pirates" was operating, so a watch had to be kept on the area. Otway reported Captain Wilson's observations to the Admiralty in London, so now the British government knew that there was a settlement from Buenos Aires in the Falklands.

At Port Louis on 18 May 1829 a man who was to become famous in Falklands history makes his first appearance in Emilio Vernet's diary:[2]

Simon[,] S. Centurion and Antº Rivero slaughtered 2 cows in the camp and brought hides and meat.

That date makes it highly unlikely that Rivero took part in the fighting surrounding the Lavalle coup, as asserted by Martiniano Leguizamón Pondal (section 6.33), and impossible that he arrived in the *Betsey* since she did not leave Buenos Aires till June 1829 (section 5.16). The PLSR records nine ships arriving at Port Louis between the Lavalle rising in December 1828 and the arrival of the *Betsey* in July 1829, but the only one from Buenos Aires was the British frigate *Tribune*, which will hardly have brought Rivero.

When Rivero arrived in the islands is not recorded; he may perhaps have been present in 1828, but the fact that Emilio does not record him before May 1829 suggests that he arrived in one of half a dozen ships that touched at Port Louis in the first few months of 1829, several from "Cape Horn" including five sealers, which will not have spent much time at Cape Horn itself, but no doubt worked up and down the Patagonian coast.

In early 1829, in the chaotic civil war, the Federalists closed in on Buenos Aires, which was held by the insurgent Unitarian government under General Lavalle. José de San Martín, the great "Liberator" who had led the independence struggle against Spain, arrived back from Europe in February 1829, but was so disgusted by the chaos in Buenos Aires that he sailed back to Europe. Then Lavalle was defeated on 25 April at Conchas, 15 miles from Buenos Aires. This caused panic, and for two months the city was under siege.

Despite the chaos, on 10 June 1829 Vernet managed to get hold of General Martín Rodríguez, Lavalle's governor of Buenos Aires, and at Vernet's request Rodríguez made the Falklands into a "comandancia", the political entity below a "gobernación" in the old Spanish imperial hierarchy. A gobernación would have had a governor, but a comandancia only rated a "Comandante Político y Militar" (CPM). Vernet was thus duly appointed as (unpaid) CPM; the original appointment document is now very faded and affected by damp and mould, but Vernet made copies of it.[3]

While he was in Buenos Aires Vernet had a circular printed in English to give to captains of ships visiting the Falklands. On one side it bore Vernet's translation of the comandancia decree and on the other a warning against "fishing" (mainly sealing) and shooting cattle – since almost all ships visiting the islands had English-speaking crews, English was the only usable language. Both texts are illustrated by Kohen and Rodríguez (pp. 157, 161), who fail to point out that they contain several distortions of history. The decree states that Spain was the "first occupier" of the islands, which was not true – France was the first occupier, and Britain had occupied Port Egmont before Spain's arrival. Secondly, it states that in possessing the islands Spain had "the consent of the

---

[1] Reported in Otway's despatch to the Admiralty, 2 April 1829, in PRO Adm 1/31, fol. 2 *recto* and *verso*. All the women and children were black; the first white women and children arrived in July 1829 (section 5.16).

[2] Emilio Vernet's diary, 18 May 1829. Simon later became the capataz (head gaucho); Santos Centurion was a gaucho; Antonio Rivero later murdered Simon.

[3] Original (in very poor condition, with paper seal attached) in AGN VII, 128 (no doc. no.); copies in Vernet's hand in AGN VII 127, doc. 42, and in AGN VII 129 after doc. 10.

principal powers of Europe", which is also untrue – none of them ever recognised Spain's possession of the islands. In his warning on the other side, Vernet promotes himself to governor, though he was only a CPM (a mere commandant), and he warns that offenders against the laws governing the "fisheries" may become "a lawful prize", but that of course was something that only a prize court could decide. He says the cattle on East Falkland were "private property", but no country except Argentina recognised that he had any rights there, so his ownership of the animals was not recognised either. Thirteen years later in 1832, in his "Report" to Vicente Maza, Vernet wrongly stated that David Jewett had issued a similar warning in 1820, and his inaccurate account of Jewett's actions became a tenacious myth (section 4.7). At any rate, the date of the decree, 10 June, was noteworthy in the history of the Falklands – it was the date on which the British had been expelled from Port Egmont in 1770 (section 2.3). It was surely a pure coincidence, but it provides two events to be commemorated in Argentina on "Malvinas day" each year on 10 June.

5.12 Mathew Brisbane's rescue of the castaways from the *Hope*

Meanwhile Mathew Brisbane had arrived at Buenos Aires on 2 May 1829 after an epic ordeal of shipwreck and survival. He had set sail from London on 5 January 1828 as captain of the sealing schooner *Hope*, 146 tons, with a crew of 22 men; they intended to kill seals on South Georgia (a major centre of the sealing industry), but they were shipwrecked there on 23 April 1828, and spent almost a year on that frozen Antarctic island. Their story is recounted in the "Protest" made by Brisbane at the British Consulate in Buenos Aires on 20 May 1829,[1] and in a despatch to London by Woodbine Parish dated 1 June 1829, from both of which our account is taken. Brisbane and his crew built a house out of an old wreck, and after some months they found an incomplete shallop some 60 miles from their base. They managed to repair it and some of them set sail in it on 7 March 1829, leaving 10 men on the island. On 5 April they reached the coast near Rio Negro, 1,200 miles away, and reached Buenos Aires on 2 May. On 4 May Brisbane visited the British consulate and reported the shipwreck to Woodbine Parish, who wrote in his despatch to London:[2]

He volunteered immediately to return to South Georgia, in the hope of saving the remainder of his men,… and the accidental departure of a Vessel freighted for the Falklands, enabled me at once to make an arrangement with the Master, which I trust Lord Aberdeen will be pleased to approve of, and which may yet enable him I hope to save the lives of his unfortunate Companions… I have also taken upon myself to furnish Mr Brisbane with such articles as may be absolutely necessary for their immediate Relief,… for… which… – £75. 13. 9. Sterling I drew a Bill upon the Lords of His Majesty's Treasury…, for which disbursement, as well as for the further Sum which will be to be paid for the Voyage of the Vessel to South Georgia, I have to request that you will move Lord Aberdeen to give his Sanction in the usual manner…

Parish paid the £75 13*s* 9*d* (seventy-five pounds, thirteen shillings and ninepence) at once to Brisbane for his crew's immediate needs in Buenos Aires, and on 30 May wrote to the Treasury in London asking for approval of the payment, which was granted.[3]

The "Vessel freighted for the Falklands" was the American brig *Betsey* of Boston, Captain Oliver Keating, which Louis Vernet had chartered ("freighted") to go to the Falklands and Statenland with 57 prospective settlers including himself and his family. On 15 May Parish drew up a contract with Keating, signed by Vernet and Brisbane, arranging that Vernet was to charter the ship to Mathew Brisbane for 1,000 Spanish dollars (pesos) a month on the leg from Statenland to Port Louis, rescuing his men on the way, and on his return to Buenos Aires Brisbane was to draw up a certificate of performance for the rescue. It was naturally quicker and cheaper to use a vessel that was already going to the South Atlantic – there was no need to find and equip a vessel from

---

[1] "Protest" made by Mathew Brisbane and two crewmen to record the loss of the *Hope*, disclaiming responsibility for the shipwreck and hence obliging the ship's insurers to pay up, PRO FO 6 28, fols. 49 *recto* – 50 *verso*, authenticated by Vice-Consul Charles Griffiths on 5 June 1829 on fol. 50 *verso*.

[2] Woodbine Parish to John Bidwell, Superintendent of the Consular Service, 1 June 1829, PRO FO 6 28, fols. 47 *verso* – 48 *recto*, in the hand of a copyist, with Parish's autograph signature.

[3] Copy of letter from Parish to "The Right Honble the Lords Commrs of H.M. Treasury", dated 30 May 1829, asking for approval of his payment of £75 13*s* 9*d* to Brisbane, in PRO FO 6 28, fol. 188 *recto*; unsigned draft of reply dated 5 September 1829, in PRO FO 6 28, fols. 190 *recto* – 191 *recto*, accepting the payment.

scratch, and the charter fee could be divided between Vernet and the British government, saving money for both. The agreement was authenticated by Vice-Consul Charles Griffiths; the original was presumably retained by Keating (and has not survived), but a copy, including a copy of the authentication, was made by a professional scribe working for the British consulate. That copy was sent to London by Parish,[1] since the agreement entailed expenses to be paid by the British government. That had not been the case with the authentications of Louis Vernet's concessions in 1826 and 1828 – the two vice-consuls, Poussett and Griffiths, had not informed London about them, so the British government never found out about them (sections 5.2, 5.3, 5.7).

On 19 May Brisbane gave Parish a list of the further amounts required to supply his men on their return journey: 1040 pesos for provisions (bread, flour, sugar, beans, coffee and tea, and also 40 gallons of rum and 4 dozen bottles of port wine), and 690 pesos for clothing, a total of 1,730 pesos. Under the contract, the rescue part of the charter (for the two legs from Statenland to South Georgia and from South Georgia to Port Louis) was to be paid at the monthly rate of 1,000 pesos by the British Treasury to Brisbane, ultimately of course for Vernet. On 20 May Brisbane visited the consulate again to receive the 1,730 pesos,[2] and on that visit, with two of his crewmen, he made a formal "Protest" (i.e. a legal declaration; see footnote above) describing the wreck of the *Hope*, for the purpose of absolving his crew and the shipowners of any blame for the mishap, thus obliging the ship's insurers to pay compensation to the owners. The *Betsey* left Buenos Aires around 21 June 1829 with the 57 settlers including Vernet, his family and Brisbane, and reached Port Louis on 14 July. Brisbane then rescued his nine surviving men and brought them to Port Louis in October 1829 (section 5.13).

5.13 Incorrect account by Kohen and Rodríguez of Brisbane's rescue of the men of the *Hope*

Kohen and Rodríguez give a false account of the rescue of the *Hope*'s castaways from South Georgia – they say (p. 163) that "The settlement at Port Luis was very useful for seamen of all nations… and an essential relief for the survivors of shipwrecks in those desolate areas. It is worth noting in this connection the rescue of shipwreck survivors in South Georgia", and they also state (p. 260): "One of the first recorded official activities concerning South Georgia is the dispatch, by Political and Military Commandment of the Malvinas Commander of the Falklands/ Malvinas [*sic*!], Luis Vernet, of a team to rescue castaways who found themselves in South Georgia. This happened between August and October 1829."

That is a total distortion of the facts. As we pointed out in section 5.12, the rescue was organised by the British Consul-General Woodbine Parish, more than three weeks before Vernet was appointed Civil and Military Commandant of the Malvinas; it was financed by the British government, and Vernet's role was merely to transfer part of his charter to Brisbane (i.e. from Statenland to South Georgia and thence to the Falklands). Vernet had chartered the ship for a round trip: Buenos Aires – Falklands – Statenland – Falklands – Buenos Aires, but the rescue meant he did not have to pay for the third leg from Statenland to the Falklands (including the diversion to South Georgia), which was paid for by Britain, so it saved him money. That is the true story of Brisbane's rescue of his men in 1829.

The arrangements for that rescue began the association between Louis Vernet and Mathew Brisbane. Brisbane boarded the *Betsey* together with Vernet and his family (his wife María, known as "Mariquita", and their three small children Emilio, Luisa, and Sofía); the children's British governess Miss Robinson; two British families; one Spanish-speaking family; five German families and 16 bachelors – 57 people in all.[3] The "colonists" or "settlers" were almost all British or

---

[1] Scribal copy of agreement made at British consulate 15 May 1829, authenticated by Charles Griffiths, Vice Consul, 15 May 1829, in PRO FO 6 28, fols. 51 *recto* – 52 *recto*.

[2] Copy of letter from Brisbane to Parish, 19 May 1829, PRO FO 6 28, fol. 53 *recto*; itemised list of supplies fols. 55 *recto* and *verso*; receipt of 1730 pesos confirmed by Brisbane at foot of fol. 55 *verso*, dated 20 May 1829.

[3] List of the *Betsey*'s passengers dated 16 June 1829, in AGN VII 741; it lists 49 settlers plus Vernet's group of 8 people (Louis, his wife, three children and three servants including Mathew Brisbane). The 49 settlers are made up of 30 Germans (12 men, 5 women and 13 children), 15 British people (11 men, 2 women, 2 children), and one Spanish-

German; Vernet did not want South Americans except as gauchos.

Vernet's charter remained valid and was merely interrupted by the rescue, after which it continued – the ship left Port Louis again for Buenos Aires on 9 November 1829 with a cargo from the Falklands, returned on 12 December and left again for Buenos Aires on 26 December 1829,[1] still under charter to Vernet.

5.14 Vernet's offer to Woodbine Parish; private versus public functions

Aboard the *Betsey* off Buenos Aires on 19 June 1829, Vernet wrote a private letter to Woodbine Parish offering him a fifty-fifty partnership in his establishment and asking Parish to arrange for settlers to come from England;[2] two days later, still aboard the *Betsey*, he wrote to Parish again with the same offer of half shares, but now saying he would like to obtain inhabitants "of the Shetland Islands, of Norway, of the northern parts of Holland and Germany, of Switzerland or the highlands of Scotland and the bays of Ireland."[3] Those two letters express his concerns at the time – he did not have the funds to develop his colony himself and thought his best chance of success was to obtain British funds and British settlers, plus others from northern Europe. Kohen and Rodríguez (pp. 168-9) mention Vernet's letter to Parish, giving Caillet-Bois as their source;[4] they comment that such an investment would have had to be made within the framework of Argentine sovereignty, under which Vernet operated – but they fail to draw the obvious conclusion, namely that that was the reason why Parish declined to participate. It was ludicrous to imagine that a British consul could invest as a private individual in what Britain regarded as British territory, under the auspices of a government whose rights in that territory Britain denied. So it was natural that Parish politely declined to become involved, in his reply of 25 September 1829.[5]

Kohen and Rodríguez say it was "quite normal" at the time to combine the functions of public official and businessman; they mention a despatch sent by the American envoy Francis Baylies to Edward Livingston, the US Secretary of State (i.e. foreign minister), and say that as he left Buenos Aires Baylies referred to his "double position, public and private."[6] But in that despatch Baylies actually said (referring to the Buenos Aires government):[7]

With respect to myself personally the Government had neither the liberality or magnanimity to separate my private from my public character, and having offended them[8] in my official capacity by refusing to lay at their feet the humiliating apologies which they chose to require from the United States, they adopted a system of petty insults and vexations indicating a spirit alike mean and malignant.

Those "petty insults and vexations" against Baylies included threatening to imprison a teacher he had employed to teach his 9-year-old daughter Spanish, and falsely accusing US consul George Slacum of having fought a duel. The attitude of Buenos Aires was indeed "mean and malignant".

Baylies wrote that despatch just as he was breaking off diplomatic relations between the United States and Argentina because of Louis Vernet's seizure of three US ships and the refusal of Buenos Aires even to discuss the case (section 6.15). In the same despatch he sharply attacks the behaviour of Buenos Aires, accusing Vernet's men of "the most flagrant acts of violence and piracy", and referring to the Buenos Aires government as "this wayward people". So Buenos Aires does not come very well out of his remarks. It is odd that Kohen and Rodríguez use that example – it fails to illustrate any combination of public and official functions, and the shabby behaviour of the Buenos Aires government hardly helps their case.

---

named man with a daughter and two grandchildren. Nine of the British and 7 Germans were single men. Gómez Langenheim prints (1939, vol. I, p. 260) a similar list, but Hispanicised and partly mangled.

[1] Dates from PLSR, entries 54, 57.
[2] Keeping-copy of Vernet to Parish, 19 June 1829, in AGN VII, 129, doc. 70.
[3] Keeping-copy of Vernet to Parish, 21 June 1829, in AGN VII, 129, doc. 71.
[4] Caillet-Bois 1948, p. 224; 1952/82, pp. 226-7.
[5] Reply from Parish to Vernet, 25 September 1829, in AGN, VII, 129, doc. 74.
[6] Kohen and Rodríguez 2015, p. 169, giving as source Baylies to Livingston 26 September 1832, in Manning 1932.
[7] Baylies to Livingston 26 September 1832, in Manning 1932, p. 164.
[8] I.e. "I having offended them…".

5.15 The presidio; the *Tiburtina* wrecked; Parish informs London of Vernet's concessions

Some time in early 1829 the Buenos Aires government decided to set up a "presidio" in the Falklands, which was presumably why it had reserved ten square leagues for itself around San Carlos under Louis Vernet's concession of January 1828. A presidio was the last thing Vernet wanted – it was a frontier garrison, something between a military outpost and a prison settlement, since much of the army was made up of convicts guarding other convicts. Vernet wrote to the government to protest, saying that a presidio would dissuade many families who would otherwise go to his establishment.[1] The government, however, ignored his protest.

Hardly had Vernet got the *Tiburtina* ready to return to the Falklands than she was wrecked near Colonia in the River Plate. She was insured, but he did not obtain the full value.[2] He struggled on by mortgaging an estate he owned near Buenos Aires.

The British consul-general in Buenos Aires, Woodbine Parish, got wind of the plans for a presidio and on 15 March 1829 wrote to the British Foreign Secretary, the Earl of Aberdeen, reporting an article in the Buenos Aires newspapers to the effect that "In a Sentence lately passed upon some Convicts, and signed by the acting Government of Buenos Ayres it was expressed that they were to be banished to Martin Garcia 'until the Establishment at the Falkland Isles should be ready for their reception'." Parish went on to say that Buenos Aires had at various times granted "privileges" in the islands to form temporary settlements for sealing and cattle-killing, and he had therefore felt obliged to inform the British government of "the pretensions of this Government" to sovereignty over the islands.[3]

Parish also asked to see Vernet; he paid a third visit to the British consulate in late April 1829, and this time he met Parish, showed him his concession documents and gave him a translation of his 1828 petition and concession, plus a memorandum dated 20 April 1829 listing the people living at Port Louis or about to go there (see section 5.1). Parish sent copies of all these documents to London on 25 April 1829, so now the British government at last found out about the concessions awarded to Vernet by Buenos Aires. In his despatch Parish also reported to Lord Aberdeen his conversation with Vernet about the Falklands, describing him as "a very intelligent Person who has passed three Winters there", and adding: "He would I believe be very happy if His Majesty's Government would take his Settlement under their protection."[4] In letters to the British government written 27 years later in 1856, Vernet confirmed that in 1829 he would have preferred British sovereignty in the Falklands.[5]

On 26 June 1829 Parish sent another despatch to London, enclosing a copy of the comandancia decree of 10 June, revealing the new involvement of the Buenos Aires government, which had now given Vernet an official post in the service of the state.[6] But before receiving it, the British Foreign Office reacted to Parish's earlier despatches, and on 8 August Aberdeen wrote telling him that the government were now considering the question of the Falklands, where a British base might be vital in the event of "War in the Western Hemisphere", and instructing him to inform Buenos Aires of Britain's claim to the islands.[7]

That did not mean that Britain was about to become actively involved in the Falklands. Britain had extensive rights there, derived from 65 years of continuous economic involvement, plus the rights of exploitation and settlement that the former colonial power Spain had been forced to agree to in the Nootka Sound Convention (section 1.7), but to imagine that Britain was keen to occupy the Falklands in the 1820s and 30s would be to misunderstand the ideology of that time. Half a century later in the 1880s and 90s, European colonial empires were at their height and were enthusiastically supported, but before 1880 the atmosphere was quite different: Britain had command of the sea and

---

[1] Rough draft of a letter in AGN VII, 131, doc. 147 (in which he calls himself "D[on]. Luis Bernet").
[2] AGN VII, 131, doc. 84.
[3] Parish to Aberdeen, "Dispatch 17", 15 March 1829, in PRO FO 6 499, fols. 1 *recto* to 2 *verso*.
[4] Parish to Aberdeen, "Dispatch 24", 25 April 1829, PRO FO 6 499, fols. 4 *recto* to 5 *recto*; Vernet's memorandum fol. 13 *recto*.
[5] AGN, VII, 131, doc. 46; letter from Vernet to Lord Harrowby dated 5 May 1856.
[6] Covering letter from Parish to Aberdeen, 26 June 1829, in PRO FO 6 499, fol. 17 *recto* and *verso*.
[7] Draft despatch no. 5 from Aberdeen to Parish, 8 August 1829, in PRO FO 6 499, fols. 23 *recto* to 26 *recto*.

could intervene anywhere if problems arose, so British foreign policy was reactive (sections 6.14, 6.27). If no problems arose, British governments did nothing and hoped for peace and quiet. British policy in the 1830s was against acquiring colonies and was animated by strategic considerations. At that time Britain and the United States were far from friendly; they had fought against each other only 15 years earlier in the War of 1812, which had ended in 1814 leaving a legacy of mistrust and suspicion which lasted over 30 years – as late as the 1840s fortifications were being built in Bermuda in case of war between Britain and the United States. And it was suspicion of the United States that led Britain to send HMS *Clio* to the Falklands in 1832. Strategic worries meant that Britain could not allow any other power to become established in the Falklands, in much the same way as strategic concerns had led Spain to demand the handover of Bougainville's colony in the 1760s. The British response to Buenos Aires was supported with the assertion of Britain's "just rights of sovereignty", applying the principle of *nullum tempus occurrit regi* ["to the king, no time passes"], implying that sovereign rights are eternal (sections 8.11, 10.25). That was untrue of course, but Britain still had extensive rights and a constant presence in the Falklands.

5.16 Louis Vernet's five years in the Falklands: Phase III, 1829-1831

The *Betsey* left Buenos Aires around 21 June 1829 (section 5.13) and reached Port Louis on 14 July (PLSR entry 51). During the voyage Louis Vernet got to know Mathew Brisbane; the two men became firm friends, and Brisbane served as Vernet's righthand man and pilot for the South Atlantic. On 15 July María Vernet began a diary, which she kept for five months until 22 December.[1] Kohen and Rodríguez say (p. 163) "The best way of describing life in the islands during the period of Argentine colonisation is by reading the diary of María Sáez de Vernet", but better accounts are given in Louis Vernet's papers and in Emilio Vernet's diary, which runs for over three years (1 January 1828 to 13 February 1831) and records much more activity – María clearly had little to do.

The *Betsey* sailed again for Statenland on 16 August 1829 under Captain Keating, with Brisbane aboard, first to establish a sawmill to supply the settlement in the Falklands with timber and then to rescue Brisbane's men from South Georgia. At Statenland on 17 September Brisbane took over command of the ship for the third leg of the voyage, paid for by the British government (sections 5.12, 5.13), sailed to South Georgia, rescued his nine surviving men (one of the ten had died), and arrived back at Port Louis with them on 19 October. All were in good health except one who had lost both feet to frostbite.[2] Some left again, but some stayed on at Port Louis, including Brisbane himself.

The arrival of the *Betsey* inaugurated Phase III of Vernet's settlement in the Falklands – the colony proper, with its three groups of people: the gauchos, the blacks, and now the settlers. The *Betsey* brought 57 people; 16-20 of them sailed on to Statenland but eventually went back to Buenos Aires. Only about 40-45 of the settlers, mostly Germans or British, remained for a while at Port Louis and temporarily brought its population up to around 95-100 – the exact number is not recorded, though it is clear that the population did not rise much above 100 at this time. Even that figure was not maintained for long, as tensions arose among the Germans and the Spanish speakers. About 9 Germans left for Buenos Aires on 29 October 1830 aboard the brig *María Antonia* (PLSR entry 75), and others left during the next couple of years – out of the 57 people, only 3 were still at Port Louis two and a half years later in December 1831: Karl Kussler, Andreas Sperl and Mathew Brisbane. The comings and goings demonstrate the impermanent nature of Louis Vernet's settlement and the constant turnover of its population.

---

[1] Full text in Gómez Langenheim 1939, vol. I, pp. 265-284, and (with slight differences) in Lastra 1946, pp. 125-156.
[2] Details from Emilio's diary 16 July 1829; PLSR entries 51 and 54; María Vernet's diary, 16 August and 20 October 1829, in Lastra 1946, pp. 132, 145; and copy of statement signed "20th October 1829 Mathew Brisbane" in AGN VII 127, doc. 33, G No. 3.

5.17 Britain protests against the comandancia decree, 19 November 1829

Having received Parish's despatch of 26 June 1829, Lord Aberdeen wrote to him on 17 September instructing him to protest to Buenos Aires against the comandancia decree and its implied claim to the Falklands.[1] Accordingly, on 19 November 1829, Parish delivered an official British diplomatic protest to Buenos Aires foreign minister Tomás Guido. It ran in part as follows:[2]

… in issuing this Decree, an Authority has been assumed incompatible with His Britannick Majesty's Rights of Sovereignty over the Falkland Islands. … The Undersigned therefore in execution of the Instructions of his Court formally protests in the name of His Britannick Majesty, against the pretensions set up on the part of the Argentine Republick in the Decree of the 10th of June above referred to, and against all Acts which have been, or may hereafter be done to the prejudice of the just Rights of Sovereignty which have heretofore been exercised by the Crown of Great Britain.

That official protest upheld Britain's rights, as they existed at that time. Six days later Guido acknowledged receipt of the protest, and on 5 December Parish sent Lord Aberdeen the text of the protest and of Guido's acknowledgement of receipt,[3] but Buenos Aires never actually replied.

Kohen and Rodríguez (p. 166) criticise us for implying in *Getting it right* (we do not say so in so many words) that as long as only a private enterprise was being undertaken in the Falklands, the British government did not need to react, and only had to react when the activity became official; they also say (p. 171) that the British protest of 1829 was "belated, limited and made in bad faith". They say it was belated and limited because Britain knew of the previous official acts by Buenos Aires in the islands between 1820 and 1829 but did not protest. In fact Britain did not know of Vernet's concessions before 1829, since the British vice-consuls who authenticated his documents in 1826 and 1828 did not inform the British government (sections 5.3, 5.7).

But the decree of 10 June 1829 was a new departure, and Britain protested at once; it is not true that the British protest was late. Kohen and Rodríguez mention Parish's despatch of 15 March 1829, in which he informed the British government that the Spaniards had maintained a garrison in the islands, and that "the Buenos Ayreans" had, ever since the Spaniards left, considered the territory to belong to them, and they also say that in his despatch of 25 April 1829, Parish had sent the British government copies of Vernet's concessions that the British vice-consul had certified in January 1828 (sections 5.7, 5.15).[4] They imply that Britain failed to respond after seeing the documents, but the British government had not seen the documents earlier, and as soon as it saw them, it moved fast – the despatch was received near the end of June, and Britain replied to Parish a mere six weeks later on 8 August (section 5.15).

Kohen and Rodríguez say (p. 171) that the British protest was "in bad faith" because it was made despite the presence of Spain in the islands till 1811 and later Argentine acts of which Britain "could not be ignorant". But Britain cannot have known about such internal Argentine matters as the 1816 letter and the other insignificant things they mention (sections 4.1, 4.3, 4.4), and Britain remained ignorant of Vernet's concessions. The British protest of 19 November 1829 was made in response to Britain's first knowledge of involvement by Buenos Aires – it was neither late, nor limited, nor made in bad faith. The contentions by Kohen and Rodríguez are false.

5.18 So-called acts exercising a public function and/or Argentine sovereignty

Kohen and Rodríguez list (p. 160-161) what they call "acts in exercise of public authority and other demonstrations of Argentine sovereignty" performed by Louis Vernet during this part of his time in the islands, but none of these is of any serious relevance. The first item on their list is the circular (see section 5.11), with the comandancia decree on one side and Vernet's warning to sealers on the other. That was of course not recognised as valid by any other country.

Number 2 on their list is Vernet's possession-taking ceremony on 30 August 1829 (which was

---
[1] Draft despatch no. 9 from Aberdeen to Parish, 17 September 1829, in PRO FO 6 499, fol. 27 *recto* to 27 *verso*.
[2] Text from copy in PRO FO 6 499, 19 November 1829, fols. 33 *recto* to 35 *recto*.
[3] Parish to Aberdeen 4 December 1829, in PRO FO 6 499, fols. 31 *recto* to 32 *recto* (covering letter), 33 *recto* to 35 *recto* (text of protest), 37 *recto* to 39 *verso* (acknowledgement of receipt in Spanish and English).
[4] I.e. Parish to Aberdeen, "Dispatch 24", 25 April 1829, PRO FO 6 499 (above).

no more valid than any such ceremony), while no. 3, "Criminal proceedings", refers to an incident mentioned in María Vernet's diary, when Vernet imprisoned a man who had been drunk and had threatened another man. However, such disciplinary actions were also performed by the captains of privately owned ships and are not a proof of state authority. Emilio Vernet's diary records just such a case on 17 February 1828, when Captain Kenney of the American sealer *Sarah Atkins* stopped a gunfight between two gauchos:

Dionisio Ortiz came tonight to our house with a loaded pistol to shoot Jacinto [Correa], who realised it in time to jump aside and grab a pistol too, when Captain Kenney intervened and ended the dispute.

That is Emilio's last reference to Dionisio Ortiz; it seems he was soon sent back to Buenos Aires.

Number 4 on the list by Kohen and Rodríguez is the conduct of civil weddings performed by Vernet – but in remote territories such as the Falklands that was a normal function of whoever was in charge, indeed even today in the islands weddings and funerals on settlements in the Camp are performed by the local farm manager. That does not indicate a "demonstration of sovereignty".

Number 8 on the list ("Use of inhabitants for military service and custody of prisoners") is an absurdly inflated interpretation of a passage from Caillet-Bois,[1] who quotes a brief account by Vernet, written around 1832-5, in which he lists the pay rates of his employees, saying that "on the occasions when I employed the inhabitants for military service, I paid them the same as they earned in their respective jobs... The gauchos... earned the same for the custody and supervision of prisoners...". Looking back after leaving the islands, Vernet was idealising his activities in retrospect – in fact there was absolutely no "military service" in his settlement. There were a few occasions on which some armed gauchos were sent to arrest ships' captains, and to stand guard on the houses in which they were being held, but no more (section 6.3). The bare mention by Kohen and Rodríguez of "military service and custody of prisoners" gives a wrong impression to readers who do not know the facts – they would naturally tend to imagine that there was proper military service in the islands under Vernet. There was no such thing.

Several items on their list are repeats: number 7, "Fishing and hunting controls", is already covered by the circular, and 10 (the application of the decree of 5 January 1828) simply provides a basis for the other actions. Numbers 9 and 11 are "land concessions" and "Promotion of European and American immigration", but they were two sides of the same coin – the land concessions (such as that to William Langdon, section 6.8) were to promote immigration.

And their list contains two absurdities, which also appear in other Argentine sources. They are no. 5, the "patente de Navegación" [commission] of the schooner "Águila" (as they call the ship) and no. 6, the issuing of money. They are typical examples of the grossly overidealised Argentine view of Vernet's activities in the Falklands, and each deserves more detailed treatment.

5.19 The "Águila" myth

The first of the absurdities on the list by Kohen and Rodríguez (p. 160) is no. 5:

5. Navigation Licence for the National Schooner 'Águila', built in the Falklands/Malvinas and owned by Luis Vernet himself, dated November 6th, 1831.

They claim this was one of Vernet's "acts in exercise of public authority and other demonstrations of Argentine sovereignty", but that is nonsense. Like several other authors, they followed Gómez Langenheim 1939 (vol. I, p. 284), not realising that his work is so riddled with crass errors and distortions that it is worthless as history. We shall first tell the story of what actually happened, then reveal what Gómez Langenheim (and Cresto, and Kohen and Rodríguez) made out of it.

Here is the true story of the so-called "Águila", severely shortened.[2] On 18 December 1829 the

---

[1] Caillet-Bois 1948, p. 211; 1952/82, p. 213.
[2] Unless otherwise indicated, our account of the "Águila" (i.e. the *Eagle*), greatly abbreviated here, is based on documents including eight sworn statements (affidavits) in English, in AGN VII, 136, fols. 1 to 141; Vernet's "Report" to Vicente Maza, 10 August 1832, in *BFSP 1832-1833*, pp. 385-386; Vernet's contract with the *Belleville* men plus six affidavits by Captain Davison of the *Harriet*, in Manning 1932; the log of the USS *Lexington*, in US National Archives (USNA), Washington DC, RG 24, in E. 118, Pt 123; and Duncan's despatch to Woodbury, 3 February 1832 (below).

American sealing schooner *Belleville* of Newburyport, Massachusetts, arrived at Port Louis[1] under one of her co-owners, Captain Nehemiah Bray; also aboard was another American co-owner, Henry Metcalf. At the Jason Islands and Swan (now Weddell) Island, Bray had left two large boats, named *General Jackson* and *Black Prince*, to start sealing and operate as "tenders" to the *Belleville*. Each had a crew of half a dozen, mostly Americans, whom we call "the *Belleville* men". Bray told no one at Port Louis about those men – to him the islands were open to all; he was happy to cooperate with Vernet but did not see him as possessing any kind of monopoly.

In January 1830 Vernet chartered the *Belleville* to go first to Statenland with provisions for the men landed there by the *Betsey* in September 1829 to cut timber for the Falklands (section 5.16), and then to take a cargo of salt fish to Brazil.[2] Mathew Brisbane was to act as pilot, so Vernet gave him some circulars (section 5.11), and instructed him on what to do:[3]

… Enclosed I hand you the decree pass'd by the Buenos Ayrean Government, which authorises me to see the Laws executed on this coast. You will please to shew the same to all masters of fishing Vessels as also my notice on the subject, allowing them to take a copy of the same if they wish it…

It was of course absurd for Vernet to claim that he had authority "to see the Laws executed on this coast" – he possessed no authority recognised by any other country, and the United States and Britain had long-standing rights in the area that he could not simply abolish. Both countries had customary rights derived from 65 years' presence on the Patagonian coast and around the Falklands, and Britain had in addition rights deriving from the 1771 Anglo-Spanish agreement (in which Spain had tolerated Britain's claim to the Falklands) and the Nootka Sound Convention of 1790, in which Spain had accepted that Britain (but no other country) had extensive rights of exploitation including "fishing" (i.e. mainly sealing) in a vast area of the Patagonian coast and in most of the Falklands, and the right of settlement in parts of those areas (section 1.7).[4]

On 5 February 1830 the Vernets' fourth child, Matilde, later nicknamed "Malvina", was born at Port Louis,[5] and on 7 February the *Belleville* set off under charter to Vernet, captained by Bray and piloted by Brisbane (PLSR entry 61). But on 22 February she was wrecked on Tierra del Fuego. The crew all survived, as did their dog, and they built a "shallop" (a small schooner) out of the wreckage, which they named *Matilde* after the new baby at Port Louis. On 1 May 1830 they set off for the Falklands in the shallop, which leaked badly. They had nothing to eat but hide; one wonders how the dog survived. Two men died, but on 7 May, after a violent storm, they ran into a cove on the south coast of East Falkland, and recorded in their log: "Killed numbers of geese; thanked God for our safety."[6] They got back to Port Louis on 30 May 1830 (PLSR entry 69), and several of the men stayed in the islands working for Vernet, including Henry Metcalf.

Meanwhile the *Belleville* men had been sealing around the western Falklands in the *General Jackson* and the *Black Prince*. Some time in July 1830 they heard of the loss of the *Belleville*, and went on sealing in the islands for their own profit instead of for the ship's owners. Some men deserted from various sealing ships and joined them, attracted by the idea of working for

---

[1] PLSR entry 58; it says the *Belleville* arrived from "these Islands" and gives her occupation as "sealer".
[2] Charter agreement, dated Port Louis, 30 January 1830, in AGN VII, 127, no doc. no.
[3] Keeping-copy of Vernet to Brisbane 3 February 1830, in AGN VII, 132, doc. 80, in Vernet's hand.
[4] Buenos Aires had breached Britain's rights under the Nootka Sound Convention by imposing a tax of five pesos per ton on foreign vessels taking seals on the Patagonian coast (mentioned in Vernet's papers in AGN VII, 127, doc. 44), and had also issued a prohibition on all "fishing" on 28 October 1829, revised on 31 July 1831 to apply only to non-Argentinians (Mario Tesler, *Malvinas: como EE.UU. provocó la usurpación inglesa* ["Malvinas: how the USA provoked the English usurpation"] Buenos Aires 1979, pp. 116-121). Article 3 of the comandancia decree of 10 June 1829 instructed Vernet to implement the fishing laws in the Falklands, hence his instruction to Brisbane to "see the Laws executed on this coast", but it infringed Britain's long-standing rights.
[5] Matilde Vernet y Sáez (1830-1924) left the Falklands with the rest of the Vernet family in November 1831, aged 1¾. She married the American naval officer Greenleaf Cilley in Montevideo on 13 May 1861; they lived for a while in the United States, and were both present in Ford's Theatre in Washington DC on 14 April 1865 when Abraham Lincoln was assassinated by John Wilkes Booth. They later moved to Argentina, where they both died. Some of Matilde's female descendants were given the name "Malvina", which in her case was only a nickname. When she died on 24 September 1924 aged 94 she had about 100 descendants.
[6] FitzRoy 1839, vol. II, p. 334, quoting from the shallop's log.

themselves, while others went back to their original ships, only to "re-desert" and join the *Belleville* men again. They built themselves a house on a small island off West Falkland now called Governor Island,[1] and in August 1830 they were joined by five men who deserted from the American sealer *Thaddeus*, taking one of her boats. One of them was William Horton Smyley (1792-1868), from Rhode Island, who later served as United States commercial agent from 1850 to 1868 in Stanley, where his three children went to school. The British authorities saw him as rather a rogue, but he was also a courageous seamen who saved many lives after shipwrecks.

By early 1831 the *Black Prince* had been "stove" (smashed in), so the *Belleville* men were left with the *General Jackson* plus a boat from the American sealer *Hope* and the one Smyley took from the *Thaddeus*. They built a shallop out of the wreckage, but broke it up and built another, which was also unsatisfactory, so they broke that up too and began building a third, larger one of about 20-30 tons, on Eagle (now Speedwell) Island at the south end of Falkland Sound. They called her *Eagle* after the island where she was built – this was the vessel about which Gómez Langenheim wrote complete nonsense, which was followed by others including Kohen and Rodríguez.

They continued sealing around the islands in their other boats, and around 17 August 1831 five of them (Isaac Waldron, William Smyley, John Jones, William Davenport and the Englishman George Lambert) sailed round to Port Louis to get supplies. They were in for a shock: Louis Vernet arrested them, accusing them of sealing "illegally", and locked them up for five weeks, during which he seized three American sealing ships (section 6.3). Then he devised a way of turning them to his own advantage, and on 20 September he released them and drew up a contract specifying that together with the other five men still on Eagle Island, they were to finish their shallop, and they were to hand over as "security" the sealskins which they had acquired.[2] They were to come to Port Louis in the completed shallop on or before 1 December 1831, and would then seal the Falklands on Vernet's behalf; they were to take copies of his warning circular and inform the captain of any ship found sealing that he ran the risk of "losing his vessel". If they caught him sealing again and the ship was condemned as prize, they were to have half the proceeds.

But Vernet had lost touch with reality – it was ludicrous to expect a shallop crewed by 10 Americans to prevent a crew of 20-30 other Americans in an armed sealing ship from pursuing their livelihood. Francis Baylies later pointed out the absurdity of what Vernet expected them to do:[3]

… he would have seduced them to the commission of acts of violence and robbery on their own countrymen, by engaging to share with them the profits arising from the plunder of the vessels which they should capture!

The men signed the contract in order to get out of Vernet's clutches, and returned in their boat to Eagle Island, where they and the other *Belleville* men continued work on the shallop. That took them another couple of months, and in the meantime Vernet sold some of their sealskins and confiscated a ton of valuable whalebone they had collected (section 6.7).

He then abandoned his earlier conciliatory policy and seized some American ships for his own use, which required him to go to Buenos Aires to have them adjudged legal prize and therefore his property (section 6.3). So, on 6 November 1831, the day before he left the islands, he drew up an elaborate commission or "patente de Navegación" for the *Belleville* men's shallop, in which he called the ship "Águila" (Spanish for *Eagle*, the ship's name). He himself was not going to be at Port Louis when they arrived around 1 December, so he left the original of the commission at Port Louis with Mathew Brisbane and Henry Metcalf, who were to manage the settlement in his absence. The original does not survive, but it no doubt had blanks for the men to sign their names and to fill in the details of the ship. He also made a keeping-copy of it for his archives, which he took with him to Buenos Aires (fig. 5.19a). He himself wrote all the names on the keeping-copy, as the men were still on Eagle Island. The next day, 7 November 1831, he left the islands in the seized American sealer *Harriet* (section 6.9).

Faithfully fulfilling their contract with Vernet (if a little late), the *Belleville* men sailed round to

---

[1] Details from affidavit by Isaac Waldron, AGN VII, 136, fol. 63 *recto*.
[2] Text of contract dated 20 September 1831 printed in Manning 1932, fn. pp. 94-96.
[3] Baylies to Maza 20 June 1832, in Manning 1932, p. 102. For Baylies see section 6.15.

Port Louis in the finished shallop – PLSR (entry 106) records the arrival of the "Schooner Eagle" from Eagle Island on 24 December 1831. But to their amazement Vernet had gone! And only a couple of days later on 27 December the American corvette *Lexington* arrived under Captain Silas Duncan, who was under orders to prevent the establishment from capturing American ships (section 6.10, 6.12). Duncan towed the *Eagle* up Berkeley Sound to Port Louis, set his carpenters to work for a week making her shipshape, and gave her crew supplies and an American flag and papers – he reported to US Navy Secretary Levi Woodbury in a despatch on 3 February 1832:[1]

I also found a small schooner on the coast of East Falklands, navigated by a part of the crew of the American schooner "Belville", wreck'd on the coast of Patagonia. These men had built this small vessel or shallop of 20 to 30 tons after the loss of their vessel, and were seized and made prisoner by Vernet and his associates, and compelled to enter into their service. I supplied them with such articles as they were in want of…

They soon dropped the name *Eagle* and called their vessel the *Chaloupe* (an older form of "shallop"; see section 6.32), and continued sealing around the Falklands for their own profit for some six years. That, then, was the true story of the shallop *Eagle*.

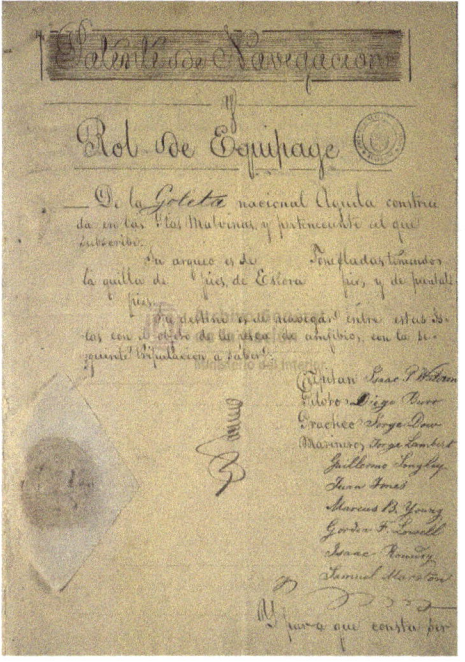
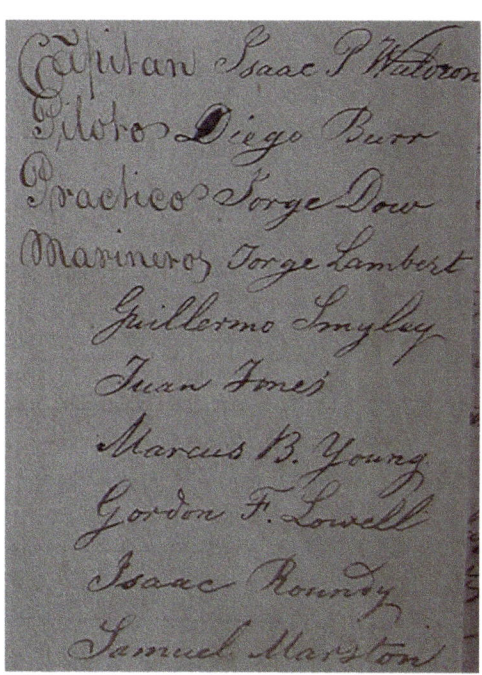

5.19a Vernet's keeping-copy of his commission for the ship that he (but no one else) called the "Águila", dated 6 November 1831 (the day before he left the islands for good). The names (right) are not signatures but are all written by Vernet in his own hand. He Hispanicises the names, though the men were all Americans or British. Vernet himself never saw the ship. (AGN VII, 136, doc. 77)

But Antonio Gómez Langenheim found Vernet's keeping-copy of the shallop's commission in the AGN in Buenos Aires (fig. 5.19a) and printed its text in his book in 1939, at the same time inventing a fictitious background:[2]

Vernet is a governor with initiative; one thing demonstrates that: the requirements of navigation and fishing on the coasts of the Colony require a larger number of vessels; Vernet loses no time but seeks out the necessary equipment, beams, ironwork, etc., brings together carpenters and has a schooner constructed on the spot and under his direction, then he christens her with the name *Águila*, crews her with ten men, draws up for her the appropriate patent or sailing list, and sends her to fish for amphibians… Thus there sailed from puerto Luis, with the Argentine flag at her masthead, the first ship built in such modest shipyards, which carried our flag among the immense sails of ships of other countries…

That is nonsense, but it has acquired a hallowed place in Argentina's fictitious picture of its involvement in the Falklands. It was followed by Juan José Cresto in 2011, who says:[3]

---

[1] Despatch in USNA, Naval Record Group 45, M147, microfilm 16, doc. 28; also microfilmed in the "Area File of the Naval Collection" 1775-1910 Area 4 1832, ref. M 625 Roll 6 (not in Manning 1932). It was first printed in Spanish translation in Fitte 1966, pp. 111-112.
[2] Gómez Langenheim 1939, vol. I, p. 284.
[3] Cresto 2011, p. 277 and footnote, same page; he gives no source for his remarks.

> ... the greatest achievement was represented by the building of the schooner called "Águila"... There was constant communication with Buenos Aires in voyages of six days and for that purpose he constructed the... "Águila". [Cresto's footnote:] One can only admire the activity displayed by this active man of business, who... smoothed down tree-trunks, made frames and planks and prepared them for the construction of ships.

It was echoed by María Angélica de Vernet, a great-great-granddaughter of Louis Vernet, speaking for Argentina at the United Nations in New York on 20 June 2013 before the Decolonisation Committee, the "Committee of 24" or "C24"; she said that Vernet's establishment possessed:[1]

> ... a schooner named *Águila*, built on the Staten Island to facilitate communications with Buenos Aires and the Malvinas Islands. This was the first piece of work manufactured in the Malvinas Islands.

It was a sheer guess that the shallop must have been built where there was wood, i.e. on Staten Island. She was actually built on woodless Eagle Island.

All those Argentine accounts are untrue. The truth is that far from directing the building of the so-called "Águila", Louis Vernet never clapped eyes on her – when he left the Falklands on 7 November 1831 she was still unfinished on Eagle Island at the southern end of Falkland Sound, about 80 miles from Port Louis. She was actually called *Eagle* (only Vernet called her "Águila"); she was not built to facilitate communications but to kill seals; she never belonged to Vernet's settlement, and Vernet played no part in her construction except that he supplied some equipment and provisions to her builders, some of whom he had imprisoned for five weeks (not exactly a good way of promoting the shallop's construction). She never flew an Argentine flag; she sailed under the United States flag, and she was still in the Falklands in 1837, with her mainly American crew.[2]

Through his historical ignorance and his unscrupulous use of evidence both here and elsewhere, Antonio Gómez Langenheim did the history of the Falklands a serious disservice. Much of his work is fiction, and like other Argentine authors, Kohen and Rodríguez fell victim to his manipulations.

5.20 The money myth – Vernet's truck system

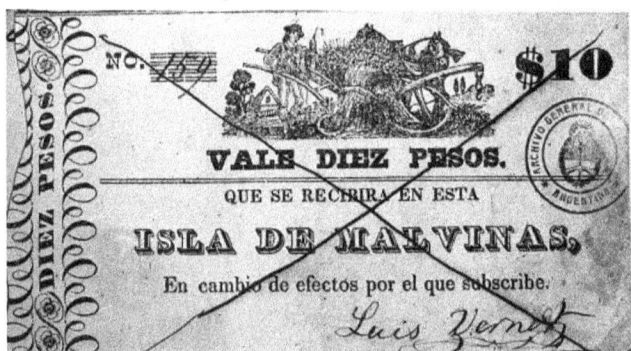

5.20a IOU: Vernet's "currency" (a paper token serving as a promissory note). The text reads "En esta isla de Malvinas" ["In this island of Malvinas"] – Vernet's concession only operated in East Falkland, but the tokens were only valid within his truck system, not throughout the island. Kohen and Rodríguez (p. 165) illustrate this same token – but photoshopped so as to omit the crossed lines indicating cancellation. (AGN)

Kohen and Rodríguez give "Currency issuance" as number 6 on their list (p. 160) of Vernet's "acts in exercise of public authority and other demonstrations of Argentine sovereignty", but this shows they also fell victim to another misunderstanding, in common with other Argentine authors. We call it "the money myth". It actually proves the opposite of what they claim – far from indicating a well-regulated establishment, it confirms that Vernet's settlement was not viable. The "currency" notes were merely his own "IOUs" – they were promissory notes not backed by real currency. In short, he was signing bouncing cheques. That does not constitute "Currency issuance".

Vernet refers to the notes as "paper tokens" in a letter of 22 August 1839 in the Jane Cameron National Archives (JCNA) in Stanley, written to the resident British Lieutenant at Port Louis,

---

[1] María Angélica Vernet at the C24, 20 June 2013, English translation transcribed as televised live from the UN.
[2] William Smyley later became her captain, and says in a letter to Louis Vernet that she was broken up in 1837 by the crew of HMS *Cleopatra* (Smyley to Vernet 24 March 1838, AGN VII 132, doc. 281); *Cleopatra*'s captain George Grey (section 6.19), says in his journal that he had the ship broken up in the San Carlos River, East Falkland.

Robert Lowcay, thus confirming that they were not real money.[1] On their p. 165 Kohen and Rodríguez illustrate the very same token that we illustrate in fig 5.20a (10-peso token no. 159) – but they have manipulated it so as to remove the crossing-out cancellation, which nonetheless remains visible on closer examination of their illustration. Most of the tokens were printed in Montevideo in November 1830 and were taken to the islands by Mathew Brisbane, with copies of Vernet's warning circular. The bill came to 28 pesos (10 pesos for 100 circulars, and 18 pesos for 1300 "billets" at 1, 5 and 10 pesos each).[2]

Far from being a sign of good government and prosperity, those tokens were a symptom of a deep malaise. Vernet's accounts show that his establishment in the Falklands was not paying its way and was running short of money,[3] so he resorted to paper tokens to keep going. If he had been making a profit from providing ships with beef, sealskins, cowhides and other supplies, he would have had real cash in hand in the form of the Spanish silver coins called pesos or "Spanish dollars";[4] he could have paid the gauchos in cash and would not have needed tokens. But the pay he had agreed (one peso a day for herding cattle, plus one per night out in the Camp, plus payments for the hides obtained), combined with the limited price he was able to charge for beef (10 pesos per animal was the standard price around the South Atlantic) ate up any profit. If he had agreed a lower rate of pay with the gauchos he might have been able to pay them in real silver money which they could have spent as they wished, but as it was, he operated at a loss.

That was confirmed in 1835 by the British naval lieutenant Henry Smith and his son Hugh, who ran the establishment at Port Louis for Vernet after he left; they continued to send him statements of account (fig. 5.20b, below) and to keep hides and sealskins reserved for him as his property. They continued his payment system but needed constant injections of cash from British funds – Hugh Smith wrote on 17 December 1835 from Port Louis to Vernet in Buenos Aires complaining that the pay for the gauchos was too high: "the way they are paid is exhorbitant, which is according to your contract; in fact it eats up all the sales of beef."[5]

Understandably, the gauchos worked better under the Smiths for real money than they had under Vernet for mere paper – Commander William Robertson of HMS *Snake* reported in January 1835 that the three remaining gauchos plus one British seaman had brought in over 200 cattle in a year,[6] not much less than had been achieved by two dozen gauchos under Vernet. Thus more than four years after Vernet left the islands, his establishment was still being run on his behalf and on the lines he had laid down, though still of course without a profit since the rate of pay he had agreed with the gauchos was too high from the start.

What Kohen and Rodríguez (and other Argentine authors) fail to note is that in introducing the paper tokens, Vernet was setting up a "truck system", a closed economy in which employees were not paid in freely negotiable cash but in goods or tokens. Such systems were common on Argentine "estancias" (cattle ranches), and had formerly been common in European countries including Britain.[7] From an employer's point of view a truck system had advantages – he did not have to obtain real cash from outside but could create his own; he could set his own prices; and his workmen were tied to him since they had no cash of their own and were thus economic captives. They could only redeem the tokens for goods in their employer's own store, and of course he could set the prices of goods and the rate at which he redeemed the tokens for cash (if at all).

---

[1] Vernet to Lowcay 22 August 1839, in JCNA, vol. H1, original in Vernet's hand.
[2] Bill dated Montevideo, 3 November 1830, in AGN VII, 132, doc. 79.
[3] Several sets of accounts, the earliest dated 1832 and 1833, in AGN VII, 130, doc. 2 (and see section 6.2).
[4] The peso (the "peso fuerte"), first issued as a silver coin by Spain in 1497, was the universal currency in South America from the 16th to the mid-19th centuries. It was known in English as a "Spanish dollar" or "piece of eight", since it was worth 8 reales. For a long period a peso was worth about 4s 4d sterling (four shillings and fourpence, i.e. about 4.6 pesos to the pound).
[5] Letter from Hugh Smith to Vernet, 17 December 1835, in AGN VII 132, doc. 223.
[6] Robertson's report January 1835, PRO Adm 1/43, no doc. no.
[7] In Britain truck systems were progressively abolished by a series of Truck Acts beginning in the 15th century. In 1831 these Acts were consolidated in the Truck Act 1831 (1 & 2 Will. 4, c. 37), though further Acts were still required in the 19th century to get rid of the practice. Their modern equivalent is the Employment Rights Act 1996.

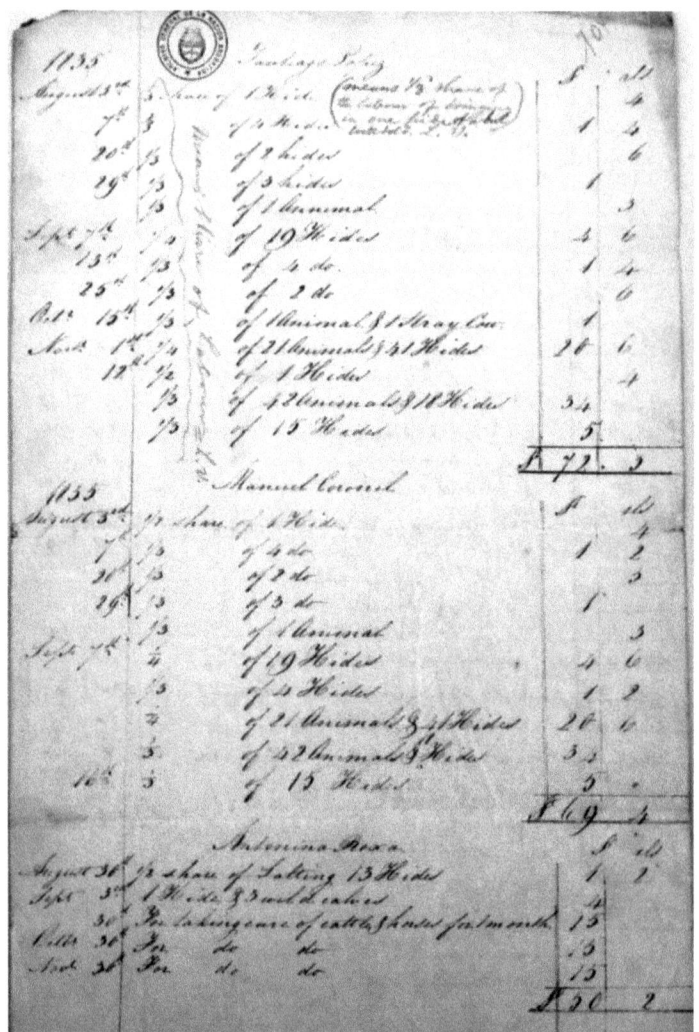

5.20b Accounts at Port Louis, 1835: the pay of the gauchos Santiago López, Manuel Coronel and Antonina Roxa, 3 August to 16 December 1835, sent by Hugh Smith (son of Henry Smith), acting as Louis Vernet's agent, to Vernet in Buenos Aires, 17 December 1835 (the first of 3 pages). The gauchos were paid in pesos (Spanish silver dollars, symbol: $) and reales (a real was ⅛ of a peso); the brown annotations are by Vernet. (AGN VII 130, doc. 104, fol. 1 *recto*)

In 1831 Vernet was only offering 40% of the face value of his tokens, as the British settler Joseph Addyman found out to his cost. Addyman had arrived at Port Louis with his wife and children around 1830, and was the kind of settler Vernet needed – active and enterprising, skilled at house-building and horse-training, and with a family, but he and his wife Jane became so incensed at Vernet's treatment of them that they left for Rio in mid-1831 in the British brigantine *Elbe*. Vernet's behaviour was in fact very different from the idealised picture painted by Argentine authors such as Ricardo Caillet-Bois, who says "The colony was a true example of order and respect for property",[1] and Juan José Cresto, who says "Vernet was an excellent administrator of 'his' islands".[2]

The people who lived there saw him differently, and Joseph Addyman described him as tyrannical: "to remonstrate was out of the question, his will being the law".[3] The Addymans found that Vernet would not pay them any cash at all for the tokens they held, and would only give them two money orders for 40% of their face value, payable in Rio by Vernet's agents, Messrs Rostron and Dutton. But when the Addymans reached Rio, Rostron and Dutton refused to honour the money orders, saying they did not hold sufficient funds of Vernet's to pay him, and the value of the *Elbe*'s cargo did not cover the cost.[4] The Addymans got nothing.

---

[1] Caillet-Bois 1948, p. 211; 1952/82, p. 215.
[2] Cresto 2011, p. 277.
[3] Addyman (in Rio) to Rear Admiral Sir Michael Seymour, 13 May 1833, PRO FO 118/31, fols. 155 *recto* to 157 *verso*.
[4] Copy of certificate from Rostron and Dutton, 4 May 1833, in PRO FO 118/31, fol. 159 *recto*.

That was not all. When Mathew Brisbane returned from Buenos Aires to Port Louis as settlement manager in March 1833 (section 6.31), he was under instructions from Vernet to not even pay the inhabitants with paper tokens, but merely to record in the account book what work they had done and what supplies he issued to them.[1] That meant that the tokens had ceased to have any value – before, they had been worthless outside the settlement, but the inhabitants could at least exchange them at the store for anything they chose (at inflated prices), and could pass them from hand to hand in payment for favours. But now they would have nothing in their hands to show how much work they had done, and nothing that they could use in exchanges among themselves. And the gauchos were illiterate, so they could not check the accuracy of the list of debts. In short, they were reduced to the status of slaves – slaves had no money and lived in a barter economy, providing labour in exchange for goods. Some of the gauchos became bitterly angry at the way they were being treated, and their anger cost the lives of six men including Mathew Brisbane (section 6.32).

5.21 Conclusion

The historical documents presented in this chapter reveal the serious errors and distortions in the account by Kohen and Rodríguez, who paint a false picture of the history and legal situation of the Falklands in the 1820s and 1830s. Their account is distorted by their simplistic "legitimist" view of sovereignty, which leads them to write as if Argentina rightfully possessed 100% sovereignty in the Falklands, whereas the real position was confused and complex – there were three mutually contradictory claims to the islands by Spain, Britain and Argentina, each of which claimed 100% rights of sovereignty, whereas the United States denied all three claims and held that the islands were open to all, like Antarctica, and that no country held sovereignty over them. In other words, there existed no clear title to the islands.

Kohen and Rodríguez failed to check some of their central assumptions against actual documentary sources – thus they automatically assume, like other Argentine authors (and Louis Vernet himself) that the British government was informed by its consular staff in Buenos Aires in 1826 and 1828 that Vernet had been given concessions in the Falklands. They therefore go on to assert that Britain's failure to protest showed lack of commitment, or of confidence, in maintaining the British claim to the islands. In fact the records of the correspondence from the British consulate in Buenos Aires (sections 5.3, 5.7) show that there was no mention of Vernet's concessions – the British government remained ignorant of their existence till mid-1829, and then protested promptly.

Uncritically following other Argentine authors, Kohen and Rodríguez also paint a false picture of Vernet's settlement at Port Louis, implying that it was much larger and much better run than it actually was. That settlement gave Argentina for the first time the beginnings of solid rights in the islands, which might have matured over time into sovereignty accepted by other countries. Title to the islands was disputed between several countries, and the very existence of a title was denied *in toto* by the United States, but in the fullness of time it might have come to be accepted that there was indeed a title to the islands and that it belonged to Argentina. That this did not happen was the result of Vernet's financial difficulties and his political incompetence, which led him to seize ships belonging to another country and thus enter the realm of international law, under which he had no rights whatever in the islands. Those developments will be examined in the next chapter, along with the errors in Kohen's and Rodríguez's account of them.

---

[1] Draft of instructions to Brisbane, in Vernet's hand, in AGN VII, 132, doc. 155, fol. 3 *recto*.

CHAPTER SIX: the Second Falklands Crisis, 1831-1833[1]

We now come to a crucial episode in the history of the Falkland Islands, which we call the Second Falklands Crisis (following the First Falklands Crisis of 1770-71 and preceding the Third Falklands Crisis, the Falklands War of 1982).

Kohen and Rodríguez devote 16 pages to this vital part of the islands' history, but as always their account of what actually happened is distorted and their description of the legal position is incorrect. Like all Argentine writers, they make the basic mistake of taking it for granted that the Falkland Islands belonged to Argentina in the 1830s. That was not the case; no other country accepted that Argentina had any rights of sovereignty whatever in the islands. Britain regarded the Falklands as British, Spain held them to be Spanish, while the United States denied that any country held any rights of sovereignty and the islands were part of the high seas, open to all. At that time no clear title to the islands existed, and there was no international body like the International Court of Justice that was entitled to rule on questions of territorial title and sovereignty. Kohen and Rodríguez assume that Louis Vernet had the right to restrict access to the islands' resources, but only Argentina accepted that. Thus it is historically and legally untrue to say that there were ships killing seals "illegally" in the islands – to all countries except Argentina, it was Vernet's actions that were illegal.

The Second Falklands Crisis had three parts: Part I was the dispute between the United States and Argentina caused by Louis Vernet, who seized three US ships in what the US government regarded as international waters; the seizures led to Part II, an act of reprisal by the United States (the "*Lexington* raid"), in which Master Commandant Silas Duncan of the corvette *Lexington* took some inhabitants of Port Louis prisoner, induced many others to leave the islands, and greatly reduced the size of Vernet's establishment – it still continued, though Vernet and his family had left several weeks earlier. As a result of Vernet's actions the United States broke off diplomatic relations with Argentina for twelve years, and the US Supreme Court ruled in 1839 that Vernet's seizure of the three ships was illegal in US law and Vernet was guilty of piracy (section 6.39). The increased American activity in the South Atlantic worried the British government and led to Part III of the Second Falklands Crisis: the reassertion of British sovereignty, which began a dispute between Argentina and Britain which lasted until it was ended by treaty in 1850 (chapter 7). We shall now recount what really happened and show where Kohen and Rodríguez are wrong.

6.1 Vernet's "Advertisement", 1831

Louis Vernet's downfall, and the end of the Argentine involvement in the Falklands, came about because he changed from a positive to a negative policy towards visitors. In early 1831 he continued his previous welcoming policy, and produced a document which we call Vernet's "Advertisement" (it is actually untitled), aimed at attracting trading ships and promoting Port Louis as a place to settle. Kohen and Rodríguez were seemingly unaware of this important document, which reveals much about Vernet's behaviour in 1831. It is in English and has three parts: a notice to mariners by Vernet dating from mid-March 1831, praising the advantages of the settlement for ships and settlers; secondly a list of 18 British ships that called between 1826 and March 1831; and a third part dated "Montevideo 2 September 1831", with sailing directions for Berkeley Sound and Port William written by the Scottish sealing captain William Low. No original or printed copy seems to have survived, but a version was sent to London and a handwritten copy was made by an Admiralty clerk and sent on 7 May 1832 by John Barrow, Second Secretary to the Admiralty, to Sir George Shee at the Foreign Office, for the information of Foreign Secretary Lord Palmerston.[2]

The first two parts of the "Advertisement" were evidently taken to Buenos Aires by Louis

---

[1] Unless otherwise mentioned, our account of the Second Falklands Crisis is based on: Vernet's "Abridged statement of the operations of the schooner Harriet", in AGN VII, 136; his "Answers to a 1st Interrogatory", AGN VII, 130, doc. 178 (of 1836-7); Vernet's "Report" of 1832; the *Harriet*'s crew list (AGN VII, 129, doc. 79); the *Breakwater*'s captain's log (AGN VII, 139); Davison's 6 affidavits, and the "*Harriet* affidavits" (AGN VII, 136, fols. 15 *recto* to 23 *recto*).

[2] Scribal copy of Vernet's untitled "Advertisement" in PRO FO 6 499, fols. 152 *recto* to 155 *verso*, enclosed with letter from Barrow to Shee 7 May 1832, *ibid.*, fols. 148 *recto* to 148 *verso*.

Vernet's brother Emilio, who left Port Louis on 26 March 1831 in the British brigantine *Elbe*, chartered by Vernet (PLSR entry 90), which sailed with a cargo for sale and with Mathew Brisbane also aboard, plus two gauchos. Emilio had been at Port Louis since June 1826, and had run the settlement during Louis's long absences, but he was now leaving for good, and was about to perform some important errands. On 13 April the *Elbe* arrived at Montevideo, where the port register records Brisbane as landing with 2 gauchos, but Emilio Vernet travelled on to Buenos Aires,[1] where he presented a letter dated 19 March from Louis Vernet to British Consul-General Woodbine Parish claiming that Parish owed him 250 pesos for rescuing Brisbane's men back in 1829 (sections 5.12, 5.13).[2] Parish replied to Vernet on 10 May 1831, clearly surprised by the request for 250 pesos – he said he would forward the request to Britain, but could not advance any money.[3]

Some kind of original of Vernet's "Advertisement" was sent by Rear Admiral Sir Thomas Baker to the Admiralty in London a year later in March 1832, though only a copy of that original has survived. How Baker received the document is unrecorded – it may be that Emilio Vernet gave a copy to Woodbine Parish, who sent it to Baker, but the records are silent. Its first part begins:

> The Owner of the East Falkland Island, who has formed a settlement there in 1826 at the head of Berkley sound, hereby informs all Masters of Vessels bound round Cape Horn and the shipping in general, that said Sound is of the easiest access and affords the safest places for Vessels to lay and where they can fill their water with the greatest facility…

Vernet's description of himself as "The Owner of the East Falkland Island" must have raised a few eyebrows in London. He goes on to say that "Vessels may rely upon the most reasonable treatment on his part", and adds that "for more particulars they are referred to the following English Vessels, that have called in there to the middle of March last."

Then follows the second part, a list of 18 ships, with their captains, previous port of call, and purpose of voyage; the list is copied from the "Port Louis Shipping Record" (PLSR), but lists only the British ships, in the order of their first visits, beginning with the *Star* in June 1826 (PLSR entry 1) and ending with the *Tula* in November 1830 (entry 78); all the 18 British ships that called in that time are listed except the *Elbe* (perhaps because she was listed in PLSR as "belonging to this Expe[ditio]^n"), and the list does not include the British cutter *Rose*, which arrived on 13 April 1831 after Emilio had left (entry 93). In that time there had also been 17 American ships, 5 French, 4 from Buenos Aires and 1 Swedish, but only the British ships are listed. In other words, Vernet was treating the British ships as "multipliers" to spread his message – he regarded them as allies. He favoured the British both as mariners and settlers, and clearly had no objection to their sealing in the islands – there were 7 British sealing ships among the 18, and he would otherwise hardly have used them as vehicles to advertise his settlement. That is more evidence of his pro-British preference.

The third part of the "Advertisement", the sailing directions for Berkeley Sound and Port William, dated "Montevideo 2 September 1831", was written by William Low, who had been at Port Louis in May 1831 – he is recorded in PLSR, entry 97, as arriving on 25 May in the "Adeona Brig of Liverpool" from "The Andes" (a likely story!), and his activity is given as "sealing"; he left for Montevideo on an unstated date.[4] We therefore presume, though without proof, that it was at Port Louis in May/June 1831 that Vernet asked Low to write the sailing directions.

The peregrinations of the "Advertisement" can be partly reconstructed: it did not leave South America until after 2 September 1831, the date of Low's sailing directions; it would seem unlikely that Louis Vernet's original handwritten text came into the hands of the British official who sent it

---

[1] Dates of the *Elbe*'s movements from Montevideo port records, in the Archivo General de la Nación, Montevideo, Uruguay, Capitanía del Puerto, "Entrada y Salida de Buques de Ultramar 1829-1835" ["Port Authority, 'Entry and Departure of Foreign Vessels'"], Libro 546 (henceforth "AGNM 546"), entry 177.
[2] Vernet to Parish 19 March 1831, in AGN VII, 129, doc. 88 (draft).
[3] Parish to Vernet 10 May 1831, in AGN VII, 129, doc. 93.
[4] It was also around that time that he left the *Adeona* and became part-owner of the *Unicorn*, which was later bought by Robert FitzRoy, renamed *Adventure*, and took part in Charles Darwin's famous voyage; Low and some of his crew remained at Port Louis, where they narrowly avoided being murdered in August 1833 (section 5.32), while the ship was engaged on some important surveying work around the South Atlantic including the Falklands.

to London, so there were evidently other versions, apparently printed ones, since Admiralty Secretary Barrow says in his covering letter of 7 May 1832 to the Foreign Office that it had been "published" by Vernet, which suggests that the Admiralty copyist was working from a printed example. No such example survives, and nothing came of the "Advertisement" since Vernet changed his policy, but the chance survival of its contents shows what might have been, if he had pursued a peaceful instead of an aggressive line.

6.2 Emilio Vernet's movements; more people for Port Louis

Emilio Vernet's movements can be reconstructed from letters, port records, and from his financial accounts: after visiting Woodbine Parish, he took passage in the River Plate packet *Flor del Rio* back to Montevideo, where he made a statement of accounts dated 24 June 1831, in English, listing payments made by Messrs Stanley Black & Co., the Vernets' Montevideo agents, for the settlement at Port Louis, and for him and Mathew Brisbane personally.[1] The accounts show that the Vernet brothers were in debt to Black & Co. to the tune of 14,390.7½ pesos, i.e. £2,398 sterling at the rate given (1 peso = 40 old pence, i.e. 3 shillings and fourpence or $^1/_6$ of a pound), while Emilio's own financial account shows a debt of 5814 pesos 3¾ reales (about £969 sterling). The Vernet brothers were thus indebted by a total of some 20,204 pesos or about £3,367 sterling. Those were large sums – they should be multiplied by around 100 to obtain a rough modern equivalent.

Emilio's next task was to recruit people for the settlement at Port Louis, and the accounts record payments he made at Montevideo to that end. On 18 June 1831 he paid 35 pesos 5 reales for "Passport for 28 Passeng^{rs} to the Falkl^d Islands", and entries in his own accounts record "Passport for Gauchos and women for Faklds" (35 pesos 6 reales), and "Advances to 23 Gauchos & sundry women engaged for the Falklands" (416 pesos 2 reales).[2] There would thus appear to have been 23 men and 5 women who were paid for. They went to the Falklands aboard the *Elbe*, which was still under charter to Louis Vernet, so we call them "the *Elbe* group".

Among the *Elbe* group were five Charrúa Indians. The Charrúas were a tribe who lived in and around Uruguay until a campaign of genocide against them was launched in the 1820s and 30s by Uruguayan leaders. Large numbers were killed in battle or murdered, and the survivors were marched to imprisonment or slavery in Montevideo, where few survived.[3] Some of them, though, were released by the Uruguayan government at the request of various interested people, who took them as servants or slaves.[4] The genocide put an end to the Charrúas as a cultural entity; any groups or individuals who survived the massacres died without trace. Their language has entirely died out, and there are said to be no living people of pure Charrúa descent. The five Charrúas who were taken to Port Louis were the only people who remained loyal to the murderer Antonio Rivero in 1833 – they had nothing to lose, since their land had been taken and their families butchered.

On 26 June 1831 the *Elbe* left Montevideo for the Falklands (AGNM 546, entry 177) under her new captain John Burt, without Emilio Vernet but with Mathew Brisbane aboard again, plus the new people for the settlement, who seem to have included the following 18 individuals:

---

[1] Twelve-page financial accounts entirely in English, a copy made in July 1841, perhaps by a clerk at Messrs Black & Co. of Montevideo, in AGN VII, 127, doc. 33, fols. 57 *recto* to 71 *verso*, in two parts: (1) Messrs Black's account from 31 October 1826 to January 1 1833, dated Montevideo 31 December 1832; (2) Emilio Vernet's account dated "Montevideo 24th June 1831 / Emilio Vernet". Emilio's journey from Buenos Aires to Montevideo is on fol. 71 *recto*: 13 pesos 4 reales for "My Passage p^{er} Flor del Rio from B^s A^s to Mont^o".

[2] Details from Louis Vernet's accounts 1841, fol. 58 *verso*, and Emilio Vernet's accounts 1831, fol. 71 *verso*.

[3] Account here mostly from Eduardo F. Acosta y Lara, *La Guerra de Los Charrúas*, Montevideo 1969-70.

[4] Acosta y Lara 1969-70, part II, pp. 60-61, 71. In 1832 and 1833 some Charrúas were taken to France, including four taken by a former officer, François de Curel, who was permitted by the Uruguayan government to take them, ostensibly because of their interest in science. They were Senaca, Vaimaca-Piru, and a young couple called Tacuabé and Guyunusa; Guyunusa was also pregnant. They were taken to Paris and put on show as a kind of circus exhibit, but they did not survive long. Guyunusa gave birth to a baby daughter, but by the end of 1834 all the Charrúas taken to France were dead. There is a statue of four of them in Montevideo, including Guyunusa and her baby, entitled "Los Últimos Charrúas" ["The last Charrúas"]. In 2002 the French government returned the remains of Vaimaca to Uruguay for burial in the Uruguayan National Pantheon. The two Charrúas known as "Luciano Flores" and "Manuel González", the last survivors of the five taken to Port Louis in July 1831, were released at Montevideo in October 1835 after being taken to Britain and back (section 6.30). They were among the very last members of the Charrúa nation.

(a) the eleven gauchos Joaquín Acuña, José Báez, Juan Brasido, Manuel Coronel, Mateo González, Mariano López, Telésforo Moreno, Sylvestre Núñez, Manuel Ruiz, Pedro Salinas and Domingo Valleja;[1]

(b) five Charrúa Indians known by the Spanish names "Luciano Flores", "Manuel Godoy", "Manuel González", "Latorre" and "Felipe Salazar" (their original Charrúa names are unrecorded); and

(c) two women, Juana and Marica (whose surnames are unrecorded).

All were new to the islands except Manuel Coronel, who had been one of the original gauchos who landed with Vernet in June 1826, but he had left aboard the *Idris* on 19 June 1827 and was now returning. He remained in the islands well into the British period; by the late 1830s he was the capataz (head gaucho), and died at Port Louis on 5 November 1841.[2] In addition to those 18 nameable individuals there may perhaps have been 10 others who went to the Falklands aboard the *Elbe* (there were passports for 28 people), but there is no record of them, so they may never have gone at all. In any case all the unnamed 10 (if there were any) left again before January 1833, either aboard one of the last ships recorded in PLSR or in one of 9 ships that visited Port Louis in 1832.[3]

The *Elbe* arrived at Port Louis on 15 July 1831 (PLSR entry 98), with the "*Elbe* group" of at least 18, possibly up to 28 more people. Emilio Vernet no doubt thought the Charrúa Indians looked promising as workers, and a later visitor, G. T. Whitington, described them as "very powerfully made men".[4] But what awaited them at Port Louis was unexpected. Colonel Belford Hinton Wilson, in his report on Port Louis in January 1833, says "they live peaceably and do nothing",[5] and Whitington also says "They were employed making lassos for the gauchos", implying that they were made to do menial tasks for the gauchos and hence that they were regarded as inferior to the "proper" gauchos. That is supported by a much-altered draft letter from Louis Vernet to Thomas Helsby dated 16 May 1834,[6] in which he makes it clear that the Charrúas had been forbidden to ride horses, though they were of course fine horsemen. That converted them from useful workers into useless mouths to feed, so why were they not allowed to ride? We can only presume it was because the "proper" gauchos were prejudiced against them – the gauchos wanted to reserve gaucho work for gauchos, and in their view the Indians were not gauchos. Racism was clearly involved too; whites looked down on non-whites and regarded them as inferior. The Indians were unhappy with their situation – Robert FitzRoy calls them "the discontented, downcast Indian prisoners".[7] The gauchos may also have feared exposure as slackers by contrast with them – under Lieutenant Henry Smith in 1834 a mere three gauchos plus a British seaman brought in over 200 cattle in a year (section 5.20), which makes the performance of the much larger number of gauchos under Vernet seem remarkably feeble. The arrival of those last gauchos, women and Charrúas aboard the *Elbe* brought the population of Port Louis to approximately 128, its highest-ever figure under Vernet.

The stage was now set for the Second Falklands Crisis. The arrival of the new people placed an immediate strain on resources at Port Louis. Houses had to be built or extended – on a later sketch-map of the settlement, Vernet noted: "The height of building was going on in 1831".[8] His accounts reveal that he was running seriously short of money, and his new plan of advertising the settlement

---

[1] Telésforo Moreno was an extremely violent man who terrified the other inhabitants and was murdered by Pedro Salinas and Mariano López in June 1832 (stated by Juan Simon in AGN VII, 130, docs. 62 and 238); Pedro Salinas was dismissed in 1833 and left the islands; Domingo Valleja died of illness on 15 June 1833 (details in the 1833 Port Louis Log, see section 6.31); Juan Brasido was murdered by Rivero's gang in 1833.

[2] Entry in the hand of Lieutenant John Tyssen in the Port Louis Settlement Log, in JCNA, Stanley, vol. H1.

[3] The visits of 9 ships to Port Louis from January to around September 1832 (on 11 visits; 2 ships visited twice) are mentioned in a statement dated Buenos Aires 30 January 1833, made by the 5 gauchos Joaquín Acuña, José Báez, Mateo González, Mariano López and Manuel Ruiz (English translation, in Vernet's hand, in AGN VII, 130, doc. 54); all except Báez had certainly, and Báez probably, returned to Buenos Aires in the *Sarandí*. See section 6.24.

[4] From article "A Visit to the Falkland Islands", in *The United Service Journal...*, London 1832, Part III, p. 312.

[5] Belford Hinton Wilson, report in PRO CO 78/1, fols. 211 *recto* to 212 *recto*.

[6] Draft letter in English dated 16 May 1834 from Louis Vernet to Thomas Helsby, with many crossings-out and alterations, in AGN VII, 133, docs. 409 and 408 (in that order).

[7] FitzRoy 1839, vol. II, p. 279.

[8] Map in his letter to the British commander-in-chief on the South American station, 22 December 1834, PRO Adm 1/43, no doc. no.

so as to attract more ships would take too long to produce results, so he took a fateful decision: he decided to monopolise the sealing trade in the islands and take it into his own hands.

A factor in his decision may well have been a scene he witnessed at Port Louis in early May 1831.[1] On 26 April the schooner *Colossus* of Boston (Captain Fales) had arrived, having had a very poor sealing season, with only 7 sealskins to show for a voyage of 10 months. Then on 7 May another American sealer, the *Breakwater* of Stonington, Connecticut (Captain Daniel Carew) also anchored at Port Louis, having had a bumper season, her hold full with 1,631 sealskins, worth about 8 US dollars each. The two captains arranged that the *Colossus* would take 1,000 skins from the *Breakwater* and return to the United States, freeing the *Breakwater* to carry on sealing. On 8 May the 1,000 skins were transferred to the *Colossus*, which left on 10 May for Boston. The *Breakwater* remained till 19 May, taking on stones for ballast and buying half a ton of bread and a bullock from Vernet, partly paying in kind with a barrel of molasses, 50 pounds of coffee and some clothing.[2]

In an account Vernet wrote about 6 years later,[3] he represented his part in the transaction as having "permitted" Carew to transfer his sealskins to the *Colossus*, but it is impossible to believe Carew asked for permission or saw himself as being in any way bound by what Vernet said. Vernet could not prevent the transfer, so he "permitted" it; it must have been galling for him to see what a profit the *Breakwater* had made taking sealskins from "his" islands and "his" Patagonian coast, so he became determined to reserve the resources of the area for himself.

But he had no ships, so he hit on the simple idea of taking ships as prizes. Simple perhaps, but it was fatal to his venture in the Falklands.

6.3 The Second Falklands Crisis, Part I: Vernet seizes three American ships

In late July 1831 Vernet began Part I of the Second Falklands Crisis by seizing three American sealing ships at gunpoint: the *Harriet* (Captain Gilbert Davison), the *Breakwater* (Captain Daniel Carew) and the *Superior* (Captain Stephen Congar). He took their crews prisoner, sold some of their cargo, and later sailed in the *Harriet* to Buenos Aires hoping that the prize court would declare her lawful prize and hence his property.

Vernet was told by a deserter (probably James Hamblet) that the *Harriet* was sealing in the islands and was anchored in Salvador Water (sometimes called Port Salvador) north-west of Port Louis, so on 29 July he gave Mathew Brisbane a slip of paper authorising him to detain "for examination" any vessel suspected of breaching the "sealing regulations" (which no country except Argentina accepted as valid).[4]

The next day Brisbane walked overland with an armed party to Salvador, where they found Davison ashore shooting geese. Brisbane ordered him and his six-man boat's crew at gunpoint to go to Port Louis; they all walked there overland, and Vernet told Davison that if it was found that he had been sealing in the islands, his ship would be sent to Buenos Aires as a prize. He then sent Brisbane back with the same armed party to bring the *Harriet* to Port Louis – the party consisted of the gauchos Sylvestre Núñez, Juan Brasido, Domingo Valleja, Dionisio Eredia and the Portuguese Jacinto Correa, and also the Charrúa Indian "Manuel González". They were merely an *ad hoc* party of men collected for the purpose; the impression given by Kohen and Rodríguez (p. 161), that Vernet employed the inhabitants on "military service" is nonsense (section 5.18). The armed party seized the ship, put most of the crew ashore to walk overland to Port Louis, and with four men Brisbane sailed the ship round to Port Louis and anchored around 3 August. He searched the ship and found the personal log of the *Breakwater*'s second mate Richard Coffin, who had moved to the *Harriet*. It revealed that both the *Breakwater* and the *Harriet* had been sealing in the islands, and

---

[1] The timing makes it impossible that Vernet was reacting to a change in the Buenos Aires fishing laws on 31 July 1831, which thereafter only applied to non-Argentinians (Tesler 1979, pp. 116-121).
[2] Account in this paragraph from the *Breakwater*'s captain's log (AGN VII, 139); from an account written in 1896 by one of the *Breakwater*'s crew, Daniel Lamb (by then in his 80s), printed in *Penguin News* 20 September 2013, p. 7 (for which see below); and the Port Louis Shipping Record ("PLSR"; AGN VII 129, doc. 61), entries 74, 95 and 96.
[3] Vernet's "Answers to a 1st Interrogatory", in AGN VII, 130, doc. 178.
[4] Unsigned draft of instructions to Brisbane 29 July 1831, AGN VII, 129, doc. 96.

from it Vernet wrote a summary of the ship's operations.[1] From then on, events came thick and fast.

A fortnight later Vernet seized the *Breakwater*. The activities of this ship and the circumstances of her seizure are well recorded, both in her captain's logbook, which was confiscated by Vernet;[2] in the log kept by her first mate Oliver York (part of which was later printed in the United States and caused outrage against Vernet's actions);[3] and in a memoir written 65 years later in 1896 by a crewman, Daniel Wightman Lamb (1809-1903), whose account was published in *Penguin News* in Stanley in 2013.[4] Captain Carew anchored in Salvador Water around 15 August looking for the *Harriet* – the two ships had been working together – but she was not there, so on 17 August he and second mate John Adair landed in a boat with some others and walked overland to Port Louis to see if the *Harriet* was there.

As recounted in section 6.2, Vernet had seen something of the activities of Captain Carew and the rich haul of sealskins he had obtained from what Vernet saw as "his" territory. So a rude surprise awaited Carew and his men when they arrived at Port Louis – Vernet arrested them and gave Brisbane written instructions to seize the ship and to put most of her crew on an island in Salvador Water with supplies and bedding, leaving one or two men aboard.[5] So Brisbane went overland to Salvador, with a different armed party, found Carew's boat and sailed it to the *Breakwater*. They captured the ship and Brisbane removed the crew except for first mate Oliver York and crewmen Tom Kennedy and Matthew Flores. Brisbane gave York a certificate stating that he had "taken by force of arms" the ship, her papers and the captain's logbook. That certificate was printed in the Philadelphia *United States Gazette* on 1 November, and amounted to an admission of piracy against US vessels. Brisbane walked back to Port Louis with some of his armed men; the *Breakwater* was left at anchor in Salvador Water with York, Kennedy and Flores aboard, guarded by some of Brisbane's men, while most of her crew spent that night in a tent on a nearby island.

Hardly had Captain Carew and his boat's crew been arrested at Port Louis than some of the *Belleville* men arrived there. There were now about ten men in the group, and since June 1831 they had been on Eagle Island building their third shallop, of 20-30 tons, which they named *Eagle* (section 5.19). In mid-August five of them (the four Americans Isaac Waldron, William Smyley, John Jones and William Davenport, and the Englishman George Lambert) sailed round to Port Louis in a small boat looking for supplies. They arrived around 17 August – and Vernet arrested them and locked them up for five weeks till about 20 September, accusing them of "illegal" sealing.[6] It was illegal only in Argentine law, of course; no other country saw it as illegal.

Then on 19 August 1831 the schooner *Superior* arrived (PLSR entry 100), commanded by Stephen Congar. He was taken prisoner and the *Superior* was seized by another armed party led by Brisbane. Vernet now held three American sealing ships, the *Harriet* and *Superior* at Port Louis and the *Breakwater* in Salvador Water, plus some of the crew of a fourth (the five *Belleville* men). Kohen and Rodríguez mention the seizure of the *Harriet*, *Breakwater* and *Superior* (p. 176), but like all Argentine authors they say nothing about the *Belleville* men; instead they follow the absurdly untrue story about the "Águila", as they call the *Belleville* men's ship.

The first reaction of all the men Vernet arrested must have been speechless amazement. Vernet had traded with them and had permitted them to carry on their activities; he had given them copies of his circular warning them not to kill seals in the islands, but they knew he could neither stop them from sealing nor exploit the seals himself, so they thought it was just a matter of form. His behaviour towards the Americans was illogical – he wanted them to buy supplies from his

---

[1] Summary of the *Harriet*'s movements, in Vernet's hand, in AGN VII, 136, fols. 25 *recto* to 26 *recto*, headed "An Abridged statement of the operations of the schooner Harriet...", taken from the personal log of Richard Coffin; some *Harriet* crewmen added corrections on fols. 26 *verso* to 28 *verso*.
[2] The *Breakwater*'s captain's log is in AGN VII, 139.
[3] Extract from log printed in the *United States Gazette*, Philadelphia 1 November 1831.
[4] "History of A Sealing Voyage / On board the Schooner / *Breakwater* of Stonington / Connecticut in the year AD / 1830 and 31: by Daniel W Lamb", printed in *Penguin News*, Stanley, under the heading "A Sealing Voyage to the Falklands", in three parts, on 13, 20 and 27 September 2013.
[5] Unsigned letter to Brisbane in AGN VII, 129, doc. 116.
[6] Details from the *Belleville* affidavits (AGN VII, 136, fols. 59-64), and Vernet's contract with the *Belleville* men.

settlement, but he was trying to stop them from taking seals, which was why they were there in the first place. He was not motivated by any concern to protect wildlife (that notion lay far in the future) – he wanted the seals to be killed, but by his own men, not by the Americans.

Almost at once, Vernet's plans began to come unstuck. Aboard the *Breakwater* in Salvador Water around midnight on 20-21 August, Oliver York surprised the guard on deck, locked him and the other guards below decks, and sent Flores and Kennedy in a boat to collect the rest of the crew from the island. They all returned to the ship; York released the guards, put them ashore and sailed the ship out of Salvador Water early on 21 August. After dawn the guards walked across to Port Louis and sheepishly reported to Vernet what had happened.

As soon as he had got safely away, York headed south-west for Statenland to rescue seven crewmen of the *Superior* who had been left there in March 1831 to kill seals – he knew they were there, as the *Breakwater* and *Superior* had been working in company. He found them on 15 September; they put a note in a bottle under a cairn of stones for their captain, Stephen Congar (not knowing he had been arrested),[1] then York took them aboard and sailed the *Breakwater* back to her home port of Stonington, Connecticut, arriving around 23 October 1831. The news of the seizure of the ship caused outrage in the United States (section 6.10), and the Americans were particularly infuriated by the fact that Vernet seized only American ships, leaving British ones unmolested.

6.4 Britain's warning to Vernet not to molest British ships

Kohen and Rodríguez (p. 174) take us to task for saying in *Getting it right* (p. 15) that Britain had warned Vernet not to seize any British ships, and they complain that we give no proof of that. So here is the proof: Mathew Brisbane visited Woodbine Parish in Buenos Aires in November 1830, and showed him Vernet's warning circular. Parish reported to London:[2]

Upon seeing the Notice signed by Vernet, I thought it right to… acquaint him [i.e. Brisbane] with the Protest I had been instructed to enter here against the Decree of the Buenos Ayrean Government of June 1829, and I desired him as he was about to return immediately to the Falklands to communicate the tenor of it to Mr Vernet as a warning against his interfering with any of His Majesty's Subjects frequenting those Coasts:– Mr Brisbane promised me he would take care that my caution should be attended to;– that the truth was, the Notice was more intended to draw Vessels to Soledad for Supplies, than to hinder their coming there, which in fact they had no means whatever at their disposal to prevent.

In other words, Brisbane assured Parish that his warning would be heeded, and that there would be no "interfering with any of His Majesty's Subjects frequenting those Coasts".

Kohen and Rodríguez then make the absurd assertion that British ships had been instructed by the British government (!) not to seal in the islands. They say (pp. 174-5) that Vernet announced that British ships respected his prohibition against sealing because "they had been warned to do so by authorities in London", and they even add that there was no reaction from the British representative in Buenos Aires to Vernet's "public assertion that the owners of the British vessels received orders from London to respect the settlers and the prohibition on hunting in the islands."

All that is nonsense – Kohen and Rodríguez have misunderstood their source, which was a statement by Vernet in English in a proclamation he issued on 3 May 1832. What he said was:[3]

… the British brig Tula, Captain Biscoe, and the Lively, from London, touched at the Falklands in November 1830; the cutter Rose, Capt. Davis, also from London, in April 1831. The Masters of these three vessels were ex-pressly enjoined, on their sailing from England, to respect the Colonists, and not to seal on the Islands.

The text means of course that the masters of the three vessels were ordered *by Vernet himself* that when they *next* sailed from England, they were to respect the colonists and not seal in the islands. The idea that "authorities in London" could have warned British ships not to seal in British territory

---

[1] It was found, not by Congar but by Captain Oliver Keating, now of the sealing schooner *Dash*, around February 1832; Keating sent it from Valparaíso on 1 June 1832 to Silas Duncan, who sent it to US Navy Secretary Levi Woodbury on 16 January 1833. Text in US National Archives, Washington DC, Naval Record Group 45, M147, microfilm 18.
[2] Parish to Lord Aberdeen 20 November 1830, in PRO FO 6 499, fols. 41 *verso* to 42 *recto*.
[3] Proclamation in English, headed "To the Public", dated 3 May 1832, illustrated in Muñoz Azpiri 1966, vol. III, p. 61, given by Kohen and Rodríguez as their source on their p. 175, fn. 131.

is ludicrous, and once again reveals the unrealistic conception of many Argentine authors (including Kohen and Rodríguez) of the plain facts. The fact is that Parish warned Brisbane that there was to be no interference with British ships, and Brisbane said the warning would be heeded – Vernet was well aware that he was not to interfere with British ships.

Kohen and Rodríguez quote (p. 175, fn. 132) a passage from Vernet's "Report" in which he says that at the time of the seizure of the *Breakwater*, *Harriet* and *Superior* there was no British ship sealing in the islands, so that he would have had no opportunity to seize them; he says he had the logbooks of the *Harriet*, *Breakwater* and *Superior*, and other documents, that say there was no British ship sealing in the islands from 1829,[1] but their testimony is not conclusive, since the islands are far too large for anyone to have known what ships were there at any given time. In fact there may well have been British ships sealing there, but Vernet knew nothing about them; his own record of ships (PLSR) was limited to Port Louis.

6.5 Vernet's illegal contract with Captains Congar and Davison

On 8 September 1831 Vernet did a bizarre deal with Captains Congar and Davison, who signed a contract under which the *Superior* was to go sealing under Vernet's orders while the *Harriet* went to Buenos Aires for adjudication by the prize court. The fate of both ships was to be bound by the court's judgement: the profits would go to Vernet if the ships were condemned for sealing in the Falklands, but to the owners of the two vessels if they were not condemned.[2] Kohen and Rodríguez briefly mention this contract (p. 176), without further comment, but it was of course entirely illegal in international law, so we call it Vernet's "illegal contract". Its illegality was different from what Vernet (and Argentina) claimed was "illegal" sealing by British and American ships – that was illegal only in Argentine national law, but Vernet's contract with Congar and Davison was illegal in international law. No laws or practices permitted the commercial use of a captured civilian vessel in peacetime without prior court adjudication, as the *Harriet*'s owner Silas Burrows reminded Vernet's American agent Lewis Krumbhaar in a letter on 14 September 1832 (section 6.13). Failure to comply with the legal norms made the perpetrator guilty of piracy.

Captain Silas Duncan of the USS *Lexington* described the contract acidly in his report to the US consul in Buenos Aires, George Slacum, on 2 February 1832:[3]

Vernet and Brisbane… had not the means of fishing, themselves, but their plan was to fish by proxy; and, whilst they laid claim to all the fish in the Southern Ocean, they were to compel our citizens to catch them for their use.

Vernet disregarded the legal regulations, stole some of the *Harriet*'s cargo and 989 sealskins from the *Superior* (which he said were "deposited as security"), entered into private commercial relations with the ships' captains, and sent the *Superior* to collect profits for himself. If his plans had worked out, he would have become the owner of the *Harriet* and *Superior*, but he was reckoning without his victims – the sealing captains, the American sealing ports, and the United States government, whose commercial interests he harmed and whose citizens he imprisoned and coerced without authority. Kohen and Rodríguez fail to note that Vernet's actions were illegal under the international law of that time, so their account of the legal position is defective.

6.6 The United States Supreme Court rules that Vernet's seizures were illegal

The seizure of the three American ships eventually resulted in a court case in the United States brought in 1837 by Charles L. Williams, a part-owner of the *Harriet* and the *Breakwater*, on behalf of the owners of the ships against the Suffolk Insurance Co. of Boston, Massachusetts.[4] The insurers claimed the seizures were lawful and that Captain Davison of the *Harriet* had been negligent in failing to heed Vernet's warnings (thus relieving the insurers of having to pay), but the shipowners claimed that since the United States did not recognise Argentine sovereignty, the islands were

---

[1] Kohen and Rodríguez p. 175, fn. 132, quoting Vernet's "Report" from *BFSP* 1832-1833, p. 388 (Perl 1983, p. 230).
[2] Text of contract in Manning 1932, vol. I, fn. pp. 68-69; also in Vernet's "Report 1832".
[3] Duncan to Slacum 2 February 1832, in Manning 1932, pp. 93-94, fn.; "fishing" meant sealing.
[4] Statement by Theophilus Parsons (counsel for Suffolk Insurance Co.), 7 October 1837, AGN VII 130, doc. 153.

international waters and Vernet's warnings were without force, so Davison was not bound to heed them and the seizures were unlawful. The judges referred the case to the US Supreme Court, where it was heard in January 1839. The Supreme Court upheld the authority of the US government to decide questions of territorial recognition, and therefore held that in US law the Falklands were not part of the "dominions within the sovereignty of Buenos Aires"; Buenos Aires had no "competency to regulate, prohibit, or punish" any activities in the islands, so Davison was not bound to respect Vernet's warnings. The Supreme Court thus ruled that in US law Vernet's actions had been illegal;[1] he had seized US ships on the high seas and had taken some of the *Harriet*'s cargo for himself, so in US law he had operated as a pirate, for which statutes of 1790 and 1820 had imposed the death penalty.[2] But by 1839 the case had become irrelevant, so nothing came of it. See also section 6.39.

6.7 The *Superior* sails; Vernet's contract with the *Belleville* men

On 15 September 1831 Captain Stephen Congar left Port Louis in the *Superior* (PLSR entry 100) to go sealing under Vernet's illegal contract, carrying "Maria of Magellan", an important leader of the Patagonian Indians, who had been a guest of the Vernet family for six months and was now landed by Congar at the Magellan Strait at her request. Kohen and Rodríguez (p. 162) mention her stay with Vernet; they call her "the Queen of the Strait" ("la Reina del Estrecho"), though in his "Memoirs", written in English (section 4.9), Louis Vernet calls her "Maria of Magellan".[3] Congar then fulfilled his contract with Vernet, and returned to Port Louis around April 1832 with sealskins worth US$8,500. But Vernet had gone and there was no one literate there, so he did not land the skins – there would have been no proof that he had done so and he would have returned home with an empty ship. So he took his cargo back to New York, arriving in early June (section 6.13).[4]

On 20 September 1831, five days after the *Superior* left, Vernet continued his plan of setting up his own sealing fleet, and released the five *Belleville* men he had imprisoned for five weeks (section 5.19) – he now had a use for them. He drew up a contract, which four of them signed: Isaac Waldron, John Jones, William Smyley and George Lambert. It laid down that together with the other *Belleville* men on Eagle Island, they were to finish their shallop (later named *Eagle*), and they were to hand over as security the sealskins which they had acquired.[5] They would then seal the Falklands in the shallop for Vernet's profit; they were to hand a copy of his circular to any ship's captain found sealing and warn him that he risked "losing his vessel". If they caught him sealing again and the ship was condemned as a prize, they were to have half the proceeds. Under Article 3 of the contract the shallop was to be "under the flag of the Republic of Buenos Ayres, with regular papers from the authority on these islands"; under Article 4 Vernet would in June 1832 buy her and her equipment for 670 silver dollars (pesos), and the men would then be free. Article 2 lists some supplies Vernet gave them, including provisions and a spar for a foremast, and also a pistol, "one bag of Shot, one Keg of Powder, six dozen musket & pistol flints, some percussion caps" – if they were to stop American ships, they had to be armed!

But it was absurd to expect ten Americans to prevent other American sealing crews from pursuing their livelihood. Vernet took from them "as security" 198 sealskins and over a ton (2744 pounds) of whalebone, and the four men sailed back to Eagle Island to work on the shallop. Under Article 5 they were to go to Port Louis in the finished shallop on or before 1 December 1831. They did so, but they were in for a surprise (section 6.12).

---

[1] Richard Peters [ed.], *Reports of Cases Argued and Adjudged in the Supreme Court of the United States. January term, 1839...*, vol. 38 ("Peters 13"): case of Charles L. Williams *versus* The Suffolk Insurance Company, summary of whole case p. 415; summary of judgement in *ibid.*, p. 422.

[2] [Anon.], *Revised Statutes of the United States..., 1873-'74...*, 2nd ed., Washington DC, 1878, p. 1042.

[3] Vernet's account of "Maria of Magellan" is in his "Memoirs", pp. 83-89.

[4] Date of arrival in New York from letter to Vernet from his US agent Lewis Krumbhaar, 20 October 1832, AGN VII, 130, doc. 40; other details in Krumbhaar to Burrows, 10 September 1832, AGN VII, 132, doc. 146.

[5] Full text in Manning 1932, vol. 1, fn. pp. 94-96; it was enclosed in Duncan to Slacum 2 February 1832, and then enclosed in Slacum to Livingston 20 March 1832; not in *Colección* 1832 or *BFSP 1832-1833*. The shallop's crew (i.e. the *Belleville* men) are listed in Vernet's keeping-copy of his commission for the ship, AGN VII, 136, fol. 77 *recto* (our fig. 5.19a); inferior copy in AGN VII, 131, doc. 185.

6.8 Vernet's land-contract with William Langdon; Vernet's English map

6.8a What the Argentinians don't mention: Vernet's English map, "East Falkland-Island 1831", labelled in English. Like the Spanish map (above, fig. 5.10a), it silently omits part of West Falkland at top left. (AGN VII, 134, doc. 21)

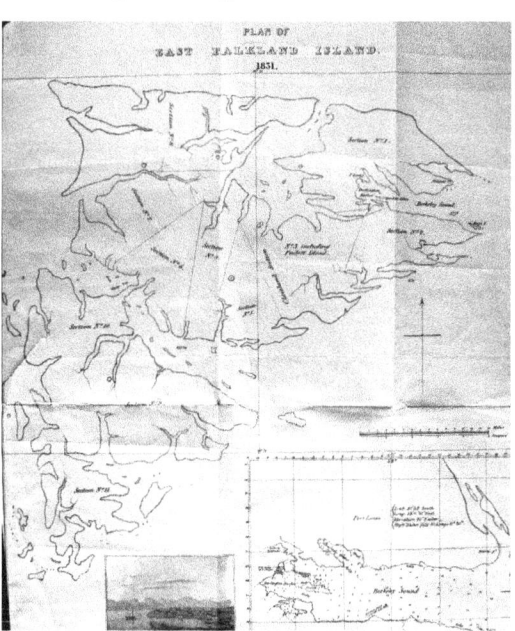

6.8b "Plan of East Falkland Island 1831" in George Whitington's prospectus, 1834, based on Vernet's map of "East Falkland-Island 1831"; Langdon's Berkeley Sound chart is at bottom right. (PRO CO 78/2, fol. 120 *recto*)

In October 1831 the retired Royal Navy lieutenant William Langdon (section 5.4) paid his second visit to the Falklands in his ship *Thomas Lawrie*, with the London merchant George Thomas Whitington as a passenger. Vernet entertained them to dinner in his house on 23 October[1] and interested them in the potential of the islands; they arranged that when Langdon got home he would recruit British settlers. At this time Vernet also made another map of East Falkland – Kohen and Rodríguez illustrate (p. 152) his earlier map labelled in Spanish (above, fig. 5.10a), but like other Argentine authors they suppress the fact that he later made another map labelled in English, entitled "East Falkland-Island 1831" (fig. 6.8a); we call it his "English map". They cannot have been unaware of it, since it is in the same folder as the Spanish map in the AGN, but they chose not to mention it since it gave clear evidence of Vernet's dealings with the British.

On 29 October, nine days before he himself left the islands, Vernet granted Langdon "Section "Nº 3" on the English map, running from Salvador Water down to where Fitzroy now stands (previously sections II, IV and V of the Spanish map), and wrote Langdon a 16-page land-grant contract, entitling him to sell land to settlers in his own section and/or in other sections. In a covering letter he granted Langdon ten square miles "as your property for ever", plus a third of all proceeds of land sales made before 1 January 1833 and a quarter of the proceeds of land sales made after that date.[2] He gave Langdon a copy of the English map, and Langdon made a chart of Berkeley Sound, of which a copy was later in the hands of Captain Francis Mason of the frigate HMS *Blonde*, which visited Port Louis from 15 to 20 July 1834.[3] George Whitington too received copies of Vernet's English map and Langdon's chart of Berkeley Sound, and had them printed in London in August 1834, in a prospectus he issued for potential settlers in the Falklands (fig. 6.8b).

---

[1] Details from article "A Visit to the Falkland Islands", anonymous but clearly by G. T. Whitington, in *The United Service Journal...*, London 1832, Part III, p. 310.

[2] Vernet's keeping-copy of Langdon's land-grant contract is in AGN VII, 129, doc. 120, following the covering letter. Langdon showed the covering letter and the contract to the British Foreign Office – a copy of his own covering letter of 20 January 1832 to the Foreign Office is in PRO FO 6 499, fols. 102 *recto* to 103 *recto*, which is followed by scribal copies of both Vernet's covering letter to him and the land-grant contract, in the hand of a Foreign Office clerk; Vernet's covering letter is fols. 104 *recto* to 107 *verso*, and the land-grant contract fols. 108 *recto* to 138 *recto*.

[3] Captain's log of HMS *Blonde*, PRO Adm 51/3063, 15 July 1834: "The only Chart we had of the Sound I got from Lieut Langdon". Captain Mason was not impressed by the chart's accuracy.

Kohen and Rodríguez (p. 168) briefly mention Langdon's visit and his comment that Vernet would raise "no objection" to the occupation of the islands by Britain (section 5.7), and they also state that Langdon failed to obtain recognition of his land-grant from the British government. That is true of course – the British government could hardly recognise the legality of a document issued on what they regarded as British territory by someone acting without British authority.

As we pointed out in section 1.7, Kohen and Rodríguez criticise us (p. 46) for saying in *Getting it right* (p. 8) that Britain had the right to settle anywhere in the islands as soon as Vernet purported to sell land to the south of Port Louis, since the secret article in the Nootka Sound Convention of 1790 entitled Britain to set up an "Establishment" south of places occupied by Spain if "the Subjects of any other Power" had done so. Kohen and Rodríguez assert that Vernet was simply continuing Spain's rights and thus did not count as a "subject of another power". Whether the Nootka Sound Convention was still in full force is debatable, and whether the Vernet operation was under the auspices of a successor state to Spain is debatable too. But what is not debatable is that if Argentina were a successor state, as Kohen and Rodriguez claim, it inherited Spain's obligations as well as rights. That would mean that Vernet's activities violated Britain's rights under Article 6 of the Convention. But if Argentina was not a successor state to Spain, that would make Vernet a "subject of another power" and by purporting to sell land to the south of Port Louis he would have activated the secret article in the Convention.

What Kohen and Rodríguez do not mention is that the meeting between Vernet and Langdon led to the arrival of the ancestors of some of today's Falkland Islanders. Langdon decided not to settle in the Falklands; he wrote to Vernet on 4 December 1833 announcing that he wished to pass his land concession to George Whitington,[1] and on 31 May 1834 Vernet wrote accepting the arrangement.[2] In the end G. T. Whitington's younger brother John Bull Whitington settled in the islands, with his servants James and Mary Watson, who arrived at Port Louis on 17 November 1840. The Watsons soon had three children; their descendants have lived in the islands ever since, and the family now includes 7th-generation Falkland Islanders. They held a party in Stanley on 17 November 2015 (the 175th anniversary of the family's arrival), attended by several dozen descendants of James and Mary Watson, hosted by Dave and Carol Eynon (née Watson).[3] The presence of those people in the Falklands is a result of arrangements made by Louis Vernet.

6.9 Vernet leaves the Falklands; he appoints William Smyley

Louis Vernet had decided to go to Buenos Aires in the seized *Harriet*, expecting (rightly) that the prize court would declare her his property. In early November 1831 the ship was loaded with cargo, including the ton of whalebone confiscated from the *Belleville* men, plus some of Vernet's possessions, including most of his archive of documents. Vernet appointed the American Henry Metcalf as settlement manager in his absence, and the Scot Mathew Brisbane as fisheries manager. And on 5 November 1831, four days after Langdon left in the *Thomas Lawrie* and two days before he himself left, Vernet wrote out a formal, official-looking document appointing William Smyley as "Branch Pilot" i.e. officially certified pilot, "for Port Louis, Port William and Choiseul Bay, and for all other ports Bays and waters under my Jurisdiction". That document is now one of the earliest documents in the Jane Cameron National Archives (JCNA) in Stanley (fig. 6.9a). Smyley was at that time on Eagle Island with the other *Belleville* men building their shallop, so the document was no doubt left at Port Louis for him to collect when he arrived in the shallop in December 1831, in fulfilment of the contract of 20 September (section 6.7).

On the same day Vernet drew up a list of 12 men who were to crew the *Harriet*, including her captain Gilbert Davison; in addition, Davison's clerk John Trumbull was aboard, plus John Gardner as a passenger, so there were 14 men in all. They were a scratch crew of men who happened to be at

---

[1] Langdon to Vernet 4 December 1833, in AGN VII 130, doc. 72; G. T. Whitington to Vernet 6 December 1833, in AGN VII 132, doc. 182.

[2] Vernet to G. T. Whitington 31 May 1834, keeping-copy in AGN VII 132, doc. 188.

[3] See article "175 years of Watsons" in *Penguin News* 20 November 2015, p. 3, with photo showing 29 descendants of James and Mary Watson (most with other surnames since the descent passed through daughters). See also editorial in *ibid.*, p. 2, by deputy editor Sharon Jaffray (who, like editor Lisa Watson, is descended from James and Mary Watson).

Port Louis, some of whom had been resident for some time; no members of the ship's original crew were aboard except Davison and Trumbull.[1] Most were Americans, including William Drake, but John Edmonds and Charles Brasier were British, Anton Vaihinger was German, and Antonio de Silveria was South American. Vernet also listed 15 passengers: himself, his wife, his four children, four unnamed black female slaves, and five named white male servants, making 29 people in all.[2]

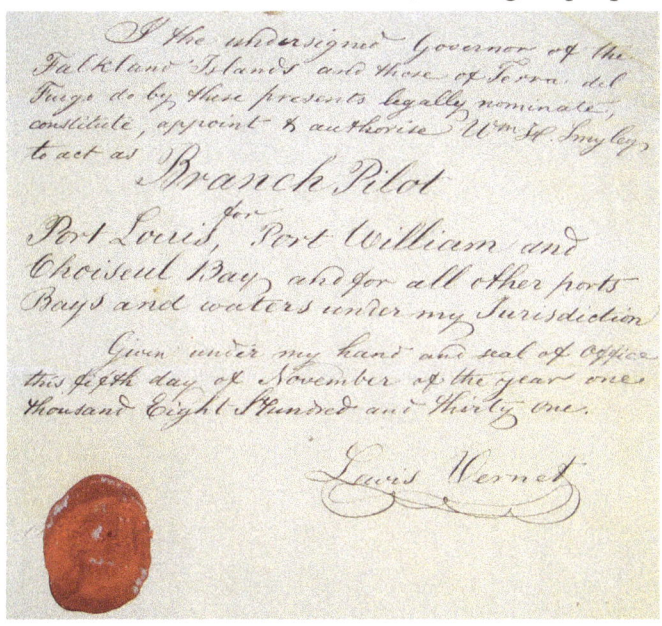

6.9a Louis Vernet appoints William Smyley, 5 November 1831. (JCNA)

The next day, 6 November, he drew up a commission for the *Belleville* men's shallop, calling her "Águila" ["Eagle"]. The extraordinary myths around this ship invented by Argentine writers were mentioned in section 5.19. The original of the commission was evidently left at Port Louis for her crew to sign, and Vernet made a keeping-copy for his own archives (fig. 5.19a). He himself never saw the ship, which was actually called *Eagle* after the island where she was built. He thought the *Superior* and the shallop would work for him while he was away, and that he would return to the islands as owner of the *Harriet* and *Superior*, and later become owner of the *Eagle* – he would possess a handsome sealing fleet. But he had lost touch with reality.

The *Harriet* sailed for Buenos Aires on Monday 7 November 1831 (PLSR entry 102), taking away over a quarter of the population of Port Louis – from mid-July 1831 there had been roughly 128 people there, the largest number ever, but in September the *Elbe* had taken just over a dozen away, leaving about 114-115, and after the 29 people departed aboard the *Harriet* there remained about 85 residents.

Louis Vernet never saw the Falkland Islands again.

6.10 The United States reacts to Vernet's seizures of American ships

Commanded by her first mate Oliver York, the schooner *Breakwater* arrived back at her home port of Stonington, Connecticut, on or around 23 October 1831 (the day when Langdon and Whitington had dinner with the Vernets at Port Louis). In its two editions of 29 October and 1 November the Philadelphia *United States Gazette* described the seizure of the ship and her recapture, and quoted a passage from York's logbook, plus the "certificate" Brisbane gave York stating that he had "by force of arms" taken possession of the ship and her papers, which amounted to an admission of piracy (section 6.3), since the US regarded the Falklands as international waters.[3]

---

[1] List of original crew, dated New London 9 August 1830, confiscated by Vernet, in AGN VII, 129, doc. 79.
[2] List in Vernet's hand, headed "Rol de Equipage De la Goleta Harriet de Stonington…", AGN VII, 129, no doc. no; payroll in AGN VII, 131, doc. 222.
[3] *The United States Gazette*, Philadelphia 1 November 1831, p. 1, cols. 5-6. Vernet's cutting in AGN VII, 129, doc. 105, and a handwritten copy in Vernet's hand, in AGN VII, 132, doc. 112, are both dated 29 October.

The *Breakwater*'s crew were paid salvage money for rescuing her from Vernet's clutches.[1]

The seizure of the ship drew an angry reaction from the United States government. President Andrew Jackson (President 1829-37) mentioned the affair in his State of the Union Address to the US Congress in Washington on 6 December 1831, in which he complained that:[2]

In the course of the present year one of our vessels, engaged in the pursuit of a trade which we have always enjoyed without molestation, has been captured by a band acting, as they pretend, under the authority of the Government of Buenos Ayres. I have therefore given orders for the dispatch of an armed vessel to join our squadron in those seas and aid in affording all lawful protection to our trade which shall be necessary…

So far Jackson only knew of one US ship seized by Vernet (the *Breakwater*), since the *Harriet* was at Buenos Aires and the *Superior* was still sealing in the Pacific. But he added that if more damage was done to US interests in the Falklands, a larger force might be sent.

Like other Argentine authors, Kohen and Rodríguez gloss over the American reaction; they say (p. 176) that "The American Consul Georges [sic] Slacum interceded in favour of the American hunters and denied any authority for Vernet and the government of Buenos Aires to proceed as they did" – they suppress the fact that the US government itself expressed anger at Argentina's aggression and that it flatly denied that Vernet and the Argentine government had any authority in the islands. They say that Slacum's action began a dispute between Buenos Aires and Washington:

… whose crowning point was the destruction and pillage of public and private property and the arbitrary arrest of settlers at Puerto Luis, carried out by the American war corvette "Lexington"…

In fact the *Lexington* only destroyed weapons and took away some property belonging to Captain Davison that Vernet had taken from the *Harriet*, plus some chickens, barrel staves and iron bars, but nothing else of note, and the arrests were not arbitrary – Duncan arrested the seven men guilty of the seizure of the *Harriet*, but no others (section 6.12).

Kohen and Rodríguez exaggerate the damage but play down the seriousness of the dispute between Argentina and the US – on p. 176 they say that it "led to recalling diplomatic officials", omitting to mention that it caused the United States to break off diplomatic relations with Argentina for twelve years (1832-1844), owing to the Argentine government's refusal to negotiate on the dispute (section 6.15), and on p. 205 they even say "In 1833, Argentina did not break off diplomatic relations [i.e. with Britain], contrary to its actions in respect of the United States over the Lexington incident", which is the reverse of what happened – in 1832 it was the United States that broke off diplomatic relations with Argentina, not the other way round. Here yet again, the two authors distort the history of what happened. They also distort the legal situation – following their simplistic view of sovereignty, they write as if it was an established fact that the islands were Argentine territory, where Argentina could prosecute those who transgressed its laws. That is untrue; the status of the islands was unclear, and Argentina had no right to claim a monopoly of title or sovereignty.

Like Britain (from 1808) and later Spain (from 1845), the United States kept a squadron of ships in South American waters to protect its national interests. On 10 June 1831, before anything happened in the Falklands, US Navy Secretary Levi Woodbury had ordered Master Commandant Silas Duncan,[3] commanding the 24-gun corvette USS *Lexington*, to sail to Rio de Janeiro and await orders from the commander of the US South Atlantic squadron, "to protect the commerce and the citizens of the United States".[4] Duncan arrived at Rio on 17 October 1831, and on 31 October Master Commandant Benjamin Cooper arrived in the corvette USS *Warren* and took over as senior officer present. On 1 November Cooper gave Duncan orders to sail south to protect US interests:[5]

You will proceed with the U.S.S. Lexington under your command, to Monte Video and Buenos Ayres in the

---

[1] Note dated 7 October 1837 by Theophilus Parsons (counsel for the Suffolk insurance company), in AGN VII 130, doc. 153, on the payment of salvage money by the underwriters to the crew of the *Breakwater* for rescuing her from seizure.
[2] Text from *Messages and Papers of the Presidents*, ed. James D. Richardson, e-book version, 2008, p. 181.
[3] Silas Duncan (1788-1834) had a distinguished career in the US Navy; his rank, "Master Commandant", between captain and lieutenant, was later called commander. Master Commandants were addressed as "Captain".
[4] Text of orders in typescript on the USS *Duncan* website, www.ussduncan.org.
[5] US National Archives (USNA), Washington DC, Naval Record Group (NRG) 45, M147, microfilm 16.

Rio de la Plata… You will use the utmost vigilance, energy, and activity, consistent with the neutral character of our country, in protecting the rights & commerce of the United States in that quarter.

Those orders were issued before anything was known at Rio about Vernet's seizure of American ships, but the US government knew in general terms that American trade and rights in the South Atlantic needed protection. On 3 November 1831 Duncan left Rio for Buenos Aires.[1]

While the *Lexington* was still sailing south from Rio, the *Harriet* anchored at Buenos Aires on 20 November. Vernet disembarked with his family and released Captain Gilbert Davison and the crew, and the next day Davison went to the American consul, George Slacum, and told him what had happened in the Falklands. Slacum wrote to the Buenos Aires foreign minister, Tomás Manuel de Anchorena, saying he was "at a loss to conceive upon what possible ground a bona-fide American vessel, while engaged in a lawful trade, should be captured by an officer of a friendly Government".[2] Two days later on 23 November, at the US consulate, Davison made the first of six affidavits describing the seizure of the *Harriet*, *Breakwater* and *Superior*, and he gave Slacum a copy of Vernet's circular of October 1830 and of Vernet's illegal contract by which he sent the *Superior* sealing for his own profit. Slacum sent the documents to US Secretary of State Edward Livingston, with a letter saying he suspected Buenos Aires would avow Vernet's actions (i.e. take responsibility for them), and that he would then make a formal protest.[3]

Anchorena replied to Slacum on 25 November that "the business of the Schooner Harriet… will be laid before the Government…".[4] That was mere fobbing-off, but it also made clear that the matter would not be decided by a court but by the government, i.e. by General Juan Manuel de Rosas, governor of Buenos Aires province, who was the central figure in the wealthy landowning oligarchy which ruled the province and dominated the Argentine Confederation.

The next day Slacum made a formal protest to Anchorena on behalf of the United States government, saying that Anchorena's reply amounted to:[5]

… a virtual avowal… of the right of Mr. Lewis Vernet to capture and detain American Vessels engaged in the Fisheries at the Falkland Islands… It… only remains to him[6] to deny, *in toto*, any such right, as having been, or being now, vested in the Government of Buenos Ayres… and to add his most earnest remonstrance against… the Decree issued on the 10th of June, 1829, asserting a claim to the before-mentioned Islands and Coasts… The Undersigned… request[s] that His Excellency… will… receive this Communication as a formal Protest on the part of the Government of The United States against that of Buenos Ayres…

Anchorena did not answer for a week, during which Duncan arrived at Buenos Aires in the *Lexington* on 29 November 1831, to find the town buzzing with the news of the arrival of the seized *Harriet*. Duncan wrote to Slacum asking for details,[7] and on 30 November Slacum sent Duncan a copy of Davison's first affidavit and of Vernet's contract with the *Belleville* men.[8] Duncan replied the next day saying he had resolved to sail to the Falklands to protect US ships and citizens, and asking Slacum to send the Buenos Aires government a copy of his letter.

At the US consulate on 2 December Davison made his second affidavit, in which he said Vernet had remarked that *"he could not take an English Vessel with the same propriety that he could an*

---

[1] Sailing date of 3 November given in Duncan's despatch of 7 December 1831; date given as 4 November in Cooper's despatch of 12 November 1831, in USNA, NRG 45, M147, microfilm 16.
[2] Slacum to Anchorena, 21 November 1831; Spanish translation in *Colección* 1832, fol. 2 *verso*; English in *BFSP 1832-1833*, p. 313, and in Manning 1932, p. 65.
[3] Slacum to Livingston, 23 November 1831, in Manning 1932, pp. 66-70, with Davison's first affidavit and the contract of 8 September 1830 in enormous fns.; not in *Colección* or *BFSP*.
[4] Anchorena to Slacum, 25 November 1831; Spanish in *Colección* 1832, fol. 3 *recto*; English translation in *BFSP 1832-1833*, p. 314, and in Manning 1932, p. 70.
[5] Slacum to Anchorena, 26 November 1831; Spanish translation in *Colección* 1832, fol. 3 *verso*; English in *BFSP 1832-1833*, pp. 314-316 and in Manning 1932, pp. 71-72; text here from *BFSP*, reparagraphed.
[6] I.e. to Slacum himself, writing in the third person as "the Undersigned".
[7] Duncan to Slacum, 29 November 1831, in Manning 1932, pp. 76-77, fn.; not in *Colección* 1832 or *BFSP*.
[8] Slacum to Duncan, 30 November 1831, in Manning 1932, p. 77, fn.; not in *Colección* 1832 or *BFSP*.

American".[1] That infuriated the Americans; they knew he had not seized any British ships, and they did not feel that the British had better rights in the islands than they themselves. They would have been even more annoyed had they known that Mathew Brisbane had assured British consul Woodbine Parish in November 1830 that there would be no "interfering with any of His Majesty's Subjects frequenting those Coasts" (section 6.4).

On 3 December Anchorena replied to Slacum's protest of 26 November, stating that "the Government of the United States has no right to the said Islands and Coasts, nor to exercise the Fishery in them, seeing that it is unquestionable in this Republic".[2] Only Argentina believed that, of course; no other country accepted that Argentina had any sovereignty in the Falklands. Anchorena added imperiously that Slacum, as a mere consul, was not entitled to protest at a diplomatic level. Slacum had sent Anchorena a copy of Duncan's letter,[3] so there could be no doubt of Duncan's intention to go to the islands himself. It should have been clear to Anchorena that unless he reacted, the situation was going to escalate, but the Buenos Aires government kept up its haughty tone and was so dilatory that Duncan simply went ahead.

6.11 Louis Vernet's misunderstanding of the *Lexington*'s purpose

Louis Vernet heard that the *Lexington* was about to leave for the Falklands – but assumed that Duncan was going to help him in his campaign against American sealers! On 6 December, he wrote letters to Mathew Brisbane and Henry Metcalf to go by the *Lexington* to the Falklands, which reveal the extent of his misconception. To Henry Metcalf he wrote:[4]

… Captain Duncan… it is said goes to relieve the boats crew of the Sch[oone]ʳ *Superior*, and to apprise american fishing vessels of the danger they run if they persist in the same.

The idea that the United States government would send a warship to assist him in stopping American sealers from pursuing their livelihood is ludicrous. It shows how far Vernet was from understanding the issues at stake. He says in the letter to Brisbane[5] that he was sending the letters with "Antonio the German", i.e. Anton Vaihinger, who was trusted by Vernet and returned aboard the *Lexington* to the Falklands, where he was murdered in January 1833 by the group led by the villain Antonio Rivero (section 6.32).

6.12 The Second Falklands Crisis, Part II: the *Lexington* raid[6]

Having got nowhere with Anchorena, Silas Duncan sailed for the Falklands in the *Lexington* on 9 December 1831, under orders to use "the utmost vigilance, energy, and activity" to protect US trade. He had the *Harriet*'s captain Gilbert Davison aboard to identify the men who had seized his ship – Duncan intended to take them to the United States to be tried for piracy. Duncan's actions in the Falklands ("the *Lexington* raid") formed Part II of the Second Falklands Crisis.

The *Lexington*'s logbook records that the ship arrived off the Falklands early on 27 December 1831; PLSR entry 107 records her arrival on 26 December (perhaps assuming that she had arrived before midnight), and gives the purpose of the visit as "To Protect the American Fisheries", which is precisely accurate. The log records that at 6.30 a.m. a "small sail" was sighted: it was the shallop *Eagle*, built by the *Belleville* men on Eagle Island, which was now based at Port Louis in fulfilment

---

[1] Davison's second affidavit of 2 December 1831, in Manning 1932, pp. 75-76, fn.; italics in Manning. Not in *Colección 1832* or *BFSP 1832-1833*.

[2] Anchorena to Slacum, 3 December 1831; Spanish in *Colección* 1832, fol. 4 *recto* and *verso*; English translation in *BFSP 1832-1833*, pp. 314-315; different translation in Manning 1932, p. 73, text here from Manning.

[3] Spanish translation of Duncan's letter of 1 December 1831, as copied to Anchorena, in *Colección* 1832, fol. 5 *verso*; *BFSP 1832-1833*, pp. 317-318; not in Manning 1932.

[4] Vernet to Metcalf, 6 December 1831, AGN VII, 136, fol. 103 *recto* and *verso* (keeping-copy).

[5] Vernet to Brisbane, 6 December 1831, AGN VII, 136, fol. 102 *recto* and *verso* (keeping-copy).

[6] Account here mostly from the *Lexington* log, in USNA, RG 24, Records of the Bureau of Naval Personnel, Logs of US Naval Ships 1801-1915, "Lexington 31.5.1831 to 13.8.1833", in E. 118, Pt 123 (extracts, in Spanish, with some misreadings, in Fitte 1966, pp. 85-88); from Duncan's reports; and from the 11 affidavits made afterwards by Dickson, Brisbane, Metcalf, Grossy and others, in Manning 1932, pp. 211-222), translated from the Spanish texts in *Colección* (Supplement) 1832, fols. 3 *recto* to 6 *verso*; not in *BFSP 1832-1833*.

of Article 5 of her crew's contract with Vernet of 20 September (section 5.19). They had arrived on 24 December (PLSR entry 106), to find that Vernet had gone; they then left to do some sealing, and were in Berkeley Sound on 27 December, just as the *Lexington* arrived. The *Lexington* towed the *Eagle* halfway up the Sound, where both vessels waited for three days of squalls and hail, before on 31 December they both moved up to Port Louis and anchored.

Captain Duncan sent a party ashore to bring aboard the men who had seized the *Harriet*. The first two they brought were Henry Metcalf and Mathew Brisbane; Duncan put Brisbane in "irons" [shackles] in the hold, but Metcalf was soon released, and Brisbane was later allowed on deck. Then the *Lexington*'s boats brought 20 men and a woman with a small child from the settlement. Davison identified the six men in Brisbane's party who had seized the *Harriet* (Sylvestre Núñez, Juan Brasido, Domingo Valleja, Dionisio Eredia, Jacinto Correa, and the Charrúa "Manuel González"); they were put in irons and held prisoner. Dionisio Eredia was one of the last remaining two out of the 25 men who had landed with Vernet in 1826 (the last one, Juan Gregorio Sánchez, decided to leave too and boarded the *Lexington* a few days later). But of course those seven men had merely been following orders; the central culprit, Louis Vernet, who had ordered the capture of US vessels, had gone. In the end the US Supreme Court ruled that he had committed piracy, for which in US law the penalty was death (sections 6.6, 6.39), so Vernet was lucky not to get caught.

All who had not been involved in seizing the *Harriet* were put ashore again, and were back at the settlement by the evening of 31 December, and from 2 January 1832 the *Lexington*'s carpenters worked on the shallop *Eagle* every day for a week. In statements made later, Antonio Rivero, Santiago López and Faustino Martínez complained that Henry Metcalf gave a good deal of wood to the shallop.[1] Captain Duncan gave the shallop's crew supplies and American papers; they soon renamed their vessel *Chaloupe* and went on sealing for their own profit as a US vessel under the United States flag; they were still in the islands in 1837. Vernet's departure was their lucky break.

Duncan's purpose was to end interference with American ships; William Dickson stated later in an affidavit that he "spiked the guns, burnt the powder… took various arms, and after having broken them up, threw them into the water…" Spiking entailed hammering metal spikes into the touch-holes of muzzle-loading cannons, rendering them useless until the holes had been bored open again, which required special hardened drills. The destruction of the weapons prevented the establishment from mounting armed attacks such as the seizure of the *Harriet*.

By 18 January Duncan had fulfilled his purpose. The seven men guilty of seizing the *Harriet* were confined aboard; now he wanted to further weaken the establishment, so he spread the rumour that the settlement had no future – he applied a "stick-and-carrot" policy, issuing threats but also warmly welcoming aboard anyone who wished to leave. All the family groups took the opportunity to go: the first to go aboard the *Lexington*, with his wife and child, was Vernet's trusted former fisheries manager Julio Grossy, who had been wanting to leave for some time (he had put a notice on his house saying that he "was leaving this forsaken country in order not to die of want"[2]), and another was Vernet's settlement manager Henry Metcalf, as revealed by Juan Simon, the capataz, in a statement made later.[3] According to Simon, Metcalf said that Vernet owed him "two thousand and something" pesos ("dos mil y tantos"),[4] and had taken whatever he felt he had a right to – Simon says that after Metcalf boarded the *Lexington* there was not a single hide left at the settlement, and Metcalf even took plates, forks and knives.

Simon's bitter comments on Metcalf's behaviour in 1832 during the *Lexington* raid and during

---

[1] Statements in AGN VII, 130, made in April 1833 by Antonio Rivero (doc. 242), Santiago López (doc. 244) and Faustino Martínez (doc. 245).
[2] The text of his notice is partly preserved in Grossy's replies to questions put to him in Buenos Aires on 10 February 1832, printed in Manning 1932, p. 216; Spanish text in *Colección* (Supplement) 1832, fols. 5 *recto* to 6 *verso*.
[3] AGN VII, 130, doc. 62, a letter to Vernet dated 2 April 1833 (henceforth "Juan Simon's letter to Vernet"; see also section 6.31). It was dictated at Port Louis by the illiterate Juan Simon to Ventura Pasos; it was first printed (in modernised spelling and with some misreadings) in [Anon.], *El Episodio Ocurrido en Puerto de la Soledad de Malvinas el 26 de Agosto de 1833…*, Buenos Aires 1967 (henceforth "*Episodio Ocurrido* 1967"), pp. 122-128.
[4] Vernet accepted that he owed Metcalf money – cf. note in lead pencil above Metcalf's statement in Vernet's copy of *Colección* (Supplement) 1832, AGN VII, 141, no doc. no., fol. 3 *recto*: "… Mr Metcalf is one of my creditors…".

the visit of HMS *Clio* in 1833 show that Metcalf was disaffected with Vernet and was not expelled against his will. Simon had never claimed his wages, so Vernet owed money to him too.[1] Vernet's debts to Simon, amounting to £550 (some 2,500 pesos), were paid by the British government in 1858 to José Simon, Juan Simon's son by the black slave Carmelita (section 10.3).

On 20 January 1832 three German families boarded the *Lexington*, 14 people in all, followed by the gaucho Juan Gregorio Sánchez (who had been, with Dionisio Eredia, the only remaining man who had landed with Vernet in 1826), with his wife and child, then 13 black slaves and a black child, taken aboard by Henry Metcalf. A single English-speaking man called Knight and a single German man called Sperl also embarked. The people are listed in Table 6.12a.

	Totals
"Non-prisoners" who later made affidavits:	
William Dickson, Henry Metcalf,	
"Mr Julien" (Julio Grossy), with wife and child	
[and his nephew Agustín, not listed]	6
Germans who later made statements:	
Carlos (Karl) Feurer (if not "Finn")	1 (?)
"David Smith" (David Schmidt), with wife and 4 children	6
"Non-prisoners" who made no statements:	
"Charles Cline" [Karl Klein], wife and son	3
Charles "Finn" (= Feurer?), wife and 3 children	5
"John G. Sanches" [Juan Gregorio Sánchez], wife and child	3
Knight (a carpenter)	1
Phillip [or Andreas] Sperl	1
Charlotte (sent by Dickson)	1
Total of settlers:	27 (26 if Finn = Feurer)
Slaves taken aboard by Metcalf:	
10 men, 3 women and 1 child[2]	14
Total with slaves but without prisoners:	41 (40 if Finn = Feurer)
Prisoners, all of whom later made affidavits:	
Mathew Brisbane, Domingo Valleja, Jacinto Correa,	
"Manuel Antonio González", Dionisio Eredia,	
Silvestre Nuñez, Juan Brasido	7
Overall total (if Finn not the same as Feurer):	48 (47 if Finn = Feurer)

Table 6.12a Roll call: the 47 or 48 people who left Port Louis aboard the USS *Lexington*, 22 January 1832, from the *Lexington*'s log (with additions). Carlos Feurer may have been the same person as Charles Finn.

Some authors, British and American as well as Argentinian, state that Duncan "razed" or "sacked" the settlement, but that is clearly untrue – in their statements made later, none of those taken aboard mentioned any damage to the buildings of the settlement. When the store manager William Dickson was asked whether Duncan did any damage to the establishment, he mentioned only the spiking of the guns and the destruction of the small-arms; if any damage had been done to the buildings, Dickson or Metcalf would scarcely have omitted to mention it. Metcalf said Duncan gave all who remained at the settlement a certificate "so that no American vessel would do them injury, to the end that they would supply meat when necessary to those arriving at the Island" – Duncan intended the settlement to continue, though reduced in strength and incapable of harming US interests. It was useful to visiting ships, so it would have been absurd to "sack" or "raze" it.

One of the myths launched by Julius Goebel in 1927 was that Duncan declared the islands "free of all government".[3] That statement arose from misinterpreting English translations of the

---

[1] Stated in Vernet's draft letter to Mathew Brisbane, 19 November 1833, in AGN VII 130, doc. 70.

[2] The child was presumably the black woman Francisca's little son, born on 10 December 1829.

[3] Goebel 1927, p. 444. That myth, and Goebel's phrase, has been repeated by several later writers, e.g. Adrián Hope in "Sovereignty and Decolonization of the Malvinas (Falkland) Islands", in *Boston College International and*

statements made by three of the prisoners taken away aboard the *Lexington* and by José Báez. They said Duncan posted "handbills" (Spanish "carteles") declaring that the islands were "free". Duncan's original text was no doubt in English, but is only known through the Spanish translations in *Colección* (Supplement) 1832; the prisoners did not see the "handbills" since they were arrested at once, and they were illiterate and knew little or no English. Juan Brasido said that the handbills declared the island "to be free from all sovereignty"; Jacinto Correa said that they declared the island "to be free so that anybody who so desired might live there"; Dionisio Eredia said that he had "learned" (i.e. from others) that they declared the island "free for anybody who wished to live there",[1] and José Báez stated that Duncan had said "that Señor Vernet would not return again to the Island, and that it and all that was in it belonged to the whole world".[2] Louis Vernet himself later wrote that "Duncan's proclamations… declared the Islands common property of all nations".[3] In other words, Duncan declared that the islands were open and free to all; they were part of the high seas, not the property of Buenos Aires. He did not imply that he had himself brought about any change in the islands such as ending their "government", but merely underlined the existing American policy, that no country possessed sovereignty over the Falklands.

The *Lexington*'s business in the Falklands was now complete. On Sunday 22 January 1832 she left for Montevideo, taking 47 or 48 people (over half the remaining roughly 85 inhabitants of Port Louis) including almost all the settlers and slaves – the *Lexington* log lists 47 people (or 48 if the otherwise unrecorded "Charles Finn" is an extra person, not merely a misspelling of the well attested Karl Feurer), eleven of whom are named (Dickson, Brisbane, Metcalf and eight others). The slaves and all women and children are enumerated but not named; in Table 6.12a we have added the names of the other six prisoners plus Agustín Grossy. The people included some who are known to have been keen to leave the islands such as Julio Grossy and Metcalf; others may have been happy to leave too, but no one was forced to leave except the seven prisoners who had seized the *Harriet*. About 33-35 people remained at Port Louis, mainly gauchos but also a few settlers such as the German Karl Kußler (Kussler), as well as the black women Carmelita and Gregoria, Carmelita's small son José Simon, and the black boy "Octubre" – the blacks seem to have been allowed to stay if they wished, whereupon their indentures clearly lapsed and they ceased to be slaves. Of those remaining, the gaucho Telésforo Moreno was murdered in June 1832, and roughly 8 people left during the remainder of 1832 (the exact numbers are unrecorded). Carmelita and Gregoria stayed in the islands for the rest of their lives, and presumably chose to do so.

After the *Lexington* raid the settlement was smaller but still functioned; Louis Vernet corresponded with Port Louis and sent supplies and people from Buenos Aires, and the work of killing cattle and supplying ships went on – the Antarctic explorer John Biscoe bought beef at Port Louis several times between April and August 1832,[4] and Vernet's establishment was still being run on his behalf in 1835 (section 5.20). But interference with American ships had ended; Duncan had been successful.

The *Lexington* reached Montevideo on 2 February 1832, and the next day Duncan released all except the seven prisoners, some 40 people. Most boarded the Uruguayan river packet *Flor del Río* for Buenos Aires, presumably paying for their passage, and the Uruguayan government arranged with the US commercial agent that the same ship should transport the black slaves, who of course had no money.[5] On 7 February the *Flor del Río* reached Buenos Aires; the slaves were put aboard the Buenos Aires government schooner *Sarandí* pending a decision on their fate, while the others

---

Comparative Law Review, vol. VI no. 2, Spring 1983, p. 415; and (following Adrián Hope) by Lawrence Freedman and Virginia Gamba-Stonehouse in *Signals of War: The Falklands Conflict of 1982*, London 1990, pp. xxxi-xxxii, and by Sir Lawrence Freedman in *The Official History of the Falklands Campaign*, Abingdon 2005/2007, vol. I, p. 7.

[1] Quotes from *Colección* (Supplement) 1832, fols. 10 *recto* to 11 *verso*; Manning 1932, pp. 219-221.
[2] José Báez's statement, in AGN VII, 136, fol. 135 *recto*.
[3] Fair copy of Vernet's file of evidence against Juan Simon, 6 February 1833, in AGN VII, 130, doc. 55, fol. 1 *recto*.
[4] Details in Biscoe's journal in BL Add. MS 15716.
[5] A small slip of paper in AGN VII, 132, doc. 136, records payment of passage for 13 blacks in the schooner *Flor del Río* by "Dⁿ Luis Bernet", 15 February 1832, each costing 5 patacones [as pesos were sometimes called in Uruguay], total 65 patacones. One of the women [i.e. Francisca] had a small child, who evidently travelled free of charge.

were released.¹ Sadly, the slaves, and most of the others, then disappear from history.

Equally sadly, it got forgotten that it was not Britain but Louis Vernet and the United States that removed most of the civilian population, and during the Falklands War on 22 May 1982, Argentine deputy foreign minister Enrique Ros stated at the UN that in 1833 Britain "imprisoned our inhabitants and expelled them to Montevideo" (section 10.24). It was of course the United States, not Britain.

In his report to US Navy Secretary Levi Woodbury, Duncan said about the people he had brought: "I have consulted their own wishes…, and they appeared [to] greatly rejoice at the opportunity thus presented of removing, with their families…".² On 15 February he sailed for Rio with the seven prisoners.

On 14 February 1832 Slacum's despatches of 23 November and 9 December 1831 arrived in Washington announcing the arrival of the seized *Harriet* at Buenos Aires.³ The lawyer Francis Baylies had been appointed by President Jackson to look into the welfare of US ships in the South Atlantic, and Secretary of State Edward Livingston instructed him to justify Duncan's action:⁴

> … you are to justify it not only on the general grounds in your instructions, but on the further facts disclosed in the protest of the Captain of the Harriet, which show the lawless, and indeed piratical, proceedings of Vernet and his band… These facts… show clearly that it is an establishment, dangerous to our commerce, which it is necessary in self-defence that we should break up.

However, Baylies still took over five months to get to Buenos Aires.

On 16 February 1832 the Buenos Aires prize court ruled that the three ships seized by Vernet were lawful prize;⁵ in fact the *Breakwater* had escaped and the *Superior* was busy sealing, so only the *Harriet* was present, but this judgement confiscated the ships from their American owners and ruled that they were legally held by the Buenos Aires government (though only under Argentine law, of course, not in international law). But then nothing happened; the *Harriet* remained at anchor under government supervision, and Vernet could do nothing. It would have been normal for the government to arrange a sale, the proceeds of which would be paid to those involved in proportion to their rank, but the government did nothing and the ship lay rotting. She later failed to sell at two auctions, and in November 1833 she was still unsold.⁶ Vernet's plan to use her as his own sealing ship had collapsed, and by seizing her he had brought disaster upon his venture in the Falklands.

Prudent action by Buenos Aires could have ended the Second Falklands Crisis before it escalated – Buenos Aires could have released the *Harriet* and disavowed the seizure, but the government neither released the ship nor sold her. That reduced Vernet to desperation, but General Rosas also refused to disavow Vernet's actions, which caused a diplomatic crisis.

On 2 March 1832 Duncan arrived back at Rio in the *Lexington* and reported to Commodore George Rodgers of the sloop USS *Warren*, commander of the US South Atlantic squadron. Duncan

---

¹ Statement by Uruguayan foreign minister Santiago Vásquez, Montevideo 6 February 1832, in *Colección* (Supplement) 1832, fol. 7 *verso*, and introductory statement, Buenos Aires 7 February 1832, fol. 8 *recto*, signed by Francisco Linch, "Enrique Metealf" [*recte* Henry Metcalf] and Guillermo Dickson; English translations in Manning 1932, pp. 211, 213. Not in *BFSP 1832-1833*. The *Sarandí* later played an important role in the Falklands (section 6.16).

² Duncan to Livingston 3 February 1832, despatch in USNA, NRG 45, M147, microfilm 16, doc. 28; also in the "Area File of the Naval Collection" 1775-1910 Area 4 1832, ref. M 625 Roll 6 (not in Manning 1932). This despatch was first printed in Spanish translation in Fitte 1966, pp. 111-112.

³ Slacum to Livingston, 23 November 1831 (Manning 1932, pp. 66-70), enclosing Davison's first affidavit and Vernet's contract of 20 September 1831 with the *Belleville* men; and 9 December 1831 (Manning 1932, pp. 75-78), enclosing Davison's second affidavit and the text of Slacum to Duncan 30 November 1831 and Duncan to Slacum 1 December 1831; none of these is in *BFSP 1832-1833* or *Colección* 1832.

⁴ Livingston to Baylies 14 February 1832, in Manning 1932, pp. 12-13. Not in *BFSP 1832-1833* or *Colección* 1832, but most of it is quoted in John Bassett Moore, *Digest of International Law*, 7 vols., Washington DC 1906, vol. I, pp. 884-885, with summaries of further correspondence, pp. 885-888.

⁵ Statement by the Buenos Aires Prize Court judge Dr Jacinto Cardenas, 16 February 1832, in AGN VII, 13, doc. 8.

⁶ Details from draft letter by Vernet to the Buenos Aires government dated 31 January 1833, AGN VII, 130, doc. 53; another auction of the *Harriet*, on 26 September 1833, for 8900 pesos, was reported by the *BPAN*, 28 September 1833, but in a letter to Brisbane of 19 November 1833 (after Brisbane's death), in AGN VII 130, doc. 70, Vernet says the *Harriet* was even then still unsold.

then left for the United States, and was succeeded as commander of the *Lexington* by Isaac McKeever (1791-1856). Duncan's report of 3 February from Montevideo reached Washington around 3 April, so the US government now knew what he had done in the Falklands back in January. Secretary of State Livingston then sent Baylies more instructions, in which he said:[1]

... the President has signified to Captain Duncan that he entirely approves of his conduct... the proceedings of Vernet and his band, have no circumstance that can distinguish them from piratical acts... The nature of the establishment... made it proper and necessary to break it up, and deprive it of the means of annoying our commerce. You will, therefore, justify the acts of Captain Duncan to the Buenos Ayres Government...

On 4 April Navy Secretary Levi Woodbury wrote to Duncan, saying "the President of the United States approves the course which you pursued, and is much gratified at the promptness, firmness and the efficiency of your measures".[2]

On 30 March Commodore Rodgers left Rio in the *Warren* together with the *Lexington* and the schooner USS *Enterprise* for Montevideo, where they arrived on 11 April. On 16 April the *Warren* took the prisoners aboard and sailed to Buenos Aires, arriving on 24 April. Rodgers then released the prisoners, who went ashore and made affidavits describing their treatment by Duncan.[3] Sadly, Rodgers died at Buenos Aires on 21 May after a brief illness, perhaps appendicitis.[4]

6.13 Captain Congar returns to New York

Captain Stephen Congar of the *Superior* fulfilled Vernet's illegal contract of 8 September 1831 (section 6.5), and collected sealskins worth 8,500 US dollars. Around April 1832 he returned to Port Louis, but Vernet, Brisbane and Metcalf had gone and there was no one literate there to sign for the cargo, so he took it back to New York and delivered it to the ship's owner, Silas Burrows, in early June 1832.[5] On 10 September 1832 Vernet's US agent Lewis Krumbhaar wrote to Burrows, informing him of the contract with Vernet and the decision of the Buenos Aires prize court that the vessel was lawful prize, so vessel and cargo were now Vernet's property. Burrows replied:[6]

Your very extraordinary letter on a very extraordinary subject is received this morning... I am surprised that any Gentleman in the US could suggest to a Merchant that his property has been taken from him by a Capture where it was not followed by any legal Condemnation. The flag, the papers, the Captain, the officers, the men of my Vessel have never been changed, they went to Sea and return'd to this port as I shipped them... Captain Congar... returnd as he agreed to the Faulkland islands where he found that Gov[erno]ʳ Vernet and his Companions had flown, and was he then to go an exploring voyage in search of them? or was he not very properly to return to his owner in the US...

There was no answer to that; it demonstrated that the contract had no legal basis, and the lack of "legal Condemnation" (court adjudication) made it piracy. Nevertheless, five years later in 1837 Vernet even attempted to have one of Burrows's ships seized in Montevideo, which had important consequences for the Falkland Islands (section 10.1).

6.14 Britain reacts to reports of American activity in the Falklands

On 16 March 1832 Rear Admiral Sir Thomas Baker, commander-in-chief on the Royal Navy's South American station at Rio de Janeiro, sent a despatch to London that must have worried the Admiralty and the Foreign Office.[7] He reported that the dispute between the United States and Buenos Aires was causing a naval build-up in the South Atlantic – he mentioned Consul Slacum's

---

[1] Livingston to Baylies 3 April 1832, in Manning 1932, pp. 14-15. Not in *BFSP 1832-1833* or *Colección* 1832.
[2] Woodbury to Duncan 4 April 1832, in USNA, NRG 45, M147, microfilm 18; quote also given on the website of USS *Duncan*, www.ussduncan.org/silasbio.
[3] Details in this paragraph from the prisoners' affidavits and other statements in Manning 1932; they are mostly in *Colección* (Supplement) 1832, but not in *BFSP 1832-1833*.
[4] Date from USS *Duncan* website, www.ussduncan.org.
[5] Details in letter to Vernet from his US agent Lewis Krumbhaar, 20 October 1832, AGN VII, 130, doc. 40.
[6] Copies in Vernet's hand, in English, of Krumbhaar to Burrows, 10 September 1832 and Burrows's reply, 14 September 1832, AGN VII, 132, doc. 146; Vernet's summary of both in Spanish in AGN VII, 130, doc. 16, fol. 4 *verso*.
[7] Despatch dated 16 March 1832 from Sir Thomas Baker, in PRO FO 6 499, fols. 150 *recto* to 151 *recto*, scribal copy.

threat of "an early accession of Naval force, to demand justice & a suitable reparation for the injuries inflicted upon his Countrymen at the Falkland Islands", and listed the warships currently at Rio: the large French frigate *Herminie* and the US squadron of *Warren*, *Lexington*, and *Enterprize*, which might be planning a further move against Buenos Aires in the Falklands, possibly affecting British interests. He also enclosed a copy of Vernet's "Advertisement", in which Vernet called himself "the Owner of East Falkland" (section 6.1) – another challenge to British interests.

In due course the British government reacted to all this. Britain had had extensive rights in the Falklands for over 60 years, beginning in 1765 and strengthened by the Nootka Sound Convention of 1790; there had been a constant presence of British ships, and the Falklands were important to Britain – they lay on the route to the Pacific, along which passed a growing volume of British trade. Britain could not permit a presence by any other power, nor the existence of any "nest of pirates". On 7 August 1832 Captain the Honourable George Elliot of the Admiralty wrote to Sir George Shee at the Foreign Office, enclosing an order to be sent to Rear Admiral Baker, that he was "to cause the Falkland Islands to be visited annually by one of H:M: Ships on the South American Station, for the purpose of keeping up and maintaining the Sovereign Rights of His Majesty over those Islands."[1]

So Britain was not going to send a garrison or any kind of permanent presence; there was to be merely an annual visit by a ship. That was typical of the British policy of "informal empire", a complex, haphazard network of commercial activity with minimal use of military power. In the 16th century Spain and Portugal had occupied territories in South America by military force before exploiting them commercially, a process in which "trade follows the flag". By contrast, Britain for centuries mostly operated the opposite policy, "the flag follows trade", under which merchants and settlers began trading with overseas peoples but no formal rule was imposed on the territories involved. Until the 1880s British policy was minimalist – the cheapest option was chosen and was ended as soon as possible. Kohen and Rodríguez (p. 188) criticise us for referring in *Getting it right* (pp. 17-18) to "the visit by HMS Clio to Port Louis, January 1833", but that was exactly what it was: the first of what was intended to be a series of brief annual visits – no more and no less.

On 30 August 1832 King William IV signed the order to send a ship to visit the Falklands,[2] whereupon Palmerston informed the Admiralty it was the King's pleasure that the Admiralty should take steps "for causing the Falkland Islands to be visited annually by one of His Majesty's ships". The orders were sent the next day, so the die was cast, but the sheer distance meant that the decision to reassert British sovereignty in the Falklands took almost three months to reach Rio.

6.15 Impasse in Buenos Aires – Francis Baylies breaks off US-Argentine diplomatic relations

On 13 June 1832 the lawyer Francis Baylies took up his post as United States chargé d'affaires in Buenos Aires.[3] On 20 June he sent a long despatch to the acting Buenos Aires foreign minister Vicente Maza, in which, following his instructions from Washington, he stated that neither Louis Vernet nor Buenos Aires had any authority in the Falklands; he demanded compensation for the losses to American ships, and concluded by stating that the United States government "utterly deny the existence of any right in this Republic to interrupt, molest, detain or capture any vessels belonging to citizens of the United States of America… engaged in taking seals or whales", and he demanded the return of all US property.[4] Maza replied on 25 June, saying that he had placed Baylies's note before Governor Rosas, and that Rosas had asked Vernet for explanations.[5]

To pass Baylies's diplomatic communication to a private individual (Vernet) without asking Baylies was of course a breach of etiquette – the government were introducing the private interests

---

[1] George Elliot to Sir George Shee 7 August 1832, PRO FO 6 499, fols. 168 *recto* to 169 *recto*.
[2] Draft order, unsigned but no doubt by Palmerston, to the Admiralty, 30 August 1832, in PRO FO 6 499, fols. 170 *recto* to 171 *recto*, to which William IV has added at the top "App[rove]ᵈ" and his signature.
[3] Baylies to Livingston 18 May 1832, in Manning 1932, pp. 98-99, and 20 June 1832, in Manning 1932, pp. 105-6; neither is in *BFSP 1832-1833* or *Colección* 1832.
[4] Baylies to Maza 20 June 1832, in Manning 1932, pp. 99-105 and *BFSP 1832-1833*, pp. 330-336; Spanish in *Colección* 1832, fols. 14 *recto* to 16 *recto*.
[5] Maza to Baylies 25 June 1832, in *Colección* 1832, fol. 16 verso; English translation in *BFSP 1832-1833*, p. 336 and Manning 1932, pp. 106-107.

of a third party into an international dispute between the United States and Buenos Aires. In the end, Baylies sent Maza on 10 July 1832 a long despatch in which he questioned the rights claimed by Buenos Aires to the Falklands (see chapter 3), pointing out that Spain had still not abandoned its claim, stating that Argentina could not claim the full rights of the former Viceroyalty of the River Plate, and pointing out that the United States had acquired customary rights in the Falklands by "long and uninterrupted use and possession".[1] There was still room for a solution – Buenos Aires could have apologised for those incidents while also repeating its claim to sovereignty. The US would not have recognised Argentine sovereignty, or the sovereignty of any country, but might have accepted an Argentine role in the islands if Americans had been permitted to exploit them.

But Buenos Aires was not disposed to back down one jot or show the slightest flexibility – Rosas did not even deign to reply for five weeks. At long last, on 14 August 1832, the Buenos Aires government replied to Baylies, with a long note from Maza[2] enclosing an immensely long response by Louis Vernet dated 10 August justifying his actions (i.e. Vernet's "Report").[3] On Vernet's behalf Maza mildly pleaded for moderation, but as soon as he came to Duncan, his language became intemperate, vituperative, almost hysterical – vintage Rosas, in fact. He referred to:

... the daring and cruel outrage committed in said Islands by M![r] Duncan... destroying, in the midst of the most profound peace, with black anger and in the most perfidious and ferocious manner, a settlement which this government had publickly formed... outrage and violence so inhuman as has been committed by Captain Duncan... attacking, as he did, by surprise and deception, like a highway-robber or a pirate, a settlement which was unprotected and unprepared...

In fact Duncan committed no "violence so inhuman" (there were no casualties), and the settlement was not destroyed; it was left virtually undamaged. And it was Vernet, not Duncan, who had acted "in the midst of the most profound peace" in seizing American ships; Duncan's actions were a reaction to that sudden assault by an agent of Buenos Aires. Maza made it clear that Buenos Aires refused point-blank to consider the American protests until the United States had paid full compensation both to the Argentine Republic and to Vernet, and added that "until... this Government obtains both things, it will not enter into discussion on any of the other points comprehended in the aforesaid notes of His Honor". That was pure Rosas – petulant, unyielding, pig-headed. The United States was the original injured party, so it was unreasonable to expect compensation for the reaction before the original grievance had even been discussed.

That note of 14 August 1832 from Maza ended any chance of an amicable solution, and Vernet's long "Report" only made matters worse. The question was one of sovereignty, to be discussed between governments, not with a private individual. Francis Baylies had been instructed by the United States government to uphold the original American grievance, so on 18 August he returned the "Report" to Maza unread. He reminded Maza that he had been "expressly directed by his own Government" to justify Duncan's actions, so he was requesting his passports.[4] On 19 August Baylies sent Secretary of State Livingston a private letter in which he called the Buenos Aires government "these wayward & petulant fools", and said of them "they have all the vices of men and all the follies of children".[5]

On 3 September Baylies received his passports – he had broken off diplomatic relations between Buenos Aires and the United States. The Argentine government had refused to consider the complaints of the United States against the losses caused to US citizens by Vernet; that was the root cause of the dispute, and a more flexible and more realistic leader than Rosas might have seen

---

[1] Baylies to Maza 10 July 1832, in Manning 1932, pp. 111-126 and *BFSP 1832-1833*, pp. 338-355; Spanish translation in *Colección* 1832, fols. 18 *recto* to 24 *recto*.
[2] Maza to Baylies 14 August 1832, in *Colección* 1832, fols. 30 *recto* to 31 *recto*; English translation in *BFSP 1832-1833*, pp. 364-369 and in Manning 1932, pp. 147-152.
[3] Louis Vernet's report to Maza of 10 August 1832, entitled "Informe del Comandante Político y Militar de Malvinas" ["Report of the Political and Military Commandant of Malvinas"], henceforth "(Vernet's) 'Report'"; full English translation in *BFSP 1832-1833*, pp. 369-436; facsimile of *BFSP* text in Perl 1983, pp. 153-283.
[4] Baylies to Maza 18 August 1832: *Colección* 1832, fol. 55 *verso*; *BFSP 1832-1833*, pp. 436-7; Manning 1932, p. 152.
[5] Private letter from Baylies to Livingston 19 August 1832, in Manning 1932, pp. 153-5; not in *BFSP 1832-1833* or *Colección* 1832 (see also section 5.14).

advantages in a diplomatic withdrawal and apology. But Rosas could tolerate no *quid pro quo* and no admission that his side had been in the wrong; only total victory was acceptable. A breach of diplomatic relations with the United States was preferable to the slightest humiliation.

On 26 September 1832 Francis Baylies, his wife and daughter, and ex-consul George Slacum boarded the corvette USS *Warren*. From on board the ship Baylies sent a last despatch to Livingston, concluding: "The Government having positively refused to treat or to discuss any question until reparation was made to Louis Vernet – his band of pirates and the Argentine Republic,– no course was left for me but to demand my passports…".[1] As pointed out in section 6.10, Kohen and Rodríguez imply (pp. 176 and 205) that it was Argentina that broke off diplomatic relations with the United States, but it was the other way round. For over two years there were no relations whatever between the United States and Argentina, until Eben Ritchie Dorr took up the post of US consul in Buenos Aires on 27 November 1834; full diplomatic relations between the US and Argentina were only restored a decade later on 14 June 1844.[2]

6.16 Argentina sends a ship and a commandant

Far from making any concessions to the United States, Rosas was determined to hammer his point home – that no one crosses Juan Manuel de Rosas with impunity. So he decided to send a military force to the Falklands, well aware that this could only worsen the dispute with the United States. On 10 September 1832 he signed a decree appointing an interim commandant (standing in for Vernet) to go to the islands with a military garrison[3] – just after the British government had on 30 August ordered that a warship should visit the islands (section 6.14). So, eleven days apart, unknown to each other, the British and Argentine governments each sent a ship to the Falklands to counteract moves by the United States. In the event the two ships did not meet with the Americans but with each other, and the consequences of their meeting are with us today.

The new interim Argentine commandant, a brevet major in the Argentine army, was originally French; his date of birth is unknown, but he was born in Blois.[4] He signed his name "Estevan Jose F^{co} Mestivier", which suggests that his French name was Étienne Joseph François Mestivier. On 14 September 1832 General Rosas drew up 26 orders to him,[5] and the two-masted topsail-schooner *Sarandí*, of 9 guns, was now loaded up for the voyage that ensured her a place in all Falklands histories. She was to be commanded by Lieutenant-Colonel José María Pinedo (1795-1885), and was to be piloted by Mathew Brisbane; her crew of 59 were mainly British or American, but they included 13 Argentine marines, and she also carried a military garrison of 28 soldiers including Commandant Mestivier, his second-in-command capitán Enrique Guinne, and an adjutant, Captain José Antonio Gomila.[6] Major Mestivier was accompanied by his wife Gertrudis, aged about 22; about a dozen men were accompanied by a woman, and there were 8 children. Including all the men, women and children, the garrison consisted of 49 people. There was a prisoner aboard, Maximo Warnes, whose surname suggests he was of English-speaking origin. It seems he was the first prisoner for the "presidio" (frontier garrison and penal colony) which had been planned in 1829, and which Vernet had protested against (section 5.15).[7] The garrison was to provide military support for the claim of Buenos Aires to the Falklands against any reaction by the Americans, but the presence of a garrison and prisoners would have deterred civilian settlers.

Pinedo's instructions included orders that he was to patrol the islands' coasts as far as New Island, and inform "foreign" ships that the Commandant of the islands forbade "fishing" (i.e.

---

[1] Baylies to Livingston 26 September 1832, in Manning 1932, pp. 161-165; Not in *BFSP 1832-1833* or *Colección* 1832.

[2] William Brent Jnr served as US chargé d'affaires from 14 June 1844 to 6 July 1846 (Manning 1932, p. 22, fn.).

[3] Decree published on 15 September in the official *El Lucero* and in *BPAN* p. 1, col. 1, and on 17 September in the *Gaceta Mercantil*; text in Fitte 1966, p. 347; details in Caillet-Bois 1948, pp. 284-285 and fn. 6; 2nd ed. 1952/1982, pp. 286-287 and fn. 6. Text also in Alfredo Becerra, *Protestas por Malvinas (1833-1946)*, Buenos Aires 1998, p. 38.

[4] Details from letter by Captain Guérin in *Le Moniteur Universel*, Paris, 5 August 1833, and Fitte 1974, p. 365.

[5] Orders to Mestivier printed in full in Fitte 1974, pp. 355-361, quoting from AGN X, 3-4-5.

[6] Crew list dated 2 August 1832 in AGN III, 27-8-2, doc. 32, giving functions and ranks but no names (printed in Fitte 1974, p. 352, from AGN III 27-8-3, doc. 17); partial list in AGN III, 27-8-4, doc. 38 (Fitte 1974, pp. 363-364).

[7] Draft of Vernet's protest against a presidio in AGN VII, 131, doc. 147, fols. 1 *verso* and 2 *recto*.

sealing).[1] In other words, he was ordered to continue the harassment that the United States was complaining about. He fulfilled those orders – and caused a predictable American reaction.

Louis Vernet put supplies aboard the *Sarandí* for his colonists, mainly clothing but also wine and spirits,[2] and he also sent several people (section 6.18). On 22 September 1832 he wrote Mestivier a letter in French and two in Spanish.[3] In the Spanish letters he enclosed some documents: copies of the illegal contract with the captains of the *Superior* and the *Harriet* of 8 September 1831; of the court certificate condemning the *Harriet* (he wrote "the cargo of the Superior is mine" and instructed Mestivier to take charge of the *Superior* if she returned); and of the contract with the men of the "goletita Aguila" (the "little schooner Aguila", i.e. the *Belleville* men's shallop, section 5.19). The letter in French was personal; he concluded "Give my compliments to your lady wife, and from my wife too, and tell her to bear with courage the inconveniences of the voyage, and that time will reward her sacrifices". Sadly, she was to have no reward; her husband was brutally murdered by the Argentine garrison and she returned a widow.

Pinedo left Buenos Aires in the *Sarandí* on 23 September, after an unscheduled stop to put ashore the second-in-command, capitán Enrique Guinne, who had got drunk and injured two soldiers.[4] Most of those aboard returned to Buenos Aires four months later, but not Mestivier himself; he lies in an unmarked grave somewhere near Port Louis.

6.17 Britain protests against the appointment of Mestivier

On 28 September 1832 the British Minister (ambassador) in Buenos Aires, Henry Fox, protested to Maza against the decree appointing Mestivier:[5]

… as soon as the Decree of the 10th of June 1829,… containing certain provisions for the Government of the Falkland Islands, had been made known… an official Protest against any assumption of any right of Sovereignty over those Islands, on the part of the Argentine Republick, was… presented to the Government of Buenos Ayres, by the Chargé d'Affaires of His Britannick Majesty.–… But, lest the silence of the Undersigned should by possibility be considered as implying an abandonment on the part of his Government, of the Rights of His Britannick Majesty, it becomes his duty now again officially to declare to the Government of Buenos Ayres, that the Sovereignty of the Falkland Islands… is vested in the Crown of Great Britain; and that no act of government or authority can be exercised over those Islands, by any other Power, without infringing upon the Just Rights of His Britannick Majesty.–

In protesting against decrees by the Argentine government, in 1829 (section 5.17) and in 1832, Britain preserved its rights to the Falklands, which were extensive and longstanding. Maza acknowledged receipt and stated that the government would reply in due course.[6] But yet again, as in 1829, there was no reply.

6.18 Commandant Mestivier arrives; the *Clio* and the *Tyne* set off for the Falklands

After a stormy voyage from Buenos Aires, Lieutenant-Colonel José María Pinedo reached Port Louis in the *Sarandí* on 6 October 1832. Before the ship's arrival there were 27 residents at the settlement, and the *Sarandí* now brought the Argentine garrison, which after the departure of capitán Enrique Guinne totalled 48 people (Commandant Mestivier and his young wife Gertrudis; 26 soldiers including adjutant José Antonio Gomila; 12 soldiers' women and 8 children), and there were also 7 people who were not part of the garrison. Of those 7 people, 3 had lived at Port Louis earlier and were now returning: Henry Metcalf (now Vernet's official agent), the storekeeper William Dickson, and Anton Vaihinger. Four of them were newcomers: José Viel and Juan Quedy

---

[1] Copy of instructions, 14 September 1832, in AGN VII, 60, fols. 6-10; Muñoz Azpiri 1966, vol. 1, pp. 432-434.
[2] Lists of goods signed by Vernet 13 September 1832, AGN VII, 130, doc. 52.
[3] Vernet to Mestivier, in AGN VII 130, doc. 35 in French; 36 and 37 in Spanish, 37 apparently superseding 36.
[4] Details from Fitte 1974, p. 369, quoting from *Defensa del Teniente Coronel de Marina José María Pinedo...*, Buenos Aires, 1833, p. 4, in AGN III, 27-8-3. We have not located this document; the AGN staff told us that they suspected it was removed from the archives by the Argentine military during the Falklands War of 1982.
[5] Text from PRO FO 6 499, fols. 195 *recto* to 196 *recto*.
[6] Maza to Fox 1 October 1832, in PRO FO 6 499; Spanish text fols. 197 *recto* to 197 *verso*; English translation in *ibid.*, fols. 198 *recto* to 199 *recto*.

(both otherwise unrecorded; their reason for coming to the islands is unclear); the clerk Ventura Pasos (a Buenos Airean related to Vernet's wife, and nephew of Juan José Pasos, one of the leaders of the Argentine independence movement in 1810);[1] and the prisoner Maximo Warnes, who was in the custody of the garrison. In addition to those 7, there were 2 men in the ship's crew who deserted at Port Louis and remained behind when the ship left: Charles Brasier and William Drake, who had lived at Port Louis in 1831 and had been in the crew of the *Harriet* (section 6.9); they deserted in January 1833 and were taken aboard HMS *Clio* on 6 January.

As well as those 9 men, one of the 12 women who had arrived "attached" to the garrison decided to remain behind: she was Antonina Roxa, who was to live in the islands for 36 years and played a notable part in their development.[2] Those 10 people brought the number of non-members of the garrison at Port Louis up to 37 on 1 January 1833, before Warnes, Viel and Quedy left in the *Sarandí*, Metcalf and Pasos left in the schooner *Rapid* and Brasier and Drake left in the *Clio*. Of the 10 non-garrison arrivals, only 3 (Dickson, Vaihinger and Antonina) were still at Port Louis after all three ships had left (see Table 6.24c).

Pinedo waited for the weather to calm down, then he landed the garrison and the 7 other people, and on 10 October 1832 he drew up a formal act of possession of the islands.[3]

On 14 November the 165-ton British whaling schooner *Rapid* of Liverpool put in to Port Louis for urgent repairs. Like most merchant ships at that time, she was armed: she had two cannons, plus rifles and muskets for her 30-man crew, and carried at least two logbooks: the "ship's log", entered mostly by the mate, and the "captain's log" entered by her captain, John Ross. The original logs are lost, but Louis Vernet later chartered the ship; he evidently borrowed both logs and copied out the passages on the ship's visit to the Falklands;[4] we base much of our account on them. Pinedo offered Ross the help of the *Sarandí*'s carpenters (who were apparently English-speaking), and on 24 November the *Rapid* was hauled into the inner basin next to the settlement for repairs.

Some time in November Pinedo took two gauchos aboard the *Sarandí*, Mariano López and Manuel Ruiz, as "incorrigible and idle",[5] drafted them into the ship's crew, and took them back to Buenos Aires in January 1833. It seems highly likely that a third gaucho was also taken aboard: José Báez, who had apparently arrived with the other two in the *Elbe* in July 1831, had certainly been in the islands for most of 1832 and was with López and Ruiz in Buenos Aires in January 1833 after the ship arrived back (section 6.24), but Pinedo does not mention him.

After the new garrison had been in the islands for six weeks, Pinedo judged that they were properly settled in, so on 21 November he set off around the islands in the *Sarandí* looking for ships "illegally" killing seals, as required by his orders. He wrote in his report that at Arch Island he found two American whalers, one of them the *Uxor*, to which he lent some men to assist with repairs – Buenos Aires did not object to whaling since whales were seen as the produce of the high seas, whereas seals were the produce of the islands. To the United States government, of course, the islands were part of the high seas too, so Buenos Aires had no right to them.

---

[1] Details from note by Vernet in AGN VII, 130, doc. 54.

[2] Marcelo Beccaceci gives a completely false account of Antonina in *Gauchos de Malvinas*, Buenos Aires 2017, p. 31: he asserts that Vernet in 1829 (!) appointed her housekeeper of his house and official midwife to the settlement. That is fiction – she was indeed a midwife and an expert animal-tamer and farmer (as Beccaceci says), but Vernet never met her since he left the islands before she arrived, and it was only later that she worked as a gaucho (see fig. 5.20b). She was a remarkable and extremely useful person (she was also expert with a gun), but she is not mentioned once in Louis Vernet's papers or in the diaries of María or Emilio Vernet, which would be inconceivable if she had been present. The evidence is perfectly clear that she arrived in the *Sarandí* in October 1832, after Vernet and his family had left (sections 5.20, 6.18, 6.19). Like many Argentine books on the Falklands, Beccaceci's work mixes truth (e.g. with reference to the Argentine gauchos who arrived in the 1840s) with fiction. See our review in *Penguin News*, 17 May 2019, pp. 12-13.

[3] "Acta / Celebrada en el Puerto de la Soledad en las Yslas Malvinas"; one original is in Academia Nacional de Historia, Colección Enrique Fitte, Sección III, no. 83; it is illustrated in Muñoz Azpiri 1966, vol. 1, p. 102. Kohen and Rodríguez (p. 197, fn.) mention this document, without exact source; a slightly different original is illustrated, without source, in Caillet-Bois 1948, between pp. 216 and 217; in 2nd ed. 1952 opp. p. 209 (no illustrations in 3rd ed. 1982).

[4] Passages from two logs, the "captain's log" and the "ship's log", in AGN VII, 130, doc. 45, all in Vernet's hand.

[5] Note by Pinedo in AGN III, 27-8-4, doc. 33, Buenos Aires 16 January 1833, saying he had two men aboard whom he had assigned to the ship's crew in November 1832, "as incorrigible and idle": "the Mulatto Mariano López and the individual Manuel Ruiz"; the latter had lost his left hand. "Mulatto" was a racist term for a person of mixed race.

At Rio in November 1832 Rear Admiral Baker received the Admiralty order to send a ship to visit the Falklands. In the event he sent two small frigates: HMS *Clio* of 18 guns, 382 tons, and HMS *Tyne* of 28 guns, 598 tons.[1] On 28 November he drew up instructions to the *Clio*'s commander, John James Onslow (1785-1856), ordering him to proceed to Port Egmont and "immediately restore" the blockhouse and flagstaff, hoist the Union Flag and repair Fort George; if he found any British subjects he was to "call them publickly" before him and "register their names, Ages, and occupations, together with the time they may have been residing in the Falkland Islands"; if he found any "foreigners" (non-British people), "occupied in peaceable pursuits", he was to ascertain their numbers and nationalities, but was "not to disturb them in their agricultural or other inoffensive employments". If he found any "foreign" (non-British) military force, he was to order them to withdraw, but if they were "decidedly superior to the Force of the Clio" (only possible if they had been American or French) he was to protest against their presence and return to Rio.[2]

That same day HMS *Tyne*, Captain Charles Hope, arrived at Rio from Britain, taking a new British consul, Colonel (later Sir) Belford Hinton Wilson (1804-1858), to his post in Lima, so Baker sent the *Tyne* too, and gave Onslow more orders,[3] informing him that the *Tyne* was following him to the Falklands and instructing him to wait 10 days for her, or 20 days if he found a "decidedly superior" foreign force. Once Onslow had set up a flagstaff and fort he was to leave again, but under the system of "informal empire" that was enough. The rights of sovereignty included the right to come and go as one pleased, and an annual visit by a ship was enough to make that point – Onslow and Hope were to *reassert* British sovereignty, but not to *establish* it by occupation.

Britain sent them to visit the Falklands in response to a perceived threat from the buildup of United States forces in the South Atlantic. The British government at the time under Charles, Earl Grey,[4] was anti-colonialist and did not wish to expand the empire (section 6.27), but feared that some move by the US might affect British trade round Cape Horn and British "fishing" (i.e. sealing) in the Falklands and the South Atlantic, so the *Clio* was sent in order to forestall any possible advance by the United States. And that was exactly what the *Clio* did: her visit to the Falklands forestalled a second visit by the USS *Lexington* (section 6.23).

On 29 November 1832 Commander Onslow left Rio in the *Clio* for the Falklands.

6.19 Mestivier murdered; the Argentine garrison goes on the rampage

The next day, Friday 30 November 1832, while Onslow was sailing down the Brazilian coast and Pinedo was busy around the western Falklands looking for "foreign" ships, Commandant Mestivier was brutally murdered at Port Louis by some soldiers of the Argentine garrison.

This is a highly embarrassing episode for Argentine writers, all of whom play down the awfulness of what happened. Kohen and Rodríguez (p. 179) say only: "In the meantime, a mutiny broke out in Puerto Soledad and Mestivier was murdered on November 30th, 1832." Playing down the mutiny allows the two authors to make absurd assertions about the expulsion of the "population" of the islands (sections 6.24, 6.25). Here is what happened.

The schooner *Rapid* was now immobile on the mud in the inner harbour (the "basin") at Port Louis, and in his log her captain John Ross recorded the murder and the chaos that followed:[5]

At 8 AM the troops of the Island mutinied against their Commander, stabbed & shot him dead in his own kitchen, dragged him out to the green and buried him about two hours after they committed the deed – his

---

[1] Details of the two ships' visits to the Falklands here from *Clio*'s "ship's log", PRO Adm 53/258 (the captain's two logs, PRO Adm 51/3117 and Adm 51/3118, are copied from the ship's log and are less detailed), and from the logs of HMS *Tyne* (the captain's log in PRO Adm 51/3512 and the ship's log in PRO Adm 53/1409, virtually identical).
[2] Baker's orders of 28 November 1832, in PRO Adm 1/2276; copy in PRO, FO 6 500, fols. 96 *recto* to 103 *verso*, plus a copy of Version G of Onslow's report on his visit to Port Louis, fols. 116 *recto* to 124 *recto* (see section 6.30).
[3] Baker's further orders of 28 November 1832, also in PRO Adm 1/2276.
[4] The 2nd Earl Grey (Charles Grey, 1764-1845), Prime Minister 22 November 1830 to 9 July 1834, during whose term the Great Reform Act of 1832 was passed and after whom Earl Grey tea is named (a kind of tea unpleasantly scented with bergamot oil). His fourth son (out of 16 children, 6 daughters and 10 sons), Captain the Hon. George Grey (1809-1891), visited the Falklands in command of HMS *Cleopatra* in 1836-7 (section 6.19).
[5] The *Rapid*'s captain's log, AGN VII, 130, doc. 45, fol. 3 *recto*, copy in Vernet's hand.

wife was in a deplorable case but [I] could not render any assistance whatever at the time – I charged all our small arms and one of our guns as they threatened to murder us and take the Schooner ——

A few weeks later several inhabitants gave Belford Hinton Wilson details of the gruesome murder:[1]

They then dragged forth the body of the unfortunate Governor, and after cutting and mutilating the face, put raw meat and tobacco into his mouth, jumped upon it and treated it with every possible indignity, his Wife, by birth a Buenos Ayrean, described to be a young and amiable woman of twenty two, being within hearing and almost within sight of these proceedings.

The instigator of the mutiny was none other than the adjutant José Antonio Gomila – Pinedo stated in a letter to a Buenos Aires government newspaper that "all the disorder, murdering and everything that happened on the Island was due to him [Gomila], and that he alone is the guilty party".[2] That was confirmed by Mestivier's widow Gertrudis, who wrote in a letter published in a different government newspaper: "I consider Adjutant Gomila the principal perpetrator of the death of my late husband; he incited those who encompassed it".[3]

Even before the murder there had been disorder in the garrison – Mestivier had imprisoned the main culprit, Private Manuel Sáenz Valiente, for stealing spirits, and had had Private Bernardino Cáceres flogged with 75 strokes for wounding a soldier and two civilians, but Sáenz Valiente was freed early on 30 November by his companions.[4] The murder was not a spontaneous outburst; it was planned beforehand, as was confirmed to Belford Hinton Wilson:

… by a woman who at the time of the murder was living with one of the murderers, and who according to her own statement, was informed the night previous by her companion of the intention to kill the Governor in the morning, but was afraid to advise him of his danger…

That woman was Antonina Roxa, as is confirmed by a letter written in February 1837 by one Mr Harger, the purser of HMS *Cleopatra*, which was in the islands from November 1836 to January 1837, commanded by Captain the Hon. George Grey, fourth son of former Prime Minister Charles, Earl Grey. Harger refers to Antonina as a "Spanish woman", and says "The Spanish woman's first husband was a soldier, he was concerned in a murder and executed at Buenos Ayres".[5] So she was in a sense an accessory before the fact – she knew but failed to warn Mestivier. That may be why she stayed in the islands when the garrison left. In short, there is no doubt that the killing of Mestivier was a premeditated act of cold-blooded murder.

For days, anarchy reigned at Port Louis as the Argentine troops went on the rampage. Some of the other soldiers joined the seven principal mutineers, terrifying the inhabitants and robbing their houses – Pinedo says in his report that the troops still at the settlement when he returned had "some accomplices in the mutiny and the plundering".[6] Gomila was now the acting commander of the garrison, but he joined in their excesses, exulting in Mestivier's death, moving into the room of his widow and repeatedly showing her the watch he had stolen from Mestivier's body (as Pinedo stated in his report). Probably Gomila sexually abused her as well; no account mentions that, though he is surely unlikely to have taken up quarters in her room but respected her person.

The Argentine troops intended to capture the *Rapid* in order to leave the islands, and it is clear from Ross's log of the first day, 30 November, that more than the seven murderers were involved:

All hands on board ready to defend ourselves and vessel – Nothing but soldiers flying about fixed bayonets & horsemen flying in every direction… at 9.30 P.M. saw the troops muster with their arms and come down

---

[1] All the quotes from Colonel Belford Hinton Wilson are from his report written at sea aboard HMS *Tyne*, 24 January 1833, in PRO CO 78/1, fols. 205 *recto* to 206 *verso*. He spoke fluent Spanish.

[2] Letter by Pinedo in *La Gaceta Mercantil*, Buenos Aires 11 February 1833, p. 2; part quoted in Fitte 1974, pp. 381-382.

[3] Letter signed "Gertrudis Sánchez, viuda [widow] Mestivier", in *El Lucero*, Buenos Aires 9 February 1833.

[4] Details from statement of Gomila's defence counsel at his trial, Major-General Nicolás de Vedia, 5 February 1833, in *Diario de la Tarde, Comercial, Político y Literario*, Buenos Aires 7 February 1833, p. [1], cols. 1 and 3.

[5] Partial copy of letter in PRO CO 78/3, section G, no doc. no., dated "Rio 28th Feb. 1837", fol. 1 *recto*. In his journal (parts transcribed in *FIJ* 1969, pp. 54-68, and in *FIJ* 1980, pp. 4-9) Grey describes how he sent a party of men ashore from the *Cleopatra* on 2 January 1837 to break up a small schooner manned by "runaway seamen", which was clearly the shallop *Chaloupe*, formerly *Eagle*, as William Smyley confirmed in a letter to Louis Vernet (section 5.19).

[6] Pinedo's report dated 16 January 1833, in AGN VII, 60, fols. 11-27 (all *recto*).

towards us – called all hands to be in readiness to jump the moment they discharged one shot. They crossed our bows, halted… and marched up again leaving a guard of 7 men close ahead of us~

Then, that evening, a French whaler arrived, the *Jean-Jacques* of Saint-Malo, Captain Guérin. The next morning, 1 December 1832, Ross told Guérin what had happened, and Ross recorded in his log that Guérin took Mestivier's widow Gertrudis aboard, she being in a "pitiful condition" (after spending a day in Gomila's clutches). Ross also recorded that Gomila, Henry Metcalf and the storekeeper William Dickson likewise took refuge from the Argentine troops "for the safety of their lives" aboard the *Jean-Jacques*. So Gomila, the acting commander of the garrison, was forced to take refuge from his own troops aboard a foreign ship.

Guérin, who spoke fluent Spanish, went ashore and told the garrison that he would land with 50 armed men and have them all shot if they resisted him, as he recounted in a letter to the French government newspaper *Le Moniteur Universel*, written at Port Louis on 8 December 1832, published in Paris on 5 August 1833.[1] He says the murderers then fled into the Camp with 30 horses, 4,000 cartridges and many weapons.

But even without the main culprits the troops ashore were still threatening, and on the evening of 1 December again looked as if they wanted to capture the *Rapid*, so Captain Ross had both his cannons loaded, and armed his men to keep watch all night. At midnight some of the troops approached the ship, "but did not molest us". On the afternoon of 2 December Ross and Guérin went ashore again with a large party of men, collected the property belonging to Mestivier and his widow, and put it aboard the *Jean-Jacques*. At 8 a.m. on 3 December the *Sarandí's* carpenter appealed to Ross to take him and his assistants aboard the *Rapid* "to save his property from the violence of the soldiers", which Ross did.

That day Guérin called the remaining troops together and told them that all who thought themselves innocent should give up their arms and go aboard his ship. Ross recorded: "Part of the troops surrendered and were put on board the whaler"; some of them took their women and children with them, so with Metcalf, Dickson, Gomila and Gertrudis Mestivier there must have been well over a dozen people sheltering aboard the *Jean-Jacques*.

Guérin thus split the Argentine soldiers into three groups: the main culprits out in the Camp; the "surrenderers" in the *Jean-Jacques*; and the dozen or so unrepentant mutineers still at Port Louis, who were armed to the teeth and continued to terrify the inhabitants, eight more of whom took refuge aboard the *Rapid* on 5 December – the ship's log records: "8 men belonging to the Island came on board for safety", joining the *Sarandí*'s carpenters sheltering aboard.

6.20 Pinedo carries on harassing American ships; Joseph Trott's revenge

Meanwhile, ignorant of the mutiny at Port Louis and the murder of Mestivier, Pinedo sailed on around the islands in the *Sarandí*, obeying the Buenos Aires government's orders to continue the harassment of "foreign" sealing vessels (they were only foreign to Argentina, of course; to all other countries active in the Falklands, it was Argentine ships that were foreign). On 7 December 1832 at New Island he found the American sealer *Sun* of New London. Her captain, Joseph P. Trott, stated later at the US legation in Montevideo that the commander of the *Sarandí* had ordered him "to depart immediately from those fisheries and return to the United States, threatening to capture and send him to Buenos Ayres in case he was again found engaged in them, and declaring his intention to deal in like manner with all American vessels in similar circumstances".[2]

Kohen and Rodríguez (p. 179) recount that incident and summarise the quote, presumably as an example of Argentina's "acts of sovereignty" in the Falklands – but what they do not mention is that Trott ignored Pinedo's orders, carried on sealing around the islands for a month before leaving for Montevideo on 4 January 1833, and then returned to the islands on 5 March (section 6.31). They also omit the fact that Trott's report made Captain Isaac McKeever of the USS *Lexington* decide to

---

[1] Letter in the French government newspaper *Le Moniteur Universel*, Paris 5 August 1833, p. 2, cols. 1-2, dated « Baie de la Soledad (îles Malouines), 8 décembre 1832 ».
[2] Despatch from John D. Mendenhall, Montevideo, 16 January 1833, to George Slacum, in Slacum's letter of 13 July 1833 to US Secretary of State Louis McLane, in Manning 1932, p. 184, fn.

take the ship for a second visit to the Falklands and even to contemplate capturing the *Sarandí* (section 6.23).

Pinedo says Trott told him that an American and a Uruguayan ship had fired at him and had then left for the Magellan Strait, a highly unlikely story (we have found no record of anything comparable). He was telling a cock-and-bull story, sending Pinedo on a wild-goose chase to remove him from the islands for a while, and the result was dramatic. Pinedo sailed to the Strait and spent two weeks on a fruitless search for the offending ships – he could otherwise have been back at Port Louis around 14-16 December; he would have sorted out the chaos and would probably have left for Buenos Aires in late December 1832 taking the murderers of Mestivier for trial, so the meeting in January 1833 between him and Commander Onslow of the *Clio* would never have taken place.

6.21 The murderers caught; the garrison prepares to leave; Argentina reneges on its debts[1]

In the Falklands the *Rapid* was still on the mud in the inner basin at Port Louis, and still had eight inhabitants plus the *Sarandí*'s carpenter and his assistants all sheltering aboard, while the *Jean-Jacques* lay at anchor out in Berkeley Sound with Gertrudis Mestivier, Henry Metcalf, William Dickson, José Gomila and some of the soldiers with their women and children. There were thus some two dozen people (including a third of the civilian population of some 3 dozen) who had taken refuge from the violence of the Argentine garrison, who were still threatening – on 5 December Captain Ross kept "All hands in readiness for defence". At last on 7 December the *Rapid* was hauled off the mud and anchored out in Berkeley Sound, with the refugees still aboard – Ross wrote in his log that day: "the people onshore still in an unsettled condition".

It was the capataz Juan Simon, as Pinedo recounted in his letter to the *Gaceta Mercantil*, who took the initiative in catching the seven leading murderers. He formed an armed posse of gauchos and some French crewmen from the *Jean-Jacques*, and on 7 December 1832 they captured them and brought them back to Port Louis. They were put in irons aboard the *Rapid*, while those who had taken refuge in the two ships went ashore, apart from Gertrudis Mestivier in the *Jean-Jacques*.

On 8 December Captain Guérin of the *Jean-Jacques* presented Adjutant Gomila with a bill for his expenses in accommodating the refugees from the mutiny and for his losses in delaying his voyage. His bill was for 2,503 francs in silver; Gomila accepted his claim and signed a payment order drawn against the government of Buenos Aires in favour of the French consul-general. The next day the *Jean-Jacques* sailed for Buenos Aires, carrying Mestivier's effects and his widow.

By late December Pinedo had been away for over five weeks; Gomila assumed that the *Sarandí* had been wrecked, so Pinedo was not coming back. Gomila therefore assumed full command and decided to evacuate the entire Argentine garrison to Buenos Aires, and on 29 December, as part of his settling of accounts before they left the islands, he signed a receipt for 29 cows and three hides.[2] That day he made an agreement with Captain Ross of the *Rapid*: Ross was to take to Buenos Aires not merely the prisoners, who were already aboard, but the whole garrison with their women and children, their weapons and equipment, plus any civilians who wished to go. Ross had abandoned his voyage to help Gomila and the inhabitants of Port Louis, so he was to get £660 sterling for the loss of profits, plus 40 pesos a day for sheltering the people for the first 21 days. Accordingly, the weapons and tools were placed aboard the *Rapid* in preparation for leaving, and Gomila arranged with Ross that the ship would sail on 31 December 1832. In other words, if things had gone according to Gomila's plan, the Argentine garrison would have left, and only the civilian inhabitants would have remained at Port Louis.

Buenos Aires later reneged on its debts to Guérin and Ross, leaving them both with a major loss from their voyages. Guérin delivered Gomila's payment order to the French consul-general, but on 17 May 1833 Gomila refused to confirm the arrangement he had made with Guérin; as late as July

---

[1] Details in this section on the expenses of Ross and Guérin, and their non-payment, from Ernesto J. Fitte, *Crónicas del Atlántico Sur: Patagonia, Malvinas y Antártida*, Buenos Aires 1974, pp. 380-381 and 386-387, quoting from documents in AGN X, 3-4-5 and 24-1-4, which are apparently now missing – the staff at the AGN told us they suspected that the documentation on this episode was among materials removed from the archives by the Argentine military in 1982.

[2] Separate receipt for 29 cows and 3 hides dated 29 December 1832, i.e. while Gomila was in command, intending to remove the whole garrison to Buenos Aires (AGN VII, 130, doc. 52, "Nº 7", in Gomila's hand).

1835 no payment had been made, and there apparently never was any. The same happened to Ross – in Buenos Aires on 6 February 1833 he presented his claim for compensation for abandoning his whaling voyage and bringing the murderers of Mestivier from Port Louis, but he did not wait to be paid; he accepted a charter from Louis Vernet to return to the Falklands, and left again for Port Louis on 13 February, with supplies and people for the settlement (section 6.31). But his claim for loss of his voyage was not honoured. Pinedo himself was consulted; by then he was on trial, and on 25 February he said he thought the price was excessive. He accepted the claim for 40 pesos per day, but said the claim for £660 should be regarded as null and void, since he had had the weapons and tools removed from the *Rapid* on 1 January 1833 and there had been no reason to evacuate the whole garrison as Gomila had arranged to do. Pinedo was being dishonest – Ross was entitled to compensation for losing his voyage as well as for transporting the people; he did not actually transport the whole garrison or the weapons and tools, but he lost his voyage all the same. Gomila (likewise on trial) said the price was more than twice the value of the ship herself. That was dishonest too – a good whaling voyage might have brought twice the value of the ship. The Argentine historian Ernesto Fitte criticises the Argentine government for not paying its debts; the whole episode is highly embarrassing to Argentina, so if the Argentine military did remove the relevant documents from the AGN in 1982 (see footnote), that may explain why.

The events of November and December 1832 at Port Louis reflect credit on Juan Simon, on the civilian residents of the settlement, and on the captains and crews of the two ships, British and French, who helped restore order and perhaps even saved the lives of the people they sheltered. By contrast, the Argentine troops had behaved abominably – they had brought death, terror and chaos, and had been brought under control by local civilians and outsiders. For any military force, nothing could be more shameful. In addition, the refusal of the Argentine government to pay the agreed compensation to the ships' captains was dishonourable. No wonder Argentine authors, including Kohen and Rodríguez, gloss over this episode.

6.22 The Second Falklands Crisis, Part III: the *Clio* arrives; Pinedo returns to Port Louis[1]

What happened at Port Louis in January 1833 forms the backdrop to Argentine claims to the Falklands, and is described with indignation by many Argentine writers, but their version of events is distorted and erroneous. Kohen and Rodríguez go yet further than other Argentine authors and commit various absurdities, which we discuss below.

Having left Rio in HMS *Clio* on 29 November 1832 (section 6.18), Commander Onslow went first to Port Egmont, where he anchored on 20 December. On 23 December he sent some men ashore to erect a flagstaff and hoist the Union Jack, and following his orders from Rear Admiral Baker, he waited for exactly 10 days for HMS *Tyne*, but she failed to appear, so on 30 December he set sail again. He sailed east along the north coast of the islands towards Port Louis – as Kohen and Rodríguez remark (p. 181), Baker's orders said nothing about going to Port Louis; they say Onslow himself decided to go there, but Baker may of course have told him orally to do so. He sailed east all day on 31 December 1832 and 1 January 1833, and on the evening of 1 January he turned west and began tacking up Berkeley Sound towards Port Louis at its western end.

Without knowing it, he was only two days behind Pinedo in the *Sarandí*, who was also heading towards Port Louis, having been delayed by the wild-goose chase to the Magellan Strait. On 29 December he anchored in Berkeley Sound, where on the 30th a boat arrived from the *Rapid* and another with Gomila and two inhabitants, bringing the shocking news of the mutiny and the murder of Mestivier. Pinedo recorded in his report that Gomila told him seven men were being held prisoner, "and the rest of the troops were in disorder, and he had chartered the Schooner Rapid to go to Buenos Aires, which was due to set Sail the next day".

Pinedo at once moved the *Sarandí* to Port Louis and went ashore. He cancelled the order to remove the whole Argentine garrison – if he had returned two days later, they would no longer have been there. He investigated the murder and Gomila's role in it, consulting Ventura Pasos, Juan

---

[1] Unless otherwise indicated, the details in this section are from Pinedo's report in AGN VII, 60, and/or from the *Clio*'s ship's log (PRO Adm 53/258); her captain's log (PRO Adm 51/3118) is less detailed.

Simon, Henry Metcalf and others. Having established the facts, he confined Gomila aboard the *Sarandí* and on 1 January 1833 he put two privates, Manuel Delgado and Mariano Gadea (who had abused Mestivier's body), aboard the schooner *Rapid*, at the same time putting ashore the weapons and tools, which had been placed aboard the ship in preparation for the whole garrison to leave.

And then, soon after noon on Wednesday 2 January 1833, HMS *Clio* arrived. The arrival of the *Clio* was not the start of a crisis but its continuation: Louis Vernet began the Second Falklands Crisis by seizing three American ships (Part I); the American reaction was the *Lexington* raid on Port Louis (Part II), which led the British government to fear an American threat to Britain's trade and to send the *Clio* to begin a series of annual visits (Part III), which forestalled a proposed second visit by the *Lexington* (section 6.23), so there was no Part IV.

Onslow had perhaps been expecting to find the Americans at Port Louis, but instead he found the "Buenos Ayrean flag" flying and the schooners *Sarandí* and *Rapid* at anchor. He boarded the *Sarandí* and told Pinedo that he intended to raise the British flag the next day, and Pinedo was to withdraw his forces. Pinedo (who spoke good English) protested that he could not leave without orders from his government, and asked Onslow to present his orders in writing. Onslow duly returned to the *Clio* and sent Pinedo a written copy of his message:[1]

I have to acquaint you that I have received directions from His Excellency the Commander-in-Chief of His Britannic Majesty's Ships and Vessels of War, on the South American Station, to exercise the rights of Sovereignty over these Islands, in the name of His Britannic Majesty.

It is my intention to hoist, to-morrow morning, the National Flag of Great Britain on shore; when I request you will be pleased to haul down your Flag, and to withdraw your Forces, taking with you all the stores, &c., belonging to your Government.   I am, &c. / J. J. ONSLOW, *Commander.*

Pinedo's first thought was to resist, but he soon saw it would be impossible – the *Clio* was much more heavily armed, with 18 guns (sixteen 32-pounders and two 6-pounders) against the *Sarandí*'s 9 guns (one 16-pounder, two 12-pounders, two 8-pounders and four short carronades), and many of his own crew were British (only one officer apart from himself was a South American); for British subjects to fire on a British warship would of course have been treason.

The civilian establishment at Port Louis was still functioning, and that day, 2 January 1833, more beef was delivered to the Argentine troops ashore and to the *Sarandí*.[2]

Pinedo began to play for time – at 10 p.m. he sent a delegation to the *Clio* to inform Onslow that "I would resist at all costs… and that he should think his orders over…" That was a silly suggestion – a naval officer was not entitled to "think his orders over". The delegation was also charged with a face-saving exercise, to ask Onslow to delay raising the British flag until Pinedo had left in the *Sarandí*.[3] That would allow him to claim later that he had left the Argentine flag flying. But Onslow was asleep and could not be disturbed, so the delegation returned to the *Sarandí*.

Pinedo released Gomila and gave him arms for the troops, and gave the capataz Juan Simon arms for the eight men he said he could command. After a sleepless night Pinedo visited Onslow on 3 January. Pinedo recorded that Onslow told him that he had been ordered to raise the English flag and that the "officers, troops, inhabitants and property of our State" were to be taken to Buenos Aires, but "those inhabitants who freely wished it should remain". Onslow was also going to lower the Argentine flag; Pinedo acquiesced, seeing how few men he had, and that his orders were not to fire on a foreign warship but "solely to defend my ship if attacked by the enemy; and I was not authorised to do so to defend the Islands nor for this case". He said he would embark his troops, but leave the Argentine flag flying. He took the soldiers aboard to defend the ship and had the Argentine flag raised ashore, "and charged the Capataz of the Islands, D[on] Juan Simon, with that task, whom I authorised by a document which I gave him, nominating him political and military Commandant of the Malvinas Islands…". So when the villain Antonio Rivero shot Simon dead in cold blood in August 1833 (section 6.32), he murdered the official representative of Argentina.

---

[1] Text from *British and Foreign State Papers 1832-1833* (*BFSP*), vol. XX, London 1836, p. 1197; italics in *BFSP*.
[2] Account in AGN VII, 130, doc. 52, "Nº 8", in Henry Metcalf's hand, 27 January 1833, recording deliveries of cattle, oil, hides and other supplies to the troops and the *Sarandí* from 9 October 1832 to 2 January 1833 inclusive.
[3] Testimony of Guillermo Mason at Pinedo's trial (in AGN VII, 60, fols. 34-35).

Onslow landed with some men and raised two Union Jacks at the settlement, then lowered the Argentine flag and sent it back to Pinedo. Pinedo completed his water supply, collected some Argentine government property and embarked the garrison's possessions, their women and children and any inhabitants who wished to leave. Onslow had said that any who wished to remain could do so, as Juan Simon confirmed in a letter to Vernet written for him by Ventura Pasos: "Command[r] Pinedo told the people that anyone who wished to go to B[ueno]s ay[re]s.[,] he would take him[,] and he took some gauchos…".[1] That was also stated by some who chose to stay (Antonio Rivero, Anton Vaihinger, Santiago López, José María Luna, Pedro Salinas, Pascual Diaz and Manuel Coronel).[2] Their statements demonstrate that the British did not expel the civilian residents.

On the morning of 4 January Onslow bought beef (and paid for it in silver), and at 4 p.m. Pinedo sailed – in his report he said "the following day", using the nautical day, in which the date and day changed at noon; by the civil day the date was 4 January, as confirmed by Onslow's report and the *Clio*'s ship's log, which records the sailing of the *Sarandí* on the 4th.[3]

That same day Captain Joseph Trott left the western Falklands in the schooner *Sun*, to report at Montevideo that he had been harassed by Pinedo at New Island on 7 December 1832 (section 6.18). So for the next two weeks the *Sun* and the *Sarandí* were both heading northwards; both bore the explosive news that they had been expelled from the Falklands, and the *Sarandí* also bore the awful news of the mutiny of the Argentine garrison and the murder of Commandant Mestivier.

Several witnesses at Pinedo's trial in January and February 1833 said some people who arrived in the *Sarandí* did not return in her to Buenos Aires – the *Sarandí*'s surgeon John Clark said there were four men and a woman.[4] There had indeed been four men and a woman who stayed behind: William Dickson, Henry Metcalf, Anton Vaihinger, Ventura Pasos and Antonina Roxa. In addition to those five people, two crewmen deserted from the ship:[5] the American William Drake and the Englishman Charles Brasier, who were taken aboard the *Clio* on 6 January 1833. Clark did not of course know that Metcalf and Pasos left again aboard the *Rapid* after he himself left in the *Sarandí*, and Drake and Brasier left in the *Clio*. So, of the 7 people who stayed behind from the *Sarandí*, only Dickson, Vaihinger and Antonina were still at Port Louis after all three ships had left.

At Port Louis on Saturday 5 January, the day after the *Sarandí* left, Juan Simon and Henry Metcalf visited Commander Onslow aboard the *Clio* and asked him how they should carry on. Onslow said work should go on as usual[6] – he was fulfilling Baker's order that if he found any "Foreigners" in the islands, he was "not to disturb them in their agricultural or other inoffensive employments". Later that day the *Rapid* left Port Louis for Buenos Aires, carrying nine of the ten principal culprits in the murder of Mestivier (the tenth, Gomila, had already left in the *Sarandí*).

On 7 January, following his orders, Onslow called the residents into the main room of what had been Vernet's and Mestivier's house and drew up a list of "the people", as Juan Simon recounted, or "the Settlers", as Onslow called them. Onslow listed only the 18 men (fig. 6.22a); for him the three women and the child (fig. 6.22b) did not count as "settlers".

And on 10 January 1833, Onslow sailed in the *Clio* – without two letters to Louis Vernet dictated by the illiterate Juan Simon to William Dickson, in which Simon told Vernet about the ugly mood of the gauchos and said he would not be able to get them to work for him much longer. In bitter frustration at seeing the ship sailing away without the vital letters, Simon tore them them up at the kitchen door of the main house.[7]

---

[1] Juan Simon's letter to Vernet, 2 April 1833, in AGN VII, 130, doc. 62.
[2] Group of statements by the gauchos in AGN VII, 130, docs. 235-249.
[3] Misled by ignorance of the nautical day, Governor Balcarce and foreign minister Maza assumed in their Message to the Buenos Aires legislature that Pinedo sailed on 5 January (followed in Fitte 1974, p. 384).
[4] Pinedo trial evidence, AGN VII 60, fol. 50. Other witnesses gave slightly different numbers of people who remained.
[5] Stated at Pinedo's trial by one of the *Sarandí*'s lieutenants, Roberto Elliot (statement in AGN VII, 60). They were clearly Drake and Brasier (there is no record of any others); the *Clio*'s ship's log (PRO Adm 53/258) and her captain's log (PRO Adm 51/3118) both record that they were taken aboard on the afternoon of Sunday 6 January 1833. Drake and Brasier had been at Port Louis in 1831; they had gone to Buenos Aires as crewmen of the *Harriet*, then returned to the Falklands in the *Sarandí* as crewmen.
[6] Juan Simon's letter to Vernet, 2 April 1833, AGN VII, 130, doc. 62, fol. 2 *verso*.
[7] Juan Simon's letter to Vernet, 2 April 1833, AGN VII, 130, doc. 62, fol. 3 *recto*.

Tables 6.22a and 6.22b: Onslow's list of settlers, 7 January 1833[1]

A List of the Settlers at Port Louis, Berkley Sound, East Falkland

Names	Age	Nativity	Occupation	Length of time in the Islands	Remarks
Wm Dickson	28	Ireland	Merchant	5 Years	In charge of the Flag
Jean Simon	31	France	Agriculturalist[2]	6 do	
Ant° Rivero	26	Buenos Ayres	Gaucho	2 do	
Jose Luna	30	do	do	2 do	
Santigo Lopes	31	do	do	2 do	
Manuel Coronel	28	do	do	2[3] do	
Piedro Firmyn[4]	22	do	do	2 do	
Luciano Flores	25	do	do	2 do	M^r. Vernet's Establishment
Manuel Galon[5]	22	do	do	2 do	
Phillip Phillipes[6]	25	do	do	2 do	
Lataro St. Juan[7]	28	do	do	2 do	
Fautino Martinez	30	do	do	2 do	
Piedro Allecio[8]	23	do	do	2 do	
Pascual Diez	30	do	do	2 do	
Benjⁿ Pearson	40	Jamaica	Carpenter	1 do	
Ant° Werner[9]	38	Germany	Agriculturalist	2 Years	Pursuing their respective Employment.
Wm Jones	20	London	Sailor	6 months	
Ch^s Kusserler[10]	32	Germany	Tailor	2 years	

6.22a The population that stayed, (i) (above).
The 18 adult male inhabitants remaining at Port Louis, 7 January 1833, as listed by Commander Onslow.

Antonina Roxa	*35?*	*Buenos Aires*	*Various*	*3 months (since arrival in the Sarandí)*
Gregoria Madrid	*25?*	*Buenos Aires*	*Servant (former slave)*	*4 years (since 1828)*
Carmelita –	*25?*	*Buenos Aires*	*Servant (former slave)*	*4 years (since 1828)*
José Simon	*2?*[11]	*Port Louis*	*Son of Carmelita*	*(born at Port Louis)*

6.22b. The population that stayed, (ii) (above).
People also present but not listed by Onslow, January 1833.

After HMS *Clio* left there followed what we call "the year of limbo" – exactly a year between 10 January 1833 and the raising of the Union Jack at Port Louis by Lieutenant Henry Smith on 10 January 1834, during which time there was no official British presence in the islands (section 6.31).

6.23 The Second Falklands Crisis, Part III (con.): no Part IV (no second *Lexington* raid)

Neither Kohen and Rodríguez, nor any other author as far as we know, notes an important consequence of the *Clio*'s visit to the Falklands: the Second Falklands Crisis had no Part IV – there was no second visit to the islands by the USS *Lexington*. As described in sections 6.20 and 6.22,

---

[1] Fair copy in PRO Adm 1/2276; another similar fair copy in PRO FO 6 500, fol. 195 *recto*.

[2] Juan Simon was the capataz (foreman) of the gauchos; as a cattle-herder he could be described as "Agriculturalist".

[3] Coronel had arrived in the islands in 1826, but had left in 1827 and returned in 1831.

[4] Pedro Firmin (Fermin, Firmyn) had been ill for several months, was bedridden from about February and died on 8 July 1833 (date given in the 1833 Port Louis Log, PRO Adm 1/42, no. 2).

[5] This was no doubt Manuel Godoy, one of the four remaining Charrúa Indians.

[6] This was no doubt Felipe Salazar, another Charrúa.

[7] This was clearly the Charrúa described in other lists as "Lattore"; he and "Luciano Flores", "Manuel Galon" [Godoy] and "Phillip Phillipes"[Salazar] were the four remaining Charrúas. The fifth Charrúa, "Manuel González", had been taken away in the *Lexington*; he returned in March 1833.

[8] This was no doubt Pedro Salinas – the soft, somewhat retracted pronunciation of "s" in Spanish may not have been heard as such by an English-speaking clerk, who heard the name as beginning with "A-".

[9] Spellings in other documents suggest that his name was actually Anton Vaihinger.

[10] His name was actually F[riedrich?] Carl Kußler (Kussler), as is confirmed by the 1837 Port Louis census.

[11] José's name and age taken from the Port Louis census of January 1842, which gives his age as 11 at that time.

Captain Joseph Trott of the American schooner *Sun* had been stopped by Pinedo in the *Sarandí* at New Island on 7 December 1832 and ordered to leave the islands; he ignored the order and sent Pinedo on a wild-goose chase to the Magellan Strait while he himself continued sealing around the Falklands for another month. He left the islands on 4 January 1833 (the same day as Pinedo), and on 16 January 1833 he arrived at Montevideo.

At Montevideo was the USS *Lexington* under her new captain Isaac McKeever, who was under orders to defend US interests in the South Atlantic. Throughout the time the Argentine garrison spent at Port Louis, while Pinedo was looking for "foreign" ships to expel from the Falklands, the *Lexington* had been there in the South Atlantic to prevent him from doing precisely that. Trott went straight to McKeever and told him that he had been harassed and expelled from the Falklands by Pinedo in the *Sarandí*; the US legation's secretary, John Mendenhall, sent US consul George Slacum an account which Slacum forwarded to US Secretary of State Louis McLane. McKeever decided to sail to the islands to put an end to the harassment of American ships by the Argentinians – he even thought he might have to capture the *Sarandí*.[1] The same day, 16 January 1833, he began writing a despatch to US Navy Secretary Levi Woodbury, informing him of his intentions, but before he could finish it he received a message that the previous day the *Sarandí* had sailed past Montevideo up the River Plate towards Buenos Aires, and was thus no longer in the Falklands, so he cancelled his trip[2] – the threat to American ships from the Argentine garrison had gone. Britain had sent the *Clio* to visit the Falklands in order to forestall any American moves to become involved in the islands, and the visit had exactly that effect – the *Clio*'s expulsion of the *Sarandí* forestalled a second visit to the islands by the *Lexington*.

But McKeever told Navy Secretary Woodbury that at his suggestion "the schooner Sun will return to the fisheries and continue her occupation in defiance of the illegal warning received." Whatever happened, the Americans were not going to allow the Argentinians to harass their ships; to the US government, any such actions by Argentina were illegal. And the *Sun* did return to the Falklands: she arrived at Port Louis on 5 March 1833 under Captain Trott, and was still in the islands in mid-August, as recorded in the "1833 Port Louis Log" (section 6.31).[3]

Kohen and Rodríguez were evidently unaware of American intentions – they say (p. 186):

If the British eviction had not occurred, the population would have remained on the islands, and the reestablishment of order would have permitted the return of the population sent scattering by the "Lexington" in 1831 [*sic*; the *Lexington* actually left in January 1832].

That is untrue – if Britain had not sent the *Clio*, the *Lexington* would have returned to the islands and prevented the Argentine garrison from remaining, and might have captured the *Sarandí*. And the Americans would not have allowed Louis Vernet to be there – he was wanted in the United States for piracy. Those important aspects of the story have hitherto been ignored in works on Falklands history. Neither Britain, nor the United States, nor Spain accepted that Argentina had any right to exercise sovereignty in the islands.

6.24 The Second Falklands Crisis, Part III (con.): those expelled and those not expelled

The *Sarandí* and the *Rapid* both reached Buenos Aires on 15 January 1833, and all passengers and prisoners were taken ashore. The next day Pinedo drew up a list of 53 people brought from Port Louis in the two ships (apart of course from the ships' crews, who included himself and the pilot, Mathew Brisbane, who only became resident in March 1833, section 6.31).

---

[1] Details in despatch from John Mendenhall, secretary of the US Legation in Montevideo, to US Consul George Slacum, 16 January 1833, enclosed in Slacum to McLane, 13 July 1833, printed in Manning 1932, p. 184, fn.
[2] Despatch by McKeever to US Navy Secretary Levi Woodbury, 16 January 1833, in US Archives, Naval Record Group 45, microfilm 18, doc. 20. Not in Manning 1932.
[3] The *Sun* is mentioned in the 1833 Port Louis Log (PRO Adm 1/42, nos. 1 and 2) on 5 and 14 March; 1, 6 and 7 April; and on 9, 14 and 17 August, mostly at Port Louis but also at Johnson's Harbour; Captain Trott is named on 5 March and 9 August. The *Sun* is not mentioned in PLSR, so she never visited Port Louis between 1826 and December 1831.

Table 6.24a. Pinedo's list of 53 people brought from Port Louis[1]

Lista de la Tropa sus familias y peones de la Ysla
Malvinas que vienen de pasaje en la Sarandy.[2]

Capitán D. Juan Antonio Gomila – **[banished & placed on half pay]**[7]

Batallon de Artilleria

Cavo 1º - - Miguel Hernandes, y su muger Maria Romero.
Soldados- - Jose Barrera
          Jose Gomes
          Manuel Franco Fernandes
          Toribio Montesuma

Baton del Rio de la Plata

Sargto-2º- Santiago Almandos
Soldados- Jose Soto
         Jose Rodrigues

Patricios de Bs Ayres

Soldados- Juan Castro y su muger Manuela Navarro
         Antonio Garcia

Guardia Argentina

Cavo - - Daniel Molina
Soldados- Juan J. Rivas y su muger Maria J. Beldaño.
         Dionisio Godoy
         Ypolito Villarreal y su muger Lucia Correa y dos hijos
         Gregorio Duran y su muger Carmen Manzanares con dos hijos
         Benito Vidal y su muger Maria Saisa

Yndividuos de la Ysla

Juaquin Acuña su muger Juana[3]
Mateo Gonsales su muger Marica

Estrangeros[4] { Jose Viel - - -
            Juan Quedy
            Franco Ferreyra [= Freire]

y el preso **M**aximo **W**arnes. que fue destinado.[5]

                        Sigue ["Continues"]

Mugeres pertenecientes a los militares qe vienen presos en la Goleta Ynglesa Rapid. y qe vienen en dha Sarandy[6]

Maria Rodrigues con tres hijos
Anastacia Romero
Encarnacion Albares
Carmen Benites
Transita Gonsales con un hijo.

Militares que vienen presos en la Goleta Ynga Rapid.[7]

Batallon de Artilleria

Soldado- Jose Antonio Dias **[shot]**

Rio de la Plata

Soldados- Manuel Delgado **[100 lashes, 6 yrs army]**
         Mariano Gadea   **[200 lashes, 8 yrs army]**
         Manuel Suares **[shot]**

Patricios de B Ays

Cavo 1º - - Franco Ramires **[shot]**
Soldados- - Bernardino Caceres **[shot]**
           Manuel Saenz Valiente[8] **[shot]**
           Antonio Moncada **[shot]**

Guardia Argentina

Sargto-2º- Jose Maria Diaz **[shot]**

Bs A. Enº 16 de 1833 —— Jose M.. de Pinedo

Summary [added here]:

26 soldiers (including 9 as prisoners in the *Rapid*)
11 soldiers' women
8 soldiers' children
45 belonging to the military garrison

4 civilian residents (two couples)
4 "foreigners" (including the prisoner Warnes)
8 civilians

Total listed: 53 (32 men, 13 women, 8 children; 44 aboard *Sarandí*, 9 aboard *Rapid*).

7 civilians omitted: Mariano López and Manuel Ruiz, aboard the *Sarandí* since November 1832 (+ José Báez); Henry Metcalf and Ventura Pasos in *Rapid*.
(also Charles Brasier and William Drake in *Clio*)

---

[1] In AGN III, Marina, Rendiciones de Cuentas 1830-1851, legajo 1320 (old-style reference Sala III, legajo 17-6-5), list in Pinedo's hand; extra-thick letters are here in bold type; all in Pinedo's original spelling; summary in bold print at end added by us. Pinedo's list was first published (in modernised spelling) in Ernesto J. Fitte, *La Agresión Norteamericana a las Islas Malvinas*, Buenos Aires 1966, pp. 372-373, who gives an incorrect old-style reference ("AGN, Sala III, 16-6-5", which is followed in Kohen and Rodríguez 2015, p. 185, fn.), but Fitte gives the correct old-style reference in *Crónicas del Atlántico Sur...*, Buenos Aires 1974, p. 385. Fitte omits Pinedo's bracket, thus obscuring the distinction between the "Individuals from the Island" and the "Foreigners". "Muger": "woman"; "Con un / dos / tres hijos": "With one / two / three children". Summary in bold print at end added by us.

[2] "List of the troops their families and farmhands [i.e. "gauchos"] from the Ysla Malvina who came on passage in the Sarandy". "Cavo" (= cabo): corporal; "Soldado": private; "Sargento Secundo": lance-sergeant, sergeant 2nd class.

[3] In their statements for Vernet of February 1833, in AGN VII 136, Acuña and González describe themselves as bachelors (so Juana and Marica were "common law wives"). Acuña was a native of Brazil, González of Uruguay.

[4] "Foreigners"; these three are bracketed together with a large swung (curly) bracket at left. Viel and Quedy presumably arrived aboard the *Sarandí* in October 1832; "Ferreyra" (i.e. Freire) was a Galician seaman who had been in the islands for some time and had been resident at Port Louis at times in 1832.

[5] "and the prisoner Maximo Warnes. who was sent". Lynch's list includes Warnes among the "Estrangeros".

[6] "Women belonging to the soldiers who came as prisoners in the English Schooner Rapid, and who came in the said Sarandy." All had of course arrived in the *Sarandí*, but only the 9 culprits returned to Buenos Aires in the *Rapid*

[7] These 9 were the mutineers who (with Gomila) were involved in the murder of Mestivier; the 7 here marked "**[shot]**" were shot on 8 February 1833; the others' sentences are as given (*BPAN*, Buenos Aires 9 February 1833).

[8] Ringleader of the mutineers [and murderers; shot and hanged like the others, but his right hand was cut off as well.

We reproduce Pinedo's list in Table 6.24a (with notes and brief summary) and add a summary table (Table 6.24b). In Table 6.24c we list the 37 people not belonging to the garrison who were at Port Louis immediately before the ships left, and mark in bold type the 22 who remained there; the nationalities of all those people are tabulated in Table 6.24d.

The 53 people listed by Pinedo comprised 45 who belonged to the garrison and 8 who did not. In addition, there were 7 people he did not list: 3 in the *Sarandí*, 2 in the *Rapid*, and 2 in the *Clio*. So in addition to the ships' crews, exactly 60 people left the islands in the three ships: the garrison plus 15 others. The Buenos Aires harbourmaster Francisco Lynch drew up a list based on Pinedo's but omitting a few details;[1] Kohen and Rodríguez illustrate the first page of Pinedo's list (p. 186),[2] and list the people (p. 185), but they partly follow Lynch's list without saying so, and they manipulate the evidence and grossly distort the facts.

Table 6.24b Summary of Pinedo's list: our categories of people

Aboard the *Sarandí*:

	Total
Pinedo's page 1 (our left-hand column in fig. 6.24a):	
(a) soldiers and their women and children (17 soldiers, 6 women and 4 children);	27
(b) residents and their women (2 men and 2 women);	4
(c) foreigners (3 men);	3
(d) a prisoner (1 man);	1
Pinedo's page 2 (our right-hand column in fig. 6.24a):	
(e) mutineers' women and children (5 women and 4 children);	9

Aboard the *Rapid*:

(f) mutineers under arrest (9 men).	9
Overall total of those listed by Pinedo:	**53**

Table 6.24b summarises the categories into which Pinedo divided the people. All were aboard the *Sarandí* except the 9 principal culprits in our category (f), who were in the *Rapid*, though their 5 women and 4 children were in the *Sarandí*. Some of the soldiers in category (a) had also been involved in the mutiny, as had Adjutant Gomila – the log of Captain John Ross of the *Rapid* makes it clear that a large part of the garrison were involved.

The 4 people in our category (b), Pinedo's "Individuals from the Island", i.e. civilian residents, were Joaquín Acuña (Brazilian) and Mateo Gonzáles (Uruguayan), with their respective women Juana and Marica; Acuña had apparently been put aboard the *Sarandí* as a slacker by Mathew Brisbane.[3] Pinedo brackets 3 men together as "Foreigners" (our category c): José Viel and Juan Quedy (who had seemingly arrived in the *Sarandí*) and Francisco "Ferreyra" (spelt "Freire" in other documents), a seaman from Galicia, Spain, who had been in the islands for some time. Pinedo placed the residents and the "Foreigners" in different categories – to him, the residents belonged to the islands whereas the "Foreigners" did not. Pinedo's first page (Table 6.24a, left-hand column) ends: "and the prisoner Maximo Warnes, who was sent", which places him in a separate category, i.e. our (d) in Table 6.24b; his English surname suggests he was a "Foreigner" too, but Pinedo brackets only Quedy, Viel and "Ferreyra" as "Foreigners", excluding Warnes.

---

[1] Lynch's list follows Pinedo's list in the same folder, AGN III, 1320, and is clearly derivative of it. Lynch does not name the Foreigners' women, and brackets 6 men together (Acuña, Gonzáles, Viel, Quedy, "Ferreyra" and Warnes) under the heading "Individuos de la Ysla" labelling all 6 as "Extrangeros". Lynch thus drops Pinedo's distinction between the "Individuals from the Island" and the "Foreigners", and places Warnes among the Foreigners without saying he was a prisoner. Kohen and Rodríguez refer only to Pinedo's list but give only Fitte as their source, though Fitte prints Pinedo's details on Warnes ("y el preso… que fue destinado"), which they suppress.

[2] The same first page, in colour, is in their English translation; we illustrated it too in *False Falklands History*, p. 4.

[3] Letter from Vernet to Brisbane (by then dead), 18 November 1833, in AGN VII 130, doc. 70.

Table 6.24c: People not belonging to the garrison, at Port Louis on 1 January 1833[1]

Men	Origin	Fate
Joaquín Acuña	Brazil (*Elbe* group)	Removed in *Sarandí* Jan. 1833
[José Báez]	Uruguay (*Elbe* group)	?Taken aboard *Sarandí* Nov. 1832?
[Charles Brasier]	Britain (arrived in *Sarandí*)	Removed in *Clio* Jan. 1833
Manuel Coronel	Buenos Aires (*Elbe* group)	**Remained**; d. Port Louis 5 Nov. 1841
Pascual Diaz	Buenos Aires	**Remained**
William Dickson	Ireland (arrived back in *Sarandí*)	**Remained**; *murder victim 26.8.1833*
[William Drake]	USA (arrived in *Sarandí*)	Removed in *Clio* Jan. 1833
Pedro Fermin	Buenos Aires	**Remained**; died 8 July 1833
"Luciano Flores"	Uruguay (Charrúa Indian, *Elbe* group)	**Remained; murderer**
Francisco Freire	Galicia, Spain	Departed in *Sarandí* Jan. 1833
"Manuel Godoy"	Uruguay (Charrúa Indian, *Elbe* group)	**Remained; murderer**
Mateo González	Uruguay (*Elbe* group)	Departed in *Sarandí* Jan. 1833
William Jones	Britain	**Remained** (left before Aug. 1833)
Carl Kussler	Germany	**Remained**
"Latorre"	Uruguay (Charrúa Indian, *Elbe* group)	**Remained; murderer**
[Mariano López]	Uruguay (*Elbe* group)	Taken aboard *Sarandí* Nov. 1832
Santiago López	Buenos Aires	**Remained**
José María Luna	Chile	**Remained; (murderer)**
Faustino Martínez	Buenos Aires	**Remained**
Henry Metcalf	USA (arrived back in *Sarandí*)	Departed in *Rapid* Jan. 1833
Ventura Pasos	Buenos Aires (arrived in *Sarandí*)	Departed in *Rapid* Jan. 1833; *murder victim 26.8.1833*
Benjamin Pearson	Jamaica	**Remained** (left before Aug. 1833)
Juan Quedy	?South America (?arrived in *Sarandí*)	Departed in *Sarandí* Jan. 1833
Antonio Rivero	Buenos Aires	**Remained; leading murderer**
[Manuel Ruiz]	Uruguay (*Elbe* group)	Taken aboard *Sarandí* Nov. 1832
"Felipe Salazar"	Uruguay (Charrúa Indian, *Elbe* group)	**Remained; murderer**
Pedro Salinas	Uruguay (*Elbe* group)	**Remained**; sent away March 1833
Juan Simon	France / Argentina	**Remained**; *murder victim 26.8.1833*
Anton Vaihinger	Germany (arrived back in *Sarandí*)	**Remained**; *murder victim 26.8.1833*
José Viel	?South America (?arrived in *Sarandí*)	Departed in *Sarandí* Jan. 1833
Maximo Warnes	Prisoner (arrived in *Sarandí*)	Removed in *Sarandí* Jan. 1833
Women		
Carmelita	Africa (slave brought by Vernet 2 Sept. 1828)	**Remained**; died Stanley 27 Oct. 1845
Gregoria	Africa (slave brought by Vernet 2 Sept. 1828)	**Remained**; died Stanley 11 Apr. 1871
Antonina Roxa	Argentina (arrived in *Sarandí*)	**Remained**; died Stanley 14 Feb. 1869
Juana	Uruguay (*Elbe* group)	Departed in *Sarandí* Jan. 1833
Marica	Uruguay (*Elbe* group)	Departed in *Sarandí* Jan. 1833
Children		
José Simon	Born at Port Louis, 1831	**Remained**; left 1858-9?

Total: 37 on 1 January 1833   After *Sarandí*, *Rapid* and *Clio* left: **22 remained**

---

[1] Names in quotes: assumed names (the Charrúa Indians); "Departed": left voluntarily; "Removed": taken away without choice. Mathew Brisbane was not resident; he came back in the *Sarandí* as pilot and left again. The "*Elbe* group" = the remaining 13 out of those who arrived in the British brigantine *Elbe* on 15 July 1831, including 4 Charrúas; only 18 names out of a maximum of 28 people are recorded, but none of the unnamed 10 were still present in January 1833. Of the 18 nameable people in the *Elbe* group, Telésforo Moreno was murdered in June 1832, and 4 had been taken away by the USS *Lexington* (Sylvestre Núñez, Juan Brasido, Domingo Valleja and the 5th Charrúa, "Manuel González"). Mariano López and Manuel Ruiz were taken aboard the *Sarandí* as "slackers" by Pinedo in November 1832, and probably José Báez too; they were at Port Louis in January 1833 but aboard the *Sarandí*, not resident on land (names in square brackets). Charles Brasier and William Drake arrived in the *Sarandí*, but deserted and were taken away by the *Clio*. Juan Quedy and José Viel are mysterious; they seem to have arrived in the *Sarandí* but are not recorded in any other document, and their role is unclear. Antonina Roxa had arrived attached to one of the men of the garrison, but decided to remain, so we count her as not belonging to the garrison. **Bold print**: the 22 who remained at Port Louis after the *Clio* left on 10 January 1833, with their fates to August 1833; "arrived back in *Sarandí*": the 3 who had lived at Port Louis and had left in the *Harriet* (Vaihinger) or *Lexington* (Dickson, Metcalf); "**murderer**": Rivero and his group (Luna escaped from Rivero – **murderer** in brackets); see section 6.36; "*murder victim 26.8.1833*": those murdered by Rivero and his group; the 5th victim, Mathew Brisbane, left and returned later with Pasos.

Kohen and Rodríguez conflate Pinedo's categories and state (p. 185) that among those taken to Buenos Aires there were "17 inhabitants of the islands that worked there", but that is not how Pinedo saw them. Kohen and Rodríguez lump together all those in our categories (b) to (e) in table 6.24b, who actually comprised 4 civilian residents, 3 "foreigners", 1 prisoner, and also what Kohen and Rodríguez call "a female group" of 5 women and 4 children, whom they include among the civilian workers! In fact those last 9 people belonged to the garrison – they were the "camp-followers" of the murderers, not ordinary residents of the islands. To Pinedo those people belonged in several different categories – they were not simply "17 inhabitants of the islands". The nationalities of the people in both lists in Table 6.24c are tabulated in Table 6.24d:

Table 6.24d: Nationalities and numbers of civilians at Port Louis on 1 and 11 January 1833[1]

	1 Jan	departed	11 Jan
Africa	2	-	2
Argentina	10	2	8
Brazil	1	1	0
Britain incl. Ireland	3	1	2
Chile	1	-	1
Falklands	1	-	1
Germany	2	-	2
Jamaica	1	-	1
South America?	2	2	0
Spain	1	1	0
Uruguay	11	6	5
United States	2	2	0
Total:	37	15	22

As mentioned above, Pinedo does not list all those who left; he names only 8 of the people not belonging to the garrison: José Viel, Juan Quedy, Francisco Freire, Maximo Warnes, Joaquín Acuña, Mateo González, Juana and Marica. He omits 7 people who left at the same time, namely:

(i) the 3 men he took aboard the *Sarandí* in November 1832 (Mariano López, Manuel Ruiz and probably José Báez), who were taken away by Argentina without any British involvement;

(ii) Henry Metcalf and Ventura Pasos, who left by their own choice in the *Rapid*, and

(iii) the American William Drake and the Englishman Charles Brasier, who had arrived as crewmen of the *Sarandí*, deserted, and were taken aboard the *Clio*.

So, to sum up, including all those mentioned and not mentioned by Pinedo, there were in all 60 people who had been for a time resident on land and left the islands aboard the three ships *Sarandí*, *Rapid* and *Clio*: 53 people mentioned by Pinedo plus 7 not mentioned. Of those 60 people, 45 belonged to the garrison and 15 did not (14 civilian residents and the prisoner Warnes). Of the 15 people not connected with the garrison, 7 clearly or possibly left of their own free will: Metcalf and Pasos clearly left by their own decision, while Mateo González and his woman Marica, Francisco Freire, José Viel and Juan Quedy seem to have chosen to leave.

There were *at most* 8 people not belonging to the garrison who were taken away against their will. Of them, 6 were removed from the islands by Argentina without British involvement: Mariano López, Manuel Ruiz, Joaquín Acuña plus his woman Juana, the prisoner Maximo Warnes, and no doubt also José Báez, who is not mentioned in the documentation on the *Sarandí*'s voyage but was in the islands for much of 1832[2] and clearly returned to Buenos Aires in the *Sarandí* with the

---

[1] In Table 6.24d we give the origin of Juan Simon as "Argentina" (he was of French origin but was presumably born in Argentina), of the Charrúas as "Uruguay", Maximo Warnes as "Argentina", Juan Quedy and José Viel as "South America?", Carmelita and Gregoria as "Africa", and José Simon as "Falklands".

[2] Of 17 gauchos Báez owed Vernet the largest amount, according to a list signed "Enrique Metcalf", Buenos Aires 27 January 1833, in AGN VII, 130, doc. 52, "Nº 9 CC". The debts, in pesos and reales (eighths of a peso) are: Mateo González 272-7; Pedro Salinas 415-2; Joaquin Acuña 398-7; Mariano López 359-7; Santiago López 231-2; José Báez 491; Antonio Rivero 214-4; Manuel Ruiz 227-1; José Luna 280-2; Pascual Diaz 155-3; Manuel Martínez [a slip for Faustino Martínez] 76-2; Manuel Coronel 60-6; Pedro Fermin 45-5; Dionisio Eredia 320; Jacinto Correa 335; Domingo

others.¹ Of the 2 men removed by the *Clio*, William Drake was presumably taken away against his will, but Charles Brasier may have been taken away at his own request since he is described in the *Clio*'s ship's log and muster book as "distressed".²

On 1 January 1833 there had been (apart from the ships' crews) a total of 82 people at Port Louis: 45 who belonged to the garrison and 37 who did not; on 11 January, after the ships had left, 22 people remained there, as confirmed by Commander Onslow and Colonel Belford Hinton Wilson (Table 6.24c and sections 6.22, 6.28).

Only the garrison were expelled from the islands by the British, and it would be unrealistic to assume all of them were sorry or angry at being ordered to leave – after the murder of Mestivier the first thought of many of the soldiers had been to capture the schooner *Rapid* and escape from the islands. They had come from warm, sociable Buenos Aires, whereas the Falklands were cold, windy and very lonely. The soldiers' women and children went where their menfolk went, of course, but it is hard to believe that if given a choice they would all have chosen to remain. And of course if Pinedo had returned only a few days later the whole garrison would have left before he got back.

Not only that: even if the *Clio* had not gone to the islands Pinedo would have removed almost half the garrison anyway – of the 26 soldiers, 10 were taken to Buenos Aires, put on trial and punished (7 shot, 2 flogged, 1 banished), and Pinedo's list shows that they had with them 5 women and 4 children, who would have been taken to Buenos Aires with their menfolk. In other words, 19 people (42% of the 45 people belonging to the garrison) would have been taken away in any case by Argentina. In effect, Britain only expelled just over half the garrison.

6.25 The Expulsion Myth

The documentation shows that in January 1833 neither Onslow nor Pinedo applied pressure on any civilians to leave; only the Argentine garrison was expelled, while the civilian inhabitants – the genuine residents – were encouraged to remain. Some of the gauchos, though, wanted to leave – Onslow stated in Version A of his report (for the different versions see section 6.30):

I had great trouble to pursuade 12 of the Gauchos to remain on the Settlement, otherwise cattle could not have been caught, and the advantages of refreshments to the shipping must have ceased.

So the only pressure Onslow applied was for the gauchos to remain. Nevertheless, Argentine authors have regularly asserted that Britain "expelled the Argentine population". That assertion is repeated every year by Argentina at the United Nations before the UN Decolonisation Committee, the "Committee of 24" or "C24" (sections 10.14, 10.24). But it is a myth, which we called the "Expulsion Myth" and refuted in our paper *Getting it right* (pp. 19-20). Henry Metcalf's reason for going back to Buenos Aires was to recover the money Louis Vernet owed him, and Pasos accompanied Metcalf; the motives of the others who went voluntarily are unknown, but they were not expelled – the choice was theirs.

Kohen and Rodríguez (pp. 185-6) invent a spurious reason for that choice:

It does not require a great deal of intelligence to understand that the 'choice' was motivated by the British occupation and the subsequent expulsion of Argentina… to place a population taken to the islands by the actions of Argentina under the authority of a British subject acting to maintain British control over the islands is a typically colonial action.

Valleja 35; Juan Brasido 91; total "4,008 pesos" (*recte* 4,010), about £868 sterling at 4.615 pesos to the pound.

¹ In Buenos Aires on 30 January 1833 five gauchos (José Báez, Manuel Ruiz, Mariano López, Mateo González and Joaquín Acuña), all illiterate, dictated a statement to Ventura Pasos recounting the problems at the settlement in 1832, thus justifying their debts; English translation by Vernet in AGN VII, 130, doc. 54; full text in Spanish in Vernet's collected statement of accounts, AGN VII, 127, doc. 33, fols. 130 *recto* to 131 *recto*, in Vernet's hand.

² The *Clio*'s ship's log (PRO Adm 53/258) states: "Received onboard Ch<u>s</u> Brasier, a distressed British Subject, and W<u>m</u> Drake an American, an improper person to be left on the Island…"; the captain's log (PRO Adm 51/3118) merely says "Rec[eive]<u>d</u> 2 Seamen onb[oar]<u>d</u> for passage." The *Clio*'s muster book, PRO Adm 37/7969, records them both as "East Falkland distressed subject for passage", and gives Drake as "given up to the American Consul" at Montevideo on 20 January, Brasier as discharged on 22 February 1833 at Rio. Why the ship's log describes Brasier as "distressed" but Drake as "improper" is not clear; as deserters they were both "improper", but perhaps Brasier told a better "sob story".

That is nonsense – there was no "British occupation" and no "British subject acting to maintain British control": the *Clio* sailed a week later and left no British presence in the islands. And like other Argentine authors, Kohen and Rodríguez automatically assume that South Americans would have preferred Argentine rule to British rule, but that is an anachronism – at the time, many South Americans saw British rule as safer and more reliable than rule by Argentina. The gauchos who remained at Port Louis would have been happy to work under British rule – they asked Commander Onslow for instructions just before he left (section 6.22), and Belford Hinton Wilson recorded that "These Gauchos would cheerfully remain on the Island under any Englishman whom the Government may please to appoint".[1] Those who left voluntarily had their own reasons for leaving, one of which was no doubt the memory of anarchy and terror when the violent Argentine garrison were present, and another was the insecurity resulting from the continued absence of Louis Vernet and the lack of proper payment.

Many Argentine authors, and Argentine speakers at the United Nations (section 10.24) speak of "the original Argentine population" of the Falklands, who, they wrongly say, were expelled by the British. But of the 37 civilians remaining on 1 January 1833, only 10 were Argentinians anyway, of whom only 2 were taken away (Table 6.24d), and of all the people in the Falklands that day, the longest-established whose arrival date is known were the two black African former slaves Carmelita and Gregoria, who had been there for 4 years and 4 months since 2 September 1828. Not a single person is known to have been in the islands longer than that.

Of the Argentinians at Port Louis on 1 January 1833 (Table 6.24c), Juan Simon had worked for Vernet in Argentina (section 5.4), though both he and Antonio Rivero are unrecorded in the Falklands until both are first mentioned in May 1829 in Emilio Vernet's diary (section 5.8). After that, Emilio mentions Simon another 16 times, Rivero another 7 times, which suggests they were not present earlier and therefore presumably arrived in one of half a dozen ships that touched at Port Louis in the first few months of 1829. However, the evidence is not conclusive; they may perhaps have been in the islands in 1828 or not. Emilio never mentions the other 4 Argentinians Pascual Diaz, Pedro Fermin, Santiago López and Faustino Martínez. Three of them, López, Martínez and Diaz, made statements about the *Lexington* raid (section 6.12),[2] so they were at Port Louis in January 1832, but are not recorded earlier, while Fermin is not recorded before January 1833. Emilio naturally mentions none of those who arrived in the *Elbe* or the *Sarandí*, since they arrived after he left. Those statistics show that it is a crass distortion of history to refer to an "original Argentine population" of the islands.

The distortions of the events of January 1833 by Kohen and Rodríguez begin with their heading (p. 184): "The expulsion of civilian residents by the British authorities" – but the soldiers of the garrison were not civilian residents! They accuse us of "a gross manipulation of numbers" in our paper *Getting it right*, but it is they who manipulate the numbers. They lump together Pinedo's distinct groups of people (our categories (b), (c), (d) and (e) in Table 6.24b), obliterating his distinction between residents and foreigners, and call them "17 inhabitants of the islands that worked there". They then say "the group of civilians was composed of the following workers", and list another 17 names – including Warnes (suppressing the fact that he was a prisoner, not a worker[3]) and also a "female group with their children", though they were the 5 women and 4 children of the main culprits, whom Pinedo listed separately. And they print all the names in one paragraph (p. 185), which further obscures the distinctions between the groups.

The greatest absurdity they commit is to include the garrison among the civilian residents, which no other author does. They say that the expulsion resulted in the departure of almost 70% of the "existing population", since "53" people left the islands [actually 60] and 22 remained there, and they attack us for saying in *Getting it right* that the "genuine residents" were not expelled. They say we indulge in "evident manipulation", since we distinguish between "genuine residents" and

---

[1] Colonel Belford Hinton Wilson, report of 24 January 1833 in PRO CO 78/1, fol. 212 *recto* (see sections 6.19, 6.28).
[2] Group of statements in AGN VII, 130, about the *Lexington* raid, docs. 238, 242-249.
[3] As mentioned in section 6.24, Lynch's list includes Warnes with the "Foreigners", but Kohen and Rodríguez quote and illustrate only Pinedo's list and nowhere mention the existence of any other list.

those who were not genuine (i.e. the garrison).

But to describe the garrison as residents of the islands is ludicrous. In the first place, the garrison twice came near to leaving before the *Clio* arrived: first after the murder of Mestivier, when they made hostile moves aimed at capturing the *Rapid* with the clear intention of escaping from the islands, and again when Gomila chartered the *Rapid* to take the entire garrison back to Buenos Aires – he planned that they would all embark on 30 December 1832 and leave the islands the next day. Their weapons and tools were already aboard the ship, and Gomila had signed for the beef and hides he had received up to 29 December (section 6.21). If Pinedo had returned only a couple of days later, he would have found no garrison but only the civilian residents. The garrison had no roots whatever in the islands; they had been there less than three months and were about to leave. To call them residents is a gross distortion of the truth.

And secondly, the soldiers had behaved abominably. They were a violent rabble who had brutally murdered their commanding officer; they had rampaged plundering through the settlement and had terrified and traumatised the residents, many of whom fled for their lives to the *Rapid* or the *Jean-Jacques*. The distinction we make between the garrison and the genuine residents reflects the facts of history, which Kohen and Rodríguez constantly misrepresent.

6.26 Kohen and Rodríguez confuse two *Rapids*

They then make the extraordinary assertion (p. 185) that "The British schooner 'Rapid' escorted the 'Sarandí' for the British" – in their Spanish version they even say "The English schooner 'Rapid' accompanied the 'Sarandí' in the role of a military escort of the British" ("en carácter de escolta militar de los británicos"). We suspect the two authors have got muddled up between the whaling schooner *Rapid* of Liverpool and the 10-gun British warship HMS *Rapid*, which was in the Falklands from 21 May to 20 July 1834, was at Rio in January 1835, and was at Buenos Aires in January-February 1836.[1]

The schooner *Rapid* was a mere commercial whaling schooner, a much smaller ship with only two guns, which had run to the Falklands for repairs in November 1832 and left again on 5 January 1833 with the murderers of Mestivier. And she had been helping the Argentinians, not the British – she had been chartered by Gomila to carry the garrison away before the British arrived.

6.27 Britain in the 1830s was anti-colonialist

Kohen and Rodríguez also misrepresent Britain's general policy as well as its policy towards the Falklands. They say (p. 187) that Britain used its old "long-abandoned" claim "in the framework of its policy of colonial, commercial and maritime domination", but in fact Britain had not abandoned its claim and there was no such policy of domination; the two authors seem unaware of the enormous difference between British policy in the 1830s and the 1890s. The 1890s were the age of "Classic Imperialism", when colonial powers (above all Britain, but also France, Italy, Germany and Belgium) did indeed follow a policy of colonial, commercial and maritime domination, and the public mood in those countries was enthusiastically imperialistic (section 8.29). But 60 years earlier in the 1830s British government policy was totally different. The government's central philosophy was free trade, so all non-trading expenses had to be cut, including colonies, though British trading interests had to be protected. Until around 1880 British foreign policy was reactive; Britain generally remained passive and only acted in response to specific problems.

The Whig government in power from 1830 to 1834 under Charles, Earl Grey, was even more sceptical towards colonies than its Tory predecessors, and Britain's lack of interest in actually occupying the Falklands is shown by the fact that in May 1835 the Colonial Office suggested to the

---

[1] HMS *Rapid* was a 10-gun brig-sloop launched at Portsmouth on 17 August 1829, wrecked off Tunisia 12 April 1838 (see the Naval Database on website www.pbenyon.plus.com). The logs of HMS *Rapid* reveal her actual movements at this time: in 1832-3 she was surveying in the Mediterranean; on 30 November 1832 (the day of the Argentine garrison's mutiny at Port Louis) she was at Malta, and on 16 January 1833 (the day after the sealing schooner *Rapid* arrived at Buenos Aires) she was at Napoli di Romania (modern Nafplio) in the Peloponnese, Greece. She left for South America in late 1833, arriving at Rio de Janeiro on 23 December 1833, and was later at Buenos Aires, from 4 January to 2 February 1836. Details from the two ship's logs of HMS *Rapid*, PRO Adm 53/1157 and Adm 53/1158.

Foreign Office that "the Naval officer and his boat's Crew should be withdrawn from Berkeley Sound" (section 6.38). The Colonial Office thought there should be no permanent British presence but merely regular visits to the islands by British warships, to trigger a British reaction to any moves by any other power. Nothing came of that proposal, but it demonstrates the falsity of all assertions or implications that in the 1830s Britain was keen to occupy the Falklands.

Kohen and Rodríguez say (p. 187) that Argentina "had succeeded in establishing a human settlement on the islands and in proving its feasibility". That is incorrect in two ways: first, the United States would never have allowed the Argentinians to continue harassing American ships; it would sooner or later have broken the settlement up. And secondly, Louis Vernet's accounts show that the settlement was not viable – it ran at a constant loss, causing him to run up serious debts and leading him to order Mathew Brisbane in March 1833 to stop issuing even paper tokens as payment (section 6.31). The Argentine settlement in the Falklands was doomed from the start.

6.28 HMS *Tyne* arrives and leaves again

HMS *Tyne* under Captain Charles Hope arrived at Port Egmont on 10 January 1833, the same day as the *Clio* left Port Louis. Hope found a letter in a bottle by the flagstaff, informing him that Onslow had left in the *Clio* for Port Louis, so on 12 January Hope sailed round to Port Louis, where he arrived on 14 January.[1] The Falklands were a stopover in his voyage to take Colonel Belford Hinton Wilson to his post as British Minister to Peru in Lima.

Wilson had impeccable South American credentials: he spoke fluent Spanish, had served from 1823 as aide-de-camp to the liberator Simón Bolívar (1783-1830), had attended Bolívar on his deathbed and on 10 December 1830 was one of the seven witnesses of his will, in which Bolívar mentions him with gratitude. At Port Louis Wilson established that there were 22 inhabitants, confirming Onslow's figure. William Dickson and the gauchos told him about the murder of Mestivier on 30 November 1832 (section 6.19); Wilson recorded their complaints about Vernet, that he did not pay them in silver but in "Paper of his own coining", and their approval of the fact that on the arrival of HMS *Clio* they were paid in silver, and he added:[2]

These Gauchos would cheerfully remain on the Island under any Englishman whom the Government may please to appoint…

The motives for their approval are clear – Britain paid in silver, not paper, and they had been traumatised by the mutinous Argentine garrison; some of the gauchos had helped to sort out the chaos and capture the mutineers, and they no doubt felt the best guarantee of order (and of payment in cash) would be for Britain to take the establishment over. One of the gauchos was Antonio Rivero; Belford Wilson does not mention him by name but says he heard their "unanimous statement", so Rivero clearly agreed that they would cheerfully live under an English administrator. The gauchos were in principle well disposed towards the British, but Britain let them down and failed to take charge – on 18 January 1833 the *Tyne* sailed away again just as the *Clio* had done. That was typical of "informal empire" – the two British warships left no governor, no garrison, not even a token guard. Once the *Tyne* had gone, the 22 residents of Port Louis were on their own.

6.29 Argentine protests begin, 1833 – and end, 1849; silent vs. overt acquiescence

The day after the *Sarandí*'s return, Buenos Aires protested officially to Britain at the actions of HMS *Clio*. For the next 17 years, from 1833 to 1849 inclusive, Argentina maintained a two-pronged campaign against Britain's possession of the Falklands, on the one hand by three sets of formal diplomatic protests (1833-4, 1841-2 and 1849),[3] and on the other hand by annual protests in the "Mensajes", the official Messages at the ceremonial opening of the legislature of the province of Buenos Aires, which dealt with the whole Argentine Confederation's foreign policy (section 7.15).

The first diplomatic protest was a note on 16 January 1833 by Manuel Maza, acting foreign

---

[1] Details from captain's log of HMS *Tyne*, in PRO Adm 51/3512.
[2] Details and quotes from Belford Hinton Wilson's report in PRO CO 78/1, fol. 212 *recto*; Wilson's underlining.
[3] Printed in Spanish in Alfredo Becerra, *Protestas por Malvinas (1833-1946)*, Buenos Aires 1998; his title implies that the protests were regular from 1833 to 1946, which was not the case.

minister of the province of Buenos Aires, to Captain Philip Gore, the British chargé d'affaires, demanding explanations of the incident at Port Louis. Gore replied feebly on 17 January that "he has received no Instructions" on the matter (his instructions had been sent to Rio by mistake).[1] Maza then prepared a more detailed protest, delivered to Gore five days later on 22 January.[2]

It is universally accepted among jurists that official protests are essential in maintaining a claim by one government against another. Acceptance of an existing state of affairs without protesting at some perceived injustice is termed "acquiescence", and the presence or absence of acquiescence is inversely dependent on the absence or presence of protests. There are self-evidently two kinds of acquiescence, which we term "silent" and "overt". Silent acquiescence means doing nothing for a length of time and thereby abandoning a claim, while overt acquiescence involves doing something specific that ends a claim. In both cases it is not the mere passage of time that ends a claim (time does nothing by itself), but the behaviour of the claimant state in either doing nothing or performing actions that indicate that its claim has ended. Silent acquiescence can only be made clear by the passage of a significant length of time during which protests could have been made but were not, as summed up in the saying "Silence gives consent". Overt acquiescence, by contrast, can be shown by appropriate actions within any space of time, long or short. Argentina performed several actions in the 19th and 20th centuries which either directly indicated or implied overt acquiescence in Britain's possession of the Falklands (see especially sections 7.8, 7.9, 7.15, 7.19, 8.7, 8.8, 8.18, 8.22, 8.28, 9.1, 9.3, 10.22).

It is clearly an embarrassment to Kohen and Rodríguez that Argentina's protests ceased entirely after the ratification of the Convention of Peace in 1850. They refer briefly (pp. 196-7) to Argentina's protests from 1833 to 1849, and go into more detail (pp. 207-209) on the protest of 27 December 1849, but they do not mention that it was Argentina's last protest for 38 years, nor do they make the vital connection between the ratification of the Convention of Peace and the cessation of Argentina's protests (section 7.15).

However, Kohen naturally accepts that acquiescence may play a decisive role in effectively transferring title to a territory from one state to another – he says:[3]

… the critical issue regarding transfer of territorial sovereignty in cases other than formal cession is not only the fact of possession *à titre de souverain*, but also essentially the conduct of the dispossessed holder of title… acquiescence will play a decisive role in this regard. […]
… case law shows that tribunals… focus on state conduct by both sides to the dispute to determine whether there has been an abandonment of title and recognition of the other state's sovereignty through acquiesence.

The Argentine title to the Falklands had been imperfect from the outset and was ended by the Convention of Peace in 1850; the behaviour of Argentina in failing to protest throughout the 1850s, 1860s, 1870s and early 1880s, while Britain administered the islands, indicated silent acquiesence by Argentina in Britain's possession of the islands, and it was made overt by various acts such as statements by Argentine leaders (section 8.18) and the publication of maps showing the Falklands as outside Argentina (section 8.22). All that meant that by the early 1880s no trace of an Argentine title to the islands survived. For all this see chapters 7 and 8.

6.30 The *Clio* reaches port; 4 versions of Onslow's report; trials of Pinedo and the mutineers

The *Clio* reached Montevideo on 19 January 1833, and Commander Onslow wrote a report on his actions in the Falklands, in four different versions, which we call "Version A" (to the Admiralty in London), "Version B" (to Rear Admiral Sir Thomas Baker in Rio), "Version G" (to chargé d'affaires Philip Gore in Buenos Aires), and "Version W", given by Onslow to G. T. Whitington and printed in 1840.[4] Versions A and B differ considerably, but Kohen and Rodríguez seemingly

---

[1] Both notes in English in *BFSP 1832-1833*, London 1836, pp. 1197-1198, and in Spanish in Becerra 1998, pp. 44-46.
[2] Text in Becerra 1998, pp. 46-48.
[3] Marcelo Kohen, in Marcelo G. Kohen and Mamadou Hébié (eds.), *Research Handbook on Territorial Disputes in International Law*, Cheltenham (UK) and Northampton (USA), 2018, pp. 155, 156.
[4] Secretarial copies of versions A, B, and G in PRO Adm 1/2276, without separate doc. nos.; errors in A and B suggest they were dictated orally; G uses the wording of A with very slight differences; Gore's copy of G is in PRO FO 6 500,

only knew of the version printed by Whitington, since they mention no other version in the footnote on their p. 182 (it is close to Version B).

In Version A (but not in B or W) Onslow says Pinedo recounted the recent events to him:[1]

> He informed me a mutiny had taken place whilst he was at Sea, amongst the soldiers, they had killed their commander, and were in a state of great insubordination, so much so, that the settlers were afraid to pursue their avocations, and all appeared anarchy and confusion.

That description, by Pinedo himself, reveals how the garrison terrified the civilian inhabitants, who were "afraid to pursue their avocations". That reveals the absurdity of the attempt by Kohen and Rodríguez to count the garrison as part of the population (section 6.25).

In Buenos Aires in January and February 1833 courts held trials of the mutineers for mutiny and murder, and of Pinedo for dereliction of duty in not resisting the British.[2] The trial of Pinedo lasted from 19 January to 14 February, during which a court martial met for a single day on 5 February and tried the ten men most guilty of the mutiny and the murder of Commandant Mestivier. The court martial found all ten guilty and passed sentence of death on the seven principal culprits: Private Manuel Sáenz Valiente (the ringleader), Corporal Francisco Ramírez, and Privates Bernadino Cáceres, Antonio Moncada, José Antonio Díaz, Manuel Suares and José María Díaz, all of whom were publicly shot by firing squad in the centre of Buenos Aires on 8 February. Privates Manuel Delgado and Mariano Gadea were sentenced to floggings and an extension of their army service (which suggests they were already criminals serving their time in the army), while Gomila was lucky to have a good lawyer (Major-General Nicolás de Vedia) and got off with being banished from Buenos Aires and placed on half pay. De Vedia suggested that Gomila had merely been irresponsible, an "unfortunate youth" (he was 22), but both Pinedo and Gertrudis Mestivier say he was the instigator of the mutiny (section 6.19). The eyewitness accounts of the mutiny make it clear that the ten men were not the only ones involved; other members of the garrison participated in plundering the settlement and made moves to capture the *Rapid* and escape from the islands.

On 7 March the governor of Buenos Aires province, Juan Ramón Balcarce, pronounced the final sentence on José María Pinedo: dismissal from the Navy and four months' suspension from employment.[3] Nevertheless, some 19 months later Pinedo was again given command of a naval ship.[4] The rest of his career was undistinguished. During his brief visit to the Falklands he had had to act in two major crises in rapid succession, in which he displayed competence and humanity, and his decision not to fight against superior odds no doubt saved many lives. It is pleasant to record that he lived to the ripe old age of 90 and died peacefully in 1885.

6.31 The year of limbo, 1833-4; Charles Darwin's first visit, 1833; the "1833 Port Louis Log"

We refer to the year between the departure of HMS *Clio* on 10 January 1833 and the raising of the Union Jack at Port Louis on 10 January 1834 as "the year of limbo" – for exactly a year there was a complete power vacuum. It was a dramatic year in Falklands history, but it is important to remember that there was no official British presence in the islands; the *Clio* and the *Tyne* simply sailed away. Kohen and Rodríguez (p. 185) talk of the "British occupation", but there was none. They also repeat (p. 187) what we call "the Implantation Myth" – the notion that Britain did not allow any of those removed from the islands in "1831" [i.e. by the *Lexington* in January 1832] to return, and that Britain replaced the former "Argentine inhabitants" with British people (section 10.14). That is untrue – with zero presence in the islands Britain was not in a position to prevent the return of civilians, and anyway Britain did not object to their returning.

In fact several people did return, which Kohen and Rodríguez suppress, and during the year of limbo there were some important arrivals and returnings. On 1 March 1833 HMS *Beagle* arrived on

---

fols. 116 *recto*-124 *recto*. Onslow gave G. T. Whitington a copy of W and of Baker's orders; Whitington printed them in *The Falkland Islands &c. &c....*, London 1840, pp. 12-18 (used by Kohen and Rodríguez).

[1] Version A of Onslow's report, fol. 1 *verso*, PRO Adm 1/2276.
[2] Details of the trials from the volume of evidence for Pinedo's trial, including Pinedo's report, in AGN VII, doc. 60.
[3] Pinedo trial evidence 1833, AGN VII, 60, fols. 208-210.
[4] *BPAN* Saturday 25 October 1834.

her epoch-making round-the-world voyage (1831-6), with Charles Darwin aboard, who visited the islands twice, in March 1833 and March 1834, and spent almost twice as long in the Falklands as on his more famous visit to the Galapagos Islands. The voyage was recorded in detail by the *Beagle*'s captain Robert FitzRoy[1] and in Charles Darwin's diary.[2]

Having delivered the murderers of Mestivier to Buenos Aires, the schooner *Rapid* returned to Port Louis on 3 March 1833, now under charter to Louis Vernet, bringing supplies and six more people Vernet had sent: Mathew Brisbane, Ventura Pasos, the Charrúa "Manuel González" and the gauchos Juan Brasido (from Uruguay) and Domingo Valleja, all of whom were returning to the islands, plus the Englishman Thomas Helsby, a newcomer.[3] Brisbane, Brasido, Valleja and "González" had all been taken away by the *Lexington* in January 1832; Brisbane had been the pilot of the *Sarandí* in January 1833, under contract to the Argentine government, from which post he resigned on 5 February 1833[4] in order to return to the Falklands to work again for Vernet. He thus became once more a civilian resident.

The arrivals increased the population of Port Louis from 22 after the *Clio* left to 28, which fell to 27 with the dismissal of Pedro Salinas in March, rose to 28 in May with the birth of Manuel Coronel junior, and dropped in June to 27 and in July to 26 with the deaths of Domingo Valleja and Pedro Fermin. Of the six arrivals, only Helsby and "González" were still alive ten months later – Valleja died of illness, while Brisbane, Pasos and Brasido were murdered by Antonio Rivero's gang (Brisbane and Pasos in August, Brasido later).

On the day the *Rapid* arrived, 3 March 1833, a brief but important record of events at Port Louis during the year of limbo was begun. It is a tattered, anonymous and untitled journal in the Public Record Office in London (PRO), which we call the "1833 Port Louis Log".[5] From March to August 1833 it records the weather, the sailings of ships and boats, and the activities of the little community of people living at Port Louis. It is in two handwritings: the storekeeper William Dickson wrote it from 3 March to 6 April (with several gaps), during which Charles Darwin visited the settlement twice, but both times Dickson failed to catch his name: on 21 March he left a blank, and on 23 March he refers to the visit of "M^r ~~~~~~~~~ the Naturalist". Dickson's second entry, on 5 March 1833, records the arrival of the schooner *Sun*: Captain Trott was returning to the islands, as arranged by Captain Isaac McKeever of the USS *Lexington*, to "continue her occupation [i.e. sealing] in defiance of the illegal warning received" (i.e. received at the meeting with José María Pinedo on 7 December 1832: sections 6.20, 6.22).

Mathew Brisbane returned to Port Louis aboard the *Rapid* as Vernet's settlement manager. He was clearly unhappy with the way William Dickson had been keeping the 1833 Port Louis Log, and on 6 April he took over the writing of it himself. He wrote it every day from then until 26 August 1833, when he was murdered by Antonio Rivero (fig. 6.32a). The log has never been printed in English; it was printed in Spanish in Buenos Aires in 1967, with some omissions and misunderstandings.[6] The whole will appear in English for the first time in *The Falklands Saga*.

As mentioned in section 5.20, Vernet had instructed Brisbane not to pay the gauchos with paper tokens, but merely to record in the account book what work they had done and what supplies he issued to them. That was necessary because the settlement was not paying its way – contrary to what Kohen and Rodríguez say, it was not in fact viable. But this reduced the men to the status of slaves, which made them even more dissatisfied.

Vernet also ordered Brisbane to arrest the capataz Juan Simon. Basing his instructions on false information given to him by Henry Metcalf, Vernet says Simon had not run the establishment

---

[1] Robert FitzRoy, *Narrative of the Surveying Voyages of His Majesty's Ships Adventure and Beagle...*, London 1839. He always signed his name "FitzRoy", and this spelling is used in all authoritative works.
[2] Full text in Richard Darwin Keynes (ed.), *Charles Darwin's Beagle Diary*, Cambridge 1988. By a slip Kohen and Rodríguez refer (p. 191) to "HMS Darwin" (corrected in their English edition).
[3] Details from the 1833 Port Louis Log and from FitzRoy 1839, vol. II, pp. 225-227.
[4] His letter of resignation is in AGN Sala III, 9-1-3.
[5] PRO Adm 1/42, nos. 1 and 2: slim untitled sewn booklets, grubby and stained: no. 1 running from 3 March to 8 May 1833 inclusive, no. 2 from 9 May to 25 August 1833 inclusive, both written in English, *recto* and *verso*.
[6] In *Episodio* 1967, pp. 29-36. It wrongly ascribes the whole log to Dickson (followed in Tesler 1971, pp. 250-255).

properly, had made "very considerable advances" of money to the men without getting them to work and had worked for his own account; Vernet calls him "that traitor" and says that he had been wrong to trust him – "In fact I nursed a viper in my bosom" – and stresses that Simon should be arrested at once before he had a chance to escape.[1]

One feels sorry for Juan Simon. He had actually performed his job with commitment and energy; he led the posse that captured the murderers of Mestivier in December 1832 (section 6.21); he stoutly defended Vernet's property from various claimants including Metcalf; he was appointed as Argentina's representative in the islands by Pinedo; he kept the gauchos working – and he never claimed his wages. He explained things to Brisbane, who did not arrest him; in April 1833 Simon sent Vernet a letter (dictated to Ventura Pasos as Simon was illiterate) justifying his conduct,[2] and he obtained testimonials from Captain Robert FitzRoy of HMS *Beagle*[3] and another signed jointly by Brisbane, FitzRoy and Captains John Ross of the *Rapid* and Nehemiah Bray, formerly of the US sealers *Belleville* and *Transport*,[4] but in vain – Vernet realised too late what a good servant he had been. Simon's reward was to be murdered in cold blood by the villain Antonio Rivero.

6.32 The Port Louis murders, 26 August 1833

What happened at Port Louis in August 1833 is another embarrassing episode for Argentine authors, following the murder of Mestivier nine months earlier in November 1832. Kohen and Rodríguez say simply (p. 191) that on 26 August 1833 "eight 'gauchos' led by Antonio Rivero" killed Brisbane, Dickson and three others – and the two authors leave it at that, without details.

But even their brief mention is not correct as it stands. There were not eight gauchos – by that time there were only seven gauchos left in the islands, and only two of them followed Rivero: José María Luna (a Chilean) and José Brasido (a Uruguayan). The other four gauchos were Argentinians (Manuel Coronel, Pascual Diez, Santiago López and Faustino Martínez), but they refused to join Rivero's group and actually fled from them. Moreover, both Luna and Brasido later tried to leave the group; the group murdered Brasido but Luna managed to get away and "turn King's Evidence" (i.e. change sides from being one of the culprits to being a witness against them). The only ones who continued to follow Rivero were the five Charrúa Indians, who had not been allowed to ride horses (a very hard fate), and who had nothing to lose since their entire nation had been massacred in Uruguay (section 6.2).

Kohen and Rodríguez say nothing about the murderers' motives; they do not repeat the "Rivero Myth", as we call it (the absurd idea that Rivero led a rebellion against Britain, see section 6.33), but they fail to make it clear that the main motive was to get money and escape – Lieutenant Henry Smith recorded in his journal on 8 January 1834 that the settlement was ruinous, "the Murderers having burnt and destroyed some of the houses for money and nails". Nails were traditional trade goods on the coast, and they may have been for boat-building – Rivero's plan was to murder the leading inhabitants, plunder the houses and seize the money, and then get a boat and escape from the islands. The eyewitness Henry Channen recounted: "I observed the murderers dividing the

---

[1] Rough draft of instructions to Brisbane, in Vernet's hand, in AGN VII, 132, doc. 155, fol. 3 *recto*.
[2] Letter to Vernet dated 2 April 1833, in AGN VII, 130, doc. 62 ("Juan Simon's letter to Vernet"; see section 6.12).
[3] Letter by FitzRoy, 20 March 1833, in AGN VII, 130, doc. 59, addressed to Brisbane and forwarded to Vernet, saying "I see much to regret in the removal of Simon;– whose conduct has evidently been much misrepresented;– and whose services, here, are at present essentially necessary. It appears that the Gauchos are attached to, and confide in him…".
[4] Letter in FitzRoy's hand, in AGN VII 132, doc. 181, dated "March 1833", no addressee, signed by Brisbane, FitzRoy, Bray and Ross, and forwarded to Vernet, saying "… the conduct of M[r] Jean Simon had been much misrepresented to his employer", and they were "… fully satisfied of M[r] Jean Simon's honesty,– activity, and knowledge of his business". Bray's ships *Belleville* and *Transport* had both been wrecked on Tierra del Fuego, the *Belleville* on 22 February 1830 (section 5.19), and the *Transport* in the great South Atlantic storm of 12 January 1833 (when the French *Magellan* was wrecked in Berkeley Sound, in what is now Magellan Cove). The second time Bray and his crew were rescued by the British schooner *Unicorn*, whose captain William Low had visited the Falklands several times in 1829-31 in the *Adeona*; the *Unicorn* was bought by FitzRoy, renamed *Adventure* and used with the *Beagle* for surveying, leaving Low and some of his crew at their own request at Port Louis, where they just avoided being murdered by Rivero (section 6.32). This testimonial was clearly written after Bray and his men reached Port Louis in the *Unicorn* on 22 March 1833.

money[,] Santiago being present with money in his hand".[1] In any account of the Port Louis murders, that needs to be made clear.

The events of 26 August 1833, and the months before and after it, are extensively documented: in the 1833 Port Louis Log; in Thomas Helsby's journal from August 1833 to January 1834;[2] in Henry Smith's journal; and in eyewitness statements made at Port Louis in March 1834 and at Sheerness near London in 1835. Our account is taken from those documents, heavily abbreviated – the full texts of all of them will appear in *The Falklands Saga*.

What happened was, very briefly, that on the evening of 25 August 1833, Henry Channen and George Hopkins, two former members of the crew of William Low's sealer *Unicorn* (11 of whose crew had stayed at Port Louis and worked as a boat's crew after Robert FitzRoy bought the ship), were invited to dine at Antonio Rivero's house, where they found Rivero, Juan Brasido, José María Luna, and the Charrúas "Manuel González" and "Latorre". Channen later told Henry Smith that the conspirators had asked him if there was "any chance of their getting away" – like the murderers of Mestivier, they wanted to get away from the islands, and they later kidnapped Channen (a carpenter) to force him to help them. Channen told them that if they went to the western part of the islands, "they might fall in with the Chaloupe", i.e. the shallop formerly called *Eagle*, built by the *Belleville* men on Eagle Island (section 5.19). They also asked for bullets – Rivero later boasted to José María Prado (another former crewman of the *Unicorn*) that "the night before the murders the English had given him fifty bullets and that that night he had been in the house of the English until ten o'clock waiting for the making of the bullets to be finished".[3] Henry Smith added a note in faint lead pencil on the back cover of Thomas Helsby's journal: "They had the Carpenter & George Hopkins cast balls and gave powder to Rubio the night previous to the murder" (the carpenter was Henry Channen; "Rubio" ["Blond"] was José María Luna). The help given to the murderers by the British members of the boat's crew led Smith to see them as accomplices and to send them to Britain as suspects and/or witnesses together with Rivero and the other murderers – far from rebelling against the British, Rivero asked them for help. Those important facts are omitted from all Argentine accounts of this episode.

Mathew Brisbane filled in the date for Monday 26 August in the 1833 Port Louis Log, but he never got any further (fig. 6.32a). Early that morning he went down to the landing-stage to see off Captain William Low and his boat's crew (Francisco Machado, José María Prado, the black crewman Antonio Manuel and the gaucho Faustino Martínez), who left at 7 a.m. on a sealing trip around Berkeley Sound – by being away, they avoided being murdered.

Brisbane walked back up to his house (built for Louis Vernet, see fig. 5.4a), and then Rivero put his plan into action. Followed by two (non-Argentine) gauchos and five Indians, he first shot dead Juan Simon as he was busy salting hides, then took his group to Brisbane's house (where Mestivier had been murdered nine months earlier). He himself shot Brisbane dead in the main room, then they seriously injured Ventura Pasos and left him for dead before going to the house of the German Anton Vaihinger (whom Vernet trusted), where William Dickson happened to be visiting. They killed Dickson with shots and cutlass-blows, Rivero firing the final shot, then they killed Vaihinger with shots and blows. They then returned to Brisbane's house, where they found Ventura Pasos was not dead, but had only been badly wounded – Thomas Helsby says he had been "wounded by a ball thro' his throat, his head cut open, and some of his fingers off, by a sabre" – and he had managed to get to Antonina Roxa's house. So they followed him and Rivero finished him off.

In view of the heroic role later ascribed to Antonio Rivero by Argentine hardliners, it is worth recording his part in the murders as recounted by the eyewitnesses. In addition to being the ringleader of the murderers, Rivero personally shot dead Juan Simon, Mathew Brisbane, William Dickson and Ventura Pasos; Dickson was also struck on the head with a sword by "Felipe Salazar";

---

[1] Channen's statement to Smith, Port Louis, in Smith's letter of 8 March 1834, PRO Adm 1/42, doc. 9, fol. 2 *recto*.
[2] Helsby's original is in the Public Record Office (PRO) in London (PRO Adm 1/42 doc. 4, "the PRO text"), but the last 8 folios have been cut out; there is a complete contemporary copy in the Jane Cameron National Archives (JCNA) in Stanley ("the JCNA copy"), but it contains some misreadings. The PRO text as far as it goes, and the JCNA copy from that point to the end, will appear in full for the first time in *The Falklands Saga*.
[3] From log of José María Prado, PRO Adm 1/42, doc. 3, fol. 12 *verso*.

6.32a The murder of Mathew Brisbane: the last two pages of the 1833 Port Louis Log, PRO Adm 1/42 doc. 2, fols. 6 *verso* (left) and 7 *recto* (right), written by Mathew Brisbane. He wrote the entries for Thursday 15 August 1833 to Sunday 25 August (left) and the heading for Monday 26 August (right), but he never wrote the entry for 26 August – at around 10 a.m. that morning he was murdered by Antonio Rivero. (The symmetrical brown marks are later damp-stains.)

Pasos was struck with a sword by "Luciano Flores" and "afterwards" shot with a pistol by Juan Brasido; Vaihinger was wounded by several members of Rivero's gang, but the witnesses leave it unclear who actually killed him.

Kohen and Rodríguez take pains to point out (p. 191) that Brisbane and Dickson were of British nationality, but they do not make it clear that neither of them represented Britain. Both were working for Louis Vernet, who was still running the establishment from Buenos Aires. Brisbane (a Scot) was Vernet's settlement manager, while the storekeeper Dickson (an Irishman) had been entrusted by Commander Onslow with raising the Union Jack on public holidays and whenever a ship arrived, but otherwise did nothing connected with Britain. None of the eyewitnesses said Rivero rebelled against the British.

Juan Simon was the official representative of Argentina, having been appointed "political and military Commandant of the Malvinas Islands" on 3 January 1833 by Pinedo, and Ventura Pasos was from a Buenos Airean family distinguished in the Argentine independence struggle. The men Rivero killed represented Argentina, not Britain.

6.33 The Rivero Myth

However, a campaign began in Argentina in the 1950s to raise Rivero to the status of a hero. The campaign was launched and developed by hardline Argentine "Malvinists" (supporters of Argentina's claim to the Falklands), who constructed the untrue story that Rivero had been an Argentine patriot who rebelled against the British. We call this fiction "the Rivero Myth".

The initial impetus for the Rivero Myth came in 1956 from Martiniano Leguizamón Pondal, who created the fiction that the murderers were motivated by Argentine patriotism and that Rivero "captured the islands from the British". His account of 26 August 1833 is ludicrous. He implies that Rivero made an "appeal" to Buenos Aires (which is not true), and continues:

… Buenos Aires did not hear Rivero's appeal, the gallop of his colts [*sic*], the crackle of his camp fire, the shudder of the anticolonialist idea, and the Buenos Aires squadron did not go to the unhappy islands… On the verge of trance, Antonio Rivero, in a superb expression of life and spontaneity, without hesitating, ordered the uprising...

In fact the documentation shows that the attacks had been planned for some days, and the day before the murders Rivero had asked the British boat's crew to make him some bullets.

Leguizamón Pondal then goes on to give a fictitious and laughably overdone account of the gauchos' actions after murdering Simon, Brisbane and Pasos:[1]

The English flag on the flagpole in front of the Irishman's store... was visible some five hundred metres to the south; towards it, with a sort of gigantic, epic energy, the rebels made their way. Dickson... emerged from the store shooting, and received a shot that stopped him. The gauchos, carried almost to frenzy, with patriotic fury, pulled down the English flag and, delirious, raised that of Belgrano, and, certainly rejoicing, pulled more than one cork...

That is nonsense, as the eyewitness accounts demonstrate. In the first place, 26 August 1833 was a Monday, so the British flag would not have been flying (it was hoisted only on Sundays); Dickson was unarmed; the murderers were not Argentine patriots – only Rivero was Argentinian, and his followers were Luna (Chilean), Brasido (Uruguayan), and the five Charrúa Indians, who felt no loyalty towards Buenos Aires. The idea that they raised an Argentine flag is absurd to start with, and there is not a scrap of evidence that they even had one, let alone that they raised one. There is not even any evidence that they pulled any corks to celebrate their success – in fact they seem to have remained sober.

Nevertheless, Leguizamón Pondal's book led to the foundation of a new organisation, the "Comisión pro Monumento a Antonio Rivero", on 11 November 1965,[2] which agitated for a monument to be raised to Rivero as a patriotic Argentine hero. The "Comisión" held a ceremony at the Casa de la Provincia de Buenos Aires on 3 January 1966, at which Leguizamón Pondal assserted that Antonio Rivero had been a captain in the army of Manuel Dorrego fighting against Lavalle (section 5.11) in the uprising in December 1828 before "fleeing" in 1829 to the Malvinas, where he headed the "rebellion of 26 August 1833", and that he died fighting in the battle of the Vuelta de Obligado in 1845 (see section 7.4).[3] There is in fact no evidence for any of that; Leguizamon Pondal presented none, and Rivero cannot have been a captain since he was illiterate.

The Rivero Myth was discredited in a "dictamen" (official opinion) written by the Argentine historians Ricardo Caillet-Bois and Capitán Humberto Burzio, adopted unanimously by the Academía Nacional de la Historia and published on 19 April 1966, pointing out that Rivero and his group did not rebel against Britain and that they killed representatives of Argentina. They stated:[4]

The motive was that Rivero and his men were being paid, not in British money but in paper chits... it should be emphasised that at no time did either Rivero or any of his companions declare that the act committed by them had the aim of rebelling against British domination.

The publication of the Academy's opinion at once unleashed a storm of protest in Argentina. There were furious attacks on the "dictamen", such as the following:[5]

... To comprehend the quality of the impulse that inspired the struggle of Antonio Rivero, the boldness of his bravery, the driving force of his patriotism, it is necessary to begin by being Argentinian... With his qualities and his defects, his roughness and his tenderness, his triumphs and his defeats, Argentina is in Rivero and

---

[1] This and previous quote from Martiniano Leguizamón Pondal, *Toponimía Criolla en las Malvinas* ["Native South American toponymy in the Malvinas"], Buenos Aires 1956, pp. 50-51. Manuel Belgrano (1770-1820) was an important Argentine independence leader, who designed the pale blue and white Argentine national flag in 1812.
[2] Date given (but misprinted as "11-11-1945" in Mario Tesler, *El Gaucho Antonio Rivero: La Mentira en la historiografía académica*, Buenos Aires 1971, p. 28.
[3] Details from Tesler 1971, p. 28, and *La Nación*, Buenos Aires, 4 January 1966.
[4] Quote from the "Dictamen", Buenos Aires, 19 April 1966. The facts of the case are considered by Mario Tesler in *El Gaucho Antonio Rivero...*, Buenos Aires, April 1971, with the dictamen in full on pp. 51-53.
[5] Declaration entitled "Dictamen que agravia la soberanía" ["Dictamen that offends sovereignty"], in the Buenos Aires weekly *Propósitos*, 5 May 1966, signed by Enrique V. Corominas (former president of the council of the Organization of American States), army general Oscar A. Uriondo, and an ex-minister, a senator and some professors, printed in full in Tesler 1971, pp. 36-38; Tesler also prints some other similar attacks on the "dictamen".

Argentina is Rivero, as a supreme protagonist of the drama of our lives, struggling against powers and empires, a vibrant will for justice which extols the native community of Argentinians, on the stages of that same human and political journey on which we travel and on which travelled Antonio Rivero…

Such rubbish can only arise out of a completely uncritical, factproof nationalism, which was all too powerful in Argentina in the 1960s and has by no means disappeared – the Rivero Myth has been repeated many times by successive Argentine governments and Argentine authors.

It was repeated in 1966 by the crackpot DC4 hijackers, who announced that Stanley was to be renamed "Port Rivero" (section 10.19). And in April 1982 during the Argentine occupation of the Falklands, Stanley was for a while named "Puerto Rivero" in his honour. There were suggestions that it should be called "Puerto Mestivier", but neither name was finally adopted. It is a moot point whether it would have been better to name the town after a man who murdered Argentinians, or after one who was murdered *by* Argentinians. In the end, on 22 April 1982, the junta issued decree no. 757 naming Stanley "Puerto Argentino". That name is still used in Argentina, and the fact that "Puerto Rivero" was once used is suppressed. To Argentinians the use of "Puerto Argentino" may obscure the fact that Stanley is a British foundation; it is, and always has been, English-speaking and in 1995 it celebrated its 150th anniversary. It is the oldest town in the world so far south.

6.33a The Rivero Myth in action, 2015: detail of the Argentine 50-peso banknote issued in March 2015, with the legend: "GAUCHO ANTONIO RIVERO (Entre Ríos 1808 – Buenos Aires 1845) First defender of national [i.e. Argentine] sovereignty in the Malvinas Islands, restored the fatherland's sovereignty in the year 1833. He fought for the social rights of the workers in the islands." The crosses under his horse are the ones in the Argentine cemetery near Darwin in the Falklands; the ship is the *General Belgrano*. It is nonsense to say that he restored Argentine sovereignty or that he fought for the social rights of the workers. The banknote is now being withdrawn.

The height of absurdity was reached on the 50-peso Argentine banknote issued in March 2015, which portrayed Rivero as a hero who defended Argentine sovereignty (fig. 6.33a; it was steadily withdrawn from late 2017). In fact Rivero was a villain who merely led a few non-Argentinians in a revolt over pay; he murdered representatives of Argentina, not Britain, and later betrayed his companions to the British (section 6.35). The survival of the Rivero Myth demonstrates the bizarre nature of the Argentine claim to the Falkland Islands.

6.34 The inhabitants struggle to survive, August 1833-January 1834; several captured

After the murders the surviving inhabitants remained at Port Louis for three more days before fleeing for their lives to the small barren islands in Berkeley Sound, first to Hog Island, then to Turf Island, now called Peat Island or Peat Islet. In his journal Thomas Helsby records the sufferings of the men, women and children for the desperate four months after the murders, and near the end, on 3 January 1834, he describes the capture of himself and José María Prado, Carl Kussler, Santiago

López and Pascual Diez by the murderers, who seized their boat to escape from the islands in – Helsby says "They told us they would force us to carry them in the launch to Patagonia, or they would kill us". Once again the inhabitants went in fear of their lives at the hands of Rivero and his gang, though Prado and Kussler managed to get away in another boat and reach Kidney Island at the mouth of Berkeley Sound. But at that dramatic juncture Lieutenant Henry Smith arrived.

6.35 Henry Smith arrives

In August 1833 the British government had at long last decided to do something about the Falklands (section 6.14). By that time the islands had been in a state of limbo for eight months, and although British sovereignty had been reasserted in January, it had not begun to exist on the ground. Several British ships' captains including Onslow, Hope and FitzRoy, and also Colonel Belford Hinton Wilson, had paid brief visits to the islands, and in their despatches to London they had all recommended the sending of a military force to preserve law and order, but for months the British government did nothing. That slowness in reacting to their warnings led to the deaths of six men, but at least when Britain did eventually make a move, it came in the nick of time to save several more inhabitants, who were running for their lives a second time when the arrival of Britain's representative ended the danger.

That representative was Henry Smith (1797-1854), who had visited the Falklands in January 1833 as First Lieutenant of HMS *Tyne*. He was officially appointed on 14 August 1833,[1] but the British government was not prepared to send more than the absolute minimum force to the islands. There was to be nothing like a garrison – Smith was to be assisted by a mere four-man boat's crew. On his way to take up his new post he reached Rio in December 1833, and only then did he receive his detailed orders, from Rear Admiral Sir Michael Seymour, commander-in-chief on the Royal Navy's South American station.[2] His boat's crew (John Dowdell, Joshua Lee, Charles Melville and John Thomas), were volunteers from the crew of HMS *Tyne*. Charles Melville spent the rest of his life in the islands, married into the Biggs family, had five children and died aged 70 in 1876.

Smith still knew nothing of the murders at Port Louis in August 1833, since the news had not reached the outside world. He and his four men left Rio on 20 December 1833 in the 28-gun corvette HMS *Challenger*, which was to drop them off on her way to the Pacific. The moment he landed near Port Louis on 7 January 1834 he was faced with a major crisis – there was a band of heavily-armed and ruthless murderers at large, who had killed the leaders of the settlement and taken all the tame horses; Port Louis was deserted, the houses had been wrecked by the murderers, and two dozen destitute and starving people including three women, a 3-year-old child (José Simon) and a 7-month-old baby (Manuel Coronel junior) were living on tiny islands in Berkeley Sound.

From his arrival, Smith kept a journal in which he wrote a laconic account of events.[3] Like so many other important documents in the history of the Falklands, it was first published in Argentina in Spanish translation, first in 1956 (a few brief quotations only),[4] and most of it in 1967, minus the weather details and with some misreadings;[5] the two surviving sections of it (Parts I and III) will appear in full in the original for the first time in *The Falklands Saga*.

At long last, on 10 January 1834, Smith raised the Union Jack at Port Louis and set up a regular authority in the Falklands, ending the year of limbo. The lack of authority had cost the lives of six people (the five victims of 26 August plus Juan Brasido). After heroic efforts Smith succeeded in getting the murderers captured: Antonio Rivero sent a messenger offering to do a deal with Smith, by which Rivero would betray his companions in exchange for clemency for himself. Smith says in

---

[1] Letter from Captain George Elliot of the Admiralty dated 14 August 1833, informing the Foreign Office, for the information of Lord Palmerston, that the Admiralty had authorised an officer, a servant, and a four-man boat's crew to reside at the Falklands, in PRO CO 78-1, fol. 257ff. Details in Gough 1992, p. 109. Smith never got the servant.

[2] Copies of Seymour's orders and the Admiralty instructions are in PRO Adm 1/42, no doc. nos., dated December 1833; both partly quoted, with omissions, in John Skelly, "The Falklands Story" in *FIJ* 1984, p. 4.

[3] The first part (7 January to 14 April 1834) is in PRO Adm 1/42, no doc. no.; the second part (15 April to 19 July 1834) now appears to be lost; the third part (20 July 1834 to 16 January 1835) is in PRO Adm 1/43, no doc. no.

[4] Leguizamón Pondal 1956, pp. 17-18 (parts of Smith's entries of 4, 5, 10 and 14 February 1834).

[5] In *Episodio* 1967, pp. 67-75.

his journal on 27 January 1834 that he received "a message from Antonio Riveiro the principal of the Murderers saying if I would promise him pardon… he would give up the horses and himself and assist in capturing the others…".[1] Smith gave no guarantees, but on 7 March Rivero surrendered and betrayed his companions (by now only the five Charrúa Indians) by handing all their horses over to Smith. The four active Indians then surrendered – by that time "Felipe Salazar" was lying helpless out in the Camp, having broken his thigh in a fall.

6.36 Charles Darwin's second visit, 1834; the murderers' odyssey

Smith wanted to send the murderers, suspects and witnesses to Britain for trial, but for that he needed a ship that was heading for Britain. No such ship appeared, so the men were put aboard ships going in the wrong direction, and were sent on an extraordinary odyssey whose sheer complexity was first partly revealed by Andrew David in the *Falkland Islands Journal* (*FIJ*) in 2007.[2] The first ship was HMS *Beagle*, which paid a second visit to the Falklands from 10 March to 7 April 1834. Smith put three men aboard: the principal murderer, Antonio Rivero; José María Luna, who had decided to "turn King's Evidence", i.e. testify against his former fellow accomplices and become the principal witness against Rivero; and the British carpenter Henry Channen, who had incriminated himself in his statement to Smith and was thus a major suspect.

The *Beagle* left Port Louis on 7 April, with Charles Darwin, Antonio Rivero, José María Luna and Henry Channen aboard. Then, on 11 April, the 28-gun corvette HMS *Conway* arrived on her way to the Pacific. Smith put the remaining ten prisoners aboard: five culprits (the five Charrúa Indians) "Luciano Flores", "Manuel Godoy", "Manuel González", "Latorre" and the severely injured "Felipe Salazar"; four British suspects: George Hopkins, Patrick Kerwin, Daniel McKay and John Stokes; and also the gaucho Faustino Martínez, who was neither a culprit nor a witness and was released at Rio. On 17 April 1834 the *Conway* left for the Pacific.[3]

The journey of the two groups of prisoners from the Falklands to Britain began in the wrong direction. Both groups were first taken separately up the west coast of South America to Valparaíso in Chile, and were repeatedly transferred from one British warship to another, sometimes to the next ship going in the right direction, but when no such ship was available they were "parked" aboard ships that were going nowhere. Both groups were taken separately back round Cape Horn and up the east coast to Rio de Janeiro in Brazil, where Faustino Martínez was released in July 1834, and on 18 October 1834 "Felipe Salazar" died aboard HMS *Spartiate* from the effects of his broken thigh suffered some eleven months previously.[4] Rivero, Luna and Channen arrived at Rio on 20 November 1834 and were put with the others aboard the *Spartiate*, where they all spent four months before being sent on to Britain. In the event the men were not put on trial (section 6.37); the British prisoners were released after making eyewitness statements, and the other survivors (Rivero, Luna, "Manuel González" and "Luciano Flores") were returned to South America and released. In all, 15 Royal Navy warships were involved, but different goups of prisoners were aboard different ships.

Of the 13 men taken from Port Louis in April 1834, one was released early (Faustino Martínez), one died at Rio ("Felipe Salazar"), and two died in Britain ("Manuel Godoy" and "Latorre"). The main British suspect Henry Channen was aboard 10 ships, in the order *Beagle*, *Blonde*, *Samarang*, *Spartiate*, *Snake*, *Ocean*, *Messenger*, *San Josef*, *Netley* and *Astraea*, with a month's interval

---

[1] Henry Smith's journal, 27 January 1834, in PRO Adm 1/42. The murderers had taken all 53 tame horses from the settlement, preventing Smith and his men from following them. Smith tried unsuccessfully to catch the murderers, but eventually, on 6 March 1834, he made contact with Rivero again. As Smith later wrote in a letter: "…he [Rivero] determined the following morning to betray his companions, and deliver the horses (fifty three) being his turn to take care of them, which he accordingly did, and the four Indians seeing the course things had taken, surrendered" (Smith to Rear Admiral Sir Michael Seymour, 30 June 1834, PRO Adm 1/42, doc. 12). The next day Smith wrote in his journal: "Friday 7th [March 1834] … the Marines with Santiago came in with all the horses [,] Antonio Riveiro having betrayed them into their hands". Most of this last journal entry by Smith was printed in Buenos Aires in Spanish in *Episodio* 1967 (p. 72), so it was theoretically known in Buenos Aires from late 1967 that Rivero had betrayed his companions.
[2] Andrew David, "The Massacre of Matthew Brisbane and his Companions at Port Louis in 1833 and the Fate of their Murderers", in *FIJ* vol. 9 (1), 2007, pp. 110-123, but our account is drawn directly from the original documents.
[3] Date of sailing from the *Conway*'s captain's log, PRO Adm 51/3108.
[4] Date from letter from Captain Robert Tait to the Admiralty, 26 November 1834, PRO Adm 1/43, no doc. no.

(between *Ocean* and *Messenger*) ashore at his father's house in London. The other British suspects George Hopkins, Patrick Kirwan, Daniel McKay and John Stokes were in 9 ships: *Conway, Dublin, Spartiate, Snake, Ocean, Messenger, San Josef, Netley* and *Astraea*, and also spent a month in London with Channen. The Charrúa culprits "Luciano Flores" and "Manuel González" were aboard 12 ships: *Conway, Dublin, Spartiate, Snake, Ocean, Messenger, San Josef, Netley, Astraea, Swallow, Dublin* [again], *Cockatrice* and *Talbot*. The leading murderer Antonio Rivero and the chief witness against him, José María Luna, were aboard 14 of the 15 ships: *Beagle, Blonde, Samarang, Spartiate, Snake, Ocean, Messenger, San Josef, Netley, Astraea, Swallow, Dublin, Cockatrice* and *Talbot*. During that time they had probably neither set foot on dry land nor been told what was happening to them.

6.37 Why was Rivero not put on trial? Kohen's and Rodríguez's false assumption

The point of the exercise was to put on trial the murderers of six men at Port Louis in 1833. The surviving prisoners arrived in the Thames aboard HMS *Snake* on 14 May 1835 – over a year after leaving the Falklands. The British prisoners were allowed to go ashore, but the others were transferred to HMS *Ocean*, the flagship at Sheerness near London. They were the culprits Rivero, "González", "Godoy" and "Flores" (the three surviving Charrúas), and the Chilean witness Luna, who were left aboard for six weeks while the British government considered what to do with them.

The government consulted the Crown's law officers (the Advocate-General, Attorney-General and Solicitor-General), asking them whether the prisoners had been British subjects at the time of the crimes, i.e. whether a statute of 1828, the 9th year of the reign of George IV (9 Geo. IV, Chapter 31, Section 7) was operative here.[1] This Act applied to "any of His Majesty's subjects" charged with murder or manslaughter committed on land outside the United Kingdom, or with being an accessory to such crimes, but it did not apply to foreigners. The Home Office (responsible for justice in Britain) drew up a file of evidence for the law officers, including extensive eyewitness statements, making it clear that the government held the men to be British and stating:[2]

… it is submitted that after the possession taken by Commodore Onslow the settlement in Berkeley Sound became a part of and within the Dominions of His Majesty and thus these individuals (altho' Foreigners and originally settled there under a Foreign Dominion) being residents within the King's Dominion and therefore entitled to the King's protection and owing allegiance to him became subjects of His Majesty within the meaning of the Statute.

The file ended with three questions, with spaces left in which the lawyers wrote their answers. They agreed with the Home Office's view of the case, but were doubtful of the wisdom of proceeding. The questions and answers ran as follows (with the law officers' answers here in italics):[3]

1ˢᵗ Whether these Prisoners are liable to be prosecuted under the provisions of the Act 9 G. 4. C.31 S.7 or by any other means for the murder of all or any and which of the Individuals above stated?

We are of opinion that under 9 Geo. 4 C.31 these prisoners might be prosecuted in England for the murder of all the individuals above mentioned.

2ᵈ Whether the evidence will be sufficient to lead to their Conviction?

We think the evidence would be sufficient to warrant a conviction.

3ᵈ Whether under the circumstances, and with reference to whether it might be fit to execute judgement upon them in case of a Conviction they would recommend a prosecution?

But under all the circumstances it appears to us that in the case of a conviction the sentence could not fitly be carried into execution & ~~for them~~ *we cannot recommend a prosecution.*

On the first question the law officers agreed with the Home Office that the prisoners were British subjects and were thus amenable to prosecution, and to the second question they answered that they

---

[1] The Offences Against the Person Act, passed 27 June 1828 (9 Geo. 4 c. 31), also known as "Lord Lansdowne's Act" after Henry Petty-Fitzmaurice, 3rd Marquess of Lansdowne (1780–1863), Home Secretary July 1827-January 1828.
[2] File of evidence for the case, in PRO HO 48-30, Case 5, fol. 22.
[3] PRO HO 48-30, Case 5, fols. 22-23: roman print here = scribal copperplate; italics = scrawl.

thought the evidence was sufficient for a conviction. So the legal position was clear – the government and its law officers agreed that the islands were British, the men were British and the evidence was adequate to convict them.

But on the third question, whether "it might be fit to execute judgement", the law officers said they felt that "the sentence could not fitly be carried into execution". Here their concerns were not legal but practical: three of the four men ("Godoy", "González" and "Flores") were Charrúa Indians, whom the government described in its file of evidence as "nearly approaching Savages"; if convicted they and Rivero would have been publicly hanged (executions in Britain were carried out in public until 1868), and the spectacle of "savages" being hanged in the middle of London would have been highly embarrassing for the British government. Though the men were British in legal theory, none of them spoke English and the three Charrúas did not even speak much Spanish – they were among the last speakers of the Charrúa language, for which there were of course no interpreters. Moreover, in Uruguay they had been prisoners of war, the last survivors of a brutal genocide, and in the Falklands they were still in effect prisoners – they were not allowed to ride horses and were reduced to doing menial tasks (section 6.2), and unlike the gauchos they were not free to leave. The British public – and any jury – would have seen them as exotic victims and would have had great sympathy for them; a trial would have attracted extensive press coverage, and the impossibility of conducting a fair trial of such men would have made the proceedings highly questionable. Furthermore, until 1836 defence lawyers had to be paid by the defendant; the right of poor people to be represented in court by lawyers had been discussed in Parliament since 1833 but did not become law until 1836, by the Prisoners Counsel's Act,[1] which provided defence lawyers at public expense for prisoners who could not afford one. The Tory government (in power since July 1834, succeeding Earl Grey's Whigs) had been opposing the Bill in Parliament on grounds of cost, but a spectacular trial of "savages" would have been seen as a farce and a mockery of justice since the men would have had no defence counsel. The government's case in Parliament against the Prisoners Counsel's Act would have been undermined, and the opposition Whigs would have been handed a textbook case with which to embarrass the government. A trial would also have drawn public attention to the failure by successive governments to provide for the security of the Falkland Islands, on which British governments of both parties wished to spend as little as possible.

So no trial took place; nothing got into the newspapers, and the government ordered that the men should be sent back to South America. On 27 June 1835 they were put aboard HMS *Messenger*, a paddle-steamer, which took them to Plymouth, where on 30 June they were transferred to HMS *San Josef* – a famous ship.[2] By then "Manuel Godoy" was seriously ill and was taken to Plymouth hospital, where he died on 5 July. The three surviving culprits, Antonio Rivero, "Luciano Flores" and "Manuel González", plus the witness José María Luna, were taken to Falmouth, where on 10 July they were put aboard the naval packet HMS *Swallow*, which arrived at Rio on 3 September 1835. They were eventually transferred to HMS *Talbot*, the last of the 15 ships, and at Montevideo on 28 October 1835, a year and a half after leaving Port Louis, the four men were allowed to disembark. They then disappear from history.

"Luciano Flores" and "Manuel González" (as they were called in Spanish) were the last of the five Charrúa Indians from Port Louis, and were now back in Uruguay, the country where their ancestors had lived for millennia but whose government had massacred their nation. One fears they did not have much of a future. Rivero's and Luna's chances were better; they were not Indians but white South Americans, so they may well have found work as gauchos. But on their fate history is silent, in contrast to pseudo-history, in which Antonio Rivero plays a heroic but entirely fictional part (section 6.33).

---

[1] Prisoners Counsel's [*sic*] Act 1836 (6 & 7 Will. 4, c. 104).
[2] The 114-gun three-decker HMS *San Josef*, originally Spanish, was one of the two personally captured by Nelson at the Battle of Cape St Vincent on 14 February 1797, when he led a boarding party that climbed through a stern window into the 84-gun *San Nicolás*; the *San Nicolás* surrendered after a fierce fight, during which the *San José* drifted up against the *San Nicolás*; Nelson led his men across the deck of the *San Nicolás* (using her as "Nelson's Patent Bridge for boarding First Rates", as was later said) and captured the *San José* too. The *San Josef* later briefly served as Nelson's flagship from 17 January to 1 February 1801.

Kohen and Rodríguez mention (pp. 192-3) our very brief treatment of the murders in *Getting it right* (p. 21); they call our account:

… a pitiful attempt to ignore the simple fact that British justice system [*sic*] failed to bring to trial the authors of serious crimes against British citizens in territories that were supposedly British, using the argument that…[1] the perpetrators were not British! This is absurd. In other words, according to Pascoe and Pepper, if the perpetrators of the murders had been British and not Argentine, they would have been brought before a judge and most likely sentenced to death. Instead, as they were Argentine,[2] they were sent back to South America and freed! In actual fact, the British justice system simply did not consider British legislation to be applicable in the islands at the time the acts occurred.[3] It is well known that criminal law is essentially territorial in nature and can only exceptionally be personal. The absence of a trial and the surreptitious freeing of Rivero and his gang of gauchos is better seen as evidence of the weakness of the British legal position regarding sovereignty.

That is entirely incorrect. Kohen and Rodríguez give Caillet-Bois and Canclini as their sources,[4] but they all get the wrong end of the stick – Canclini questions why putting the murderers on trial "was considered inconvenient if there was no doubt of the status of British possession of the islands".

In fact it was not the status of the *territory* that was doubtful but the status of the *culprits*. All the documentation makes it perfectly clear that the British government held the Falklands to be British territory without question – in the letter to Captain George Elliot at the Admiralty (quoted below in section 6.38), Colonial Secretary Thomas Spring Rice says "the Falkland Islands are an undoubted possession of Great Britain". The question was only whether the *culprits* were British.

Kohen and Rodríguez say that "criminal law is essentially territorial in nature", which is generally true (crimes are nowadays usually judged by the authorities of the place where they were committed, irrespective of the nationality of the perpetrators), but the situation in the 1830s was different, and some countries asserted the right to try their own citizens for serious crimes wherever they had been committed. That practice has not entirely died out – South Korea still asserts the right to try its own citizens for offences committed anywhere in the world, even for actions (such as smoking marijuana) which are legal where committed (e.g. in Canada) but illegal in South Korea.[5]

In much the same way, the 1828 statute (9 Geo. IV, Chapter 31, Section 7), asserted the British government's right to try British subjects for murder or manslaughter committed anywhere in the world outside the United Kingdom. So it was quite simply true that if the murderers were British, they could be tried and, if convicted, hanged.

It is important to realise that the statute applied everywhere outside the United Kingdom, and therefore applied in British territories overseas as well as in foreign countries. The United Kingdom consisted of England, Scotland, Wales, the whole of Ireland, *and nothing else*. Britain's policy on the status of its overseas territories has always been maximally restrictive – they have never counted as part of the United Kingdom, in contrast to Portugal and France, where overseas territories were treated as parts of the metropolitan countries, with representatives in the national parliaments. Thus the French « Collectivités d'Outre-Mer » [Overseas Communities] are currently (2022) represented by 27 members in the French parliament in Paris. That has never been the case in Britain; the

---

[1] These suspension points in original, not added by us.

[2] In fact only Rivero was Argentinian; the Charrúas were from Uruguay and Luna was Chilean.

[3] The myth that Britain did not view itself as having jurisdiction in the Falklands is widespread in Argentina – Marcelo Beccaceci says the murderers were imprisoned in Newgate prison (another myth) and that "the presiding judge considered that the Court of London 'has no jurisdiction whatever over the Malvinas islands'." (*Gauchos de Malvinas*, Buenos Aires 2017, p. 27). That is untrue – there was no trial, so there was no judge anyway, and Britain regarded its sovereignty and jurisdiction in the islands as incontestible.

[4] They give Caillet-Bois, p. 379, fn.6 (i.e. in the 1952 and 1982 editions; it is pp. 376-377 in the 1948 ed.), and Arnoldo Canclini, *Malvinas 1833: antes y después de la agresión inglesa* ["Malvinas 1833: before and after the English aggression"], Buenos Aires March 2007, p. 56.

[5] See e.g. article by Benjamin Haas on the *Guardian* website, 23 October 2018: "Bong arm of the law: South Korea says it will arrest citizens who smoke weed in Canada". The article states: "South Korean law is based on the concept that laws made in Seoul still apply to citizens anywhere in the world, and violations, even while abroad, can technically lead to punishment when they return home. Those who smoke weed could face up to five years in prison." Canada legalised marijuana on 17 October 2018, but it remains illegal in South Korea.

United Kingdom consists exclusively of England, Scotland, Wales and Northern Ireland, i.e. only places with Members of Parliament (MPs) in the British Parliament at Westminster. The Isle of Man, the Channel Islands, Gibraltar, the Falklands, St Helena and various other territories are British but are not part of the United Kingdom; they have no MPs at Westminster but have their own legislatures.

Thus the 1828 statute applied alike to all non-British parts of the world and also to all British overseas territories including the Falklands. It did not empower the government to try foreigners for the same crimes, so it was essential to establish whether the Port Louis murderers were British. The Home Office and the Crown's law officers agreed that they were, but decided for domestic political reasons not to proceed. The assertion by Kohen and Rodríguez that "the British justice system simply did not consider British legislation to be applicable in the islands" is disproved by the facts.

6.38 The British government considers withdrawing the British presence

We now come to an important aspect of the story which has been misunderstood by Argentine writers, including Kohen and Rodríguez, perhaps partly because they themselves or their sources (i.e. other Argentine writers) were unable to read some central documents. Those documents reveal how unimperialistic Britain was in the 1830s and 40s, contrary to what is usually stated or implied by Argentine authors. At that time British governments, far from being aggressively imperialistic (which they did become half a century later), were against the acquisition of overseas possessions, as shown by a speech by Sir William Molesworth in the House of Commons in 1848 which is quoted by many Argentine authors including Kohen and Rodríguez (see section 7.3). So keen was the British government to save money, and so certain of its sovereignty over the Falklands, that in 1834 and 1835 British ministers debated whether to withdraw the British presence entirely, and the Colonial Office advocated a return to the policy of simply having the islands visited annually by "one of His Majesty's ships".

Colonial Secretary Thomas Spring Rice was alarmed for the safety of the boat's crew stationed in the islands after the Port Louis murders, and initially ordered the Undersecretary at the Colonial Office, Robert William Hay, to prepare a letter to the Admiralty recommending an increase in the British presence: instead of a mere boat's crew it would be better to send a small force of Marines, with some convicts as labourers. That letter was copied out by a Colonial Office clerk and presented to Spring Rice for signature, but on 5 August 1834 he had second thoughts and recommended a cheaper and safer policy: to withdraw the British presence completely, on the grounds that it was not necessary for maintaining British rights in the islands since those rights were incontestible. He instructed Undersecretary Hay to rework the letter, leaving out the Marines and simply saying the boat's crew should be withdrawn. Hay crossed out most of the text, scrawled the alterations in lead pencil, and sent it back to the clerk for copying. The resulting much-altered letter reveals the dramatic policy change at the Colonial Office, from reinforcing the British presence in the Falklands to withdrawing it completely.[1]

Unfortunately for Kohen and Rodríguez, Arnoldo Canclini (one of their sources) was unable to read the pencil additions to that letter, and could only read the original text in ink, so he remained unaware of the total reversal of Colonial Office policy towards the Falklands. Canclini prints part of the letter (in Spanish), but he thoroughly misunderstands it. In the first place, he says "George Elliot wrote from Downing Street his opinions on what to do with the prisoners" – but Elliot was the addressee, not the writer; the letter is *from* Robert William Hay in Downing Street on behalf of Thomas Spring Rice *to* Captain George Elliot. And secondly he prints the part of the letter that was crossed out, but not the part that replaced it, thus falsifying what it finally said. Here is the part of the letter Canclini printed, but using the text of the English original (except for his misspelling of

---

[1] Letter from Colonial Secretary Thomas Spring Rice to the Admiralty, PRO CO 78/1, fols. 92 *recto* to 94 *verso*, addressed at foot of fol. 92 *recto* to "Captain / The Hon<u>b</u> George Elliot CB" [CB: Companion of the Most Honourable Order of the Bath], with crossings-out and pencil additions in the hand of Robert William Hay (1786-1861), Undersecretary at the Colonial Office (at that time housed in Downing Street, which Canclini did not know).

Spring Rice's name); we enclose in double round brackets a passage Canclini omits, and indicate by strikethrough the passages which he prints but which are actually crossed out:[1]

((I am directed to request that, in expressing to the Lords Commissioners of the Admiralty M[r] Spring Rice's concern at the outrage in question, you will)) state his opinion that as the Falkland Islands are an undoubted possession of Great Britain, there can be no question as to the right which His Majesty possesses of ordering the Murderers to be sent home and to be submitted to the ordinary course of the Law in this Country. This is a measure, however, which should be avoided, if possible, and Mr. Sprung Rice [*sic* in Canclini] hopes that the Admiral on the South American Station may be enabled to devise some other means for disposing of the prisoners in the event of their apprehension.[2]

Mr. Sprung Rice is desirous of taking this opportunity of conveying to the Lords Commissioners his opinion that, ~~instead of retaining a Ship of War at the Falkland Islands, or allowing a boat's crew to be left ashore there, at the risk of their lives, it will be more expedient to send out a small body of marines, with a certain number of convicts under their charge, who may be employed in the construction of such works and public buildings as are absolutely required for the security of the place, and for its establishment as a port of refit for shipping proceeding from the Pacific~~.

Canclini does say the text was a draft and that the second part had been cancelled and replaced by "generalidades difícil a leer" ["generalities difficult to read"], i.e. the remarks in pencil, but of course those "generalities", which he was unable to decipher, were the intended message from Spring Rice: that the British presence should be withdrawn.

The operative part of the letter actually said the opposite of what Canclini prints – it reads as follows (pencil here in italics, crossed-out passage omitted):

M[r] Spring Rice is desirous of taking this opportunity of conveying to the Lords Commissioners his opinion that, *as the Rights of the British Crown to the possession & Sovereignty of the Falkland Islands have been fully asserted, & are incontestible, it is not necessary for the preservation of these rights that a Boat's Crew should be left ashore there at the risk of their lives, he therefore recommends that this small force should be altogether withdrawn.*

That reveals the British government's certainty as to Britain's sovereignty over the Falklands, and at the same time its lack of any intention to fortify or occupy the territory. On 18 April 1835 Spring Rice was succeeded as Colonial Secretary by Lord Glenelg, who continued the policy of withdrawing the British presence from the Falklands, and on 19 May 1835 instructed Undersecretary Hay to communicate that view again to the Foreign Office:[3]

Lord Glenelg,… being confident that the military occupation of the Falkland islands, is not necessary in order to the preservation [*sic*] of His Majesty's Rights of Sovereignty his Lordship would propose, as has been already recommended that the Naval officer and his boat's Crew should be withdrawn from Berkeley Sound, but that the Rear Admiral commanding on the South American Station should be instructed to order his Squadron to pay frequent visits to the Falkland islands, for the purpose of preventing their occupation by another Power…

For over a year the discussion went back and forth within the British government as to whether the lieutenant and boat's crew should be withdrawn, leaving the islands without any official British presence, but in the end, in August 1835, the view of Lord Palmerston at the Foreign Office prevailed, and Smith and his 4-man boat's crew were left in place (but without any Marines).

6.39 The US Supreme Court rules, 1839: Vernet's seizures of ships were illegal in US law

The court case in the US in 1837 (section 6.6), concerning Louis Vernet's seizures of the American sealers *Harriet*, *Breakwater* and *Superior* in 1831 was eventually heard before the United States Supreme Court, which in January 1839 delivered a final authoritative ruling, namely:[4]

---

[1] Canclini 2007, p. 56. The full text, with ink and pencil crossings-out indicated, will appear in *The Falklands Saga*.
[2] Even as late as August 1834 it was not known in London that the culprits had been caught in March.
[3] Hay to Backhouse, 19 May 1835, PRO FO 6 501, fols. 149 *recto* to 151 *verso*. Charles Grant (1778-1866), from 5 May 1835 1st Baron Glenelg, was Secretary of State for War and the Colonies, 18 April 1835 to 20 February 1839.
[4] Richard Peters [ed.], *Reports of Cases…*, vol. 38 ("Peters 13"), January 1839, p. 415. Statement of final judgement in *ibid.*, p. 422: "… it is the opinion of this Court, 1st, That, inasmuch as the American government has insisted and still

... that the Falkland islands do not constitute any part of the dominions within the sovereignty of Buenos Ayres, and that the seal fishery at those islands is a trade free and lawful to the citizens of the United States, and beyond the competency of the Buenos Ayres government to regulate, prohibit, or punish...

The court stated the position under the US constitution, which was that "When the executive branch of the government, which is charged with the foreign relations of the United States, shall, in its correspondence with a foreign nation, assume a fact in regard to the sovereignty of any island or country, it is conclusive on the judicial department". In other words, no US court could question the Falklands policy of the US government, which recognised no territorial sovereignty over the islands. So in United States law the purported "sovereignty" of Argentina in the Falklands was invalid and always had been.

6.40 Conclusion

This chapter has exposed and corrected many individual errors of fact in the arguments presented by Marcelo Kohen and Facundo Rodríguez, and has also revealed their basic underlying error: the notion that the legal position of the Falklands in the 1830s was clear. As Argentinians, they naturally start from the assumption that the islands belonged to Argentina, but that was the case only in internal Argentine law, not in international law. There was in fact no international consensus on the question at that time, and no clear holder of title over the islands. The countries involved held mutually contradictory views on the matter: Argentina held the islands to be Argentinian, Britain held them to be British and Spain held them to be Spanish, while the United States denied all those claims and held that they belonged to no country and were open to all.

That situation changed during the 19th century, as Argentina dropped its claim to the Falklands by treaty in 1850 and accepted that the islands were British, Spain abandoned its claim in 1863 at the latest, and the United States accepted in the 1870s that the islands were British territory. Those developments will now be examined.

---

does insist, through its regular executive authority, that the Falkland islands do not constitute any part of the dominions within the sovereignty of the government of Buenos Ayres, the action of the American government on this subject is binding on the said Circuit Court, as to whom the sovereignty of those islands belongs...". Whole text of case reprinted (without original page nos.) in Perl 1983, pp. 335-342 (summary on Perl's p. 335, final judgement p. 342).

CHAPTER SEVEN: the years 1840-1850; the end of Argentina's partial title

We now come to a vitally important decade in the history of the Falkland Islands: the years 1840-50. It was in those years that Argentina's title to the islands (which was only partial anyway) was definitively extinguished by the Convention of Peace between Britain and Argentina, signed in 1849 and ratified in 1850. At Argentina's insistence, it was a full peace treaty (Britain would have preferred a lower-level agreement), and it not only ended all Argentine title but initiated a total change in Argentina's actions with respect to the Falklands. The account of this period by Kohen and Rodríguez (their pages 193-214)[1] contains serious distortions and falsifications, some of which have been repeated for years in Argentine accounts, while others are new, including several responses to our internet papers *Getting it right* and *False Falklands History*. In this chapter we demonstrate that we were right in our papers, but we begin with a little history to set the scene.

7.1 Population developments; lands granted to both British and non-British inhabitants

Throughout the year of limbo (January 1833 to January 1834) there was no resident British authority in the islands. Then, from 1834 to 1841, British authority was exercised by a mere naval lieutenant with a boat's crew of four men. They did not form a separate force in their own right but counted as part of the crew of the British flagship at Rio de Janeiro on the Royal Navy's South American station, which reveals Britain's lack of commitment to the islands – there was no aggressive campaign of imperial expansion at work.

During those years there were some significant developments among the tiny population of Port Louis, which fell to a dozen inhabitants by 1837, though it rose to about three dozen by 1840. As mentioned in section 6.35, Charles Melville arrived in January 1834 as one of Henry Smith's boat's crew; he married into the Biggs family, lived in the islands for the rest of his life and had five children. A noteworthy arrival in 1838 was Andrez Pitaluga (1822-1878), who was born in Gibraltar, though his family were originally Italian, from Sestri di Ponente near Genoa.[2] He still has descendants in the islands today, and his family has now lived there for 180 years. In 1840 James and Mary Watson arrived, the ancestors of many of today's Falkland Islanders (section 6.8).

And on 1 January 1841 three people took the Oath of Allegiance to Queen Victoria and became naturalised British subjects. They were Antonina Roxa from Argentina, "Ieergen" (Jürgen) Dettleff from Germany, and Thomas Rolon from "South America". That began a slow trickle of people who took British nationality – there were only 31 grants of British nationality in the Falklands in the entire 19th century. The origins of those 31 people were as in Table 7.1a:[3]

Argentina	2	Italy	2	United States	2
Denmark	3	Norway	1	Uruguay	2
France	2	Portugal	4	"South America"	1 (Thomas Rolon)
Germany	8	Spain	1		
Holland	1	Sweden	2	Total:	31

Table 7.1a Naturalisations in the Falklands in the 19th century.

That disproves the contention of Kohen and Rodríguez (p. 195) that it was compulsory to swear an oath of loyalty to the British Crown, on pain of being expelled from the islands. By the mid-19th century there were far more than 31 non-British people in the islands, few of whom swore an oath of loyalty – for a time in the 1840s there were over 150 of them, including at least 17 Argentinians (sections 7.7, 10.1). Kohen and Rodríguez base their assertion on a work by Hipólito Solari Yrigoyen,[4] though they give some wrong page-references. They say on the same page that it was at this time that the distribution of lands began, "exclusively to the subjects of Her Majesty," and on

---

[1] As explained in the Introduction, we quote from the English translation of Kohen and Rodríguez, but we give page-numbers from the paper Spanish version of 2015.

[2] Details on Andrez Pitaluga from entry by Nicholas Pitaluga in *DFB*. In the Falklands the surname is pronounced "*Pitt*alooga", with a short stressed first syllable (Saul Pitaluga, pers. comm.).

[3] List in [Anon.], *Revised Falklands Ordinances 1915*, Stanley 1915, p. 202 (copy in JCNA).

[4] Hipólito Solari Yrigoyen, *Malvinas: lo que no cuentan los ingleses (1833-1982)* ["Malvinas: what the English don't say (1833-1982)"], Buenos Aires 1998, p. 18.

their p. 266 they refer to "the concession of lands to British subjects only", but they are wrong.

In the first place, no individuals, British or not British, were granted the freehold (unrestricted ownership) of land; they obtained only the leasehold, i.e. they held the land under a lease which expired after a given number of years (a typically British arrangement; there are millions of leasehold properties in Britain, and more are constantly being built). When the lease ended they either had to leave the land or buy the lease again – and British subjects had to do that just the same as non-British subjects. Non-British subjects (or "aliens", as they were somewhat disdainfully called) could hold land on the same terms as British subjects and had exactly the same rights and obligations except for holding public office and being called for jury service. Some non-British subjects held quite extensive lands – by the 1870s 12,000 acres were being held by José Llamosa, who was apparently from Spain but had gone to the River Plate and was sent to the Falklands from Montevideo in 1847 (section 10.1) and was never naturalised, and the Dane Charles Hansen leased Carcass Island and the Jason Islands for ten years in the 1870s before he took British citizenship in January 1880. In addition, 10,000 acres were held by Andrez Pitaluga, who as a Gibraltarian might be classed as British, though his forebears were Italian.[1] In the holding of land there was equality of rights between British citizens and "aliens" in the Falklands – and some "aliens" were part of the land-holding elite while most British subjects were not. Yrigoyen's assertions (followed by Kohen and Rodríguez) are disproved by the documentation.

7.2 The establishment of the colony; the first Governor

Britain was slow to heed the advice of private citizens such as William Langdon and G. T. Whitington, who had both visited the islands during Vernet's time (section 6.8) and strongly urged the British government to administer the islands properly. At long last, in 1841, the British government appointed a lieutenant-governor: Richard Moody (1813-1887), who was not promoted to full governor until 1843. He arrived at Port Louis in the brig *Hebe* on 15 January 1842, accompanied by a dozen volunteers of the regiment of Royal Sappers and Miners: a sergeant, two corporals and nine privates; there were also three wives and seven children.[2] The size of Moody's party, though it consisted of a mere 22 people, marked the acceptance by Britain for the first time of a definite commitment to the islands. Among the party was Private James Biggs (1806-1853) and his wife Margaret; many of today's islanders are descended from them since they had six children, 38 grandchildren and 141 great-grandchildren. In 1992 the family produced a "Biggs badge" showing the *Hebe* and inscribed "The Biggs Family: 150 years in the Falklands 1842-1992". Some 200 descendants of James and Margaret Biggs held a family party in Stanley Town Hall on 15 January 1992, the 150th anniversary of the family's arrival in the islands. The youngest children now vary between seventh and ninth generations.[3] One other member of Moody's party, Thomas Yates, still has descendants in the islands, though they all have other surnames.[4]

The soldiers did not form much of a garrison – there were only 12 of them, fewer than half the 27 soldiers of the Argentine garrison a decade earlier, and their purpose was quite different. They were not there to suppress "illegal" sealing, and did nothing to interfere with ships of any nationality around the islands; they were there as builders, and they constructed a number of buildings at Port Louis, one of which still stands, the barrack building of 1843 (fig. 7.2a).[5] For over 160 years it has been a private house, and it is the oldest complete inhabited building so far south in the world.[6] Kohen and Rodríguez do not mention this building, but it is worth pointing out that many Argentine books, pamphlets and leaflets, including some published officially by the

---

[1] List of confirmed land grants, 1879, at end of Falklands *Blue Book* 1879, PRO CO 81/34; details on Charles Hansen from the entry by Jane Cameron in *DFB*.
[2] T.W.J. Connolly, *The History of the Corps of Royal Sappers and Miners...*, vol. I, London 1855, pp. 360, 361.
[3] Details from Jane Cameron, pers. comm.; from "My Family" by Ailie Biggs, aged 11, in *FIJ* vol. 6 (3), 1994, pp. 62-65; and from entry in *DFB* on James Biggs by Coleen Biggs.
[4] We are grateful to the Falkland Islands National Archivist Tansy Bishop for information on the Yates family.
[5] The barrack building is described in detail and illustrated in Robert Philpott, forthcoming.
[6] Some buildings in Stanley are 12 miles further south but are just a couple of years younger; Charles Barnard's house on New Island, built in 1813, is 30 years older but has been partly reconstructed.

7.2a The barrack building at Port Louis, built in 1843 by the British regiment of Sappers and Miners; photo of around 1890 (Falkland Islands Museum and National Trust). It originally had 18 loopholes for rifle fire in the south wall; by 1890 one had been enlarged into a window as seen here; now (2022) two have been enlarged, and the three loopholes in each end wall have been obliterated. The same photo has appeared in several Argentine books and publications including an official Argentine government pamphlet distributed at the United Nations in 2012, in all cases without the correct source and wrongly identified as showing Vernet's house, which actually stood 150 yards to the north-east (see chapter 5, figs. 5.4b, 5.4c).

Argentine government, erroneously describe it as having been Louis Vernet's house.[1]

In 1843 the British government decided – against the wishes of Moody and some of the leading residents – to move the seat of government from Port Louis, and work began on the first buildings of a new town, to be called Stanley after Colonial Secretary Lord Stanley. The original name was Stanley rather than Port Stanley,[2] though the longer name is still sometimes used. The Sappers and Miners erected some buildings on the new site, including the Old Central Store (which in 2014 became the Historic Dockyard Museum), then Moody and his party moved from Port Louis to Stanley, which was officially inaugurated on 18 July 1845. It is the oldest town so far south in the world, and is older than several other New World towns, such as Otago, New Zealand (founded 1848); Punta Arenas, Chile (1849); Canterbury and Christchurch, New Zealand (both 1850); Seattle, USA (1851); Vancouver, Canada (1867), or Ushuaia, Argentina (founded as a mission station in 1871 by missionaries from the Falklands, established as a town in 1884). The role of Stanley in the islands, as the capital and largest settlement, is naturally preeminent – so much so that there is a term for the whole of the islands *except* Stanley: "the Camp", derived from Spanish "campo" and also from early modern English "camp" meaning "field".[3]

Stanley has always been English-speaking, yet in Argentina it is mostly referred to as "Puerto Argentino", a name imposed by the fascist Argentine junta that invaded the islands in 1982. Initially, on 5 April 1982, the junta imposed the name "Puerto Rivero", following the erroneous

---

[1] One of them is the seriously erroneous 10-page official pamphlet produced by the Argentine foreign ministry and distributed in several languages at the United Nations in September 2012: the English version, entitled *Argentine Republic / The Question of the Malvinas Islands / A story of colonialism. A United Nations cause.* [Buenos Aires 2012], prints on p. 4 (somewhat blurred) the photo that we reproduce in fig. 7.2a, of the barrack building around 1890, with the caption "View of Governor Vernet's residence in the Malvinas Islands." The same photo, also identified as Vernet's house, is printed (murkily) in Marcelo Beccaceci, *Gauchos de Malvinas*, Buenos Aires 2017, p. 22. In fact Vernet never saw the building; it was built 12 years after he left the islands for good. His house stood some 150 yards north-east of the barrack building, and some of its walls still stand 4 or 5 feet high (see chapter 5, figs. 5.4a-5.4c).

[2] Jane Cameron, pers. comm.

[3] The most detailed history of Stanley is in a richly illustrated book by John Smith, *An Historical Scrapbook of Stanley*, Stanley 2013, while another richly illustrated book, by Joan Spruce and Natalie Smith, *Falkland Rural Heritage: Sites, Structures and Snippets of Historical Interest*, Fox Bay (West Falkland) and Stockholm (Sweden), 2018, gives an account of the many ruins, old buildings, wrecks and characters in the history of the Camp.

theory that Rivero had led an anti-British uprising, but on 22 April 1982 they issued decree no. 757 imposing the name "Puerto Argentino" (section 6.33). Argentinians now roundly reject the acts of the junta of 1976-83, but nevertheless continue to use a name which Falkland Islanders see as a deliberate insult. Argentina promised in 1999 to cease using Puerto Argentino,[1] but that promise has not been kept.

The buildings in Stanley dating to the 1840s, plus the barracks at Port Louis, are the oldest inhabited buildings in the world so far south, and form an ensemble of historic significance. It is not only the buildings that are the oldest ones at such a latitude – in the mid-1840s there were no Spanish-speaking settlements as far south as the Falklands, so that apart from a few surviving descendants of Fuegian and Patagonian tribes, the Falkland Islanders are the world's oldest community at such a deep southern latitude. Kohen and Rodríguez say nothing of all this – they are not interested in the history of the islands as such, still less in their inhabitants.

For Moody, after his disappointment at the move of the capital, there was at least the consolation that in 1843 he was promoted to the rank of full governor, under a new Charter for the Colony in the form of Letters Patent under the Great Seal dated 23 June 1843,[2] which at last set up a proper administration in the islands (not in 1845, as Kohen and Rodríguez say on their p. 193). The Charter was in effect, if not in name, a constitution for the islands, and laid down that there was to be a Legislative Council consisting of the Governor and at least two "other persons", to make all laws and ordinances for the government of the Falkland Islands and their Dependencies. Those arrangements have been altered in many ways since then, above all by the latest Falklands constitution of 2009, always in the direction of giving more power to the people of the islands.

Kohen and Rodríguez maintain (pp. 193-4) that under English law, territorial sovereignty can only be acquired by settlement, cession, conquest or annexation; they maintain that none of those applies to the situation in the 1840s, but in fact the situation then as in the 1830s and earlier was complex. At that time there was no country that possessed a perfect title to the Falklands (i.e. 100% exclusive sovereignty), but merely several overlapping and contested claims. Argentina had some rights in the islands in the 1820s and 30s, which were continued into the 1840s by regular protests, and Britain had extensive rights too, which were steadily strengthened by Britain's many acts of administration (« effectivités », sections 8.9, 8.20), but neither country could claim full *de jure* sovereignty in international law. Britain's rights were encumbered by the rights of Argentina and Spain just as Argentina's rights were encumbered by Britain's and Spain's, and Argentina had not inherited any right to restrict British activities in the islands, since Spain had surrendered that right by the Nootka Sound Convention (section 1.7). By contrast, the United States did not recognise any territorial title to the islands held by any country, but regarded them as part of the high seas. Thus there was at that time no clear title to the Falklands, but only several imperfect titles.

7.3 Sir William Molesworth's suggestion, I, 25 July 1848 – not repeated in 1849

Kohen and Rodríguez mention (p. 202), slightly out of chronological sequence, something which is referred to by several Argentine writers; we place it here in its correct chronological place, since it has a sequel of which they were unaware.

It is a suggestion made in the House of Commons by the Whig (Liberal) MP Sir William Molesworth (1810-55) on 25 July 1848,[3] which Argentine writers see as support for their case. As a Liberal, Molesworth was anti-colonialist and in favour of free trade – to him, the possession of a territory that offered no trade was anathema. The Whig government at the time under Lord John Russell (Prime Minister 1846-52) broadly agreed with him, but he wished to push the government further in the direction of reducing colonial expenditure. In his speech he distinguished between "colonies", with considerable populations and real economic value, and "military stations", whose

---

[1] Article in *Clarín*, Buenos Aires, 16 July 1999, p. 3.
[2] Full text of the "Charter for the Government of the Falkland Islands", dated 23 June 1843, printed in [Anon.], *Laws and Ordinances of the Falkland Islands from the Settlement of the Colony to the year 1884*, Stanley [1884], pp. 5-7.
[3] Speech in the Commons by Sir William Molesworth, 25 July 1848, in *Hansard's Parliamentary Debates* (henceforth "*Hansard*"), London 25 July 1848, columns 816-857.

very raison d'être he questioned:[1]

> Our military stations are Heligoland, Gibraltar, Malta, the Ionian Islands, Bermuda, the stations on the west coast of Africa, St. Helena, the Cape of Good Hope, the Mauritius, Hong-Kong, Labuan, and the Falkland Islands. What do these stations cost us? Of what use are they to this country? ...

He dealt with each of them in detail, excoriating the wastefulness of the expenditure lavished on them – for example, "those worthless rocks... the Bermudas" cost £90,000 a year.[2] The Falklands came lowest in his catalogue of imperial profligacy – in their English translation Kohen and Rodríguez quote part of his speech from *Hansard*:[3]

> I will now conclude... with the Falkland Islands. On that dreary, desolate, and windy spot, where neither corn nor trees can grow, long wisely abandoned by us, we have, since 1841, expended upwards of 35,000£[;] we have a civil establishment there at the cost of 5,000£ a year[...] What I propose to the House is this: [... to] acknowledge the claim of Buenos Ayres to the Falkland Islands.

Kohen and Rodríguez comment: "As we can see, at the time some legislators were even prepared to return the Falklands/Malvinas". Actually, few agreed with Molesworth – Mr Hawkes, replying for the government, refuted Molesworth's statistics and corrected his assertions.[4] At that time Molesworth was unaware that Buenos Aires was about to drop its claim to the Falkland Islands, which rendered his suggestion otiose. And he failed to obtain a vote – it was past midnight, the debate failed to retain a quorum of forty MPs and was adjourned without a division.

Molesworth's remarks became much more widely known than they deserved to be: the Argentine ambassador in London, Manuel Moreno, reported them to Argentine foreign minister Felipe Arana in a despatch of 1 September 1848; Violet Boyson found them in the Buenos Aires government newspaper *Gaceta Mercantil* of 22 November 1848, and gave them wide currency by quoting them in her book in 1924,[5] and they have since been quoted by various Argentine writers including Kohen and Rodríguez. But what none of them realised is that a year later in June 1849 Molesworth made much the same speech again, but with an important omission – he left out the Falkland Islands (section 7.6).

7.4 The Anglo-French intervention around the River Plate[6]

After the Spanish South American territories obtained their independence in the 1820s, confusion and chaos continued for much of the following 50 years, as the new republics competed for territorial possession. A hotly contested question was whether Uruguay should be a separate country (it had become independent in 1828) or part of the Argentine Confederation. In Argentina there were two competing factions, the Unitarians, who fought for a unitary Argentine state (including Uruguay) and the Federalists, who fought for a federal Argentina with partly autonomous provinces (likewise including Uruguay). The leader of the Federalists, and *de facto* dictator of Argentina, was General Juan Manuel de Rosas.[7] Technically he was merely the governor of Buenos Aires province (1829-32 and 1835-52), but that province was "charged" with the foreign policy of the whole Confederation, so Rosas could decide Argentine foreign policy by himself.

---

[1] *Hansard* 25 July 1848, col. 820.

[2] *Hansard* 25 July 1848, col. 822.

[3] *Hansard* 25 July 1848, cols. 828, 829; the square brackets added here by us mark silent omissions by Kohen and Rodríguez. In their Spanish version (p. 202) they use a very different text taken from the *Morning Chronicle* and *Daily News*, 27 July 1848, sent by Manuel Moreno to Felipe Arana on 1 September 1848, which is also quoted (variously translated) in Muñoz Azpiri 1966, vol. 2, p. 193; in Alfredo Burnet-Merlín, *Cuando Rosas quiso ser inglés...* ["When Rosas wanted to be British..."], Buenos Aires 1974, p. 21; in Solari Yrigoyen 1998, p. 24; and in Becerra 1998, p. 133.

[4] *Hansard* 25 July 1848, col. 874.

[5] Boyson 1924, pp. 118-119.

[6] The immensely convoluted events of this time are described in John F. Cady, *Foreign Intervention in the Rio de la Plata 1838-50*, Philadelphia 1929, and in John Lynch's biographies of Rosas mentioned in the footnote below.

[7] Juan Manuel José Domingo Ortiz de Rosas y López de Osornio; born Buenos Aires 30 March 1793, died Southampton, Hampshire, 14 March 1877; Governor of the Province of Buenos Aires 8 December 1829 to 5 December 1832 and 13 April 1835 to 3 February 1852. Biography by John Lynch, *Argentine Dictator: Juan Manuel de Rosas 1829-1852*, Oxford 1981; abridged version, *Argentine Caudillo: Juan Manuel de Rosas*, Wilmington (Delaware) 2001.

As well as the complex internecine power struggle between rival South American factions, a further complication was caused by Britain and France, which intervened with military force around the River Plate, in a series of intermittent actions over more than a decade (1838-50). The River Plate area had great potential for trade, and many British traders had settled around Buenos Aires, while French traders had settled around Montevideo. It was partly to protect them that Britain and France intervened; both felt entitled to intervene in pursuing their own interests, and regarded Argentina and Uruguay in much the same way as they regarded Africa – as somewhere without "proper" government, where military intervention was permissible. Britain and France sometimes worked together, sometimes bitterly disagreed, and sometimes withdrew altogether.

There was much skirmishing and several battles, and from 22 September 1845 Britain and France blockaded Buenos Aires, which played into Rosas's hands – he closed the River Paraná by a chain, which brought trade in the area to a standstill. Britain and France sent a joint expedition to break the chain and open the river by force, and at the bend ("vuelta") of the Paraná at a place called Obligado, there was a hard-fought battle on 20 November 1845, in which the Anglo-French forces broke Rosas's chain, raised the blockade, and escorted upriver over a hundred merchant ships that had been waiting. The Argentine defenders lost the battle, but the heroic fight against the European invaders inspired them with patriotism and united them behind Rosas, so the Battle of the Vuelta de Obligado became a defining symbol of Argentina's rise to nationhood. The Anglo-French blockade of Buenos Aires continued, but it was self-defeating since it hit British and French trade, while Argentina's simple economy was fairly immune to outside pressure. In the end Britain lifted the blockade on 15 July 1847, and France followed suit in June 1848.

7.5 Peace negotiations; Henry Southern arrives, October 1848

Once the Anglo-French blockade of Buenos Aires had been lifted, the way was clear for normal relations to be resumed between Britain and the Argentine Confederation. That required Britain to negotiate with the touchy, stubborn, pig-headed General Rosas. He was basically pro-British, but he was dictatorial by instinct; any resumption of relations between Britain and Argentina would be on his terms, so for the tricky task of negotiating with him the British government chose Henry Southern (1799-1853), who spoke fluent Spanish and had considerable diplomatic experience. The British government gave him plenipotentiary powers to negotiate on Britain's behalf – the British government would be negotiating through him.

An odd aspect of this episode was that two years later the Buenos Aires government published some of the confidential correspondence between the two sides. From 1843 to 1851 the Rosas regime published much of its own diplomatic correspondence, plus other documents, in an official compilation entitled *Archivo Americano y Espíritu de la Prensa del Mundo* ["American Archive and Spirit of the World Press"], which appeared several times a year in English, Spanish and French, in 1500 copies, 400 of which were sent abroad. It was edited by the Italian-born jurist and historian Pedro de Angelis (1784-1859), a loyal servant of Rosas, and was printed by the official Argentine government printing office "Imprenta de la Independencia". The content of each volume was personally supervised by Rosas himself, and precisely reflected his government's policies. It was a serious indiscretion to publish another country's diplomatic correspondence, but Rosas cared nothing for such niceties, and Britain did not complain; it was the price of doing business with him. The texts of 24 communications between Rosas's government and Henry Southern were printed in English, Spanish and French in *Archivo Americano* in December 1850, headed "State Documents relative to the last Convention of Peace, celebrated with England".[1] That confirms that the negotiations resulted in a peace treaty between Britain and Argentina. In the 19th century "treaty" and "convention" were synonymous, as is made clear by the official British patent appointing Henry Southern in the name of Queen Victoria, printed twice in *Archivo Americano*, giving him plenipotentiary powers "to negotiate and conclude a Treaty or Convention between Us and the Argentine Government for the purpose of putting an End to Existing differences, and of restoring

---

[1] In *Archivo Americano* vol. 21, dated at top of p. 1 "Buenos Aires, Diciembre 16 de 1850"; the correspondence and treaty texts relevant to the Convention of Peace run from p. 100 to p. 193.

perfect relations of Friendship between Us and the said Confederation".[1]

In signing a peace treaty, Britain accepted that the armed conflict around the River Plate had been an actual war, in which Argentina had been not merely the scene of conflict but a belligerent, i.e. a combatant with the same status as Britain. The treaty therefore marked Britain's acceptance of Argentina as a member of the comity of nations, on a par with such countries as France, Spain, or the United States. That was Rosas's central aim throughout.

Southern arrived at Buenos Aires on 5 October 1848. Rosas received him cordially, but only on a personal level; he said he was not receiving Southern as an official British representative but only as a negotiator; foreign minister Felipe Arana called him the "Minister Negotiator of the Peace".[2] After several meetings with Rosas, Southern reported to Foreign Secretary Lord Palmerston on 14 October in his first despatch from Buenos Aires, describing Rosas's negotiating position:[3]

He returned to His original argument: that it would be dishonorable for Him and to the Confederation, if after all that has passed, He did not terminate on a convention of peace…

Thus right at the outset Rosas made Britain's acceptance of a full, formal peace treaty a precondition of any negotiations, and made the signing of such a treaty a precondition for the official reception of Southern as British Minister Plenipotentiary (i.e. ambassador).

So Argentina was not coerced into signing a peace treaty with Britain; it was the other way round – it was Argentina that forced Britain to sign a peace treaty. Britain would have preferred a less formal agreement that merely settled specific complaints, and would have liked to reestablish full diplomatic relations beforehand. Britain was unhappy with Rosas's insistence that Britain should accept from the outset that there was first to be a peace treaty, as Southern stated to Arana on 18 October 1848:[4]

It is with great regret that I observe the Government of the Confederation considers that the continuation or resumption of Diplomatic Relations between that of Great Britain and itself at Buenos Ayres ought to be preceded by a previous arrangement between the two Governments… undertaken with the avowed object of bringing about peace…

In Britain's view, no such arrangement was needed since peace already prevailed. But Rosas would not yield on those two points: there was to be no resumption of diplomatic relations before the signing of a treaty, and the treaty was to be a full peace treaty. That had great significance for the legal status of the Falkland Islands, then as now – as explained below in section 7.12, a peace treaty has the effect of ending all disputes between countries (as Henry Southern pointed out to Rosas on 10-11 December 1849, see section 7.14), and hence of confirming any unmentioned territories in the possession of the party that held them when the treaty was signed. The Falklands were not mentioned in the treaty, so it confirmed them in the possession of Britain. That was accepted by Rosas, and it was later confirmed by many acts of commission and omission by Argentina.

But months of tough negotiations were needed to get to that point. Initially Southern tried to get Rosas to accept him as Britain's representative (i.e. to resume diplomatic relations) before the negotiations began, and to negotiate a lower-level agreement, but he failed on both counts. On another tricky point Southern was more successful: Rosas wanted to obtain Britain's support in his attempt to make Uruguay part of the Argentine Confederation, and in the end Southern managed to get him to drop that demand.

On 3 March 1849 Arana sent Southern a "project of Treaty", which was actually the final text of what became the Convention of Peace.[5] On 6 March Southern sent it to Palmerston, who received it on 15 May, and the text and correspondence were printed in London in the secret internal *Foreign*

---

[1] Official patent, printed in full twice in *Archivo Americano* 1850, on pp. 110-111 and pp. 169-170.
[2] Arana to Southern, 6 November 1849, in *Archivo Americano* 1850, p. 123.
[3] Southern to Palmerston 14 October 1848, PRO FO 6 139, fol. 64 *verso*, received at the Foreign Office 21 January 1849, recounting several meetings with Rosas. In referring to Rosas he often capitalises "He", "His", etc.
[4] This despatch is printed twice in *Archivo Americano* 1850, first on p. 111, and again on p. 118, quoted in Arana's reply to Southern of 6 November 1848.
[5] Arana to Southern, printed in English, Spanish and French in *Archivo Americano* 1850, pp. 132-135.

Office Confidential Print (*FOCP*)¹ as no. 246, now reprinted in *British Documents on Foreign Affairs* (*BDFA*).² From Britain's point of view the Falkland Islands were not involved – the islands were British and were nothing to do with Argentina, so Britain did not mention them. It would, however, have been natural for Rosas to mention them – they were one of his grievances against Britain, and in all his Messages to the Buenos Aires legislature he had made a protest against Britain's possession of them. But throughout the negotiations, Rosas never once raised the question of the Falklands, as Southern noted in a private letter to Palmerston on 13 June 1849 (section 7.7), and only mentioned them after the Convention of Peace had been signed (section 7.14).

From 15 May 1849, when Southern's despatch of 6 March arrived in London, the British government knew that Argentina had not insisted on including the Falklands in the projected treaty, and that the treaty was to include a statement that it was restoring "perfect friendship" between Britain and Argentina. In other words, Argentina was showing overt acquiescence in Britain's possession of the islands – the Argentine claim, which had been kept alive by regular protests for 17 years since 1833, was being dropped. That revelation had several immediate results.

7.6 Sir William Molesworth's suggestion, II, 26 June 1849: no mention of the Falklands

The first publicly observable consequence of the news of Argentina's acquiescence in Britain's possession of the Falklands was in a speech in the House of Commons in June 1849 by the Whig (Liberal) MP Sir William Molesworth. In July 1848 he had made a speech calling for cuts in the expenditure on Britain's overseas stations, including "the Bermudas" and the Falklands (section 7.3). He had recommended handing the Falklands to Buenos Aires, and his remarks have been quoted and their importance greatly exaggerated by several writers including Kohen and Rodríguez, though his motion never got as far as a vote.

What all those writers failed to note is that he made much the same speech in the Commons a year later on 26 June 1849 – but without mentioning the Falklands.³ He again recited a long catalogue of useless expenditure on a list of colonies and military stations, but at the place corresponding to his suggestion in 1848 that the Falklands be handed to Buenos Aires, he said:⁴

… between 1829 and 1847… 313,000*l*. have been expended… at Malta and Gibraltar, and it was estimated that a further sum of 250,000*l*. would be required to complete the ordnance works in progress in these colonies. During the same period we have expended in Bermuda 183,000*l*. on ordnance works: to complete them another 100,000*l*. will be required…

Thus although he mentioned some of the same military stations as in 1848 (Malta, Gibraltar and Bermuda), he did not mention the Falkland Islands in any part of his speech. Molesworth was a prominent member of Palmerston's governing Whig party; he probably had access to the *Foreign Office Confidential Print*, so it seems clear that he knew of Henry Southern's despatch received at the Foreign Office on 15 May, with the draft of the Convention of Peace confirming that Argentina was acquiescing in Britain's possession of the islands (section 7.5). That would explain why he dropped his reference to the Falklands in his speech six weeks later.

Molesworth proposed a motion calling for a commission of inquiry "into the whole colonial policy of the British Empire",⁵ but the other speakers (including William Gladstone, later four times Prime Minister) disagreed. In contrast to 1848 the House was well attended, there being 252 MPs present, so the motion was put to a vote, but it was defeated by 163 votes to 89.⁶

---

¹ The secret *Foreign Office Confidential Print* (*FOCP*) was a uniquely British institution that began in the 1840s; its sets of documents, some containing large numbers of papers, were numbered from 1 to over 20,000, and were circulated to the Sovereign, Cabinet ministers, major government departments and selected British embassies abroad.
² The most significant parts of *FOCP* are being reprinted in *British Documents on Foreign Affairs: Reports and Papers from the Foreign Office Confidential Print* (*BDFA*), general eds. Kenneth Bourne and D. Cameron Watt, Bethesda, Maryland, USA 1991. Doc. 246 in *FOCP* is reprinted as doc. 59 in *BDFA*, I, D, 1, pp. 106-149.
³ Speech in the Commons by Sir William Molesworth, 26 June 1849, in *Hansard*, London 1849, columns 937-1004 (Molesworth cols. 937-969; other speakers replying, cols. 969-1002).
⁴ *Hansard* 26 June 1849, cols. 954-955.
⁵ *Hansard* 26 June 1849, col. 968.
⁶ *Hansard* 26 June 1849: vote recorded in cols. 1002-4.

In short, unknown to Argentine writers including Kohen and Rodríguez, in 1849 Sir William Molesworth dropped the suggestion he had made in 1848 – he no longer proposed to hand the Falklands to Buenos Aires. The "dreary, desolate, and windy" Falkland Islands and "those worthless rocks… the Bermudas" remain British to this day.

7.7 The Chelsea pensioners; Henry Southern notes Argentine acquiescence

By 1848 almost all the detachment of Sappers and Miners (section 7.2) had left the Falklands. Four of the original 12 had proved insubordinate and were taken away aboard HMS *Philomel* on 16 April 1845, and it was decided to withdraw the rest. Three of them (James Biggs, Thomas Yates and John Herkes) purchased their discharge from the army and remained in the islands (where Biggs and Yates still have descendants), and the others left with Governor Richard Moody in HMS *Nautilus* on 15 July 1848.[1] So the islands were without any serving soldiers as a garrison, and just at that time the incoming Governor, George Rennie (Governor 4 July 1848 – 4 November 1855) was faced with a humanitarian problem that was emerging in Stanley.

He found that increasing numbers of people, some of them gauchos but also women and children, were arriving in Stanley entirely destitute, having been dismissed from their jobs out in the Camp. They had been sent to the Falklands by Samuel Fisher Lafone (section 10.1), an Englishman from Liverpool, who had emigrated to Uruguay and become a prosperous cattle-rancher. In 1837 in Montevideo he had met Louis Vernet, who had interested him in the potential of the Falklands for cattle-ranching – the killing of the "wild" (actually feral) cattle on East Falkland, the descendants of those taken to the islands by Bougainville. Hides, tallow and beef were profitable commodities, and Lafone was interested at once. In March 1846 he contracted with Governor Moody to send people and equipment to the Falklands and set up a cattle-ranching business. He despatched managers, foremen and gauchos to the islands, many with families, and a large settlement arose at Hope Place on Falkland Sound. Its extensive remains have recently been surveyed and richly illustrated by Rob Philpott.[2] Lafone himself never visited the Falklands, but for some five years he sent a stream of ships from Montevideo bringing enormous quantities of stores and roughly 150 immigrants, mostly Spanish-speaking. Among them were at least 17 Argentinians,[3] probably more. They were allowed to enter the Falklands freely, which disproves assertions by Argentine authors including José María Ruda (section 10.14) that Britain "replaced" the population with British citizens and did not allow Argentinians to go to the islands.[4]

Lafone's plans turned out to have been over-ambitious, having been based on an overestimate of the area of East Falkland and hence of the numbers of cattle. He had sent shiploads of people to the islands, but had made no arrangements for their welfare if they were no longer needed. When they proved to be too many for the work available, his managers began to dismiss people with no concern for their future; many of them walked all the way to Stanley completely destitute, where they had to be fed and clothed at the government's expense. Their presence was a potential cause of civil disturbances.

So, to regulate new arrivals, the Falklands Legislative Council under Governor Rennie in September 1848 issued the Aliens Ordinance,[5] which imposed a bond of £10 (ten pounds) per person on anyone bringing "aliens" (non-British people) into the islands without the Governor's permission, and also imposed the same bond on every "Foreigner" landing or settling in the islands without the Governor's permission. The money was not to be paid on arrival but only if the

---

[1] Details from entry on James Biggs by Coleen Biggs in *DFB*, and from Falkland Islands National Archivist Tansy Bishop, pers. comm.

[2] Robert A. Philpott, *The Early Falkland Islands Company Settlements: An Archaeological Survey*, Stanley and Liverpool 2007.

[3] List under "Miscellaneous Documents" in Volume H8, JCNA, Stanley; see section 10.1.

[4] For example, Marcelo Beccaceci, *Gauchos de Malvinas*, Buenos Aires 2017, makes it abundantly clear that Argentine gauchos were permitted to go to the Falklands in the 19th century, and illustrates the first page of a passenger list including 9 of at least 17 Argentinians who arrived in May 1847 (section 10.1).

[5] Aliens Settlement and Regulation Ordinance, in the volume "Legislation 1846-1853", signature E6, in JCNA. The ordinance was to last for three years and was to come into force from 1 September 1848.

regulations were infringed, and there seems to be not a single case in which it was actually paid.[1] The intention was to penalise unscrupulous investors like Lafone who brought people into the islands – the bonds would deter them in the first place, and could provide money to support any arrivals who became destitute. Moreover, non-British people arriving in the islands would have to prove (by accepting the £10 bond) that they had some financial resources before they were allowed to stay. The Aliens Ordinance was not of course intended to prevent foreigners arriving in the islands – they were at all times welcome and necessary – and people continued to arrive destitute (for example those who swam ashore after shipwrecks). Both before and after the Aliens Ordinance there were foreigners in the Falklands possessing the same rights as British citizens except for holding public office and being called for jury service, and some even held quite extensive lands (section 7.1).

On 21 January 1849 Henry Southern's despatch of 14 October 1848 was received at the Foreign Office (sections 7.5, 7.12), with the information that General Rosas was insisting on concluding a full peace treaty with Britain, which would change the situation in the South Atlantic, including the Falklands.

That consideration, plus the unregulated presence of many "aliens" in Stanley and the lack of a force to preserve law and order, led the British government to send another detachment of soldiers to the islands.[2] They were to be Chelsea "Out-Pensioners" from the Royal Hospital, Chelsea: there were 30 Pensioners, and with wives and families the party amounted to 120 people, who were to be colonists as well as forming the garrison. They were not elderly retired soldiers like today's Chelsea Pensioners – their average age was 42, the youngest was 26, and the oldest, aged 53, was Sergeant Major Henry Felton (1798-1879). Henry Felton had 14 children (7 born in Britain, 7 in the Falklands); he has many descendants in the islands, as do several other members of the detachment.[3] Their presence today is a result of Britain's open policy towards non-British people, including Argentinians, in allowing them to go to the islands, requiring a garrison to keep order.

The islands were without any form of garrison or force to keep law and order for a year and a quarter from July 1848, when the last Sappers and Miners left, till the Chelsea Pensioners arrived in Stanley on 8 October 1849 aboard the barque *Victory*. News of their voyage reached Buenos Aires around June 1849, and on 13 June Henry Southern added a postscript to a private letter to Lord Palmerston:[4]

PS An angry paragraph has appeared in the Gazette on the subject of an expedition of colonists to the Falkland Islands led by an officer of the British Navy. The possession of these Islands by England is always maintained in public documents as an unjust aggression and in terms of indignation, whereas I believe General Rosas really attributes no sort of importance to the question. It is a farce like so many others, which he thinks it wise to keep up. In none of the very many conversations we have had on all subjects has he ever alluded to the Falkland Islands.

It was going too far to say that for Rosas the public maintenance of the Falklands dispute was a "farce"; Rosas was a wily politician who did not concede any advantages without some tangible benefit, so he continued the practice until he saw a way of turning it to his own advantage. As H. S. Ferns puts it: "For Rosas the Falkland Islands were bargaining counters... a frozen asset in the game of diplomacy, but nothing more."[5] He saw an opportunity to obtain advantages and prestige from a peace treaty with Britain, but the price was the ending of the Falklands dispute; any attempt

---

[1] Jane Cameron, pers. comm. – she told us there was no case of the payment of the bond recorded in the Stanley archives, and we have discovered none either there or elsewhere.

[2] Letter from L. Sullivan of the War Office, 27 April 1849, in the *Globe*, London 8 June 1849, giving the requirements for the detachment to be sent to the Falklands. We are grateful to Roger Lorton for drawing our attention to this letter.

[3] Details here mostly from entry "Pensioners, The Military (or Chelsea)" by Joan Spruce in *DFB*, with list of names of the 30 pensioners and their wives and children (in all 120 people), and their dates of leaving. All left in the 1850s except 5 who stayed and 7 who died (4 of whose wives plus 1 daughter stayed).

[4] Southern to Palmerston 13 June 1849, PRO FO 6 502, fol. 266 *verso*, annotated "Received 5th September", enclosing an undated, unsourced cutting which seems to be the "angry" text of the *Gaceta Mercantil* editorial announcing the departure of the colonists; it is now pasted on to PRO FO 6 502, fol. 278 *recto*.

[5] H. S. Ferns, *Britain and Argentina in the Nineteenth Century*, Oxford 1960, pp. 232-233.

to keep it alive would have been opposed by Britain and would have endangered his victory. In fact Rosas did raise the question of the Falklands at a later stage, between the signing and the ratification of the Convention of Peace, but Southern pointed out that the convention had ended all differences between Britain and Argentina, and Rosas dropped the point (section 7.14).

7.8 Palmerston's Commons statement, 27 July 1849: Argentina's acquiescence

The Falklands were present in the background of political concern in Britain in mid-1849 as a result of the negotiations over the Convention of Peace. That explains the change in Sir William Molesworth's speech in June 1849 (section 7.6), and also a question put to Foreign Secretary Lord Palmerston[1] in the House of Commons on 27 July 1849 by an opposition member, Henry Baillie.[2] At that time the daily Parliamentary record, known as *Hansard*, only covered debates as such, so it did not record the exchange, but two newspapers reported it. *The Times* wrote:[3]

In reply to Mr. H. J. BAILLIE,

Lord PALMERSTON said, that a claim had been made many years ago, on the part of Buenos Ayres, to the Falkland Islands, and had been resisted by the British Government. Great Britain had always disputed and denied the claim of Spain to the Falkland Islands, and she was not therefore willing to yield to Buenos Ayres what had been refused to Spain. 10 or 12 years ago the Falkland Islands, having been unoccupied for some time, were taken possession of by Great Britain, and a settlement had ever since been maintained there; and he thought it would be most unadvisable to revive a correspondence which had ceased by the acquiescence of one party and the maintenance of the other.

The *Daily News* printed a slightly different text:[4]

THE FALKLAND ISLANDS.

Mr. H. BAILLIE inquired whether it was true that the government of Buenos Ayres had laid claim to the Falkland Islands, and, if so, what had been done upon the matter.

Viscount PALMERSTON said there was a claim made some time ago, which had been resisted by the British government. Great Britian [*sic*] had always denied the claim of Spain to the Falkland Islands, and the government was certainly not inclined to yield to Buenos Ayres what it had refused to Spain. The result was, that some ten or twelve years ago the Falkland Islands were taken possession of and occupied by the British, and ever since that period there had been a settlement there. He thought, under these circumstances, the hon. gentleman would see that there would be no great use in reviving the correspondence which had ceased with the acquiescence of both parties, the fact being that for the last 10 or 12 years we had occupied the Falkland Islands as a possession of the British crown.

Unlike the *Times*, the *Daily News* preserved the text of Baillie's question, but only the *Times* made Palmerston mention the "maintenance of the other" party, though both agreed that he had talked of acquiescence. In reference to Argentina, acquiescence could only mean the acceptance of an originally undesired state of affairs (Britain's possession of the Falklands), while in the case of Britain it meant merely acceptance of the *status quo*. Whatever his exact wording, Palmerston's statement was perfectly natural given what was going on behind the scenes – he knew from Southern's despatches that the negotiations with Argentina were aimed at concluding a definitive peace treaty (a "convention of peace"), and on 15 May 1849 he had received Southern's despatch of 6 March enclosing a draft of the treaty, in which Argentina accepted the reestablishment of "perfect friendship" with Britain and had not inserted a reservation on the Falklands. That was very significant owing to the principle that territories not mentioned in a peace treaty are fixed by the

---

[1] Henry John Temple, 3rd Viscount Palmerston (1784-1865), three times Secretary of State for Foreign Affairs: 22 November 1830 to 15 November 1834; 18 April 1835 to 2 September 1841; and 6 July 1846 to 26 December 1851, and twice Prime Minister: 6 February 1855 to 19 February 1858 and 12 June 1859 to 18 October 1865. He sat in the House of Commons because his Viscountcy was in the Irish peerage.

[2] Henry James Baillie (1803-1885), member for Inverness-shire, 1840-1868.

[3] *The Times*, London, Saturday 28 July 1849, p. 2, col. 6. The texts immediately preceding and following these lines are other questions, not related to the Falklands.

[4] *The Daily News*, London, Saturday 28 July 1849 (no pagination), immediately followed by another question from Baillie, about compensation for British subjects resident in Senegal. Slightly different text of Palmerston's reply (but no text of Baillie's question) in the *London Evening Mail* of Monday 30 July.

treaty in the possession of the state that held them when the treaty was signed. Palmerston's mention of acquiescence in his Commons statement truthfully represented the situation, though it had to be expressed in veiled terms since the treaty was not yet ready to be mentioned in public.

On 31 July 1849 the Argentine minister in London, Manuel Moreno, protested to Palmerston,[1] repeating Palmerston's Commons statement both from the *Times* and from the *Daily News*, and complaining that it misrepresented the case. Moreno said the Buenos Aires government, far from acquiescing in British possession of the Falklands, had repeated its protests regularly since 1833, and had thus "maintained its indisputable rights". That was true, though Argentina was not the only country with rights in the islands, and the protests only kept such rights alive as Argentina actually possessed, which were much less than 100% sovereignty. He added that Buenos Aires had also made protests every year in Messages to the provincial legislature, and repeated the texts of the Falklands protests in the Messages of 1843, 44, 45, 47 and 48, underlining the fact that those protests were an important part of Argentina's campaign against Britain's possession of the islands, though he did admit that the discussion had been "almost exhausted" ("casi agotada").

Kohen and Rodríguez criticise us for saying in *Getting it right* (p. 23) that Moreno was "unaware of what Rosas was negotiating", and their English translation says of Moreno's protest:

> It refers to the Government in London sending a messenger to Buenos Aires to negotiate a solution for the Anglo-French blockade... Pascoe and Pepper's pure speculation makes no sense... Moreno was of course aware that messengers were being sent to Buenos Aires, and had been for a year...

Here their English translator has let them down – their "emisario" in Spanish (pp. 199-200) should have been "emissary" or "envoy", not a mere "messenger". And they evade the point by saying that Moreno was aware that an envoy had been sent – he no doubt knew that, but the point is that he was unaware that the negotiations were to end in a peace treaty.

7.9 No protest from Buenos Aires; the Moreno-Palmerston exchange

On 2 August 1849 Moreno sent a despatch from London to Arana in Buenos Aires reporting Palmerston's statement of 27 July; he mentioned the different versions of Palmerston's words and gave the text of Baillie's question from the *Daily News*, but only quoted the *Times*'s version of Palmerston.[2] He may have been expecting the Argentine government to respond by instructing him to make another official protest in London.

But there was no reaction at all from Buenos Aires, since Argentina was in the process of dropping the Falklands dispute. However, on 8 August 1849 Palmerston replied personally to Moreno's letter of 31 July, and displayed a masterly skill in taking the wind out of Moreno's sails:[3]

> I have the honour to acknowledge the receipt of your note of the 31st of July, stating that the Reply which I was reported by some of the London newspapers to have made to a question put to me by Mr. Baillie in the House of Commons on the 27th of July, did not correctly describe the state of the question between the British Government and the Government of Buenos Aires respecting the Falkland Islands; and I have the honour to acquaint you that whatever the newspapers may have represented me as having said on the occasion above referred to, I have always understood the matter in question to stand exactly in the way described by you in your letter.

Palmerston's reply was mentioned in the 1849 Message to the Buenos Aires legislature (section 7.15), and Argentina mentioned it again 35 years later in 1885 with the incorrect addition that Palmerston had accepted that the issue remained "unsettled" or "pending" (section 8.23).[4] It was

---

[1] Moreno to Palmerston 31 July 1849, Spanish (in Moreno's hand?) in PRO FO 6 502, fols. 279 *recto*-280 *verso*; English translation in PRO FO 6 502, fols. 282 *recto*-285 *recto*, dated "22 Manchester Square, 31st July, 1849"; full Spanish text in Becerra 1998, pp. 136-138; summary in Bernhardt 1910, p. 398.

[2] Moreno's despatch of 2 August 1849 printed in full in Becerra 1998, pp. 134-135.

[3] Copy in PRO FO 6 502, fol. 376 *recto*; letter quoted in full in English in Muñoz Azpiri 1966, vol. 2, p. 197, and (in parallel English and Spanish versions) in Becerra 1998, pp. 139-140; summary in Bernhardt 1910, p. 398.

[4] Letter from Dr. Francisco J. Ortiz (1840-1932), later foreign minister of Argentina 1883-6, to British ambassador Sir Edmund Monson, 2 January 1885, in Becerra 1998, pp. 153-157.

also referred to in 2007, in an Argentine government pamphlet with the same incorrect addition:[1]

The issue remained unsettled and was recognised as such by the British Foreign Secretary in 1849.

Kohen and Rodríguez likewise assert (pp. 200, 241, 243) that the Falklands issue was "pending". In fact neither Palmerston nor Moreno said or implied that the question was "pending" – there is no such expression in the statements by either of them. Kohen and Rodríguez refer (p. 199) to Palmerston's phrase "whatever the newspapers may have represented me as having said", and assert that: "This formulation would make no sense if the newspapers had truthfully reflected what he said regarding the status of the situation" (i.e. if the newspapers had represented the situation as Kohen and Rodríguez would like, without Argentine acquiescence).

That is nonsense – Palmerston was not saying the newspapers had reported untruthfully; Moreno had mentioned the two versions of what he had said, from the *Times* and the *Daily News*, so Palmerston was merely saying it was immaterial that they had quoted him differently. The notion that Palmerston accepted Moreno's view that Argentina had not acquiesced in Britain's possession of the Falklands has often been repeated in Argentina, starting with foreign minister Francisco Ortiz's letter to British ambassador Edmund Monson on 19 December 1884 (which Monson at once refuted, section 8.23).

But that notion does not hold water. First, in his reply to Moreno, Palmerston can hardly have accepted a view he had roundly rejected only twelve days earlier in the Commons. Secondly, he knew from the draft treaty sent by Henry Southern that Argentina was indeed acquiescing in Britain's possession of the islands and was hence dropping the Falklands dispute.

And thirdly, Palmerston's reply cannot be understood without Moreno's letter of 31 July, to which he was replying. Kohen and Rodríguez assert (p. 199) that in his note to Moreno Palmerston did not confirm his Commons statement but confirmed that there had been no consent or acquiescence by Argentina. But it is absurd to imagine that Palmerston told Moreno in effect "you are right; I was actually lying to the House of Commons". Palmerston could not yet refer openly to the draft treaty since it was still secret, but he was a shrewd politician, so he simply turned Moreno's own statement against him. Moreno had said many things that were true – he had stated that Argentina had made repeated protests since 1833, and had thus "maintained its indisputable rights"; he had stated that the Buenos Aires government had protested every year in Messages to the legislature, and he had also quoted Palmerston's Commons statement, including Palmerston's phrase that the correspondence had ceased by "the acquiescence of one party and the maintenance of the other" or "the acquiescence of both parties". All those things were true – Argentina had protested in that way, and Palmerston had made those remarks in the Commons.

So in saying "I have always understood the matter in question to stand exactly in the way described by you in your letter", Palmerston said Moreno was right in saying that he, Palmerston, had referred to acquiescence over the Falkland Islands. In other words, in confirming Moreno's account he *confirmed* his Parliamentary statement. He did not say that he accepted Moreno's view that Argentina was not showing acquiescence. That has been asserted by Argentine writers including Kohen and Rodríguez, who say (p. 200) "the exchange between Moreno and Palmerston that took place only a few months before the treaty is key to refuting the interpretation of the treaty as Argentine acquiescence before and after Moreno's protest being formulated". That is untrue.

At Balmoral, Queen Victoria's Scottish castle, on 27 August 1849, the Queen and Palmerston both signed a splendidly worded Royal Patent under the Great Seal of the United Kingdom giving Henry Southern authority to sign the Convention of Peace;[2] Palmerston sent it to Buenos Aires, and once it had arrived, Rosas on 15 November signed an official order (which twice used the term

---

[1] Anonymous pamphlet in English, *Islas Malvinas, Georgias del Sur y Sandwich del Sur / Malvinas, South Georgia and South Sandwich Islands*, distributed on 3 December 2007 at the London School of Economics, p. 3; Spanish version in pamphlet *Islas Malvinas*, Buenos Aires March 2007, p. 7.

[2] This Patent, dated 27 August 1849, was printed in *Archivo Americano* 1850, pp. 160-161. The date may be the origin of the misconception that the peace treaty itself was signed on 27 August 1849 (asserted by some Argentine authors, e.g. Absalón Rojas in his speech to the Argentine Congress on 19 July 1950, repeated in his book *Rosas y las Malvinas*, Buenos Aires 1950, p. 12, and followed in Burnet-Merlín 1974, pp. 20-21, and Cresto 2011, p. 433; see section 7.17).

"convención de paz"), giving foreign minister Felipe Arana the same authority to sign it.[1]

7.10 Press reports of the Convention of Peace[2]

The negotiations for the Convention of Peace were widely reported in the British press, both national and regional, and even before the treaty was signed it was known in Britain that it was a peace treaty and that it was going to end the Falklands dispute. To mention only a few of many similar articles in many newspapers, on 17 May 1849 the London *Shipping & Mercantile Gazette* printed a private letter dated Montevideo, 11 March 1849, from "a gentleman of considerable influence in that quarter", who wrote:[3]

Since my last the British Minister, Mr. Southern, in Buenos Ayres, jointly with the French admiral, Lepredon [*sic*], has secretly signed a convention of peace with General Rosas...

It was not of course true that the convention had already been signed, but Felipe Arana had sent its text in his "project of Treaty" to Henry Southern on 3 March (section 7.5). There had clearly been a leak, enabling the gentleman to describe it as a "convention of peace", which was exactly accurate.

On the same day, 17 May 1849, the London daily *The Globe* reported in its columns of brief news items from around the world that:[4]

Letters from Buenos Ayres of the 7th ult. [i.e. 7 April 1849] state that treaties of peace were rumoured to have been agreed to, and that propositions to that effect had been forwarded to our government by Mr. SOUTHERN, her Majesty's Minister in that country.

That brief announcement showed that the leak had gained substance – rumours were already going round in Buenos Aires that Britain and Argentina had agreed on "treaties of peace".

And it was also realised that the negotiations affected the Falklands: the London *Evening Mail* reported in its issue for 1-3 August 1849:[5]

A late report from the Governor of the Falkland Islands, the possession of which formed one of the points of our dispute now in course of arrangement with Buenos Ayres, furnishes some interesting details of the capabilities and resources of these almost unknown settlements.

The article gave no details of the negotiations, but it says the Falklands were "one of the points of our dispute" with Buenos Aires – as we point out below in sections 7.12 and 7.16, there had been a single complex dispute between Britain and Buenos Aires, which was "now in course of arrangement", and the Falklands had formed one "point" of it. The Falklands dispute between Britain and Argentina was about to end.

7.11 The Convention of Peace: what it says – and what Kohen and Rodríguez suppress[6]

The Convention of Peace was signed by Arana and Southern in Buenos Aires on Saturday 24 November 1849.[7] The text was printed in full twice in English, Spanish and French, in *Archivo Americano* 1850,[8] first the version for the Argentine government, then the version for the British

---

[1] Original copy of Rosas's order, in a copyist's script, with autograph signature of Felipe Arana, in PRO FO 93/10/4.
[2] We are grateful to Roger Lorton for drawing our attention to these and many other similar press reports.
[3] *Shipping & Mercantile Gazette*, London, Thursday 17 May 1849, p. 1, col. 4; identical text in the London *Evening Standard* of the same date.
[4] *The Globe*, London, Thursday 17 May 1849, p. [2], col. 3; identical text in *The Scotsman*, Edinburgh, Saturday 19 May 1849 (neither has any more on this topic).
[5] *Evening Mail*, London, issue for Wednesday 1 August to Friday 3 August 1849, p. 2, col. 1.
[6] This section deals with the meaning of "perfect friendship"; section 7.12 deals with the special nature of peace treaties.
[7] There are two official archival copies of it in the Public Record Office (PRO) in London, handwritten in Buenos Aires by a professional copyist on oiled paper: the Plenipotentiaries' Copy, PRO FO 93/10/4, bound in boards and bearing at the end the autograph signatures and wax signet seals of Southern and Arana, each twice (once under each of the two languages of the text); and Rosas's Copy, PRO FO 94/408, sumptuously bound in gold-ornamented crimson velvet, bearing at the end the autograph signature of General Rosas, following a statement that he had obtained the approval of the House of Representatives to ratify it, with his attached impressed paper seal bearing his title as "Governor charged with the Foreign Relations of the Argentine Confederation". The ratification document is in PRO FO 93/10/4.
[8] *Archivo Americano* 1850, pp. 135-138.

> CONVENTION between Great Britain and the Argentine Confederation, for the Settlement of existing Differences and the re-establishment of Friendship.—Signed at Buenos Ayres, November 24, 1849.
>
> [Ratifications exchanged at Buenos Ayres, May 15, 1850.]
>
> | Convention for re-establishing the perfect Relations of Friendship between Her Britannic Majesty and the Argentine Confederation. | Convencion para restablecer las perfectas Relaciones de Amistad entre la Confederacion Argentina y Su Majestad Británica. |
> |---|---|
> | HER Majesty the Queen of Great Britain, and his Excellency the Governor and Captain-General of the Province of Buenos Ayres, charged with the foreign relations of the Argentine Confederation, being desirous of putting an end to the existing differences, and of restoring perfect relations of friendship, in accordance with the wishes manifested by both Governments; and the Government of Her Britannic Majesty having declared that it has no separate or interested | EL Exelentisimo Señor Gobernador y Capitan General de la Provincia de Buenos Ayres, encargado de las Relaciones Esteriores de la Confederacion Argentina, y Su Majestad la Reyna de la Gran Bretaña, deseando concluir las diferencias existentes, y restablecer las perfectas relaciones de amistad, en conformidad á los deseos manifestados por ambos Gobiernos; y habiendo declarado el de Su Majestad Británica no tener objetos algunos separados ó egoístas |

7.11a The Convention of Peace: the *BFSP*'s heading, the Convention's title and part of the preamble, from *British and Foreign State Papers (BFSP) 1848-1849*, vol. XXXVII (London 1862), p. 7.

---

government, and it was printed again in full in Britain, in English and Spanish, in *BFSP*.[1] It has recently sometimes been known as "the Arana-Southern Treaty", though Arana played no part in negotiating it and Rosas signed it too, on 10 May 1850 before ratification. Kohen and Rodríguez call it only "the Arana-Southern Treaty" (14 times), plus twice "the Southern-Arana Treaty", but those names are later inventions; we have found no uses of them before the 20th century. In the 19th century it was called by both sides the "Convention of Peace", in Spanish "Convención de Paz" – at that time the terms "treaty" and "convention" were synonymous, whereas nowadays "treaty" typically denotes a bilateral agreement, while a "convention" is generally multilateral.[2]

From November 1849 to May 1850 the treaty was in a kind of legal limbo, since it had been signed but not ratified – in the 19th century treaties only came into force upon ratification. Kohen and Rodríguez castigate us (p. 208) for ignorance on this point – they say:

> It is well known by any student of international law as well as by any informed person that bilateral treaties subject to ratification enter into force after the exchange of instruments of ratification, both in the 19th and 21st Centuries. This fact does not alter the interpretation of the treaty, but it does speak volumes about the intellectual quality of the British pamphlet.

They commit a tautology in saying "bilateral treaties subject to ratification enter into force after… ratification" – of course *treaties subject to ratification* require ratification! In our defence we can quote Professor John O'Brien, who says: "The 19th century view was that a treaty could not be effective unless it had been ratified. Today, many treaties do not require ratification".[3]

Kohen and Rodríguez also criticise us (p. 201) for omitting parts of the treaty, so here we reproduce all of it in figs. 7.11a, 7.11b and 7.11c, from *BFSP*, and in fig. 7.11d the beginning of it from the original Plenipotentiaries' Copy. The Convention of Peace crucially affects the Falklands in two ways: by what it says, and by what it does not say.

---

[1] *British and Foreign State Papers (BFSP) 1848-1849*, vol. XXXVII (London 1862), pp. 7-11, illustrated here.
[2] John O'Brien, *International Law*, London 2001, p. 329.
[3] O'Brien 2001, pp. 334-335.

object in view, nor any other desire than to see securely established the peace and independence of the States of the River Plate, as recognized by Treaty; have named to that effect as their Plenipotentiaries, viz.:

Her Majesty the Queen of Great Britain, Henry Southern, Esquire, Her Majesty's Minister Plenipotentiary accredited to the Court of Buenos Ayres;

And his Excellency the Governor and Captain-General of the Province of Buenos Ayres, his Excellency the Minister for Foreign Affairs, Doctor Don Felipe Arana;

Who, after having communicated to each other their respective full powers, and found them in good and due form, have agreed as follows:

ART. I. The Government of Her Britannic Majesty, animated by the desire of putting an end to the differences which have interrupted the political and commercial relations between the 2 countries, having on the 15th of July, 1847, raised the blockade which it had established of the ports of the 2 Republics of the Plata, thereby giving a proof of its conciliatory sentiments, now hereby binds itself, in the same amicable spirit, definitively to evacuate the Island of Martin Garcia; to return the Argentine vessels of war which are in its possession, as far as possible in the same state as they were in when taken; and to salute the flag of the Argentine Confederation with 21 guns.

II. By both Contracting Parties shall be delivered to their respective owners, all the merchant-vessels, with their cargoes, taken by them during the blockade.

III. The auxiliary Argentine divisions existing in the Oriental State, shall return across the Uruguay when the French Government disarms the Foreign Legion and all other foreigners who may be under arms, and form the garrison of the town of Montevideo, evacuates the territory of the 2 Republics of the Plata, abandons its hostile position, and celebrates a Treaty of Peace. Her Britannic Majesty's Government, in the event of its being necessary, offers to use its good offices in bringing about these objects, with its ally the French Republic.

IV. Her Britannic Majesty's Government recognizes the navigation of the River Paraná to be an inland navigation of the Argentine Confederation, and subject solely to its laws and regulations, in the same manner as that of the River Uruguay in common with the Oriental State.

V. Her Britannic Majesty's Government having declared, " that it is freely acknowledged and admitted that the Argentine Republic is in the unquestioned enjoyment and exercise of every right, whether of peace or war, possessed by any independent

en vista, ni ningun otro deseo que ver establecidas con seguridad la paz é independencia de los Estados del Rio de la Plata, tal como son reconocidos por Tratados; han nombrado al efecto por sus Plenipotenciarios, á saber:

Su Exelencia el Señor Gobernador y Capitan General de la Provincia de Buenos Ayres, al Ministro de Relaciones Esteriores, Camarista Doctor Don Felipe Arana;

Y Su Majestad la Reyna de la Gran Bretaña, al Exelentisimo Señor Ministro Plenipotenciario nombrado por Su Majestad cerca del Gobierno de la Confederacion, Caballero Don Henrique Southern;

Quienes, despues de haberse comunicado sus respectivos plenos poderes, y halládolos en buena y debida forma, han convenido lo que sigue:

ART. 1°. Habiendo el Gobierno de Su Majestad Británica, animado del deseo de poner fin á las diferencias que han interrumpido las relaciones políticas y comerciales entre los dos paises, levantado el dia quince de Julio de mil ochocientos cuarenta y siete, el bloqueo que habia establecido en los puertos de las dos Repúblicas del Plata, dando así una prueba de sus sentimientos conciliatorios, al presente se obliga, con el mismo espíritu amistoso, á evacuar definitivmente la Isla de Martin Garcia; á devolver los buques de guerra Argentinos que estan en su posesion, tanto como sea posible en el mismo estado en que fueron tomados; y á saludar al Pavellon de la Confederacion Argentina con veinte y un tiros de cañon.

2°. Por las dos Partes Contratantes serán entregados á sus respectivos dueños todos los buques mercantes, con sus cargamentos, tomados durante el bloqueo.

3°. Las divisiones auxiliares Argentinas, existentes en el Estado Oriental, repasarán el Uruguay cuando el Gobierno Frances desarme á la Legion Estrangera, y á todos los demas estrangeros que se hallen con las armas, y formen la guarnicion de la ciudad de Montevideo, evacue el territorio de las dos Repúblicas del Plata, abandone su posicion hostil, y celebre un Tratado de Paz. El Gobierno de Su Majestad Británica, en caso necesario, se ofrece á emplear sus buenos oficios para conseguir estos objetos con su aliada la República Francesa.

4°. El Gobierno de Su Majestad Británica reconoce ser la navegacion del Rio Paraná una navegacion interior de la Confederacion Argentina, y sugeta solamente á sus leyes y reglamentos, lo mismo que la del Rio Uruguay en comun con el Estado Oriental.

5°. Habiendo declarado el Gobierno de Su Majestad Británica, " quedar libremente reconocido y admitido que la República Argentina se halla en el goce y ejercicio incuestionable de todo derecho, ora de paz ó guerra, poseido por cualquiera nacion independiente;

7.11b The Convention of Peace: end of the Preamble and articles 1-5 (*BFSP 1848-1849*, pp. 8-9).

What it says is crucial because it three times says "perfect" friendship – in its title,[1] in the Preamble ("restoring perfect relations of friendship") and in Article VII:

VII. Under this Convention perfect friendship between Her Britannic Majesty's Government and the Government of the Confederation, is restored to its former state of good understanding and cordiality.

The words "perfect friendship" are definitive and all-encompassing; the Convention thus "wiped the slate clean" of all disputes and put relations between Britain and Argentina on a new footing.

It is a universal principle of international law that treaties are to be precisely observed, expressed by the formula *pacta sunt servanda* ["agreements are to be kept"], which Kohen and Rodríguez quote twice (pp. 59, 73). So the words "perfect friendship" mean exactly that, and the phrase "the existing differences" in the preamble means such differences as exist – all of them. If Rosas had wanted to keep the Falklands dispute open in the background, he could have said "relations of friendship", or "good friendship", or "cordial friendship", or "perpetual amity" (as did the Treaty of Amity in 1825), or he could have said "the settlement of certain differences" or "some differences", thus limiting the scope of the treaty to those specifically mentioned. In all those cases he, or future representatives of Argentina, could have maintained that the friendship restored by the Convention was not comprehensive and did not cancel the Falklands dispute. He did attempt to

---

[1] The Convention's own title is "*Convention for re-establishing the perfect Relations of Friendship between Her Britannic Majesty and the Argentine Confederation*"; the *BFSP* heading "*CONVENTION between Great Britain and the Argentine Confederation...*" was added by the editors of *BFSP* in 1862 and is thus not part of the Convention itself – see the original beginning in fig. 7.11d.

GREAT BRITAIN AND ARGENTINE CONFEDERATION.		GREAT BRITAIN AND BELGIUM.
nation; and that if the course of events in the Oriental Republic has made it necessary for the Allied Powers to interrupt for a time the exercise of the belligerent rights of the Argentine Republic, it is fully admitted that the principles on which they have acted, would, under similar circumstances, have been applicable either to Great Britain or France," it is hereby agreed that the Argentine Government, with regard to this declaration, reserves its right to discuss it opportunely with the Government of Great Britain, in that part which relates to the application of the principle. VI. In virtue of the Argentine Government having declared that it would celebrate this Convention on condition that its ally, his Excellency the President of the Oriental Republic of Uruguay, Brigadier Don Manuel Oribe, should previously agree to it,—this being for the Argentine Government an indispensable condition in any arrangement of the existing differences,—it proceeded to solicit the assent of its said ally, and having obtained it, the present Convention is hereby agreed upon and concluded. VII. Under this Convention perfect friendship between Her Britannic Majesty's Government and the Government of the Confederation, is restored to its former state of good understanding and cordiality. VIII. This Convention shall be ratified by the Argentine Government within 15 days after the	y que si el curso de los sucesos en la República Oriental ha hecho necesario que las Potencias Aliadas interrumpan por cierto tiempo el ejercicio de los derechos beligerantes de la República Argentina, queda plenamente admitido que los principios bajo los cuales han obrado, en inguales circunstancias habrian sido aplicables, ya á la Gran Bretaña ó á la Francia," queda convenido que el Gobierno Argentino, en cuanto á esta declaracion, reserva su derecho para discutirlo oportunamente con el de la Gran Bretaña, en la parte relativa á la aplicacion del principio. 6°. A virtud de haber declarado el Gobierno Argentino que celebraria esta Convencion, siempre que su aliado el Exelentisimo Señor Presidente de la República Oriental del Uruguay, Brigadier Don Manuel Oribe, estuviese previamente conforme con ella,—siendo esto para el Gobierno Argentino una condicion indispensable en todo arreglo de las diferencias existentes,—procedió á solicitar el avenimiento de su referido aliado; y habiéndolo obtenido, se ajusta y concluye la presente. 7°. Mediante esta Convencion, queda restablecida la perfecta amistad entre el Gobierno de la Confederacion, y el de Su Majestad Británica, á su anterior estado de buena inteligencia y cordialidad. 8°. La presente Convencion será ratificada por el Gobierno Argentino á los quince dias despues de	ratification of Her Britannic Majesty's Government is presented, and the ratifications shall be exchanged. IX. In witness whereof the Plenipotentiaries sign this Convention, and affix the seals of their arms thereto. Done at Buenos Ayres on the 24th of November, in the year of our Lord, 1849. (L.S.) HENRY SOUTHERN. (L.S.) FELIPE ARANA. presentada la ratificacion del de Su Majestad Británica, y ambas se cangearán. En testimonio de lo cual los Plenipotenciarios firman y sellan esta Convencion. En Buenos Ayres, á 24 de Noviembre, del año del Señor, 1849. (L.S.) FELIPE ARANA. (L.S.) HENRY SOUTHERN.

7.11c The Convention of Peace: articles 5-9 (*BFSP 1848-1849*, pp. 10-11).

make a reservation of the Falklands dispute after the treaty was signed, but Southern pointed out to him that treaties of peace ended all differences between their signatories; far from disputing the point, Rosas actually repeated it (section 7.14), and did not mention the Falklands again. The treaty remained as an all-embracing reestablishment of "perfect friendship" between the two countries.

That crucial phrase in the treaty thus put a final end to *all* disputes between Argentina and Britain – even by itself, without the many acts of omission and commission by Argentina that followed it (sections 8.7, 8.8, 8.18), it annihilated Argentina's title to the Falklands. If two countries conclude a treaty that makes their friendship "perfect", they have ended all their differences. It is not possible to continue a territorial dispute and still have "perfect" friendship.

Kohen and Rodríguez are clearly worried by "perfect" friendship, and proceed to manipulate the evidence. In the Spanish version they quote the actual title of the treaty, which includes the phrase "perfect Relations of Friendship" ("perfectas Relaciones de Amistad", see fig. 7.11a), but in their discussion they ignore the fact that the treaty says "perfect". What is more, in their English translation they suppress it altogether – they do not use its original title, but use only the explanatory heading added in 1862 by the editors of the *British and Foreign State Papers* (*BFSP*): "Convention between Great Britain and the Argentine Confederation, for the settlement of existing differences and the re-establishment of friendship"; the original title (i.e. "Convention for re-establishing the perfect Relations of Friendship…") is absent from their English version, though *BFSP* included it. The suppression of the original title may be the fault of their English translator, but it is a serious omission and invalidates their account.

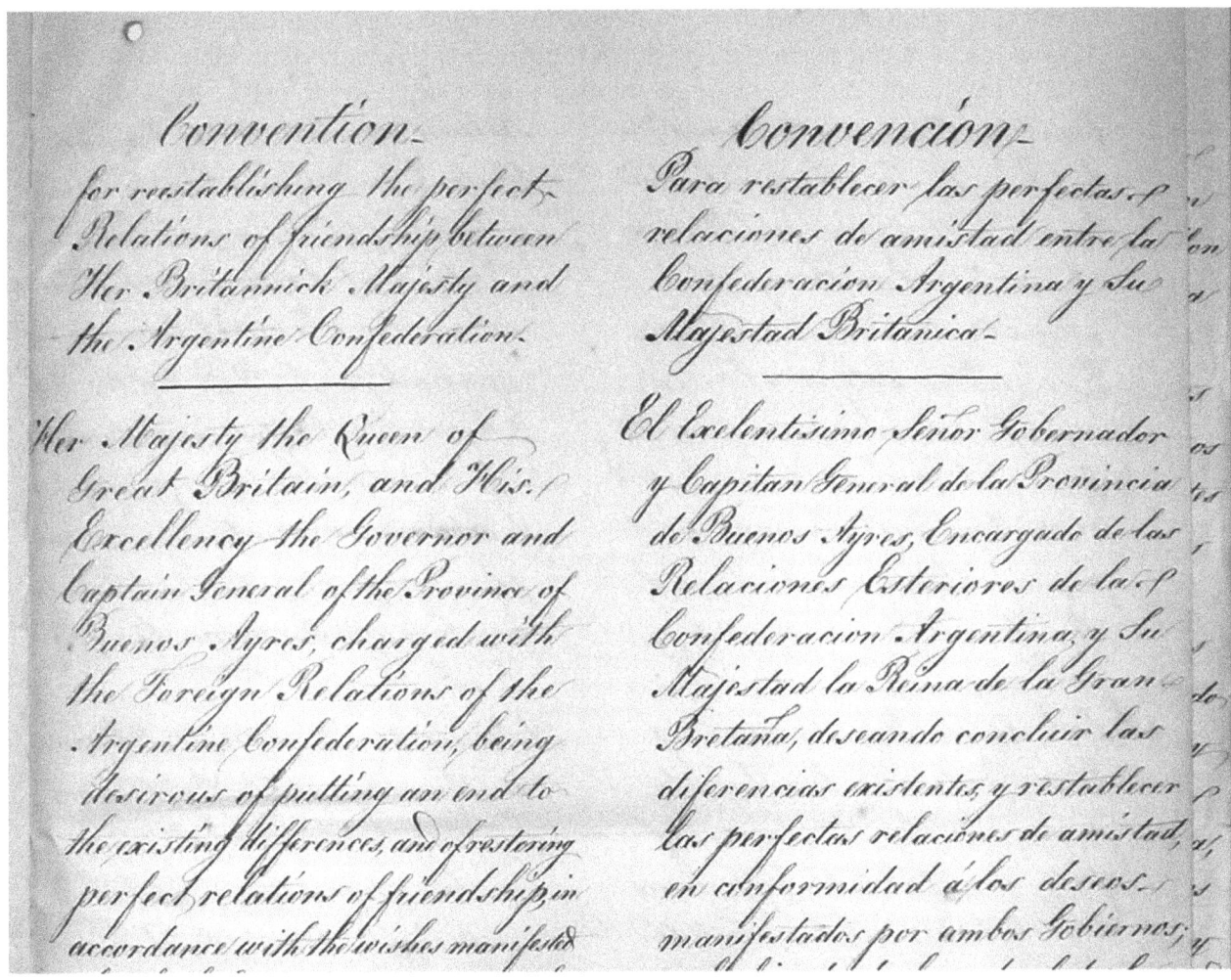

7.11d Object and purpose of the Convention of Peace: Perfect relations of friendship; title and first words of the preamble in the official Plenipotentiaries' Copy. (PRO FO 93/10/4)

We pointed out in both *Getting it right* (p. 23) and *False Falklands History* (p. 7) that the "perfect" friendship established by the Convention ended the dispute between Britain and Argentina over the Falklands; Kohen and Rodríguez (p. 201, footnote) quote our brief passage including that statement, but they nevertheless take us to task – they say:

Pascoe and Pepper manipulated the terms of the Treaty's preamble and its Article 7. They ignore the first article, which is of fundamental importance, as well as the object and purpose of the treaty, which has nothing to do with the Falklands/Malvinas.

That is a serious misrepresentation. Here Kohen and Rodríguez twice accuse us of manipulation – of "the terms of the Treaty's preamble and its Article 7", and of "the object and purpose of the treaty, which has nothing to do with the Falklands/Malvinas".

We categorically deny those accusations. In both *Getting it right* and *False Falklands History* (in figures 7 and (iv) respectively) we actually illustrated the title, part of the preamble and the whole of Article VII, from the selfsame photographs of *BFSP* of which we reproduce the whole here in our figures 7.11a and 7.11c. We fail to see how that can be seen as a manipulation.

And the treaty's object and purpose is stated in its own title, as shown in fig. 7.11a from *BFSP* and in the original in fig. 7.11d, taken from the Plenipotentiaries' Copy, one of the official archival copies in the Public Record Office in London. Its object and purpose was "for reestablishing the perfect Relations of friendship between Her Britannick Majesty and the Argentine Confederation". Its title states its purpose in comprehensive terms: to reestablish "perfect Relations of friendship", so its object and purpose was among other things to end the Falklands dispute; it is not true that it had "nothing to do with the Falklands/Malvinas".

As for "ignoring" Article I, we left it out of our two online papers because it dealt only with Britain's promise to evacuate Martín García island, return Argentine ships, and salute the Argentine flag (see the actual text in fig. 7.11b). Those promises are not relevant to the Falklands, so we did not mention them. Kohen and Rodríguez, however, criticise us again (pp. 203-4) for omitting Article I, and assert that those promises were themselves the object and purpose of the Convention:

The object and the purpose of the treaty in question clearly emerge from its Article 1 (which Pascoe and Pepper omit entirely), which states: "Art. I. ..." [they then quote Article I in full, exactly as we give above in our fig. 7.11b].

But the things mentioned in Article I were merely the actions the British government promised to carry out in order to achieve the treaty's purpose; they did not *constitute* its purpose, which is stated in its title. Here Kohen and Rodríguez are manipulating the truth.

Article I is of minor importance compared to Article V, which contained Rosas's central aim: it established Argentina as an equal to the major powers, by Britain's humiliating declaration:

V. Her Britannic Majesty's Government having declared, "that it is freely acknowledged and admitted that the Argentine Republic is in the unquestioned enjoyment and exercise of every right, whether of peace or war, possessed by any independent nation; and that if the course of events in the Oriental Republic has made it necessary for the Allied Powers to interrupt for a time the exercise of the belligerent rights of the Argentine Republic, it is fully admitted that the principles on which they have acted, would, under similar circumstances, have been applicable either to Great Britain or France..."

Article V encapsulates Rosas's victory – he had forced Britain to accept his belligerent rights as an equal partner on the world stage on the same level as Britain or France, not a mere scene of interventions. The ending of hostilities between those equal partners by a full peace treaty established "perfect friendship" between them, which naturally entailed the abandonment of Argentina's claim to the Falkland Islands.

As Henry Southern pointed out, the things Britain bound itself to do (those mentioned in Article I) could have been quickly settled without a treaty,[1] and if General Rosas had agreed to that, as Britain hoped at the beginning of the negotiations,[2] there need have been no mention of "perfect friendship". But that perfect friendship was precisely what Rosas wanted from Britain, which was why he insisted on a full peace treaty. That placed Argentina on an equal footing with Britain and forced Britain to accept that Argentina could be the object of perfect friendship between equals, not merely a place where Britain could intervene at will. That is why the object and purpose of the treaty was stated in its title: to reestablish perfect friendship between Britain and Argentina.

The distorted account by Kohen and Rodríguez is broadly followed by Professor Seokwoo Lee in his chapter on "Territorial settlements in peace treaties", in the *Research Handbook* edited by Marcelo Kohen and Mamadou Hébié.[3] Like Kohen and Rodríguez, he suppresses the original name of the convention, using only "the 1849 Arana-Southern Treaty",[4] and like them he prints the whole of Article 1 and maintains that the treaty refers only to the navigation of the rivers and the ending of the blockade – he says "There was neither a specific reference to the Falkland/Malvinas Islands in the treaty, nor any discussion about that dispute during the negotiations of it", and adds "The

---

[1] In a private letter to Palmerston, 13 December 1849, in PRO FO 6 145, fol. 180 *verso* (see section 7.14).
[2] Southern to Arana, 18 October 1848, printed in *Archivo Americano* 1850, pp. 111 and 118 (see section 7.5).
[3] Professor Seokwoo Lee, in Marcelo Kohen and Mamadou Hébié (eds.), *Research Handbook on Territorial Disputes in International Law*, Cheltenham (UK) and Northampton (USA), 2018, pp. 278-279.
[4] He also wrongly says that "This treaty is also referred to as the 1850 Convention of Settlement". To set the record straight: the name "Convention of Settlement" was invented by Graham Pascoe in April 2008, shortly before *Getting it right* appeared, as a convenient abbreviation for the treaty, based on the *BFSP* title "*CONVENTION... for the Settlement of existing Differences...*". That was 12 years ago, before we realised the sheer extent to which both sides at the time referred to it as the Convention of Peace – historical research is an ongoing process, and new evidence can always turn up which requires a revision of earlier views. It is thus untrue to say that the treaty "is also referred to" as the Convention of Settlement; it was briefly our own name for it until we had made further progress in our research. The correct name is (and always was) the Convention of Peace (and the Spanish translations of both our internet papers always used "Convención de Paz", which was used innumerable times in Argentina in 1848-9; see section 7.13).

question of sovereignty over the Falkland/Malvinas Islands remained outside the treaty".

However, it is only fair to add that Lee, Kohen and Rodríguez were all unaware that General Rosas did indeed try to raise the question of the Falklands between the signing and the ratification of the treaty, and that his attempt was quashed by Henry Southern, who stated that "All national differences are terminated by solemn and public Conventions of Peace" (see below, section 7.14), underlining the special effect of peace treaties, which we illustrate with quotations from the legal literature in section 7.12. In that connexion we find it odd that in the whole of Kohen's and Hébié's *Research Handbook* – a comprehensive overview of territorial disputes in international law – there is not a single mention of the opinion of such jurists as Grotius, Wheaton or Oppenheim on the special nature of peace treaties, not even in the chapter by Seokwoo Lee specifically on the settlement of territorial disputes in peace treaties.

Irrelevantly, Kohen and Rodríguez quote (pp. 202-3) two statements made in the British Parliament, first on 23 April 1849 in the House of Lords by the Earl of Harrowby, who complained of General Rosas's refusal to receive a British minister (i.e. Henry Southern) and asked what Britain was going to be expected to pay Argentina, including the question "Are we prepared to give up the Falkland Isles?"[1] Kohen and Rodríguez then quote the speech by Sir William Molesworth to the House of Commons on 25 July 1848, which we discussed above in section 7.3, in which he said "I propose to the House [… to] acknowledge the claim of Buenos Ayres to the Falkland Islands" (as we pointed out in section 7.3, the Spanish and English editions of Kohen and Rodríguez have different versions of his speech). They conclude: "As we can see, at the time some legislators were even prepared to return the Falklands/Malvinas". Their conclusion is wide of the mark – in fact Lord Harrowby said quite the reverse; he was not suggesting "returning" the Falklands; he was complaining about the lack of information about the negotiations in Buenos Aires and asking in aggrieved tones how high the price for Rosas's agreement might be – he was implying that the Falklands would be too high a price. And Kohen and Rodríguez were presumably unaware of Molesworth's speech on 26 June 1849, which was similar to the one in 1848 except that he omitted the Falklands (section 7.6).

Kohen and Rodríguez then (p. 204) refer to Article 31 of the Vienna Convention on the Law of Treaties (1969) and say: "This article establishes that a treaty should be interpreted in good faith in light of the ordinary meaning to be given to its terms in their context and in light of its object and purpose".[2] They comment: "Which, of course, the British leaflet does not do in the least." We beg to differ – as we said above, we printed the title, part of the preamble and the whole of Article VII in both our internet papers. In this chapter we print the whole of the Convention of Peace, and in our usage the "ordinary meaning" of the word "perfect" is "perfect", without limitation. We are interpreting the treaty in good faith, quoting all of it, and giving its terms their ordinary meaning.

It is Kohen and Rodríguez who do not interpret the Convention of Peace in good faith, by never calling it by its original name, which was "the Convention of Peace" / "la Convención de Paz" (not "the Arana-Southern Treaty"), by ignoring the fact that it says three times that it restores "perfect" friendship between Argentina and Britain (and in their English version by suppressing the fact that it says "perfect" at all), and by distorting its effect.

7.12 The Convention of Peace: what it does not say – and what Kohen and Rodríguez distort

The effect of the Convention of Peace derives also from what it does *not* say: it does not mention the Falkland Islands; they were not mentioned by either side during the negotiations, as Henry Southern stated in his letter of 13 June 1849, and Rosas's attempt to mention them after the treaty had been signed came to nothing (section 7.14). That is significant because of the nature of the Convention: both sides knew that it was a peace treaty. The expression "convention of peace" was constantly used by both sides: "convención de paz" is used twice in the order granting Arana power to sign it (in PRO FO 93/10/4); the 1849 Message to the legislature used the term five times

---

[1] Kohen and Rodríguez 2015, quoting from *Hansard*, House of Lords debates, vol. 104, p. 609.
[2] Kohen and Rodríguez 2015, quoting from the Vienna Convention on the Law of Treaties, Art. 31, para.1 - UN Doc A/CONF.39/27 (1969).

(section 7.15); the official Buenos Aires government newspaper *Gaceta Mercantil* of 26 January 1850 used it seven times in announcing that the Convention had been signed,[1] and it was used some twenty times in the texts printed in December 1850 in *Archivo Americano* 1850 (section 7.13).

Peace treaties are different from most other treaties in that what they do not say is as significant as what they do say. As long ago as 1646, the "father of international law", Hugo Grotius,[2] explained those two aspects of a peace treaty as follows:[3]

XI.... either the possession of property which was disturbed by the war is to be determined as stated by the former right... or things are to remain in the position they are in, as the Greeks say ἔχοντες ἃ ἔχουσιν ["the holders holding"].

XII. Of these two, in a case of doubt, it is better to presume the latter, since it is easier & causes no change.

By the 19th century, writers on international law all agreed that if, after a war, matters are to be returned to their former state, there has to be an explicit statement to that effect in a peace treaty – if a certain matter is not mentioned in a peace treaty, the treaty fixes it in the state it was in when the treaty was signed. Thus any territories not mentioned in the treaty are confirmed in the possession of the state that held them at the time of signing. A peace treaty thus establishes a new state of relations between countries; it "re-sets the clock" and lays down a new "critical date" from which *uti possidetis* operates, i.e. a date at which the dispute "crystallises" such that later events and actions no longer affect the possession of title. From that date the holder's possession is valid and unchallengeable (see chapter 3).

That principle was described in 1836 by the US legal writer Henry Wheaton (1785-1848):[4]

The treaty of peace leaves every thing in the state in which it found it, unless there be some express stipulation to the contrary. The existing state of possession is maintained, except so far as altered by the terms of the treaty. If nothing be said about the conquered country or places, they remain with the conqueror, and his title cannot afterwards be called in question. During the continuance of the war, the conqueror in possession has only an usufructuary right, and the latent title of the former sovereign continues, until the treaty of peace, by its silent operation, or express provisions, extinguishes his title for ever.

The principle was also stated in much the same terms by later legal writers – the British jurist Thomas Joseph Lawrence (1849-1919) wrote in 1910:[5]

As between the belligerent powers themselves, it is held that the conclusion of peace legalizes the state of possession existing at the moment, unless special stipulations to the contrary are contained in the treaty. This is called the principle of *uti possidetis,* and it is of very wide and far-reaching application. Cities, districts, and provinces held in belligerent occupation by an enemy, fall to him by the title of completed conquest, when it is not expressly stated that they are to be evacuated...

The peace treaty confirmed that Argentina and Britain had been belligerents, i.e. combatants with equal rights (see section 7.5) – Rosas forced Britain to accept that Argentina had been not merely the scene of a British intervention, but an opponent of equal status with Britain.

The special nature of a peace treaty is also stated by Hersch Lauterpacht in "Oppenheim's *International Law*", the standard work on international law, in the 7th edition of 1952:[6]

---

[1] Copy in PRO FO 6 149, fol. 132.

[2] Latinised name of Huig van Groot (1583-1645), Dutch legal commentator.

[3] Hugo Grotius, *De Iure Belli ac Pacis Libri tres...*, Amsterdam 1646, Liber III, Caput XX, Sectiones XI and XII, p. 577: "[XI.]... aut ut quarum rerum turbata bello possessio est, ex formula iuris antiqui componatur... aut ut res maneant quo sunt loco: quod Græci dicunt ἔχοντες ἃ ἔχουσιν. XII. Ex his duobus posterius in dubio magis est ut præsumatur, quia facilius est, & nullam inducit mutationem." The expression ἔχοντες ἃ ἔχουσιν is elliptical, literally "havers of what they have", i.e. the peace treaty leaves the parties in possession of what they hold – it leaves "the holders holding".

[4] Henry Wheaton, *Elements of International Law: with a Sketch of the History of the Science*, London 1836, vol. II, chapter IV, § [section] 4, p. 288. Identical text in several 1-volume later editions: in 2nd annotated ed. ("*Lawrence's Wheaton*"), ed. by William Beach Lawrence, London 1863, part II, chapter IV, § 4, pp. 878-882, and in 8th ed., ed. by Richard Henry Dana, London 1866, part IV, chapter IV, § 545, pp. 716-717.

[5] T[homas] J[oseph] Lawrence, *The Principles of International Law*, 4th revised ed. 1910, Boston (Massachusetts) 1910, pp. 571-572.

[6] L[assa] Oppenheim, *International Law: A Treatise*, 7th ed., ed. by H[ersch] Lauterpacht, London 1952, vol. II,

§ 273. Unless the parties stipulate otherwise, the effect of a treaty of peace is that conditions remain as at the conclusion of peace. Thus, all moveable State property, such as munitions, provisions, arms, money, horses, means of transport, and the like, seized by an invading belligerent, remain his property, as likewise do the fruits of immoveable property seized by him. Thus further, if nothing is stipulated regarding conquered territory, it remains in the hands of the possessor, who may annex it.

Those quotations demonstrate the complete unanimity among legal writers that a peace treaty fixes the state of territorial possession as it was when the treaty is signed – Henry Wheaton said in 1836: "If nothing be said about the conquered country or places, they remain with the conqueror, and his title cannot afterwards be called in question"; Thomas Lawrence said in 1910 that "the conclusion of peace legalizes the state of possession existing at the moment, unless special stipulations to the contrary are contained in the treaty", and Hersch Lauterpacht said in 1952 that "if nothing is stipulated regarding conquered territory, it remains in the hands of the possessor, who may annex it."

All those writers make it clear that there is a special element to a peace treaty – unlike other kinds of agreement it settles various questions of possession that it does not mention. Britain would have preferred a less formal *ad hoc* agreement that merely covered individual matters such as the return of ships, the evacuation of Martín García island, saluting the Argentine flag, and so on. The British government would have been happy to settle those matters, and would then have remained free to treat Argentina as a place where Britain could intervene at will, like parts of Africa. But General Rosas insisted that Britain recognise Argentina as a belligerent, in other words a country that fought a war against Britain and therefore enjoyed equal status with Britain. That is why he insisted on a full peace treaty and ordered it to be celebrated in such an elaborate way (sections 7.5, 7.14, 7.15, 7.16). The treaty therefore covered the unmentioned matters too, which is of great significance for the legal status of the Falkland Islands – they are not mentioned in the treaty, but it covered them nonetheless, precisely because it was a peace treaty.

Kohen and Rodríguez print (pp. 212-213) two quotations which might be taken as limiting the applicability of the Convention of Peace to the Falklands, but which do not in fact do so. First they quote the Swiss legal writer Emer de Vattel (1714-67), in an English translation of 1797:[1]

The effect of the treaty of peace is to put an end to the war, and to abolish the subject of it. (…) the effect (…) cannot be extended to things which have no relation to the war that is terminated by the treaty… The treaty of peace naturally and of itself relates only to the war which it terminates. It is, therefore, in such relation only, that its vague clauses are to be understood. Thus, the simple stipulation of restoring things to their former condition does not relate to changes which have not been occasioned by the war itself.

That in no way invalidates what we say. Like the other writers we quoted above, Vattel presumes that there had been a war, which is ended by the peace treaty, but he is the only one who says the peace treaty "relates only to the war which it terminates". The others write in more general terms of "conditions" or the "state of possession" which are fixed by the treaty; those things may or may not have been directly caused by the war, while "conquered territory" may have been conquered some time before the war and may or may not have been the cause of the war.

Vattel says a peace treaty relates "only to the war which it terminates", so the question is *what war* did the Convention of Peace terminate? Kohen and Rodríguez naturally assume that it was only the Anglo-French intervention around the River Plate – they say (p. 206): "the Arana-Southern Treaty only refers to the dispute regarding the blockade of the Rio de la Plata and the navigation of the Argentine-Uruguayan rivers". However, that dispute was not a declared war. Until the mid-20th century wars had a clear beginning and end – they began with a declaration of war by one side, and generally ended with the surrender of the losing side. Any hostilities that did not begin with a declaration of war were not a war, technically speaking, and in Britain's view there had been no war

---

Disputes, War and Neutrality, p. 611.
[1] Kohen and Rodríguez 2015, quoting Emer de Vattel, *The Law of Nations or the Principle of Natural Law* [1797], by Pitt, Nicklin & T. Johnson, Philadelphia, Liberty Fund, 1829, pp. 500, 505; also available under http://oll.liberty fund.org/titles/2246#Vattel_1519_1468.

– Southern said in his despatch to Arana on 18 October 1848 that he regretted that the Argentine government insisted on an "arrangement between the two Governments... undertaken with the avowed object of bringing about peace".[1] But Rosas told Southern that "it would be dishonorable for Him..., if... He did not terminate on a convention of peace"[2] – it was Rosas who insisted that there had been a war, by insisting on a peace treaty. Things could otherwise have been arranged piecemeal, by handing back the ships, etc., as Britain would have preferred. On Britain's behalf Southern reluctantly accepted Rosas's view that the two countries had been at war.

However, there had been no declaration of war, so there was no *terminus a quo* from which it had run. But Argentina and Britain had been continuously in dispute over the Falklands since 1833; that dispute had begun with a British military intervention (by HMS *Clio*); Argentina maintained that Britain took Argentine territory in 1833, and Britain still held it in 1849, so the dispute was continuous from 1833 to 1849. The River Plate intervention took place during that dispute and alongside it; it had no clearly-defined beginning but consisted of various actions, including the blockade of Buenos Aires in 1845-7, with gaps in between. While those intermittent and sometimes chaotic hostilities were taking place, the Falklands dispute was continuing in the background, and Rosas protested every year from 1833 to 1849 in his Messages to the legislature against Britain's possession of the islands. In Argentina's view, throughout those years Britain was holding a piece of Argentine territory that had been obtained by military force, without possessing title to that territory. In short, there was a complex dispute between Britain and Argentina from 1833 to 1849, which had various aspects including the Falklands and the River Plate intervention. That explains why Lord Palmerston in the House of Commons, various British newspapers, and the *British Packet and Argentine News* (*BPAN*) in Buenos Aires referred to "the dispute" in the singular (sections 7.8, 7.10, 8.1), and the *Evening Mail* said on 1-3 August 1849 that the possession of the Falklands was "one of the points of our dispute now in course of arrangement with Buenos Ayres" (section 7.10). So Vattel's statement in no way prevents the Convention of Peace from referring to the Falklands.

Secondly, Kohen and Rodríguez quote (pp. 212-213) three brief passages from Dana's 8th edition of Wheaton (1866), all from § [= "section"] 544 (though their footnote wrongly says that the third one is from § 545):

The effect of a treaty of peace is to put an end to the war and to abolish the subject of it. It is an agreement to waive all discussion concerning the respective rights and claims of the parties and to bury in oblivion the original causes of the war...

If an abstract right be in question between the parties, on which the treaty of peace is silent, it follows, that all previous complaints and injury, arising under such claim are thrown into oblivion, by the amnesty necessarily implied, if not expressed; but the claim itself is not thereby settled either one way or the other. In the absence of express renunciation or recognition it remains open for future discussion...

The treaty of peace does not extinguish claims founded upon debts contracted or injuries inflicted previously to the war, and unconnected with its causes, unless there be an express stipulation to that effect.

That does not invalidate what we say either. Wheaton and Dana here refer to what they call "claims founded upon debts contracted or injuries inflicted previously to the war, and unconnected with its causes"; they are not referring to titles to territory, which are dealt with in their next section, in the quote we reproduced above ("The treaty of peace leaves every thing in the state in which it found it..."). Wheaton and Dana are not being inconsistent – their treatment of territories is perfectly clear, and they are not the same thing as an "abstract right" or "debts contracted or injuries inflicted previously to the war".

It is thus highly significant that the Convention of Peace makes no mention of the Falkland Islands. They had been disputed between Argentina and Britain from 1833 to 1849; they were held by Britain throughout the hostilities, and they were held by Britain when the Convention was ratified, so it confirmed Britain's possession of them once and for all. There had been a partial Argentine claim until 1849 (see chapter 3 for its limitations), which had been kept alive by annual

---

[1] *Archivo Americano* 1850, pp. 111 and 118; longer quote in section 7.5.
[2] Southern to Palmerston 14 October 1848 (received in London 21 January 1849), PRO FO 6 139, fol. 64 *verso*; see also section 7.5.

protests in the Messages to the Buenos Aires legislature from 1833 to 1849, but the non-mention of the islands in the Convention definitively ended it – as Henry Wheaton put it in 1836: "the latent title of the former sovereign continues, until the treaty of peace, by its silent operation... extinguishes his title for ever." Henry Southern pointed that out to General Rosas after the signing of the treaty, and Rosas did not demur (section 7.14).

To sum up: by the Convention of Peace Argentina finally and unequivocally accepted that the Falklands were British territory, both by restoring "perfect" friendship between Britain and Argentina, and by omitting to mention the islands in the treaty.

7.13 The so-called "Arana-Southern treaty" was a peace treaty

— 163 —

United Kingdom of Great Britain and Ireland, granted to H. E. the Honourable Henry Southern Esq.ʳᵉ to sign and conclude the Convention of Peace.

The confidential draft of Convention of Peace, arranged with H. E. the Honourable Henry Southern Esq.ʳᵉ, and referred by him to the Government of H. B. M., and which is the same that has been accepted without any alteration by the Government of H. M., and signed by the Argentine and British Plenipotentiaries, after the exchange of their respective powers.

In the 8ᵗʰ article it is stipulated, that the Convention will be ratified by the Argentine Government, within fifteen days after the presentation of the ratification of H. B. M.

But the credential which H. M. the Queen of Great Britain has granted to H. E. her Minister Plenipotentiary, the Honourable Henry Southern Esq.ʳᵉ is absolute and unlimited. It was issued, after Her Majesty had informed herself of the literal terms of the draft of Convention of Peace. Besides, the adjustment and conclusion of treaties of peace, without the previous consultation of Parliament, is the direct and inherent prerogative of the British Crown. For these very special reasons, the Government would now proceed to ratify on its part the convention of peace that has been signed, should you deign to authorise it for the purpose.

It respectfully requests you will be pleased to take this matter into your high consideration, and decide upon it, should it be possible for you, during the first days of January 1850.

In order to facilitate it, that you may save, if you think proper, a repeated reading, it reminds you, in short, that you are informed in detail of the said correspondence, by the manifestations which the Government addressed to you in its Message of 1843, and in that of the current year; and that in the latter, the Convention of Peace and the Credential are transcribed at length. It likewise remarks to you, that in the notes of the Government you will find transcribed at length the respective communications of H. E. the Minister Plenipotentiary of H. B. M., the reason why it does not present them to you in other separate copies,

7.13a Convention of Peace: the official Argentine government publication *Archivo Americano*, vol. 21, Buenos Aires December 1850, p. 163. This text appears twice: on pp. 101-102 in the appeal by Rosas and Arana to the Buenos Aires legislature on 27 December 1849, asking them to ratify the treaty, and here repeated in their reply to Rosas. The phrase "convention of peace", underlined by us 5 times here, occurs often. The text makes it clear that "convention" and "treaty" are synonymous (oblong added here).

In view of the crucial effect of the Convention of Peace in annihilating Argentina's title to the Falklands, it is not surprising that Kohen and Rodríguez do not use the term "Convention of Peace" but only the 20th-century term "Arana-Southern treaty", and several times they place the expression "peace treaty" in quotes as if it were not genuine.

For example, in reference to our statement in *Getting it right* (p. 24) that "By that Convention, Argentina accepted that the Falklands were British", they say (p. 211):

In their attempt to find an Argentine renunciation in the Arana-Southern Treaty, the authors of the pamphlet insist on its nature as a "peace treaty" and claim that it is because of this nature that the renunciation existed.

The truth is that the agreement was indeed a peace treaty, at Argentina's insistence – Britain would have preferred a lower-level agreement (sections 7.5, 7.14), but Rosas was intransigent and the result was a full peace treaty. That can easily be demonstrated – the expression "Convention of Peace" (meaning the same as peace treaty) was used innumerable times by both sides during the negotiations, and some 20 times in the documents in the official Argentine government publication *Archivo Americano* in December 1850 (fig. 7.13a).

The attempt by Kohen and Rodríguez to deny that the so-called "Arana-Southern treaty" was a peace treaty is thus disproved by the contemporary documentation. Both sides knew throughout that they were negotiating a comprehensive peace treaty, which meant that it ended Argentina's title to the Falklands, as Henry Southern was soon to make clear to General Rosas.

7.14 What Kohen and Rodríguez did not know: Southern quashes Rosas's attempt to raise the Falklands question

Once the Convention of Peace had been signed (on 24 November 1849), Henry Southern thought it was time for Rosas to officially recognise him as Britain's ambassador in Buenos Aires, not merely as "Minister Negotiator of the Peace" as Argentine foreign minister Felipe Arana called him in a letter to him on 6 November 1848.[1] Southern asked Rosas for another meeting, and the two men met on 10 December 1849 for a conversation "which lasted the whole night nearly", as Southern reported to Palmerston in a despatch on 13 December.[2] This important meeting was never made public; it is only recorded in the original documents, and Kohen and Rodríguez were clearly unaware of it. It contradicts their view of the Convention of Peace – they say (p. 203):[3]

If at some point during the negotiations it made a verbal attempt to include the issue of the Falklands/ Malvinas, and there is no evidence of such a thing happening, it is likely that neither of the parties could impose its position on the other. There is no proof that Great Britain demanded the renunciation of Argentine sovereignty, and Rosas was not required to give up the claim to be able to conclude the treaty.

But that is exactly what did happen. Rosas *did* make a verbal attempt to "include the issue of the Falklands/Malvinas", but Henry Southern quashed it at once and Rosas made no attempt to raise the matter again; he was indeed "required to give up the claim", as Kohen and Rodríguez put it, in order to conclude the treaty. What happened is recorded in two memorandums, from Southern to Rosas on 11 December 1849 and from Rosas on 15 December replying to Southern's memorandum. Briefly, the content of those memorandums is as follows.

To Southern's surprise and indignation, Rosas would still not recognise him as ambassador – he said he wanted to wait until the treaty had been ratified and until the Argentine warships seized by Britain had been returned and he had received formal confirmation that Martín García island had been evacuated by Britain, as laid down in Article I of the Convention of Peace. In fact there had been no British soldiers on the island for some time, but Rosas wanted a formal statement of the fact. Southern pointed out that no treaty was valid until ratified, but that to leave a long interval between the signing and his official recognition as ambassador might give foreign governments an impression of a lack of good faith on the part of Argentina.

At that, Rosas began to list matters which he said demonstrated the Argentine government's good faith, including the fact that it had "dispensed with all pecuniary compensation" and had kept the Treaty of Commerce and Amity of 1825 in force throughout the hostilities. And he added:[4]

It has not introduced the grave question which is pending of the Falkland Islands.

Southern at once pointed out to Rosas that peace treaties end all differences between countries, and on 11 December, the day after the conversation, he handed a 5-page written memorandum to Rosas's daughter "Manuelita" (who acted as his secretary) summarising the previous night's conversation. It included Southern's statement that:[5]

All national differences are terminated by solemn and public Conventions of Peace…

That statement by Southern confirms what we said in section 7.12: that a peace treaty "establishes a new state of relations between countries; it 're-sets the clock'". It therefore ends all disputes. Southern thus confirmed to Rosas that any Argentine title to the Falklands had been ended by the

---

[1] *Archivo Americano* 1850, p. 123.
[2] Southern to Palmerston 13 December 1849, in PRO FO 6 145, fol. 178 *recto*.
[3] Much the same is asserted by Seokwoo Lee in Kohen and Mamadou Hébié (eds.), 2018, pp. 278-279 (see section 7.11).
[4] Memorandum from Rosas to Southern, 15 December 1849, English translation enclosed in Southern's despatch to Palmerston of 17 December 1849, PRO FO 6 145, fol. 213 *verso*.
[5] English translation of Southern's memorandum to Rosas, 11 December 1849, enclosed in Southern's despatch to Palmerston of 17 December 1849, in PRO FO 6 145, fol. 203 *recto*.

Convention of Peace. And Rosas did not demur (below).

In pursuance of Rosas's demand for the return of the Argentine ships, Southern wrote to Rear Admiral Barrington Reynolds, commander-in-chief on the Royal Navy's South American station, asking about the state of the Argentine warships in his possession.[1] In a private letter to Palmerston on 13 December reporting the delay in his reception as Britain's ambassador, Southern mentioned Rosas's insistence on the ships, which Britain would have "returned without any treaty, if he had not insisted on one."[2] That confirms that Britain had not wanted a full-scale treaty between the two countries, but would have complied with Rosas's requests promptly if they had been presented at a lower level. The delay was caused by the Argentine side's insistence on a peace treaty.

Following the nocturnal conversation on 10-11 December 1849, Rosas sent Southern a written memorandum dated 15 December 1849 replying to Southern's memorandum of 11 December. Rosas's long reply repeated the arguments in Southern's memorandum, first giving the statement by one side, then the reply by the other, and adding his own extensive additional explanations.

Significantly, Rosas merely repeated without further comment Southern's statement that "All national differences are terminated by solemn and public Conventions of Peace"[3] – that statement therefore appears twice in the exchange, first in Southern's memorandum to Rosas and again in Rosas's reply to Southern. By repeating Southern's statement without contradicting it or limiting it in any way, Rosas showed unambiguously that he accepted the ending of the Falklands dispute.

So Kohen and Rodríguez are (unwittingly) wrong in saying that there is "no evidence" that an attempt was made to include the Falklands question – Rosas made precisely such an attempt after the negotiations, but Southern quashed it by stating that "All national differences are terminated by solemn and public Conventions of Peace", which Rosas accepted and repeated. That marked the end of the Falklands dispute and the end of any Argentine title. The end was not yet definitive since the Convention was not ratified, but the ratification put the final seal on it (section 7.16).

On 17 December 1849 Southern sent a despatch to Palmerston, reporting that as a result of their conversation, Rosas had decided to submit the Convention to the Buenos Aires legislature for ratification without waiting for ratification by Britain. He also enclosed English translations of his own memorandum to Rosas and Rosas's memorandum in reply.[4]

To sum up: Britain and Argentina both accepted that the agreement later sometimes called the "Arana-Southern treaty" was a full peace treaty, and they both accepted that peace treaties ended all disputes between their signatories. Both countries therefore agreed that the Convention of Peace ended any Argentine title to the Falkland Islands.

7.15 Argentine protests, 1833-1849; Argentina's symbolic last protest, 27 December 1849

As recounted in section 6.29, Argentina maintained a two-pronged campaign for 17 years (1833 to 1849 inclusive) against Britain's possession of the Falklands, on the one hand by three sets of formal diplomatic protests (1833-4, 1841-2 and 1849),[5] and on the other hand by annual protests in the "Mensajes", the official Messages at the ceremonial opening of the legislature of the province of Buenos Aires, which dealt with the whole Argentine Confederation's foreign policy.[6]

Kohen and Rodríguez mention (pp. 196-7) the Argentine protests in those 17 years, and complain about the injustice of the British reply, which was always to say that the subject was closed. Up to a point they are right – in those 17 years Britain was indeed going too far in saying the subject was closed: as long as Argentina kept up regular protests, the subject was not closed, and Argentina's claim and rights continued unchanged (such as they were; they did not amount to 100% sovereignty, and had not amounted to 100% sovereignty in 1833 either). But the Convention of

---

[1] Southern to Reynolds 11 December 1849, in PRO FO 6 145, fols. 274 *recto* to 275 *recto*; Reynolds stated in his reply of 15 December, in *ibid.*, fols. 276 *recto* to 277 *verso*, that he held only one Argentine ship, in very poor condition.
[2] Private letter from Southern to Palmerston, 13 December 1849, in PRO FO 6 145, fol. 180 *verso*.
[3] English translation of Rosas's reply to Southern's memorandum, in PRO FO 6 145, fol. 214 *verso*.
[4] Southern to Palmerston 17 December 1849, in PRO FO 6 145, fols. 193 *recto* to 200 *verso*.
[5] The diplomatic protests are printed in Spanish in Becerra 1998.
[6] The full texts of all Messages from 1810 to 1910, which from 1833 to 1849 include protests against British possession of the Falklands, were reprinted in H[eraclio] Mabragaña, *Los Mensajes 1810-1910*, Buenos Aires 1910.

Peace changed all that.

The two Argentine authors say (p. 207) that the Message of 27 December 1849 by Rosas to the Buenos Aires legislature is of "key importance", especially because it was given a month after the signing of what they call the "Arana-Southern treaty". They say that we cannot be ignorant of the full content of that Message, since in our paper *Getting it right* we mention its existence, and they maintain that it is "absurd" that we say that Rosas renounced the Malvinas by that treaty, since in his Message on 27 December 1849 he officially repeated the Argentine claim.

They are right that we knew the full content of that Message, but they miss the point. The point is that in December 1849 the treaty was not yet ratified and so had not yet come into force. Southern and Rosas confirmed in their conversation on the night of 10-11 December 1849 that a treaty did not come into force until it had been ratified,[1] so both knew that any statements made before ratification did not contradict the treaty or cancel it. So Rosas's protest of December 1849 was merely symbolic and did not lessen the effect of the peace treaty.

Though dated 27 December 1849, the protest was not actually made until the first few days of 1850, and it was preceded by an appeal from Rosas and Arana to the Buenos Aires legislature to ratify the treaty without waiting for Britain's ratification, as Rosas had offered to Southern. The appeal used the term "Convention of Peace" many times, as shown in our fig. 7.13a, so there was no doubt as to what was being agreed to. Kohen and Rodríguez do not mention the appeal, nor the oddness of the 1849 protest compared with all preceding ones. The whole Message was immensely long – it ran in the original script to 453 pages – and was not delivered by Rosas but by a heroic secretary, who read it to the exhausted representatives over four days from 1 to 4 January 1850. Those days were proclaimed as festivals, with all work and business suspended – the conclusion of peace between Britain and Argentina, and Rosas's triumph in imposing peace terms on Britain and forcing Britain to accept Argentina as an equal, were to be properly celebrated.[2]

Like the whole 1849 Message itself, the passage protesting against Britain's possession of the Falklands was positively eccentric. Kohen and Rodríguez quote (pp. 207-208) about a quarter of it but do not draw attention to its length or its oddness. It ran to 728 words – some 15 times as long as the typical protests in the Messages in the 1830s and 40s, and almost 40 times as long as the 19 words of the 1846 protest. Not only that; three passages are each repeated almost *verbatim*. That shows that far from being of "key importance", the 1849 protest was merely symbolic – the decision to drop the Falklands claim had been made and the Convention of Peace had made it official, but the Convention had not yet been ratified, so Rosas could "go to town", as it were, and give vent to his sense of pique that he had lost that minor point. His comments about the Falklands were inconsistent with what he knew to be the case, but anything he said at that precise time was without force. That impression is strengthened by the fact that the Falklands protest was almost immediately followed in the Message by the full text of the Convention of Peace, not once but twice: first the version for the Argentine government, with Spanish before English, then the version for the British government, with English before Spanish, followed by a request to the legislature to declare whether the government should ratify it. That was a foregone conclusion of course – Rosas's authority was absolute, so he needed no one's permission to ratify the treaty, but he went through the charade of asking for authority all the same.

He was given that authority on 24 January 1850,[3] and his behaviour towards Henry Southern changed dramatically. That evening he officially received Southern as Her Britannic Majesty's Minister (i.e. ambassador) to Buenos Aires, and underlined the significance of the occasion with elaborate ceremonies. He pardoned some prisoners; orchestras serenaded Rosas and Southern at

---

[1] Confirmed in a memorandum by Southern to Rosas, 17 December 1849, in PRO FO 6 145, fols. 194 *recto* and 196 *recto*, and again in another memorandum on 20 December 1849, PRO FO 6 145, fol. 267 *verso*.

[2] Details and dates in despatch from Southern dated 19 January 1850, in PRO FO 6 149, fols. 1-5; see also Lynch 2001, pp. 129-130. The text of the Message of 1849 was printed in Buenos Aires in two booklets in Spanish and English by the official Argentine government printer, both dated 1849. Copies of both are in PRO FO 6 149; the Spanish version is 236 pages, the English version 242 pages, and it runs to 239 pages in Mabragaña 1910, vol. II, pp. 251-490.

[3] Announced in official letter of 24 January 1850 by Manuel García, President of the House of Representatives, printed in *Archivo Americano 1850*, p. 166, followed (pp. 166-169) by an account of the ceremonies that day.

their respective homes; Rosas sent his own private coach, rather than a government one, to bring Southern through cheering crowds to the reception at Rosas's private house, and there was a firework display in the evening.[1] All those things confirm that something major had happened – peace had been concluded between Argentina and Britain by the signing of a comprehensive peace treaty. If the treaty had merely made arrangements to return a few ships, evacuate Martín García Island, confirm the Argentine nature of two rivers, and order the saluting of Argentine vessels, there would have been no reason for such impressive ceremonies.

Amazingly, foreign minister Felipe Arana knew nothing of all those ceremonies! He spent the day at his private house and only learnt of Southern's reception from the next day's newspapers. Presumably Rosas was underlining his dictatorial powers and refusing to share the credit with anyone, but the snub to Arana was extreme, as Henry Southern noted: "Arana is reduced to the most absolute nullity; whatever goes through that channel might as well be thrown into the Plata."[2] The guiding spirit behind the Convention was Rosas's alone, and it was a personal triumph for him.

In concluding the Convention of Peace, Rosas was giving up the Falklands as a lost cause, but what mattered to him was that he had forced Britain to accept Argentina as an equal partner on the world stage. It is important to remember that Argentina was not coerced by Britain into signing a peace treaty – it was the other way round: Argentina had forced Britain into signing a peace treaty.

7.16 Critical date, 15 May 1850:[3] the Convention of Peace is ratified; end of the Argentine title

The Convention of Peace had been signed in November 1849, but it was not till early in 1850 that news of the signing reached Britain: on Monday 11 February 1850 the London *Evening Mail* printed a report from Argentina datelined "Buenos Ayres, Nov. 26, 1849" (two days after the signing), which stated that "Mr. Southern... signed the Convention with this Government [i.e. the Argentine government], which puts an end to all old animosities...". That article shows that it was known in Buenos Aires that the Convention ended all disputes between Britain and Argentina; its publication in Britain confirmed what British newspapers had stated back in 1849 (section 7.10).

If the Falklands had been important to General Rosas – if he had seriously regretted losing them by signing the Convention of Peace – he could have kept Argentina's claim alive simply by omitting to ratify the Convention. As he and Southern knew, treaties only came into force on ratification; failure to ratify the Convention of Peace would have left it in limbo, signed but not in force, as happened with the Le Prédour treaty (section 7.18). But he did not do that; to him the loss of the Falklands did not matter – it was the price to be paid for achieving his central aim. Rosas's authorisation to Arana to sign it twice refers to it as "la Convencion de Paz", and the ratification document, in English, says that the convention was "for the settlement of existing differences, and the reestablishment of perfect relations of Friendship"; those two documents confirmed that it was a peace treaty and that it dropped all disputes between Argentina and Britain.[4]

On Wednesday 15 May 1850 the Convention of Peace was ratified by both sides in Buenos Aires, Henry Southern signing for Britain, Felipe Arana for Argentina. Thereupon it came into

---

[1] Henry Southern described the celebrations, the circumstances surrounding the signing, and subsequent events in two despatches both dated 26 January 1850, in PRO FO 6 149: no. 5 (fols. 152ff) and no. 6, fols. 177ff – Arana's ignorance is mentioned in no. 6 on fol. 181 *recto*.

[2] Private letter from Southern to Palmerston, 11 March 1850, PRO FO 6 149 fols. 420 *verso* – 421 *recto*.

[3] There are several definitions of the term "critical date"; we follow that by L. F. E. Goldie in *International and Comparative Law Quarterly*, 1963, issue 4, p. 1251: "In international law the point of time falling at the end of a period within which the material facts of a dispute are said to have occurred is usually called the 'critical date.' It is also the date after which the actions of the parties to a dispute can no longer affect the issue. It is exclusionary, and it is terminal". Under that definition, the period in which the material facts of the Falklands dispute occurred ended on 15 May 1850 with Argentina's final dropping of its claim to the islands; that date is terminal since it brought the dispute to an end, and it is exclusionary since it excludes all later acts – nothing done by either party after that can affect the issue. Marc Shucksmith-Wesley mentions several definitions of "critical date" including that by Goldie, but oddly he does not mention the Convention of Peace (Marc Shucksmith-Wesley, *The Falklands (Malvinas) Dispute: a critique of international law and the pacific settlement of disputes*, Nottingham May 2018: doctoral thesis available online, pp. 282-3). Some critical dates are overt (e.g. in a cession treaty); in other cases it only later emerges what they were.

[4] A copy of Rosas's authorisation for Arana to sign, dated 15 November 1849, and the British original of the final ratification document, signed and sealed, 15 May 1850, are in PRO FO 93/10/4.

force; Argentina and Britain had concluded a peace treaty which settled all their differences.

That was confirmed in Buenos Aires by the *British Packet and Argentine News* (*BPAN*), which on 18 May 1850 reprinted *verbatim* the article dated 26 November 1849 from the London *Evening Mail* of 11 February 1850 (fig. 7.16a). The original article had a dateline but no headline; the *BPAN* retained the original dateline but added a headline using "dispute" in the singular, indicating that "all old animosities" were parts of the same dispute. So it was well understood in Buenos Aires, as well as in Britain, that the Convention ended all disputes between Britain and Argentina.

And then there was silence. Argentina's protests against Britain's possession of the Falklands ceased. No author offers an explanation as to why they stopped at that precise moment, after 17 years of regular annual protests. In fact there was a very good reason: the ratification of the peace treaty had ended not merely Britain's armed intervention around the River Plate but *all* disagreements between Britain and Argentina including the Falklands dispute.

> **SETTLEMENT OF DISPUTE BETWEEN ENGLAND AND BUENOS AYRES.**
>
> (FROM AN OCCASIONAL CORRESPONDENT.)
>
> Buenos Ayres, Nov. 26, 1849.
>
> On the 24th of November last Mr. Southern, having received full powers by the last packet, signed the convention with this Government, which puts an end to all old animosities, and re-establishes the former relations of friendship and good understanding. In a political point of view this convention may be productive of some good. There is a large population of British

7.16a The Convention of Peace puts an end to all old animosities:
British Packet and Argentine News (*BPAN*), Buenos Aires 18 May 1850, p. 2, col. 2;
text (except the headline) from the *Evening Mail*, London Monday 11 February 1850.

As mentioned in section 7.12, Kohen and Rodríguez attempt to maintain (p. 206) that what they call the "Arana-Southern treaty" did not refer to the Falklands but only to Britain's blockade of the River Plate. As evidence they mention a speech by Foreign Secretary Lord Palmerston in the House of Commons on 12 August 1850, in which – they say – "he constantly refers to the dispute (in the singular) resolved by the treaty, which is obviously the one mentioned in Article 1, and covers the problem arising with a third State (Uruguay), and not to the existing disputes (plural) between Argentina and Great Britain. No mention of the Falklands/Malvinas, whether implicit or explicit, was made." Here they are yet again distorting the evidence.

The facts are these: Palmerston was asked by an MP, Mr Smythe, if he would present to the House copies of the various earlier proposals for negotiations between Britain and General Rosas; Palmerston refused, and *Hansard* records him as saying:[1]

Now, however, a treaty, and, as he thought, a satisfactory treaty, having been concluded… he did not think it would be just or right to produce former proposals which had been unsuccessful.

He did not say what those "former proposals" were, but they included some sent to London on 21 July 1848 by the British vice-consul in Montevideo, Martin Tupper Hood, who had reported that Rosas was then demanding, among other things, "The Restitution of the Falkland Islands".[2] There had been other proposals too, including some from Thomas Samuel Hood (father of Martin Tupper Hood) which did not include the Falklands, but Palmerston's refusal to lay them before the House meant that they all remained internal government matters and did not become public knowledge.

Mr Smythe's second question was whether Britain's relations with France were such as to afford any hope of success from the offer of Britain's good offices in arranging for France to evacuate the republics of the River Plate and celebrate a treaty of peace, as laid down in Article III

---

[1] *Hansard* 12 August 1850, column 1028.
[2] Martin Tupper Hood to Palmerston, 21 July 1848, in PRO FO 6 140, fol. 180 *recto*.

of the treaty. Palmerston replied that they (the British government) had thought it better to conclude a separate treaty with General Rosas, to obtain a better settlement "of the entire dispute between all parties", without waiting for the conclusion of Rosas's negotiations with France. He added:[1]

According to the last accounts, these negotiations were going on satisfactorily; and no person was more likely to obtain from General Rosas those small modifications which were required to terminate the dispute, than the officer who was sent out by the French government to conduct the negotiations.

That was all. Far from referring "constantly" to "the dispute (in the singular)", as Kohen and Rodríguez say, Palmerston used the word exactly twice in his speech, in both cases involving France, the first time referring to "the entire dispute between all parties", meaning all aspects of the complex problem (including the French troops in Uruguay, the Falklands dispute with Britain, the French foreign legion, the Argentine ships held by both Britain and France, and various other matters) and the second time meaning France's part of the whole dispute with Argentina. Back in August 1849 the London *Evening Mail* had recognised that the Falklands were "one of the points of our dispute" with Buenos Aires (section 7.10), and the *BPAN* made clear in its report published three days after the ratification of the Convention of Peace (fig. 7.16a) that there had been a single complex dispute involving "all old animosities". The notion that Palmerston's singular "dispute" refers exclusively to the River Plate blockade, and therefore excludes the Falklands, is untenable.

It is impossible to reconcile the Convention of Peace with any idea that Argentina retained rights to the Falkland Islands. Echoing the Convention's title, the ratification document says that the Convention is "for the settlement of existing differences, and the reestablishment of perfect Relations of Friendship" between Britain and Argentina; that wording, even without the confirmatory acts by Argentina that followed it (section 8.18), constitutes a clear statement of the official dropping of all disputes with Britain. And as explained in section 7.12, the omission of any mention of the Falklands fixed the position as it stood when the peace treaty was ratified, thus definitively confirming Argentina's consent to Britain's possession of the islands.

So the date of ratification of the Convention of Peace, Wednesday 15 May 1850, was the critical date in the legal history of the Falkland Islands. The Falklands dispute between Argentina and Britain, which had continued since 1833, ended on that date – Argentina had ceased to dispute Britain's title to the islands and had accepted that the islands were British territory. Till then the Falklands had only been *de facto* British, and Argentina had kept her claim alive by regular protests, but the ratification of the Convention of Peace ended Argentina's partial title and made the islands *de jure* British territory from that day onwards. That was the date on which the dispute "crystallised", i.e. ceased to be fluid; it was the point at which Britain's rights to the Falklands became absolute. As Professor Giovanni Distefano says in reference to the critical date:[2]

... the critical date acts as a juridical watershed so that facts occurring after the critical date may only be taken into account as evidence of a title already constituted... state conduct accomplished before the critical date are [sic] in all regards 'vesting acts' to the extent that they contribute to create, extinguish or modify existing territorial titles.

Thus the Convention extinguished such (partial) title as Argentina had possessed up to the critical date of 15 May 1850. That left no active counter-claimant to Britain (Spain's rights had fallen into desuetude and were finally cancelled in 1863, section 8.17), so the signing and ratification of the Convention of Peace was a "vesting act" which confirmed Britain's existing rights in the Falklands and converted them into a full territorial title after having previously been a claim asserted in 1765, consolidated in 1766 and tacitly accepted by Spain in 1771, plus specific rights (landing, "fishing", constructing buildings, etc., in most of the islands, and settling permanently in some parts of them; see section 1.7), plus customary rights derived from 16 years of administration (January 1834 to May 1850).

By the Convention of Peace, full title to the Falklands was vested in Britain, so Britain acquired exclusive sovereign rights in the whole of the islands. And after the critical date several things

---

[1] *Hansard* 12 August 1850, col. 1029. The "officer who was sent out" was Le Prédour (section 7.18).
[2] Giovanni Distefano in Kohen and Hébié (eds.) 2018, p. 403.

occurred that gave conclusive evidence of that "title already constituted": Argentina's ceasing to protest from 1850 (section 7.19); Argentina's overt acquiescence indicating consent to Britain's title (section 8.18); Britain's innumerable acts of jurisdiction (« effectivités ») in the islands (sections 8.9, 8.20); and international acceptance of Britain's title, including acceptance by the United States, which had hitherto denied the existence of any title at all (section 8.15).

In legal terms, the Convention of Peace perfected Britain's title to the Falkland Islands, and subsequent events definitively confirmed that title once and for all.

7.17 Later opinions of the Convention of Peace

We are not by any means the first to have noticed that the Convention of Peace ended any Argentine title to the Falkland Islands. Over a century ago the Mexican historian and diplomat Carlos Pereyra (1871-1942) came to the same conclusion in his book *Rosas y Thiers*, written in 1917, published in 1919 in Madrid. Referring to Britain's behaviour in negotiating with General Rosas while at the same time reinforcing its position in the Falklands, he says:[1]

Rosas protested, but he did so with the patently obvious intention of ceasing to merely emphasise his indignation and instead buying with the Malvinas islands, which were already in British hands and would not be likely to leave those hands, the abstention of the British in the question of the River Plate.

After discussing the Convention of Peace and summarising the first seven articles, Pereyra adds:[2]

8th. (unwritten). Britain retained the Malvinas islands.

Pereyra is not implying that there was a full-fledged secret agreement (for which he presents no evidence), but rather that there was merely a tacit, unwritten acceptance by Argentina that the Convention confirmed Britain's retention of the Falklands. In other words, the effect of the Convention was the same as if there had been such an article.

Pereyra's book was reprinted in Buenos Aires in 1944, and contributed to several later discussions of the Convention of Peace in Argentina: in a debate in the Argentine Congress in July 1950; in a book by one of the main speakers in the debate, Absalón Rojas, published in late 1950; in books by the distinguished Argentine historian Ernesto Fitte in 1966, 1974 and 1975, and in a book by Alfredo Burnet-Merlín printed in April 1974, June 1974 and October 1976. We will now summarise those in turn.

The Argentine Chamber of Deputies held a major debate on Argentina's claim to the Falklands over several days in July 1950.[3] For all the speakers without exception, it was merely a question of territory – not one of them so much as mentioned the people of the Falklands, 90% of whom had been born in the islands, some of them in families who had lived there for five or six generations.

Several things were mentioned in the debate that seriously undermined Argentina's position, including the Convention of Peace, British arbitration in Argentine territorial disputes (see section 9.1, and for another, later, arbitration, 10.22), and the behaviour of the Argentine whaling company "Pesca" in recognising British possession of South Georgia (section 9.6). The most important of those topics was the Convention of Peace, which was treated in detail on 19 July 1950 by Deputy Absalón Rojas, member for Santiago del Estero and a hardline "Malvinist" (i.e. supporter of the Argentine claim). He said he was going to treat the question of the Malvinas as if he were a lawyer defending a case in court, and pointed out that for a lawyer it is important to know the weak point of one's own position.[4] That weak point, he said, was the actions of General Juan Manuel Rosas, whom he accused of being responsible in two ways for the loss of the Malvinas to Britain. First, he

---

[1] Carlos Pereyra, *Rosas y Thiers: La diplomacia europea en el Río de la Plata (1838-1850)* ["Rosas and Thiers: European diplomacy in the River Plate (1838-1850)"], 1st ed. Madrid 1919, new edition Buenos Aires 1944; this quote from 1919 ed. p. 202 (1944 ed. p. 217). The conservative French politician Adolphe Thiers (1797-1877) was prime minister of France, 22 February to 5 September 1836 and 1 March to 28 October 1840.
[2] Pereyra 1919, p. 206 (1944, p. 222); Pereyra's round brackets.
[3] *Verbatim* record of debate in *Diario de Sesiones de la Cámara de Diputados, Año del Libertador General San Martín, 1950, Tomo II, Período Ordinario, 6 de julio-10 y 11 de agosto*, Buenos Aires 1951 (henceforth "*Diario* 1950"); debates on 12, 14, 19, 20 July 1950 (pp. 997-1004; 1058-1064; 1093-1099; 1172-1215; 1217-1220).
[4] *Diario* 1950, 19 July, p. 1094.

asserted that Rosas's machinations in 1833 had caused the chaos in Argentina that had made the British takeover possible – that was of course incorrect: Britain's actions in 1833 were nothing to do with any chaos or other developments in Argentina; they were to forestall the possible sending of an American naval force to the islands, and HMS *Clio*'s visit did in fact forestall a second visit by the USS *Lexington* (section 6.23). Secondly, he said Rosas had failed to reserve Argentina's sovereignty in what he calls the "treaty of friendship", i.e. the Convention of Peace:[1]

[**Absalón Rojas**, in the Argentine Chamber of Deputies, Buenos Aires, 19 July 1950:] ... On 27 August 1849[2] Rosas signed his famous treaty of friendship with Great Britain, with the aim of putting an end to the differences existing between the two countries. It was a sort of general settlement of accounts with Britain, since all problems were about to be settled... this treaty... states: "By this convention the perfect friendship between Her Majesty's Government and that of the Argentine Confederation is reestablished." ... However, in that treaty nothing is said about the Malvinas islands, which is odd, since Rosas especially remembered the island of Martín García... what is serious is that in the treaty Rosas accepts our "perfect friendship" with Britain as restored, and does not formulate at least a reservation in respect of the Malvinas islands... the lack of reference to the Malvinas islands in the treaty of 1849 is of great importance. That treaty, at any rate its silence on that point, was a concession to Britain or a culpable oversight...

I do not believe that this omission, legally speaking, has injured the fullness of Argentine rights over those islands; but at all events, it is a delicate point which must be fully investigated and taken into account in future dealings with England... We must not admit any discussion about the better title to the Malvinas islands, nor raise questions about that territory, nor limit ourselves to protesting. My opinion is that the Government should study the possibility and the opportunity of bringing a case before the International Court of Justice at The Hague to demand that England hand over the Malvinas islands to the Argentine Republic... free of all occupation... thus repairing the outrage and restoring things to the state they were in before the dispossession, as in a simple possessory prohibition. That would not prevent England from discussing afterwards, if it wants to, the titles and rights of each side to sovereignty over the Malvinas islands. But it should begin by handing them over.

As an exercise in doublethink, that takes some beating. On the one hand, Rojas accepts that the Convention of Peace was a serious weakness in Argentina's case in that it restored "perfect friendship" between Britain and Argentina (hence dropping all disputes including the Falklands dispute), and he also accepts that it was "a sort of general settlement of accounts with Britain". All that is absolutely right, of course. But then he says he does not believe that the treaty had "injured the fullness of Argentine rights over those islands", which is not a logical conclusion from what he had just said. Revealingly, he also says Argentina "must not admit any discussion about the better title to the Malvinas islands, nor raise questions about that territory", which suggests he was not entirely sure of the "fullness of Argentine rights". All the more absurd, then, that he demands that Britain should "hand over the Malvinas islands to the Argentine Republic... free of all occupation" – he seriously expected Britain to remove the entire population of the islands!

Actually the loss of the Falklands was a part of Rosas's calculations in negotiating a peace treaty with Britain; he made a half-hearted attempt to raise the Falklands question after signing the treaty, but dropped his attempt when Henry Southern blocked it (section 7.14).

We mentioned Pereyra, Rojas, Fitte and Burnet-Merlín by name in *Getting it right* (p. 24), and briefly summarised their remarks accepting that the Convention of Peace was a serious weakness in Argentina's case, but Kohen and Rodríguez dismiss them all with a wave of the hand (pp. 209-211), talking of "The lack of importance of the authors cited in the British pamphlet", and employing the time-honoured lawyers' trick of omitting the names of opponents, thus making them less visible.

The only one they name is Rojas, though they do not quote him but quote only the rejoinder to Rojas by the leftwing Peronist deputy John William Cooke (1919-1968), who attempted to rebut Rojas's argument that the Convention of Peace was damaging to Argentina's case. However, Cooke

---

[1] *Diario* 1950, 19 July, pp. 1095-1096.

[2] *Sic*; the Convention of Peace was actually signed on 24 November 1849; 27 August 1849 was the date of Queen Victoria's official patent giving Henry Southern authority to sign the "Treaty or Convention" between Britain and Argentina (printed in English, Spanish and French in *Archivo Americano* 1850, pp. 160-161). The incorrect date 27 August 1849 is also given in Burnet-Merlín 1974 and 1976, pp. 20-21, and in Cresto 2011, p. 433.

did not mention that it says three times that it restores "perfect" friendship, nor the fact that, being a peace treaty, it fixed the state of territorial possession existing in 1850, nor the fact that Argentina's protests ceased for over a third of a century after its ratification. He attempted to reduce it to absurdity by saying that it required the prior assent of the Uruguayan leader Manuel Oribe (in article VI, see fig. 7.11c above), and asking whether it could be accepted that Oribe had been granted such a role of arbitrator. Cooke also said that if the treaty's omission of a mention of rights over the Malvinas indicated a renunciation of the Malvinas, then its failure to mention rights over all Argentine rivers must indicate a renunciation of those rivers, since only the rivers Paraná and Uruguay were mentioned.

Kohen and Rodríguez repeat all that (pp. 209-210), but it is nonsense. Article VI shows that it was only Argentina, not Britain, that required Oribe's assent, and that Argentina had already obtained it before the Convention was signed, so Oribe had not acted as an arbitrator; Argentina had arranged things with him beforehand. And Cooke's example of the rivers is ridiculous – as a peace treaty, the Convention fixed the existing state of territorial possession except in stated cases: in Article IV it stated the new position with the two rivers Paraná and Uruguay (namely that they were not international but respectively Argentinian and jointly Argentinian-Uruguayan), and it left Argentina in possession of all the unmentioned rivers simply by not mentioning them. There was no renunciation of the other rivers. Thus Cooke's arguments (and their repetition by Kohen and Rodríguez) are absurd and Absalón Rojas was right in saying that the Convention of Peace damaged Argentina's case.

Later in 1950 Rojas published a 50-page booklet in Buenos Aires entitled *Rosas y las Malvinas*,[1] in which he printed much of the debate in the Chamber of Deputies in July 1950, with most of his own speech, including the passage we quoted above, with his statements that the Convention of Peace established "perfect friendship" with Britain and that it was a "general settlement of accounts". The second chapter of his book contains his proposal for an official appeal by Argentina to the International Court of Justice (ICJ) at The Hague, requesting a "prohibition of dispossession" ("interdicto de despojo") which would declare that Britain's "dispossession" of Argentina in 1833 was illegal, and his third chapter calls for an official investigation in Argentina to discover whether "the treaty of 1849" (as he calls it) demonstrated a renunciation of sovereignty over the Malvinas, or simply weakness, complacency or lack of foresight by Rosas. He mentions (his p. 38) the work by "the erudite Mexican historian" Carlos Pereyra (which we quoted above) – but he seems to think that Pereyra said there was an actual secret article in the Convention of Peace, which Pereyra did not. Rojas also mentions the speech made in 1848 by Sir William Molesworth: calling him "Malesworth", he quotes Molesworth's remarks on the Falklands, and then concludes: "Public opinion spoke with the voice of deputy Malesworth". That was untrue (see section 7.3), and of course Rojas does not mention that Molesworth omitted the Falklands from his speech in 1849 (section 7.6).

In his book Rojas complains several times about the fact that the treaty established "perfect friendship" between Britain and Argentina: he repeats his complaint on pp. 12 and 13 in quotes from his own speech (in the passage we quote above), and also on pp. 33, 36 and 38. But he does not draw the obvious conclusion, namely that that "perfect friendship" ended Argentina's title to the Falklands. Instead he says (p. 16, see quote above) that he does not believe that the omission of the Falklands damaged the "fullness of Argentine rights", which is illogical.

Rojas's aims are divorced from reality. He expects the ICJ to rule that Britain's "dispossession" of Argentina in 1833 was illegal, but he says half a dozen times, on his pp. 17, 21 and 27, and several times on p. 22, that there must be no discussion of Argentina's rights to the islands, only a simple verdict that Britain's possession is illegal and Britain must hand the islands back to Argentina "free of all occupation" – as in his speech, he actually proposes that Britain should remove the population! Not many Malvinists, even hardline ones, go that far. And it is ludicrous to expect the ICJ to rule on a question of territorial sovereignty without investigating the titles of the rival claimants.

---

[1] Absalón Rojas, *Rosas y las Malvinas*, Buenos Aires 1950; preface (p. 4) dated 15 November 1950.

Rojas's final section (pp. 47-50) contains the draft of a law calling on the presidency to order the publication of a million copies (!) of the book *Causa criminal contra el tirano Juan Manuel de Rosas* ["Criminal case against the tyrant Juan Manuel de Rosas"] by the state prosecutor Dr Emilio A. Agrelo, to be distributed free of charge. That book, published in Buenos Aires in 1867, contains details of the trial of Rosas (*in absentia*) and the sentence of death passed against him on 2 December 1861 (when he was safely in exile in Britain). The central accusations against Rosas concerned his ordering of many murders while he was in power, but an important reason for Rojas's keenness to condemn Rosas all over again was that Rojas held him responsible for the "loss" of the Falklands. Nothing whatever came of Rojas's demands or projects, but his book eloquently reveals the bizarre nature of the Argentine claim to the Falklands.

The negative effect of the Convention of Peace on Argentina's claim was also mentioned in several works by Ernesto Fitte, probably the most eminent 20th-century Argentine historian. In *La Agresión Norteamericana a las Islas Malvinas* he complains that no mention of the Malvinas was made in a navigation treaty with Britain in 1853; he says that treaty showed the same weakness as Rosas had shown in the "Arana-Southern treaty" (i.e. the Convention of Peace),[1] and in the same book, with reference to the Falklands, he admits that after 1849 "many years pass, interminable and incredibly long, and no one remembers the insult inflicted on the dignity of the republic."[2] That was true, of course – during the 34 years after the Convention of Peace (1850-84) Argentina overtly acquiesced in Britain's possession of the Falklands and did not mention the matter to the British government, thus confirming the definitive ending of any Argentine title. In an essay published in *La Prensa* in 1969 Fitte criticised General Rosas for being weak over the Falklands, and "forgetting to include their cession in the Arana-Southern Convention of 1849". The whole article was reprinted in *Crónicas del Atlántico Sur*, a collection of his essays published in 1974,[3] and he said much the same yet again in another book in 1975:[4]

... what is serious is that in 1850 he forgets to demand the cession of the Malvinas, when Great Britain is ready to repair the insults inflicted and to salute our flag with 21 guns. If he obtains that much, why did he not include the captive islands?

Actually, Rosas did make an attempt to negotiate on the Malvinas after the signing of the Convention of Peace, but Henry Southern nipped it in the bud, and Rosas did not press the point (section 7.14). The truth is that he attached no importance to the islands and gave them up as part of a comprehensive peace treaty.

Both Pereyra's book of 1919 (reprinted in Buenos Aires in 1944) and Rojas's speech in the Argentine Congress in 1950 were mentioned in a book by Alfredo Burnet-Merlín published in Buenos Aires in 1974 (twice) and 1976,[5] and he also copies the error "deputy Malesworth" from Rojas's book of 1950. Burnet-Merlín says Absalón Rojas "held Rosas accountable for the islands, imputing to him a fault of commission and a fault of omission. The fault of omission referred to the 'forgetting' of the Malvinas in the treaty of 'perfect friendship solemnised with Britain...'." Burnet-Merlín then mentions Carlos Pereyra's statement in *Rosas y Thiers* that the effect of the treaty was as if there had been an 8th "secret clause" by which Britain retained the Falklands; he (Burnet-Merlín) continues: "Equally astonishing is Rosas's determination to abandon the Malvinas islands to the British, even though Britain did not have great interest in retaining them...".[6] Those things may be astonishing to a Malvinist, but the documentation shows that for Rosas the abandonment of the Falklands was not astonishing at all; it was part of his overall calculation.

Since we wrote *Getting it right* and *False Falklands History*, another Argentine historian has

---

[1] Ernesto J. Fitte, *La Agresión Norteamericana a las Islas Malvinas* ["American Aggression against the Malvinas Islands"], Buenos Aires 1966, p. 447.
[2] Fitte 1966, p. 455.
[3] Ernesto J. Fitte, *Crónicas del Atlántico Sur...*, Buenos Aires 1974, pp. 247-256.
[4] Ernesto J. Fitte, *Crónicas de Rosas*, Buenos Aires 1975, p. 8.
[5] Alfredo R. Burnet-Merlín, *Cuando Rosas quiso ser inglés...* ["When Rosas wanted to be British..."], Buenos Aires, printed April 1974, June 1974 and October 1976.
[6] Quotes here from Burnet-Merlín 1974, pp. 20-21.

confirmed the negative effect of the Convention of Peace on Argentina's claim to the Falklands – Juan José Cresto noted with irritation in a seriously erroneous two-volume work published in 2011 (when he was President of the Argentine Academy of History) that the Convention mentioned the establishment of "perfect friendship" between Britain and Argentina, but contained no "**proviso for the restitution of the iniquitously usurped islands**".[1]

In short, given the extensive discussion in Argentina since the Second World War confirming the consequences of the Convention of Peace, it is impossible to argue today that Argentina has any title whatever to the Falkland Islands.

7.18 The Le Prédour treaties, 1850

Soon after the negotiation of the Convention of Peace with Britain, Rosas negotiated a similar treaty with the French emissary Rear Admiral Fortuné-Joseph-Hyacinthe Le Prédour (1793-1866). The treaty is known as the "Arana-Prédour treaty";[2] Kohen and Rodríguez mention it once (p. 201), though they say nothing about it except that it was similar to the "Arana-Southern treaty". There was, though, a very significant difference – it was never ratified. It was signed on 31 August 1850 by Le Prédour and Felipe Arana, but the French National Assembly failed to even discuss it after it was first moved on 28 June 1851. Both France and Argentina were changing: in France political turmoil led to Louis Napoleon's coup d'état on 2 December 1851 and his assumption of imperial power as Emperor Napoleon III in November 1852, while the fall of Rosas on 3 February 1852 drastically altered the situation around the River Plate. Le Prédour also negotiated a treaty between France and Uruguay, which was signed on 13 September 1850 but was likewise never ratified.[3] The two Le Prédour treaties were overtaken by events and never came into force. It is actually misleading to call them the "Arana-Prédour treaties" (though that is the only name used for them), since they were stillborn and never actually became valid treaties.

7.19 No Argentine protests after the Convention of Peace

After the ratification of the Convention of Peace Argentina's protests against Britain's possession of the Falkland Islands ceased. Kohen and Rodríguez mention (pp. 214-215) that there were no Messages to the Buenos Aires legislature in 1850 or 1851, and maintain that the absence of Messages was the reason why there were no protests to Britain in those two years. But that is disingenuous – Rosas could easily have ordered Argentina's ambassador in Britain, Manuel Moreno, to protest again to Britain, thus continuing the diplomatic protests (the other "prong" of the Argentine campaign), and he could have sent a simple note to be read out at the opening of the Buenos Aires legislature stating that the government had not abandoned its claim to the Malvinas. But he did neither of those things – he had given up the Falkland Islands.

Kohen and Rodríguez introduce a spurious objection to the Convention of Peace, implying that its validity is dependent on its being actually invoked by the British government – they say (p. 203): "Another element undermining this new argument of the British pamphlet is the simple fact that, over the protracted history of the dispute, the British Government never once invoked the Arana-Southern Treaty." That is irrelevant; in the first place there is no such thing as a rule in international law (or any kind of law) that says that a treaty or law has to be *mentioned* in order to remain valid, and secondly there was no occasion for the British government to mention it for many decades after 1850, since Argentina was silent and had accepted that the Falklands were British. If Argentina had, say, taken the case to the International Court of Justice at some time after 1945, the British government would no doubt have mentioned the Convention of Peace along with all the many other arguments that demonstrate that the Falkland Islands are British territory. In any case, in a court of law, the rule that prevents the introduction of new, previously unmentioned evidence only begins to apply after an actual verdict – and if significant new evidence later emerges, the case may be

---

[1] Juan José Cresto, *Historia de las Islas Malvinas...* ["History of the Malvinas Islands..."], Buenos Aires 2011, p. 433; Cresto's bold print.
[2] Text printed (in French only) in Charles Samwer, ed., *Nouveau Recueil Général de Traités, Conventions et Autres Transactions Remarquables,...* vol. XV, Gottingue [= Göttingen] 1857, pp. 50-55.
[3] Text (in French only) in Samwer 1857, pp. 55-59.

reopened; the new evidence is not automatically ruled out of court.

Another invalid argument advanced by Kohen and Rodríguez (pp. 214, 223, 225) is that Argentina, faced with the British government's insistence that the Falklands question was closed, had repeatedly stated that Argentina's silence should not be regarded as acquiescence or as acceptance of the British position – as if that "cancelled" Argentina's silence! Here again they distort the evidence: all those statements were made by Argentina during the years 1833-49, when there were regular protests; such statements were part of those protests. But Argentina said no such thing during the 38 years (1849-88) when there was silence and no protests.

It is absurd to imagine that a party to a dispute has a right to lay down what significance is to be attached to his present or future silence. The significance of silence is simply the existence of silence, not anything the silent party may say before or after his silence. It is not possible to say in effect "I'm still protesting even when I'm not protesting" – the only way to keep a claim alive is to keep protesting. It is not open to a claimant to decide how long his claims are to subsist; he cannot lay down a stock of protests for the future like laying down a case of vintage port.

7.20 Conclusion

This chapter has demonstrated that Argentina consented finally and definitively to Britain's possession of the Falkland Islands by ratifying the Convention of Peace in 1850. The attempt by Kohen and Rodríguez to devalue it, or to deny that it was a peace treaty, is refuted by the documentation. The critical date in the legal history of the Falklands is Wednesday 15 May 1850; after that date Argentina no longer claimed the Falkland Islands, and for over a third of a century gave repeated overt confirmation of its acceptance that the Falklands were *de jure* British territory, as we shall demonstrate in the next chapter.

212

CHAPTER EIGHT: the years 1850-1890

For almost 38 years after Argentina dropped its claim to the Falklands in 1850, Argentine governments made no protest against Britain's possession of the islands. For 34 years – over a third of the 19th century – Argentina did not even mention the islands to Britain; there was a brief flurry of activity from 1884 to 1888, which we call "the Affair of the Map" (sections 8.23, 8.26), but then there was silence again and Argentina performed more acts of omission and commission which cemented its acceptance that the Falklands were British. Kohen and Rodríguez give a perfunctory account of this period, but fail to show that Argentina maintained any claim to the islands.

8.1 The fall of the Rosas dictatorship, 1852; Argentina breaks apart

In 1850-51 the intricate politics of the River Plate region led to war. The Argentine leader General Juan Manuel de Rosas claimed Uruguay and Paraguay, but they did not wish to become mere provinces of Argentina. Paraguay had made an alliance with Brazil on 24 December 1850, and on 29 May 1851 Brazil, Uruguay and the nominally Argentine province of Entre Ríos joined forces against the province of Buenos Aires, and were joined by Paraguay and the nominally Argentine province of Corrientes. Rosas declared war on Brazil on 18 August 1851, and for several months yet another war raged around the River Plate.[1]

Rosas's regime collapsed after his crushing defeat on 3 February 1852 at the battle of Caseros, and he himself took refuge in Buenos Aires in the house of Captain Robert Gore, the British chargé d'affaires. On 10 February Gore arranged for Rosas, his family and a few others to board the steamship HMS *Conflict*, which took them to Britain at the expense of the British government. Rosas received a semi-official welcome at Plymouth on 26 August 1852, and retired to a house near Southampton and later to a modest cottage and smallholding, where he died on 14 March 1877.[2]

After the fall of Rosas – perhaps the only man who could have held the country together – Argentina broke apart. In June 1852 a proposed new constitution for the whole country was rejected by the province of Buenos Aires. By May 1853 the other 13 provinces had ratified it, and Argentina split into two independent countries. The 13 provinces retained the former official name, the Argentine Confederation, and transferred the federal capital to Paraná, while the Province of Buenos Aires adopted a new provincial constitution in 1854 and declared itself a sovereign republic, "El Estado de Buenos Aires" ["The State of Buenos Aires"].[3] The split lasted for nine years until 1862, when Argentina became united again (section 8.6).

> It may be assumed that the seigniority of the Falkland Islands has been definitively forfeited; but that is no reason why greater extension should be given to the dissolvent principle.

8.1a The seigniority of the Falkland Islands has been definitively forfeited:[4]
BPAN, Buenos Aires 26 November 1853, editorial, p. 2, col. 2.

During those nine years neither of the two Argentine states said or did anything relevant to the Falkland Islands, and the *BPAN* concluded in an editorial in November 1853 that the Falklands had been "definitively forfeited" (fig. 8.1a). The *BPAN* wrote in English, but from an Argentine, not a British, point of view – for example "our government" always meant the Argentine government, not the British government. Thus its editorial said Argentina had forfeited the Falkland Islands.

Kohen and Rodríguez twice say (pp. 214 and 215) that the province of Buenos Aires was an

---

[1] Lynch 1981, pp. 139-155.
[2] Details from Lynch 2001, pp. 156-163. In September 1989, at the request of the new Argentine president, Carlos Saúl Menem, Rosas's remains were taken from Britain to Argentina, where they were reburied in the Recoleta cemetery (Antonius C. G. M. Robben, *Death, mourning and burial: a cross-cultural reader*, Oxford 2004, p. 135).
[3] For the foreign policy of the two Argentine states in this period see Andrés Cisneros and Carlos Escudé (eds.), *Historia General de las Relaciones Exteriores de la República Argentina*, Part I, vol. V: *1852-1860: Dos Estados Argentinos, Dos Políticas Exteriores*, Buenos Aires 1998, and Nicolas Shumway, *The Invention of Argentina*, Berkeley 1991, pp. 173-175.
[4] "**seigniority, seignority**, obs[olete]: Lordship, governance" (*OED*); the *OED*'s most recent quote is from 1598 (!).

independent state separate from the rest of the Confederation, as if that were a reason for the lack of protests against Britain's possession of the Falklands. It is in fact no reason at all – from the 1820s to 1853, Buenos Aires province was "charged" with the foreign policy of the entire Argentine Confederation, including its claim to the Falklands, and had protested to Britain on behalf of the Confederation, so there was no reason why it should not have continued to pursue the claim to the islands when it was acting alone. But it did not do so.

The two authors criticise us (pp. 215-216) for saying in *Getting it right* (p. 31) that the new Argentine constitution of 1853 apportioned seats in Congress on a territorial basis but without any mention of the Falklands, and they quote (p. 216) a passage from the separate constitution of the State of Buenos Aires, adopted on 8 April 1854, which (in their English translation) states that the territory of the republic:

… extends from North to South from the Medio stream to the entrance of the mountains into the sea, along a West to South-west line, and to the West with the flanks of the mountain range and to the North East and East by the Rivers Parana and Plata and the Atlantic, including Martin Garcia Island and the islands adjacent to its river and sea coasts.

They say that it includes the Malvinas, but we beg to differ – the text says that the boundaries of the republic are to the west the mountain range, to the north-east the rivers Paraná and Plate, and to the east the Atlantic. As regards "islands adjacent to its river and sea coasts", there are some small islands off the coast of the province of Buenos Aires, south of the town of Bahía Blanca, and a few tiny islands in the River Plate, but the Falklands cannot be said to be adjacent (they are 1,000 kilometres away from the coast of the province). At that time it was not clear whether the Argentine Confederation or the independent State of Buenos Aires claimed Patagonia (there was no agreement between them on that question, and neither of them had any presence there anyway), and in any case the Patagonian coast is some 500 kilometres from the Falklands. So the 1854 constitution of the State of Buenos Aires did not include the Falkland Islands. That can be shown by an examination of the debates on the drafting of that constitution, which we will now consider.

8.2 The Falklands not mentioned in debates on drafting the 1854 Buenos Aires constitution

The Falklands were not mentioned once during the debates on the drafting of the 1854 Buenos Aires constitution. It was debated by a special congress in March and April 1854, and the speeches made during the debates were printed *verbatim* in the separate Buenos Aires *Diario de Sesiones*, a copy of which is in the provincial archives in La Plata.[1] Martín García island was mentioned, and various matters were mentioned that did not appear in the final text adopted on 8 April 1854, but no speaker mentioned the Malvinas.

Some of those present had been closely connected with Argentina's earlier campaigns of protests against Britain's possession of the Falklands. Two members of that congress were Nicolás de Anchorena and Tomás Severino de Anchorena, respectively the brother and the son of Tomás Manuel de Anchorena, Rosas's foreign minister in 1832, who had dealt with the *Lexington* raid (section 6.12) and had died in 1847. Two other important members were Valentín Alsina and Bartolomé Mitre: Alsina wrote much of Vernet's "Report" of 1832 (see section 4.7), and was governor of what became the independent State of Buenos Aires, 31 October to 7 December 1852 and 21 December 1858 to 23 October 1859; Mitre later played a central role in the reuniting of Argentina, and was president of the whole of Argentina from 1862 to 1868. Alsina and Mitre both spoke in the debates, but neither of them, nor anyone else, mentioned the Falklands at all, though several speakers raised territorial issues: Tomás de Anchorena mentioned the loss of Tarija (a region on Argentina's border with Bolivia), and the loss of both Atacama (to Chile) and Misiones (to Brazil), and he also mentioned the loss of much of Chaco, and the division of Cuyo between Chile and Argentina, while three other representatives mentioned the claim by the province of

---

[1] *Diario de Sesiones de la Sala de Representantes de la Provincia de Buenos Aires 1854*, printed Buenos Aires 1865, held e.g. in the provincial archives in La Plata (the capital of the province of Buenos Aires); the debates from 7 March to 8 April 1854, preceding the adoption of the constitution, are printed on pp. 37-114, the text of the constitution on pp. 114-119; the territorial limits of the republic (as in Kohen and Rodríguez, see section 8.1) are on p. 114.

Mendoza to part of what Buenos Aires considered its own territory. Tomás de Anchorena even discussed whether continuous occupation was necessary to establish possession, and said "Britain occupies a vast amount of territory: but does it do so continuously? No, Gentlemen" ("Inglaterra ocupa una vasta extensión de territorio: pero ¿La ocupa continuamente? No Señores"). But even when Britain and its occupation of territory were mentioned, there was no mention of the Falklands.

In short, the 1854 constitution of the independent State of Buenos Aires did not include a claim to the Falklands. They are not mentioned in the constitution itself, and were not mentioned once by any speaker at the convention that drafted that constitution. That is very strong evidence that Argentina had abandoned its claim to the islands in the Convention of Peace. The assertions of Kohen and Rodríguez are incorrect.

8.3 The *Germantown* incident, 1854

Kohen and Rodríguez then mention the "*Germantown* incident" of 1854, but fail to draw the relevant conclusions. What happened was that in Stanley on 9 January 1854 six deserters from the US whaler *Hudson* laid information before Governor George Rennie against their captain, Hiram Clift, stating that the *Hudson* and her tender *Washington* (Captain William Eldridge) were at New Island killing pigs and geese. Rennie wished (like Louis Vernet) to reserve the resources of the islands, and wrote to Rear Admiral William Henderson, commander-in-chief on the Royal Navy's South American station, asking for help in preventing "poaching" by the *Hudson* and the *Washington*. Henderson sent Commander Henry Boys in the 6-gun brig HMS *Express* to the Falklands to take action.[1]

At the same time, William Smyley, who since 1850 had been the United States commercial agent in Stanley, wrote to US Secretary of State (i.e. foreign minister) William Marcy and to Commodore W. D. Salter, in command of the United States Brazil station, asking for a US warship to be sent to Stanley to protect US interests.[2] Salter sent the 22-gun sloop USS *Germantown* to the islands under Captain William Francis Lynch. In Stanley on 20 February Colonial Secretary James Longden issued an arrest warrant for captains Clift and Eldridge, and Boys left Stanley in the *Express* to arrest them. The *Germantown* reached Stanley late on 2 March 1854 – and at dawn the next day HMS *Express* brought the *Hudson* and the *Washington* into Stanley harbour under arrest.

Lynch and Smyley hurried to protest to Rennie, but Rennie declared that the Americans had committed depredations and handed Lynch a copy of Secretary of State Marcy's note to US vessels warning them that they might suffer the prescribed penalties. Lynch was surprised, and commented in his letter to Commodore Salter that before he saw the note he had decided to seize Rennie as a pirate and take him to face judgement, but in the face of the compliant attitude of the US authorities, he had decided to desist. On 7 March Captain Clift was fined £27 16s. for killing 22 pigs.

Lynch sent Rennie a letter of protest saying the United States raised no claim "to these inhospitable rocks & bogs", and as to British sovereignty over the islands, he was not authorised "either to admit it or deny it".[3] The American ships left again, and on 14 June 1854 Captains Clift and Eldridge drew up a claim for damages, for no less than $39,000, but it was not presented until May 1866 after the American Civil War, and was then included among the many claims by the US against Britain known as the "*Alabama* claims", which Britain paid in 1872.[4]

Secretary of State William Marcy put the United States viewpoint to the British ambassador on

---

[1] Our account is based on John Bassett Moore, *A Digest of International Law*, Washington DC 1906, vol. I, pp. 888-890; Boyson 1924, pp. 125-135; William Smyley's letters; and the entries in *DFB* on Boys and Lynch.

[2] Stated in later letter by Smyley to US Secretary of State Marcy, 4 June 1854, US National Archives, Washington DC, *Despatches from United States Consuls in Port Stanley, Falkland Islands, 1851-1906*, microfilm T480 1.43.

[3] Lynch's letter of 7 March 1854, quoted in entry on Lynch by John B. Hattendorf in *DFB*; Violet Boyson quotes it with a few differences (1924, pp. 129, 133, 135).

[4] Boyson 1924, pp. 133, 135. During the Civil War between the United States and the secessionist Confederate States of America, 1861-5, Britain had been neutral, but had failed to prevent losses being caused to the United States, including the sinking of US ships by the CSS *Alabama*, a Confederate raider built in Britain. After the war the US government claimed damages from Britain for this and other losses, all being subsumed under the name "*Alabama* claims". After international arbitration Britain paid the United States compensation of $15.5 million. Both sides accepted that the agreement settled all US claims on Britain, so the claims arising out of the *Germantown* affair disappeared.

1 July 1854: he pointed out that the US government:[1]

... while it claimed no rights for the United States, it conceded none to Great Britain or any other power... A still graver matter of complaint is the pretension set up by these authorities to exclude our citizens from fishing and taking whale in the waters about these islands.

Thereupon the British Foreign Secretary, the Earl of Clarendon, disavowed the seizure of the American ships and admitted that Rennie had exceeded his authority, but also expressed surprise that Marcy should question British rights in the islands.[2] And that was the end of the matter.

Kohen and Rodríguez (p. 217) quote a letter from Lynch to Rennie of 7 March 1854, in which Lynch says the US chargé d'affaires in Buenos Aires had told him that Argentina had not renounced, and never would renounce, its claim to the islands. That shows only what an American diplomat thought, not what the true position was – private views are irrelevant to questions of international law. What counted was the official US position as stated by Secretary of State William Marcy, that the United States claimed no rights in the Falklands and also "conceded none to Great Britain or any other power".

The significance of the *Germantown* incident is, first, that in 1854 (and for some 20 years afterwards) the United States did not recognise the rights of Britain in the Falklands nor of any other country including Argentina, and secondly that Britain, unlike Argentina in 1832, disavowed the action of its representative in the islands and apologised to the United States for the seizure of US ships. But by 1874 the United States came to accept Britain's possession of the Falklands as legitimate (section 8.15).

8.4 Non-evidence of Argentina's lack of acquiescence

Kohen and Rodríguez then mention (p. 218) a treaty between Argentina and Chile signed in 1856, in which both agreed to accept the *uti possidetis* of 1810 as the basis of their territorial possessions. It is difficult to see the relevance of this – in the first place, in 1856 there was no country called "Argentina", but two separate and mutually hostile countries, the Argentine Confederation and the State of Buenos Aires; any treaty signed by one did not bind the other. And secondly, neither this treaty nor the one of 1881 ended the border disputes between Argentina and Chile – on two later occasions the two countries even accepted arbitration by Britain on the question, in 1899-1902 and in 1964-6 (sections 9.1, 10.22).

On their p. 218 Kohen and Rodríguez refer to Welsh immigration to Patagonia in the 1860s, which resulted in a Welsh colony in Chubut province. They say this demonstrates that Argentina "did not remain silent" on the Malvinas question – but all they say is that Argentina asked the British ambassador in Buenos Aires, Sir Edward Thornton, if Britain was prepared to cede the Malvinas to Argentina, in which case there would be no objection to a Welsh population settling in Patagonia. To ask Britain to cede the islands naturally implies that Argentina regarded Britain as having title to them – to cede a territory necessarily entails possessing it legally in the first place. That request was therefore yet another indication that Argentina accepted that the islands were *de jure* British territory. Thornton merely replied that he had nothing to add to what Woodbine Parish had said in 1829, or to what the British government said in 1833. The Welsh immigrants settled, and Argentina did nothing; the link to the Malvinas was clearly irrelevant anyway.

Kohen and Rodríguez then imply that Argentina attempted to obtain compensation from the United States for the *Lexington* raid (for which see section 6.12), but that is untrue – no such attempt was ever made. They head section (e) on their p. 219 "Protests before the United States for the Lexington Incident", but in fact there was no protest whatever, and the US government was not even approached. What happened was that in 1866 the Argentine ambassador in Washington, Domingo Sarmiento (later president of Argentina), in response to a request from the Cilley family (relatives of Louis Vernet), asked the Argentine government for authority to request the payment of "millions of pesos" from the United States to the Vernet family for, among other things, the loss of

---
[1] Quoted in Moore 1906, vol. I, pp. 888-889.
[2] Brief extract from the Earl of Clarendon's letter to Washington dated 21 September 1854 given in Moore 1906, vol. I, p. 889; longer extract in Boyson 1924, p. 134.

the Malvinas as a result of the *Lexington* raid.[1] The two authors omit to mention that the Argentine government never even gave Sarmiento the authority to make the request, so nothing came of this.

They are also perhaps unaware of a rather different comment on the question of the Malvinas which Sarmiento made earlier: while in exile in Chile, he wrote in the Chilean periodical *El Progreso* on 28 November 1842, probably in response to reports that Britain had appointed a governor in the Falklands: "England is becoming established in the Malvinas. Let us be frank: this invasion is useful for civilisation and for progress."[2] And later, as president, Sarmiento made comments in his formal Message at the opening of the Argentine Congress that show he was not maintaining Argentina's claim to the Falklands, or the dispute with Britain (section 8.18).

In short, the arguments presented by Kohen and Rodríguez are so weak that they hardly count as evidence. Their attempt to show that Argentina did not acquiesce in Britain's possession of the Falklands fails completely.

8.5 The Falklands not mentioned in debates on drafting the Argentine constitution, 1860

The separation of Argentina into two states ended when they went to war with each other. The State of Buenos Aires under Bartolomé Mitre was defeated by the Argentine Confederation in the Battle of Cepeda on 23 October 1859, and preparations were made for Buenos Aires to rejoin the Confederation. A convention was set up to examine the 1853 constitution; some 70 representatives were elected in Buenos Aires, and the convention met several times during the first five months of 1860 (5 January to 12 May). Its debates were published *verbatim* in a special *Diario de Sesiones*,[3] containing some 500 pages of *verbatim* records of debates and constitutional documents including the constitution of the Argentine Confederation and the Peace Agreement ("Convenio de Paz", also known as the "Pacto de San José de Flores")[4] concluded between the Confederation and the State of Buenos Aires on 11 November 1859, which was intended to formalise the accession of Buenos Aires to the Confederation but was followed by further fighting and a different result.

As in the constitutional convention of 1854 (section 8.2), several distinguished Argentine politicians took part in the 1860 convention including the future presidents Bartolomé Mitre and Domingo Sarmiento, the future foreign minister Rufino Jacinto de Elizalde (1822-1887), the lawyer Dalmacio Vélez Sarsfield (1800-1875), who drew up the Argentine Civil Code (which came into force on 1 January 1871 and with amendments is still in force), Valentín Alsina and Tomás de Anchorena, all of whom were fully familiar with the former dispute with Britain over the Falklands, and all of whom spoke in the debates, along with many less well-known figures.

But in all that documentation of a vital phase in the development of Argentina, there is not a single mention of the Falkland Islands – the word "Malvinas" does not occur once. That is not because no islands or geographical places were mentioned: Martín García island is mentioned on pages 100 and 246, as were several places in Argentina, e.g. Bahía Blanca and Patagones on p. 246. Several speakers referred to lost territory – Elizalde referred on p. 229 to various territories the province of Buenos Aires had lost, including Uruguay, Entre Ríos and Corrientes, and said the province had protested against its losses in what he calls the "Convención de paz" (i.e. the "Convenio de Paz" of 11 November 1859 between Buenos Aires and the Confederation, not the 1850 Convention of Peace with Britain). Britain is mentioned several times, e.g. on p. 247 by

---

[1] The documentation on this non-event is contained in AGN VII, 131, e.g. doc. 131, a contract dated 21 August 1866 between Louis Vernet and Jonathan Cilley, in which Cilley undertook to apply his professional knowledge to assist Sarmiento in obtaining compensation for Vernet, in exchange for 1 per cent of all money obtained from the US.

[2] Article in *El Progreso*, Valparaíso, 28 November 1842: "La Inglaterra se estaciona en las Malvinas. Seamos francos: esta invasión es útil a la civilización y al progreso."

[3] Title on cover: *Diario de Sesiones de la Convencion del Estado de Buenos Aires Acompañado de El Redactor y el Informe de la Comision. Constitucion Federal con las enmiendas y los convenios de 11 de Noviembre de 1859 y 6 de Junio de 1860*, Buenos Aires 1860; title on title page: *Diario de Sesiones de la Convencion del Estado de Buenos Aires encargada del Examen de la Constitucion Federal*, Buenos Aires 1860.

[4] This agreement between the Argentine Confederation and the State of Buenos Aires is entitled "Convenio de Paz" ["Peace Agreement"], not "Convención de Paz" ["Convention of Peace"], though the difference is presumably not significant. Like the Convention of Peace with Britain, it ended all previous disputes between the two parties and "reset" their relations on a new basis (in this case by reunifying Argentina, though it failed to bring this about).

Elizalde, p. 254 by Vélez Sarsfield; pp. 262-3 by Sarmiento (on taxation), and p. 270 by Elizalde again, and in the first annexe on p. 11 (British law including Magna Carta, the Bill of Rights and *habeas corpus*), p. 52 (British law) and p. 56 (Britain's protection of slaves who had mutinied). But despite all those mentions of Britain and of territory, including lost territory, the Falklands were not mentioned once – they were clearly not Argentine territory.

The constitutional convention and the Convenio de Paz failed to resolve the differences between the Argentine Confederation and Buenos Aires; fighting continued, and Buenos Aires (still under Mitre) won the decisive Battle of Pavón on 17 September 1861. Mitre thereupon imposed his will on the other provinces and reunited Argentina. On 12 October 1862 a newly elected national congress confirmed Mitre as president of the whole of Argentina (the 14 provinces of which the country thereafter consisted, without the Falklands and as yet without Patagonia). The province of Buenos Aires was no longer "charged" with foreign policy; there was a central government for the whole country, and there was a national congress above the legislatures of the individual provinces.[1]

8.6 Argentina becomes reunited, but does not resume protesting

It might have been expected that once Argentina was reunited, protests against Britain's possession of the Falkland Islands would resume after a gap of only 13 years between 1849 and 1862. If the Falklands had been important to Argentina, there would have been several ways of reopening the dispute. The 1850 Convention of Peace could have been repudiated – the new Argentine government could have declared that it did not regard itself as being bound to respect the previous regime's undertakings. It could then have maintained that the dropping of the claim to the Falklands had not had time to become effective, and could have resumed protests to Britain and in the Messages to the legislature. Or the new government could have announced a reservation to the Convention, stating that it desired friendship with Britain but that this did not compromise the claim to the Falklands. Or it might simply have attempted to apply a narrow interpretation of Article VII – the return of relations to their "former state of good understanding and cordiality" could have been taken to mean "including the former claim to the Falklands", and protests could have been resumed.

But no such thing happened. Argentina made no repudiation or limitation of the Convention of Peace either then or later, and for another quarter of a century did not protest against Britain's possession of the Falklands. The changed behaviour of Argentine governments after the ratification of the Convention of Peace precludes any idea that they were applying a narrow interpretation of its Article VII. For over a third of the 19th century from 1850 onwards, all Argentine governments acquiesced in Britain's possession of the Falklands, and their acquiescence was not merely silent; it was overtly confirmed in official statements by Argentine leaders (section 8.18). Argentina's behaviour is of probative value in confirming that the Convention of Peace had ended all Argentine title to the Falkland Islands.

8.7 Argentina's acquiescence in Britain's possession of the Falklands

On their pages 214-229 Kohen and Rodríguez attempt to show that Argentina did not acquiesce in Britain's possession of the Falklands between 1850 and 1884. Their attempt fails, as can easily be demonstrated – the examples we gave in *Getting it right* (pp. 25-26; see section 8.18), showed that Argentina did overtly acquiesce in Britain's possession of the islands.

There are two kinds of acquiescence, "silent" and "overt" (section 6.29). Silent acquiescence is summed up in the Latin saying *Qui tacet consentire videtur, si loqui debuisset ac potuisset* (or ... *ubi loqui debuit ac potuit*) ["He who is silent is seen to consent, if he should have spoken and could have done"], often summarised as "Silence gives consent". Since silent acquiescence involves doing nothing, it does not become apparent until there has been a lack of activity over a considerable length of time; what indicates acquiescence is not the passage of time *per se*, but the actions of a country during that time – namely none. Overt acquiescence, by contrast, does not require the passage of any length of time and can be indicated by appropriate actions at any time. Argentina indicated overt acquiescence by a number of actions in the 19th and 20th centuries, the first of

---
[1] Shumway 1991, pp. 223-228.

which was the ratification of the Convention of Peace with Britain in 1850 (section 7.11).

Till 1849 Argentina kept up its claim to the Falklands by regular protests, which are essential to keep a claim alive. Valid international protests can only be made by one government to another government – they have to be made *by and to* official representatives of the two governments such as ambassadors or government ministers. It is immaterial whether a grievance has been aired in private, in the press, in ordinary debates in a legislature, etc. – the government of a country is the guardian of that country's territorial affairs, and only the actions of official representatives of a government have any bearing on the status of its territorial relations with other countries. As John O'Brien points out, protests have to be "sustained and made in the appropriate form".[1] That requirement was fulfilled by Argentina's protests from 1833 to 1849, but it is not fulfilled by the arguments Kohen and Rodríguez present to support their case. Some of their main arguments concern the concept of prescription, the role of protests and the nature of acquiescence.

8.8 Acquisitive prescription; protests

Protests are an essential element in "prescription" (in full "acquisitive prescription"), a principle in the private law of most countries under which claims to property lapse after a certain length of time unless the claimant does something to maintain them (see also section 8.11).

Prescription and protests are two sides of the same coin – if a claimant protests and claims a given property, there can be no prescription, but failure by the claimant to protest will in the end indicate "acquiescence" (acceptance of a given situation) and prescription will operate. Rightful title to the property then passes to the current possessor, who had until then held it by "adverse possession" (possession contrary to the claims of the previous possessor). In national law the necessary length of time for prescription varies according to the nature of the property or rights claimed; the maximum is often 30 years, usually in the form of a "blanket" term of 30 years which covers all claims not explicitly subject to shorter terms. Thus the Argentine Civil Code, drawn up between 1864 and 1869 by Dr Dalmacio Vélez Sarsfield (1800-1875), which (with amendments) has since 1871 formed the basis of Argentine civil law, states:[2]

Art. 4.016. Against him who has possessed for thirty years, without any interruption, neither the lack nor the nullity of title, nor bad faith in possession may be adduced.

In other words, a possessor of property who has held that property uninterruptedly for thirty years cannot be challenged by accusations of bad faith or by contentions that he holds no title at all to that property, or that his title is invalid.

But there is an important difference between international law and national law: international law has no fixed "blanket" time-limit for prescription to operate since the lifespan of countries and nations is in principle indefinite, and every case must be considered on its merits. The extinction of a state is rare, though not unknown – for example, Prussia was abolished on 25 February 1947 by Decree no. 46 of the Allied Control Council administering Germany.

As a result of that important difference, there is some doubt as to whether acquisitive prescription can operate at all in international law. Marcelo Kohen's definition is revealing:[3]

Acquisitive prescription would be a title leading to the acquisition of territorial sovereignty having a previous holder [*sic*], through the possession of a territory *à titre de souverain* over a prolonged lapse of time.

His use of "would be" is significant – the usefulness, indeed the existence, of acquisitive prescription in international law is subject to considerable doubt.

Kohen and Rodríguez state (p. 227) that "The simple passing of time in itself does not produce a change in a territorial situation", and quote Hugo Grotius saying that "time has no productive virtue,

---

[1] John O'Brien, *International Law*, London 2001, p. 211.
[2] Details from the text and commentary on the Code in *Código Civil de la República Argentina: Estudio preliminar del Dr. José Maria Mustapich*, Madrid 1960 (introduction dated Buenos Aires, July 1958); quote from pp. 815-816.
[3] Marcelo Kohen, in Marcelo G. Kohen and Mamadou Hébié (eds.), *Research Handbook on Territorial Disputes in International Law*, Cheltenham (UK) and Northampton (USA), 2018, p. 154; italics in original.

nothing is done through time, but rather everything happens in time".[1] What is important is what happens (or does not happen) as time passes – as Professor Giovanni Distefano says:[2]

... time neither creates nor extinguishes territorial titles. States' relevant acts *over time* may lead, either by treaty or by other means (conduct) to this result.

In the case of the Falklands, Argentina's "relevant acts" included ratifying a treaty (the 1850 Convention of Peace), failing to protest and making top-level comments indicating the absence of a dispute with Britain, all of which extinguished Argentina's territorial title.

Kohen and Rodríguez assert on their p. 226 that Argentina's silence for "34 years" without protesting was not enough for prescription to operate (it was actually over 38 years, from December 1849 to January 1888, see sections 7.15, 8.26), and they point out that it was less than the "54 years" of Britain's silence (on p. 223 they say "55 years", i.e. 1774-1829), which the British government asserted did not put an end to its claim to sovereignty in the Falklands. It is difficult to see how that serves their case – all jurists are agreed that in international law there is no precise, universal moment at which prescription "kicks in", so for Argentina's inaction for 38 years to be irrelevant to prescription, but Britain's inaction for 55 years to be relevant, would require a "cut-off point" for prescription lying exactly in the 17 years between 38 and 55 years. No jurist believes for an instant that there exists such an exact "cut-off point" (see sections 8.11, 8.24).

And that is precisely the objection to the concept of acquisitive prescription in international law. Its virtues in national law are that it has a cut-off point and that a court can easily establish that the deadline has passed and award title to a claimant. Both those features are inoperative in international law – as Marcelo Kohen says:[3]

The difficulty of this doctrine is that it tends to transpose into international law a domestic legal institution which, in order to be implemented, needs not only a fixed deadline but also the authority of a judge to declare the transfer of title from its legitimate owner to the possessor...

But that does not mean that in international law all titles are eternal; it simply means that in the absence of acquisitive prescription other factors come into play and (given appropriate circumstances) produce the transfer of title from one party to the other. Those factors include treaties and acquiescence, which transferred Argentina's title to Britain, and acts of jurisdiction (« effectivités »), and self-determination, which confirm Britain's title to the Falklands.

8.9 Court cases, I: the Beagle Channel case, 1977

Two court cases throw some light on the significance of the length of a country's silence in a territorial dispute. The first concerns the Beagle Channel case (for which see also section 8.22), in which Argentina disputed Chile's possession of Picton, Nueva and Lennox Islands ("the PNL islands" or "PNL group"), three tiny islands off the southern tip of South America (see fig. 8.22f).[4] The border between Argentina and Chile had been broadly settled in 1881 by a treaty between the two countries, and their border along the cordillera of the Andes had been laid down by the British arbitration in 1902 (section 9.1), but the question of sovereignty in other areas had not been resolved. Britain arbitrated in another border dispute between the two countries in 1964-6, and again laid down the extent of Argentine and Chilean territory (section 10.22), but the border in the

---

[1] Kohen and Rodríguez 2015, note 64 p. 227, quoting a Spanish translation of a French translation of Grotius, *Le droit de la guerre et de la paix* [1625], book II, ch. IV, I, p. 210, París 1999.
[2] Giovanni Distefano in Kohen and Hébié (eds.) 2018, p. 416; italics in original.
[3] Marcelo Kohen, in Kohen and Hébié (eds.) 2018, p. 155 ("domestic " = national).
[4] Report on the 1971-7 arbitration in "Beagle Channel Arbitration between the Republic of Argentina and the Republic of Chile" in *International Law Reports* (*ILR*) vol. 52, Cambridge 1979 (henceforth "*ILR* 1979"); extensive account in Juan K. Kobylanski, *El Conflicto del Beagle y la Mediación Papal*, Montevideo September 1987; briefer account from 1881 to 1984 in Mark Laudy, "The Vatican Mediation of the Beagle Channel Dispute: Crisis Intervention and Forum Building", chapter 11 of *Words over War: Mediation and Arbitration to Prevent Deadly Conflict*, New York 2000, also available online; detailed account up to 1980 in Karl Hernekamp, *Der argentinisch-chilenische Grenzstreit am Beagle-Kanal* ["The Argentine-Chilean border dispute on the Beagle Channel"], Hamburg 1980 (text in German with many documents in full in English and Spanish).

Beagle Channel remained unclear. Argentina and Chile signed an agreement in London on 22 July 1971 providing for Britain to act again as Permanent Arbitrator and to convene a Court of Arbitration to decide the issue. This time Britain did not arbitrate directly (as it had done in 1899-1902 and 1964-6), but only set up the arrangements, and the case was heard in 1977 before five judges from the International Court of Justice (ICJ), who sat in Geneva; their judgement was to be submitted to the British Crown, which could accept or reject it but not modify it. Both Argentina and Chile accepted the choice of judges and agreed to respect the result.

Chile asserted before the 1977 Court of Arbitration that Argentina had acquiesced in Chile's sovereignty over the PNL islands, since after the 1881 border treaty Chile performed acts of jurisdiction in the islands which Argentina did not object to until 1915 – Chile stated:[1]

In these circumstances the Argentine failure to protest for 34 years after the conclusion of the Treaty constituted an adoption or recognition of the allocation effected by its provision.

Chile stated that "the open, persistent and undisturbed exercise of sovereignty by Chile over the islands, coupled with knowledge by Argentina and the latter's silence"[2] demonstrated Argentina's acquiescence in the possession of the PNL islands by Chile. Each side submitted maps in support of its claim; the maps submitted by Chile included an official Argentine map, the "1882 Latzina map", and Chile claimed that since it marked the PNL islands in the same colour as areas outside Argentina, it demonstrated Argentina's acceptance that the islands belonged to Chile (section 8.22).

The Court agreed with Chile's interpretation of the 1882 Latzina map, and of Argentina's failure to protest at Chile's acts of jurisdiction, and stated that "the silence of Argentina permits the inference that the acts tended to confirm an interpretation of the meaning of the Treaty independent of the acts of jurisdiction themselves."[3] The final paragraph of the Court's account runs:[4]

The Court therefore, after a review of certain of the principal aspects of the matter, holds that, as with the cartography of the case, evidence of the acts of jurisdiction performed by Chile is admissible and tends to confirm and corroborate the conclusions the Court has reached, affirming her title to the PNL group.

The arguments Chile presented against Argentina's claim to the PNL islands could be used in exactly the same way to deny Argentina's claim to the Falklands. Naturally there are differences between the 1881 boundary treaty between Argentina and Chile and the 1850 Convention of Peace between Argentina and Britain, but the similarities are also striking: neither mentioned the islands which were later at issue, and after the treaties were ratified Argentina failed to protest for a long time (34 years and 38 years respectively) at acts of jurisdiction by the other party in the islands.

Acts of jurisdiction (often known in international law by the French term « effectivités ») are commonly accepted by jurists working in international law as confirming the possession of a title; Marcelo Kohen quotes the statement by arbitrator Max Huber in the well-known Island of Palmas case: "the continuous and peaceful display of territorial sovereignty is as good as a title". That, however, has to be placed in context – the role of « effectivités » varies according to the nature of the title over a territory. Where there is a clear title, « effectivités » play only a supporting role in confirming the existence of that title, but where there is no title, or a disputed or unclear one, « effectivités » come into their own and may play a decisive role in establishing a definitive title. Marcelo Kohen lists the kind of acts that may play such a role, as evaluated by the International Court of Justice in the *Nicaragua/Colombia* case in 2012:[5]

Public administration and legislation, regulation of economic activities, public works, law enforcement measures, naval visits and search and rescue operations, recognition of consular representations as applying to the islands, regulation of fishing activities and maintenance of lighthouses and buoys.

---

[1] Chilean submission in *ILR* 1979, p. 222; "the Treaty" was the 1881 border treaty.
[2] Chilean submission in *ILR* 1979, p. 223.
[3] Court's summary in *ILR* 1979, p. 224; i.e. Chile's acts of jurisdiction showed that Chile regarded the islands as Chilean, but Argentina's failure to protest at those acts implied that Argentina regarded the Treaty as implying so too.
[4] *ILR* 1979, p. 226.
[5] Quotes in this paragraph from Marcelo Kohen, in Kohen and Hébié (eds.) 2018, pp. 147, 161.

Britain held a definitive and exclusive title to the Falklands from 1850, and since then has performed all those acts innumerable times in the islands – Britain has performed immeasurably more « effectivités » in the Falklands than did Chile in the PNL islands. Britain's display of territorial sovereignty was always "continuous", as Max Huber's statement requires, and for long periods it was "peaceful" too, since it was undisturbed and uncontested by any protest by Argentina.

Argentina's failure to protest for 38 years (1849-88) against Britain's acts can thus be taken as part of the effect of the Convention of Peace – it shows that Argentina regarded the Convention as having decided the Falklands question. And significantly, the Court in 1977 awarded the PNL islands to Chile; Argentina repudiated the result (despite having agreed to accept it) and nearly went to war with Chile over the question in 1978, but in 1985 finally accepted the verdict, and the islands are now indisputably Chilean territory. Argentina's failure to protest for 34 years against Chile's acts was an important factor in that. See also section 8.20.

8.10 Court cases, II: the *Libya/Chad* case at the International Court of Justice, 1994

Another relevant court case is the *Territorial Dispute (Libyan Arab Jamahiriya/Chad)* case, heard before the International Court of Justice (ICJ) in 1994.[1] The case concerned part of the southern Sahara called the "BET region" after its constituent parts Borkou-Ounianga, Ennedi and Tibesti, which were disputed between Libya and Chad. On 3 February 1994 the ICJ awarded it to Chad by a vote of 16 to 1 (the dissenter being the Libyan judge); Libya accepted the decision and withdrew its troops, and the region is now part of the Republic of Chad.

An important factor in the Court's decision was Libya's failure to protest for 11 years against Chad's possession of the BET region after the Treaty of Friendship and Good Neighbourliness signed on 10 August 1955[2] between Libya and France (which ruled Chad till 1960). In his written opinion delivered as part of the judgement, Judge Ajibola of Nigeria makes it clear that Libya could have protested at the 1955 treaty, but failed to do so:[3]

111. There were many occasions… when Libya could have protested to Chad or even France (between 1955 and 1960) that the Treaty was invalid or had failed to create the expected boundary, yet Libya was silent. Since 1955, Libya had many opportunities to protest against this frontier but it did nothing. Instead it signed another Treaty with Chad in 1966 without making mention of any defect or presenting a case of nullity or even raising any objection whatsoever against the 1955 Treaty…

The absence of a protest by Libya for 11 years from 1955 to 1966 was taken by the Court as acquiescence by Libya in the boundary line claimed by Chad. So a period of silence as short as 11 years may be enough to indicate acquiescence.

On occasion an even shorter time has been considered to establish a *status quo*, as Pierre Klein and Vaios Koutroulis state in their chapter on the use of force in territorial disputes, in the *Research Handbook* edited by Marcelo Kohen and Mamadou Hébié – they say, referring to an arbitration by the Eritrea Ethiopia Claims Commission (EECC) in 2005:[4]

… if the EECC arbitral award on the Eritrea/Ethiopia conflict can be viewed as offering any indication, five years of inaction are enough for a *status quo* to be considered as established.

Thus those two court cases dispose of the assertion by Kohen and Rodríguez (pp. 226-7) that 34 years is too short for prescription to operate.

8.11 *Nullum tempus*: the legitimist view of sovereignty; eternal titles; limits of prescription

Argentina's claim to the Falklands is perforce based on the "legitimist" view of sovereignty, according to which a claim lasts eternally unless voluntarily given up by the claimant. In other

---

[1] Printed in *International Law Reports*, vol. 100, ed. [Sir] E[lihu] Lauterpacht, C.J. Greenwood and A.G. Oppenheimer, Cambridge 1995 (henceforth *ILR* 1995), pp. 1-114, *Libyan Arab Jamahiriya v. Chad*; also discussed in Sir Ian Sinclair, "Estoppel and acquiescence", in *Fifty Years of the International Court of Justice…*, Cambridge 1996, pp. 118-120.
[2] *ILR* 1995, paragraph 35.
[3] *ILR* 1995, paragraph 111.
[4] Pierre Klein and Vaios Koutroulis, in Kohen and Hébié (eds.), 2018, p. 259.

words, Argentina's claim is based on the medieval principle *nullum tempus occurrit regi* ["to the king, no time passes"]: the sovereign's claims are eternal unless he freely gives them up, whereas the rights and claims of lower authorities or private citizens are impermanent and subject to time-limits. This principle is still invoked occasionally in national law cases in the United States: the rights and claims of federal authorities against private citizens are permanent, whereas citizens' claims lapse after a given time. It is self-evidently not a workable principle in international law since there is no hierarchy among states – any state could maintain it with equal justice against any other state.

Nevertheless, Argentina regularly relies on *nullum tempus* in maintaining that the Argentine title to the Falklands is "imprescriptible", i.e. that it has lasted since 1833 and has not been weakened by the passage of time or by events that have happened – or not happened – since then. That was asserted twice by José María Ruda in his speech to the United Nations' decolonisation committee (the Committee of 24 or "C24") on 9 September 1964 (below, section 10.14); it was enshrined in the Argentine constitution in 1994 (below, section 10.25), and it has often been stated by Argentine speakers at the United Nations. On 18 June 2004 the then Argentine foreign minister Rafael Bielsa stated to the C24 "The passage of time and the long British occupation have not impaired our rights",[1] and an official release from the Argentine foreign ministry issued on 10 June 2017 states:[2]

… the Argentine government reaffirms the imprescriptible sovereignty rights of Argentina over the Malvinas, South Georgia, South Sandwich Islands and adjoining maritime spaces, since they are integral part of the national territory.

And the then Argentine foreign minister Jorge Marcelo Faurie stated at the C24 on 20 June 2018: "The passage of time has not diminished the validity of our claims."[3]

All those statements are straightforward assertions of *nullum tempus*: Bielsa said Argentina's rights survived intact for 170 years from 1834 to 2004; Faurie said they had survived for 184 years from 1834 to 2018, and Argentine governments say Argentina's rights are imprescriptible – all despite the effective sovereignty exercised by Britain in the islands throughout that time.[4] Their statements also imply the existence of what we call "background sovereignty" (sections 8.12, 8.13).

However, Bielsa, Faurie, Kohen and Rodríguez, the Argentine constitution, and successive Argentine governments are all tying themselves into legal knots. There are two possibilities: either (a) *nullum tempus* is valid in international law, or (b) it is not. If (a) is true, and *nullum tempus* is valid in international law, Argentina's claim would be no more imprescriptible than Britain's or Spain's, and both Spain and Britain would have much better claims than Argentina. Spain's claim would survive from 1767, and contains 44 years of occupation as against Argentina's 7 years, while Britain's claim under *nullum tempus* would be unbeatable – it would go back over a quarter of a

---

[1] English text here from the English-language website of the Permanent Mission of Argentina to the United Nations, accessed 8 November 2009.

[2] Argentina has often used similar wording, for example in a UN working paper for the C24, A/AC.109/2018/6, dated 14 March 2018, paragraph 48, p. 12: "The Government of Argentina reaffirms its imprescriptible sovereignty rights over the Malvinas Islands, South Georgia Islands and South Sandwich Islands and the surrounding maritime areas, all of which are an integral part of its national territory."

[3] Quote from official UN summary of all speeches at the C24 meeting in New York, 20 June 2018, on the UN website under https://www.un.org/press/en/2018/gacol3326.doc.htm.

[4] An odd version of this argument is found in Manuel Pedro Peña and Juan Angél Peña, *Falklands or Malvinas: Myths & Facts*, Sevilla (Spain) 2018, an adapted English version of Manuel P[edro] Peña, *Malvinas: Mito & Realidad: Desde los primeros avistamientos, hasta la consolidación de los derechos* ["Malvinas: Myth & Reality: From the first sightings, to the consolidation of rights"], Buenos Aires April 2016. The introductions to both books state (English p. 13, Spanish p. 11) that they are broadly based on the online work by Roger Lorton: "Falklands Wars: the history of the Falkland Islands…" [currently some 1150 pages; ongoing under https://falklandstimeline.wordpress.com], but both books ignore most of the vast amount of evidence presented by Lorton and also his general conclusion, which is that the Falkland Islands are British territory. Instead they present a bizarre "legitimist" argument (English pp. 281, 302-303; Spanish pp. 376-378), namely that France's perfect original title was inherited by Spain and then by Argentina, so the Malvinas are now rightfully Argentine territory. That is untenable – it is eccentric to maintain that Spain inherited France's title when at the time Spain flatly denied that France possessed any title at all (section 2.3). As pointed out in chapter 3, Argentina only inherited from Spain "part of an encumbered and restricted title", which was totally annulled by later developments including the Convention of Peace.

millennium to 1765, and Britain can also show 7 years of occupation from 1766 (antedating Spain's claim) to 1774, plus over 186 years of continuous administration since 1834. Alternatively, if (b) is true, and *nullum tempus* is not valid in international law, then Argentina's claim is not imprescriptible and lapsed long ago.

Any such debate is pointless, of course; (b) is in fact true: *nullum tempus* is not valid in international law, and it is incorrect to assert that Argentina's claim is imprescriptible, or that Argentina's rights have not been impaired by the passage of time. Those rights have been impaired by Argentina's actions – and inactions – during that time. Argentine governments regularly maintain that the British takeover in 1833 was "illegal" because the islands were rightfully Argentinian, but if *nullum tempus* is operative, then Britain can maintain that the Argentine settlement from 1826 to 1833 was illegal because the islands were rightfully British.

The very fact that *nullum tempus* is not a principle of international law makes a discussion of prescription reasonable – if *nullum tempus* were valid, there would be no prescription in international law. However, there is no clarity about the length of time required for prescription to operate – any claimant is free to assert that a given period was short enough, and any possessor to say that it was long enough, and there is some doubt as to whether acquisitive prescription operates in international law at all (section 8.8).

Kohen and Rodríguez claim that 34 years is too short for prescription to operate (section 8.8); others have sometimes claimed that writers on international law such as Hugo Grotius or Oppenheim state that 50 or 100 years must elapse before prescription becomes effective in international law,[1] but in fact neither Grotius nor Oppenheim does so. In discussing the Roman-law concept of "usucaption" (acquisition of ownership by long usage), Grotius states that he does not agree with authors who maintain that laws conferring ownership by long use or prescription also extend to the rights of sovereignty itself. He says:[2]

> ... sovereignty is not on a level with other things; instead, it far surpasses them in the nobility of its nature. I have seen no civil statute treating of prescription that either does include sovereignty or could be reasonably construed as designed to include it under its rules.

Grotius therefore removes sovereignty from any fixed time-limit, but that does not mean he is here accepting *nullum tempus* in international law, since he is only considering sovereignty within a country, not conflicts between sovereigns over territory. Moreover, he goes on immediately after that passage to state that if a transfer of territory to another sovereign is being contemplated, the people of the territory have the right to veto it – the Falkland Islanders' self-determination has a long pedigree (section 10.5).

The editors of the 9th edition of *Oppenheim* do not mention any such fixed period as 50 or 100 years; on the contrary, they make it abundantly clear in their sections 269 and 270 that in international law there can be no *a priori* fixed term for prescription to operate:[3]

§ 269 ... There is no doubt that, in international practice, a state has been considered to be the lawful owner even of those parts of its territory of which it originally took possession wrongfully, provided that the possessor has been in undisturbed possession for so long as to create the general conviction that the present condition of things is in conformity with international order...

§ 270 **Conditions for prescription** No general rule could be laid down as regards the length of time and

---

[1] For example by Jeffrey D. Myhre in "Title to the Falklands-Malvinas Under International Law", in *Millennium Journal of International Studies*, Oxford 1983, p. 34 & fns. 52-54, p. 38; and by Lowell S. Gustafson in *The Sovereignty Dispute over the Falkland (Malvinas) Islands*, New York 1988, p. 34.

[2] Hugo Grotius, *De Iure Belli ac Pacis Libri tres, in quibus jus Naturæ & Gentium, item juris publici præcipua explicantur, Editio Nova cum Annotatis Auctoris*, Amsterdam 1646, Liber II, Caput IV, Sectio XII, p. 142 (1632 edition: p. 99): "At summum imperium non est paris rationis cum rebus aliis: imo nobilitate sua res alias multum excedit. Neque ullam vidi legem civilem de præscriptione agentem, quæ summum imperium comprehenderet, aut comprehendere voluisse probabiliter censeri posset".

[3] Sir Robert Jennings and Sir Arthur Watts (eds.), *Oppenheim's International Law, vol. I, Peace, Introduction and Part I*, 9th ed. by Sir Robert Jennings and Sir Arthur Watts, Harlow 1992, §§ [= sections] 269 and 270, pp. 706-708; the past tense, e.g. at the beginning of § 270, refers to earlier editions of the work.

other circumstances necessary to create such a title by prescription. Everything depended upon the individual case. As long as other states keep up protests and claims, the actual exercise of sovereignty is not undisturbed, nor is there the required general conviction that the present condition of things is in conformity with international order. But after such protests and claims, if any, cease to be repeated, the actual possession ceases to be disturbed and thus in certain circumstances matters may gradually ripen into that condition which is in conformity with international order...

It is important to point out that in that passage *Oppenheim*'s editors do not consider what we call "overt acquiescence", but only what we have termed "silent acquiescence", i.e. cases in which the former possessor "has silently dropped the claim", as they put it later in their section **270**. In the case of the Falklands, however, Argentina's acquiescence was overtly proclaimed several times at the highest level (section 8.18). As regards the "general conviction that the present condition of things is in conformity with international order", that view was held by a number of countries that maintained consulates in the Falklands (section 8.15) – they regarded Britain's possession as an established fact, as did the official Spanish diplomatic and scientific expedition that spent six weeks in the islands in 1863 and fully accepted Britain's sovereignty (section 8.17).

In the course of their attempt to show that prescription does not apply in the Falklands case, Kohen and Rodríguez (pp. 226-7) briefly allude to an international agreement which did lay down a definite length of time for prescription to become effective, namely 50 years. They do not say what that agreement was, neither in their text nor in their source references, but it was the treaty between Britain and Venezuela concluded on 2 February 1897 to regulate the boundary between Venezuela and British Guiana (now Guyana). In laying down a length of time for prescription it may well be unique in international legal history, since it is quoted by writers on international law who give no other example.[1] Its Article IV lays down a set of rules to be applied by arbitrators charged with settling territorial disputes – Rule (a) runs as follows:[2]

(a) Adverse holding or prescription during the period of fifty years shall make a good title. The arbitrators may deem exclusive political control of a district, as well as actual settlement thereof, sufficient to constitute adverse holding or to make title by prescription.

"Adverse holding", i.e. holding in opposition to another state's rights, presumably includes holding despite the other state's protests. So if protests are irrelevant and only "exclusive political control of a district" is operative, then this would provide a clear answer to the Falklands case: Britain held exclusive political control over the Falklands for 148 years from January 1834 to April 1982, and hence acquired "good title" to the Falklands, i.e. full legitimate sovereignty.

However, Rule (a) does not stand alone; Rules (b) and (c) greatly extend the criteria:

(b) The arbitrators may recognize and give effect to rights and claims resting on any other ground whatever, valid according to international law, and on any principles of international law which the arbitrators may deem to be applicable to the case and which are not in contravention of the foregoing rule.

(c) In determining the boundary line, if territory of one party be found by the tribunal to have been at the date of this treaty in the occupation of the subjects or citizens of the other party, such effect shall be given to such occupation as reason, justice, the principles of international law, and the equities of the case shall, in the opinion of the tribunal, require.

So the term of 50 years given in Rule (a) was only one of a number of factors to be considered by the arbitrators, confirming the statement by *Oppenheim*'s editors that prescription depends on the facts of the situation. Rules (a), (b) and (c) give the arbitrators *carte blanche* to act in any way they think fit – the term of 50 years for prescription is actually rendered irrelevant by the wide range of other options for the existence of a good title. So the Anglo-Venezuelan treaty of 1897 actually supplies strong confirmation of Britain's title to the Falklands.

Some recent Argentine pronouncements have implied that Argentina's rights in the Falklands are eternal because Britain's actions in 1833 were "illegal". José María Ruda stated in his influential

---

[1] E.g. Oppenheim 9th ed. 1992, vol. I, Part I, p. 706, fn. 1.; O'Brien 2001, p. 211, fn. 52; Marcelo Kohen, in Kohen and Hébié (eds.) 2018, p. 155, with footnote quoting Rule (a) but not (b) or (c).
[2] Rules (a) (b) and (c) quoted in John Bassett Moore, *Digest of International Law*, Washington DC 1906, vol. I, p. 297.

speech in 1964 that Britain's reassertion of sovereignty in 1833 "cannot generate nor create any rights for Great Britain" (section 10.14), and much the same was asserted in an article published in July 1965,[1] at the beginning of Argentina's new campaign at the United Nations, by Carlos María Velázquez, the Uruguayan UN representative and vice-chairman of the decolonisation committee (section 10.11). Such assertions are based on the legal principle *ex iniuria ius non oritur* ["Law does not arise from injury", or "Rights cannot arise out of wrongs"].

But Britain's actions in 1833 were not illegal at all; they were a perfectly legitimate action, in a disputed territory, to defend British interests after the *Lexington* raid in 1831-2. It can of course be argued that Britain's actions in 1833 conferred no *new extra rights* on Britain *at that time*, but that is irrelevant. Britain already had important rights in the Falklands before 1833, and Argentina did not possess exclusive rights of sovereignty in the islands then or later. Britain's definitive rights arose after 1833, from Argentina's acquiescence indicated by the Convention of Peace in 1850 and the long period without protests that followed it (section 7.16); from Argentina's later actions including official pronouncements indicating consent (8.18) and the publication of maps not showing the Falklands as Argentine territory (8.22); from Britain's performance of innumerable « effectivités » (acts of sovereignty) in the islands; and from the emergence of a population native to the islands (who of course have their own rights in their country in addition to Britain's). Those factors are all operative in international law, even without invoking the controversial doctrine of acquisitive prescription, and they unambiguously confer title to the Falklands on Britain.

8.12 "Historical ties": is Argentina's claim to title or to historical title?

In his analysis of self-determination in disputed territories,[2] Jamie Trinidad discusses a special type of claim raised by some claimant countries to territories held by other countries: a claim based on "historical ties". Such a claim was raised by Morocco in the *Western Sahara* case at the International Court of Justice (ICJ) in 1975 (see also section 10.21). Morocco accepted that the territory concerned was a Spanish colony (Spanish Sahara), but asserted that there had been historical ties between Morocco and the territory that antedated Spain's takeover and therefore gave Morocco title to the territory.[3] Much the same was asserted by India in the case of Goa in western India, which was a Portuguese colony from 1505 until it was captured by India by military force in December 1961. Morocco and India both accepted that the places in question had been Spanish and Portuguese territory, but they asserted that the decolonisation of those territories could only proceed by "reintegration" into Morocco and India respectively, since the populations of those territories had always been Moroccan and Indian.

That is clearly not applicable to the Falklands since the islands were uninhabited until the French settlement was established at Port Louis in 1764 (section 2.1); there was no pre-colonial population that could be "reintegrated", and Britain's presence in the islands began in January 1766, over a year before Spain's presence began in April 1767 (sections 2.2, 2.3). Britain therefore has historical ties with the islands that always overlaid Spain's ties and hence Argentina's too.

Nevertheless, Argentine politicians and writers have frequently asserted that the Falklands are Argentine territory "illegally usurped" by Britain and that Argentina has "never consented" to that "usurpation" – for example, on their p. 187 Kohen and Rodríguez refer to "the British usurpation of 1833", and José María Ruda said in his UN speech in 1964 that "Argentina has never accepted Britain's possession of the Falklands". Those assertions are of course incorrect, but they imply that in 1833 Argentina was the legitimate territorial sovereign of the islands and remains so today since Argentina's title was never extinguished and Britain's title was never perfected. Thus Jamie Trinidad states in reference to Argentina's claim to the Falklands:[4]

… it is important to stress that Argentina's claim is not based fundamentally on the existence of historical

---

[1] Carlos María Velázquez, "Some Legal Aspects of the Colonial Problem in Latin America", in *The Annals of the American Academy of Political and Social Science*, Philadelphia July 1965, pp. 111-118.
[2] Jamie Trinidad, *Self-Determination in Disputed Colonial Territories*, Cambridge 2018, p. 139.
[3] Trinidad 2018, p. 52.
[4] Trinidad 2018, p. 139 (Trinidad's italics).

ties with the islands in the absence of territorial sovereignty… At the heart of the Argentine position is the claim that its *present-day* territorial sovereignty is at stake in the decolonization of the Falkland/Malvinas Islands, because the title claimed by Britain is defective.

That is not actually true of Argentina's claim – as mentioned above in chapter 3, Kohen and Rodríguez sum up Argentina's case as follows (pp. 21, 25):

(p. 21) The islands are Argentine by virtue of its succession to Spain's rights, the concrete display of sovereignty by the new South American nation from the beginning of the process of independence in 1810 until 1833, year of the eviction by Britain, and the lack of Argentine consent to the British occupation since 1833. The succession to Spain's rights is justified by the recognition of Spanish sovereignty by the main European maritime powers, by Spain's continuation of France's right of first occupant (1764), and by its continuous exercise of sovereignty over the islands until 1811 – an exclusive exercise between 1774 and 1811. […] (p. 25): the essence of the Spanish, and consequently Argentine, claim is based on other arguments,[1] such as: 1) recognition by maritime powers – including England – that the region, including the islands, belonged to Spain; 2) the right of first occupancy and 3) the continuous, public and peaceful exercise of sovereignty until 1811.

That shows that Argentina's case is indeed "based fundamentally" on historical ties with the islands – it would be hard to find a clearer presentation of a claim based on such ties (though every word of it is untrue). That is also shown by the constant references in Argentine works and speeches to Britain's supposed "usurpation" of the islands in 1833.

But are Argentine authors and politicians right in implying that Argentina's title was never interrupted and that Britain's title is defective? It is important to investigate the nature of Argentina's purported title, since the existence of self-determination for a given group of people depends not only on their inherent characteristics but also to a significant degree on the nature of the sovereignty under which they live. In their last section (pp. 281-2), Kohen and Rodríguez quote the distinguished British judge Dame Rosalyn Higgins on the question of self-determination and sovereignty – she says:[2]

Until it is determined where territorial sovereignty lies it is impossible to see if the inhabitants have a right of self-determination.

So does Argentina have a claim to a present-day continuing title? That requires a consideration of the deeper reaches of legitimist views of sovereignty.

8.13 "Background sovereignty": historical ties versus legal ties of territorial sovereignty

The legitimist view of sovereignty has produced a curious excrescence, which for want of a better term we have christened "background sovereignty". This is our term for the idea that despite the loss of a territory, the original possessor's sovereignty continues in the background. In the Falklands context it is thus closely related to the notion of *nullum tempus* (as that term is employed or implied by those who assert a "legitimist" Argentine claim to the Falklands). In actual fact, however, as explained in sections 8.11 and 10.25, *nullum tempus* operates only within a given country, not at international level, whereas background sovereignty is seen (by those who assert it) as operating at international level in disputes involving the sovereignty of two or more countries.

Jamie Trinidad (who is himself Gibraltarian) discusses the concept in connection with Gibraltar, though he does not use the term "background sovereignty". He heads his section 3.2.4.1 "Are There Present-Day 'Legal Ties of Territorial Sovereignty' between Spain and Gibraltar?", and mentions an argument advanced by Spain in support of its claim to Gibraltar, namely that the Treaty of Utrecht of 1713 did not effect a true cession of sovereignty. That seems an eccentric position to take, given that under Article X of the Treaty of Utrecht, the king of Spain ceded to Britain:[3]

---

[1] I.e. other arguments than discovery, the papal Bulls and the Treaty of Tordesillas, mentioned earlier in the sentence.
[2] Rosalyn Higgins, *Problems & Process: International Law and How We Use it*, Oxford 1994, p. 127 (based on her lectures to the Hague Academy). Dame Rosalyn Higgins, DBE, QC (b. 1937) is a British judge who was the first woman appointed to the ICJ (on 12 July 1995); she was reelected on 6 February 2000 and became President of the Court in 2006. She was succeeded as President on 6 February 2009 by Judge Hisashi Owada of Japan.
[3] Treaty quoted in Trinidad 2018, p. 122.

... the full and entire propriety of the town and castle of Gibraltar, together with the port, fortifications, and forts thereunto belonging, and he gives up the said propriety to be held and enjoyed absolutely with all manner of right for ever, without any exception or impediment whatever.

That wording is perfectly clear; the cession of Gibraltar to Britain was total and final. Nevertheless, Spain has sought to evade the inevitable conclusion (i.e. that Gibraltar is British territory) by maintaining that the "propriety" [i.e. property] mentioned is "something less than sovereignty" and is merely a "right of possession" over a military base.[1] Trinidad comments that it is hard to see how the wording of the Treaty of Utrecht could amount to anything less than a transfer of territorial sovereignty; he points out that "The balance of academic opinion (in Spain as well as elsewhere) supports this view",[2] and concludes that "it can be stated with reasonable confidence that Spain does not retain ties of territorial sovereignty with Gibraltar".[3] Or, as we would put it, Spain retains no background sovereignty over Gibraltar.

There are, however, a few cases in which it is justified to assume that a country's sovereignty over a given territory continues despite another country's possession of that territory. The clearest example of this is the New Territories of Hong Kong, which were merely leased by Britain from China in 1898 for 99 years. During that time Britain accepted that China was the freeholder of the territory, while Britain was only the leaseholder. That is a genuine case of background sovereignty: by agreement with Britain, China retained legal ties of territorial sovereignty over the territory. China's sovereignty over the New Territories was therefore not interrupted but merely placed in abeyance for 99 years, during which it continued in the background, and was resumed in 1997.

Argentina's reliance on the medieval principle of *nullum tempus* implies the continuance of its background sovereignty, but that has never been valid. In the first place, there is abundant evidence that Argentina's title to the Falklands never amounted to unrestricted sovereignty in the first place (i.e. that Argentina was never the sole territorial sovereign of the islands, see chapter 3). Secondly, what limited rights of title Argentina possessed continued only as long as Argentina regularly protested in appropriate form to Britain, i.e. during the 17 years 1833-49. Any Argentine title was ended by the ratification of the Convention of Peace in 1850 (section 7.11), and its ending was definitively confirmed by statements by Argentine leaders (section 8.18) and ruled out by developments such as United Nations resolutions (sections 10.8, 10.9, 10.17, 10.18) and decisions of the International Court of Justice in relevant cases (sections 8.10, 10.21, 10.30). And if any background sovereignty did exist, then it was British: Britain can just as well assert that British sovereignty continued in the background throughout the Spanish and Argentine periods.

Finally, any principle of background sovereignty (except in explicit cases such as leases, as with the Hong Kong New Territories) gets into deep water in terms of international law. If a country's sovereignty over a territory were to continue despite abundant evidence that it has ceased, then it would be impossible for any transfers of territory to be truly permanent. Mexico would be entitled to claim continuing sovereignty over California, Arizona and Texas (all ceded to the United States in the 1840s), and Germany would be entitled to claim sovereignty over Alsace-Lorraine (ceded to France in 1919) and over East Prussia (lost to Poland and Russia in 1945 without any act of cession). No territorial change would ever be final, and no treaty would ever mean what it said. That would mean the end of any meaningful international law – if international law cannot definitively regulate the possession of territory, then it is not much use. As regards the Falklands, there was never any kind of lease or other agreement by which an Argentine title continued.

In short, Argentina retains no legal ties of territorial sovereignty, no "background sovereignty" over the Falklands.

8.14 Effective territorial possession

The "exclusive political control of a district" mentioned in the British-Venezuelan treaty of 2

---

[1] Trinidad 2018, pp. 122-123.
[2] Trinidad 2018, p. 124; his implication is that though most academics, including Spanish ones, maintain that Spain's sovereignty over Gibraltar has ended, others (e.g. Spanish politicians) maintain that it continues.
[3] Trinidad 2018, p. 127.

February 1897 (section 8.11) is the basis of the principle of "effective territorial possession" put forward by the Belgian jurist Charles de Visscher in 1953 as a mode of acquisition of title:[1]

International law concedes to effective territorial possession consequences that private law would by no means admit in relation to property. A State which has ceased to exercise any authority over a territory cannot, by purely verbal protestations, indefinitely maintain its title against another which for a sufficiently long time has effectively exercised the powers and fulfilled the duties of sovereignty in it. Considerations of stability, order, and peace, analogous to those that justify acquisitive prescription, are here preponderant.

For de Visscher, a state that has held "effective territorial possession" for long enough acquires full title however long a previous possessor may protest, so protests are irrelevant. But he does not say what he would regard as "a sufficiently long time".

Here is our contribution to the concept of "a sufficiently long time": the Falklands have now been held by Britain for two-thirds of the 19th century, all of the 20th (with a brief interruption in 1982 which did not affect all the islands) and over a fifth of the 21st century. The 188 years from 1834 to now (2022) are a sizeable slice of human history, as long, say, as the period between 1658 and 1843, from the early years of Louis XIV to the first years of Queen Victoria, from the Age of Absolutism to the age of railways and photographs – and with the entire 18th century in between. Or, to put it another way, 187 years is over a twelfth of the time that has passed since the death of Julius Caesar. It would seem hard to argue that it is not "a sufficiently long time".

8.15 Foreign consulates imply recognition

Kohen and Rodríguez refer briefly (pp. 227-8) to the presence of foreign consulates in the Falklands, criticising us for saying in *Getting it right* (pp. 24-27) that those consulates implied recognition of British sovereignty in the islands. What we said was:

The opening of a consulate is significant in international law. It does not *constitute* diplomatic recognition (that is achieved by the exchange of ambassadors), but it *implies* diplomatic recognition – if a country does not recognise the legitimacy of another's government, it does not open a consulate there.

Kohen and Rodríguez say "The intermittent presence of consuls in Port Stanley is irrelevant for the issue of sovereignty", and assert that "their duties were simply of a commercial nature". That is actually true only of commercial agents, who are indeed irrelevant to sovereignty and have a purely commercial role.

Consuls, by contrast, do fulfil certain legal functions such as authenticating documents (see sections 5.2, 5.3, 5.7), and their presence does indicate *de jure* recognition of the country to which they are accredited. Kohen and Rodríguez say that several countries have consulates in Jerusalem, "without implying any recognition of the factual situation of the city", but that example proves the opposite of what they assert. Several countries have a consulate or consulate-general in the city that is not a diplomatic mission to Israel, even though in Israeli law Jerusalem is Israel's capital. For example, the Belgian Consulate-General in Jerusalem states on its website that in the text of United Nations General Assembly Resolution 181 of 1947:[2]

... Jerusalem is referred to as a "*Corpus Separatum*", a separate enclave under international jurisdiction. Thereby, the jurisdiction of the Consulate General is based on this special status… the territorial jurisdiction of the Consulate General includes both Jerusalem (the *Corpus Separatum*) and the territories occupied by Israel in 1967 (West Bank and Gaza). This jurisdiction gives to the Consulate General a special position, shared with the eight other consulates general in Jerusalem… The diplomatic relations with the State of Israel remain the exclusive competence of the Embassy of Belgium in Tel Aviv.

Likewise, the British Consulate-General in Jerusalem represents Britain in the same three places (Jerusalem, the West Bank and Gaza), which in Israel's view do not constitute a unit. The reason is that to maintain a consulate in Jerusalem accredited to Israel would demonstrate a higher degree of

---

[1] Charles de Visscher, *Théories et Réalités en Droit International Public*, Paris 1953; quote here from English translation by P.E. Corbett, *Theory and Reality in Public International Law*, Princeton 1957, p. 201.
[2] Quotes from the English-language website of the Belgian Consulate-General in Jerusalem, accessed 6 October 2021.

recognition of Israel's sovereignty in the city than those countries wish to accord it.

In short, maintaining a consulate does imply recognition of the sovereignty of the authority in place. That is why Argentina has never had a consulate in the Falklands – if consulates really were irrelevant to sovereignty, Stanley would be a natural place for Argentina to have one, but to maintain a consulate in Stanley would have given greater recognition to Britain's sovereignty than Argentina wished to accord it. In 1952 the Argentine government protested sharply against the presence of a Uruguayan consulate in Stanley, making it clear that Argentina did regard the existence of a consulate as relevant to the question of sovereignty (section 8.16).

Kate Parlett agrees that under certain circumstances "recognition of sovereignty by third states may also be taken into account in territorial disputes";[1] she goes on: "recognition by third states may be an element in the evidence to be taken into account, but it is very unlikely to be determinative of title. Nevertheless, in the context of competing claims, it may be highly relevant". There are competing claims in the context of the Falklands of course, so there is a good case for saying that recognition of Britain's sovereignty by third states is an additional element in the confirmation of Britain's title to the islands.

There were consulates of foreign countries in the Falklands for a century and a quarter from the 1850s. Opening a consulate is one of several acts which may imply international recognition – O'Brien supplies a list of some of them, and also a list of acts without such implication:[2]

... it is possible that the following acts might constitute implied recognition of a state or government:

(i) the formal establishment of diplomatic relations;
(ii) the issue of a consular exequatur;
(iii) the signing of a bi-lateral treaty between two states designed to comprehensively regulate relations;
[...]

It would seem that the following acts will not of themselves constitute implied recognition:

(i) the maintenance of unofficial contacts;
(ii) the initiation of negotiations;
(iii) the exchange of trade missions with an unrecognised state; [... ...]

William Smyley's appointment by the United States as commercial agent in 1850 (no. iii in O'Brien's second list) did not constitute recognition, but the attitude of the US gradually changed, and after a quarter of a century in which there had been no evidence of a territorial dispute over the Falklands between Britain and Argentina, the US commercial agency in Stanley was upgraded to a consulate, which was recognised by Britain in 1875 by the issue of an exequatur (a document issued by the head of state of a country recognising the status of a foreign consul, guaranteeing his or her rights and privileges and authorising him or her to act as consul).

The issue of a consular exequatur is no. (ii) in O'Brien's first list of acts which might constitute implied recognition. The appointment of a consul does not of course *constitute* recognition of a foreign government, which involves the formal establishment of diplomatic relations and the exchange of ambassadors. However, the appointment of a consul in overseas possessions is the highest level of recognition possible in a non-independent territory, and implies recognition of the authority of the metropolitan country in those possessions. The existence of a consulate *presupposes* recognition, and recognition is always mutual: in 1874 the United States appointed George Gerard, initially as commercial agent; Britain then issued an exequatur recognising his consulship, and in August 1875 the US representation in Stanley became a consulate, whereby the United States recognised Britain's possession of the Falklands. In the US consular regulations of the 1870s and later, the Falklands were included among "British dominions" in lists of US consular posts.[3]

Details of the foreign consulates in Stanley were entered in the annual *Falklands Blue Books* for

---

[1] Kate Parlett, in Kohen and Hébié (eds.) 2018, p. 179, with references to sources.
[2] O'Brien 2001, pp. 181-182.
[3] E.g. in *Revised Statutes of the United States...*, Washington DC, 1878, 2nd ed., title XVIII, chapter 2, p. 301, and in *US Consular Regulations*, Washington DC 1881, Appendix V, p. 472.

89 years from 1856 to 1944 inclusive.[1] The very first consul was appointed by Hamburg (then an independent state) on 30 May 1853;[2] Denmark was next in 1858, followed in the 1860s and 70s by Belgium, Italy, Germany, the United States, and Sweden and Norway jointly. From 1877 until the Danish consulate closed in 1895, six countries were represented (Chile, Denmark, Germany, Italy, Sweden and Norway jointly, and the United States); for 5 years from 1895 to 1900 there were consulates for five countries (Chile, Germany, Italy, Sweden and Norway jointly, and the United States), and from 1900 to 1908 for six countries again: Chile, Germany, Italy, Norway, Sweden, and the United States. Norway holds the record for length of consular representation with almost 100 years, first jointly with Sweden from 1877, then with a separate consulate from 1900 to 1974; Chile was represented in Stanley from 1877 until 1959 (with a 7-year gap from 1928 to 1935, making 75 years in all); Italy was represented for 71 years from 1869 to 1940, Uruguay for over 50 years from 1924 to 1975, and the United States for 33 years from 1875 to 1908.

In maintaining those consulates, those countries showed that they did not accept that Argentina held rightful sovereignty over the Falklands. There were ten countries (Belgium, Chile, Denmark, France, Italy, Germany, Norway, Sweden, the United States and Uruguay) which for many years accepted that the Falklands were British, and thus contributed to the validation of Britain's title to the islands. Today all those countries self-evidently accept that Argentina's claim is not old and continuous. The consulates of Uruguay and Chile are particularly significant – those two countries now pay lip-service to Argentina's claim, but their behaviour in the past means they cannot maintain that they have never regarded the Falklands as British territory.

8.16 Argentina protests against the presence of a Uruguayan consulate in Stanley, 1952

Kohen and Rodríguez say consulates are "irrelevant for the issue of sovereignty" (section 8.15), but the Argentine government saw things otherwise: in Buenos Aires on 21 October 1952 the Argentine foreign minister Dr. Jerónimo Remorino made a formal protest to the Uruguayan ambassador Dr. Mateo Marques Castro against the presence of a Uruguayan consulate in Stanley. The stimulus for the protest was a proposed flight from Uruguay to the Falklands under the Anglo-Uruguayan aviation treaty of 1947, but it seems the Argentine government had just learnt that there was a Uruguayan consulate in Stanley and assumed it was a new development (in fact Uruguay had had a consulate in Stanley for over a quarter of a century). Part of the long Argentine protest read:[3]

On the basis of legal foundations and the political circumstances which I hereby express in the name of my government and through the agency of Y[our] E[xcellency], I present the most formal protest to the government of Uruguay against the disregard for Argentine sovereignty in the Malvinas Islands implied by the agreement on aviation signed with the government of the United Kingdom of Great Britain and Northern Ireland, and against the violation of that sovereignty involved in the appointment of a consular official to act within those territories…

So in 1952 Argentina regarded the existence of a foreign consulate in Stanley as a "violation" of Argentine claims to sovereignty. Moreover, as a reaction to Uruguay's links with the Falklands including the consulate, Argentina imposed restrictions on Argentinians visiting Uruguay during the

---

[1] From the 1840s, governors of British overseas possessions were required to submit to the Colonial Office in London detailed annual returns on the territories under their authority, which were entered in books known as *Blue Books* from the blue colour of their paper. There are 99 Falklands *Blue Books*: the first was submitted by Governor Richard Moody for 1846, the 99th and last by Governor Sir Allan Cardinall for 1944. The Colonial Office originals are now in the PRO under CO 81, numbered from CO 81/1 to CO 81/99; there is an incomplete set in the JCNA, Stanley.

[2] Date of appointment of John Pownall Dale by the Hamburg Senate as Hamburg consul in Stanley from Jürgen Sielemann in *Hamburgische Geschichts- und Heimatblätter* ["*Hamburg Historical and Local Studies*"], vol. 11, 1987, pp. 8-9. Vernet was in Hamburg when Dale's appointment was announced. Details of consulates here from a variety of sources including the *Blue Books*.

[3] Text of protest in "Formuló la Argentina una protesta Ante el Uruguay" ["Argentina addresses a protest to Uruguay"] in the Buenos Aires newspaper *Noticias Gráficas* 23 October 1952, p. 5, cols. 1-5; extracts also in report "El gobierno de la Argentina formula una protesta a las autoridades de nuestro país" ["The government of Argentina addresses a protest to the authorities of our country"], in *El País*, Montevideo, Uruguay, 23 October 1952, p. 1, cols. 1-3.

southern summer of 1952-3, which seriously affected the Uruguayan tourist industry, as the *New York Times* reported in January 1953.[1]

In view of Argentina's sharp protest against the existence of a Uruguayan consulate in the Falklands, it is impossible for Argentina to deny that the consulates maintained in Stanley by several countries indicated recognition of British sovereignty. And significantly, the Argentine protest had no effect; the Uruguayan consulate remained open for another 23 years, and its coat of arms can now be admired in the Historic Dockyard Museum in Stanley.

8.17 The significance of the visit of the Spanish expedition, 1863

The account by Kohen and Rodríguez (pp. 228-229) of the visit of the Spanish diplomatic and scientific expedition in 1863 is wildly far from the truth. In *Getting it right* (p. 26) we said:

> In 1863 the islands were visited by an official Spanish diplomatic and scientific expedition commanded by Vice-Admiral Luiz Hernández de Pinzón, who in January had visited Buenos Aires and initiated negotiations for the recognition of the whole of Argentina by Spain (at that time the Province of Buenos Aires had only just become reunited with the rest of Argentina, and Spain did not have a recognition treaty with Buenos Aires). The expedition's two frigates spent six weeks in Stanley harbour from 27 February to 9 April 1863; they fired a salute to the British flag and received Governor James Mackenzie on board, and the expedition accepted gifts of scientific specimens. They were official representatives of the former colonial power, Spain, and clearly accepted the Falklands as British.

Kohen and Rodríguez say that "The truth, which once again the pamphlet conceals... is very different to the description given by Pascoe and Pepper".

Actually, the real truth is that we were right, which is easy to demonstrate. They state in a footnote on their p. 229 that their source is the Argentine historian Ricardo Caillet-Bois.[2] But everything he says is wrong, so Kohen and Rodríguez get everything wrong too. They get the governor's name wrong; they misrepresent his actions; they call the expedition merely "scientific", suppressing the fact that it had an important diplomatic role; they say the visit was to repair damage suffered in the Magellan Strait, and that the ships remained at anchor to make repairs and only stayed so long because they had to get wood and coal from Montevideo. All that is incorrect.

What really happened was this.[3] The visit of the two Spanish frigates *Resolución* and *Nuestra Señora del Triunfo* to Stanley was not to repair damage; they had suffered no damage in the Strait except that the *Resolución* had lost an anchor and a few men had been injured. Captain Enrique Croquer y Pavía of the *Triunfo* reported incorrectly that he was short of coal, which led Vice Admiral Pinzón to run to the Falklands – the zoologist Marcos Jiménez de la Espada, aboard the expedition's third ship *Covadonga* (which did not go to the Falklands), recorded in his diary: "They villainously abandoned us in the Straits, leaving us alone against weather they dared not face."[4]

The expedition's purpose was not merely scientific – indeed Captain Croquer saw the expedition's role as exclusively diplomatic; to him the scientific part was an irrelevance and a nuisance. He violently objected to the presence of the scientists, impeded their research, threw some of their specimens overboard, and posted a guard with fixed bayonet to keep them in their quarters.[5]

---

[1] Article headed "Uruguay's tourist trade blocked by Argentina" in the *New York Times*, 7 January 1953, p. 80.

[2] Kohen and Rodríguez 2015, p. 229, giving as their source Ricardo Caillet-Bois, p. 404. It is not in the 1st ed. (Ricardo R. Caillet-Bois, *Una Tierra Argentina: Las Islas Malvinas* ["An Argentine Land: The Malvinas Islands"], Buenos Aires 1948), but only in a footnote in the 2nd extended ed. Buenos Aires 1952, p. 404, and the 3rd ed., facsimile reprint of 2nd ed., Buenos Aires 1982. Caillet-Bois's very brief account also errs in saying that the Spanish ships visited "Puerto Luis"; Kohen and Rodríguez do at least omit that error.

[3] Our account is based on Alejandro Fery y Torres, *Viaje de regreso de la Resolución*, Madrid 1882, reprinted Madrid 1940; William Columbus Davis, *The Last Conquistadores: the Spanish Intervention in Peru and Chile 1863-1866*, Athens (Georgia, USA) 1950; Robert Ryal Miller, *For Science and Glory: the Spanish Scientific Expedition to America, 1862-1866*, Oklahoma 1968; Spanish translation by Antonio M. Regueiro: *Por la Ciencia y la Gloria Nacional: la expedición científica española a América (1862-1866)*, Barcelona 1983, and Miguel Puig-Samper, *Crónica de una Expedición Romántica al Nuevo Mundo*, Madrid 1988. The *Resolución*'s voyage is also briefly described in Miguel Ángel de Marco, *La Armada Española en el Plata (1845-1900)*, Buenos Aires 1981, esp. pp. 231-245.

[4] Miller 1968, pp. 23-69; 68 & fns.; Puig-Samper 1988, p. 184.

[5] Miller 1968, pp. 28, 50.

The expedition's diplomatic function was at top international level – Pinzón's mission was to promote the conclusion of a formal recognition treaty between Argentina and Spain. Buenos Aires had not been a party to the treaty with Spain signed by the Argentine Confederation in 1859, since it had at that time been a separate country. In early January 1863 Pinzón and some officers visited Argentine President Bartolomé Mitre, who gave a state banquet in their honour; Pinzón urged Mitre to send an envoy to Spain to draw up a treaty, which Mitre agreed to do.[1] The expedition then sailed for the Pacific but met heavy weather in the Strait, and the *Resolución* and the *Triunfo* turned back, ran for the Falklands and spent six weeks from 27 February to 9 April 1863 in Stanley harbour.

Kohen and Rodríguez (following Caillet-Bois) call the Governor of the Falklands "H. W. Mackenzie", but he was actually Captain James George Mackenzie (Governor 1862-6). They say he "prevented the Spaniards from making any forays into the interior of the islands", which is the reverse of the truth: he had cordial relations with the expedition, and in a despatch of 2 March 1863 to the Colonial Secretary, the Duke of Newcastle, Mackenzie emphasised "the friendly spirit evinced by the Spanish Admiral" and said the Spanish ships had fired a salute to the British flag.[2] Far from preventing forays into the interior, Mackenzie allowed the members of the expedition to move around freely, and they made many visits ashore; the scientists and chief officers were invited to several homes in Stanley, and the Colonial chaplain, Charles Bull, showed them his greenhouse full of European plants. The US commercial agent, William Smyley (sections 5.19, 6.9, 8.3), accompanied the naturalist Francisco de Paula Martínez y Sáez and the expedition's taxidermist Dr Bartolomé Puig[3] on a trip on horseback around part of East Falkland, and the expedition acquired several hundred scientific specimens from the islands, which are now in the Museo de Ciencias Naturales in Madrid.[4] They collected many of these themselves and received others from Stanley residents. The ships did not get wood or coal from Montevideo; Stanley could supply those things, and the only ship that went from Stanley to Montevideo and back during the expedition's stay was the schooner *David Ewan*, which the Falklands Shipping Register (FSR) records as leaving on 2 March and returning on 1 April.[5] She was a small ship of 115 tons with a crew of 7, so she cannot have brought much in the way of coal or supplies for two such large ships (the FSR says the *Resolución* was of 3,200 tons with a crew of 711 men, the *Triunfo* 2,800 tons, with 690 men).[6]

Kohen and Rodríguez say (p. 229) the captain of a ship was not authorised, nor did he have the capacity, to recognise sovereignty over a territory in the name of his State. Their implication is that we maintained in *Getting it right* that the visitors officially recognised British sovereignty, but a glance at our text above shows that we actually said only that the expedition "clearly accepted the Falklands as British". In other words, the legal significance of the expedition's visit is merely that it ended any possible claim by Spain. Spain's claim had faded during the 40 years since the Spanish protests to the United States in 1822 and to Britain in 1825; whether it had *de facto* disappeared completely is a moot point, but at any rate the expedition's behaviour put a final end to it. The ships had not suffered significant damage, so it would be impossible to argue that the visit was made in an emergency and was thus irrelevant in diplomatic terms. If it had been kept as short as possible and contact with the governor and local people limited to a minimum, and if they had politely declined all gifts, it might have been possible to maintain that the expedition reserved its position and did not wish its visit to be taken as implicit recognition of British sovereignty. But they did no such thing; they accepted the Britishness of the Falklands as part of the established order of things.

The expedition sailed on into the Pacific, where it started a war – on 14 April 1864 Pinzón seized the guano-rich Peruvian Chincha Islands, leading to war between Spain and Peru, which soon became the "War of the American Union" in which Bolivia, Chile and Ecuador allied themselves with Peru against Spain. The war proved an embarrassing fiasco for Spain; Pinzón sent

---

[1] Miller 1968, pp. 56-57; Davis 1950, p. 13.
[2] Copy in Governor's Letter Book, "Despatches Out", 22 November 1862 to 3 July 1866, vol. B13, in the Jane Cameron National Archives (JCNA), Stanley.
[3] A Catalan name, pronounced more or less like "putsch".
[4] Miller 1968, pp. 70; 107-166; 180.
[5] Falklands Shipping Register (FSR), "Vol. AA1", 1842-1878, in JCNA, entries nos. 12a and 19a of 1863.
[6] FSR, entries 9 and 10 of 1863, in JCNA.

his ships home by various routes, and an armistice was signed in 1871, but full peace treaties were not concluded between Spain and its former Pacific territories until 1885.

Thus it came about that the *Resolución* returned to Stanley on 22 June 1866, in distress, having lost her rudder in the Southern Ocean and been towed in by the British paddle sloop HMS *Spiteful*, which had just brought the new governor, William Robinson (Governor 1866-70). Unlike the first visit in 1863, this visit was a genuine emergency, and the ship spent almost three months in Stanley harbour till 18 September. The whole voyage, including both visits to Stanley, is described in a book published in Spain in 1882 by one of her Marines officers, Alejandro Fery y Torres (see footnote), who clearly regards the Falklands as British without question. He several times calls them "las Falklands", and though he mentions the Argentine gauchos (i.e. the ones sent by Samuel Fisher Lafone, sections 7.7, 10.1), he ignores any Argentine period or Argentine claim, and says the islands passed from Spanish into British rule.[1] His account confirms that the members of the Spanish expedition of 1862-6 regarded the Falklands as British; they gave no hint that they regarded them as still rightfully Spanish, and it never entered their heads that the islands might be Argentinian. That behaviour by officials of the former colonial power, on an international diplomatic mission involving Argentina, is significant. They treated the Britishness of the Falklands as part of the established order, and their attitude, during a period when Argentina mentioned no claim to the islands for over a third of a century, undermines contentions by Argentine writers that Argentina inherited the Falklands from Spain. In the view of some quite high-ranking Spanish officials, it was Britain that took the islands over from Spain, not Argentina.

The nature and timing of the visit meant that when Spain and the newly reunited Argentina signed a Treaty of Recognition, Peace, and Friendship in Madrid on 21 September 1863, finally formalising Spain's recognition of the independence of the whole of Argentina including the Province of Buenos Aires, Spain did not regard Argentina as including the Falkland Islands, and for many years Argentina made no such assertion either. In the 1860s the Spanish and Argentine governments both regarded the Falklands as British, as Argentina made clear in top-level statements by Argentine leaders (section 8.18).

8.18 Acts by Argentina that showed acquiescence in Britain's possession of the Falklands

In contrast to the exceedingly feeble examples given by Kohen and Rodríguez purporting to show that Argentina did not acquiesce in Britain's possession of the Falklands (section 8.4), we gave several examples in *Getting it right* (pp. 25-26) of statements by Argentine presidents or vice-presidents in their Messages at the opening of the Argentine Congress that clearly did indicate acquiescence by Argentina. Kohen and Rodríguez refrain from quoting those statements since their content is so damaging to Argentina's case, but they do allude (p. 226) to our mention of them, calling them merely "general statements of presidents and one vice-president in relation to the friendly relations of Argentina with the world in general or with the British government in particular".

In fact those statements were a good deal more than that, and derive special force from the fact that they were delivered at the yearly ceremonial opening of the national congress – a top-level international forum attended by foreign diplomats – and were printed in the Argentine press, some of them also in London in the *British and Foreign State Papers* (*BFSP*), and were all printed again in 1910 in the compilation by Heraclio Mabragaña of all the ceremonial Messages from 1810 to 1910.[2] The Messages at the opening of the Buenos Aires legislature had been a natural forum for protests to Britain over the Falklands from 1833 to 1849 (see sections 6.29, 7.15), and Argentina clearly regarded those statements as valid international protests, constituting part of Argentina's campaign to maintain its claim to the Falklands – in 1849 the Argentine ambassador in London, Manuel Moreno, pointed out to Lord Palmerston that Buenos Aires had made protests every year in Messages to the provincial legislature, and he repeated the texts of the protests in the Messages of

---

[1] Fery 1882, pp. 120, 122.
[2] H[eraclio] Mabragaña, *Los Mensajes 1810-1910*, Buenos Aires 1910.

1843, 44, 45, 47 and 48.[1] From 1862 the Argentine national congress could have been used as such a forum but that did not happen, and the Messages in the 1860s contained several statements that there was no dispute between Argentina and Britain and hence that there was no Argentine claim to the Falklands.

For example, in his Message at the opening of the Argentine Congress on 1 May 1865, President Bartolomé Mitre said that Argentina had scrupulously fulfilled undertakings with Britain and France, so "there was nothing to prevent the consolidation of friendly relations between this country and those Governments."[2] If there had been a dispute between Britain and Argentina over the Falklands, there would have been something to prevent that consolidation.

A year later, Vice-President Marcos Paz opened Congress on 1 May 1866, and in his Message mentioned some old claims for private losses by British citizens:[3]

The British Government has accepted the President of the Republic of Chile as arbitrator in the reclamation pending with the Argentine Republic, for damages suffered by English subjects in 1845. This question, which is the only one between us and the British nation, has not yet been settled.

That statement is perfectly clear – apart from the question of personal claims for damages, there was no dispute between Argentina and Britain. If there had been any outstanding problem such as a territorial dispute over the Falklands, Vice-President Paz could not have expressed himself in such a way. In other words, the Falklands were no longer in dispute between the two countries.

In his Message to the Argentine Congress on 1 May 1869 President Domingo Sarmiento expressed satisfaction at the state of Argentina's foreign relations:[4]

The state of our foreign relations fulfils the aspirations of the country. Nothing is claimed from us by other nations; we have nothing to ask of them except that they will persevere in manifesting their sympathies, with which both Governments and peoples have honoured the Republic, both for its progress and its spirit of fairness.

President Sarmiento stated unambiguously that Argentina had nothing to ask of other nations except friendship and respect. He could have said something to the effect that "apart from the question of the Malvinas Islands, our relations with all foreign nations are cordial." But he did not; his pronouncement is all-embracing and mentions no exceptions – the Falklands were clearly not in dispute between Argentina and Britain. All those top-level statements were demonstrations of overt acquiescence in Britain's possession of the islands.

When territories are in dispute between countries, comments by the leaders of one country may demonstrate acquiescence in the possession of those territories by another country. A famous example is provided by the *Eastern Greenland Case (Norway* v. *Denmark)*, heard in 1933 before the Permanent Court of International Justice (PCIJ, the predecessor of the ICJ). The Norwegian foreign minister, Nils Claus Ihlen (1855-1925), had stated on 22 July 1919 that Denmark's claim to sovereignty over the whole of Greenland "would be met with no difficulties on the part of Norway." That naturally implied Norwegian acceptance of the Danish claim to the whole of Greenland and was inconsistent with a claim by Norway to Eastern Greenland, as the PCIJ's judgement stated:[5]

---

[1] Moreno to Palmerston 31 July 1849, in PRO FO 6 502, fols. 279 *recto*-280 *verso*; see section 7.8.
[2] *British and Foreign State Papers (BFSP) 1865-1866*, (London 1870), p. 1174; Mabragaña 1910, vol. III, p. 227: "… no ha habido sino motivos para consolidar las relaciones amistosas que existen entre éste y aquellos gobiernos."
[3] This translation from *BFSP 1866-1867* (London 1871), p. 1009; Spanish in Mabragaña 1910, vol. III, p. 238: "Este mismo gobierno [= el gobierno británico] aceptó por árbitro al Presidente de la República de Chile, sobre perjuicios sufridos por súbditos ingleses en 1845. Aun no se ha resuelto esta cuestión que es la única que con aquella nación subsiste." The explanatory additions in *BFSP*: "the British government" (explaining "Este mismo gobierno", referring back to "El Gobierno de S[u] M[ajestad] B[ritánica]", i.e. "Her Britannic Majesty's Government" in the previous sentence in Mabragaña); "between us and the British nation" (explaining "con aquella nación" ["with that nation"]); and the phrase: "in the reclamation pending with the Argentine Republic" were added by *BFSP*'s editors.
[4] *BFSP 1870-1871* (London 1877), pp. 1227-1228; Spanish in Mabragaña 1910, vol. III, p. 286: "El estado de nuestras relaciones exteriores responde á las aspiraciones del país. Nada nos reclaman las otras Naciónes: nada tenemos que pedir de ellas, sino es la continuación de las manifestaciones de simpatía con que de parte de pueblos y gobiernos ha sido favorecida la República por sus progresos y espíritu de justicia."
[5] *P.C.I.J. Series A/B, No. 53*, p. 1, paragraph 103.

The Court considers it beyond all dispute that a reply of this nature given by the Minister of Foreign Affairs on behalf of his Government in response to a request by the diplomatic representative of a foreign power, in regard to a question falling within his province, is binding upon the country to which the Minister belongs.

In the *Research Handbook* edited by Marcelo Kohen and Mamadou Hébié, Kate Parlett mentions Ihlen's remarks, pointing out that in order to be binding on the state issuing them, such statements have to be made by "Persons Authorized to Bind the State through Unilateral Statements".[1]

Ihlen's remarks have become known as "the Ihlen declaration", and are obviously comparable to the official pronouncements by Argentine leaders in the 1860s to the effect that there were no disputes between Argentina and other countries. Those statements were made by Argentine leaders who were indubitably authorised to bind the state (Presidents Mitre and Sarmiento, and Vice-President Paz); they were made on a top-level occasion (the ceremonial opening of the Argentine Congress); they were witnessed not only by the whole of the Argentine Congress but by foreign ambassadors, and they were published both in Argentina and Britain. They therefore had international significance. In 1866 Vice-President Paz specifically stated that apart from the question of private compensation to British subjects, there were no outstanding questions between Britain and Argentina. In other words, there was no dispute over the Falklands and the Argentine claim to the islands had been definitively dropped. That is supported by the fact that neither then, nor for many years afterwards, did Argentina mention the Falklands at all to Britain. As Marcelo Kohen and Mamadou Hébié say in their introductory chapter to their *Research Handbook*:[2]

What generally remains crucial in territorial disputes is the demonstration that one side accepted in some way the existence and validity of the claim invoked by the other.

Kate Parlett says in the same book:[3]

Underlying all of the legal devices used to establish sovereignty to disputed territory based on state conduct examined here is the principle of consent: international courts and tribunals search for evidence that states have consented to the sovereignty of one state. In considering that question, both positive acts and omissions may be relevant, and consent need not be express, but may be tacit, provided there is compelling evidence.

And in his concluding chapter of the book Marcelo Kohen himself refers to:[4]

... the critical importance of consent in the creation and extinction of territorial sovereignty in international law.

In the case of the Falklands dispute between Argentina and Britain, it is clear that by its omissions and commissions Argentina accepted the "existence and validity" of Britain's title to the islands and "consented to the sovereignty" of Britain – indeed the evidence is overwhelming.

8.19 Another Falklands family – the Goss family

Several families have lived in the Falklands for around 180 years – the Pitaluga and Biggs families arrived in 1838 and 1840 respectively (sections 7.1 and 7.2), and the Goss family have been in the islands for 178 years: their ancestor Jacob Napoleon Goss (1825-68) arrived at Port Louis in the brig *Alarm* on 10 April 1842 aged only 16, and in 1846 he was commissioned to build a stone corral on Sappers Hill south of Stanley. The Sappers Hill corral, a typical Falklands corral consisting of a massive 5-foot-high circular drystone wall with entrances, was a favourite picnic spot for Stanleyites until it was mined by the Argentinians in 1982. It was de-mined thirty years later, and opened again to the public on 26 March 2012.[5] By 1854 Jacob Napoleon Goss and his

---

[1] Kate Parlett, chapter heading in Kohen and Hébié (eds.) 2018, p. 175; she mentions Ihlen's statement again on p. 188 (text and fn.), though without naming Ihlen.
[2] Marcelo Kohen and Mamadou Hébié, in Kohen and Hébié (eds.) 2018, p. 33.
[3] Kate Parlett, in Kohen and Hébié (eds.) 2018, p. 192.
[4] Marcelo Kohen, in Kohen and Hébié (eds.) 2018, p. 438.
[5] The original contract for this corral, dated 2 February 1846, is in the JCNA. See Eric Goss, "The stone corral – a history confirmed" in *Penguin News* 27 April 2012, p. 7, and articles "History returned as stone corral opened to public" in *Penguin News* 30 March 2012, p. 9, and "Stone Corral history worthy of preservation", in *Penguin News* 29 January 2016, p. 7. Extra details on the Goss family and Marmont Row from the late Jane Cameron, pers. comm.

8.19a Marmont Row, Stanley, October 1890; the sign "SHIP HOTEL" above the central entrance is just legible on the original; the second St Mary's church (1886) is visible at right. (FIC, album 1.e)

wife Ann had three children, were expecting a fourth, and were to have five more.[1]

On 25 March 1854 he obtained Crown Grant no. 67, of a plot on Ross Road in Stanley on which he built a row of five cottages, with an inn in the centre named the Eagle Inn, later the Ship Hotel (fig. 8.19a). The massive stone walls, over two feet thick in places, are more reminiscent of the 14th century than the 19th. In 1871 Ellaline Terriss (1871-1971), one of the most famous British actresses and beauties of the years 1890-1920, was born in the building.

By the early 1880s the second generation of native-born Falkland Islanders had begun to see the light of day, among them the first four of Jacob Napoleon Goss's grandchildren, whose parents had themselves been born in the islands: his fifth child Margaret (born 1856) had married William Bound in 1873, and their first child Richard Napoleon Bound was born in 1877 (died 1942); Jacob Napoleon Goss's second child Richard (born 1853) had married Sarah Belcher in 1881, and the first three of their nine children were William (b. 1881), Ada (1882) and Richard William Napoleon (1884), all born in Stanley. Those and other children – and their parents – were all born during the third of a century in which Argentina made no protest against Britain's possession of the islands.

By 1888 Jacob Napoleon Goss's building on Ross Road had acquired the name Marmont Row, of unknown origin; at some time the inn was renamed the Ship Hotel, and the hotel gradually absorbed the cottages. In 1969 it was bought by Des King, who renamed it the Upland Goose Hotel, under which name it became famous during and after the Falklands War, when it was often known simply as "the Goose". During the Argentine occupation its thick walls sheltered a number of people including Graham Bound, founder of *Penguin News* in 1979, and a direct descendant of Jacob Napoleon Goss.[2] The hotel closed in 2008, and the building reverted to its older name Marmont Row, which had never passed out of use among older islanders.

On 9 April 2017 some 30 descendants of Jacob Napoleon Goss gathered on Victory Green in front of Marmont Row to commemorate the 175th anniversary of their family's arrival in the Falklands. About half those present bore the surname Goss; the others had different surnames as the descent passed through daughters. The ages ranged from the oldest at 79 to the youngest at six months; some of the children are eighth and ninth-generation Falkland Islanders, and many other relatives were scattered elsewhere in the islands, the oldest being over 90.[3]

---

[1] Names of all his 9 children in entry on Jacob Napoleon Goss by Bill Featherstone in *DFB*. Family tree of Jacob Napoleon Goss to the mid-1980s in Lynda and Nicholas Pine, *William Henry Goss: the story of the Staffordshire family of Potters who invented Heraldic Porcelain*, Portsmouth 1987, pp. 248-249.

[2] Graham Bound, *Falkland Islanders at War*, Barnsley 2002, dustcover and e.g. pp. 191-2; 2nd expanded and updated ed., *Invasion 1982: The Falkland Islanders' Story*, Barnsley 2007, dustcover and e.g. pp. 199-200, quoting letters by Graham's father Nap Bound, who sheltered at the Goose with his family.

[3] See article in *Penguin News* 14 April 2017, p. 11, "Goss gathering for 175 year anniversary", and "The History of the Goss Family in the Falkland Islands", by Kelly Harris (aged 14) in *FIJ* vol. 11 (2), Stanley 2018, pp. 193-197. Kelly is an 8th-generation Falkland Islander on both her father's and her mother's side *(ibid.)*.

8.20 British acts of sovereignty (« effectivités ») in the Falklands in the 1850s, 60s and 70s

In international disputes over territory, it is of importance whether one of the claiming parties has performed « effectivités » (section 8.9), i.e. acts of sovereignty, in the disputed territory without protest from the other party. As described in section 8.9, Chile pointed out before the Court of Arbitration in 1977 that it had performed acts of sovereignty in the Beagle Channel Islands for 34 years (1881-1915) without protest from Argentina; that was a factor in the Court's decision to award those islands to Chile. In the Falklands Britain performed innumerable acts of sovereignty for 38 years (1850-1888), during which Argentina made no protest against Britain's possession of the islands.

In the 1850s Britain extended the settlement of the islands beyond East Falkland to two more islands: in 1855 Keppel Island received permanent inhabitants for the first time, and some of the buildings they built in the 1850s still stand.[1] In 1859 the British-run commercial firm of Smith Brothers of Montevideo took a lease of 160 acres on New Island; the firm rented out the island for fishing (i.e. sealing), and also sent out settlers, an activity they had experience in – they had brought about 1,000 Irish emigrants to Buenos Aires in the previous few years. In 1861 Colonial Surveyor Arthur Bailey visited New Island and found a "quiet and orderly" population of seven men, a woman and a child, plus 500 sheep, 46 head of cattle, and some horses, goats and mules. There was also a stone house (i.e. Charles Barnard's house, no doubt repaired and extended), two turf houses, and a try-works for boiling out the oil from seal blubber.[2]

Another act of sovereignty by Britain in the 1850s was the issuing of exequaturs for consuls to represent Hamburg in 1853, and Denmark in 1858, the first of ten countries to recognise British sovereignty in the islands by opening consulates (section 8.15).

For the Falklands the 1860s were even more important. We have already mentioned acts by foreign countries that confirmed British sovereignty (section 8.15), the opening of further consulates and the behaviour of the Spanish diplomatic and scientific expedition in 1863, which ended any Spanish claim to the islands (8.17), and in section 8.18 we quoted statements by Argentine leaders in 1865, 1866 and 1869 that indicated Argentina's consent to Britain's possession of the Falklands.

In addition, during the 1860s Britain performed large-scale acts of sovereignty in the islands. First, large areas were leased out on East Falkland. One of the lessees was Antonina Roxa, who had arrived aboard the *Sarandí* in 1832 and had stayed when the ship left in January 1833 (section 6.19). In 1866 she took a 10-year lease on a station of 6,000 acres around Smyley's Creek, which she worked as a cattle ranch with her second husband Pedro Varela, though she did not live for the full term of the lease and died on 14 February 1869. Among other lessees were John Bonner (who founded San Carlos in the late 1860s); John Llamosa from Spain; and Andrez Pitaluga from Gibraltar, who took up a station west of Port Salvador and by April 1862 had built a stone house, a calf corral, a pig sty and a vegetable garden, had 53 working horses, 30 mares, 59 tame cattle, 18 pigs, 7 goats, 7 sheep, 20 fowl and some ducks, and was already supplying Stanley with beef and butter.[3] All those three men have descendants in the islands today.

During the governorship of William Robinson (1866-70), Saunders Island acquired its first inhabitants since 1774, and more importantly West Falkland was settled for the first time ever – in 1866 the brothers Robert and Edward Packe leased 118,000 acres on West Falkland, at Fox Bay East, Dunnose Head, and a station near Port Howard still known as Packe's Port Howard.[4] Several

---
[1] A fully illustrated authoritative account of the history of Keppel Island is given in Robert A. Philpott, *Keppel: The South American Missionary Society Settlement 1855-1911, An Archaeological and Historical Survey*, Stanley and Liverpool 2009). By 1855 the island had been known as Keppel Island for at least 80 years; it was named after Rear Admiral Augustus Keppel (1725-86), and the name is shown on Hawkesworth's (McBride's) Falklands chart of 1773 and Edgar's chart of 1786.

[2] Wayne Bernhardson, *Land and Life in the Falkland Islands*, unpublished doctoral thesis, Berkeley 1989 (in JCNA), p. 326; letters from Smith Brothers to Governor Moore 17 September 1859 and 24 February 1860, in JCNA, H16.

[3] Bernhardson 1989, p. 324, quoting a letter from Surveyor Bailey to Moore, 21 April 1862, in JCNA, H18. The name is pronounced "*Pitt*alooga", with a short stressed first syllable (Saul Pitaluga, pers. comm.).

[4] Details from entry on Packe by Michael Stammers in *DFB*.

more of today's West Falkland farms were established in those years too: Chartres River by James McClymont; Fox Bay West by Louis and Edward Baillon with William and Bernard Stickney; Port Howard by James Waldron; Port Stephens by Montague Dean, and Shallow Bay (with Hill Cove and Roy Cove) by Ernest Holmested, William Bertrand, John Switzer and Robert Blake.[1] By 1868 the whole of West Falkland had been leased out and was being farmed – Governor Robinson said in a despatch to the Colonial Secretary, the Duke of Buckingham, on 25 May 1868:[2]

Twelve months ago there was not a settler on the island; now there is not one acre of land… unoccupied. Twelve months ago the island did not contribute in any manner to the Revenue; now the land rents… will amount next year… to over £1,300 per annum…

Kohen and Rodríguez say nothing about all that, but those things have a highly significant bearing on the legal status of the Falklands today. The settling of West Falkland and other islands took place without the slightest reaction on the part of Argentina – there had been no mention of the Falklands by Argentina to the British government since 1850, nor was there until the mid-1880s, though there was a constant coming and going of ships and people between the islands and Argentina, and the Argentine government knew what was going on. The settlement of the western Falklands was a practical demonstration of the aphorism "gobernar es poblar" ["to govern is to populate"] enunciated a decade earlier by the prominent Argentine liberal and political theorist Juan Bautista Alberdi.[3] In extending population and government to West Falkland and other formerly uninhabited islands, and performing countless acts of administration in them, Britain was exercising sovereignty over them, and Argentina failed to react at all.

Throughout the 1870s the recognition of Britain's sovereignty in the Falklands developed without any reaction from Argentina. In 1875 the United States opened a consulate in Stanley, thus abandoning the US government's earlier policy of not recognising any territorial sovereignty in the islands. In 1877 Chile opened a consulate, as did Sweden and Norway jointly (the two crowns were united till 1905), and by the end of the 1870s there were consulates of Belgium, Chile, Germany, Italy, Sweden and Norway (jointly), and the United States (section 8.15). Those seven countries clearly did not accept that there was a valid Argentine claim to the Falkland Islands, and by 1875 Argentina had not mentioned it to Britain for a quarter of a century anyway.

By the 1870s a new element began to enter the equation – the Falkland Islanders were starting to become a distinct population. Most of the people were of British origin and had gone to the islands under their own steam, but there were a number who were not British and who arrived by accident. For example, in August 1860 the British barque *Colonsay* and the German ship *Concordia* were wrecked in the islands within a few days of each other;[4] all aboard both ships were saved, and the 16-year-old Swede Frans Theodor Rylander from the *Colonsay* and the Dane Karl Hansen from the *Concordia* both stayed in the Falklands for the rest of their lives, married and had children. Rylander Anglicised his name to Francis (or Frank) Theodore Rowlands, was naturalised on 26 August 1870, died in Stanley on 15 April 1919 and is buried in Stanley cemetery.[5] In 1872 Karl Hansen bought the lease of Carcass Island and the Jason Islands, stocked them with sheep, and spent 20 years sheep-farming and sealing in the Falklands, initially as an "alien", which did not prevent him from leasing land, but on 5 January 1880 he was granted British citizenship as Charles Hansen. On 1 October 1891 he was washed overboard from the schooner *Result* and drowned. Both men have descendants in the islands today.

---

[1] Details from the entries on these people in *DFB*.
[2] Copy of despatch from Robinson to the Duke of Buckingham, 25 May 1868, in JCNA, B 14, pp. 211-212.
[3] Juan Bautista Alberdi (1810-84); his most influential political essay, *Bases y puntos de partida para la organización política de la República Argentina* ["Bases and starting points for the political organisation of the Argentine Republic"] (1st and 2nd eds. Valparaíso, Chile, 1852; 3rd ed. Buenos Aires September 1852) contains the phrase "gobernar es poblar" several times; he expanded it in the Paris ed. to "en América gobernar es poblar".
[4] Details of *Colonsay* from the large wall poster *A plan of the Falkland Islands drawn by John Smith: With details of historical and of maritime interest*, Stanley 1977, new edition Stanley 1985; details of the loss of the *Concordia* from a letter to the Admiralty by Charles Hansen dated 6 February 1882, in *The Falkland Islands Journal* (*FIJ*) 1977, p. 7.
[5] Obituary of "Capt. Frank Rowlands" in *The Falkland Islands Magazine* (*FIM*) No. II Vol. XXXI, June 1919, p. 4, ending with the Welsh phrase "Heddwch yw lwch" [*sic*],"Peace to his dust", *recte* "Heddwch i'w lwch".

By 1881 the population of the islands amounted to over 1,500, including some 150 children in full-time education, and there was a steady increase of about 40 native-born people a year.[1] And by the early 1880s the second generation of native-born Falkland Islanders had begun to see the light of day, among whom were the first four grandchildren of Jacob Napoleon Goss, all of whose parents had been born in the islands (section 8.19).[2] By now (2022) some families have been in the islands for over 180 years and for eight or nine generations.

Throughout the 1850s, 1860s, 1870s and well into the 1880s, Argentina made no protest against Britain's possession of the Falklands. Any Argentine title to the islands was well and truly dead.

8.21 International recognition: the UPU; a new Falklands industry; no Argentine protests

The second-oldest international organisation in the world after the International Telecommunications Union is the Union Postale Universelle or Universal Postal Union. It was founded on 9 October 1874 by the Treaty of Berne, signed by 22 countries including Britain. Its members now include the 193 members of the United Nations, plus the dependent territories of several of them including Britain, France, the Netherlands, New Zealand and the United States.

Britain joined the organisation on 1 July 1875, and on 1 April 1877 the dependent territories of the British Empire, including the Falklands, were also registered as members. That brought the islands a new industry: the issuing of postage stamps. The first Falkland Islands stamps, valued at 1d [a penny] and 6d [sixpence], were issued in June 1878. That provided a significant source of revenue for the islands and has spawned considerable international philatelic interest.[3]

On 1 April 1878, a year after the Falklands were included in the UPU, Argentina joined the organisation, and for the rest of the 19th century and well into the 20th accepted the inclusion of the islands in the organisation without protest or comment. The acceptance of the Falklands by the other members of the UPU provides further evidence of general international acceptance of the islands as British territory, while conversely the absence of Argentine protests is yet another sign that Argentina acquiesced in British possession of the islands.[4]

8.22 Maps; the 1882 Latzina map; Argentina's inconsistency, I

The publication of maps is a standard way of making statements on claims to territory, and in *Getting it right* (p. 29) we pointed out that during the years 1850-84 "a number of maps were published in Argentina that did not show the Falklands as Argentine territory". These are of three types: type (a) showed only the northern part of Argentina, leaving out the Falklands completely;[5] type (b) showed all of Argentina but cut out the Falklands by covering their position with empty sea or an insert, like the vegetation map in fig. 8.22a, while type (c) marked the Falklands but in a different colour from Argentina ("the non-Argentina colour"). Type (d) would be maps that unambiguously showed the Falklands as Argentine territory, but we have found none before 1886. Thus in the publication of maps, Argentina for over 30 years after the ratification of the Convention of Peace followed a policy that was inconsistent with maintaining any claim to the Falklands.

Our fig. 8.22a is taken from *Die Argentinische Republik*, by Richard Napp,[6] which was published as part of the Argentine contribution to the Centennial Exhibition in Philadelphia (5 May

---

[1] The 1881 census, in the *Blue Book* for 1881 (PRO CO 81/36), recorded a total of 1,553 (976 males, 577 females). In the early 1880s there averaged about 55 births to about 15 deaths, i.e. a natural increase of about 40 people a year.

[2] Details from family tree in Pine 1987, pp. 248-249.

[3] E.g. B.W. H. Poole, *Postage Stamps of the Falkland Islands*, London 1909; B. S. H. Grant, *The Postage Stamps of the Falkland Islands and Dependencies*, London 1952; Robert Barnes, *The Postal Service of the Falkland Islands*, London 1972; and *id.*, *The Postal Cancellations of the Falkland Islands*, Southampton 1982; Stefan Heijtz, *Specialised Stamp Catalogue of the Falkland Islands and Dependencies..., 1800-1987*, 1st ed. Stockholm, 1988; 2nd ed. 1990; 3rd 1995.

[4] The Falkland Islands are still listed (under O, for Overseas Territories of Great Britain) in the South America section of the list of UPU members on the website of the Universal Postal Union.

[5] E.g. the general map of Argentina in [Anon.], *Atlas Geográfico de la República Argentina Comprendiendo al Mapa General y los de cada Provincia...*, printed Paris 1877 (copy in British Library, Maps 2 c 7).

[6] Richard Napp [ed.], *Die Argentinische Republik. Im Auftrag des Argentin. Central Comité's für die Philadelphia-Ausstellung...* ["The Argentine Republic. Commissioned by the Argentine Central Committee for the Philadelphia Exhibition..."], Buenos Aires 1876 (Introduction dated Buenos Aires, October 1875).

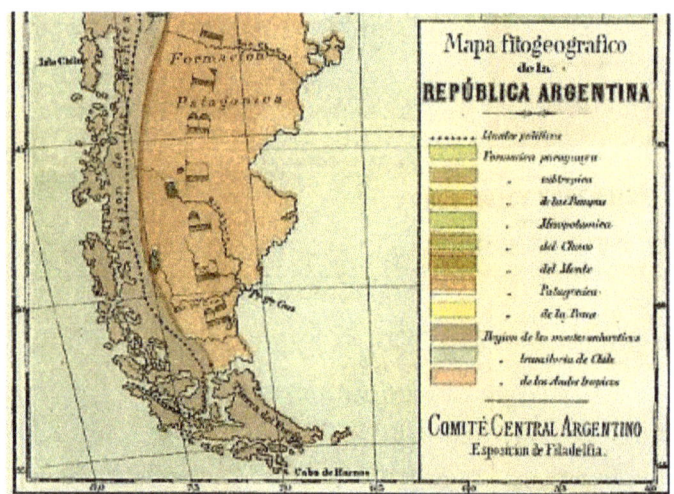

8.22a Vegetation map in Richard Napp, *Die Argentinische Republik*, Buenos Aires 1876 (detail).
A type (b) map – the position of the Falklands is empty or hidden by the legend.

to 10 November 1876), celebrating the centenary of the independence of the United States. The text of the book describes the geography, natural history and politics of Argentina, and was written largely by a group of German scientists headed by Richard Napp, the German-born head of the Argentine general commercial statistical office. The German original was translated into English, Spanish and French, and a total of 15,000 copies were distributed at the Philadelphia exhibition and to Argentine consulates all over the world.

Kohen and Rodríguez (pp. 231, 232) reproduce another map from the same book, on which they claim that the Malvinas are shown as Argentinian, but that assertion needs to be qualified. It is a large map, in outlines only, without colour; it shows the whole of Argentina and also the Falklands, but does not specifically mark them as Argentinian (which could have been done by a label such as "Arg.", but there is none). On the small reproduction by Kohen and Rodríguez it is possible to see that the islands are marked "Islas Malvinas" (unremarkable on a Spanish-language map), but no smaller names are legible. In fact all the other place-names on that map are not the original Spanish names but the English names translated into Spanish, for example:

West Falkland:	Falkland Occid^{tal}	East Falkland:	Falkland Orien^{tal}
Falkland Sound:	Estrecho de Falkland	King George Bay:	Bahía del Rey Jorge
Byron Sound:	Bahía Byron	Jason Islands:	Islas de Jason
Cape Dolphin:	Cabo Delfin	Speedwell Island:	I. Speedwell

Thus the map does not indicate an unequivocal Argentine claim to the Falklands, especially given that the vegetation map in the same book omits the islands, as shown in fig. 8.22a.

The book does not avoid territorial controversies – it goes into detail on border disputes with Bolivia[1] and describes in aggrieved tones the recently-raised Chilean claims to much of Patagonia and Tierra del Fuego, quoting the treaty by which Spain recognised Chile's independence on 1 July 1845, which according to Napp excluded any Chilean claim to Tierra del Fuego[2] (the large map in the book, printed by Kohen and Rodríguez, marks the whole of Tierra del Fuego as Argentinian).

But compared with the detailed and indignant treatment of Chilean pretensions in Tierra del Fuego and Patagonia, the book's treatment of the Falklands is noticeably muted, and they are missing where one might have expected them. They are not mentioned in the "Historical Overview" in chapter 2, nor in the description of the course of the Argentine coast, nor in the table of the latitudes and longitudes of the easternmost points of Argentina at different latitudes.[3]

---

[1] Napp 1876, p. 28 (references here are to the original German edition). The Spanish translation is available in full online under https://archive.org/stream/larepblicaarge00napp#page/476/mode/2up.
[2] Napp 1876, pp. 26-27.
[3] Napp 1876, pp. 22-23, 28-29.

The Falklands are only mentioned near the end of the book, in a single paragraph full of errors.[1] It calls Port Louis "Puerto Ruiz", and claims that Britain and the United States recognised Argentina's rights to the islands, Britain by recognising the independence of Argentina, Washington by diplomatic negotiations after the conflict with "North American seal-killers". In fact Britain's recognition of Argentina's independence in 1825 in no way implied recognition of the claim to the Falklands (section 4.12), and the only diplomatic negotiations with Washington (in 1832, section 6.15) had explicitly denied Argentina's rights in the islands. The paragraph twice says that England was occupying the islands "illegally"; it mentions that Argentina had protested in London, and adds: "Although it [Argentina's protesting] has produced no practical consequences, it has nevertheless served to protect our rights".[2] Kohen and Rodriguez quote that statement (p. 233), but of course it was true only as long as protests continued – Argentina's rights had been maintained by regular protests for 17 years from 1833 to 1849, but those protests had ceased entirely in 1850 after the ratification of the Convention of Peace, and by 1876 there had been none for over a quarter of a century. Napp does not draw attention to the fact that Argentina had not protested for a long time, nor that the Convention of Peace had ended all disputes between Britain and Argentina. So the book does not provide strong evidence for Argentina's continuing claim to the Falklands.

Kohen and Rodríguez give a seriously inaccurate account of a much more important map, the 1882 Latzina map, which we discussed and illustrated in *Getting it right* (p. 29). It is a type (c) map, i.e. one which marks the Falklands in the "non-Argentina colour", showing them as outside Argentina. The map's special significance derives from the fact that it was issued at a high official level, and that it played a role in the court case over the Beagle Channel islands dispute between Argentina and Chile in 1977, when its coloration was a factor in the court's decision to award those islands to Chile, which Argentina later accepted (section 8.9).

The 1882 Latzina map was produced after the so-called "Campaign of the Desert", in which from 1878 onwards Argentine defence minister Julio Roca (president from 1880) conducted a systematic campaign of genocide against the American Indian inhabitants of Patagonia. Most of them were killed or driven off their ancestral lands, after which the Patagonian border between Argentina and Chile was fixed by treaty on 23 July 1881. Being now "clear" of Indians, Patagonia was open for European immigration, and President Roca and foreign minister Bernardo de Irigoyen promoted the publication of a map of Argentina specifically to attract immigrants. The map, dated 1882 but published in 1883, was produced under the supervision of Dr Francisco Latzina (1843-1922), director of the Argentine national statistical office, whence it is known as the "1882 Latzina map". Its publication was authorised by the Argentine Congress and financed by the Argentine government, and it was headed on the front cover "PUBLICACION OFICIAL" (fig. 8.22b) – it was an official, definitive and up-to-date map of the country in its new borders. It was printed in 120,000 copies, which were distributed to Argentine consulates in Europe and North America.[3]

Those circumstances give this map particular significance – as the Eritrea-Ethiopia Boundary Commission said in 2002, not specifically referring to this map but to maps in general and to the way in which they may affect a territorial dispute when produced by a party to that dispute:[4]

... a map produced by an official government agency of a party, on a scale sufficient to enable its portrayal of the disputed boundary to be identifiable, which is generally available for purchase or examination, whether in the country of origin or elsewhere, and acted upon, or not reacted to, by the adversely affected party, can be expected to have significant legal consequences.

The 1882 Latzina map satisfies all those requirements for a map to have "significant legal consequences" and is thus of special importance.

---

[1] Napp 1876, pp. 479-480 (pp. 450-451 in the Spanish version). Kohen and Rodríguez say "two pages are dedicated to the Malvinas", but there is in fact only one paragraph of less than a page, which happens to run on to a second page.
[2] Napp 1876, p. 480.
[3] Details on the map's financing and publication from "Una Tradición Cartográfica Física y Política de la Argentina, 1838-1882", by Hernan González Bollo, in *Ciencia Hoy*, vol. 8, no. 46, Buenos Aires, May/June 1998.
[4] Katherine Del Mar, in Kohen and Hébié (eds.) 2018, p. 426, with footnote referring to the decision of the Eritrea-Ethiopia Boundary Commission of 13 April 2002.

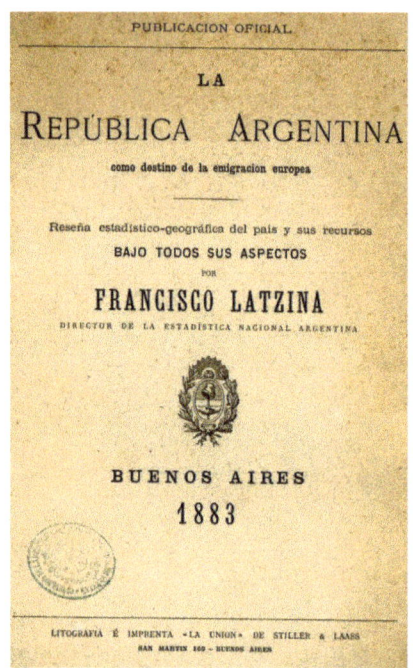

8.22b The 1882 Latzina map: the front cover, headed "Publicación oficial".

8.22c The 1882 Latzina map: the main map (Buenos Aires 1883), a type (c) map. Both inserts at bottom are beige.

8.22d No Falklands in the insert at bottom left, type (b).

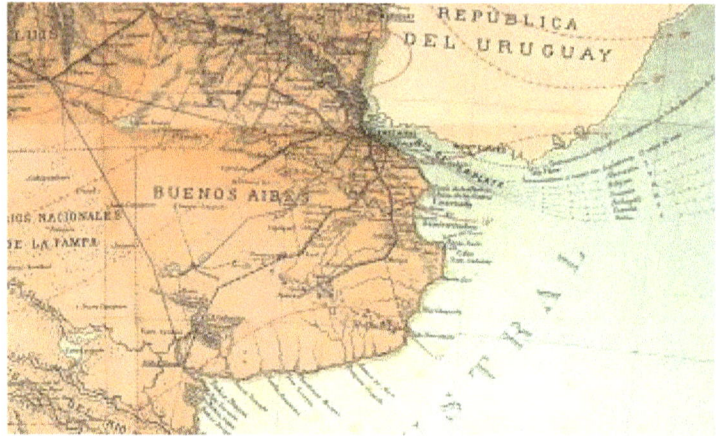

8.22e Buenos Aires from the main map, in the darker orange-brown; Uruguay is beige, the sea pale blue.

8.22f The Falklands in the non-Argentina colour on the type (c) main map. Here Argentine territory is marked in the paler orange-brown; Chile and the Falklands are beige, the sea pale blue. The PNL group are the little islands below the letters "GO" of "TIERRA DEL FUEGO". The curved lines are isotherms showing average temperatures; there are many such lines on Chilean territory.

Figure 8.22c shows the whole of the 1882 Latzina map. Printed on a single large sheet, it shows most of southern South America, labelled in Spanish; the reverse bears a long text with information for potential immigrants, which was printed in five separate versions (Spanish, English, French, German and Italian), none of which mentions the Falklands. The map's four colours are not printed in halftone (in which shapes and different colours are produced by a pattern of tiny coloured dots visible under a magnifying glass) but are block-printed; the ink is continuous and no amount of magnification shows dots. On all the originals we have seen the colours are not perfectly aligned. The outlines, relief shading and names are in black; the sea is eggshell blue; all countries outside Argentina plus both the insert maps are pale beige, and on the main map only, Argentina is in two shades of orange-brown. The orange-brown shades are keyed to two panels in the legend: the upper panel, in the paler shade, indicates "Tierras incultas" ["uncultivated lands"], and the lower panel in the darker shade indicates "id. de pastoreo" ["ditto grazing lands"]. The paler colour covers some two thirds of the country: the Gran Chaco at the top of the map, the "territorios nacionales" (i.e. areas ruled by the central government) of La Pampa and most of Río Negro, plus all of Patagonia, while the darker colour covers the province of Buenos Aires and the northern parts including Mendoza and Cordoba, though a few small parts of those provinces are in the paler colour.

The inserts at top (Santa Fe and Gran Chaco) and bottom right (Buenos Aires) are type (a), i.e. they do not show the South Atlantic; that at bottom left is type (b); the title covers the Falklands.

The Falklands only appear on the main map, which is of type (c) – it shows all areas outside Argentina (Chile, Uruguay, parts of Paraguay and Brazil, plus the Falklands and all the islands south of Tierra del Fuego) in blank pale beige, i.e. the "non-Argentina colour". The colour difference between Argentina and all areas outside Argentina (including the Falklands) is quite clear, as shown in figs. 8.22c, 8.22e and 8.22f, taken directly from an original of the map in the possession of Graham Pascoe. We have also seen two other originals, in the AGN in Buenos Aires and the British Library in London, which are identical to this one. Note that there is (or was until recently) a "doctored" version of the map on the internet in which the colours have been manipulated to make Argentina and the Falklands the same colour. It is a forgery; we suspect it was put online as a direct response to our two online papers *Getting it right* and *False Falklands History*, in both of which we illustrated the map in colour showing the difference.

The fact that the 1882 Latzina map marks the Falklands in the "non-Argentina colour" is of special significance, since almost a century later in the 1970s it played a role in the Beagle Channel dispute between Argentina and Chile over the possession of the three small islands of Picton, Nueva and Lennox (the "PNL group") south of Tierra del Fuego, on which a decision was made in 1977 by a special Court of Arbitration (section 8.9).[1] The court was convened under British auspices but sat in Geneva and consisted of an international group of judges of the International Court of Justice.[2] The 1882 Latzina map was submitted to the Court by Chile as "Chilean Plate no. 25", as evidence that Argentina had produced an official map not indicating the PNL group as Argentinian. On the basis of this and much other evidence, the Court of Arbitration unanimously awarded the PNL group to Chile on 18 February 1977. The Court rejected Argentina's contention that the 1882 Latzina map was non-official, and stated:[3]

The Argentine Congress officially approved the project and authorized the publication of a large number of copies for distribution throughout Europe... this Latzina map leaves no doubt as to the attribution to Chile of the PNL group of islands... The Latzina map of 1882-3 provides an excellent example... for the circumstances of its production and dissemination, making it of high probative value on account of the evidence afforded by this episode, namely of official Argentine recognition, at the time, of the Chilean character of the PNL group...

Argentina repudiated the Court's award in 1978, but the Argentine "Declaration of Nullity" made

---

[1] Details on this dispute from *ILR* 1979 and Kobylanski 1987.
[2] The judges were Sir Gerald Fitzmaurice (Britain; chairman), André Gros (France), Sture Petrén (Sweden), Charles D. Onyeama (Nigeria), and Hardy C. Dillard (United States) (*ILR* 1979, pp. 104 and 107).
[3] *ILR* 1979, pp. 197-198 and 212; the "Treaty" is the 1881 border treaty between Argentina and Chile.

no mention of the 1882 Latzina map and hence implicitly accepted the Court's description of it.[1] Argentina and Chile almost went to war over the PNL group in 1978, and Argentina actually opened hostilities on 22 December 1978 by starting "Operación Soberanía" ["Operation Sovereignty"], which would have involved an invasion of the PNL islands. The new Pope (John Paul II) offered mediation and sent his envoy, Cardinal Antonio Samoré, to Buenos Aires; Argentina halted hostilities but did not drop the dispute. In the end, after the Falklands War, the Vatican mediated between Argentina and Chile and in 1984 proposed an award similar to that made by the Court of Arbitration in 1977, likewise awarding the PNL group to Chile, and in 1985 Argentina and Chile both accepted the Vatican award. Argentina thus accepted the 1977 Court's analysis of the 1882 Latzina map – that in marking the PNL group in the same colour as territories outside Argentina, it officially recognised them as not being Argentine territory. The 1882 Latzina map marks the Falklands in the same colour as the PNL group, so it implies that for the Argentine government in 1882 the Falklands too were outside Argentina.

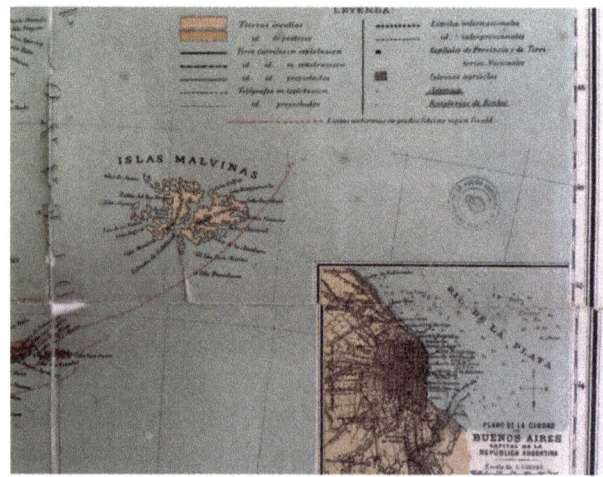 

8.22g Kohen's and Rodríguez's first excerpt from the map, omitting Argentina but including the insert map of Buenos Aires, in the same beige as the Falklands. It can be seen that the islands are not in either of the "Argentina colours", which are shown in the two oblong panels in the legend.

8.22h Kohen's and Rodríguez's second excerpt; it cuts out half of the type (b) insert at bottom left, and thus obscures its omission of the Falklands. This excerpt likewise shows the oblong panels in the legend with the two "Argentina colours", both of which are darker and more orange in hue than the colour of the Falklands.

Naturally Kohen and Rodríguez are concerned to devalue the evidence of the 1882 Latzina map, since it is so damaging to their case. They distort the evidence of the map by describing it incorrectly and illustrating it selectively (our figs. 8.22g and 8.22h). They illustrate two excerpts from it, in their Spanish version murkily in black and white as figs. 21 and 22 on pp. 234 and 235, and in colour (correctly, not falsified) as figs. 19 and 20 in their English online version. We reproduce their two illustrations here from their English version in our figs. 8.22g and 8.22h, which show that they distort the evidence of the map. The one in fig. 8.22g shows the Falklands and the insert map of Buenos Aires, which are the same colour, but they are on two separate maps (the main map and the insert); the colour attributions in the legend of the main map do not apply to the insert.

Kohen and Rodríguez do not mention that Buenos Aires appears twice, and they do not point out that on the main map (the only one that shows the Falklands) Buenos Aires is darkish orange-brown, quite different from the beige of the Falklands (figs. 8.22e, 8.22f). Their second excerpt (fig. 8.22h) cuts out most of the bottom-left type (b) insert, obscuring the fact that it covers the position of the Falklands with the title-box (fig. 8.22d). The two excerpts from the 1882 Latzina map illustrated by Kohen and Rodríguez misrepresent it so as to support what they say in their text.

And what they say is incorrect in several ways. In the first place, they say (p. 233) that we say in *Getting it right* that on the 1882 Latzina map the colour of the islands is "similar" to that of Chile or Uruguay – in fact we say (p. 29) that it is "the same as Uruguay and Chile" (it is identical).

---

[1] Argentina's "Declaration of Nullity" is given in full in *ILR* 1979, pp. 269-277; the rejection of the Court's decision was based on other considerations than the 1882 Latzina map.

Secondly, they assert on their pp. 233-4 that the Falklands and Buenos Aires are shown in the colour that indicates "uncultivated lands". That is not the case; the Falklands and the insert of Buenos Aires are both in exactly the same beige as Chile or Uruguay, not the colour that indicates "uncultivated lands", i.e. the paler "Argentina colour". The difference is slight but unmistakeable. The main map's legend does not apply to the inserts, so the insert map is not indicating that Buenos Aires is uncultivated, but nor is it placing it outside Argentina; it is in pale beige because either of the "Argentina colours" would have made the details hard to see.

And thirdly, Kohen and Rodríguez say that on the 1882 Latzina map, countries outside Argentina bear no geographical names, whereas both the Falklands and Argentina are labelled with names of bays, sounds, etc. But that needs qualification. In the first place, there are a few such names outside Argentina, e.g. in Chile south of Tierra del Fuego, as shown in fig. 8.22f; secondly, there is in general a greater density of place-names on the Argentine coast than in the Falklands, and thirdly the place-names in the Falklands are not genuine Spanish names but English names translated into Spanish, the same ones as on the large map in Napp 1876 (above). In short, Kohen and Rodríguez give an incorrect description of the 1882 Latzina map.

In fact it marks the Falklands in the same colour as the PNL group, which the 1977 Court of Arbitration ruled were Chilean territory, as Argentina later accepted. The official nature of the map gives it special authority, and it is of probative value in showing that in 1882, over 30 years after the Convention of Peace, Argentina had abandoned any title to the Falklands. In 1888 and 1890 Francisco Latzina published two works on the geography of Argentina which imply that the Falklands were not Argentine territory, or even state that they belonged to Britain (section 8.28).

And it was in 1882 that the Argentine government declared in the Argentine Congress that Louis Vernet's 1828 concession was invalid (section 5.6). In a debate during the session of 29 July 1882, the future Argentine foreign minister Francisco Ortiz reported the decision of an official commission, that the decree authorising Vernet's concession:[1]

… had no legal force, since it had not been authorised by the General Congress of the Nation, which was the power that had to regulate grants of national territories.

So in 1882 the Argentine government regarded the basis of Vernet's activities in the Falklands from 1828 as having been illegal. That retrospectively called into question the whole of Argentina's actions in the Falklands from 1828 onwards.

8.23 The Affair of the Map: Phase I, 1884-5; Britain protests

Nevertheless, in 1884 the Argentine government under President Roca decided on a change of policy and began to raise a claim to the Falklands. Argentina called it a "revival" or "reopening" of its old claim, but it was really a new claim. The old claim had lapsed completely, as a result of many things including the Convention of Peace, statements by Argentine leaders, the absence of protests by Argentina, the publication of the 1882 Latzina map, innumerable acts of sovereignty by Britain without any Argentine reaction, and the recognition of British sovereignty by governments that opened consulates in Stanley. Argentina retained no title whatsoever to the Falklands.

So the raising of a claim to the islands was a new departure. The resulting disputes, between Argentina and the US on the one hand, and between Argentina and Britain on the other, took place from 1884 to 1888, in two phases, with a gap from August 1886 to March 1887.[2] The dispute with Britain ended with Argentina's last-ever Falklands protest on 20 January 1888 (section 8.26).

Argentina began the American part of the dispute first: on 28 January 1884 foreign minister Francisco Ortiz (who in 1882 had stated that Vernet's 1828 concession had been invalid, section 8.22) instructed the Argentine ambassador in Washington, Luis Domínguez, to take up the question of compensation from the United States for losses caused by the *Lexington* raid of 1831-2 (section 6.12), since the heirs of Louis Vernet (who had died in 1871) had recently presented their claim to

---

[1] Text from *Diario de Sesiones*, Buenos Aires 29 July 1882, p. 311 (fuller quote in section 5.6).
[2] Partial summary of the correspondence on the disputes in Bernhardt 1910 and in *BDFA I, D*, vol. 1, 1991, pp. 358-406. Fuller text in Fitte 1966, pp. 455-540, Muñoz Azpiri 1966, vol. II, pp. 204-361, and Becerra 1998, pp. 145-210.

the Argentine Congress.[1] Ortiz began:[2]

> I have the pleasure to announce to Your Excellency that this government has resolved to reopen in London the discussion of its right to the Malvinas Islands, with the aim of obtaining their return.

It was presumptuous to "resolve to reopen" the discussion – history had moved on a long way in the third of a century since Argentina had dropped its claim in 1850, and the Falklands were no longer a subject on which Argentina had any right to resolve anything.

Five months later Argentina began the British part of the dispute, which we call "the Affair of the Map" since it centred on the production of a new map showing the Falklands as Argentine territory. The affair took place in two phases, which we call "Phase I", from May 1884 to February 1886, and "Phase II", from March 1887 to its final end in June 1888. In the gap between the two phases some important developments in the history of the islands took place (section 8.25).

If the Argentine government had begun by protesting to London against British possession of the Falklands, it might have claimed to be continuing where it had left off after the last symbolic protest of 27 December 1849 (section 7.15), though a gap of 34 years does not exactly make for continuity. But there was no protest, just a mere oral hint by Ortiz to Edmund Monson, the British ambassador in Buenos Aires, who reported on 30 May 1884 to Foreign Secretary Earl Granville:[3]

> ... Dr Ortiz... said... most confidentially, that the Argentine Government intended re-opening their claim to the Falkland Islands. I interrupted His Excellency at once by stating that, if his Government contemplated so serious a step, I thought that the better and more regular plan would be to cause the communication to be made to Your Lordship by the Argentine Minister in London... His Excellency replied... Now that the Country was consolidated, and was "rounding off" its territories, it seemed advisable to take advantage of the moment to settle all its territorial claims... He did not want to say more at present than that his Government thought it a question which might fairly be settled by arbitration... Although I was naturally much surprised at being suddenly made the recipient of a statement that Her Majesty's Government were to be asked to make a cession of territory to which the exercise of possession for more than half a century seems to give Her Majesty the strongest prescriptive right, I did not think it politic to resent by warm language a proposition which... savours a good deal of impertinence. The Argentine Government, having recently annexed the major part of Patagonia, now want to "round off" their territory by taking the Falkland Islands...

Kohen and Rodríguez mention this despatch (p. 240), but they suppress the secretive, almost underhand way in which Argentina raised the question; they do not mention Monson's statements that the suggestion "savours a good deal of impertinence" and that the Argentine government wanted "to 'round off' their territory by taking the Falkland Islands", nor the fact that Monson stated that Britain had "the strongest prescriptive right" to the islands after exercising sovereignty in them for over half a century. As pointed out in section 8.11, there were many factors that made the Falklands indisputably British, of which prescription was only one.

Kohen and Rodríguez mention Ortiz's suggestion that the matter should be put to arbitration and add: "It is one of the many times in which Argentina offered a peaceful solution and Great Britain rejected it", but as we said in *Getting it right* (p. 31), it was likely by 1884 that any arbitration would have awarded the Falklands to Britain. In fact Argentina was not offering a solution at all; the question had been definitively solved in 1850 by the Convention of Peace and many acts by both sides afterwards. There is naturally no solution for a dispute that has already been solved.

On 28 July 1884 the British government instructed Monson to inform Ortiz that the British government could not permit any infringement of Her Majesty's rights of sovereignty over the Falkland Islands.[4] The Argentine government still did not protest, and said nothing at all in

---

[1] Argentina pursued the aim of obtaining compensation from the United States for the *Lexington* raid from 1884 to 1887, but in the end dropped the issue (see documents 214-237 in Fitte 1966, dated between 1884 and 1887).

[2] Francisco Ortiz to Luis Domínguez 28 January 1884, quoted in full in Fitte 1966, pp. 455-457.

[3] Scribal copy in PRO, FO 6/503, fols. 1 *recto* to 8 *verso*; summary in Bernhardt 1910, pp. 398-399. Bernhardt only dealt with the official *correspondence* regarding the Falklands; there was none between the Convention of Peace and 1884, so in his account this despatch comes immediately after Lord Palmerston's reply to Manuel Moreno of 8 August 1849. The 34 years in between were in fact a vital phase in the history of the Falklands and of the Falklands dispute.

[4] Correspondence summarised in Bernhardt 1910, p. 399.

London,[1] but commissioned the Argentine Geographical Institute to publish a new atlas of Argentina, for which the Argentine Congress voted 25,000 pesos; it was to include a map showing the Falklands as Argentine territory. That was extraordinary, given that the 1882 Latzina map, which showed the islands as outside Argentina (section 8.22), had only recently been published (in 1883) in 120,000 copies and was being distributed by Argentine consulates all over the world. Work on the new atlas took several years, so during most of the "Affair of the Map" the only map being distributed by Argentina was the 1882 Latzina map showing the Falklands as *not* Argentinian.

On 8 December 1884 the Buenos Aires daily *El Nacional* reported that a planned new atlas of Argentina was to include the Malvinas in the Argentine Republic. Kohen and Rodríguez call it (p. 241) "a first map of the Argentine Republic that was to include the Falklands/Malvinas", confirming that there had been no such map before. *El Nacional* said Argentina's protests had been made annually until "1851" (*recte* 1849), and announced "a rebirth of the demonstration of the legitimacy of complaints suspended, but not abandoned."[2] Actually, Argentina's behaviour since 1850 had been a pretty convincing display of abandonment.

Edmund Monson read the article in *El Nacional*, and on 16 December he informed London that a new map of Argentina was going to mark the Falklands as Argentine territory. The Foreign Office ordered Monson to protest officially at once,[3] so on 17 December 1884 he wrote to foreign minister Ortiz asking about the status of the map – he said privately-published maps had no official relevance, but an official map might be taken to represent the view of the government. He noted that it was to include as Argentine territory the Falkland Islands, which were part of the dominions of the queen of Great Britain, and that the Argentine Congress had charged the Geographical Institute with the work and had voted to pay the costs, so he presumed that the map would be official, and asked for the Argentine government's view.[4]

Ortiz replied on 19 December 1884 that he could not say whether the map was official, but he said its publication would not alter the position regarding sovereignty over the Malvinas or Falkland Islands, and he could give the same answer as the Argentine Minister in London in 1849 had received from Viscount Palmerston, that the declarations made did not alter the state of the pending issue, which was considered by the British government to be the same as in 1843.[5]

That of course was untrue. Palmerston had not said in his reply to Manuel Moreno on 8 August 1849 that the question was in the same state as in 1843, but that it stood exactly as described in Moreno's letter of 27 July 1849, which included Palmerston's own Commons statement that the matter had lapsed by Argentina's acquiescence (section 7.9).

Ortiz assured Monson on 20 December 1884 that the funds voted by Congress were not specifically for the map, but were general funds for the Geographical Institute. But on 23 December Monson read in *La Tribunal Nacional* that the members of the Geographical Institute believed that the money had been voted for the printing of the map, so he wrote again to Ortiz saying that Her Majesty's Government would find it hard to believe that the map was unofficial.[6]

On 24 December Ortiz replied that the Geographical Institute was neither official nor an office of state; he enclosed a copy of the law passed by Congress, voting 25,000 pesos to produce the map, but asserted that the map's character did not depend on the source of its funding; it depended on whether it was afterwards declared or decreed to be official. He reassured Monson that a map did not confer or deny any rights, and said that the question should be resolved by discussing the fundamentals of the matter.[7]

---

[1] There is nothing touching the Falklands in the correspondence from the Argentine Legation in London to the British government, January to December 1884 (PRO FO 6/383).
[2] Article in *El Nacional*, Buenos Aires, 8 December 1884.
[3] Bernhardt 1910, p. 400.
[4] Summary of Monson's letter of 17 December 1884 in Bernhardt 1910, p. 400; full text (in Spanish) in Becerra 1998, pp. 141-142, but giving the date as 15 December.
[5] Ortiz's reply of 19 Dec. 1884 in full (in Spanish) in Becerra 1998, pp. 143-144; extremely brief summary, without quoting Palmerston, in Bernhardt 1910, p. 400.
[6] Monson's letter of 23 Dec. 1884 in full (in Spanish) in Becerra 1998, pp. 145-147; not in Bernhardt 1910.
[7] Ortiz's letter of 24 Dec. 1884 in full (in Spanish) in Becerra 1998, pp. 148-149.

Monson consulted London by cable, and replied to Ortiz on 26 December that his government had instructed him to make an official protest against the new map. He stated:[1]

… a Map for which a special grant of money has been voted by Congress cannot be, and will not be, regarded by Her Majesty's Gov^t and by the world at large, in any other light than as an official Map… the Undersigned cannot, in view of the positive orders which he has received from H. M. Government, afford to leave any doubt… as to the sense which they[2] would attribute to the inclusion, as National Argentine Territory, in a Map compiled by the direct sanction and on the account, of the National Congress, of a Group of Islands forming part of the Dominions of the British Crown.

The Undersigned, therefore, in execution of his instructions, has no alternative but to place on record the formal protest of H. M. Minister against any such inclusion, or any decision authorizing such inclusion…

That, then, was a formal official protest by Britain, on 26 December 1884, against the planned inclusion of the Falkland Islands in a map of the Argentine Republic. It is important to note that for 35 years, ever since the symbolic Argentine protest of December 1849, Argentina had not protested against Britain's possession of the islands – and still did not protest for another 3 years.

Ortiz replied on 2 January 1885,[3] noting the formal protest by Britain, but emphasising that the whole matter was based on mere reports in newspapers. He said the inclusion of the islands in a map did not change the way in which the Malvinas had always been regarded, namely as an issue pending and subject to solution by the governments concerned. He even asserted that Monson had personally confirmed to him that the matter was still pending[4] – that was absolutely untrue, as Monson stated angrily in his despatch to Granville on 17 January 1885 (below). Finally Ortiz said he hoped "that the postponed discussion ("la discusión aplazada") will be reopened"[5] and solved by arbitration. He enclosed a long memorandum on the history of the dispute,[6] from the Papal bulls of 1493 to Sir William Molesworth's remarks in 1848 (but not Molesworth's remarks in 1849, see sections 7.3 and 7.6), and ended by saying that the matter remained pending, according to the declaration of the Argentine representative in London in 1849.

In fact Moreno's letter of 31 July 1849 to Lord Palmerston had not said or implied that the question was pending or had been postponed (section 7.9); Moreno's letter related exclusively to the past actions of Argentina in maintaining protests every year from 1833 to 1849. He had said nothing about reserving a claim on a pending question for decision at some future date.[7]

So Argentina was now, in December 1884, asserting for the very first time that the discussion had been "postponed" ("aplazada"). But in order to be a postponement, any delay has to be agreed beforehand, whereas in 1849 neither Argentina nor Britain had mentioned any delay. Henry Southern had rebuffed the attempt by General Rosas during their discussion on 10-11 December 1849 to raise the "pending" question of the Falklands; Rosas had accepted Southern's statement that "All national differences are terminated by solemn and public Conventions of Peace", had even repeated it, and had not raised the matter again (section 7.14). Argentine writers from Ortiz to Kohen and Rodríguez have repeatedly asserted that the Falklands question was said to be "pending", but no one on the British side, from Palmerston onwards, ever stated that the question was pending. Actually, it had indeed been pending from 1833 to 1849 since it was being kept alive by Argentine protests, but after the ratification of the Convention of Peace in 1850 it was no longer pending and the British position was correct and unassailable in international law: the question was closed and the Falkland Islands were *de jure* British territory.

Monson at once refuted Argentina's new position. On 8 January 1885 he wrote to Ortiz, stating that the Argentine government could not disclaim responsibility for a map which affected the

---

[1] Copy of Monson's protest of 26 December 1884 in PRO FO 6/503, fols. 130 *recto* to 133 *recto*; Spanish translation in Becerra 1998, pp. 150-152; brief mention in Bernhardt 1910, p. 400. Kohen and Rodríguez refer (p. 242) to "the British protest of 31 December 1884"; it was actually made on 26 December.
[2] I.e. Her Majesty's Government, until recently always treated as a plural.
[3] Ortiz's reply of 2 January 1885 in full in Becerra 1998, pp. 153-157; summary in Bernhardt 1910, pp. 400-401.
[4] Becerra 1998, p. 155; Kohen and Rodríguez p. 243.
[5] Ortiz in Becerra 1998, p. 156.
[6] Ortiz's memorandum of 2 January 1885 in Becerra 1998, pp. 157-176; summary in Bernhardt 1910, pp. 401-402.
[7] Text of Moreno to Palmerston, 31 July 1849, in Becerra 1998, pp. 136-138; summary in Bernhardt 1910, p. 398.

sovereign rights of a foreign power. He added that Britain had always maintained that the question of sovereignty over the Falkland Islands had been definitively solved by Lord Palmerston's letters to Moreno on 8 January 1834, 15 February 1842, and 8 August 1849, all of which stated the government's refusal to admit any questioning of Britain's rights to the islands.[1] Secondly, Monson complained that Ortiz had gone much further than he himself had ever done, in asserting that the question of sovereignty was still pending and subject to solution by the two governments.[2]

In a despatch to Earl Granville on 17 January 1885 Monson emphasised that he had never said that the matter was "pending", and described his reply to Ortiz, in which "I repudiate the idea that the question of Sovereignty is a 'pending question'; and I rectify His Excellency's assertion that I had made an admission to that effect."[3] Ortiz replied to Monson on 13 January 1885,[4] maintaining that his statement that the matter was still pending had been taken from the correspondence of 1849, and that Monson had misunderstood Lord Palmerston's reply of 8 August 1849. The reverse was true of course – Ortiz had himself misunderstood Palmerston's reply.

Monson replied to Ortiz the same day, 13 January,[5] that he could find nothing in the correspondence indicating that he himself, or Her Majesty's Government, considered the question of sovereignty over the Falkland Islands as pending. He quoted Lord Aberdeen's letter of 5 March 1842, saying that Her Majesty's Government considered final the declaration he had made to Moreno on 15 February regarding the government's refusal to permit any violation of the rights of Great Britain to the islands. And Palmerston's reply of August 1849, that he considered the question to stand exactly as Moreno described in his letter, only accepts that the government regarded the matter as closed. Monson said he failed to understand how the Argentine government could assume that he himself, or the British government, regarded the question as pending.

That was confirmed by Lord Granville in a despatch to Monson of 8 April 1885 in which he said that the Argentine government should not be allowed to imagine that the British government might be induced to reopen the Falklands question; he therefore instructed Monson not to carry on any discussion with Argentina on the subject.[6] Monson nevertheless sent Ortiz a note on 5 May saying that the British government took it from the recent correspondence that the Argentine government disclaimed all responsibility for the new map,[7] and Ortiz replied with a note on 6 May expressing pleasure that the British government had correctly deduced that Argentina disclaimed all responsibility for the map.[8] So Argentina accepted that the proposed map did not officially indicate that Argentina regarded the Falklands as Argentine territory.

There the matter rested for nine months, during which US President Grover Cleveland mentioned the new Argentine initiative in his first State of the Union Address in December 1885:[9]

> The Argentine government has revived the long dormant question of the Falkland Islands by claiming from the United States indemnity for their loss attributed to the action of the commander of the sloop of war *Lexington* in breaking up a piratical colony on those islands in 1831 and their subsequent occupation by Great Britain. In view of the ample justification for the act of the *Lexington* and the derelict condition of the islands before and after the alleged occupation by Argentine colonials this Government considers the claim as wholly groundless.

At last, on 10 February 1886, the new Argentine ambassador in London, Dr García, asked the new Foreign Secretary Lord Rosebery for a reply to Argentina's memorandum of 2 January 1885. Rosebery informed the new British ambassador in Buenos Aires, Francis Pakenham, that Britain

---

[1] Monson was actually going too far in stating that the question was closed in 1834, 1842 or August 1849, but he was right in reference to any date later than May 1850.
[2] Monson's letter of 8 January 1885 (in Spanish) in Becerra 1998, pp. 177-181; summary in Bernhardt 1910, p. 401.
[3] Monson's despatch to Earl Granville, 17 January 1885, explaining his reply to Ortiz of 7 January, in PRO FO 6/503, p. 143ff (not in Becerra or Bernhardt).
[4] Ortiz's letter of 13 January 1885 in Becerra 1998, pp. 182-184; not in Bernhardt 1910.
[5] Monson's letter of 13 January 1885 (in Spanish) in Becerra 1998, pp. 185-188.
[6] Bernhardt 1910, p. 402; not in Becerra 1998.
[7] Monson's note of 5 May 1885 in Becerra 1998, pp. 189; not in Bernhardt 1910.
[8] Ortiz's note of 6 May 1885 in Becerra 1998, p. 190; not in Bernhardt 1910.
[9] Quoted in Julius Goebel, *The Struggle for the Falkland Islands...*, New Haven (Connecticut) 1927, p. 463.

regarded the matter as closed and would not consent to reopen it; Pakenham thereupon informed the Argentine foreign minister orally, and on 6 August 1886 reported to London that he had done so.[1] Then there was silence again from Buenos Aires for over seven months till March 1887.

What exactly had happened? Very little in fact; all that had happened was that instead of making a formal protest to Britain, or a diplomatic approach, the Argentine government had casually mentioned that it was intending to raise a claim to the Falklands and to include the islands in a proposed map of Argentina. Britain had at once formally protested, thus maintaining its position that the question of sovereignty over the Falklands was closed. Argentina had thereupon confirmed that the map had no official character. That was all.

The new departure represented by the proposed map in showing the Falklands as Argentinian territory shows that the islands had not been thus shown before – an "Affair of the Map" would have been impossible earlier since there were no official maps that marked the islands as Argentinian. Argentina had still made no protest to Britain since 1849, but Britain had now protested against Argentina's attempt to raise the issue. It was not even raised in the Messages to the Argentine Congress – the symbolic protest in the Message of 27 December 1849 was not only the last protest in the Messages over the Falklands; it was the last time the word "Malvinas" occurred in a Message to Congress for over ninety years up to 1941.

Britain's protest of 26 December 1884 stood on much firmer ground than its previous protest of 19 November 1829 against the Buenos Aires government's presumption of sovereignty over the Falklands (section 5.16). Back in 1829 Buenos Aires clearly had rights in the islands as well as Britain, but the position in 1884 was radically different – not only had half a century passed in which Britain had exerted sovereignty in the islands, performing innumerable acts of administration and jurisdiction (« effectivités »), but Argentina had ratified a comprehensive peace treaty in 1850 which ended all differences with Britain and thus also any Argentine title to the islands. Ever since then, Argentina had not only refrained from raising the matter, but had on several occasions overtly indicated that there was no dispute between the two countries. There are therefore good grounds for presuming that there was an actual legal obstruction to Argentina's attempt to raise the question of the Falklands in 1884: the principle of "estoppel".

8.24 Estoppel

"Estoppel" is a legal principle under which a party to a dispute may not go back on its previous acts or statements if the other party would thereby suffer detriment.[2] Those previous acts or statements may imply acquiescence, so acquiescence and estoppel are closely related. We mentioned a clear case of estoppel in *Getting it right* (p. 30) which precluded Argentina's raising the question of the Falklands in 1884; Kohen and Rodríguez ignore our example and mention three other cases which they say constitute estoppel, but which are not.

Their first case (p. 223) contrasts Britain's silence for 55 years (1774-1829) with Argentina's silence of "34 years" (i.e. 1849-1884) – that would require a "cut-off point" lying exactly between 38 and 55 years without protests, which is absurd (see section 8.8). They maintain that Britain cannot claim that Argentina's 34 years of silence can be considered acquiescence, "particularly when preceded by a clear rejection of any possibility of acquiescence, and containing other expressions of the persistence of Argentina's claim." They say this is a "textbook case of the technical concept of estoppel", but we beg to differ. As we pointed out in section 7.19, it is not open to a claimant to say that his future silence will not indicate acquiescence – silence is silence. And what they call "other expressions of the persistence of Argentina's claim" during those 34 years are nothing of the sort – the "expressions" that they mention are trivial (sections 8.4, 9.2, 9.4). The only such expression with any weight in international law would have been an official protest to Britain, but there was none. Britain's policy did not change – it held the Falklands to be 100% British territory, as arranged by the Anglo-Spanish agreement of 1771 (section 2.3), and what changed was not Britain's behaviour but the situation in the territory: Spain departed, Argentina arrived, and the

---
[1] Correspondence summarised in Bernhardt 1910, p. 402.
[2] O'Brien 2001, p. 215.

United States started to make threatening moves. The British action in 1833 was a response to those changes; Britain's behaviour was consistent and there was therefore no estoppel.

Secondly, they say (p. 230) "Pascoe and Pepper's pamphlet also ventures to imagine that, by virtue of cartography, Argentina recognised Britain's alleged sovereignty, and that for that very reason Argentina is now prevented from claiming its sovereignty by virtue of the rule of estoppel." That is untrue; in *Getting it right* we discussed evidence from maps in our section 32 and estoppel in section 33, but we nowhere said that the maps constituted an estoppel against Argentina.

And thirdly, they say (p. 261) "Another estoppel can be opposed to the United Kingdom. The British government did not consider that its silence over the Argentine concessions of 1823 and 1828 in the Falklands/Malvinas prevented it from reclaiming its sovereignty." However, Britain remained ignorant of those concessions until 1829 (section 5.7), and then protested promptly; there was therefore no estoppel in those cases either.

But there was an estoppel against Argentina in the early 1880s – the one we mentioned in *Getting it right*. For estoppel to exist, one side must attempt to change its behaviour despite causing disadvantage to the other side. Sir Ian Sinclair discusses the relationship between estoppel and acquiescence, and the way in which arguments founded on them are advanced before international tribunals by the two sides in territorial disputes. He says lawyers for both sides:[1]

... will in all probability have uncovered evidence of inconsistency of conduct on the part of one or both states parties to the dispute. That evidence may demonstrate that, on the occasion of some incident in the past, state A will have taken a position *vis-à-vis* state B at variance with the position it is now asserting in proceedings against state B. It may equally demonstrate that state A has entered into international agreements with state B or indeed with other states, the terms of which are incompatible with the position it is now asserting in proceedings against state B. The evidence may also disclose that state B has failed to protest against a previous act of state A challenging the title of state B to a given territory or parcel of territory. Any evidence of inconsistency of conduct of this type is likely to be prayed in aid as providing grounds for a finding by the tribunal of estoppel or acquiescence.

In using the letters "A" and "B" Sinclair was presumably not thinking of any actual dispute, but if for "A" and "B" one reads "Argentina" and "Britain", the arguments fit the Falklands case in 1884 remarkably well.

Thus A now asserts a claim to the Falkland Islands, but from 1849 to 1884 accepted B's possession of the islands without comment or protest and thus took a position at variance with what it asserted in 1884. Secondly, A entered into an international agreement with B (the Convention of Peace) the terms of which are incompatible with what it is now asserting. The third argument, that B failed to protest at some act by A challenging B's title to the territory in question, is relevant but unlike the first two arguments is false: B did protest in 1829 against A's act in appointing Louis Vernet as civil and military commandant, again in 1832 against the appointment of Mestivier, and yet again in 1884 against a map showing the Falklands as Argentine territory.

And crucially for the existence of estoppel, during the 34 years of Argentina's silence from 1850 to 1884, the Falklands were for Britain a loss-making concern that required constant financial support – Britain invested in the islands without any return until 1885, when they became self-supporting for the first time (section 8.25). In asking Britain to hand the islands over during the Affair of the Map in 1884-8, Argentina was demanding to take over a going concern with a newly profitable economy that had been established by loss-making actions on the part of Britain. Kate Parlett says "incurring expenses may constitute detrimental reliance",[2] which precisely describes the case here: Britain had relied on Argentina's acceptance of British sovereignty and had suffered a financial loss as a result. Since Britain had incurred that loss during a long period without any territorial claim from Argentina, there are good grounds for believing that Argentina was "estopped" [blocked, prevented] from raising a claim in the 1880s.

We presented all those arguments in *Getting it right*, but Kohen and Rodríguez completely

---

[1] Sir Ian Sinclair, "Estoppel and acquiescence", in *Fifty Years of the International Court of Justice…*, Cambridge 1996, pp. 104-105. "Prayed in aid" = used as a supporting argument.
[2] Kate Parlett, in Kohen and Hébié (eds.) 2018, p. 189.

ignore them. That makes us suspect that they know they are strong evidence.

So, to the already conclusive arguments for the existence of acquiescence by Argentina in the Falklands case may be added a strong case for an estoppel from the mid-1880s onwards. From then on, any attempt by Argentina to raise a claim to the Falklands was legally inadmissible.

8.25 Arthur Barkly in the Falklands, March-December 1886

8.25a Arthur Barkly (1843-90), Lieutenant-Governor of the Falkland Islands, March-December 1886. (JCNA)

8.25b The second Stanley peat slip, 2 June 1886. Photo taken a day or two later after some clearing had been done. Probably the last photo of the Exchange building (completed 1854) containing Holy Trinity church and the school, on the site of the present Cathedral. (FIC 5.057)

For most of the year 1886 the administration of the Falklands was headed by Arthur Cecil Stuart Barkly (1843-90; fig. 8.25a), who took office as Lieutenant-Governor on 4 March when Governor Thomas Kerr left for Britain to recover from ill health. Kerr returned on 17 December, and Barkly sailed for Britain the same day.[1] Arthur Barkly provided a personal link between the Falklands and two other small British overseas territories: he served two brief tours of duty as Governor of the Seychelles, which like the Falklands had probably been discovered by the Portuguese in the early 16th century and were first settled by the French in the late 18th century, and he was the last British Governor of Heligoland, a small island in the North Sea which had been British from 1807 and was ceded to Germany against the wishes of its inhabitants in August 1890 (section 8.29).

Arthur Barkly's tenure of office in the Falklands was brief, but was noteworthy for three things. First, it fell to him to report that the islands had begun to pay their way, an important milestone in their history which constituted a clear estoppel against Argentina's raising a claim to them (section 8.24).[2] Secondly, on 2 June 1886 there was a second serious peat slip in Stanley, following the first one in November 1878. The second slip killed two people and damaged the 30-year-old Exchange building (fig. 8.25b) so badly that it had to be demolished. The disaster forced the school to move from the Exchange into the government store and the old theatre for 20 years until a new school was opened in 1906.[3] But it brought two improvements: the peat banks behind the town were drained to prevent further peat slips, and the Exchange was replaced by a better school and by Christ Church Cathedral, built from some of the materials of the Exchange, consecrated on 21 February 1892.

And thirdly, in September 1886 Carlos María Moyano, governor of the newly-formed Argentine

---

[1] Details from Governor's Letter Book "Letters Out", 8 January 1884 to 2 January 1888, p. 254, in JCNA.
[2] In his *Report on the Blue Book* for 1885, Barkly stated: "The year 1885 is memorable in the history of the Colony as being the first in which no pecuniary aid has been received from the Imperial Government…" (statement dated 20 March 1886, in *Reports on Blue Books, 1883, 1884, and 1885*, London 1886, p. 200), confirmed by the *Colonial Report* for 1927, which stated (p. 3): "The Colony received a regular grant-in-aid from the Imperial Treasury until 1880 and a special grant for a mail service until 1885, since which date it has been wholly self-supporting".
[3] Details from the entry on Frederick Durose (1855-1933), headmaster of the school, by Annie Gisby in *DFB*.

province of Santa Cruz in Patagonia, sent a ship to Stanley to collect his fiancée Ethel Turner and take her back to Santa Cruz, where they were married on 12 September. In late 1884 Moyano had been instructed by the Argentine government to visit the Falklands to get settlers and sheep for his province; he travelled to the islands in January 1885 and in Stanley saw Ethel coming out of church. It was love at first sight; one John Richmond interpreted between the couple, who initially had no common language but still became engaged.[1]

Argentine governments were well aware that Britain was exercising sovereignty in the Falklands, and far from protesting against it, Argentina obtained settlers and sheep from the islands to populate and stock Patagonia. Argentina accepted that the Falklands were British.

8.26 The Affair of the Map: Phase II, 1887-8; Argentina's last protest

Kohen and Rodríguez ignore our example of estoppel that disqualified Argentina from raising the Falklands issue in 1884, but they criticise us for omitting the second part of the Affair of the Map – they say (p. 243):

It is interesting to note how Pascoe and Pepper then skip forward to 1888... the British authors "forget" to mention that on March 11th, 1887 the Argentine Minister of Foreign Affairs, Dr Quirno Costa, ordered the Argentine Ambassador in London, Luis Domínguez, to remind the British Government about the memorandum on the issue presented by Dr Ortiz on January 2nd, 1885, which remained unanswered.

In their turn, Kohen and Rodríguez omit events in the two years between January 1885 and March 1887. They omit to mention that Britain had indeed answered the Argentine memorandum of 2 January 1885 – British ambassador Edmund Monson replied to Argentine foreign minister Ortiz on 8 January 1885 (section 8.23). The new British ambassador to Argentina, Francis Pakenham, had reported to London on 6 August 1886 that he had informed Ortiz that Britain regarded the subject as closed.[2] That marked the end of Phase I of the Affair of the Map, and there was silence again from Buenos Aires for the rest of 1886 and early 1887.

Then, on 11 March 1887, the new Argentine foreign minister, Norberto Quirno Costa, instructed yet another new Argentine ambassador in London, Luis Domínguez, to obtain a reply from Britain.[3] Thus began Phase II of the Affair of the Map, though Domínguez did nothing till November 1887. By that time the Marquess of Salisbury[4] was Prime Minister, and from January 1887 Foreign Secretary too. On 3 November 1887 Domínguez asked Salisbury for an answer, pointing out that the Argentine memorandum of 2 January 1885 was still unanswered (by the British government, though Edmund Monson had answered it).[5]

On 9 November 1887 the British government first replied to Quirno Costa in a letter from Pakenham, who said that he had been charged with reminding the Argentine foreign minister of the British notes to M. Moreno of 8 January 1834, 15 February 1842, and especially Lord Aberdeen's note of 5 March 1842, which indicated that for Britain the matter was closed.[6]

A second British reply, to ambassador Domínguez in London, was made on 14 November 1887 by Sir Thomas Lister, Undersecretary of State at the Foreign Office, who likewise drew attention to the British notes of 8 January 1834, 15 February 1842 and 5 March 1842, informing Moreno that in the British view the discussion was closed.[7] Domínguez wrote to Quirno Costa on 18 November 1887 enclosing both his request to Salisbury and Lister's reply.[8]

---

[1] Arnoldo Canclini, *Malvinas: Su historia en historias* [The Malvinas: their history in stories], Buenos Aires 2000, pp. 244-246; some details on Moyano from entry by Canclini in *DFB*.
[2] Correspondence summarised in Bernhardt 1910, p. 402.
[3] Quirno Costa to Domínguez of 11 March 1887, in Becerra 1998, pp. 191-192.
[4] Robert Cecil, third Marquess of Salisbury (1830-1903), Prime Minister from 23 June 1885 to 26 January 1886, from 25 July 1886 to 11 August 1892, and from 25 June 1895 to 11 July 1902. His family name is pronounced "sissl".
[5] Quirno Costa to Salisbury, 3 November 1887, in Becerra 1998, pp. 193-194; summary in Bernhardt 1910, p. 403.
[6] Pakenham to Quirno Costa of 9 November 1887, in Becerra 1998, pp. 197-198; brief mention in Bernhardt 1910, p. 403; Bernhardt states that Pakenham's text was approved by Lord Salisbury.
[7] Sir Thomas Lister's note of 14 November 1887 in Becerra 1998, pp. 194-196; summarised in Bernhardt 1910, p. 403.
[8] Domínguez's covering note of 18 November 1887 in Becerra 1998, pp. 192-193; not in Bernhardt 1910.

On 20 January 1888 Quirno Costa sent a long letter to Pakenham,[1] first recapitulating the preceding correspondence of 1834, 1842 and 1849, and quoting Moreno's letter of 31 July 1849 to Lord Palmerston, plus Palmerston's Commons statement that "the correspondence had ceased by the acquiescence of one party and the perseverance [*sic*] of the other." He then quoted Palmerston's reply of 8 August 1849 to Moreno, in which Palmerston stated that he had always understood the matter to stand exactly as Moreno had described it in his letter. Quirno Costa asserted that those two letters proved that the matter had not been closed in 1842 but merely interrupted, and that once it had been raised in 1849, Lord Palmerston had solemnly declared that the matter remained in the situation indicated by the Argentine representative, which could not mean otherwise than the return of a territory which had always formed part of the Argentine Republic.

But just like Francisco Ortiz, Quirno Costa had interpreted Palmerston's reply of 8 August 1849 incorrectly (sections 7.9, 8.23). In mid-1849 Palmerston knew Argentina was acquiescing in Britain's possession of the Falklands by establishing "perfect friendship" with Britain in the proposed peace treaty and without mentioning the islands, so in saying in the Commons on 27 July 1849 that the correspondence had ceased by acquiescence, he was stating a simple fact. Moreno had repeated Palmerston's statement in his letter of 31 July 1849, and had listed the earlier protests, which enabled Palmerston to state in his reply to Moreno of 8 August 1849 that the matter stood exactly as Moreno had described it (including Palmerston's own statement of the position). Perhaps Palmerston's reply was too subtle, or too arrogant, or too slapdash; at all events it was misunderstood by the Argentinians, and the misunderstanding continues to this day, as shown by various Argentine authors including Kohen and Rodríguez.

Quirno Costa concluded his letter of 20 January 1888 by declaring that the Argentine government maintained, "as before", its protest in respect of the "illegitimate" occupation of the Malvinas Islands, that it did not abandon nor would ever abandon its rights to those territories, and would always consider them as an integral part of the territories of the Argentine Republic, founded on the priority of discovery, priority of occupation, on possession undertaken and exercised, and on the tacit and explicit recognition of rights, also acquired by treaty, which belonged to Spain.

In its outward form, that letter of 20 January 1888 was an official protest by Argentina against British possession of the Falkland Islands. It was the first official Argentine protest to Britain over the Falklands since December 1849, over 38 years earlier. But although it fulfilled the outward conditions which any protest must satisfy, it was without legal force. The grounds on which Quirno Costa said the Argentine title was based were invalid: Spain had not had priority of discovery (though no one knew that), nor of occupation; Argentina had not inherited exclusive sovereignty in the islands from Spain (sections 1.7, 2.7), and Spain had accepted the Falklands as British in 1863 (section 8.17).

And above all, *it was not true* that Argentina was maintaining its protest "as before". Argentina had not maintained its protests but had abandoned its title to the Falklands by the Convention of Peace in 1850 and had not protested for two generations, during which time Argentine leaders had made several top-level statements that there was no dispute with Britain (section 8.18). The British protests of 19 November 1829 and 28 September 1832[2] against Argentina's presumption of sovereignty in the Falklands had suffered from much the same weaknesses: Britain had not maintained an official presence in the islands and had not mentioned its claimed rights for some 55 years, so Lord Aberdeen's assertion to Woodbine Parish in 1829 that Britain had "constantly asserted" its rights to the islands[3] was untrue in exactly the same way as the Argentine protest of 1888. The length of time was longer than in the case of Argentina's protest (55 against 38 years), but the acquiescence by Britain had been silent and Britain possessed extensive rights and retained a constant presence in the islands, whereas Argentina overtly proclaimed acquiescence by a number of significant instruments including a peace treaty, statements by leaders, and an official map

---

[1] Quirno Costa to Pakenham, 20 January 1888 in Becerra 1998, pp. 199-206; mentioned in Bernhardt 1910 only in Pakenham's report of it (pp. 403-404).
[2] Copies in PRO FO 6/499, fols. 33 recto to 35 *recto* and 195 *recto* to 196 *recto* respectively.
[3] Draft despatch no. 5 from Lord Aberdeen to Woodbine Parish, 8 August 1829, in PRO FO 6 499, fols. 23 *recto* to 26 *recto*; Spanish summary in Ferrer Vieyra 1993, p. 387.

showing the Falklands as outside Argentina (the 1882 Latzina map). In short, Argentina's protest in 1888 was devoid of substance, so it was invalid.

On 13 April 1888 Mr Jenner of the British Foreign Office informed Quirno Costa that the British government refused to enter into discussion of the rights of Her Majesty to the Falkland Islands, rights which in the government's view presented no doubts or difficulties of any kind.[1] That view was indisputably correct.

On the same day, 13 April 1888, Argentine ambassador Domínguez wrote to Lord Salisbury expressing the hope that the Falklands question would be "reopened"; Salisbury replied on 21 April that as far as Britain was concerned the matter was closed.[2] Quirno Costa replied to Jenner's note on 12 June 1888,[3] saying that the President had charged him to make it clear to the British Foreign Secretary that despite Britain's refusal to discuss any rights it might have to the islands, the government of the Republic did not regard its own rights as being compromised by that declaration, nor by the silence of the British government towards suggestions of arbitration made by the Argentine government, which maintained and always would maintain its rights to the sovereignty over the Malvinas Islands, of which it was violently deprived in peacetime. On 14 June 1888, Jenner reported Quirno Costa's reply to the British government.[4] And that was that.

Britain did not reply; Argentina never again made a formal protest to Britain on the Falklands, and on several occasions in the following years accepted the strength of Britain's position (sections 9.2, 9.4). Argentina also twice accepted British arbitration in a territorial dispute with Chile (sections 9.1, 10.22), which was incompatible with maintaining a territorial dispute with Britain.

In short, Argentine foreign minister Quirno Costa's statement in his letter to Lord Salisbury of 12 June 1888, that Argentina "maintained and always would maintain its rights to the sovereignty over the Malvinas Islands" was wrong in two ways: Argentina had not maintained its rights to the islands but had dropped them by the Convention of Peace in 1850 and abandoned them thereafter, and in addition would not maintain them either – to this day there has never been another official Argentine protest to Britain since the protest of 20 January 1888.

8.27 The foundation of the *Falkland Islands Magazine*, 1889

8.27a Cover story: a selection of issues from the first decade of the *Falkland Islands Magazine*:

May 1889	May 1893	October 1895	July 1898
November 1890	August 1893	January 1896	March 1899
April 1891	June 1895	November 1896	
November 1892			

---

[1] Jenner's note of 13 April 1888 (in Spanish) in Becerra 1998, p. 208; Bernhardt 1910, p. 405.
[2] Correspondence briefly summarised in Bernhardt 1910, p. 405; not in Becerra 1998.
[3] Quirno Costa's letter of 12 June 1888 in Becerra 1998, pp. 209-210.
[4] Bernhardt 1910, p. 405; not in Becerra 1998.

Life in the Falklands continued completely independently of diplomatic disagreements between Britain and Argentina. There was an important new development in May 1889, when the first issue of the monthly *Falkland Islands Magazine* (*FIM*) appeared, printed in Stanley. It was destined to become the islands' hitherto longest-lasting publication, apart from the *Falkland Islands Gazette*, which has appeared several times every year since 1 January 1891 but contains mainly official announcements. The *Falkland Islands Magazine* appeared for 41 years from 1889 to 1930, with a temporary revival in 1932-3 after a two-year break. It showed that the islands had come of age, in that there was now a regular forum in which islanders could air their opinions and read local and international news. It is a major source for historians of the islands, and has now been put online in full on the website of the Jane Cameron National Archives (JCNA) in Stanley. It may be accessed under http://www.nationalarchives.gov.fk, "Online Collections", "Periodicals".

8.28 More Argentine maps and books fail to claim the Falkland Islands

Kohen and Rodríguez print (pp. 236, 237, 238) excerpts from three Argentine maps which show the Falklands as Argentinian, but dating from 1888, 1886 and 1888 respectively, i.e. the period of the Affair of the Map, so it is not surprising that they mark the Falklands as Argentinian.

What is surprising, though, is that during those years – and afterwards – books and maps were still being published in Argentina that did *not* treat the Falklands as Argentine territory. In 1888 Francisco Latzina, director of the Argentine national statistical office (who had published the 1882 Latzina map showing the Falklands as outside Argentina; see section 8.22), published a 750-page work in Spanish on the geography of Argentina, of which an updated, shortened French translation of 486 pages appeared in 1890.[1] These books were published just after the end of the Affair of the Map, and show that the change of policy in Argentina towards raising a claim to the Falklands had been brief and temporary. Books written by such a high-ranking state official, whose position gave him a central role in the description of Argentina's territory, can certainly be described as semi-official; one might expect that they would reflect the new policy and treat the Falklands as Argentinian, but both Latzina's books are highly equivocal on the matter. In the text of the 1888 Spanish edition, the detailed chronological table mentions the islands only in two short entries, which do not suggest that Argentina was now raising a claim to them:[2]

1771 I 22   Spain implicitly recognises the right of the English to the Malvinas.

1832 X 10   José María Pineda [*sic*], commander of the Argentine frigate *Sarandi*, takes possession of the Malvinas islands in the name of the Argentine Republic.

And that is all. There is no mention of the islands at all after 1832 – but there is a brief mention of the Convention of Peace between Argentina and Britain of 24 November 1849.[3]

Both editions contain several maps: a "Mapa General" of Argentina; a map of Buenos Aires; a large communications map of the country showing railways, posts and telegraphs, and some province-maps, and the 1890 French edition also contains a rainfall map (fig. 8.28a). The Mapa General (not illustrated here) marks the Falklands as Argentine territory, with a white background like Argentina, while areas outside Argentina are a pale cream colour.[4] That is what one would expect after the Argentine decision to start a Falklands dispute in 1884 after a third of a century of silence. But apart from that one map, which is not so much as alluded to in the text, and the two brief references in the chronology in the 1888 edition, the Falklands are not mentioned once in either edition, under any name; in 1890 the « île *de los Estados* » [*sic*] is stated to be part of the territory of Tierra del Fuego, but there is no reference to the Falklands.

---

[1] F[rancisco] Latzina, *Geografía de la República Argentina*, Buenos Aires 1888 (preface October 1887); *Géographie de la République Argentine*, Buenos Aires 1890 (updated and adapted French translation of the preceding).

[2] Latzina 1888, pp. 665, 676.

[3] Latzina 1888, p. 679.

[4] This map is identical in both editions except for one difference: in 1888 the PNL group of islands are assigned to Chile (as on the 1882 Latzina map), while in the 1890 ed. (dated 1889) they and Cape Horn are marked as Argentinian.

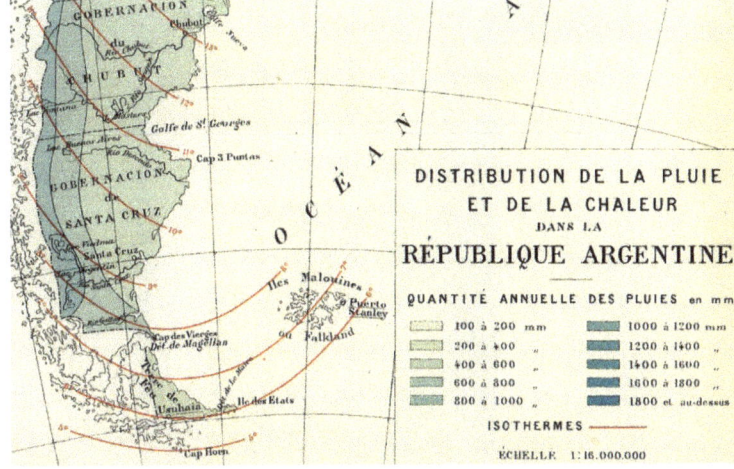
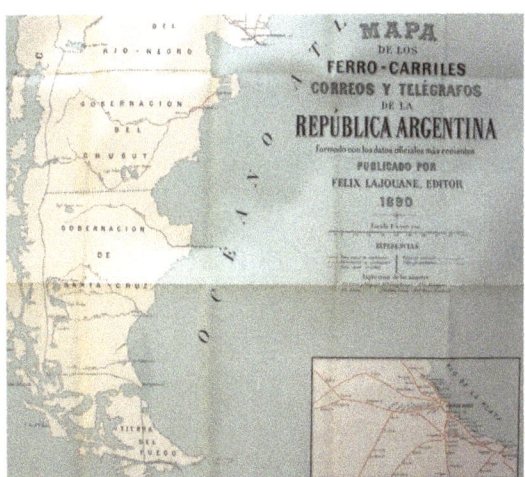

8.28a No Argentine rain, 1890: the Falklands shown blank like areas outside Argentina on a type (c) rainfall map, from Francisco Latzina, *Géographie de la République Argentine*, Buenos Aires 1890, opp. p. 90. The whole of Argentina is coloured in shades of green, including areas with 100-200 mm of rain; Chile, the Falklands and the sea are all colourless.

8.28b No Falklands in 1890: the southern part of Argentina on a type (b) communications map: Francisco Latzina, *Géographie de la République Argentine*, Buenos Aires 1890, opp. p. 484. The Falklands are completely omitted.

What is more, two maps in the 1890 edition clearly imply that the islands are *not* Argentine territory. The rainfall map is of type (c), i.e. it marks the Falklands as outside Argentina (fig. 8.28a). They are named « Iles Malouines ou Falkland » and are blank like all areas outside Argentina – Argentine rain stops precisely at the borders of the republic. The "PNL group" of Beagle Channel islands are blank too; they received no Argentine rain any more than did the Falklands. The communications map is of type (b), i.e. it omits the Falklands entirely (fig. 8.28b), but not because they had no railways; Tierra del Fuego had no railways but is shown. Where the islands should be, the map shows empty ocean and the corner of an insert of Buenos Aires.

Those omissions are significant, but they were not the only ones in the 1890s – in 1891 Latzina published the first edition of his large *Diccionario Geográfico Argentino*, in which he listed all the geographical places in Argentina, "with the names of all the rivers, streams, lakes, mountain ranges, valleys, plateaus, capes, bays, gulfs, islands, etc.".[1] But his list does not include the Falkland Islands, neither under "Isla", "Islas" nor "Malvinas" (nor under "Falkland"). Not only that; Latzina added the islands to his third edition in 1899, not as Argentine territory but British – he says:[2]

> The islands belong today to England, even though, geographically speaking, they are a dependency of Patagonia. They were seen for the first time by Sebald in 1599, and then by Strong in 1688, who gave them the name of *Falkland Islands*. The Malvinas remained uninhabited until 1764, at which time France occupied them. Bougainville took to these islands an expedition which he had formed in Saint-Malo, whence comes the name of Malvinas. Spain then claimed these islands and France returned them. The Argentine government, successor to that of Spain and heir to its rights, sent to these islands in 1820 a señor Vernet as governor, who was displaced from his position by England in 1833. The Malvinas offer ports for shelter and for supplies of provisions, coal and water.

Several of Latzina's dates are wrong (1599, 1688 and 1820 should be 1600, 1690 and 1829), as is the idea that John Strong called the islands "Falkland Islands" (it was Woodes Rogers in 1708, see section 1.4) and that the name "Malvinas" comes from the fact that Bougainville set off from St-Malo. But it is noteworthy that the director of the Argentine national statistical office stated baldly in 1899: "The islands belong today to England".

---

[1] Francisco Latzina, *Diccionario Geográfico Argentino*, 1st ed. Buenos Aires 1891, introduction p. [v].
[2] Francisco Latzina, *Diccionario Geográfico Argentino*, 3rd ed. Buenos Aires 1899, p. 391.

8.28c The Falklands in the "non-Argentina colour", 1918, from a type (c) map of Argentina issued by the Argentine ministry of agriculture: the Falklands are colourless, exactly like Chile (and also like Uruguay and the sea) – but the PNL islands are in the "Argentina colour" (sections 8.9, 8.22).

Even more remarkably, Argentine governments dropped the topic of the Falklands entirely. No Argentine government mentioned the subject to Britain for several decades after 1888, and in 1899 Argentina even asked Britain to arbitrate in a border dispute between Argentina and Chile, which was incompatible with maintaining a territorial claim against Britain (section 9.1). Some later Argentine maps likewise omitted the Falklands or marked them as being outside Argentina, such as the type (c) map issued in 1918 by the Argentine ministry of agriculture (fig. 8.28c).

By contrast, Britain was completely consistent – we have seen many post-1850 British maps that show the Falkland Islands, and every single one marks them as British.

8.29 The Heligoland Connection; Classic Imperialism, 1890: land before people

Heligoland is a small island in the North Sea whose history offers interesting parallels to the Falkland Islands.[1] Both Heligoland and the Falklands are cool, windy, almost treeless islands with similar population numbers – the Falklands now have around 3,200 people and Heligoland 1,400; in 1890 the Falklands had 1,900, Heligoland 2,300 – and Arthur Barkly added a personal connection between them, as Lieutenant-Governor of the Falklands in 1886 (section 8.25) and Governor of Heligoland in 1888-90. Kohen and Rodríguez do not mention Heligoland, but it is one of three examples which illuminate the legal status of the Falklands (with the Chagos Islands in the 1960s and Kuwait in 1990-91: sections 10.28, 10.29).

Heligoland lies off the German coast, but it was never German territory in any real sense; it was ruled for centuries by Denmark, by the Hanse or the Duchy of Schleswig-Gottorp; it was Danish from 1714 until occupied by Britain in 1807 during the Napoleonic Wars (when the island's settlement was named "Falkland Town"), and was ceded to Britain in 1814. Its inhabitants originally spoke Frisian, a Germanic language related to English and German; they now normally speak German, but still cultivate Frisian. In the 19th century the Heligolanders approved of British sovereignty, since Britain, unlike Denmark, exacted no yearly tribute.[2] In 1890 Britain ceded it to Germany together with its inhabitants, against their wishes.

---

[1] Account here mainly from Jan Rüger, *Heligoland: Britain, Germany and the Struggle for the North Sea*, Oxford 2017; George Drower, *Heligoland: the True Story of German Bight and the Island that Britain Betrayed*, Stroud 2002; and Michael Herms, *Flaggenwechsel auf Helgoland: Der Kampf um einen militärischen Vorposten in der Nordsee* ["Changing flags on Heligoland: the struggle for a military outpost in the North Sea"], Berlin 2002.
[2] Drower 2002, pp. 10-11, 19, 21, 27.

It was Heligoland's misfortune to become a very small pawn in the great chess-game of late 19th-century empire-building. At a vital stage in that game, the most important player was the Marquess of Salisbury, a Conservative statesman who was Prime Minister and Foreign Secretary at the same time. In foreign policy he favoured the traditional British policy of "informal empire", under which "the flag followed trade" and British governments were against annexing overseas territories, but events in the 1880s forced Britain to change its policy. In 1882 Britain was impelled to act in Egypt against a French threat to the Suez Canal; from 1884 Germany became another rival, and Kaiser Wilhelm II (ruled 1888-1918) began to apply an aggressive foreign policy. The period from 1880 to 1914 is often called the age of Classic Imperialism: in that new, expansionist phase of imperialism "trade followed the flag"; the ideology was "land before people", and European colonial powers took over many territories without the agreement of the people who lived there. Argentina's current claim to the Falklands shows that that way of thinking has not died out.

Lord Salisbury saw Britain as the landlord of Heligoland – to Britain and Germany, and all colonial powers in the age of Classic Imperialism, overseas territories were *possessions* which could be handed over at will together with their populations. What mattered was to possess the *land*; the people who lived on it had no say in affairs.

In the late 1880s, in his landlordly way, Salisbury became worried about Africa, and in June 1889 he was perturbed to hear of the activities of the German empire-builder Carl Peters (1856-1918). Just as Cecil Rhodes brought much of southern Africa under British control, Peters was preparing a German takeover in East Africa. Peters was as ambitious as Rhodes but even more racist and much more brutal – he set out to exterminate the Warombo people "like the redskins of North America, to win their broad and fertile lands for German cultivation". He punished Africans savagely, which earned him the nickname „Hänge-Peters" ["Hanging Peters"].[1]

Salisbury resolved to put a stop to Peters's doings – as Prime Minister and Foreign Secretary he could decide the foreign policy of the British Empire by himself. On 13 May 1890, in a conversation with German ambassador Graf Paul von Hatzfeldt, he demanded the retreat of Germany from the newly occupied territory in East Africa, and said that in return Britain might hand Heligoland to Germany. The German government was interested at once, and Wilhelm II sent Hatzfeldt several telegrams emphasising Heligoland's importance, since it could threaten the new Kiel Canal. Negotiations between the two governments were brief and agreement was swift. In a draft treaty on 5 June 1890 Salisbury offered exchanges of territory in Africa: Germany would get the empty "Caprivi strip", Britain would get the territory opened up by Carl Peters in East Africa and would set up a British protectorate over Zanzibar (whose sultan was only told later) – and Germany would get Heligoland.[2] The rights, wishes and interests of the peoples of all those territories played no part whatever. Land came before people.

Some people in Britain did think the wishes and rights of the people were important. On 8 June 1890 Salisbury informed Queen Victoria by telegram that the Cabinet had approved the draft Anglo-German agreement, but Victoria telegraphed her disapproval of the handover of Heligoland:[3]

I very much deprecate it and am anxious *not to give my consent* unless I hear that the people's feelings are consulted and their rights are respected.

At the Cabinet meeting on 10 June 1890 there was considerable opposition to ceding the island to Germany, but in another telegram to the queen Salisbury said that to ask a colonial people to express their wishes would set a bad precedent and might lead people in Gibraltar, Malta, Cyprus and even India to expect the same. In two telegrams on 11 and 12 June Victoria reluctantly signified her assent, and the die was cast.

A preliminary agreement on Africa and Heligoland was initialled in Berlin on 17 June 1890; Salisbury deposited a copy in the Vote Office at the Houses of Parliament, hoping it would not be noticed, but it was spotted by some *Times* correspondents, who rushed out a special edition the next

---

[1] Drower 2002, pp. 64ff; Herms 2002, pp. 76-77.
[2] Drower 2002, pp. 68-74, and Rüger 2017, p. 104.
[3] Drower 2002, 77, quoting Buckle, *The Letters of Queen Victoria 1862-1901*, vol. I, p. 614, and CAB 41/21/42.

morning. Arthur Barkly was staying at his father's house in London and was shocked to read the news; he at once returned to Heligoland, where he arrived on 21 June and called an emergency meeting of the island's Executive Council. On 26 June he left for Berlin, where he vainly urged Sir Percy Anderson of the British Foreign Office to make some amendments.[1]

The Heligolanders heard the news from the newspapers on the same day as their governor, and sent a telegram to William Black, a strong supporter in Britain,[2] asking him to do everything he could to put their case against the cession of their homeland to Germany. Black consulted Lord Rosebery, the leader of the Liberal Party in the House of Lords, one of the few British politicians who had visited the island (as Foreign Secretary in 1886). Rosebery asked Salisbury in the Lords on 19 June 1890 "If any steps have been taken, or are in contemplation, to ascertain the wishes of the Heligolanders themselves with regard to the transfer."[3]

Lord Rosebery's use of the word "wishes" as long ago as 1890 is noteworthy, since one of the disagreements between Argentina and Britain in the 1970s was that Britain wanted to consider the "wishes" of the Falkland Islanders, whereas Argentina only recognised their "interests" (section 10.16). Lord Salisbury gave an evasive answer, maintaining that "the plebiscite is not among the traditions of the country".[4] The Heligolanders would undoubtedly have voted to remain British had they been permitted to do so – Jan Rüger says "all dispatches from the colony indicated that the islanders were opposed to German rule". Salisbury knew that, and ruled that there was to be no official plebiscite, but as Rüger says, "British journalists... were busy conducting an unofficial plebiscite... the result... a clear vote for remaining British".[5]

Lord Rosebery was not alone in his concern for the Heligolanders' wishes – several MPs had asked in Parliament whether the views of the inhabitants had been obtained. The magazine *Review of Reviews* compared Britain's behaviour to that of Russian aristocrats: "It reminds one of the transactions between Russian grandees of olden times, when, to pay a gambling debt, an estate with all its serfs would be made over from one noble proprietor to another." The *Pall Mall Gazette* quoted a telling comment: "'You may give away a cat or a dog,' said an indignant Heligoland dame, 'but not a whole people'." Nevertheless, the Anglo-German Agreement was signed in Berlin on 1 July 1890 by British ambassador Sir Edward Malet and the new German Imperial Chancellor Leo von Caprivi.[6]

In his report on the *Heligoland Blue Book* for 1889, Arthur Barkly had written: "the prosperity of Heligoland at the present time is probably greater than at any former period. The people are contented and orderly...";[7] and in a telegram to Lord Salisbury on 10 July he pointed out the wishes of the Heligolanders: "They are perfectly contented and happy under British rule and desirous of no change."[8] In the House of Lords Salisbury ignored all that; by contrast Rosebery stressed the importance of the wishes of the islanders.[9] But the government had a large majority in the Lords, so the Bill was passed despite Rosebery's criticisms.

The Heligolanders drew up a petition to Queen Victoria, in which they said "we shall never forget the manifold reasons we have experienced to feel contented and happy under your Majesty's government." On 21 July they presented the petition to Arthur Barkly, who forwarded it to Britain. Victoria was touched, and sent a gracious reply saying she sincerely desired the islanders' "sustained prosperity and contentment".[10]

In the House of Commons debates on 24 and 25 July an MP named Storey commented caustically on the morality of the exchange of territories:[11]

---

[1] Drower 2002, pp. 79-85, 107.

[2] William George Black was the author of *Heligoland and the Islands of the North Sea*, Edinburgh 1888.

[3] Drower 2002, p. 88, quoting *Hansard* 19 June 1890, col. 1311.

[4] Drower 2002, p. 88.

[5] Rüger 2017, pp. 85, 87, 88.

[6] Details and quotes in this paragraph from Drower 2002, pp. 90-93.

[7] *Heligoland, Report on the Blue Book for 1889*, London 1890, p. 5.

[8] Drower 2002, p. 109.

[9] Drower 2002, pp. 97-98, quoting *Hansard* 10 July 1890, cols. 1275, 1287.

[10] Drower 2002, pp. 109-110.

[11] Drower 2002, pp. 98-99, quoting *Hansard* 24 July 1890, col. 957. Dick Turpin (1705-39) was a famous highwayman.

Since the day Dick Turpin and Tom King met to divide the plunder of Hagley Hall I do not know of any more atrocious thing that has been done by those two great civilising powers in Africa.

On 25 July the Commons passed the Bill, and the fate of Heligoland and large parts of Africa was sealed. Salisbury was in such a hurry that the handover of Heligoland to Germany took place before the Act of Parliament had received the Royal Assent.[1] All opposition had been steam-rollered, and no thought was given to the people involved. The Heligolanders, the Africans and the Sultan of Zanzibar did not count at all.

The cession of Heligoland by Britain to Germany took place on 9 August 1890. Arthur Barkly and other British officials received the German representatives, then the two flags were raised side by side, and the British flag was lowered at sunset. Barkly, his wife and their five children left the island that evening aboard HMS *Calypso*,[2] and never saw Heligoland again. Seven weeks later on 27 September 1890, Arthur Barkly died of diabetes aged only 47.[3]

The Kaiser's government turned Heligoland into a giant fortress; in 1914 its inhabitants were forcibly evacuated to Germany, and when they returned home in December 1918 they found their houses wrecked by the German military. In desperation a group of them, all born under British sovereignty, addressed a petition to the Allied Commissioners in Berlin, to Prime Minister David Lloyd George, and to the League of Nations, asking to be taken back under British sovereignty.[4] It was the second Heligoland petition to Britain, but this one did not even get a reply.

The Nazis refortified the island, and in the Second World War it was heavily bombed by the RAF. On 17 April 1945 a group of conspirators failed in a courageous attempt to hand the island over to Britain and were caught by the Gestapo; seven of them were shot for treason on 21 April 1945, a fortnight before the end of the war.[5] Most of the remaining inhabitants were then evacuated to Germany; some returned after the war, but the British government ordered the total evacuation of the island, and the last inhabitants were removed on 16 May 1945.

On 1 January 1946 some islanders addressed a third Heligoland petition to Britain, asking to be taken once more under British sovereignty – there were still about 250 Heligolanders who had been born under the British Crown. The Foreign Office did not answer, so they sent a fourth petition asking for readmission to the British realm, failing which they would prefer Danish sovereignty to German. Their plea yet again went unanswered.[6]

Britain had other ideas about the future of Heligoland. The British government showed the same callous disregard for the inhabitants of Heligoland in 1946 as it had in 1890 (and as it later did in the case of the Chagos Islanders, section 10.28). The tunnels and bunkers in the island were filled with bombs, shells, mines and torpedo warheads, and on 18 April 1947, watched by a dozen British warships, the "Big Bang", as it was called, took place: 6,700 tons of explosive were set off.[7] It was one of the largest non-nuclear explosions in history, and changed the shape of the island. In the end Britain handed Heligoland back to Germany on 1 March 1952.

The case of Heligoland is an example of Classic Imperialism at its most atrocious. And today, in demanding that Britain should hand over the Falklands against the wishes of their people, Argentina expects Britain to behave like Lord Salisbury in the heyday of Imperialism. But in 1890 there was nothing to stop Lord Salisbury, whereas the situation today is different – the International Covenant on Civil and Political Rights (ICCPR), passed by the United Nations General Assembly in 1966, imposes an obligation on states reponsible for non-self-governing territories to promote "the

---

[1] The *Anglo-German Agreement Act*, 53 & 54 Vict, ch. 52, passed in the Commons on 25 July by 209 votes to 61, Royal Assent 18 August 1890 (details in *Hazell's Annual for 1891*, ed. E. D. Price, p. 593).

[2] By a slip Rüger says Barkly left aboard HMS *Enchantress* (2017, p. 89), but the report by Captain Frederick C. Metaxa of HMS *Calypso* to Vice Admiral Curme, PRO CO 537-17, fols. 96 *recto* – 97 *recto*, makes it clear that the Barklys were aboard *Calypso*.

[3] His death certificate, dated 29 September 1890 (copy in Graham Pascoe's possession), gives "Coma Diabetes" as the cause of death; the death notice in the *Falkland Islands Magazine* for December 1890 also gives "Diabetes".

[4] Herms 2002, p. 71.

[5] Details and names in Herms 2002, pp. 98-99.

[6] Drower 2002, pp. 253-254.

[7] Details and illustrations in Herms 2002, pp. 102-104.

realization of the right of self-determination" for the peoples of those territories (section 10.17). Handing the Falklands to Argentina would breach that obligation.

8.30 Conclusion

Argentina did not mention the Falklands to the British government for 34 years after ratifying the Convention of Peace in 1850, and confirmed that it consented to Britain's possession of the Falklands by many official acts including top-level statements by Argentine leaders and the publication of official maps showing the islands as outside Argentina. Ten countries showed that they agreed with that position by opening consulates in Stanley, and Britain performed innumerable acts of sovereignty in the islands without protest from Argentina. There was an estoppel preventing Argentina from raising the question in the 1880s, but nevertheless Argentina began to press the matter from 1884. Britain protested formally against a proposed Argentine map showing the Falklands as Argentine territory; Argentina accepted that the map would not be official, and protested on 20 January 1888 for the very last time against Britain's refusal to discuss the issue. By then, though, that protest was without substance, since Argentina no longer had the slightest title to the Falklands – they were *de jure* British territory beyond question.

Britain's cession of Heligoland to Germany against the wishes of the Heligolanders was a particularly egregious example of Classic Imperialism, and it was highly controversial even in 1890. There were many demands for the wishes of the Heligolanders to be respected, from figures as diverse as Queen Victoria, Lord Rosebery and various Members of Parliament, as well as petitions and an informal plebiscite from the Heligolanders themselves. Argentina's demand for Britain to cede sovereignty over the Falkland Islands is totally anachronistic in the 21st century.

CHAPTER NINE: the years 1890-1955

Kohen and Rodríguez devote their pages 245-254 to what they call "Argentina's consistent conduct between 1888 and 1941", but in those years Argentina was consistent only in its continuing abandonment of its claim to the Falklands. They say:

... the truth is that the Argentine Government took every opportunity to demonstrate its sovereignty over the islands, both internally and internationally. It is also incorrect to state that no formal protests were made during the period, as we shall now see.

The examples they give are feeble in the extreme (section 9.2). The only effective way of maintaining a claim to a territory is to protest to the current possessor, but Argentina failed to perform that essential act. Not only that; during those years some of Argentina's acts (which Kohen and Rodríguez naturally omit) indicated the exact opposite of the maintenance of a claim. The first of those acts was the acceptance of Britain as an arbitrator over Argentina's territory.

9.1 Argentina's inconsistency, II: British arbitration over Argentina's territory, I, 1899-1902[1]

If country A wishes to maintain a claim to territory held by country B, the last thing it should do is to allow B to decide on what is, and what is not, A's territory. To do so would be to show inconsistency, as described by Sir Ian Sinclair, of the kind when:[2]

... state A has entered into international agreements with state B or indeed with other states, the terms of which are incompatible with the position it is now asserting in proceedings against state B.

As explained in section 8.24, Sinclair's "state A" and "state B" correspond closely to Argentina and Britain in the Falklands dispute: Argentina entered into international agreements with Britain which are incompatible with the position it is now asserting, first in ratifying the Convention of Peace in 1850, and then again twice in appointing Britain as a territorial arbitrator, in 1899-1902 and in 1964-6 (section 10.22). And in 1971-7 Argentina accepted the territorial jurisdiction of a court convened under British auspices, though Britain acted as mediator, not arbitrator (section 8.9).

The British arbitration of 1899-1902 concerned a dispute between Argentina and Chile over the position of their mutual border. The question arose once Argentina had occupied most of Patagonia in 1878-9 after massacring the Indians, and it was settled by a border treaty in 1881. But disagreements continued, and in the late 1890s the two countries came close to war. In an attempt to defuse the situation, President Julio Argentino Roca of Argentina and President Federico Errázuriz Echaurren of Chile met on 15 and 16 February 1899 aboard naval ships in the Magellan Strait; both made flowery speeches extolling the virtues of peace, and are said to have embraced, in what was called "The Embrace at the Strait" ("El Abrazo del Estrecho"). They agreed that the dispute was to be settled by arbitration – and that the British Crown was to be the arbitrator. From Chile that was natural enough, but for Argentina to accept Britain as arbitrator over Argentina's territory was incompatible with maintaining a territorial dispute with Britain over the Falkland Islands.

In his official Message ("Mensaje") to the Argentine Congress in May 1899, President Roca announced that the question of borders with Chile in the north had been solved, "while the Government of Her Britannic Majesty is studying the question of the South, submitted by both countries to its august judgement".[3] But relations between Argentina and Chile deteriorated, and both began to strengthen their armed forces: Argentina ordered two armoured cruisers in Italy, to be named *Rivadavia* and *Moreno*, in response to which in December 1901 Chile ordered two light battleships in Britain, to be named *Constitución* and *Libertad*.[4]

On 28 May 1902 Argentina and Chile signed a treaty in Santiago (Chile), under which the arbitrator charged with drawing the border between Argentina and Chile was to be either Britain or Switzerland. As well as the eminently neutral Switzerland there would have been various other

---

[1] Account here mainly from the *Cordillera of the Andes Boundary Case*, available on the United Nations website, in *Reports of International Arbitral Awards / Recueil des Sentences Arbitrales*, vol. ix, pp. 37-49.
[2] Sinclair 1996, pp. 104-105; longer quote and discussion in section 8.24.
[3] H[eraclio] Mabragaña, *Los Mensajes 1810-1910*, Buenos Aires 1910, vol. V, p. 343.
[4] Oscar Parkes, *British Battleships: A History of Design, Construction and Armament...*, London 1957, p. 437.

potential territorial arbitrators with no involvement in the Falklands (in 1895 the President of the United States had arbitrated between Argentina and Brazil), but both countries appointed the British Crown as Permanent Arbitrator.

Argentina and Chile agreed that their mutual border along the cordillera of the Andes in southern Patagonia between latitudes 41° and 52° South was to be laid down by a British surveying commission. The commission, a group of British officers led by Colonel Sir Thomas Holdich, had already set sail on 31 January 1902, and spent several months in both Argentina and Chile. In his book about the mission Holdich emphasises the friendliness of the Argentinians:[1]

From the President of the Republic..., from members of the Argentine Government..., from senators and scientists, from soldiers, sailors, missionaries, priests and people, there was but one word of kindly welcome, backed by one obvious desire to make all things plain and easy for the peace-makers.

It would have been contradictory to appoint a territorial arbitrator with whom Argentina had a territorial dispute, so Argentina's acceptance of Britain as an arbitrator over Argentina's territory indicated acceptance of Britain's possession of the Falklands – 14 years after the end of the Affair of the Map, Argentina had abandoned its newly-raised Falklands claim.

On 19 November 1902 the commission reported its ruling to King Edward VII, who signed it on 20 November, making it official and binding on both parties. For a while it seemed the dispute had ended; Chile cancelled its order for the *Constitución* and the *Libertad*, and in December 1903 both ships were taken into the Royal Navy and renamed *Swiftsure* and *Triumph* respectively.[2] However, that was not the end of British arbitration between Argentina and Chile (see section 10.22).

The British arbitration of 1899-1902 is of probative value in showing that Argentina was not maintaining a claim to the Falkland Islands. After definitively consenting to Britain's possession of the islands by ratifying the Convention of Peace in 1850, Argentina had performed many acts of omission and commission that ruled out the continuance of any Argentine title to the islands. Then, for four years in 1884-8, it had looked as if Argentina was going to raise a claim to the islands and perhaps start regular protests (though they would have been devoid of force and were rendered invalid by an estoppel, section 8.24), but not even that happened. After one last protest on 20 January 1888 (section 8.26) Argentina dropped the question again, and after a 14-year break without mentioning the Falklands to Britain, accepted Britain as an arbitrator over Argentine territory. If Britain had acted merely as a mediator tasked with bringing the two sides together and presiding over their discussions without active involvement, the British role would have been less relevant, but in 1902 and again in 1964-6, Britain was a territorial arbitrator with authority to lay down the extent of Argentina's and Chile's territorial sovereignty.

We mentioned the British arbitration of 1899-1902 in *Getting it right* (p. 31), but Kohen and Rodríguez say nothing about it, nor about the second arbitration in 1964-6. No doubt they thought it better to keep quiet about them, realising their destructive effect on Argentina's case. That destructive effect is known in Argentina; it was mentioned with anger in the Argentine Congress on 20 July 1950, during a major debate on the Falklands (section 7.17) by a member for Buenos Aires, Dellepiane, who pointed out the absurdities and contradictions in Argentina's behaviour:[3]

We make clear our rights against Britain, of sovereignty over the Malvinas islands and over a sector of the Antarctic – and His Britannic Majesty is the arbitrator in a border dispute which we still have with Chile...

Dellepiane mentioned an earlier proposal that the United States should serve as arbitrator, which had come to nothing, and called for an end to the "errors and omissions" committed by Argentina on the Malvinas issue. By that time, though, there had been so many errors and omissions by Argentina that no vestige of an Argentine title to the Falklands survived. The British arbitration confirmed yet again that Argentina had dropped all claim to the islands – Argentina accepted Britain as being entitled to decide what was Argentine territory and what was not. That is incompatible with a claim to the Falklands.

---

[1] Col. Sir Thomas Hungerford Holdich, *The Countries of the King's Award*, London 1904, pp. 91-92.
[2] Parkes 1957, pp. 436, 437.
[3] *Diario de Sesiones de la Cámara de Diputados,... 6 de julio-10 y 11 de agosto*, Buenos Aires 1951, p. 1181.

9.2 Feeble examples from Kohen and Rodríguez

In contrast to the abundant evidence of Argentina's acquiescence in Britain's possession of the Falklands, Kohen and Rodríguez present no serious evidence to the contrary. They print (pp. 236-8) parts of three Argentine maps showing the Falklands as Argentine territory, but that is not surprising since they were all printed during the Affair of the Map (one in 1886, two in 1888), when Argentina briefly attempted to open the question (sections 8.23, 8.26). They do not mention that Argentina published detailed descriptions of its territory omitting the Falklands (Latzina 1891 and 1899; see section 8.28), and also accepted British territorial arbitration in 1899-1902.

The two authors jump from 1888 to 1908, when Argentina objected to the inclusion of the Falklands in a communication by the Italian ambassador in Buenos Aires. What happened was actually that in early 1908, the Italian ambassador in Buenos Aires sent a communication to the Argentine government in connection with the Rome Postal Union Convention, listing the Falklands among British territories that had joined that Convention. Thereupon the Argentine foreign minister sent a formal protest to Italy against the inclusion of the Falklands, asserting that they were part of Argentina. The British ambassador in Buenos Aires, Walter Townley, learnt of the affair and on 25 February 1908 informed the Foreign Office in London, saying that he would avoid raising it in discussion with the Argentine foreign minister, but if it were raised by the Argentine side he would say that the British government could not discuss the question. The Foreign Office approved.[1]

And that was the end of the matter. Nothing whatever came of it; Argentina did not raise the affair with Britain, and continued to tolerate the presence of the Falklands in the UPU, as she had done since April 1877 (and still does; the Falklands are still listed on the UPU's website as an overseas territory of Great Britain). So there was in 1908 no protest to Britain over the possession of the Falklands, and in 1914 and again in 1915 Argentine foreign minister José Luis Murature specifically stated that there had been no Argentine protest over the Falklands since 1888.[2] The long period without Argentine protests to Britain over the Falklands continued unbroken from the time of the last protest in 1888, which had been devoid of substance anyway – in Alfredo Becerra's *Protestas por Malvinas*, Buenos Aires 1998, there is nothing between 1888 and 1919.

In the whole of Kohen's and Rodríguez's work, the Falkland Islands as such are absent; they are not interested in the islands' own history, nor in their people. By contrast, we might here mention something that happened in the islands in 1908 that still has an important effect today: in 1908 the Stanley Sports Association was founded. Its history is described by Patrick Watts in *The Christmas Sports*, a richly illustrated work with tables of competition results going back over more than a century.[3] Patrick says in his introduction that the book was inspired by Falklands children, who often asked for information about sports for their work on the local history of their country. His book records an important aspect of that history.

Kohen and Rodríguez mention (p. 246) an Argentine map produced in 1910 for the centenary of Argentina's independence, which included the Falklands as Argentine territory; they state that the British representative in Buenos Aires was instructed to take no notice of it. Townley successfully ignored the map, Argentina did not mention it, and there were no repercussions.

9.3 No mention of the Falklands in the Argentine Messages to Congress

That map was not the only publication commemorating 100 years of Argentine independence; another was a six-volume compilation by Heraclio Mabragaña of all the Messages at the ceremonial openings of Argentine legislatures from 1810 to 1910 (from 1810 to 1849 at the legislature of the province of Buenos Aires, and after a break in 1850 and 1851 when there was no Message, at the legislature of the Argentine Confederation, and from 1862 of the newly united Argentina).[4] That

---

[1] Bernhardt 1910, pp. 405-406; Ferrer Vieyra 1993, p. 468, quoting (in Spanish) John Field's Foreign Office memorandum of 29 February 1928.

[2] Stated in despatches from British ambassador Sir Reginald Tower to British Foreign Secretary Sir Edward Grey, 23 December 1914, in *BDFA* Part II, D, vol. I, 1989, p. 18; and 20 March 1915, in *ibid.*, p. 20.

[3] Patrick J. Watts, MBE, *The Christmas Sports: a History of the Stanley Sports Association 1908-2012*, Stanley 2012.

[4] H[eraclio] Mabragaña, *Los Mensajes 1810-1910*, Buenos Aires 1910.

publication reveals the total change in Argentina's behaviour over the Falklands after the ratification of the Convention of Peace in 1850 – it prints the texts of the protests against Britain's possession of the Falklands every year in the Messages from 1833 to 1849, but thereafter there are none. One might have expected that protests would be resumed at some time in the 19th century, for example during the Affair of the Map in 1884-8, or perhaps after the last protest of 20 January 1888 following the failure of the Argentine attempt to open the question. But no; the word "Malvinas" does not occur at all in any of the Messages after 1849 (and nor does "Falkland"). There might have been a simple explanation for that – the Messages might have become mere statements of the government's intentions, or brief formulaic opening statements without political content. It would not then have been surprising if they had not mentioned a dispute over the Falklands.

But they did not change; the Messages remained detailed accounts of the current state of Argentina, including territorial disputes with other countries. For example, in 1882 President Julio Roca said that many problems including border disputes with Chile had prevented the settlement of Patagonia, but that the laws of the Republic were now recognised down to 52° South on the Atlantic coast; in 1886 Roca said the final border agreement with Brazil was about to be signed, and that since the dispute with Chile over the seizure of the French barque *Jeanne Amélie* had been solved, "the last remnant of our old border dispute with that nation had disappeared"; in 1895 President José Uriburu announced that on 5 February 1895 the President of the United States had made his decision on the borders between Argentina and Brazil; in 1896 Uriburu went into detail on a new territorial dispute developing with Chile; in 1899 Julio Roca (president once again) was able to announce that the question of borders with Chile in the north had been solved, "while the Government of Her Britannic Majesty is studying the question of the South, submitted by both countries to its august judgement"; in 1901 he stated that there was no border dispute outstanding, since the dispute between Chile and Argentina was about to be decided by an impartial judgement (i.e. by Britain); in 1902 he stated that the question of borders with Chile was about to be solved, and that a distinguished representative of the arbitrators (i.e. Sir Thomas Holdich) was studying the disputed territory preparatory to the judgement, and in 1906 President José Figueroa Alcorta announced that some progress had been made in border discussions with Chile, but further work was needed in some areas including the Beagle Channel.[1]

Those are only a small selection of the many territorial and border questions that were mentioned in the Messages to Congress after the ratification of the Convention of Peace in 1850. They are enough to show that Argentina's territory continued to be a regular and significant topic in the Messages, but the existence of a dispute between Britain and Argentina over the Falklands was never so much as alluded to, and the islands were not mentioned once.

Not only that; various presidential and vice-presidential statements in the Messages rule out the existence of any such dispute. As we pointed out in section 8.18, in 1865 President Bartolomé Mitre said there was no obstacle to friendly relations between Argentina and Britain and France;[2] in 1866 Vice-President Marcos Paz mentioned some private claims for damages raised by British subjects, and added that "This question, which is the only one between us and the British nation, has not yet been settled";[3] in 1869 President Domingo Sarmiento said Argentina had nothing to ask of other nations except their goodwill,[4] and in 1906 President Figueroa Alcorta said: "Since the ending of the border conflicts, the Republic, without serious problems to resolve, and satisfied with her own inheritance, has limited her diplomatic activity to spreading ideas of international justice…".[5] If border conflicts had ended and the Republic was satisfied with her inheritance, she clearly had no territorial dispute with any other country.

In fact the Falklands were not mentioned in any Message to the Argentine Congress for 91 years between 1849 and 1941. That was a significant change, since the Messages had been a natural

---

[1] Examples and quotes in this paragraph from Mabragaña 1910, vol. IV, pp. 37, 161; vol. V, pp. 214, 236-240, 343; vol. VI, pp. 1, 22, 168.
[2] Mabragaña 1910, vol. III, p. 227.
[3] English translation here from *BFSP 1866-1867* (London 1871), p. 1009; original in Mabragaña 1910, vol. III, p. 238.
[4] Mabragaña 1910, vol. III, p. 286.
[5] Mabragaña 1910, vol. VI, p. 167.

forum for protests against Britain from 1833 to 1849, but together with the denials of any dispute with Britain, the references to good relations with Britain, and the complete dropping of the subject by Argentina in 1888 after the Affair of the Map, it demonstrates that successive Argentine governments failed to maintain any claim to the islands. As Professor Giovanni Distefano points out (sections 7.16, 8.8), the conduct of a state after the "juridical watershed" in a territorial dispute (i.e. the critical date) is significant as "evidence of a title already constituted". Argentina's total lack of activity, and Britain's continuous activity as sovereign of the Falklands, confirmed Britain's title beyond doubt.

The trivial examples of Argentine activity mentioned by Kohen and Rodríguez do nothing to change that – as O'Brien says, protests have to be "sustained and made in the appropriate form",[1] or they have no legal force. Argentina has not sustained its protests, and has not protested to Britain over the Falklands for over 130 years since 20 January 1888. There is thus no legal force whatever in any Argentine claim to the islands.

9.4 More feeble examples from Kohen and Rodríguez

Kohen and Rodríguez say (p. 247) that Argentina made what they call a "formal protest" to Belgium on 20 December 1926, having been informed by the Belgian ambassador that the Falklands had been included in the "Brussels sanitary convention". They are presumably referring to the International Sanitary Convention signed in Paris on 21 June 1926,[2] which however contains no reference to the Falklands, though it includes a number of reservations by several countries, including one by Egypt of sovereignty over "the Soudan", but no reservation by Argentina, though Argentina signed the convention too. The British representatives merely declared that their signatures did not bind any part of the British Empire that was a separate member of the League of Nations (e.g. Canada), nor any British territories that might not have the resources to arrange for declaration of serious diseases. That is all. The Falklands were covered by Britain's signature and were not mentioned separately – the reference to Belgium seems to have been a misunderstanding.

The two authors mention that we referred in *Getting it right* (p. 32) to a meeting between Argentine foreign minister Dr Angél Gallardo and British Foreign Secretary Sir Austen Chamberlain in 1927, in which Gallardo said that the British claim to the Falklands was "exceedingly strong". They criticise us for not mentioning Sir Austen Chamberlain's further remarks (we had no room), so here is a longer quote from his despatch of 31 December 1927 to ambassador Sir Malcolm Robertson in Buenos Aires about the conversation with Gallardo:[3]

2. I ... made use of the opportunity to speak to him on the subject of the Falkland Islands... I made it plain to Dr. Gallardo that I did not wish to embarrass the Argentine Government by forcing them to any embarrassing retractation[4] of their claim, but this was a very different thing from being compelled by indiscretion on their part – *i.e.*, by the action taken at Berne,[5] which I would hope was only the result of an *excès de zèle* on the part of an irresponsible postal official – to rebut their ill-founded claim in a manner which might prove as embarrassing to them as detrimental to good relations on either side. I asked his Excellency... to desist from such useless and provocative action...

3. Dr. Gallardo said that he had been recently looking into the question of the Falkland Islands, and had come to the conclusion that our position and claim there were exceedingly strong...

4. Dr. Gallardo said that in any case he would at once telegraph to his Government urging that no action should be taken or contemplated with regard to the Falkland Islands pending his return...

Kohen and Rodríguez quote part of that, but omit Chamberlain's passage about not wishing to be compelled "to rebut their ill-founded claim in a manner which might prove as embarrassing to them as detrimental to good relations on either side", and they also omit Gallardo's admission that Britain's "position and claim there were exceedingly strong". Those statements do not support any

---

[1] O'Brien 2001, p. 211.
[2] Text online under https://www.loc.gov/law/help/us-treaties/bevans/m-ust000002-0545.pdf.
[3] Printed in 1928 as document A 7276/381/2 in *FOCP*, reprinted in *BDFA* Part II, D, 5, 1989, pp. 104-105.
[4] **retractation 2.a.** Withdrawal or recantation of an opinion, statement, etc., with admission of error" (*OED*).
[5] The Argentine claim had been asserted in a statement to the Universal Postal Union and included in a UPU circular of 14 October 1927 on territorial claims (Becerra 1998, p. 237), but Argentina made no protest to Britain.

idea that Argentina was maintaining a claim to the Falklands. And in 1936 another Argentine foreign minister, Ibarra García, had a series of meetings with J. H. Leche, a British embassy official, and said the last thing he wanted was a sovereignty dispute with Britain over the Falklands, adding that Argentina could never publicly abandon its claim because some politicians were able to exploit public opinion on the subject.[1]

Argentina's actions during the *Uruguay* affair in July 1932 cast further doubt on the existence of a territorial dispute between Argentina and Britain. The Uruguayan cruiser *Uruguay* had received on board the Argentine general Toranzo, an opponent of the Argentine military government. In response to Argentine complaints, and to general astonishment, Uruguay broke off diplomatic relations with Argentina. Argentine President Agustín Justo thereupon issued a decree breaking off relations with Uruguay, including the following: "Article 3. Request the Government of Great Britain to take charge temporarily of the Argentine interests in the Uruguayan Republic."[2] The fact that in such a diplomatic emergency Argentina asked Britain to represent Argentine interests, rather than, say, Switzerland or the United States, again calls into question Argentina's seriousness in maintaining a dispute with Britain over the Falklands.

As Kohen and Rodríguez also say (p. 253), Argentina mentioned its claim to the Falklands in various international forums including the United Nations, the Interamerican Conference on the Maintenance of Peace and Security in Rio in 1947, the 9th Panamerican Conference in Bogotá in 1948 and the Havana conference of the American Commission on Dependent Territories in 1949, but of all those meetings the only ones of any importance were those at the United Nations. Argentina has raised the issue of the Falklands every year at the United Nations since 1946, only with brief notes for the first 18 years, but since 1964 with a presentation before the UN decolonisation committee, the "Committee of 24" (C24) – a clear misuse of the C24 since its mission is to promote self-determination for non-self-governing territories, not to assist third-party countries to take them over (section 10.11). All those meetings merely called for dialogue on the issue; the UN has never pronounced on the merits of Argentina's claim. But there is one UN resolution that Argentina never mentions – Resolution 1541 (XV) of 1960. That resolution annihilates any possible claim by Argentina to the Falklands (section 10.9).

To sum up: Argentina's doubts over its claim to the Falklands were directly expressed to Britain, and in 1932 Argentina entrusted Britain with the representation of Argentine interests, all of which indicates a lack of seriousness in Argentina's claim to the Falklands. Argentina did inform other countries and postal authorities about its claim, but that is irrelevant.

9.5 Two faulty books: Groussac 1910 and Goebel 1927

Kohen and Rodríguez conclude their section (p. 254) by saying "The British pamphlet then claims to disregard the studies and publications of non-Argentine writers such as Paul Groussac and Julius Goebel". They are referring to Groussac's book of 1910[3] and Goebel's of 1927,[4] and there are good reasons for "disregarding" both those works.

Paul Groussac (1848-1929) was French; he emigrated to Argentina, and thanks to connections with Argentine president Julio Roca became director of the national library. His book *Les Iles Malouines*, published as part of the 100th anniversary celebrations of Argentine independence, gives a seriously faulty account of Falklands history: he misinterprets the events of 1770-71, he understates the involvement of American sealing ships and the foreign recognition of Britain's

---

[1] Report by the "Insight team" in *The Sunday Times*, London, 20 June 1982, p. 20.
[2] Details of this incident, including the full text of an article from the *Review of the River Plate* and a statement from the Argentine Foreign Office, in *BDFA* Part II, Series D, vol. 8, pp. 332-338.
[3] Paul Groussac, *Les Iles Malouines: nouvel exposé d'un vieux litige* ["The Malouine Islands: a new account of an old legal dispute"], Buenos Aires 1910.
[4] Julius Goebel, *The Struggle for the Falkland Islands: A study in legal and diplomatic history*, New Haven (Connecticut) 1927 (with 14 illustrations); the 2nd ed., Port Washington (N.Y.) 1971, is a facsimile reprint of the 1927 ed. with all illustrations; the 3rd ed., New Haven and London 1982, is also a facsimile reprint of the 1927 ed., but text only, no illustrations, with a different map of the islands (frontispiece) and with a preface (dated May 1982) and an introduction (dated July 1968) by Professor J. C. J. Metford.

possession of the islands, he says hardly anything about Louis Vernet, who played such a central part in the story, and he omits the vitally important Convention of Peace. Groussac's work is therefore of little value, though for some time it was the only full-length book on the Falklands dispute, and thanks to its publication and distribution in Argentina as a result of the efforts of Alfredo Palacios,[1] it made a significant contribution to the raising of an Argentine claim to the Falklands in the 1930s.

Julius Ludwig Goebel, jun. (1892-1973), son of a German immigrant to the United States, is mainly remembered for *The Struggle for the Falkland Islands*, which has had an influence out of all proportion to its content. It is actually an examination of the 18th-century legal and diplomatic history of the Falklands dispute, and has little to say on later periods. Out of the 468 pages of text he takes 425 to get to the Nootka Sound controversy of 1790, to which he devotes six pages, full of errors; he mentions Louis Vernet for the first time on page 434, and devotes only 16 pages to the vital years from 1823 to 1834. Apart from a footnote on the *Germantown* affair in 1854 and a brief mention of affairs in 1884-5 including US President Grover Cleveland's State of the Union Address,[2] he mentions no history after 1842 – he hardly deals with the 19th century, let alone the 20th. Parts of it are still useful, especially some of the documents he quotes and his bibliography, but it has severe shortcomings: his account of the discovery of the islands has been superseded; he wrongly states that Spain knew more than Britain about the Falklands in the 1760s; he muddles the question of Spain's acquisition of France's rights; he wrongly assumes that there was a secret promise by Britain in the 1770s to vacate the islands; he wrongly states that Spain made a reservation of Spanish rights in 1771; he totally misinterprets the Nootka Sound Convention of 1790 (see section 1.7); he confuses Jewett's and Vernet's letters; he fails to mention the Spanish claim of 1822 to all South American possessions (though he had mentioned it in his doctoral thesis),[3] or the Spanish protest in 1825 to Britain against the recognition of South American countries; he gives an inaccurate account of the *Lexington* raid of 1831-2, and he misrepresents Britain's motives for sending HMS *Clio*. Quite apart from all his errors, his version of the legal and diplomatic history of the Falklands dispute in the 18th century has now been superseded and corrected by the much more detailed research of Jean-Étienne Martin-Allanic.[4] The Swiss historian Jörg Fisch has analysed Goebel's accounts of several 17th and 18th century treaties, and concludes that Goebel confuses and conflates the treaties themselves and the Spanish intentions behind them.[5] Neither Groussac nor Goebel is in any way reliable – they should both be disregarded.

9.6 South Georgia and the Falkland Islands Dependencies[6]

Some 800 miles east-south-east of the Falklands lies the mountainous island of South Georgia, with an area of some 3,755 sq. km., mostly under permanent snow cover. The highest of its many mountains, Mount Paget, at 2,934 metres, is over twice as high as Britain's highest mountain Ben Nevis at 1,344 metres. Some 200 miles east-south-east of South Georgia lie the South Sandwich Islands, while below 60° South lie the South Orkney and South Shetland Islands, all of which, as well as a sector of Antarctica, are claimed by Britain, though all claims below 60° are "frozen" by

---

[1] In 1934 the Argentine Senator Alfredo Palacios got the Argentine Congress to finance a Spanish translation (*Las Islas Malvinas por Paul Groussac…*, Buenos Aires 1936) and its distribution to all Argentine schools and colleges.
[2] Goebel 1927 p. 462, fn. 11 and p. 463, fn. 16.
[3] Julius Goebel, Jr., *The Recognition Policy of the United States…*, New York 1915; facsimile reprint Buffalo, New York, 2001; Spain's 1822 protest mentioned on pp. 136-137. He does not mention the Falklands, but his argumentation casts some doubt on his conclusions in his later book. In medieval Europe, he says, the basis of recognition was legitimacy, which contrasts with the new, democratic principle of *de facto* recognition given to governments actually exerting authority, independently of questions of legitimacy. He approves of a "defacto-ist" policy as being more modern and more democratic than the old legitimist policy, but there is no trace of that in his 1927 book on the Falklands, in which he supports Spain's and Argentina's exclusively legitimist claims to the islands.
[4] Jean-Étienne Martin-Allanic, *Bougainville navigateur et les découvertes de son temps* ["Bougainville as navigator and the discoveries of his time"], 2 vols., Paris 1964 (see section 2.2).
[5] Jörg Fisch, "The Falkland Islands in the European Treaty System 1493-1833", in *German Yearbook of International Law / Jahrbuch für Internationales Recht*, Berlin, vol. 26, 1983 (see section 1.1).
[6] Background details in this section mostly from Robert Headland, *The Island of South Georgia*, Cambridge 1984.

the Antarctic Treaty of 1959. For over a century some of them, especially South Georgia, have had an effective British administrative presence, and for some 120 years they were all known as the Falkland Islands Dependencies, with the Governor of the Falklands as *ex officio* governor.[1]

South Georgia was apparently discovered in 1675 by the British merchant Antoine de la Roché, born in London to a French father. It is marked as "Roche I." on maps dating from c. 1745, and may have been sighted again in 1756 by the Spanish captain Gregorio Jérez, in the ship *León*, chartered by French merchants from St-Malo.[2] What is certain is that it was charted in 1775 by Captain James Cook, who also made the first recorded landing on 17 January 1775, when he "took possession" of the island for Britain. Cook also discovered the South Sandwich Islands, on 31 January 1775; the South Shetlands were discovered on 19 February 1819 by the British captain William Smith, who "took possession" of them in October that year (section 4.6), and the South Orkney Islands were discovered on 6 December 1821 by another British captain, George Powell, who "took possession" of them for Britain the next day.[3] All the island territories in the Falkland Islands Dependencies were discovered by British captains, who claimed them for Britain.

Kohen's and Rodríguez's account of these islands (pp. 259-263) is a thorough mix-up. On their p. 259 they illustrate two details of a map, of which they say in their running text on pp. 258-9:[4]

A map of South America published in 1790 in London by the renowned cartographer Thomas Bowen describes South Georgia as having been discovered by the Spanish in 1756 and explored by Cook in 1775. This contradicts the British statement of the island's likely discovery by De La Roche in 1675 and its "re-discovery" (sic) by Cook in 1775. This is an official map. It states: "Published by Royal Authority".

However, the caption to their illustration runs: "Map of South America of 1790 performed by Thomas Brown. This is a British official publication".

All that needs correction. In the first place, there were in 1790 no published official British maps of places outside Britain; the British government did not begin to print such maps until after the foundation of the Admiralty Hydrographic Office in 1795.[5] Before that, all published maps and charts were mere commercial ventures. Secondly, they confuse two mapmakers: Thomas Bowen and Thomas Brown. The map they illustrate was in fact engraved by Thomas Bowen (d. 1790, date of birth apparently unrecorded), but the map is not from 1790; it was printed in Middleton's *Geography* in 1779.[6] Thirdly, the map they illustrate nowhere states that it is "Published by Royal Authority".[7] And fourthly, the mapmaker Thomas Brown (1764-1820) was an ordinary publisher, bookseller, printseller, stationer and engraver in Edinburgh; his maps had no special authority and he did not print this map. In short, Kohen and Rodríguez provide no official British evidence that disproves the discovery of South Georgia by Antoine de la Roché in 1675.

Kohen and Rodríguez maintain (p. 260) that one of the first official acts concerning South Georgia was "the dispatch, by Political and Military Commandment of the Malvinas Commander of the Falklands/ Malvinas [*sic*!], Luis Vernet, of a team to rescue castaways who found themselves in South Georgia". That too is nonsense; the rescue was organised and arranged by the British consul-general Woodbine Parish, over three weeks before Vernet was appointed Civil and Military Commandant of the Malvinas, and it was financed by the British government; Vernet's role was

---

[1] A summary of British involvement in all these territories from the 19th century, of Argentina's attempts from around 1925 to raise a claim to them, and of the resulting dispute, is on the ICJ website, entitled *Pleadings, Oral Arguments, Documents: Antarctica Cases (United Kingdom v. Argentina; United Kingdom v. Chile); Orders of March 16th 1956; Removal from the List*, under https://www.icj-cij.org/en/case/26, henceforth "British ICJ application 1955". See also E. W. [Bill] Hunter Christie, *The Antarctic Problem*, London 1951, and Klaus Dodds, *Pink Ice: Britain and the South Atlantic Empire*, London 2002.

[2] For the discovery of the island in 1675 by de la Roché, and the 2nd sighting in 1756, see Headland 1984, pp. 21-22. Headland comments (pp. 22, 23) that the coordinates in both accounts are inaccurate, but typical for those times.

[3] Details of discoveries from the British ICJ application 1955, pp. 11-12; date of discovery of the South Shetlands corrected from R.J. Campbell, *The Discovery of the South Shetland Islands, 1819-1820...*, London 2000, p. 46.

[4] The "British statement" they refer to is in the British application to the ICJ in 1955 (below).

[5] See Vice Admiral Sir Archibald Day, *The Admiralty Hydrographic Service 1795-1919*, London 1967, pp. 12-13.

[6] Charles Theodore Middleton, *A New and Complete System of Geography...*, [London] 1778-9.

[7] Its cartouche (partly visible in Kohen's and Rodríguez's illustration) runs in full: "An accurate Map of South America, from the best Modern Maps and Charts, By Thos Bowen, Geog.^r[apher]". There is no other legend.

merely to transfer part of his charter to Mathew Brisbane, who performed the rescue (sections 5.12, 5.13). The castaways were British, the rescuer was British, the rescue was paid for by Britain, and the arrangements were made by Britain – and it saved Vernet money since the British government paid part of the charter fee for the *Betsey*. The rescue was nothing to do with Argentina; it showed the involvement of Britain and British citizens in the affairs of South Georgia.

British authority in the Dependencies was asserted in the Charter for the Falklands dated 23 June 1843 and also in Letters Patent of 28 April 1876 and 25 February 1892. In April 1896 a Norwegian captain, Carl Anton Larsen,[1] wrote to Falklands Governor Sir Roger Goldsworthy in Stanley requesting sole rights to erect a whaling station and accommodation on South Georgia;[2] he clearly regarded the island as British. That and various other enquiries for permission to exploit the island led to the publication in the *Falkland Islands Gazette* on 2 October 1900 of the offer of a 21-year lease of the island, but there were no takers. In 1901-3 Larsen captained the Swedish Nordenskjöld expedition, which visited the Falklands and South Georgia – on South Georgia a shore party named a bay "Grytviken" ["The Pot Bay"] after some old trypots they found there. In 1904 Larsen tried to raise capital to found a whaling company in Norway, but failed. He obtained the capital in Buenos Aires, where he founded a whaling company, the "Compañia Argentina de Pesca" (known as "Pesca" for short), which was constituted by Argentine government decree on 29 February 1904 and registered in Buenos Aires on 8 April 1904.[3]

Kohen and Rodríguez say (p. 260) that the aim of the "Norwegian businessmen" was:

... to settle in South Georgia, and with that aim the business was set up under Argentine legislation. Once settled, they received the assistance of Argentine war ships that for decades supplied fuel to the islands without any British reaction. Argentina also installed a telegraph station, and members of Argentine military crews conducted various deployments on the island, without ever being disturbed by British authorities.

Yet again the two authors omit many vital details. They do not mention that British warships also took supplies and personnel to the island; the Argentine military "deployments" were mere landings by sailors without significance for sovereignty, and above all, they suppress the fact that Pesca recognised British sovereignty, which can easily be demonstrated.

Larsen arrived at Grytviken on 16 November 1904 to set up a whaling station, but a Chilean company had been formed in Punta Arenas and was also aiming to exploit the island. The British cruiser HMS *Sappho* was sent to South Georgia to sort matters out; Captain Hodges of *Sappho* had cordial relations with Larsen, and Britain granted the lease to Pesca. That gave the island its first residents – some 60 Norwegians including some wives and Larsen's five daughters and two sons.

In January 1905 Pesca set up a meteorological station at Grytviken, staffed by Norwegians,[4] and on 2 November 1905 the president of Pesca, Hermann Schlieper, and Capitán Guillermo Nuñes, Director of Armaments of the Argentine ministry of marine, applied through the British Legation in Buenos Aires for a whaling licence from the Governor of the Falklands. A contract between the Falkland Islands Government and Pesca was drawn up in Stanley and signed in Buenos Aires on 8 March 1906. It included a lease of land at Grytviken – the first-ever Antarctic whaling lease.[5]

Further Letters Patent issued by the British government on 21 July 1908 defined the Falkland Islands Dependencies as South Georgia, the South Sandwich Islands, the South Orkney Islands, the South Shetland Islands, Graham Land (part of the Antarctic Peninsula), and all land in the South Atlantic lying south of 50° South and between 20° and 80° West; the Letters Patent were published in the *Falkland Islands Gazette*, a copy of which was sent to the Argentine foreign ministry on 20

---

[1] Detailed history of Larsen's involvement in South Georgia and the company "Pesca" in Ian B. Hart, *Pesca: A History of the Pioneer Modern Whaling Company in the Antarctic*, Salcombe 2001; brief account in Headland 1984, p. 110.
[2] Hart 2001, p. 20, quoting letter from Larsen to Goldsworthy, April 1896, in the Royal Geographical Society archives.
[3] Hart 2001, p. 39.
[4] Hart 2001, p. 90 and fn. 43 on p. 358, with names of Norwegian observers. The meteorological station was originally maintained by the Oficina Meteorológica Argentina under the terms of Pesca's British lease, but it was Pesca that paid the Norwegian observers and the station was also included in the terms of leases granted to Pesca by the Falkland Islands Government. The station was taken over in 1948 by the Falkland Islands Dependencies Survey, 1952-69 by the Falkland Islands Government and finally by the British Antarctic Survey (*ibid., loc. cit.*).
[5] Account here from Hart 2001, pp. 20-88, and from Headland 1984, esp. pp. 64-65, 112-113.

February 1909; Argentina acknowledged receipt of it on 18 March 1909, but did not protest or take any other action. A copy was also sent to the Chilean foreign ministry, which likewise acknowledged receipt but took no action.[1] New Letters Patent were issued on 28 March 1917, defining the extent of the Dependencies so as to exclude any possibility that they might have referred to Patagonia (as had been wrongly asserted in Argentina), and to include all islands and territories south of 58° South and between 50° and 80° West.[2]

Ian Hart points out the complete lack of any Argentine reaction to the British administrative measures, and also the unquestioning acceptance by Pesca of British sovereignty over South Georgia. The Argentine historian Ernesto Fitte criticises Pesca for acting in an "unpardonable, submissive manner" in accepting British jurisdiction over its activities,[3] and confirms that the Argentine government knew what was going on but still failed to protest – he says:[4]

... nor does the passivity shown by the government of the Nation offer any mitigating circumstances in view of that primary fact and others that followed later... there are no excuses for what happened...

Fitte explains that there was a government crisis – President Manuel Quintana died suddenly on 12 March 1906 and the entire cabinet resigned. But that does not excuse Argentina's inactivity, however serious the crisis – there were civil servants in office throughout, and a failure to protest is a failure to protest; no reasons however powerful can convert it into a "non-failure". In any case a protest could always have been made later once things had settled down in Buenos Aires, but none was made.

Argentina had not as yet raised a claim to South Georgia, and the actions of Pesca and the total inaction of the Argentine government in the face of known administrative acts by Britain ruled out any Argentine claim then and for the future.

Despite all that, Kohen and Rodríguez assert (p. 261):

The fact is that Argentina continued to exercise acts of authority over South Georgia during the period in question, for example through the aforementioned presence of war ships, its declaration before the Universal Postal Union in 1927, considering that it exercised *de jure* and *de facto* sovereignty over South Georgia, and the dispatch of an official of the Ministry of Inland Revenue in 1947.

That is nonsense; there were no "acts of authority" by Argentina at all. Throughout that period there was a resident British magistrate at King Edward Point (the island's administrative headquarters) with full legal authority over the island – the first magistrate, James Innes Wilson, was appointed on 20 November 1909, and from May 1910 a Falkland Islands police officer was appointed to serve on the island. During December 1909 Wilson inspected all the South Georgian whaling stations and established that the total population was 720, of whom 670 (93%) were Scandinavians; the population of Grytviken was 150.

Pesca's second lease was signed at the British Consulate in Buenos Aires on 22 July 1909 by company president Schlieper and by Falklands Governor William Allardyce and the Falklands Colonial Secretary W. A. Thompson, both representing the British Crown.[5] When it expired in 1927, the lease reverted to the Falkland Islands Government. The recognition of British sovereignty by Pesca was lamented by several speakers in the Argentine Congress on 20 July 1950 in the course of a major debate on Argentina's claim to the Falklands (see section 7.1). One of the speakers was Miguel Ángel Zavala Ortiz (later foreign minister, 1963-6), who said:[6]

... I might refer, for example, to what goes on with the Compañia Argentina de Pesca... A company... which recognises a concession granted by the British government... the Argentine government, through that

---

[1] Hart 2001, pp. 94-95; British ICJ application 1955, pp. 22-23, with text of Argentine acknowledgement of receipt of the *Falkland Islands Gazette*.
[2] Full texts in Hunter Christie 1951: Letters Patent of 1908 on pp. 301-302, those of 1917 on pp. 302-303.
[3] Ernesto Fitte, *La disputa con Gran Bretaña por las islas del Atlántico Sur*, Buenos Aires 1968, p. 114.
[4] Fitte 1968, pp. 116-117. Detailed account of Argentina's failure to protest in Hart 2001, pp. 88-90.
[5] Leases listed in Headland 1984, Appendix I, p. 257; the Jason Harbour lease is illustrated in Hart 2001, frontispiece. Hart also illustrates (2001, p. 93) a Falkland Islands Government Licence issued to Pesca for the season 1959-60.
[6] *Diario* 1950, 20 July, pp. 1178-1179.

company's compromising, appears to recognise British sovereignty. That is deplorable.

Zavala Ortiz might have been even angrier with "Pesca" if he had known that its representatives had not only visited the Falklands on occasion, but even contributed to Falklands sporting activities – the *Falkland Islands Magazine* (*FIM*) reported in December 1925 that Capitán Guillermo Nuñes, an advisor to Pesca, who was then visiting Stanley, had agreed to present a cup for a sailing challenge race in the islands.[1] As mentioned above, Nuñes had in 1905 been Director of Armaments of the Argentine ministry of marine and had visited the British legation in Buenos Aires with Pesca's president Hermann Schlieper to apply for a whaling licence from the Governor of the Falkland Islands. The behaviour of Nuñes, and of "Pesca" over several decades, together with the complete lack of any Argentine reaction to Britain's administration of South Georgia and the other Falkland Islands Dependencies, prevented any possible Argentine claim to those territories.

The magistrate on South Georgia from 1914 to 1927 was Edward Binnie (1884-1956), a Falkland Islander born in Stanley, and in the 1920s there were some 20 British government personnel permanently stationed on the island.[2] In the 1950s the resident British officials included the magistrate, a customs officer and assistant, a couple of policemen, and a government naturalist and sealing inspector, as well as government-employed staff such as mechanics, radio operators, weather forecasters and observers, a cook and a steward, mostly recruited from Britain, the Falklands or Ireland, several with their wives and children.[3] There were no Argentine officials on the island; to say that Argentina exercised sovereignty is laughable.

There have been many British scientific and exploratory expeditions that visited the island, the most famous being the emergency visit of Sir Ernest Shackleton in 1915-16,[4] and there have been many visits by British warships since HMS *Sappho* in 1906, including by HMS *Dartmouth* and *Weymouth* (1920 and 1921), HMS *Ajax* and *Exeter* (1937 and 1938), and many more since 1945.[5] Argentine ships sometimes visited the island, and always complied with British customs and immigration procedures without mentioning any sovereignty dispute.[6] Argentina accepted British sovereignty without question.

To sum up: Britain discovered South Georgia, the South Orkneys, the South Sandwich Islands and the South Shetlands and administered them with magistrates and other officials from 1909, with Argentina's knowledge and without protest. There is no possible Argentine claim to have inherited South Georgia from Spain, since the Treaty of Tordesillas "allocated" it to Portugal, and Spain never had any presence there. Nonetheless, from about 1925 onwards Argentina slowly began to suggest that it was raising a claim to all the Falkland Islands Dependencies, and on 1 June 1937 for the very first time mentioned a claim to them.[7] From 1946 onwards Argentina also often mentioned its claim to the Falklands, but no moves were made which might have led to an open dispute, and in conversation with British Foreign Secretary Ernest Bevin, Argentine foreign minister Dr Bramuglia denied that any such measures were contemplated,[8] though an Argentine observation post had been erected on Deception Island, at which Britain had protested in April 1946.[9]

President Perón slowly intensified Argentina's territorial disputes with Britain, and by a decree of 2 September 1946 he extended the western boundary of Argentina's Antarctic claim to longitude 74° West.[10] Britain sent official Notes to both Argentina and Chile on 17 December 1947, inviting them to challenge Britain's sovereignty by invoking the International Court of Justice (ICJ), and stating that Britain would accept the decision of the Court. In its reply of 28 January 1948 the

---

[1] *FIM* No. VIII Vol. XXXVII, Stanley December 1925, p. 6.
[2] Hart 2001, pp. 69, 95-100.
[3] Headland 1984, p. 136; list of magistrates from 1909 to 1969 p. 137; since November 1969 the powers of the magistrate, customs officers, etc., have been exercised by the British Antarctic Survey (BAS).
[4] Headland 1984, pp. 73-75.
[5] Headland 1984 pp. 67, 76, 91-92.
[6] Headland 1984, p. 241.
[7] Details from British ICJ application 1955.
[8] Reported in *BDFA*, IV D 6, p. 33.
[9] *BDFA*, IV D 6, p. 4.
[10] British ICJ application 1955, p. 9.

Argentine government stated that it was convinced of the unquestionable rights of Argentina and Chile (!) over the disputed areas, adding that it would not be right for Argentina to appear before the ICJ as a country requesting what already belonged to it. In its reply of 31 January 1948 to the same British Note, the Chilean government claimed that Graham Land and the South Shetlands were Chilean territory, and calling them "a territory over which she [i.e. Chile] holds irrefutable juridical, political, historical, diplomatic and administrative titles".[1] But no matter how "irrefutable" Argentina's and Chile's titles may have been, they conflicted with each other as well as with Britain's, and neither country had a title anything like as good as Britain had.

The slowly worsening dispute over the Falkland Islands Dependencies threatened to impair relations between Britain and Argentina, so Britain sent further Notes to Argentina on 30 April 1951 and 16 February 1953 repeating the offer to go to the ICJ, but Argentina did not accept. On 21 December 1954 Britain invited Argentina and Chile to join Britain in referring the dispute to an independent *ad hoc* tribunal for a ruling, but both countries rejected the offer.

So Britain made a unilateral application to the ICJ for a ruling in the case, declaring that Britain accepted the jurisdiction of the Court. Britain asked the Court to rule:[2]

(1) that the United Kingdom, as against the Republic of Argentina, possesses, and at all material dates has possessed, valid and subsisting legal titles to the sovereignty over all the territories comprised in the Falkland Islands Dependencies, and in particular South Sandwich Islands, South Georgia, the South Orkneys, South Shetlands, Graham Land and Coats Land;

(2) that the pretensions of the Republic of Argentina to the territories comprised in the Falkland Islands Dependencies, and in particular South Sandwich Islands, South Georgia, the South Orkneys, South Shetlands, Graham Land and Coats Land, and her encroachments and pretended acts of sovereignty in or relative to any of those territories are, under international law, illegal and invalid;

(3) that the Republic of Argentina is bound to respect the United Kingdom's sovereignty over the territories comprised in the Falkland Islands Dependencies, and in particular South Sandwich Islands, South Georgia, the South Orkneys, South Shetlands, Graham Land and Coats Land, to cease her pretensions to exercise sovereignty in or relative to those territories and, if called on by the United Kingdom, to withdraw from them all or any Argentine personnel and equipment.

The application, dated 4 May 1955, was communicated by the Registry of the ICJ to the Argentine foreign minister and to the Secretary-General of the United Nations.[3]

By coincidence, on the same day, 4 May 1955, Argentine foreign minister Jerónimo Remorino received British ambassador Sir Francis Evans and gave him the official Argentine rejection of the earlier British proposal of 21 December 1954 to refer the question to an *ad hoc* tribunal.[4] That reply had been expected, and Britain had already taken the case to the ICJ. Without giving any evidence, the Argentine rejection of the proposal for a tribunal stated baldly that:[5]

The Malvinas islands, together with the lands situated in our Antarctic sector, are Argentinian, as are the South Georgias and the South Sandwich Islands.

It went on to say that since the Malvinas islands were Argentinian, the islands which were associated with them, by repeated British declarations, were Argentine territory too. That, however, underlined that Argentina's claim to South Georgia is contradictory, as Alfred Rubin points out:[6]

South Georgia has its own history, and the basis for the Argentine claim to it appears to be merely succession to British administrative powers exercised from the Falkland/ Malvinas. The steady Argentine rejection of

---

[1] British ICJ application 1955, p. 35; text of British Note of 17 December 1947 in Hunter Christie 1951, pp. 305-308; text of Argentine reply of 28 January 1948 in *ibid.*, pp. 309-313; Chilean reply, 31 January 1948, in *ibid.*, pp. 314-316.

[2] British ICJ application 1955, pp. 35-36, 38.

[3] Details from the ICJ Order of 16 March 1956 removing the case from the list of cases before the Court, on the ICJ website entitled *Reports of Judgments, Advisory Opinions and Orders: Antarctica Case (United Kingdom* v. *Argentina: Order of March 16th, 1956*, under https://www.icj-cij.org/en/case/26, henceforth "ICJ Order 1956".

[4] Fitte 1968, p. 257.

[5] Quoted in Fitte 1968, p. 258.

[6] Alfred C. Rubin, "Historical and Legal Background of the Falkland/Malvinas Dispute", in Alberto R. Coll and Anthony C. Arend (eds.), *The Falklands War: Lessons for Strategy, Diplomacy and International Law*, Boston 1985, p. 20 (fn.).

the legal effect of that British administration as a basis for establishing rights even in the Falkland/ Malvinas group itself would seem to justify rejection of the Argentine claims to South Georgia without further analysis.

The Argentine Note ended by saying that until the Malvinas had been transferred to Argentina, there was no reason for referring the remaining cases to an international tribunal.

Kohen and Rodríguez criticise us for our treatment of South Georgia in our paper *Getting it right* (pp. 35-36) – they say on their pp. 262-263:

The British pamphlet also ignores the main reason invoked by Argentina for refusing the British offer to submit those territories to the decision of the Hague Court: the absence of any reference to the issue of the Falkland/ Malvinas Islands. In the Note that the Argentine Ministry of Foreign Affairs sent to the British Embassy in Buenos Aires on May 4, 1955 in response to the British proposal, it is highlighted that:

(...) Her Majesty's Government excises the bottom issue, as if all could be reduced to a single aspect, mentioning as the sole problem that needs solution the one referring to the Antarctic territories it demands and those that qualifies as dependencies of the Malvinas Islands (...) The Argentine Government cannot conceive nor accept as friendly nor juridical a proposal that has as its heart to sustain that usurpation (...). Consequently, while there is no resolution in the indicated direction on the pre-existing issue that has just been mentioned, it is not correct to propose, as Great Britain does, the subject of the issue to the International Court of Justice in Hague or an ad hoc arbitration tribunal.

Kohen and Rodríguez fail to point out that there was nothing to stop Argentina from taking the Falklands dispute to the ICJ, with or without the Dependencies – the lack of any such move suggests that Argentina was not optimistic that the Court would uphold the Argentine claim.

As the two authors say (above), Argentina's Note of 4 May 1955 to the British embassy made a connection between the Falklands and the Falklands Dependencies, stating that Argentina did not regard an approach to the ICJ over the Dependencies as "correct" without including the "pre-existing issue" (i.e. the Falklands themselves), but Argentina did not make any such connection in its official reply to the ICJ (which is not mentioned by Kohen and Rodríguez). Argentina simply refused to accept the Court's jurisdiction in the case – the reply from the Argentine foreign minister to the Court on 1 August 1955 stated:[1]

… the Argentine Government has several times had occasion to indicate in notes addressed to Her Britannic Majesty's Embassy in Buenos Aires that it cannot consent to the question of sovereignty over the Antarctic territories of Argentina which it is sought to raise being referred for decision to any international Court of Justice or Arbitration Tribunal. By this present note, my Government reaffirms its refusal in the most express way with regard to the jurisdiction of this Court and with regard to any possibility that it should be seised as such to deal with this case.

The British government stated on 31 August 1955 that it regarded the Argentine reply of 1 August "as amounting to a rejection of the International Court of Justice for the purpose of the present case", and on 16 March 1956 the Court itself issued an Order stating that it:[2]

… has not before it any acceptance by the Government of Argentina of the jurisdiction of the Court to deal with the dispute which is the subject of the Application submitted to it by the United Kingdom Government and that therefore it can take no further steps upon this Application…

The Court therefore removed the case from its list of cases to be heard. Argentina's refusal to accept the authority of the ICJ ended Britain's attempt to submit the Dependencies dispute to judicial arbitration, and Argentina has never submitted the Falklands case to the ICJ either. One is entitled to suspect that the Argentine government is not entirely sure of the justice of its cause.

9.7 Conclusion

This chapter has documented Argentina's acquiescence in Britain's possession of the Falkland Islands from 1890 to 1955. During those years, in 1899-1902, Argentina accepted Britain as an

---

[1] Details and quote from ICJ Order 1956, p. 13; "seised" (pronounced like "seized") = "endowed with authority".
[2] ICJ Order 1956, p. 14.

arbitrator entitled to lay down how far Argentina's territory extended, and accepted without question Britain's decision on the extent of that territory. That behaviour is incompatible with maintaining a territorial dispute with Britain, but it was repeated in 1964-6 (section 10.22).

Kohen and Rodríguez assert that Argentina "exercised acts of authority over South Georgia", but that is untrue. It was (and is) Britain that has exercised sovereignty over South Georgia and the other South Atlantic islands, and far from performing acts of authority, Argentina accepted British sovereignty without question. The Argentine whaling company "Pesca" held leases in South Georgia granted by Britain, which were signed at the British embassy in Buenos Aires by Pesca's representative and British officials including the Governor of the Falklands, and the company accepted Britain's authority over the island, as did the crews of visiting Argentine ships.

For over 130 years from 1888, Argentina has never made a formal protest to Britain over the possession of the Falklands or the other islands; the examples given by Kohen and Rodríguez purporting to show "Argentina's constant claim" are insignificant and prove nothing. At the end of their chapter (p. 264) they say it is the British government that is responsible for keeping the controversy "pending", but as we have shown in this and the previous chapter, the controversy is not pending at all; it was definitively ended by Argentina's ratification of the Convention of Peace with Britain in May 1850, and for decades in the 19th century Argentina demonstrated overt acquiescence in Britain's possession of the islands. That acquiescence has also been demonstrated on various occasions since then, as this chapter has shown. Ever since 1850 the Falklands have been both *de facto* and *de jure* British territory, by Argentina's agreement. The attempt by Kohen and Rodríguez to prove the contrary fails completely.

CHAPTER TEN: the people; self-determination; the Falklands at the United Nations

We concluded our 40-page internet paper *Getting it right* in 2008 with three sections entitled "Self-determination", "The people" and "The Falklands dispute in the international field". In their last chapter Kohen and Rodríguez address those topics too, and attempt to refute what we say. But their argumentation is fallacious and their conclusions are incorrect, as can easily be shown.

10.1 The people, I

In discussing the people of the Falklands, the Argentinians have a problem: the Falkland Islanders do not wish their country to be taken over by Argentina. In other words, Argentina has no political claim to the islands, which it would have if the islanders were clamouring to become Argentinian but Britain was stopping them. And authors on international law agree that "contiguity" (geographical closeness) does not constitute a root of title and applies only to territories with land borders, not to islands; at best it is merely a technique to assist in drawing borders.[1] So Argentina's claim is exclusively historical, and Argentine authors, including Kohen and Rodríguez, present an untrue version of history as the basis for their assertion that the islands are rightfully Argentine territory.

Argentine writers and politicians attempt to get round the problem of the resistance of the Falkland Islanders by asserting that they do not have the right of self-determination because they are an "implanted population", or as Kohen and Rodríguez put it (p. 265, twice), a "population established by the United Kingdom".[2] That is untrue, and even if it were true, it would be no bar to self-determination – the populations of all the Caribbean islands were established by the colonial powers Spain, France, the Netherlands and Britain. And the Seychelles, for example, were uninhabited when discovered by the Portuguese in the 16th century; France established the first population there from the 1770s, and Britain took more people there from 1814 onwards. No one would dream of saying that the peoples of those places do not enjoy the right of self-determination.

In fact Britain never had any population plan for the Falklands and in 1834-5 considered withdrawing the British presence entirely (section 6.38); the population grew haphazardly, mostly without any involvement of the British government, and included people not of British origin.[3] Far from establishing an English-speaking population to justify Britain's possession of the islands, Britain allowed large numbers of Spanish-speaking people to go there; in the late 1840s they formed almost a third of the population, and some still have descendants in the islands (below).

---

[1] Jamie Trinidad, *Self-Determination in Disputed Colonial Territories*, Cambridge 2018, pp. 168-169, 175, quoting opinions by A. Rigo-Sureda in *The Evolution of the Right to Self-Determination...*, Leiden 1973, and by M. Shaw, *Title to Territory in Africa...*, Oxford 1986.

[2] As explained in the Introduction, we quote from the English translation of Kohen and Rodríguez, but we give page-numbers from the paper Spanish version of 2015.

[3] In the 19th century many countries including Argentina (section 8.22) encouraged immigration from Europe, and in Britain the Colonial Land and Emigration Commission was established in 1840 to promote immigration into all British possessions by the "Land Order System": a purchaser investing £100 in land could bring five labourers from Britain at government expense. This system was important in settling Australia and New Zealand, but in the Falklands it only started around 1858, and the Falkland Islands Company (FIC) was almost the only beneficiary – it actively discouraged immigration to preserve its near-monopoly of landholding. The people agreed to spend 5 years working for the FIC, but the system was extensively misused: many then returned to Britain, so did not become permanent immigrants; some came twice or more, with each passage paid under this system, and some passages were paid for native-born Falklands children returning from visits to Britain. In "Emigration into the Falkland Islands", in *FIJ* vol. 10 (2), 2013, pp. 107-127, David Tatham lists 327 people "sponsored by the Falkland Islands Company, 1859-1878", but given the abuses, that does not mean that 327 people were added to the islands' population. The abuses led Governor Jeremiah Callaghan to terminate the system in March 1879. Wayne Bernhardson says several dozen people were brought in between 1864 and 1877, but the total immigration figures recorded in Stanley and London differ: records in Stanley give 71 men, 30 women and 37 children under 15 (total 138), while London records give 101 men, 38 women and 54 children (total 193). The discrepancy reflects the fact that in Stanley it was known which people were new immigrants and which were returnees, and the figures include some who came under their own steam. Details from Bernhardson 1989, pp. 338-341, quoting from Emigration Commissioners' Accounts, in JCNA, Stanley, vol. H22, and Colonial Land and Emigration Commissioners accounts, 1859-1878, PRO CO 386/5. In any case, the Falklands *Blue Books* record a total population of 539 in 1859 and 1,461 in 1879 (PRO CO 81/14, CO 81/34), an increase of 922, of which 123 were births, so the number brought in by the Colonial Land and Emigration Commission was not significant.

Kohen and Rodríguez say not a word about that; they say (p. 266) that the present population of the islands is "essentially the result of the arrival of new British citizens from the metropolis after the colony was officially constituted in 1843, the concession of lands to British subjects only, and the appointment of officials from Great Britain. Any temporary South American workers were never considered part of the permanent population"; they also (p. 268) say the population in 1851 was "287 people, most of whom had arrived in at [*sic*] the close of the previous decade, upon the establishment of the British colony in 1843."

All that needs correction. We do not know where they got their figures from, but the 1851 Falklands census (in JCNA) actually records a population of 383, and the 1851 *Blue Book* records a total of 423 people, made up of 190 "white" and 2 "coloured" males, 130 "white" and 1 "coloured" female, and "about 100 aliens and resident strangers" – some of the figures are clearly approximate, and the discrepancy of 40 no doubt arose from under-recording at Hope Place. The population of the islands was slowly increasing: in 1851 there were 5 marriages, 6 births, 3 deaths, and 38 "scholars" in full-time education.[1] The population figure given by Kohen and Rodríguez is wrong.

Secondly, it is untrue that there was "distribution of land exclusively to the subjects of Her Majesty" (Kohen and Rodríguez p. 195), or that there was "concession of lands to British subjects only" (their p. 266) – as we pointed out in section 7.1, there was equality of rights in land-holding in the Falklands between British citizens and "aliens", and the examples of Llamosa and Hansen, who acquired large areas of land without having British nationality, disprove what Kohen and Rodríguez say – José Llamosa held extensive lands but never took British nationality, and the Dane Charles Hansen leased several islands for ten years before becoming naturalised British. And thirdly, as we said in section 5.1, Louis Vernet never regarded gauchos as permanent settlers.

In fact the largest contingent of people who went to the Falklands in the entire 19th century were mostly Spanish speakers, sent to the islands in 1846-50 by Samuel Fisher Lafone, whose association with the Falklands derived from Louis Vernet. That connection came about in a roundabout way: in March 1837 Vernet heard that the New York shipowner Silas Burrows was at Montevideo; Vernet went there at once hoping to have Burrows's ship seized, since he still believed Burrows owed him money from the voyage of the *Superior* (which Burrows owned) back in 1831. That was absurd, of course; the contract under which she had sailed had no legal validity (sections 6.5, 6.13). In Montevideo he missed Burrows but by chance met Samuel Fisher Lafone (1805-71), an Englishman from Liverpool, whose originally Huguenot name is pronounced with two syllables: "La Fonn", not with three as if it were Spanish. He had emigrated to Uruguay and become a prosperous cattle-rancher; at their meeting in 1837 Vernet interested him in the potential of the Falklands for cattle-ranching, and suggested a partnership to exploit the islands. On 9 April 1837 Vernet wrote him a long letter recounting the story of his involvement in the Falklands,[2] but in the end the partnership idea came to nothing, though Vernet continued in friendly correspondence with Lafone as late as October 1843. Lafone no doubt found it hard to see any advantage in a partnership, since Vernet had no rights in the Falklands that were recognised outside Argentina (nor even in Uruguay) – why should a partnership be a better proposition than proceeding alone?

So Lafone did proceed alone, which Vernet saw as a betrayal. Lafone's Falklands venture contributed to the foundation of the Falkland Islands Company and led to the arrival of the ancestors of some of today's Falkland Islanders.[3] The southern part of East Falkland is called Lafonia after him, and his activities resulted in a number of ruined buildings that dot the landscape,

---

[1] *Falklands Blue Book* 1851, PRO CO 81/6; the "coloured" males were Carmelita's two sons (she died in 1845), and the one "coloured" female was Gregoria Parry (née Madrid), who died in Stanley on 11 April 1871. She was one of the black slaves Louis Vernet took to the islands in September 1828; she had no children but married Francis Henry Parry from Bermuda, who in 1846 was appointed Chief Constable of the new police force in Stanley; he was still the jailer and courthouse-keeper in 1883 and died in Stanley in 1885 aged 75 (details from Jane Cameron, pers. comm.).

[2] Vernet to Lafone 9 April 1837, in English, in AGN VII, 130, no doc. no., after doc. 146.

[3] Unless otherwise stated, our account of Lafone's activities is taken from Vernet's letter to Lafone, 9 April 1837, Vernet's "Memoirs" and his "2nd Memorial", London 6 September 1852, AGN VII, 132, doc. 378.

as well as expressions derived from Spanish that are still sometimes used in Falklands English.[1]

As described in section 7.7, Lafone sent ships from Montevideo with stores and roughly 150 immigrants, mostly Spanish-speaking, who set up a large settlement and cattle-ranch at Hope Place on the eastern shore of Falkland Sound.[2] The *Falklands Shipping Register* (*FSR*) gives no numbers or origins for the new arrivals,[3] but for the 350-ton Norwegian ship *Napoleon*, which reached Stanley from Montevideo on 10 May 1847 with a total of 117 people, there is a passenger list, which names 104 people with their countries of origin.[4] There were 77 men, 18 women and 9 children, including 12 Argentine men, with 4 women and 1 child; there were 15 Uruguayan men, with 6 women and 3 children, and 24 "Spanish" men with 4 women and 2 children (some of whom may have been South Americans). Thus out of those 104 people, 71 were Spanish-speaking. There were also 16 French men, with 2 wives and 1 child; 3 Brazilian men; 1 German with his wife; and 6 British men with 1 wife and 2 children. Such details are not recorded for the other ships Lafone sent, so it is likely there were more Argentinians. Of those people, 78 were still there in 1851, including 17 Argentinians and 15 Uruguayans,[5] which suggests that the original total had been more than 17 Argentinians. The documentation disproves assertions by Argentine authors (and speakers at the United Nations, section 10.14) that Argentinians were not allowed to go to the islands.

Most of those people worked for Lafone at Hope Place, while others worked at Port Louis, including a few for George Whitington (whom Kohen and Rodríguez call "Withington", p. 266). When Lafone's operations failed to prove profitable, some people were dismissed by Lafone's managers; entirely destitute, they made their way to Stanley and were an immediate concern to the new Governor George Rennie (section 7.7). Nevertheless, contrary to what Kohen and Rodríguez say, some of them did become part of the permanent population, and in 1870 the Spaniard José Llamosa, who arrived in 1847 with the others from Montevideo, leased 12,000 acres of East Falkland without taking British nationality; there were Llamosas at Port Howard on West Falkland until at least the 1960s.[6] The surname has now died out in the islands, but there are still descendants of the Llamosas with other surnames.

The only people Britain took to the Falklands in the 19th century were soldiers (some of them with families), but they all arrived over 140 years ago: the Sappers and Miners in 1842 (section 7.2), the Chelsea Pensioners in 1849 (section 7.7) and several parties of Marines from 1855, the last of whom arrived in 1878. They themselves could be said to have been "transplanted", "transferred" or "implanted", but almost all soon left again, and the present-day descendants of the few who stayed were not taken to the islands but were born there. In the Falklands most of the population are descended from civilians who arrived under their own steam (or sail), to take up specific posts such as shepherds, or to seek their fortunes. Some of them were not British, such as Joseph Alazia (French), Joseph Lellman (German), Anton Richard Larsen (Norwegian), or Johannes Henricksen (from Russian Finland). A number of non-British Falklands ancestors arrived accidentally, such as

---

[1] Falklands English is described in a book by three native Falkland Islanders, Sally Blake, Jane Cameron and Joan Spruce: *Diddle Dee to Wire Gates: A Dictionary of Falklands Vocabulary*, Stanley 2011.

[2] Described in Robert A. Philpott, *The Early Falkland Islands Company Settlements…*, Stanley and Liverpool 2007.

[3] *Falklands Shipping Register* (*FSR*) vol. 1 (ex vol. AA1) 1842-1878, in the JCNA, Stanley, now available online under https://www.nationalarchives.gov.fk/online-collections/shipping/shipping-registers (though sadly without the entry-numbers, which begin in the 1860s and are useful for reference). *FSR* records several ships bringing unspecified numbers of passengers, e.g. the *Vigilante* and the *Paloma*, which reached Stanley from Montevideo on 20 and 22 November 1846 respectively and are listed jointly as "Two of Mr Lafone's vessels with his agent Messrs Martinez and Williams, stores and passengers"; the *Vigilante* came again on 11 November 1847 "with Emigrants for Mr Lafone", and the Russian brig *Marie* came from Montevideo and arrived at Hope Place on 26 October 1850 "With Mr Williams… and peons as passengers", reaching Stanley on 8 November 1850; the numbers of "passengers", "emigrants" and "peons" are not stated.

[4] List under "Miscellaneous Documents" in Volume H8, JCNA, Stanley. The first page, listing 36 people including 9 of the 17 Argentinians, is illustrated in colour in Marcelo Beccaceci, *Gauchos de Malvinas*, Buenos Aires 2017, p. 38. The remaining 13 out of the 117 people were evidently crewmen.

[5] Figure from the 1851 Falklands census, held in JCNA, Stanley.

[6] The *Falkland Islands Magazine* (*FIM*) mentions members of the Llamosa family living in the islands in issue No. II Vol. XXX, Stanley, June 1918, p. 5; No. II Vol. XXXV, June 1923, p. 4; and No. X Vol. XXXIX, June 1928, p. 10; and the *Falkland Islands Monthly Review*, Stanley 5 July 1965, p. 18, mentions Llamosas then living at Port Howard.

the two Swedes Frans Theodor Rylander (shipwrecked in the *Colonsay* in 1860) and Axel Pettersson (shipwrecked in the *Samoa* in 1899), or the Dane Karl (Charles) Hansen, shipwrecked in the *Concordia* in 1860. Descendants of all those men still live in the islands today.

In 1859 the British-run commercial firm of Smith Brothers of Montevideo arranged the transport of about 10 people to New Island – and of 1,000 people to Buenos Aires.[1] Argentina was one of the countries that benefited from European immigration – the 1882 Latzina map (section 8.22) was part of a long Argentine campaign to obtain more people. Some went to Argentina from the Falklands, including some born in the islands. In those years many thousands left Europe to seek their fortunes, in Argentina, Australia, Canada, Chile, New Zealand, Uruguay, the United States and elsewhere, and those who chose to go to the Falklands were part of the same trend. They were not taken to the islands by Britain, they did not replace any original population, and they and their descendants had the same rights in the Falklands as immigrants and their descendants elsewhere.

For the best part of 150 years, the majority of the inhabitants have arrived in the Falklands by a short biological route: they were born there. They are as much natives of the Falklands as the Seychellois are of the Seychelles. Several families have been in the Falklands for nine generations; there are quite a few seventh and eighth-generation Falkland Islanders, and many in the fifth and sixth generations. The Pitaluga and Watson families have now (2022) been in the islands for over 180 years, the Biggs and Goss families for over 175 years, those of Bonner, Felton, Gleadell and Short for over 150 years, and many other families have been in the islands for over a century.

The emergence of a population native to a given territory changes the distribution of rights over that territory. Such rights arise gradually over time – in New Zealand in the 1830s, and in the Falklands in the 1840s, inhabitants who were British nationals were simply British people living in another country; in addition to their British nationality they were ethnically English, Scottish, Welsh, Irish, etc., and had not yet acquired a new ethnicity. But a century and a half later, the descendants of those British people are New Zealanders and Falkland Islanders respectively. They are no longer English, Scottish, Welsh or Irish – their ethnicity has changed. In the case of the people of New Zealand, their ethnicity had changed after a century or so but their nationality had not – until 1948 they were simply British subjects living in New Zealand. They held British passports, as did people in other Commonwealth countries and British territories. On 1 January 1949 the British Nationality and New Zealand Citizenship Act came into force,[2] creating a separate New Zealand nationality – from then on, the people were New Zealanders, not British subjects. The fact that Falkland Islanders hold British passports says nothing about their ethnicity – they are ethnic Falkland Islanders.

By contrast, Ascension Island has no native inhabitants; the British people living there remain English, Scottish, Welsh, Irish, etc.; their ethnicity is not distinct from that of the colonial power, so they do not enjoy the right to self-determination under Resolution 1541 (section 10.9).

Falkland Islanders have been a unique community since at least 1890,[3] and their history in their country is almost as long as that of the English-speaking communities in New Zealand or California. They have evolved their own variety of English, which has been described by Andrea Sudbury, both in a highly detailed account[4] and also in a briefer account in which she places Falkland Islands English among "Lesser-Known Varieties of English" (LKVEs) – in other words, it is not a dialect but a distinct variety of English.[5]

The Falkland Islanders are a people in their own right, as was made clear by the British

---

[1] Bernhardson 1989, p. 326, quoting letters from Smith Brothers to Governor Moore of 17 September 1859 and 24 February 1860, in JCNA, vol. H16.

[2] *British Nationality and New Zealand Citizenship Act*, Act of the General Assembly of New Zealand 1948, No. 15 (Royal Assent 6 September 1948).

[3] Bernhardson 1989, p. 398.

[4] Andrea Sudbury, *Dialect Contact and Koineisation in the Falkland Islands…*, unpublished doctoral thesis, University of Essex, July 2000, ix + 249pp., on the Internet until 2002 (accessed 12 October 2002). A "koiné" is a standard form of a language (Greek κοινή, "common", "ordinary"); "koineisation" means "the development of a standard language".

[5] David Britain and Andrea Sudbury, "Falkland Islands English", in Daniel Schreier *et al.*, (eds.), *The Lesser-Known Varieties of English…*, Cambridge 2010, pp. 209-221, with bibliography of works on lesser-known varieties of English.

Nationality Act 1981,[1] which was introduced by the Thatcher government in pursuance of a restrictive policy on immigration (but was superseded for the Falklands in 1983, see footnote). Its main purpose was to prevent millions of Hong Kongers from coming to Britain before and after the return of Hong Kong to China in 1997, but it also removed full British citizenship from some 600-700 native-born Falkland Islanders who were not "patrial", i.e. who did not have at least one British-born parent or grandparent. Those 600-700 people were precisely those whose families had lived longest in the islands, and they made up about half the native-born population, which showed that the islanders were already a distinct people. They had the right of abode in their own country (the Falklands), but not in Britain, the country whose passports they held – they were not British people living in another country. It is self-evident that Falkland Islanders therefore have the full right of external self-determination.

To call the Falkland Islanders an "implanted population" betrays a misunderstanding of the islands' population history – the Falklands have long been a "people factory", and for a century and a half their story has been one of emigration, not immigration. In the 19th century and again after 1945 many Falkland Islanders emigrated to Argentina, Australia or New Zealand, and Mateo Martinic shows that between 1880 and 1930 over 300 emigrated to southern Chile.[2]

In the early 20th century immigration into the islands slowed and emigration was almost confined to non-natives, which together with a fairly high birth rate resulted in a steady increase both of the total population and the percentage of natives. The *Blue Books* and the *Falkland Islands Magazine* record that there were several hundred children in the islands over a century ago – in 1912 there were 426 children at school and several dozen pre-school children.[3] Virtually all those children were born in the islands, many to parents and grandparents who had themselves been born there. In 1911 natives formed 62.5% of the population; by 1926 the percentage had risen to 76.7%, and in 1931, when the total population reached 2,392, it had reached 80.3%. The Second World War prevented a census in 1941, but in 1946 the total population of 2,239 was 89.4% native-born.[4] At that time native-born Falkland Islanders thus constituted almost 90% of the inhabitants of the islands; their country was the Falklands.

But from the 1950s there was a constant outflow of people born in the islands, partly because of the climate and the lack of opportunity resulting from chronic under-investment by Britain, but also because of constant harassment by Argentina (sections 10.13, 10.19).

10.2 Louis Vernet's problems; the Lavalleja connection

At this point in their account (pp. 267-8), Kohen and Rodríguez discuss Britain's prohibition on Louis Vernet's returning to the islands, and quote a letter of 2 November 1836 from the Permanent Undersecretary of State for War and the Colonies, James Stephen, to the British ambassador in Buenos Aires, John Henry Mandeville (original in PRO FO 6 501, fols. 205-6), in which Stephen informs Mandeville that any attempt by Vernet "to carry into execution the intention announced to you of returning to the Falklands Islands" would not be permitted.

Stated like that, it might look as if Britain was treating Vernet harshly, but as usual Kohen and Rodríguez omit the background (though perhaps they were unaware of it). As recounted in section 6.9, Vernet left the Falklands by his own decision on 7 November 1831 in the American sealer *Harriet*, which he had seized along with the sealers *Breakwater* and *Superior*. He hoped to acquire his own sealing fleet, but seizing the ships was a disastrous mistake – he never obtained the ships, and the United States broke off diplomatic relations with Argentina for 12 years (section 6.15).

---

[1] British Nationality Act 1981 (1981 chapter 61; Royal Assent 30 October 1981, came into force 1 January 1983, but was superseded for the Falklands by the British Nationality (Falkland Islands) Act 1983, passed 28 March 1983, retrospectively in force since 1 January 1983). Both now superseded by the British Overseas Territories Act 2002.

[2] In Mateo Martinic, "Falkland Islands Immigration to the Magellanic Region", in *FIJ* vol. 6 (5), 1996, p. 83.

[3] From the Education report for 1912, printed in the *Falkland Islands Magazine*, vol. XXV, no. 3, July 1913, p. 5.

[4] Figures from Wayne Bernhardson, *Land and Life in the Falkland Islands*, unpublished doctoral thesis, Berkeley (California) 1989, pp. 538-541 and 604 (photocopy in JCNA), with table of numbers and percentages from census reports at St Catherine's House, London; in PRO 78/81 and PRO 78/100; and in FIG *Reports* on censuses; also given in the *Shackleton Report* 1976, vol. I, p. 10.

Initially Britain did nothing to prevent Vernet from returning to the Falklands. He explained to the British consul-general Woodbine Parish in July 1834:[1]

> I would long since have returned to the Islands... had I possessed the means of doing it... without exposing myself to the displeasure of this Government [i.e. the Buenos Aires government], who then would certainly desist from her offers of supporting my private claims against the United States...

He could naturally expect no support from Buenos Aires against the United States for the losses caused by the *Lexington* if he cooperated with Britain in a territory claimed by Buenos Aires.

Moreover, he knew the US government was incensed at his actions, and that if he returned to the islands any American ship could arrest him and take him to the United States to be tried for piracy, for which the punishment was death. For a while, though, his affairs in the islands seemed to be under control – as recounted in section 5.20, his cattle-ranching establishment at Port Louis was run on his behalf by Lieutenant Henry Smith and his son Hugh, who sent him statements of account (fig. 5.20b). Vernet wrote long letters to Henry Smith full of what he thought was helpful advice, but much of it was absurd, for example he said in his first letter, of 2 July 1834, that the preservation of the houses was the "object of the least importance"[2] – it was ridiculous to tell Smith it was not important to preserve the houses, six months after he arrived (Smith had repaired them at once). Vernet told Smith the three remaining gauchos would not be enough, and said "you could afford the assistance of two or three good english lads", whom he was proposing to send out – he assumed that more gauchos were needed and that British gauchos would be acceptable. But the few gauchos at Port Louis were managing perfectly well, and Britain did not object to their Argentine nationality. The real problem was something Vernet never grasped: at that time the British government were not interested in the Falklands at all, not even as a naval base, and would not allow them to be made into a settlement, not even a British one. That would have required expenditure which no British government would contemplate in the days of "informal empire". From Britain's point of view the few people at Port Louis were enough to serve as a tripwire to prevent any other power from establishing itself in the islands, and they were supplying ships satisfactorily at minimal cost, so no change was needed.

Britain initially even advised him to go to the islands himself if he wished to carry on his affairs there – Rear Admiral Sir Graham Hamond (commanding the Royal Navy's South American station) told British ambassador Mandeville that he had informed Vernet "that if he wished to continue any mercantile speculation until the orders of the British Government shall be received, he would do well to proceed thither himself, or send some responsible person to act for him."[3]

Vernet felt encouraged by that, but he did not go to the islands; instead he made yet another disastrous mistake. In February 1836 he made an agreement with a Uruguayan general, Juan Antonio Lavalleja, to take horses and gauchos to the Falklands. And he kept the agreement secret, which made it even worse – the British authorities were aghast when they found out. Lavalleja was a famous and disruptive figure who had fought for Uruguayan independence in 1825 and aspired to be president, but was defeated in 1830 by Fructuoso Rivera, who then conducted a campaign of genocide against the Charrúa Indians (section 6.2). Lavalleja refused to accept defeat and repeatedly attempted to overthrow Rivera, acquiring a reputation as a conspirator and insurrectionist. At various times he commanded an army, but at other times, as the fortunes of Uruguayan battles and politics ebbed and flowed, he fled to Brazil or Argentina. It was during one of those periods of exile that Vernet met him in Buenos Aires and was convinced that the general could supply horses and gauchos and that he was prepared to go to the Falklands and supervise the cattle-killing.

Vernet then wrote to the British ambassador to Brazil, Hamilton Hamilton [*sic*!], asking if he thought the British government would object to his arranging to supply cattle to British ships.[4] He said he was now able "to obtain assistance from friends to enable me to furnish the necessary

---

[1] Vernet to Parish 23 July 1834, PRO FO 6 501, fol. 148 *recto*.
[2] Vernet to Smith 2 July 1834, PRO Adm 1/43, no doc. no., fol. 1 *verso*.
[3] Mandeville to Palmerston 14 July 1836, PRO FO 6 501, fol. 184 *recto*, referring to an earlier letter from Hamond to Vernet which we have not traced.
[4] Vernet to Hamilton, 12 February 1836, in AGN VII, 132, doc. 228.

supplies of cattle to H. M. Ship's of war & to the settlers who might come from England to the Falkland Islands" – but he did not mention the connection with Lavalleja. Hamilton replied saying that he could only express his own private opinion, but "I cannot anticipate any opposition whatever on the side of my Gov^t."[1] But Hamilton knew nothing of the Lavalleja connection; Britain would have strongly objected to any involvement in the Falklands of such a notorious figure, who, for all the British government knew, might take a whole army there.

Vernet naturally saw Hamilton's reply as encouraging; on 10 March 1836 he wrote to his former business partner Lewis Krumbhaar in Philadelphia outlining his plan,[2] and on 22 March he wrote to Messrs Dickson & Co., a British trading firm in Buenos Aires, informing them that:[3]

I Lately made a contract with General Lavallega [*sic*], in which he obligates himself to undertake at his sole expence the domestication of all the wild Cattle I possess on the East Falkland Islands; the cows & calves of which he is to deliver to me at the end of 4 years in Estancias, at the price of one Spanish Dollar for each head, for his trouble & Expences, & to kill during the 4 years all the Oxen in a Saladero [i.e. a meat-salting establishment]…

The Dicksons were the first people to be told of Vernet's agreement with Lavalleja, and he still did not tell the British government. It was absurd to speak of "the wild Cattle I possess" – no country except Argentina accepted that he possessed them. He also requested an unspecified loan, and as security he offered cattle, horses, cattle hides and sealskins, and "a few houses", which he said he owned at Port Louis. That too was absurd – those houses had been wrecked by the Port Louis murderers in 1833 and knocked about by the weather, and had been uninhabitable till Henry Smith repaired them. Vernet could not claim that any of the value of those houses belonged to him.[4]

Vernet did not inform Rear Admiral Hamond of the Lavalleja connection, but went behind his back by writing a private letter to one E. Vidal, who however showed it to Hamond. Hamond and Vidal were astounded to discover that Vernet was proposing to send General Lavalleja – of all people! – to the Falklands. In his reply on 21 June 1836, Vidal told Vernet of Hamond's reaction:[5]

Nothing has been <u>said</u> to <u>him</u> of General Lavalleja and he was astonished when he read your letter. I am very sorry for your misfortunes, but… I repeat to you that <u>if you write</u> at once to the British Secretary $^{\text{of State}}$ for the Colonies and ask permission to follow up any plans you may state to him, you will adopt the <u>only</u> likely means of Success.

Most people would have read that as discouraging, but Vernet felt his plans were going well – he had no conception of the horror Lavalleja's colourful reputation would arouse in London. He described his scheme orally to British ambassador Mandeville, including the proposed involvement of Lavalleja, as Mandeville reported to Lord Palmerston on 14 July 1836.[6] Mandeville warned Vernet not to proceed without Britain's agreement, but Vernet was not to be put off, and on 9 July 1836 he sent Mandeville more details and announced that he was preparing a "memorial" to the British government.[7] That letter of 9 July 1836 was Vernet's first written mention to Mandeville of his intention to send gauchos and horses to the Falklands, but he still said nothing in writing about General Lavalleja (though Rear Admiral Hamond now knew about it from Vernet's private letter to Vidal). Mandeville replied on 12 July, warning Vernet that he should not proceed without the British government's permission, but mentioning a comment by Rear Admiral Hamond, that "he says that with regard to your proposal of again forming an establishment on those islands, he is by no means sure that such a measure will meet the wishes of His Majesty's Government".[8] To Vernet the mild phrase "he is by no means sure" again sounded encouraging – he ignored the warnings by Hamond and Mandeville not to proceed without Britain's permission.

---

[1] Hamilton to Vernet 14 February 1836, in AGN VII, 127, doc. 45.
[2] Vernet to Krumbhaar, in AGN VII, 130, doc. 111.
[3] Draft letter from Vernet to Messrs Dicksons, 22 March 1836, in AGN VII, 130, doc. 112.
[4] For the building of the houses, by the crews of the British ships *Star* and *Sprightly*, see section 5.4.
[5] E. Vidal to Vernet, 21 June 1836, in AGN VII 132, doc. 235; underlining as in original.
[6] Mandeville to Palmerston 14 July 1836, PRO FO 6 501, fols. 182 *recto* to 185 *verso*.
[7] Vernet to Mandeville 9 July 1836, in PRO FO 6 501, fols. 187 *recto* to 188 *verso*.
[8] Mandeville to Vernet 12 July 1836, AGN VII 130, doc. 121; copy in PRO FO 6 501, fols. 190 *recto* to 191 *recto*.

Part of the problem was that Vernet made no move to deny the legality of his concession from Buenos Aires. Britain had never recognised the right of Buenos Aires to do anything in the Falklands, but Vernet lived in Buenos Aires, so it was impossible for him to deny the legality of the concession under which he had operated (though in 1882 the Argentine government retrospectively declared it to have been invalid from the outset, see sections 5.6, 8.22). It might have been different if he had solemnly declared that all rights and concessions granted to him by Buenos Aires had been invalid, and that he had operated purely as a private individual on British territory. That might have made him less suspect in British eyes, but it would not have moved the British government any closer to undertaking, or permitting, any involvement in the islands. At that time Britain regarded the Falklands much as Spain had regarded them earlier, as a necessary evil; they were of no intrinsic interest but had to be protected from occupation by any other power. Vernet had not only involved General Lavalleja, "a man of some notoriety", as Mandeville put it drily in his report to Palmerston of 14 July 1836, but had kept his scheme secret from Britain. To the British government, Vernet had revealed himself as deceitful and a serious security risk.

In the end Vernet realised what an obstacle Lavalleja was to any project of returning to the Falklands. He replied to Mandeville on 16 July saying he had resolved to give up his arrangement with Lavalleja,[1] but the damage had been done – Britain could never trust him again. But he pressed on, and on 5 August he wrote his elaborately obsequious "memorial" to Lord Palmerston asking for British aid and protection for his possessions in the Falklands.[2] Palmerston himself normally scrawled brief notes on scraps of paper, so it is hard to believe he ever read Vernet's turgid screed. It appealed for "two to three thousand pounds" (a large sum) to be paid to Vernet himself, but it was ludicrous to expect the British government to pay such a sum in taxpayers' money to set a foreigner up in business, and his claim that "the british nation will… be injured" if he were not assisted with a loan was laughable. He failed to realise that Britain was not prepared to devote more than the most minimal expenditure to the tiny British presence in the Falklands; nothing he could do would induce the British government to spend any more on the islands, still less on him.

That, then, is the background to Britain's refusal to allow Louis Vernet to return to the Falklands. The letter of 2 November 1836 quoted by Kohen and Rodríguez (p. 267) from James Stephen to John Henry Mandeville, prohibiting "the intention announced to you of returning to the Falklands Islands" was a reaction to Vernet's long-concealed plan to send General Lavalleja to the islands, potentially with a whole army under his command. That would have thoroughly mixed up the politics of the whole of South America, and involved Britain in incalculable expenses and problems. No wonder the British government would have none of it.

10.3 Vernet eventually claims, and receives, compensation from Britain

From 1834 to 1839 Vernet bombarded British officials, including Henry Smith, Rear Admiral Hamond and Lord Palmerston, with letters full of irrelevant advice and also requests for money, but the one thing he did not do was to submit a simple statement of what he believed the British government owed him for his property in the islands. Hamond was irritated by Vernet's constant importunity and his ever-changing projects, but he made him a reasonable offer, that he could remove his horses, or else state his price for the government's use of them. In May 1837 Vernet did eventually tell Hamond (by now promoted to Vice Admiral) how much he wanted for his horses, namely £5,500,[3] but he still did not submit a full account of what he claimed.

In August 1839 Vernet wrote to Hamond's successor, Captain Thomas Ball Sulivan, asking for "one thousand pounds sterling, which I consider the value of said property and with which this matter will be fully settled."[4] The British government would have done well to pay him the £1,000, since in the end, after long delays, they paid him over twice as much: in 1858 they awarded him £2,400 in compensation. However, when he left the islands in 1831 he had owed money to Henry

---

[1] Vernet to Mandeville 16 July 1836, in AGN VII 132, doc. 237; copy in PRO FO 6 501, fols. 194 *recto* and *verso*.
[2] Vernet to Palmerston, 5 August 1836, in AGN VII, 130, doc. 122.
[3] Vernet to Hamond 25 April 1837, AGN VII, 132, doc. 258, fol. 2 *verso*.
[4] Vernet to T. B. Sulivan 29 August 1839, in AGN VII, 132, doc. 291, draft in Vernet's hand, fol. 2 *recto*.

Metcalf and to the capataz Juan Simon, who was later murdered by Antonio Rivero. Juan Simon's son José, born at Port Louis around 1831, was still in the islands in 1858, and Britain insisted that Vernet's debts to Juan Simon were to be paid to José. Accordingly, £550 was deducted from the £2,400; Vernet was paid £1,850 in London on 17 May 1858, and Governor Thomas Edward Laws Moore paid the £550 to José Simon in Stanley on 13 December 1858.[1]

Kohen and Rodríguez say (p. 268) that Vernet's settlement at Port Louis was "the greatest development of civilization in the entire history of the islands", but that is nonsense; Bougainville's settlement at Port Louis was larger (with 135 people by the end) than Vernet's ever was (with briefly 128 people at most), and Bougainville's was much better run than Vernet's settlement, which was inhabited by constantly changing and mutually suspicious groups of people under a dictatorial proprietor. The greatest development of civilisation in the Falklands is of course the present population of the islands, who now have a history of over 180 years in their country and are civilised and prosperous as never before.

10.4 The people, II

Kohen and Rodríguez (pp. 268-72) quote some statistics from Falklands censuses, in such a way as to make it appear that the population-changes over the past 25 years are so great that the islanders "hardly constitute a separated 'people' in the international legal sense of the term." That is far from the truth, and some facts will clarify the picture. In 1946 almost 90% of the population had been born in the islands (section 10.1) and many had never set foot outside them at all, others only for war service,[2] but the story from the 1950s to the 1980s was one of steady emigration, as Britain allowed the islands' economy to stagnate – the population declined from 2,239 in 1946 to 1,813 in 1980. The *Shackleton Report*,[3] published in May 1976 by a research team headed by Lord Shackleton ("Eddie" Shackleton, 1911-94, son of the explorer Sir Ernest Shackleton), revealed that between 1951 and 1973 the net outflow of money from the Falklands to Britain was £9,310,000 at 1974 prices – and the islands had been bringing Britain a profit since the 1880s (section 8.25). That was the reason for the economic stagnation that blighted the lives of the Falkland Islanders and forced so many to emigrate – absentee landowners in Britain were bleeding the islands white.

From the low base figure of a mere 1,800 people in the early 1980s, the only way the population could go was up if the islands were to remain viable. After the Falklands War of 1982 immigration was vitally important to put the islands back on their feet, and has continued steadily since then, though slowly. The economy has expanded largely thanks to fishing and tourism, and the 2016 census recorded a population of 3,200, the largest ever. Of those, 1,371 (42.9%) were born in the islands, while 1,544 (49%) regard themselves as Falkland Islanders.[4] The difference is natural, since many people nowadays move several times in their lives, and it is anachronistic to say that only people born in a certain place are "natives" of that place – such an attitude is based on "crude notions of identity based on blood and soil" as the *Economist* put it recently.[5]

Kohen and Rodríguez say (p. 271): "The population of the Falkland/Malvinas Islands is mainly temporary, constantly renewed, and has a completely artifical demographic growth". That is incorrect – almost half the present population were born in the islands. The two authors seem to assume that all people who left the islands never returned, but that is far from the truth. Whereas formerly all young people who sought to expand their horizons had to leave, nowadays increasing numbers of islanders go abroad for training or university studies and return to live in the islands – they make up part of the figure for people leaving and arriving.

---

[1] Details of these payments from PRO CO 78/43, near the end – the file is entirely without folio numbers!
[2] There were 94 Falkland Islanders who fought in the British armed services in the First World War, of whom 18 were killed on active service; in the Second World War 174 Falkland Islanders (145 men and 29 women) served in the British armed services, of whom 20 (all of them men) were killed on active service (Jane Cameron, pers. comm.).
[3] Its full title is *Economic Survey of the Falkland Islands, presented to the Secretary of State for Foreign and Commonwealth Affairs*, 2 vols., London May 1976, usually known as the *Shackleton Report*.
[4] Figures from the 2016 Falkland Islands Census of 9 October 2016, from the Falkland Islands Government website, www.fig.gov.fk.
[5] In an editorial on dual nationality (not mentioning the Falklands), in *The Economist* 19-25 August 2017, p. 19.

The Falklands are a small country with a high standard of living, so they require experts in many fields, such as medicine, engineering, communications, and so on. The islands supply a surprising number of those people themselves, but the balance has to be made up from outside, as with all small countries. In 1945 their simple economy could be run more or less exclusively by the native-born population, but the greater complexity of modern life makes that impossible. To say that the islanders therefore "hardly constitute" a people is nonsense. People born in the islands are by far the largest group of residents today, as always since the late 19th century.

Kohen and Rodríguez say (p. 270): "The United Kingdom implements migration policies to ensure that emigrants are constantly replaced," but that is incorrect. The United Kingdom plays no part in Falklands immigration policies; the islands are self-governing and decide their immigration policy themselves. The two authors go on to say:

> ... Argentine citizens are discriminated against. Immediately after the 1982 war, Argentine residents on the islands who worked in the oil and transport services were expelled. For 17 years no Argentine passport holder had the right to visit the islands, not even as a tourist.

On the one hand, it is true that the Argentine oil workers and employees of the Argentine state airline LADE were expelled from the islands in 1982, though that was natural in the circumstances (they had helped to prepare the Argentine invasion).

But it is untrue that Argentine citizens are discriminated against – at the time of the 2013 Falklands referendum (section 10.6) there were 22 people of Argentine origin in the islands, of whom 16 had obtained Falkland Islands Status as "Argentine Incorporated Islanders" and were thus entitled to vote in the referendum. Five Argentine Incorporated Islanders identified themselves as Argentine citizens, so since there were only 3 "No" votes they cannot all have voted No.[1]

It is also untrue that no Argentine passport holder had the right to visit the islands for 17 years after 1982. The first visit by Argentine passport holders after the Falklands War occurred in October 1986, when the funeral of Lieutenant Miguel Ángel Giménez (whose body had just been found in the wreckage of his Pucará) was attended by his father Isaías and Isaías's daughter Carolina.[2] That was an exception, but in any case the interruption of Argentine visits actually lasted less than 9 years (June 1982 – March 1991), not 17, and Kohen and Rodríguez omit the reason, which was that Argentina refused to accept that the war had ended. From 1982 to 1989 Argentina refused to declare an end to hostilities, so there were no diplomatic relations between the two countries and therefore no possibility of visits.

After diplomatic relations were resumed in 1989, a visit for relatives of Argentine war dead was arranged through the International Committee of the Red Cross: 354 Argentinians arrived by sea on 18 March 1991 and visited the Argentine military cemetery near the Stanley-Darwin road. The next visit, by 11 Argentine next-of-kin, was on 31 October/1 November 1995, and there were three Argentine next-of-kin visits each year in 1997, '98 and '99, each with 15 family members plus a priest. In the end the July 1999 agreement between Britain and Argentina provided for regular international flights to the Falklands, which Argentine passport holders can use without restriction.[3]

10.5 Plebiscites; referendums

Self-determination, the right of a people to decide by whom it wishes to be governed, lies at the root of democracy and has its origin in the Greek city-states of the 5th century BC. Though self-determination has only recently become a central part of international law, it is not solely a modern concept. In the early 17th century Hugo Grotius, the "father of international law", discussing the right of a ruler to "alienate" (cede) his territory, stated that before a sovereign can cede part of his

---

[1] Details from Professor Peter Willetts's analysis of the Falklands referendum results (see section 10.6).

[2] Details from internet paper by Peter Willetts and Filipe Noguera, "Prospects for a Settlement of the Falklands/ Malvinas Dispute: An Analysis of Public Opinion in Britain and Argentina", March 1992, online under http://www.staff.city.ac.uk/p.willetts/SAC/OP/ICAROP04.PDF, p. 11, and from Argentine veterans' website http://www.3040100.com.ar/un-piloto-un-destino/.

[3] Statistics from account by Councillor Mike Summers in *Penguin News* 2 October 2009, p. 12.

territory to another sovereign, the people who inhabit that part must consent to the cession:[1]

[Heading] IV.   Impossibility of ceding rule over part of the people from the people as a whole against the will of that part [...]

[Text] IV.   In the case of the cession of a part, something more is required: that the part whose cession is being considered shall consent.

In other words, the people of part of a sovereign's territory have a right of veto over any proposed cession of their territory to another sovereign. Grotius's opinion was shared by Samuel von Pufendorf (1632-94), the second great 17th-century authority on international law:[2]

But in the cession of a part, in addition to the king's consent, there is required not only the consent of the people who remain under the original king, but especially the consent of that part whose cession is being considered.

Both those 17th-century jurists discuss cession in terms of the people involved rather than of mere territory; the Falkland Islanders are British citizens, so to cede their territory to Argentina would be "ceding part of the people from the people as a whole against the will of the part," which is precisely what Grotius and Pufendorf declare to be impossible.

In the Middle Ages, rulers occasionally permitted local representatives to express opposition to the cession of their territories,[3] but that practice died out during the so-called "Age of Absolutism" (roughly 1660 to 1790), when many territories – among them the Falklands in 1767 – were ceded from one country to another without the consent of the people who lived in them.

The practice of obtaining the inhabitants' consent to territorial cessions did not become common until the late 18th century, when the American War of Independence and the French Revolution brought a change in the way governments treated their citizens: the people of a territory were gradually accorded (or took for themselves) the right to decide what country their territory was to belong to – they exercised what is now known as external self-determination. That decision was often taken in the form of a territorial plebiscite or referendum.[4] In her magisterial work on plebiscites, Sarah Wambaugh (1882-1955) discerns two periods in which that right was often exercised: during the French Revolutionary period of 1791-8 there were votes in several places including the papal territory of Avignon and the Sardinian territory of Nice, which both chose to join France.[5] The rise of Napoleon and the reactionary Congress of Vienna in 1814-15 ended the regular exercise of external self-determination until the popular uprisings of 1848 ushered in a second period of some 30 years when it became quite common, for example Italy was finally unified by plebiscites in various regions between 1848 and 1870.[6]

Sarah Wambaugh also mentions several territorial plebiscites between the 1860s and 1880s. For

---

[1] Hugo Grotius, *De Iure Belli ac Pacis Libri tres...* ["Three Books on the Law of War and Peace..."], Amsterdam 1646, Liber II, Caput VI, Sectio IV, heading and text p. 170; heading: "Imperium in partem populi alienari parte invita à populo non posse"; text: "In partis alienatione aliud insuper requiritur, ut etiam pars de qua alienanda agitur consentiat." Both heading and text are identical in the 1st edition of 1625 and in the re-edition of 1632. Louise Loomis translates it (in *Hugo Grotius, The Law of War and Peace...*, New York 1949, p. 110): "For the alienation of a section of the people something more is required, namely, the consent of the section whose alienation is being considered"; she takes the word "people" from the heading, which however she omits.

[2] Samuel von Pufendorf, *De jure naturæ et gentium*, Lund (Sweden) 1672, lib. VIII, cap. V, sec. IX: "Sed in alienatione partis praeter consensum regis requiritur non solum populi, qui sub pristino rege remanet, sed vel maxime consensus illius partis, de qua alienanda agitur."

[3] Sarah Wambaugh, *A Monograph on Plebiscites* (1087 pp.), New York 1920, pp. 2-3.

[4] There is no clear distinction in meaning between "plebiscite" and "referendum", though "plebiscite" has generally been used to refer to votes on the totality of a territory's situation (e.g. on what country it belongs to), whereas "referendum" generally refers to decisions on specific matters. However, "referendum" is the more modern term, and is now also used for matters of "totality" e.g. the Falklands referendum in 2013, the Scottish independence referendum in 2014, or the UK-wide EU referendum in June 2016, all of which could also corrrectly be called plebiscites.

[5] Wambaugh 1920, pp. 33-57; 172-369; see also *id., Plebiscites since the World War*, 2 vols., Washington DC 1933.

[6] Wambaugh 1920, pp. 58-101 (discussion), pp. 370-725 (documents). The last place to join Italy was Rome itself, whose male citizens on 2 October 1870 voted by 133,681 to 1,507 to be united with the kingdom of Italy rather than to remain under papal sovereignty (Wambaugh 1920, p. 717).

example, in the 1860s the governments of Denmark and the United States contemplated a purchase of the Danish Virgin Islands by the US, but Denmark insisted in 1867 that the consent of the people of the islands must first be obtained by a free vote. That vote was obtained on 9 January 1868: on the island of St Thomas, 1,039 votes were cast for annexation by the United States, with 22 against, while on St John 205 votes were cast for annexation, with none against.[1] After many delays the transfer eventually took place half a century later in 1917, when the islands became the American Virgin Islands.[2] In August 1877 a plebiscite was held on the Swedish-ruled Caribbean island of St. Barthelémy, which had been ceded to Sweden in 1784 by King Louis XVI of France, by a mere stroke of the pen as it were, in exchange for trading privileges in Göteborg. In the 18th century such a cession had been quite normal; during the Age of Absolutism the king's right to do as he pleased with his subjects was untrammelled by any consideration of their wishes. In the St. Barthelémy plebiscite in 1877, 351 votes were cast, of which 350 were for reunion with France and exactly one against, and Sweden accordingly ceded the island back to France.[3] As pointed out in section 8.29, the Heligolanders would have voted overwhelmingly to remain British in 1890 had they been allowed to; Lord Salisbury knew that, and gave them no chance.

The holding of territorial plebiscites was opposed by autocratic rulers, who increased their pressure against liberal and democratic ideas, so self-determination lost ground again. One setback occurred during the unification of Italy, in which Emperor Napoleon III of France supported the Italians against the Austrian occupation of parts of northern Italy. Having defeated Austria in 1859 and secured the freedom of Lombardy, Napoleon III attempted to include the phrase "according to the wishes of the population" in the agreement ceding the province to France and thence to Italy; the local people's wishes had been taken into account many times in the unification of Italy, but on this occasion Austria was involved, and Emperor Franz Joseph would have none of it:[4]

Francis Joseph... refused, saying that "he was unable to attach any importance to the will of the people"...

That is exactly the thinking that Argentina applies in attempting to deny the relevance of the wishes of the people of the Falklands (section 10.16).

After the First World War there was a hopeful period when it seemed that a new age of peace and justice was about to begin. Sarah Wambaugh, an American writing in 1920, was still full of hope, and what she says sounds eminently modern:[5]

The war has rescued the principle of self-determination from its academic retirement... One hears no longer that it is a doctrine which does not concern international law; for it grows obvious to the world that everything which concerns sovereignty concerns international law... History would seem to prove that, in questions of territorial sovereignty, public opinion bases its judgment on an unexpressed major premise, namely, that no title acquired either through treaty, conquest or occupation, or based on economic, racial or historical arguments, or arguments of military necessity, is valid, no matter how many centuries it has run, unless it has behind it the consent of the majority of the inhabitants of the territory.

During that hopeful period the borders between Germany and Denmark, and between Germany and Poland, were laid down after plebiscites in the relevant areas, and somewhat later the Saarland chose by plebiscites on 13 January 1935 and 23 October 1955 to join Germany rather than France.[6]

---

[1] Details in Wambaugh 1920, pp. 149-155; 945-976; 975-976.

[2] *Whitaker's Almanack* 2006, pp. 1038-1039.

[3] Wambaugh 1920, pp. 155-156; 977-984.

[4] Wambaugh 1920, p. 13 (Franz Joseph I, b. 18 August 1830, emperor of Austria-Hungary 2 December 1848 to his death on 21 November 1916).

[5] Wambaugh 1920, pp. 30-31.

[6] The inter-War plebiscites are described in detail in Wambaugh 1933; for the plebiscites in the Danish-German border region see Franz Kock and Wolf von Buchwald, *Die Volksabstimmungen im Landesteil Schleswig: Weg und Wandel deutsch-dänischen Ringens um die Grenze 1920-1970* ["The plebiscites in the Schleswig region: direction and changes in the German-Danish struggle for the border 1920-1970"], Neumünster, n.d. but *c.* 1970.

10.6 The Falklands referendum, March 2013[1]

It was thus perfectly normal that a territorial plebiscite was held in the Falklands to establish the views of the inhabitants on whether they wished to continue being a British Overseas Territory. In other words, Falkland Islanders were asked to exercise their right of external self-determination (to choose the way in which their country should relate to other countries), which they undoubtedly enjoy under UN resolutions 1514, 1541, 2625 and the International Covenant on Civil and Political Rights (see sections 10.8, 10.9, 10.18 and 10.17). Their views were of course broadly known, but the extent of feeling had never been measured by an actual vote – there might have been a low turnout indicating apathy, or a surprisingly large number of No votes, or other unexpected results.

So, in response to constant Argentine calls for negotiations on sovereignty over the islands, the Falkland Islands government held a referendum on 10 and 11 March 2013 – it was a classic territorial plebiscite, but was universally (and perfectly correctly) referred to as the Falklands referendum. It was held entirely under the authority of the Falkland Islands government; the British government played no part in it. To be entitled to vote, electors had to be resident in the islands, aged 18 or over, and have Falkland Islands Status, which includes the right of abode in the Falklands. They were asked to vote on the question "Do you wish the Falkland Islands to retain their current political status as an Overseas Territory of the United Kingdom?"

The result was conclusive, to say the least. There were 1,650 people on the electoral register; 1,518 votes were cast; there were 1,513 Yes votes, 3 No votes, 1 rejected ballot paper and 1 ballot paper "unaccounted for" (apparently blank). The turnout was extremely high (92%), and an overwhelming majority of 99.8% voted to remain a British Overseas Territory.[2] The conduct of the referendum was unimpeachably democratic: it was observed by the Referendum International Observation Mission, which was led by Brad Smith from the United States and included representatives from Canada, Chile, Mexico, New Zealand, Paraguay and Uruguay. The mission released an official statement afterwards, confirming that the referendum was "in accordance with international standards and local laws" and was "technically sound, with a systematic adherence to established voting procedures", and was thus "free and fair".[3]

The presence of an observer from Uruguay, Jaime Trobo, a member of the Uruguayan Chamber of Deputies, drew a sharp reaction from Julián Domínguez, the president of the Argentine Chamber of Deputies, who said "It is treason to the whole of Latin America that a lawmaker from Uruguay should attend... a referendum on sovereignty over the Malvinas Islands, a territory that belongs to the Argentinians", but his remarks had no consequences whatever.

On the composition of the electorate, Professor Peter Willetts comments:[4]

Both the history of the Falklands and the 2012 census data demonstrate that it is an inaccurate simplification to describe the people as British settlers. Among the census population of 2,840, 8.9% do not have British citizenship; 24.8% were neither born in the Islands nor born in the United Kingdom; and 24.0% do not choose British or Falkland Islander when asked to "describe their national identity". These figures cover both people who could vote, and immigrants on work or residence permits, who could not vote.

Even the electorate included people that I have called "Incorporated Islanders", who were neither born in the Falklands nor born in the UK. New immigrants, who have been in the Islands long enough, can be granted Falkland Islands Status and can become naturalised as British citizens. The census population includes 703 people from 58 other countries, with about 150 of them having gained the vote. These Incorporated Islanders provided up to 9.6% of the electorate. The largest minorities were St Helenians and

---

[1] The most detailed account of the referendum is by Professor Peter Willetts, *A Report on the Referendum on the Political Status of the Falkland Islands*, June 2013, online under http://www.staff.city.ac.uk/p.willetts/SAC/OP/ OCCPAP12.HTM. Professor Willetts was in the islands during the referendum period and watched the process closely, though he was not one of the official observers. His report contains comments, statistics and references, and is an essential source for discussion of the Falklands referendum.

[2] Figures from Willetts 2013, table 9.

[3] The Referendum International Observation Mission / Misión Internacional de Observación del Referendo (RIOM / MIOR), *Final Report*, 23 March 2013 (www.falklands.gov.fk/assets/105-13P.pdf and www.riom-mior.com).

[4] Willetts 2013, "Short Summary" before Introduction to his Report.

Chileans, but there were also people of Argentine origin on the electoral register. The high turnout could only have been obtained by a large proportion of these Incorporated Islander electors voting Yes.

Near the end of his "Short Summary" Willetts comments on the islanders themselves:

The Falklands is a small, distinct, cohesive, political community and the referendum increased the cohesion. We should now call the Falkland Islanders a "micro-nation".

Willetts quotes the former Falklands Councillor and MLA (Member of the Legislative Assembly) Mike Summers, who said at the UN Decolonization Committee (the "C24") in June 2012:

We are a successful country. I intentionally use the word country, because Falkland Islanders have a distinct and clear identity, and consider the islands to be our country, our home.

And among his final conclusions Willetts has this to say, after reporting on a fifty-minute interview with Nigel Haywood, the then Governor of the Falklands:[1]

The Governor is correct to suggest the referendum has finalised the process of bringing together a diverse range of people as a new nation – perhaps we should say a micro-nation. Consequently, the referendum is the start, not the end, of a debate about what the place of the Falklands could be in the global political system.

Finally, Marcelo Kohen and Mamadou Hébié state in their *Research Handbook*:[2]

... from the establishment of self-determination as a principle of international law, peoples that have not yet achieved statehood are also holders of territorial sovereignty.

All those statements support what we say in this book – that the Falkland Islands are a country and the Falkland Islanders are a people in the full sense of the word, "holders of territorial sovereignty" with the full right of external self-determination, i.e. the right to determine their place in the global political system.

The fact that the islanders are holders of territorial sovereignty means *ipso facto* that the Falklands are not in a colonial situation. In a colonial situation the holder of territorial sovereignty is the colonial power, but that is no longer the case; under current international law Britain is the "administering power", not the colonial power. Britain holds rightful and exclusive title to the islands; in addition the Falkland Islanders possess the right of external self-determination and therefore have the right to decide how their country is decolonised. At present they freely choose to remain in partnership with Britain.

10.7 The Falklands at the UN, I

The foundation of the United Nations (UN) in 1945 gave Argentina a new forum in which to present a claim to the Falklands, though that claim had been devoid of legal validity for a very long time. For some 20 years it was all very low-key: in September 1945 Argentina made a reservation concerning territories that might be placed under trusteeship, but not mentioning the Falklands. Britain deplored the Argentine act, and Argentina replied that it only intended to express a reservation of right, hoping to settle the matter with Britain in the future.[3] And that was all.

On 24 February 1946 Juan Domingo Perón (1895-1974) was elected president of Argentina, and remained in office until on 16 September 1955 he was ousted in a military coup, the third of six military coups in Argentina in the 20th century.[4] Perón soon saw the Falklands and Antarctica as an

---

[1] This and previous quote from Willetts 2013, end of his Report before the Appendix.
[2] Marcelo Kohen and Mamadou Hébié, in Marcelo Kohen and Mamadou Hébié (eds.), *Research Handbook on Territorial Disputes in International Law*, Cheltenham (UK) and Northampton (USA), 2018, p. 25.
[3] Brief correspondence in *British Documents on Foreign Affairs...* (*BDFA*), Part IV, Series D, vol. 1, pp. 88-90. Texts of Argentine speeches, reports and letters to the UN and other international organisations are printed in [Anon.], *Malvinas, Georgias, y Sandwich del Sur: Diplomacia Argentina en Naciones Unidas* (henceforth *MGSS*), Buenos Aires, 8 vols., 1983-2008 (and ongoing), of which vols. VI, VII and VIII are each bound in two parts, making 11 bound volumes. The steady escalation of the Falklands dispute at the UN and the OAS is shown by the fact that in vols. I-III the 19 years 1945-63 fill 80 pages, while those on the 17 years 1964-81 fill 608 pages (over 7 times as long), and far more since then. The 11 vols. plus a small Addendum contain a total of 4,829 pages of running text. It is one-sided and distorts things, e.g. by printing UN Resolution 1514 but not 1541, but it is useful as there is no British equivalent.
[4] There were military coups in Argentina, resulting in short- or long-lived military dictatorships, in 1930, 1943, 1955,

external cause with which to rally support, and Argentina began to press a claim to both those territories, though initially the mild tone continued. On 11 December 1946, at the first session of the UN General Assembly, both Britain and Argentina made brief reservations of their rights of sovereignty over the Falklands.[1] Since then, Argentina has raised the topic every year, at the UN, at the Organization of American States (OAS) and other international organisations, and in contacts with Britain and other countries. It is important to note that this was a new development, not the maintenance of a continuing old claim. Argentina's title to the Falklands was ended in 1850 by the ratification of the Convention of Peace (chapter 7); Argentina did not mention the islands to the British government at all for over a third of a century from 1850 to 1884, and made no mention of them in the Messages to the legislature for 91 years from 1849 to 1941, whereas Britain protested to Argentina in 1829, 1832 and 1884 against Argentine presumptions of sovereignty.

Nevertheless, from 1946 onwards Perón began to use the Falklands issue to distract attention from Argentine domestic problems, and he also raised a new Argentine claim to part of Antarctica and escalated the hitherto halfhearted claim to the Falkland Islands Dependencies (section 9.6). The first Argentine school geography book to mention any claim to South Georgia was published in 1946-8, and since 1948 all Argentine school geography books have mentioned the claim to South Georgia, the South Orkneys and the South Shetlands.[2]

For almost 25 years, at the United Nations and elsewhere, Argentina made only brief formulaic references to its "reservation of right" over the Malvinas. But 1960 brought a profound change at the UN: in what Mikulas Fabry calls "the famed 1960 session",[3] 17 new independent states (16 in Africa plus Cyprus) were admitted as members of the UN on a single day (20 September 1960). That began a transformation of the UN, and the new members were keen to extend the benefits of independence to the remaining colonial territories. On 23 September the Soviet leader Nikita Khrushchev made a speech at the UN General Assembly calling for a statement of intent to end colonialism, and on 14 December 1960 the General Assembly unanimously passed Resolution 1514 (XV), the "Declaration on Decolonization" (see section 10.8).

The next day, 15 December 1960, the General Assembly passed Resolution 1541 (XV),[4] which like 1514 has central relevance to the Falklands: Resolutions 1514 and 1541 state definitively that the peoples of all non-self-governing territories have the right to self-determination, and the UN includes the Falklands on its list of non-self-governing territories, the "Chapter XI territories" (i.e. those covered by Chapter XI of the UN Charter), thus expressly confirming that they are covered by resolutions 1514 and 1541. Those Resolutions, together with 2625 (section 10.18), rule out Argentina's aim of taking over the Falklands, but Argentina misuses the first Resolution and disregards the others. We examine them below in sections 10.8, 10.9 and 10.18.

10.8 The resolution Argentina misuses – UN Resolution 1514 (XV), 14 December 1960

United Nations Resolution 1514 (XV), passed by the General Assembly on 14 December 1960, is entitled "Declaration on the Granting of Independence to Colonial Countries and Peoples", or for short the "Declaration on Decolonization". Its first two operative paragraphs read as follows:[5]

(1) The subjection of peoples to alien subjugation, domination and exploitation constitutes a denial of fundamental human rights, is contrary to the Charter of the United Nations and is an impediment to the

---

1962, 1966 and 1976 – see Deborah L. Norden, *Military rebellion in Argentina*, Nebraska 1996.
[1] Text of the Argentine reservation (but not the British) in *MGSS*, vol. I, 1983, p. 11.
[2] Carlos Escudé, "Contenido nacionalista de la enseñanza de la geografía en la República Argentina 1879-1986" ["Nationalist content in the teaching of geography in the Republic of Argentina 1879-1986"], in *Malvinas hoy: herencia de un conflicto* ["Malvinas today: legacy of a conflict"], Buenos Aires 1989, pp. 411-454.
[3] Mikulas Fabry, *Recognizing States...*, Oxford 2010, p. 154.
[4] UN document number A/RES/1541(XV).
[5] UN doc. no. A/RES/15/1514; full text on the UN website. The roman numeral in brackets is the session number: XV was the 15th session of the UN. After session XXX in 1975 the numbering system was changed, and from session 31 (1976) the session number has been written in arabic numerals and placed first. In UN resolutions, an operative paragraph is a piece of text that indicates what the UN resolved (as distinct from e.g. a merely introductory paragraph). By "paragraphs" of UN resolutions we always mean operative paragraphs. Some UN documents are only available under https://documents.un.org/prod/ods.nsf/home.xsp.

promotion of World peace and co-operation.

(2) All peoples have the right to self-determination; by virtue of that right they freely determine their political status and freely pursue their economic, social and cultural development.

Those declarations are obviously relevant to the Falklands. To the Falkland Islanders, Argentina is an alien country, so the cession of the islands to Argentina would place them under "alien subjugation and domination" as mentioned in paragraph 1. As Mikulas Fabry puts it:[1]

... the ideas of self-determination and sovereignty were always the opposite of government by foreigners.

Falkland Islanders have unpleasant memories of Argentina's attempt in 1982 to impose "government by foreigners" upon them, and that memory is not limited to those islanders who remember it personally – the younger generation are well informed about the experiences of their families during the Argentine occupation.[2] The Resolution continues:

(3) Inadequacy of political, economic, social or educational preparedness should never serve as a pretext for delaying independence.

(4) All armed action or repressive measures of all kinds directed against dependent peoples shall cease in order to enable them to exercise peacefully and freely their right to complete independence, and the integrity of their national territory shall be respected.

(5) Immediate steps shall be taken, in Trust and Non-Self-Governing Territories or all other territories which have not yet attained independence, to transfer all powers to the peoples of those territories, without any conditions or reservations, in accordance with their freely expressed will and desire, without any distinction as to race, creed or colour, in order to enable them to enjoy complete independence and freedom.

Paragraph (3) is not relevant to the Falklands – the islanders have a high standard of education and development, and there is no lower limit to the number of people a territory has to have before it can become independent. That is shown by the case of Tokelau, a group of small Pacific atolls at present administered by New Zealand, and one of the countries on the UN's list of non-self-governing territories, the "Chapter XI territories". Though the total population of Tokelau is only 1,500 (half the population of the Falklands), the United Nations has constantly pressed the Tokelauans to accept independence, although they have repeatedly made it clear, including in two referendums in 2006 and 2007, that they are happy with their present status and do not wish for independence.[3] Since the UN clearly does not regard a population of 1,500 as a bar to complete independence, it is illogical to maintain that the Falklands cannot obtain independence because their population is too small.

Paragraph (4) clearly made illegal not only the Argentine invasion of the islands in 1982 but all the repressive measures employed by Argentina since then, including attempts to suppress trade between the Falklands and other South American countries.

Paragraph (5) is important – it calls for "immediate steps" in all non-independent territories to transfer "all powers" to their peoples "without any conditions or reservations, in accordance with their freely expressed will and desire". The phrase "without any conditions or reservations" is all-embracing, so the existence of a sovereignty dispute is irrelevant. Paragraph (5) thus calls on Britain to transfer power to the Falkland Islanders, which Britain has been doing ever since 1960, mainly

---

[1] Fabry 2010, pp. 206-207.

[2] See, for example, "What did the Jaffray family experience at Goose Green in 1982?", by Keon Kennedy (aged 14) in *FIJ* vol. 11 (2), Stanley 2018, pp. 198-200, with an alphabetical list of the 115 people who were imprisoned by the Argentinians in the Goose Green community hall for four weeks during the Argentine occupation of the islands from 1 May 1982; they included 12 members of the Jaffray family, 5 members of the Anderson family and 4 members of the Goss family. There were 72 adults and 43 children; of those, 32 children were under 15, two adults were over 80, and Matthew McMullen was 3 months old. They were without food for the first 36 hours. More details in Graham Bound, *Falkland Islanders at War*, Barnsley 2002, pp. 142-144; and *id.*, *Invasion 1982: The Falkland Islanders' Story*, Barnsley 2007, pp. 151-154). The imprisonment of those people was a breach of the Fourth Geneva Convention, 12 August 1949, Chapter II, Article 85, which regulates the treatment of Protected Persons, including civilian internees.

[3] The repeated attempts by the United Nations to impose independence (!) on Tokelau are described authoritatively and with resigned humour by Judith Huntsman and Kelihiano Kalolo in *The Future of Tokelau: Decolonising Agendas, 1975-2006*, Auckland and Honolulu 2007.

through a succession of new Falklands constitutions in 1985, 1997 and 2009, each of which further increased the extent of islander control over the islands' politics and economy. Britain has thus been fulfilling the central demand of Resolution 1514. The speed has been less than "immediate", but progress has been considerable and has been directed by the Falkland Islanders themselves, "in accordance with their freely expressed will and desire", as the United Nations puts it. Significantly, paragraph 5 was specifically referred to in UN Resolution 1810 (XVII) of 17 December 1962, without reference to any other paragraphs of Resolution 1514 (see section 10.11). In giving Falkland Islanders the right to "freely determine their political status" and the right to "complete independence", Resolution 1514 unambiguously gives them the full right of external self-determination. Those paragraphs therefore rule out an Argentine takeover of the islands.

Argentina is left with paragraph (6), which reads:

6) Any attempt aimed at the partial or total disruption of the national unity and the territorial integrity of a country is incompatible with the purposes and principles of the Charter of the United Nations.

To apply that paragraph to the Falklands is a distortion of its object and purpose – the phrase "Any attempt aimed at" refers unambiguously to moves *after 1960* aiming to break up a country or territory. Paragraph (6) was included in Resolution 1514 to preserve newly independent countries from the kind of danger that was just emerging in Africa: the Belgian Congo had become independent on 30 June 1960 as the Republic of Congo (Léopoldville), but had almost at once been dismembered by the secession of the mineral-rich province of Katanga under its leader Moïse Tshombe (1919-69), who declared the "Republic of Katanga" independent on 11 July 1960; after a series of military operations and interventions, the secession was defeated on 15 January 1963. The purpose of paragraph (6) was to deter any such secessions *in the future*.

That was confirmed at the C24 by the British "alternate representative" Cecil King[1] on 9 September 1964 – he said paragraph 6 of Resolution 1514 "clearly referred to possible attempts at disruption in the future and not to issues of sovereignty dating back to distant history" (section 10.12). That is also underlined by Jamie Trinidad, who sums up the tenor of the discussion in the UN General Assembly in December 1960 as follows: "One derives the impression from the debate that the purpose of paragraph (6) was indeed to address situations like Katanga and West Irian".[2] He quotes J. E. S. Fawcett, saying that "the language of 'attempts' in paragraph 6 'can hardly be apposite to describe an already existing and indeed long-established situation'."[3] Trinidad also quotes the submission by Algeria in the *Western Sahara* case at the International Court of Justice in 1975 (see section 10.21), stating that paragraph (6) of Resolution 1514 does not cover "the case of territories *formerly or at one time* illegally detached from a State and which are the subject of a territorial claim by that State on the basis of the principle of integrity".[4] In short, paragraph (6) was exclusively prospective: it applied only to breaches of territorial integrity that took place after 1960.

It is a general legal principle that laws cannot apply retroactively (i.e. they cannot apply to events that happened before the laws were enacted), and this principle is stated with specific reference to international treaties in Article 28 of the Vienna Convention on the Law of Treaties, signed at Vienna on 23 May 1969:[5]

Article 28. NON-RETROACTIVITY OF TREATIES

Unless a different intention appears from the treaty or is otherwise established, its provisions do not bind a

---

[1] Cecil Edward King, CMG (1912–81), Britain's "alternate representative" at the UN. Britain's Permanent Representative (ambassador) to the UN, 1960-64, was Sir Patrick Henry Dean, GCMG (1909–1994).

[2] Trinidad 2018, p. 37. West Irian (or West Papua) is the western part of the island of New Guinea, inhabited by Papuan peoples, formerly part of the Dutch East Indies, which was invaded and detached from the rest of New Guinea by Indonesia in 1962, claiming that its retention by the Netherlands "breached Indonesia's territorial integrity". The peoples of the territory were not allowed any meaningful exercise of self-determination (Trinidad 2018, pp. 28-29).

[3] Trinidad 2018, p. 49, quoting J.E.S. Fawcett, "Gibraltar: The Legal Issues", in *International Affairs*, 1967, pp. 236, 249.

[4] Trinidad 2018, p. 49, quoting the *Western Sahara* case, ICJ Pleadings 1975, p. 321 (in French; italics in original, translation here by Graham Pascoe).

[5] Text from UN website under https://treaties.un.org/doc/Publication/UNTS/Volume%201155/volume-1155-I-18232-English.pdf.

party in relation to any act or fact which took place or any situation which ceased to exist before the date of the entry into force of the treaty with respect to that party.

The non-retroactive principle has also been confirmed in several judgements of the International Court of Justice, for example in the Lockerbie Case of 1998 and the Genocide Case in 2003.[1] It is therefore abundantly clear that paragraph 6 of Resolution 1514 cannot apply to any events that took place before 1960, so it does not apply to Britain's actions in 1833.

By contrast, Britain's treatment of the Chagos Islands in the 1960s was indeed a breach of paragraph 6 of Resolution 1514 – it took place after 1960 and involved the dismemberment of a newly emerging country: Britain detached the islands from Mauritius, breaching Mauritius's territorial integrity (section 10.28). That was confirmed by the International Court of Justice (ICJ) in their landmark advisory opinion delivered on 25 February 2019. The Court stated that the purpose of paragraph 6 of Resolution 1514 was "to prevent any dismemberment of non-self-governing territories".[2] That made it clear beyond doubt that it referred only to non-self-governing territories on the road to independence, not to any cases from past history or in order to protect existing independent countries from dismemberment. The Court's ruling therefore means that paragraph 6 of Resolution 1514 cannot be used by Argentina to claim that its territorial integrity is being breached by Britain's possession of the Falklands – and it incidentally also means that it cannot be used, for example, by China to criminalise calls for the secession of Hong Kong, Tibet, Taiwan or East Turkestan.

The drafting history of paragraph (6) reveals that it was not intended as a dilution of the right of self-determination.[3] Jamie Trinidad says "Guatemala was concerned that paragraph 6, as originally drafted, placed insufficient restrictions on the exercise of self-determination in territories that were the subject of dispute or litigation"; Guatemala had a long-standing claim to British Honduras (now Belize), and proposed the insertion of a new paragraph (7), as follows:

The principle of the self-determination of peoples may in no case impair the right of territorial integrity of any State or its right to the recovery of territory.

That would have been useful for countries claiming that their territorial integrity would be breached by the exercise of self-determination in certain specific territories. Argentina could have referred to it over the Falklands, Spain over Gibraltar, and Guatemala over British Honduras, though in fact all those claims were devoid of validity as well as being contrary to the wishes of the people of the territories concerned.

In the event, as Trinidad states, "the Guatemalan amendment received little support in the General Assembly", and the Soviet Union made its opposition abundantly clear:[4]

... the Soviet delegation is unable to support these amendments since they provide for a limitation of the fundamental right of all peoples to self-determination and are thus contrary to paragraph 2 in the... draft resolution, which quite rightly states that 'All peoples have the right of self-determination'... no attempt should be made to raise private claims to the level of a general principle restricting the inalienable right of every people to self-determination.

In the event, seeing the lack of support for its proposed paragraph (7), Guatemala withdrew its proposal and it was never put to a vote. Despite the failure of that attempt to upgrade the principle of territorial integrity so as to trump self-determination, Argentina made an attempt in 2008 to "move the goalposts" in the same way, but its proposed amendment was defeated in the UN General Assembly (see sections 10.26, 10.28).

---

[1] Lockerbie Case (ICJ), Libya v. USA, Preliminary Objections Judgment, 27 Feb 1998, p. 25, para 43; Genocide Case (ICJ), Bosnia & Herzegovina v. Serbia, Application of Revision of Judgment of 11 July 1996, Press Release 2003/8, 3 Feb 2003, para 10 (details from letter by Stephen Potts in *Penguin News* 7 June 2019, p. 5).

[2] International Court of Justice (ICJ), Advisory Opinion on "Legal Consequences of the Separation of the Chagos Archipelago from Mauritius in 1965", Year 2019, General List No. 169 (2019, 25 February), available in full on the ICJ website under www.icj-cij.org, 169-20190225-01-00-EN.pdf. Quote here from p. 37, paragraph 153.

[3] Details here from Trinidad 2018, pp. 30-38.

[4] Trinidad 2018, pp. 32, 33.

Jamie Trinidad's conclusion supports the view that paragraph (6) of the "Declaration on Decolonization", i.e. UN Resolution 1514, applies only to new developments after 1960, not to earlier events (such as Britain's reassertion of sovereignty in the Falklands in 1833). He says:[1]

> The wording of paragraph 6 of the Colonial Declaration [*sic*], which prohibits any 'attempt' to interfere with the territorial integrity of a State or country, suggests that the provision was designed to address *prospective* action that poses a threat to *uti possidetis* boundaries. The provision does not appear to have been intended to apply retrospectively as a basis for reconstituting dismembered pre-colonial territorial formations… It does not appear to have been the intention of the drafters that irredentist claims… should have a special status in the decolonization process…

That was confirmed in 1975 in the *Western Sahara* case by the International Court of Justice, who rejected any notion of the primacy of irredentist claims based on territorial integrity over the wishes of the people of a territory (section 10.21).

Argentina always applies the irredentist approach, claiming that the Falklands are rightfully a part of Argentina's territory that was "usurped" by Britain and which should be "returned" to Argentina. That is also precisely the "legitimist" approach – it is impossible to be an irredentist without also being a legitimist. Argentine speakers and writers customarily claim that paragraph (6) of Resolution 1514 is relevant to the Falklands and that Argentina's territorial integrity is being violated by Britain's possession of the islands, but that is of course untrue; the Falklands have not been Argentine territory since May 1850 at the latest, and all paragraphs of Resolution 1514, as well as Resolution 1541 (section 10.9) definitively invalidate any Argentine claim to the islands.

10.9 The resolution Argentina never mentions – UN Resolution 1541, 15 December 1960

United Nations Resolution 1514 was followed the next day, 15 December 1960, by Resolution 1541 (XV). Once 1514 had enunciated the basic principles behind decolonisation, 1541 listed the forms it could take. In a long Annex it lists "Principles which should guide Members in determining whether or not an obligation exists to transmit the information called for in article 73e of the Charter of the United Nations". Those principles include:[2]

[Resolution 1541 (XV)]:

Principle IV

Prima facie there is an obligation to transmit information in respect of a territory which is geographically separate and is distinct ethnically and/or culturally from the country administering it.

Principle V

Once it has been established that such a *prima facie* case of geographical and ethnical or cultural distinctness of a territory exists, other elements may then be brought into consideration. These additional elements may be, *inter alia,* of an administrative, political, juridical, economic or historical nature. If they affect the relationship between the metropolitan State and the territory concerned in a manner which arbitrarily places the latter in a position or status of subordination, they support the presumption that there is an obligation to transmit information under Article *73* e of the Charter.

Principle VI

A Non-Self-Governing Territory can be said to have reached a full measure of self-government by:

(*a*) Emergence as a sovereign independent State;

(*b*) Free association with an independent State; or

(*c*) Integration with an independent State.

Principle VII

(*a*) Free association should be the result of a free and voluntary choice by the peoples of the territory concerned expressed through informed and democratic processes. It should be one which respects the individuality and the cultural characteristics of the territory and its peoples, and retains for the peoples of the territory which is associated with an independent State the freedom to modify the status of that territory through the expression of their will by democratic means and through constitutional processes.

---

[1] Trinidad 2018, p. 239; italics in original.

[2] UN document A/RES/1541(XV); text from *General Assembly – Fifteenth Session: Resolutions adopted on the reports of the Fourth Committee*, United Nations, New York 1960, pp. 29-30 (also available on the UN website).

(*b*) The associated territory should have the right to determine its internal constitution without outside interference, in accordance with due constitutional processes and the freely expressed wishes of the people. This does not preclude consultations as appropriate or necessary under the terms of the free association agreed upon.

Principle VIII

Integration with an independent State should be on the basis of complete equality between the peoples of the erstwhile Non-Self-Governing Territory and those of the independent country with which it is integrated. The peoples of both territories should have equal status and rights of citizenship and equal guarantees of fundamental rights and freedoms without any distinction or discrimination; both should have equal rights and opportunities for representation and effective participation at all levels in the executive, legislative and judicial organs of government.

Principle IX

Integration should have come about in the following circumstances:

(*a*) The integrating territory should have attained an advanced stage of self-government with free political institutions, so that its peoples would have the capacity to make a responsible choice through informed and democratic processes;

(*b*) The integration should be the result of the freely expressed wishes of the territory's peoples acting with full knowledge of the change in their status, their wishes having been expressed through informed and democratic processes, impartially conducted and based on universal adult suffrage. The United Nations could, when it deems it necessary, supervise these processes.

Resolution 1541 indubitably applies to the Falklands: they are included in the UN's current list of non-self-governing territories (the "Chapter XI territories"), and since 1960 Britain has regularly submitted reports on the islands to the United Nations, fulfilling Article 73e of the UN Charter as required by Resolution 1541. Those British reports have been accepted by the UN for almost 60 years, and the information in them has often been used in UN working papers.[1] Britain's reports were mentioned by Lucio García del Solar (1922-2010; Argentine UN ambassador 1962-6), at a meeting of the C24 on 17 November 1965 – he said "the United Kingdom transmitted information on the Malvinas Islands to the United Nations every year under Article 73 of the Charter, which clearly showed that they constituted a Non-Self-Governing Territory."[2] In other words, the Falklands are a territory to which Resolution 1541 applies and Argentina accepts the fact – neither Argentina nor any other country has ever called that into question.

Principles VI and VII of Resolution 1541 mention free association, an example of which is provided by the Republic of Palau, a small country in the Pacific with a population of around 21,000. It was the last remaining UN Trust Territory (out of the original 11), but in 1982 signed a Compact of Free Association with the United States. The Compact came into force on 1 October 1994, making Palau *de jure* independent. The Compact enshrines the free and voluntary association of the two governments in matters of economic relations, security and defence; defence is provided by the United States since Palau has no military of its own. Though in free association with the US, Palau is a sovereign country and has diplomatic relations with a number of countries. It became a member of the United Nations on 15 December 1994 under UN Resolution 49/63.[3]

---

[1] This is regularly confirmed in the Reports of the C24, e.g. in UN document A/5800/Rev.1, Annex 8, p. 29, stating that Britain had transmitted reports on the Falklands to the UN on 3 July 1963 and 23 June 1964; and in UN document A/AC.109/2008/13 (a working paper on the Falklands by the UN Secretariat, New York 2008), p. 3 fn.1, which states that the details given are from "Information provided by the administering Power, 9 January 2008"; it contains many paragraphs beginning "According to the administering Power". That Secretariat working paper formed part of the basis of the UN *Report of the Special Committee on the Situation with regard to the Implentation of the Declaration on the Granting of Independence to Colonial Countries and Peoples for 2008* (UN doc. A/63/23, General Assembly Official Records, Sixty-third Session, Supplement No. 23, New York 2008), as stated on its p. 48. And UN working paper A/AC.109/2018/6, dated 14 March 2018, prepared for the C24, states on its p. 1: "The information contained in the present working paper has been derived from information transmitted to the Secretary-General by the administering Power under Article 73e of the Charter of the United Nations on 18 December 2017".

[2] Text here from speech as reported (hence the past tense) in UN document A/C.4/SR.1559; Spanish text in *MGSS* vol. 1, 1983, p. 255.

[3] Details mostly from the website of the Government of Palau, http://palaugov.pw/.

As to whether the Falklands are a territory "distinct ethnically and/or culturally from the country administering it" (as Principle IV puts it), the terms "ethnic" and "cultural" are famously nebulous and indefinable – all definitions of "ethnicity" or "culture" are tailor-made to fit some predefined political agenda. They are "loaded terms", and there is no universally acceptable neutral definition of either. Ethnicity is sometimes used in a racial and/or national sense (e.g. "ethnic minorities"), and sometimes in a family-historical sense (e.g. "ethnic Germans", the descendants of Germans from eastern Europe, in particular Russia, whose native language is often Russian or another east European language, though they count in German law as German). There are many other uses and definitions of the word. Applied to Falkland Islanders, "ethnically distinct" could mean that while they have British passports, they are not English, Scottish, etc., and are thus clearly distinct from British people living in Britain. In any case the ancestry of the Falkland Islanders is by no means exclusively British; they are a unique mixture, with many ancestors who arrived in the 19th and 20th century from Scandinavia, South America, France and Germany (section 10.1).

There are also many non-British nationals living in the islands – as well as 1,544 Falkland Islanders, the 2016 Falklands census records 148 Chilean citizens, 53 with Philippines citizenship, 18 Peruvians, 17 Australians and 16 New Zealanders, plus people with some three dozen other nationalities including 4 Argentinians and 2 Paraguayans. Many of the non-British nationals have lived in the islands for a long time, and some have children born in the islands, several with one parent who is a native-born Falkland Islander and one who is not of British origin – the census records 8 people who are both Chilean and Falkland Islander, 5 who are St Helenian and Falkland Islander, and several other combinations including Falkland Islander/ British/ Chilean. The inhabitants of the islands self-evidently constitute a unique community that is indisputably a people – a "micro-nation", as Professor Peter Willetts calls them (section 10.6).

The use of the terms "nation" and "national" in reference to the Falklands has greatly increased during the last decade – the former Falkland Islands Archives in Stanley were renamed the Jane Cameron National Archives (JCNA) in 2010 after the tragic death of archivist Jane Cameron; the title of her successor Tansy Bishop is Falkland Islands National Archivist; the annual address by the governor to the Falklands Legislative Assembly is called the State of the Nation Address (it is delivered by the Governor but written by the elected members of the Legislative Assembly), and the Falkland Islanders clearly have the right to be regarded as a nation. Jamie Trinidad says of them:[1]

Although the islanders are British and identify as such, it would be difficult to argue against their claim that a distinctive society has developed there over the past 200 years… there is no requirement laid down anywhere that the population of a Non-Self-Governing Territory must have suffered alien subjugation or racial discrimination in order to qualify as a 'people'.

Trinidad rejects the view of S. K. N. Blay, who says of the Falklands and Gibraltar that the "inhabitants are, in effect, beneficiaries of colonial rule",[2] and Trinidad denies several times that there is any relevance in Professor Marcelo Kohen's proposed distinction between "beneficiaries" and "victims" of colonialism.[3]

As the *Shackleton Report* showed (section 10.4), Britain exploited the Falklands for decades and made a handsome profit out of them, while at the same time strangling their growth and increasing the hardship of the Falkland Islanders. For over a century British officials filled the important executive positions and treated the Falklands like any other colonial territory in the British Empire, discriminating against the native-born islanders and keeping them out of participation in decision-making. In the 1920s and 30s the British expatriates had their own club in Stanley, the Falkland Club, which Howell Evans calls "a select institution, membership exclusive to expatriate, white-

---

[1] Trinidad 2018, p. 150.

[2] Trinidad 2018, p. 207, quoting S. K. N. Blay, "Self-Determination versus Territorial Integrity in Decolonization", in *New York University Journal of International Law and Politics*, vol. 18 (1985-6), p. 464.

[3] Trinidad 2018, p. 148 (criticising Kohen's view that self-determination for the Falkland Islanders is "an insult to genuine peoples who have had to fight to liberate themselves from the colonial yoke"), and pp. 150-151, 207, 209, 218-219, 242.

collar workers. It became known as the Snobs Club."[1] The colonial power, Britain, treated the native islanders (almost 90% of the population in 1946, and still 80% in 1962; see sections 10.1, 10.14) as second-class citizens. To call them "beneficiaries" of colonialism is absurd; they were exploited just as much as the inhabitants of any other colonial territory. It is only since the Falklands War that they have come to play a central role in the government of their country.

Resolution 1541 (like Resolution 1514, see section 10.8) uses neither "population" nor "inhabitants"; it refers nine times to the "peoples" of non-self-governing territories (and once to "people"). Furthermore, it states that there has to be a "free and voluntary choice by the peoples of the territory concerned", and refers three times to the "wishes" of those peoples, making it abundantly clear that their wishes are paramount in the decolonisation of their homelands. Thanks to the steady development of their democratic institutions, the Falklands have moved a long way towards "free association" with Britain, the status described in Principle VII of UN Resolution 1541. Whether they will actually make a "free and voluntary choice" to formally adopt that status remains to be seen; if they did, that choice would express their wishes under Resolution 1541. Thus Resolution 1541 annihilates Argentina's case, and (with Resolution 1514) gives Falkland Islanders not merely the right to internal self-determination (the right to administer their country internally), but the full right to external self-determination (the right to choose how their country relates to other countries, including independence and other forms of association with other countries).

Small wonder, then, that Argentina carefully avoids mentioning Resolution 1541. We have conscientiously worked through 11 volumes of the official compilation of Argentina's activities at the United Nations and other international forums, *Malvinas, Georgias, y Sandwich del Sur: Diplomacia Argentina en Naciones Unidas* (henceforth *MGSS*), Buenos Aires 1983-2008; we have turned every one of its 4,829 pages (up to 2008), and have failed to find a single mention of UN Resolution 1541, though *MGSS* contains many lists of UN Resolutions.[2] Naturally those 11 volumes were not exactly a riveting read, and we may have nodded at times, so we are not quite certain that we have not missed 1541 somewhere or other. But if mentioned at all, it is well hidden and occupies no significant position in that otherwise comprehensive publication.

At a mere 300 pages the work by Kohen and Rodríguez is much less comprehensive, but it displays the same lordly disdain for Resolution 1541 as other Argentine publications. The two authors refer (p. 278) to "the more than 40 resolutions passed by the General Assembly and the Decolonization Committee of the United Nations", and in a huge 18-line footnote on the same page they list 41 resolutions: 11 by the UN General Assembly, 28 by the C24, and 2 by the UN Security Council, whose resolutions are generally seen as binding, including no. 502 of 3 April 1982 ordering Argentina to withdraw its forces from the Falklands (which Argentina disregarded). But Resolution 1541 is missing from their list.

The constant suppression of any mention of UN Resolution 1541 in Argentine works including that by Kohen and Rodríguez is a blatant distortion of history and of the legal situation. The reason for that omission is clear: 1541 enshrines the "wishes" of the Falkland Islanders as paramount in discussions of the future of the Falklands, and hence destroys Argentina's case.

To sum up: neither Resolution 1514 nor 1541 permits what Argentina is seeking to impose on the Falklands: the transfer of sovereignty *against* the wishes of the people of the territory. Those two resolutions were further strengthened by UN Resolution 2625 in 1970 (section 10.18).

10.10 The territoriality of self-determination

A "people" is naturally defined in the first instance by the characteristics of the individuals it is composed of, but it is also partly defined by its geographical position and its territory. Individuals living dispersed among another population, e.g. French or Pakistani citizens living in Britain, cannot be a "people" entitled to external self-determination (i.e. the right to decide their relations with other countries and peoples), since they have no piece of physical territory that they can

---

[1] Howell Evans, *The Falkland Islands I Knew*, Oswestry 2001, p. 54. Howell Robert ("Bobby") Evans (1914-2001) was born in the Falklands as the fourth of eight children of John David Evans and Matilda Letitia, née Betts.
[2] *MGSS* lists Resolution 1514 many times, and also contains its full text (vol. I, pp. 90-94), but 1541 is omitted.

collectively call their own.

By contrast the Falkland Islands are a compact geographical unit, where the Falkland Islanders have lived as a settled community for well over a century and a half. The islands are an immense distance from Britain – the islanders' geographical apartness from other British passport holders could hardly be more extreme. In reference to Argentina's population-based attempt to deny that the Falkland Islanders are a people, Jamie Trinidad comments:[1]

The resulting 'ethno-centric' discourse… misconstrues external self-determination as a right defined primarily by the human characteristics of the affected population, rather than the territorially defined right that it is.

He had pointed out earlier in his work:[2]

… the 'people' entitled to determine the political destiny of a colonial territory is *territorially defined*.

The territorial location of the Falkland Islanders within a specific territory far from other territories underlines the fact that they are a distinct and unique people – a "micro-nation", as Professor Peter Willetts puts it.

In view of that, the question of sovereignty over the territory is of central importance to the question of self-determination. As we pointed out in section 8.12, Kohen and Rodríguez quote (their pp. 281-2) the British judge Dame Rosalyn Higgins on the question of self-determination and sovereignty – she says:[3]

Until it is determined where territorial sovereignty lies it is impossible to see if the inhabitants have a right of self-determination.

Jamie Trinidad clearly agrees – in considering the UN resolutions on the Falklands, he says:[4]

Rather than call for a transfer of the islands or otherwise endorse the Argentine territorial claim, the resolutions appear to treat the territorial claim (rather than self-determination) as a prior question that needs to be resolved before the appropriate modalities of decolonization can be agreed internationally. The question of 'peoplehood' and self-determination is inseparable from, and consequent to, the question of the validity of the underlying territorial claim.

By "prior question" Trinidad means a logical precondition, rather than a mere chronologically preceding question. In any case, that question was definitively resolved by the Convention of Peace in 1850 and the many acts of omission and commission by Argentina that followed it (sections 7.16, 8.18). Trinidad does not mention any of that; his treatment of the Falklands issue (his pp. 133-152) is marred by his being (like other authors) unaware of many of its central aspects, such as the Convention of Peace, statements by Argentine leaders, foreign recognition and Argentina's acceptance of Britain as a territorial arbitrator, as well as older aspects such as the effect of the Anglo-Spanish agreement of 1771 and the Nootka Sound Convention. The truth is that Argentina has no title to the islands whatever.

10.11 Argentina's worries; the C24[5]

In the early 1960s Argentina began to become concerned at the way things were going. As the Argentine historian Martín Abel González shows, the Argentine government saw the independence of former colonial territories as a danger to its claim to the Falklands – if decolonisation continued, the Falklands might end up as an independent country, foiling Argentina's aim to take them over. González says: "Argentina perceived the acceleration of British decolonisation and the UN intervention… as a potentially lethal menace to its historical claim to the islands"; he adds "Argentina's consideration of the Falklands as an integral part of its territory was at loggerheads

---

[1] Trinidad 2018, p. 135.
[2] Trinidad 2018, p. 71; Trinidad's italics; he says much the same on his p. 209.
[3] Rosalyn Higgins, *Problems & Process: International Law and How We Use it*, Oxford 1994, p. 127.
[4] Trinidad 2018, p. 149.
[5] We are grateful to Professor Peter Willetts for his assistance in clarifying technical points connected with the C24. Any remaining errors are entirely our own.

with the UN's categorisation of them as a colony", and he refers to "the fiction of the archipelago as an integral part of Argentina"[1] – an accurate description, but rare from an Argentine writer.

Argentina's worries soon faded. On 27 November 1961 UN Resolution 1654 (XVI) set up a Special Committee of 17 UN member countries to investigate and report on progress towards decolonisation as demanded by Resolution 1514. Seven more countries were added by Resolution 1810 (XVII) of 17 December 1962, which brought the number to 24. Significantly, though, paragraph 6 of Resolution 1810, referring to the "Declaration on Decolonization", i.e. Resolution 1514 of 14 December 1960 (see section 10.8), states that the UN General Assembly:[2]

[Resolution 1810] 6) *Urges* all administering Powers to take immediate steps in order that all colonial territories and peoples may accede to independence without delay in accordance with the provisions of paragraph 5 of the Declaration.

Resolution 1810 mentions only paragraph 5 of Resolution 1514, which is abundantly clear:

[Resolution 1514] 5) Immediate steps shall be taken, in Trust and Non-Self-Governing Territories or all other territories which have not yet attained independence, to transfer all powers to the peoples of those territories, without any conditions or reservations, in accordance with their freely expressed will and desire, without any distinction as to race, creed or colour, in order to enable them to enjoy complete independence and freedom.

That paragraph lays down that "all powers" shall be transferred to the peoples of "Trust and Non-Self-Governing Territories or all other territories which have not yet attained independence" (thus including the Falklands), and that it shall occur "without any conditions or reservations, in accordance with their freely expressed will and desire" – as we pointed out in section 10.8, paragraph 5 of Resolution 1514 unambiguously gives Falkland Islanders the full right of external self-determination and rules out an Argentine takeover of the islands. In referring specifically to that paragraph two years later in Resolution 1810, which increased the membership of the Special Committee to 24, the UN General Assembly expressly confirmed the direction in which the C24 was to go. Sadly, in the case of the Falklands it has actually gone in the opposite direction.

Since 1962 the decolonisation committee has been known as the "Committee of 24" or "C24", though the membership now (2022) stands at 29;[3] its purpose is related to that of the UN's Fourth Committee, though the two are distinct. The C24 holds seminars in various places, which have included several non-self-governing territories (though never the Falklands or Gibraltar); it meets in June in New York to hear presentations from "petitioners", some of whom represent non-self-governing territories; the others always include some from Argentina. The Committee produces a yearly report to the UN General Assembly in November or December.

For the first three years of the C24, Argentine representatives made only the same brief statements as in the years from 1946, until in September 1964 Argentina made its first detailed presentation on the Falklands (section 10.14). Since then its diplomatic activity has greatly increased – in *MGSS* the topic of the Falklands fills only 7 pages in 1963, but 102 pages in 1964.[4]

That increase in activity from 1964 inaugurated a new stridency in Argentina's presentation of its Falklands claim at the UN. It was possible largely thanks to Carlos María Velázquez (Uruguay's UN ambassador 1962-5), a strong supporter of Argentina's claim. On 25 February 1964, at the

---

[1] Martín Abel González, *The Genesis of the Falklands (Malvinas) Conflict...*, Basingstoke 2013, pp. 20, 28, 32. Sadly, González died aged 37, with his twin brother Ariel, an Argentine diplomat, in a tragic accident on 4-5 August 2011 caused by a carbon monoxide leak.

[2] Report of the 1195th session of the UN General Assembly, p. 73, from the UN website; italics in original.

[3] The current 29 members of the Committee of 24 are (2022): Antigua and Barbuda, Bolivia, Chile, China, Congo, Côte d'Ivoire, Cuba, Dominica, Ecuador, Ethiopia, Fiji, Grenada, India, Indonesia, Iran, Iraq, Mali, Nicaragua, Papua New Guinea, Russia, Saint Kitts and Nevis, Saint Lucia, Saint Vincent and the Grenadines, Sierra Leone, Syria, Tanzania, Timor-Leste, Tunisia and Venezuela. Of its members, 6 are Spanish-speaking (Bolivia, Chile, Cuba, Ecuador, Nicaragua and Venezuela), while 11 mostly small members belong to the Commonwealth (Antigua and Barbuda, Dominica, Fiji, Grenada, India, Papua New Guinea, Saint Kitts and Nevis, Saint Lucia, Saint Vincent and the Grenadines, Sierra Leone and Tanzania). Several (China, Congo, Cuba, Iran, Iraq, Mali, Russia, Venezuela) are not exactly models of democratic governance.

[4] *MGSS* vol. I, pp. 119-125 (for 1963); pp. 129-230 (for 1964).

C24's first meeting that year, Velázquez was elected First Vice-Chairman and became a prime mover in the Committee. On that day the Committee decided to divide the non-self-governing territories into three groups, with a special Sub-Committee of the C24 responsible for each; the territories in the Americas fell under Sub-Committee III.[1] And the chairman of Sub-Committee III was none other than Carlos María Velázquez. He was thus able to focus support for Argentina's Falklands claim.

The importance of Velázquez's support was underlined by the Argentine diplomat Dr Lucio García del Solar at a seminar entitled "The Role of the Falkland Islanders in the Dispute Over Sovereignty with the Argentine Republic" at St. Antony's College, Oxford, on 25 May 1993, which Peter Pepper attended. Argentina's new strategy naturally breached the remit of the C24, which was to *promote* self-determination, not to *abolish* it, but thanks to Velázquez Argentina was able to go ahead and has pursued its colonialist agenda at the C24 ever since – it has presented its territorial ambitions under the guise of decolonisation.

In pursuit of its aim of taking the Falklands over, Argentina has misused and disregarded not only UN Resolutions 1514 and 1541 (see sections 10.8, 10.9), but also Resolution 2625 and the UN's International Covenant on Civil and Political Rights, ICCPR (see sections 10.18, 10.17).

10.12 The Falklands at the UN, II: Britain's and Argentina's statements, 8 September 1964

At the UN in 1964, decisively assisted by Carlos María Velázquez (sections 8.11, 10.11), Argentina made important progress in gathering international support for its ambition to take the Falklands over, in direct opposition to the purpose of United Nations Resolutions 1514 and 1541 and of the C24 (the decolonisation committee).

The 19th session of the United Nations (1964-5) was anomalous since the UN was suffering a financial crisis due to the refusal of a number of countries to pay their contributions. Some countries were two years in arrears, which meant that under Article 19 of the UN Charter they lost their right to vote. To avoid a confrontation, and while discussions were held on resolving the crisis, it was agreed that no contentious votes would be taken during the session.[2] That is reflected in the number of "Resolutions and Decisions adopted" by the UN in the 19th session, which was only a tenth of the average number at that time,[3] and the reports of the sessions of the C24 jump a year and three quarters from 13 December 1963 to 22 September 1965.[4] That also explains the hiatus between the presentation of a draft resolution on the Falklands on 18 September 1964 (see section 10.14) and the actual vote on what became Resolution 2065 (XX) on 16 December 1965 (section 10.15).

The first session of the C24 in 1964 began unremarkably enough, with an opening statement on 25 February 1964 by its chairman, Sori Coulibaly of Mali. He briefly described the role of the C24, as reported in the UN's official summary of his speech:[5]

In… the small, sparsely populated Territories, the Special Committee could help the administering Powers in overcoming many difficulties to the extent that the real and sincere objectives of those Powers was [*sic*] to lead the peoples under their administration to independence… Under the provisions of the United Nations Charter and the Universal Declaration of Human Rights, the international community could not remain indifferent to the tragic fate of millions of people deprived of their inalienable rights. He therefore appealed again to the colonial Powers to co-operate sincerely with the Special Committee, so that the latter might be in a position to submit to the General Assembly at its nineteenth session a complete report, including recommendations regarding the accession to independence of every colonial Territory in conformity with the wishes of the populations concerned.

Coulibaly thus underlined the central purpose of the decolonisation committee: to lead every

---

[1] UN document A/5800/Rev.1, Annex 8, p. 18, paragraph 109.
[2] For clarification on this point we are grateful to Professor Peter Willetts.
[3] The numbers of "Resolutions and Decisions adopted" on the UN website in the mid-1960s are: 17th session (1962-3): 137; 18th session (1963-4): 134; 19th session (1964-5): 14; 20th session (1965-6): 165: 21st session (1966-7): 154.
[4] The series of reports on the sessions of the C24 jumps from the 1515th meeting (13 December 1963, UN doc. A/C.4/SR.1515), to the 1516th meeting (22 September 1965, UN doc. A/C.4/SR.1516); the intervening meetings are recorded in UN doc. A/5800/Rev.1, Annex 8.
[5] UN doc. A/5800/Rev.1, Annex 8, p. 6, paragraph 16.

colonial territory to independence "in conformity with the wishes of the populations concerned".

Sadly though, the committee's debates on the Falklands that year took a very different direction, and ended in a blatant breach of the committee's remit. Those debates took place in the newly-established Sub-Committee III (covering territories in the Americas), whose chairman was Carlos María Velázquez. Its debates were summarised in a UN report, document A/5800,[1] which reveals how the C24 was "hijacked" by Argentina into denying the Falkland Islanders' right to external self-determination and instead supporting Argentina's colonialist aim of taking the islands over. The debates were a one-sided "dialogue of the deaf" – the British delegation refuted several of Argentina's assertions with factual statistics, but the Argentine side completely ignored the British corrections and presented its own untrue statements, of which one, by José María Ruda, has had an influence entirely out of keeping with its total incompetence (section 10.14).

The national delegations to Sub-Committee III had submitted written statements of their positions, and debates on the Falklands began on 8 September 1964 with a statement by the deputy head of the British UN delegation, Cecil King, who said that in the British government's view:[2]

10. It was for the Islanders to determine what their ultimate constitutional status should be… the Islanders had made it clear that they did not want independence… the people of the Islands… had expressed their desire to retain and strengthen their links with the United Kingdom. They had asserted in the strongest possible terms that any constitutional association with a foreign Power would be repugnant to them…

11. Consequently, the United Kingdom Government's position with regard to the Falkland Islands was fully consistent with the principle of self-determination.… The claim advanced by the Argentine Government to sovereignty over the Falklands Islands [*sic*] was in effect a bid to annex those islands in defiance of the clearly expressed wishes and interests of the people of the Territory. According to the United Nations Charter and the Declaration on the Granting of Independence to Colonial Countries and Peoples, those wishes and interests should be paramount. In the view of his Government, the Special Committee and therefore the Sub-Committee were not competent to discuss territorial claims. … It might be suggested… that paragraph 6 of the Declaration in resolution 1514 (XV) constituted a mandate for the Committee to consider questions of sovereignty. But, in his delegation's view, that interpretation was not borne out either by the wording of the paragraph itself, which clearly referred to possible attempts at disruption in the future and not to issues of sovereignty dating back to distant history, or by the remainder of the Declaration, which stated specifically that "all peoples have the right to self-determination". No fairminded observer could therefore construe paragraph 6 as imposing a limitation on the universal application of the principle of self-determination, which was guaranteed under the Charter itself.

That statement was entirely in line with the UN's aim of bringing independence to non-self-governing territories according to their peoples' wishes under resolutions 1514 and 1541 (see sections 10.8, 10.9). However, what actually happened was far removed from that aim.

10.13 Amateur Argentine invasions of the Falklands: Miguel Fitzgerald, 8 September 1964

By coincidence, on the very day on which Sub-Committee III of the C24 started discussing the Falklands in New York, 8 September 1964, there occurred the first "amateur invasion" of the islands. At various times since then, private individuals in Argentina have staged further "amateur invasions", all of which were deliberately unfriendly, and several were positively dangerous, though to date (2022) no one has been killed. There have been over a dozen such invasions; they are just one aspect of the bizarre nature of the Argentine claim to the islands. We have no room here to recount them all, but the first three came just as Argentina was escalating its Falklands claim at the United Nations, so we shall briefly mention them here and in section 10.19.

The first one was mounted by Miguel Lawler Fitzgerald (1926-2010), a first-generation Argentinian whose parents had both been born in Ireland. On 8 September 1964 (his 38th birthday) he flew across from Argentina and landed on Stanley racecourse in a single-engined Cessna 185

---

[1] UN document A/5800/Rev.1, Annex 8, all in reported speech and past tenses; it prints the C24's final discussions and conclusions first (pp. 434-9), then the Sub-Committee's long report (pp. 439-49), with the same conclusions at the end.
[2] UN document A/5800/Rev.l, Annex 8, p. 440, paras. 10-11; substance briefly repeated on p. 449, paras. 117, 118; speech partly quoted in *Falkland Islands Monthly Review* (*FIMR*), Stanley 5 October 1964, p. 4.

provocatively named "Don Luis Vernet".[1] He had with him an oddly-phrased declaration that he had composed in English (his native language was Spanish), which he handed to Falkland Islander Jim Shirtcliffe before flying back to Argentina. It was printed a month later in the *Falkland Islands Monthly Review*.[2] In it Fitzgerald said "Today my country, awakened from a long sleep, conscious of her moral and material grandeur, has decided to recuperate [*sic*] her island territory", but in saying his country had "awakened from a long sleep" he unwittingly conceded that Argentina had acquiesced in Britain's possession of the islands. If a country falls into a "long sleep" on a territorial claim, it will find when it awakes that its claim has lapsed.

10.14 The Falklands at the UN, III: José María Ruda's erroneous speech, 9 September 1964

The next day, 9 September 1964, the Argentine UN ambassador, Dr José María Ruda,[3] made a speech to Sub-Committee III of the C24 on the Argentine claim to the Falklands. It ran to over 8,100 words (four times as long as later Argentine speeches) and has come to be called "El Alegato Ruda" ["The Ruda Statement"]. It was riddled with errors – in fact it would be hard to beat for sheer concentrated inaccuracy – but its erroneous account of the history of the Falklands has become the standard Argentine version, the basis of all Argentine presentations to the UN, and of UN Resolution 2065 of 1965 (see section 10.15). It has often been reprinted,[4] most recently by the Argentine government in 2014 to commemorate the 50th anniversary of its delivery (below).

In brief, its (incorrect) central argumentation ran in its own wording as follows:[5]

… the islands in question are an integral part of Argentine territory… Under the threats of its guns, the British fleet evicted a peaceful and active Argentine population that was exercising the legitimate rights that the Argentine Republic possessed as the Heir of Spain. The British… lowered the Argentine flag and by force, occupied Port Soledad… Almost all the Argentine inhabitants were then evicted… this act of force, this arbitrary and unilateral act was never and shall never be consented to by the Argentine Republic; and… it cannot generate nor create any rights for Great Britain… the rest of the settlers who resisted the invaders, were taken and sent to London for trial under different pretexts and never returned… The Malvinas Islands are in a different situation from that of the classical colonial case. De facto and de jure, they belonged to the Argentine Republic in 1833 and were governed by Argentine authorities and occupied by Argentine settlers. These authorities and these settlers were evicted by violence and not allowed to remain in the territory. On the contrary, they were replaced, during those 131 years of usurpation, by a colonial administration and a population of British origin. … it is basically a temporary population that occupies the land and one that cannot be used by the colonial power to claim the right to apply the principle of self-determination… the territory… has been wrested – against the will of its inhabitants – by an act of force… without there being any subsequent international agreement to validate the de facto situation…

Virtually every word of that is untrue, as anyone will know who has read this book this far, but it has been repeated again and again by Argentine speakers and writers, including of course Kohen and Rodríguez, and for example by Argentine foreign minister Jorge Marcelo Faurie, who said at

---

[1] Information from entry on Fitzgerald by Edmundo Murray in *DFB*; account of Fitzgerald's flight by Alberto Fernandez D [*sic*] in *FIJ* 2012, p. 249.
[2] *FIMR*, Stanley 5 October 1964, pp. 1-3.
[3] José María Ruda (1924-94), member of the United Nations International Law Commission, 1964-72; Argentine UN ambassador, 1966-70; judge at the International Court of Justice (ICJ), 1973-91, and President of the ICJ, 1988-91. But he was not a historian, hence his many historical errors.
[4] Full text e.g. in *MGSS* vol. I, pp. 197-217, and in José Muñoz Azpiri, *Historia Completa de las Malvinas*, Buenos Aires 1966, vol. II, pp. 446-469, and in English (in facsimile from the UN English translation) in Raphael Perl, *The Falkland Islands Dispute in International Law and Politics*, London / Rome / New York 1983, pp. 351-372; most of text (in English) in Rudolf Dolzer, *Der völkerrechtliche Status der Falkland-Inseln (Malvinas)…* ["The international-law status of the Falkland Islands (Malvinas)…"], Heidelberg 1986, pp. 161-176, and its English translation, *The Territorial Status of the Falkland Islands (Malvinas)…*, New York / London / Rome 1993, pp. 223-235, from UN Doc. A/AC 109/106, dated 13 November 1964; full text also in Manuel Pedro Peña, *Malvinas: Mito y Realidad…*, Buenos Aires April 2016, pp- 381-404, and in English in Manuel Pedro Peña and Juan Angél Peña, *Falklands or Malvinas: Myths & Facts*, Sevilla (Spain) 2018, pp. 306-325 (see section 8.11); UN summary in UN document A/5800/Rev.l, Annex 8, pp. 440-442, paras. 15-34.
[5] Extracts from UN text from Perl 1983, pp. 363, 364, 368; also in Dolzer 1993, pp. 230, 233, 234.

the C24 on 20 June 2018:[1]

... the dispute had originated in the disruption of Argentina's territorial integrity in 1833, when the United Kingdom had occupied the islands, expelling both the Argentine population and the legitimate Argentine authorities. It had then populated the territory with its own settlers and impeded the settlement of Argentine citizens.

The assertions of Ruda, Faurie and other Argentine writers and speakers are untrue. It is not true that the Falklands "are an integral part of Argentine territory", nor that they "De facto and de jure… belonged to the Argentine Republic in 1833" – only Argentine national law treated them as belonging to Argentina, and they were not Argentine territory in international law. The islands were not "occupied by Argentine settlers" – the settlers were of several nationalities (of 37 civilian residents of Port Louis on 1 January 1833, only 10 were Argentinian, and only 2 of them were taken away, see section 6.24 and Tables 6.24c, 6.24d), and the British did not occupy Port Louis but sailed away. There were no "Argentine authorities" present – that phrase suggests the presence of a proper government, with a full government structure, administrative organs, etc., but there was no such thing – the only authority was exercised in emergency by José María Pinedo as the highest-ranking military officer present; there was no government as such at all. Above all, Britain did not "expel the Argentine population", though Ruda asserted five times that they did (Table 10.14a, below), and has been followed by many Argentine authors and politicians[2] – in fact the civilians were not removed by Britain but by Louis Vernet and by the United States, as explained in sections 6.9 and 6.12. Only the murderous garrison was expelled, and the civilian residents of Port Louis were no doubt relieved to see them depart. The garrison had terrorised and robbed them, and a third of the civilians fled for their lives from the rampaging Argentine soldiers – it is nonsense to say Britain expelled "a peaceful and active Argentine population". The territory was not "wrested – against the will of its inhabitants" – in fact the gauchos would gladly have served "under any Englishman whom the Government may please to appoint"[3] (sections 6.19, 6.25). And Britain did not impede the settlement of Argentinians – in the 1840s at least 17 Argentinians settled in the islands (section 10.1), and there are Argentinians living in the islands today (section 10.4).

Taken together, Ruda's statements constitute the Argentine case for possession of the Falklands, but as we have made abundantly clear, they are untrue – Britain did *not* expel the Argentine population; Britain did *not* replace the Argentine population with British subjects; the present population was *not* implanted by Britain; there *was* an "international agreement to validate the <u>de facto</u> situation" (the 1850 Convention of Peace); Argentina *did* accept Britain's possession of the islands and *did* cease to protest; Argentina's claim is no more imprescriptible than Britain's; the Falkland Islanders are *not* a temporary population but by 1964 had been in the islands for 120 years; Britain's possession of the Falklands does *not* violate the territorial integrity of Argentina since the islands are not Argentine territory, and Britain did *not* seize South Georgia and the South Sandwich Islands from Argentina. Two of Ruda's untrue statements have been repeated particularly often in Argentine books and at the United Nations: no. 4 (that Britain expelled the Argentine population in 1833) and no. 11 (that the present Falkland Islanders are a temporary population; the term used at the UN has usually been "transient", which is equally untrue, see section 10.15). And Table 10.14a is not exhaustive; there were many more historical errors in Ruda's speech.[4]

---

[1] Text from report, "Argentina Reiterates Validity of Claims to Falklands/Malvinas Islands", on website https://www.indepthnews.net/index.php/global-governance/un-insider.

[2] For example, this false assertion was also made at the UN by Argentine foreign minister Dr Nicanor Costa Méndez before the UN Security Council on 3 April 1982 (Perl 1983, p. 433) and by Argentine foreign minister Dr Jorge Taiana before the C24 on 12 June 2008 (text on the website of Argentina's Permanent Mission to the United Nations).

[3] Colonel Belford Hinton Wilson, report of 24 January 1833 in PRO CO 78/1, fol. 212 *recto*.

[4] In all, Ruda's speech contained about 70 historical errors of various kinds. As well as those listed in Table 10.14a, some other errors were e.g.: that Britain "took" St. Helena in 1815 (it was 1659); that Bougainville found Port Egmont and called it « Port de la Croisade » (he did not); that the USS *Lexington* visited the Falklands in May 1831 (it was December); that knowledge of the existence of the Falklands was uncertain in Britain until the mid-18th century (it was not); that 17th and 18th century Anglo-Spanish treaties excluded Britain from the Falklands (they did not); and that in 1820 David Jewett announced that Argentine fishing regulations would apply in the islands (he did not).

Ruda repeated some of his false assertions several times. Table 10.14a lists the more important of them; the number in brackets at right indicates how many times he stated each one.

Table 10.14a Concentrated inaccuracy: José María Ruda's principal errors at the UN, 9 September 1964.

1. That only Spain reserved its sovereignty in the Anglo-Spanish agreeement of 22 January 1771;   (6)
2. That the Nootka Sound Convention of 1790 prohibited British settlement in the Falklands;   (1)
3. That Argentina put a governor in the Falklands in 1823;   (1)
4. That Britain expelled the Argentine population from the Falklands in 1833;   (5)
5. That the Argentine inhabitants resisted the British "invaders";   (2)
6. That Britain replaced the Argentine inhabitants with British subjects;   (2)
7. That there has been no international agreement to confirm Britain's possession of the Falklands;   (1)
8. That Argentina has never accepted Britain's possession of the Falklands;   (3)
9. That Argentina has never ceased to protest at Britain's possession of the Falklands;   (6)
10. That Argentina's claim is imprescriptible, i.e. eternal unless freely given up;   (2)
11. That the present Falkland Islanders are a temporary population;   (2)
12. That Britain's possession of the Falklands violates the territorial integrity of Argentina;   (4)
13. That Britain seized South Georgia and the South Sandwich Islands by force from Argentina.   (2)

But it would be wrong to accuse Ruda of deliberately misleading the United Nations. Neither he nor anyone else at that time was in possession of the facts, since they had never been published. Ruda simply said what was (wrongly) believed in Argentina at the time, but Argentine researchers were already at work in the Archivo General de la Nación in Buenos Aires and in the Public Record Office in London, copying documents for publication. Those documents invalidated much of what Ruda said, and some were published in Fitte 1966 and 1968 and in *Episodio Ocurrido* 1967, but too late for the UN debates in 1965, so UN Resolution 2065 (see section 10.15) was passed as a result of false evidence submitted by Argentina in 1964. The excuse that the truth had not been published disappeared after the publication of the documentation, but Argentina continued to present the same false evidence in later debates (section 10.24), and still does so today.

From 2011 we worked for some time analysing and refuting Ruda's errors, and in May 2012 we placed on the Internet a 10-page paper in English and Spanish, entitled *False Falklands History at the United Nations: How Argentina misled the UN in 1964 – and still does / Historia falsa sobre las Falklands/Malvinas ante la Organización de las Naciones Unidas: Cómo la Argentina engañó a la ONU en 1964 – y sigue haciéndolo*. In that paper we listed Ruda's major errors (much as in Table 10.14a), and refuted them with extensive documentary evidence. We have reason to believe that the Argentine government was well aware of our paper, but chose to ignore the truth and instead to propagate Ruda's historical untruths: a ceremony was held at the Argentine foreign ministry on 4 September 2014 to commemorate the 50th anniversary of Ruda's speech: Argentine foreign minister Héctor Timerman and ex-senator Daniel Filmus, head of the "Secretaría de Asuntos Relativos a las Islas Malvinas" ["Secretariat for Affairs Relative to the Malvinas Islands"], presented a 50-page pamphlet in Spanish and English, entitled "*Soberanía Argentina en Malvinas a 50 años del "Alegato Ruda" / Argentine Sovereignty over Malvinas 50 years after the Ruda Statement*, also on the website of the Argentine foreign ministry press office, http://www. cancilleria.gov.ar/userfiles/ alegato_ruda. pdf. It reprints the whole of Ruda's speech (with all his errors of course), and Timerman repeated some of them in his introductory speech, including the untrue assertions that the British expelled the Argentine population and that Argentina has never ceased to protest. Against such high-power repetition of errors, the truth has a hard struggle.

On 10 September 1964, the day after Ruda's speech, "The Chairman, speaking as the representative of Uruguay" (i.e. Carlos María Velázquez) supported Argentina's line.[1] He maintained that the "*uti possidetis* principle of 1810" meant that there were no territories in the Americas that were *res nullius* (for the untruth of that, see sections 1.7, 4.8 and chapter 3), and

---
[1] UN document A/5800/Rev.l, Annex 8, pp. 442-3, paras. 35-57.

claimed, as his central assertions, that:

> 53. ... the strict application of the principle of self-determination... would place the fate of the territories in question in the hands of a small group of settlers brought in by the conquering Power... Those considerations were particularly true in the case of the Malvinas, which had been originally uninhabited and where the present population came almost entirely from the mother country and fluctuated with the seasons.
>
> 54. Paragraph 6 of resolution 1514 (XV) had made the American doctrine of "occupied territories" universal by drawing the same distinction as did the doctrine between colonies or possessions, to which the principle of self-determination applied, and *de facto* occupied territories, whose situation should be governed by the procedures of pacific settlement provided for by the Charter and other international instruments...

His assertion that the islands' "present population came almost entirely from the mother country and fluctuated with the seasons" was of course untrue (sections 10.1, 10.4), and was refuted by the British representative in a later session of Sub-Committee III (below). Velázquez's interpretation of paragraph 6 of UN resolution 1514 was entirely fallacious – that paragraph only prohibited future dismemberments of colonial territories in the course of decolonisation, and did not introduce a distinction between colonies subject to self-determination and what he called "de facto occupied territories" (section 10.8). Nevertheless, his false assertions formed the basis for UN resolution 2065 (section 10.15). Velázquez worked his speech up into an academic article tailor-made to support Argentina's claim to the Falklands, which was later published in a learned journal.[1]

The Venezuelan delegate to Sub-Committee III supported Argentina here as elsewhere:[2]

> 84. ... In the case of an uninhabited territory or one in which the original population had been expelled, sovereignty should be restored to the State which had exercised it and from which it had been taken away by force. From the legal point of view, usurped sovereignty could not be restored to a minority of settlers or to an imported population.

The Venezuelan had swallowed the myths that the population of the islands had been expelled (see sections 6.24, 6.25); that the islands had been Argentine territory (which had never been accepted by any country except Argentina), and that the Falkland Islanders were "an imported population".

Towards the end of Sub-Committee III's discussions, the British representative Cecil King made some telling comments and refutations of Argentina's assertions:[3]

> 104. The representative of the United Kingdom in reply, said that while his delegation... could not recognize the competence of the Sub-Committee to consider the question of sovereignty over the Falkland Islands..., he wished to correct a number of misconceptions about conditions in the Islands...
>
> 105. The Argentine representative had suggested that the status of the Falkland Islands as a British colony was an anachronism; the Sub-Committee might consider whether it was the United Kingdom Government's clearly stated policy of allowing the Falkland Islanders to choose their constitutional future or the Argentine Government's desire to annex a small Territory against the wishes of its inhabitants that was more in keeping with modern thought...
>
> 106. The people of the Islands were not temporary settlers; 80 per cent of the resident population in 1962 had been born in the Islands, and many of them could trace their roots there for more than a century...
>
> 109. His delegation could not agree with the interpretation placed upon paragraph 6 of the Declaration on the granting of independence to colonial countries and peoples by the representative of Uruguay... That paragraph was clearly an injunction to all countries to take no action in the future which would result in splitting existing territories or States or would infringe their sovereignty in a manner inconsistent with the Charter, especially Article 2. There was no justification for regarding the paragraph as a limitation on the principle of self-determination set out in paragraph 2 of the Declaration...
>
> 110. ... Argentina had not continually protested since 1833, as stated by its representative, but had remained silent for periods of up to thirty-five years...

He thus refuted three of Argentina's central contentions: (1) that the population of the Falklands was transient; (2) that paragraph 6 of resolution 1514 could be applied to past history so as to limit

---

[1] Carlos María Velázquez, "Some Legal Aspects of the Colonial Problem in Latin America", printed in *The Annals of the American Academy of Political and Social Science*, Philadelphia July 1965, pp. 111-119.
[2] UN document A/5800/Rev.1, Annex 8, p. 446, para. 84.
[3] UN document A/5800/Rev.1, Annex 8, p. 448, paras. 104-106; 109-110.

the right to self-determination; and (3) that Argentina had never ceased to protest against Britain's possession of the islands. But his factual corrections to Argentina's account were ignored.

Instead, on 18 September 1964 the members of Sub-Committee III discussed some "conclusions and recommendations" to be presented to the whole C24. They had been drafted in all essentials by Carlos María Velázquez, and included the following operative paragraphs:[1]

(c) The Sub-Committee notes the existence of a dispute between the Government of the United Kingdom and that of Argentina concerning sovereignty over the Falkland Islands (otherwise known as the Malvinas Islands);

(d) The Sub-Committee recommends that the Special Committee should invite the Governments of the United Kingdom and Argentina to enter into negotiations with a view to finding a peaceful solution to this problem, bearing in mind the provisions and objectives of the United Nations Charter and of Resolution 1514 (XV), the interests of the population of the islands, and the opinions expressed during the course of the general debate;

(e) The Sub-Committee recommends that the Special Committee should invite the two above-mentioned Governments to inform the Special Committee or the General Assembly of the results of their negotiations.

A year later those recommendations became draft resolution A/C.4/L.802, which was introduced into the whole C24 by the Venezuelan delegate Leonardo Díaz González on 15 November 1965, and in due course became Resolution 2065, passed by the UN General Assembly on 16 December 1965 (section 10.15).

On 13 November 1964 the whole C24 considered Britain's report on the territory, supplied under Resolution 1541 and Article 73e of the UN Charter.[2] Cecil King stated yet again that Britain:[3]

29. ... considered that the Special Committee [i.e. the whole C24] was not empowered by its terms of reference to consider territorial claims or disputes over territory, and it would therefore not regard itself as bound by any recommendations of the Committee on those subjects...

30. Where the future of the islands was concerned, his Government would be guided by what it regarded as the interests of the Falkland Islanders themselves, as required by Article 73e of the Charter.

Britain thus kept strictly and correctly within the limits of the C24's remit.

But the head of the Argentine delegation to the C24, Lucio García del Solar, wound up the debate, and made a brief but typical statement of Argentina's position:[4]

32. ... The problem had arisen from an act of military force by the United Kingdom in 1833 against a part of the Territory of Argentina... following which the Argentina [sic] authorities and inhabitants had been expelled from the islands and later replaced by settlers from the United Kingdom. The... United Kingdom could invoke no international instrument giving it any rights over the Malvinas Islands... . Argentina had never ceased to press its claim for reparation of the injury done to it, which no lapse of time could validate. [...]

36. ... since the Islanders were not the original inhabitants, but had simply replaced those expelled by force, paragraph 5 of General Assembly resolution 1514 (XV) could not be blindly applied, and the terms of paragraph 6 must be taken into account.

In referring to the Argentine "authorities" who had been expelled in January 1833, García del Solar implied that there had been a settled, stable government, but that was far from the truth – in fact there had only been a violent, murderous garrison who had terrified, traumatised and robbed the civilian inhabitants, and there had been no government as such at all; emergency authority was being exercised by Pinedo, but there was no government structure whatever.

Everything else del Solar said was untrue too: the Falklands had never been internationally recognised as a part of Argentina (see chapter 3 and sections 5.5, 6.3, 6.10); the civilian Argentine inhabitants were not expelled by Britain but were removed by Louis Vernet in 1831 and by the

---

[1] UN document A/5800/Rev.1, Annex 8, at end of Sub-Committee III report, p. 449, para. 121; repeated (with slight changes) in report of whole C24, in *ibid.*, p. 439, para. 59.
[2] UN document A/5800/Rev.1, Annex 8, pp. 434-436, paragraphs 1-25.
[3] UN document A/5800/Rev.1, Annex 8, p. 436, paras. 29, 30.
[4] UN document A/5800/Rev.1, Annex 8, pp. 436-7, para. 32.

United States in 1832, including a group of black African slaves (6.9, 6.24, 6.25); the 37 civilian settlers on 1 January 1833 were not all Argentinians but were of 12 different nationalities including Argentinian, Brazilian, British, Chilean, German and Uruguayan; there were 11 Uruguayans but only 10 Argentinians, of whom only 2 were taken away (Table 6.24d). All were temporary inhabitants since there had been a constant turnover of population (5.1, 5.16), and by January 1833 not a single inhabitant had been in the islands as long as five years (Table 6.24c); most had only been there for a couple of years. No inhabitants were replaced by settlers from Britain, and later settlers were from many countries including Argentina (10.1); the United Kingdom can indeed invoke an international instrument giving it rights over the Malvinas (the 1850 Convention of Peace; sections 7.10-7.14); Argentina did cease to press its claim (7.15, 7.19), and that claim was not imprescriptible (8.11), so Britain's title to the islands was indeed validated by Argentina's inaction and actions during the lapse of time since then, because Argentina ceased to protest and made top-level statements that there was no Falklands dispute with Britain (7.19, 8.18).

García del Solar also said in his paragraph 36 that paragraph 5 of Resolution 1514 "could not be blindly applied" since (he claimed) the Falkland Islanders had "simply replaced those expelled by force". That was of course untrue (sections 6.21-6.25), though the details were as yet unknown at the United Nations. But it was just one of many cases in which Argentina attempted to construct a link between the purported "replacement" of the population and paragraph 6 of Resolution 1514, which Argentina claimed (and still claims) was relevant to the Falklands, though many authorities deny that it is (section 10.8). In any case, paragraph 5 of Resolution 1514 leaves no doubt as to its universal applicability – it says that "Immediate steps shall be taken" in all non-independent territories "to transfer all powers to the peoples of those territories, without any conditions or reservations, in accordance with their freely expressed will and desire…". That text is absolute and all-embracing; it rules out García del Solar's attempt to limit its applicability. And as mentioned above (section 10.11), in UN Resolution 1810 of 17 December 1962 the UN General Assembly enjoined all powers administering non-independent territories to apply paragraph 5 of Resolution 1514, and made no mention of paragraph 6.

Argentina's false characterisation of the present population of the Falklands as "transient" or "temporary" was echoed by several delegations despite Cecil King's refutation of that description on 10 September 1964 (above) and his clear statement that "The people of the Islands were not temporary settlers; 80 per cent of the resident population in 1962 had been born in the Islands, and many of them could trace their roots there for more than a century." Thus the Italian delegate said:[1]

60… his delegation felt that the national origin of the islanders and the annual or seasonal fluctuations in the population gave rise to serious doubts as to whether the principle of self-determination could be strictly applied.

And the delegate from the Ivory Coast said:

65… It was tempting, in view of all the colonialist abuses that had been observed, to seek to apply the Declaration on the granting of independence to colonial countries and peoples strictly to the letter. But, in the case of the Falkland Islands, the territory was almost empty of permanent settlers…

As we said in section 10.12, the C24 debates were a one-sided "dialogue of the deaf"; Britain's factual refutations of Argentina's assertions went completely ignored.

Where political interests were concerned, the truth of history, the factual state of the territory and the wording of UN resolutions did not matter. The Sub-Committee, and after it the whole C24, was "hijacked" by Argentina, with the connivance of Uruguay, into following Argentina's line, that it was time for Britain and Argentina to start negotiating on the islands' future. That could only mean negotiating a transfer of sovereignty to Argentina, which was the ultimate aim of UN Resolution 2065.

---

[1] Quotes from the Italian and Ivorian delegates from UN document A/5800, p. 444.

10.15 UN Resolution 2065 (XX), 16 December 1965; Bonifacio del Carril's specious theory

As related in section 10.11, Carlos María Velázquez, the Second Vice-Chairman of the UN decolonisation committee (the C24) from 1964, and chairman of Sub-Committee III which dealt with territories in the Americas, bent the rules and flouted the Committee's remit. The C24's remit is of course to *promote* self-determination for the peoples of all non-self-governing territories, not to *abolish* it, but since 1964 Argentina has been allowed to present false versions of the history of the Falklands as justification for taking over the islands against the wishes of their inhabitants, thus *depriving* them of self-determination.

After the anomalous 19th session of the United Nations in 1964-5, during which no contentious votes were taken (section 10.12), the 20th session of the UN began in September 1965, with long speeches to the General Assembly by several national representatives ranking from presidents down to mere delegates. On 27 September 1965 the General Assembly was addressed by President Habib Bourguiba of Tunisia, by ambassador David of Czechoslovakia, and finally by foreign minister Miguel Ángel Zavala Ortiz of Argentina, who of course mentioned Argentina's Falklands claim. He repeated some of the central untruths in Argentina's version of what he called:[1]

    151. ... the case of our Malvinas Islands. There, the United Kingdom of Great Britain and Northern Ireland is illegally administering an integral part of our national territory, which it occupied by violence after it had evicted the Argentine authorities peacefully exercising the right of sovereignty there as the indisputable heirs to the territorial rights of the Spanish mother country.

    152. ... the Malvinas Islands never formed part of the territory of the United Kingdom. Nor can they ever have constituted a colony, in the conventional sense of the term, since no legal rights could be created which would give validity to occupation of the Islands or affect Argentina's right to the restoration of its territorial integrity.

    153. In these circumstances, there is no legal basis for speaking of self-determination;... it is a pre-condition of self-determination that it takes place in one's own territory and not in territory obtained by dispossessing others. To allow the future of the Malvinas archipelago to be decided by those occupying it would mean leaving it in the hands of people who were placed there by the United Kingdom. It would mean leaving it exclusively to the United Kingdom to resolve the problem. It would be as if one were to allow a person who had dispossessed another to confirm his own rights of ownership. For, clearly, the settlers are representatives of British power. Why so? Simply because Britain drove out the original population, replaced it and isolated the Islands. It fenced them off from the world. It placed them out of bounds, behind a British padlock.

The only true part of that statement is that the Falklands never formed part of the United Kingdom.

The rest of it is nonsense. It is not true that the Falklands are an integral part of Argentine territory, as we have demonstrated in this book, and it is absurd to say that Britain "evicted the Argentine authorities peacefully exercising the right of sovereignty there" – the mutinous Argentine garrison had murdered their commanding officer in cold blood and had robbed and terrorised the civilian inhabitants, whom Britain encouraged to remain. And as we pointed out in chapter 3, the "territorial rights of the Spanish mother country" fell far short of 100% sovereignty; Argentina had inherited only part of a restricted and encumbered title to the islands, and Britain possessed extensive rights there. It is not true that no legal rights could be created which would give validity to Britain's possession of the islands: Britain's possession of the islands was validated by the continuous British presence in the islands from the 1760s, by the 1771 Anglo-Spanish agreement, by the Nootka Sound Convention of 1790, and above all by the Convention of Peace of 1850, by Argentina's many acts of omission and commission thereafter, and by extensive foreign recognition of the islands as British (see sections 1.7, 2.3, 7.11, 7.12, 7.16, 7.19, 8.15, 8.16, 8.18). The territory belongs of course to the Falkland Islanders (they are "holders of territorial sovereignty"; see section 10.6), so their self-determination does take place in their own territory, and it is not true that Britain "drove out the original population", or "replaced it", or "isolated the islands", or placed them "behind a British padlock" (!). In 1833 Britain allowed the civilian inhabitants to remain, and never prevented Argentinians from going to the Falklands – in fact Britain allowed so many non-British

---

[1] Verbatim texts of speeches to the General Assembly, 27 September 1965, in UN document A/PV.1337.

people, including Argentinians, to go to the islands that they became a problem (sections 7.7, 10.1). But those untruths have been repeated again and again at the UN by Argentine speakers and apologists for Argentina.

Discussion of the Falklands resumed at the C24 on 9 November 1965.[1] Again a false account of history was presented by speakers for Argentina (Bonifacio del Carril) and Uruguay (Carlos María Velázquez). In his speech giving the background to the dispute, del Carril gave the usual Argentine version of the events of the 1820s and 30s, and simply stated that from 1810, under the principle of *uti possidetis*, Argentina inherited the territory from Spain (for the limitations of that see chapter 3). Referring to the Argentine historian Ricardo Caillet-Bois, he stated that Britain had a problem in judging the perpetrators of the Port Louis murders, since "No British law existed that is applicable to a territory obtained by violence", but that is untrue; there has never been any legal distinction between British territories on the basis of the method by which they were obtained, and the real reason why the Port Louis murderers were never tried was essentially party-political (section 6.37).

Del Carril then advanced a specious argument to justify Argentina's insistence on obtaining the islands despite the fact that UN resolutions 1514 and 1541 clearly give the right of external self-determination to the peoples of all non-self-governing territories. He said:[2]

> 10. The United Kingdom representative had insisted that paragraph 6 of resolution 1514 (XV) was applicable only for the future. He had thought thus to obtain a bill of indemnity against the territorial dismemberment carried out before the United Nations Charter had been signed. He had been mistaken, however, for although the United Kingdom had seized the Malvinas before the Charter had been signed, it was a question of preventing the legalization of a de facto situation that had never been accepted. The possible decolonisation of the islands through the handover of the territory to the sovereignty of a State that is not the Republic of Argentina would be, according to this concept, without the least doubt, an act of disintegration of the territory of a member state executed not *before* but *after* the signing of the Charter of the Organisation, that is to say, it would be the execution of an act prohibited by Resolution 1514 (XV), as the representative of the United Kingdom has recognised.

Del Carril thus implicitly accepted that paragraph 6 of Resolution 1514 did actually prohibit only future breaches of territorial integrity after 1960. But since that would prevent its application to the Falklands, he asserted that handing the islands "to the sovereignty of a State that is not the Republic of Argentina" would be a breach of Argentina's territorial integrity carried out *after 1960*!

That is of course absurd. There was no plan of any kind to hand the islands to any country; his implication is that any other solution than handing the islands to Argentina would breach Resolution 1514 by infringing Argentina's territorial integrity, but as we have shown with abundant evidence, the islands were never 100% Argentine territory at any time (sections 4.9, 5.21, 7.2, 7.8), and to hand them to Argentina would completely negate the principle of self-determination enshrined in UN Resolutions 1514 and 1541. It would also, for example, deprive the Chagos Islanders (section 10.28) of self-determination – the detaching of their islands from Mauritius by Britain in the 1960s was a clear breach of paragraph 6 of UN Resolution 1514, so if applied to them, it would prevent any solution except the reintegration of the islands with Mauritius. The Chagossians would not be allowed to choose independence, or free association with Britain, or free association with Mauritius, or any other option. Argentine writers including Kohen and Rodríguez are (quite rightly) sharply critical of Britain's treatment of the Chagos Islanders, but the application of del Carril's theory would deprive them of self-determination too. The absurdity of the theory is obvious.

The theory was finally laid to rest ten years later, in the *Western Sahara* case at the International Court of Justice (ICJ) in 1975 (see sections 8.12, 10.21). Morocco maintained that there had been historical ties between Morocco and the Western Sahara territory which antedated Spain's possession of the territory and gave Morocco title to it, so that decolonisation could only proceed by

---

[1] Summary of the debate in English on the UN website under "documents", doc. no. A/C.4/SR.1552 (9 November 1965), with numbered paragraphs; the speeches by Argentine speakers in 1965 also in *MGSS*, vol. I, pp. 213-267.

[2] Text to "… had never been accepted" from UN document A/C.4/SR.1552; rest of text to "… as the representative of the United Kingdom has recognised" is our own translation from the Spanish original in *MGSS*, vol. I, p. 246, since the UN document contains an incorrect translation of that part of the Spanish text, namely: "… it was therefore a question which had to be resolved at the present time, and not before the signing of the United Nations Charter."

"reintegration" into Morocco.

The ICJ did not accept that view, and ruled that though there were various historical ties between the Western Sahara and Morocco, there were no legal ties of territorial sovereignty. By "historical ties" the ICJ meant only such ties as fall short of legal ties of territorial sovereignty (i.e. a valid claim to title); the ties that existed therefore did not invalidate the Saharawis' right to self-determination. Argentina's historical ties to the Falklands are thus no proof of title. The Court also made it clear that self-determination applied to *all* non-self-governing territories and required a "free and genuine expression of the will of the peoples concerned". That disposes of Bonifacio del Carril's theory that the Falklands can only be decolonised by "reintegration" into Argentina.

When discussion of the Falklands continued at the C24 on 15 November 1965,[1] the Venezuelan delegate, Leonardo Díaz González, spoke first, in support of Argentina, followed by the Argentine representative Lucio García del Solar. Díaz González gave the standard, untrue account of the islands' history, and then added a few new but equally untrue statements, such as:

7. ... The United Kingdom had recognized the new Argentine State in March 1822, without making any territorial claim to the Malvinas, and in 1825 had concluded with Argentina the Treaty of Amity, Commerce and Navigation, in which reference was made to the territories of the United Provinces, presumably including the Malvinas. [...]

10. ... the islands had the special feature of being an occupied Territory inhabited by a transient population, composed almost exclusively of United Kingdom nationals who had come to work for the Falkland Islands Company...

And the Argentine delegate repeated two of the standard untruths:

64. Mr. GARCIA DEL SOLAR (Argentina) recalled that he had clearly explained to the Special Committee that the Argentine population of the Malvinas Islands had been dispersed after the occupation of the islands by the British in 1833 and had since been replaced by a population of British origin, most of whom lived there for part of the year only.

To set the record straight: Britain did not recognise Argentine independence in March 1822 but on 15 December 1823 with the appointment of Woodbine Parish as consul-general (section 4.8), and the 1825 Treaty of Amity made no mention of the territories of the United Provinces (sections 4.10, 4.12). The population of the islands is not "transient", nor do they live there "for part of the year only", as stated by del Solar. Cecil King had made that clear at the C24 on 10 September 1964 – he said "The people of the Islands were not temporary settlers; 80 per cent of the resident population in 1962 had been born in the Islands, and many of them could trace their roots there for more than a century..." (section 10.14). And del Solar referred to "the Argentine population" of the islands, though only a few of them were Argentinians (sections 6.24, 6.25). But in the one-sided "dialogue of the deaf" that Carlos María Velázquez conducted at the C24, Argentine apologists repeated those myths again and again, ignoring Britain's statements of the truth.

Díaz González then introduced, on behalf of fifteen South American delegations, draft resolution A/C.4/L.802, drawn up by the Uruguayan representative Carlos María Velázquez (see section 10.14) and which became, almost unchanged, UN Resolution 2065.[2] Various delegations spoke supporting it, most either explicitly endorsing Argentina's claim or at least recommending the draft as a good way forward. Only an occasional voice was raised in defence of the islanders and their right of self-determination, for example:

54. Mr. EASTMAN (Liberia) was sorry that draft resolution A/C.4/L.802 did not mention the views and aspirations of the Territory's inhabitants. He therefore suggested that the words "and the population of the islands" should be added after the words "Argentine Republic", in operative paragraph 1. Subject to that amendment, the Liberian delegation was prepared to support the draft resolution. [...]

63. Mr. EASTMAN (Liberia) observed that resolution 1514 (XV) was concerned with the independence of colonial countries and peoples, and not with the territorial sovereignty of Member States. As the Malvinas

---

[1] Quotes from this debate from summary in English on the UN website under "documents", doc. A/C.4/SR.1556; two paragraphs spoken by Argentine delegate García del Solar also in *MGSS*, vol. I, p. 254.
[2] UN doc. A/C.4/SR.1556, paras. 54, 63.

Islands had a population, that population ought to be consulted when its fate was being decided.

That was entirely true of course – but was ignored. The C24 had been subverted by Argentina into becoming a vehicle for the realisation of Argentina's territorial claim, against the rights and wishes of the people of the territory concerned.

So, after several further discussions, and following the UN's labyrinthine procedure, Draft Resolution A/C.4/L.802 on the Falklands became Draft Resolution 1 (out of eight on different territories) in UN document A/6160 of 13 December 1965,[1] which came before the United Nations General Assembly on 16 December 1965 and was voted on without further discussion. Draft resolution 1 on the Falklands was passed unanimously by 94 votes to none, with 14 abstentions including Britain. It was now UN Resolution 2065 (XX); its full text runs:[2]

2065 (XX). Question of the Falkland Islands (Malvinas)

The General Assembly,

Having examined the question of the Falkland Islands (Malvinas),

Taking into account the chapters of the reports of the Special Committee on the Situation with regard to the Implementation of the Declaration on the Granting of Independence to Colonial Countries and Peoples relating to the Falkland Islands (Malvinas), and in particular the conclusions and recommendations adopted by the Committee with reference to that Territory,

Considering that its resolution 1514 (XV) of 14 December 1960 was prompted by the cherished aim of bringing to an end everywhere colonialism in all its forms, one of which covers the case of the Falkland Islands (Malvinas),

Noting the existence of a dispute between the Governments of Argentina and the United Kingdom of Great Britain and Northern Ireland concerning sovereignty over the said Islands,

1. *Invites* the Governments of Argentina and the United Kingdom of Great Britain and Northern Ireland to proceed without delay with the negotiations recommended by the Special Committee on the Situation with regard to the Implementation of the Declaration on the Granting of Independence to Colonial Countries and Peoples with a view to finding a peaceful solution to the problem, bearing in mind the provisions and objectives of the Charter of the United Nations and of General Assembly resolution 1514 (XV) and the interests of the population of the Falkland Islands (Malvinas);

2. *Requests* the two Governments to report to the Special Committee and to the General Assembly at its twenty-first session on the results of the negotiations.

1398th plenary meeting, 16 December 1965.

Significantly, Britain did not vote against the resolution; the election of a Labour government under Harold Wilson on 15 October 1964 had brought to power a modernising government intent on redefining Britain's role in the world, which included a withdrawal from areas east of Suez and a new attitude towards overseas territories. During the 1960s and 70s Britain repeatedly negotiated with Argentina in a forlorn attempt to "solve" the Falklands "problem" in a way that would not abandon the islanders to being ruled by a foreign power – after all, to permit an Argentine takeover would have been to establish colonialism in the islands, not end it. The Falkland Islanders fought back, staunchly supported by Governor Sir Cosmo Haskard (1916-2017; Governor 1964-70), who is still remembered with affection in the islands. The islanders made their voice heard so eloquently that all attempts at negotiating away their rights failed.

UN Resolution 2065 displayed the masterly drafting skills of its originator, the Uruguayan vice-chairman of the C24 and chairman of Sub-Committee III, Carlos María Velázquez. He was well aware that no resolution that unequivocally supported Argentina's claim to the Falklands would be passed (or at least not without amendments that would negate its purpose), so he drew up a fairly anodyne text that sounds eminently reasonable – it merely calls for negotiations to begin, and lays down that their result should be a peaceful solution to the problem. Expressed like that, it sounded like a mild, positive call for peaceful progress, so it is not surprising that no country voted against it (including Britain, whose heart was not in the job of defending the Falkland Islanders).

But in fact resolution 2065 is anything but reasonable. It calls for negotiations – but not

---

[1] UN doc. A/6260, 13 December 1965; draft resolution 1 on p. 16.
[2] Full text of Resolution 2065 (XX); also available on the UN website and in Raphael Perl, *The Falkland Islands Dispute in International Law and Politics*, London / Rome / New York 1983, p. 373.

negotiations involving the Falkland Islanders, the people whose fate was at stake. Instead it calls for the same kind of negotiations as took place in London and Berlin in July 1890 over handing Heligoland to Germany (section 8.29): negotiations between the two governments over the heads of the people of the territory, whose wishes and interests were ignored, as was typical in the age of Classic Imperialism. And secondly, the resolution calls for a peaceful solution, which implies that a solution was required. As we pointed out in chapter 7, in reality the Falklands dispute between Britain and Argentina was definitively and finally solved by the Convention of Peace in 1850.

10.16 Interests versus wishes: UN resolution 2065 misused by Argentina

Much play has been made by Argentina and pro-Argentine apologists of the fact that Resolution 2065 speaks of the "interests" of the Falkland Islanders rather than their "wishes". That wording sounds imperialistic, indeed colonialistic; it seems to imply that the current colonial power, Britain, and the aspiring colonial power, Argentina, should decide the islanders' fate over their heads, just as the Heligolanders' fate was decided by the two colonial powers Britain and Germany in 1890 (section 8.29).

However, the difference between "wishes" and "interests" is spurious, as pointed out by the former British Foreign Secretary Michael Stewart:[1]

To put people under a form of government that they will heartily detest from the start, it's rather difficult to argue that that is in their interests.

It is of course impossible to rule a people according to their interests but against their wishes, since their wishes define what their interests are. Interests are not an objective reality; they are defined by the perspective of the person defining them. And since Argentina constantly insists that there are only two parties to the Falklands dispute – Argentina and Britain – and resolutely refuses to have any contact with the Falkland Islanders (the people whose interests Argentina claims to be defending), Argentina evidently arrogates to itself the right to decide what the islanders' interests are, just as colonial powers in the age of Classic Imperialism claimed that they were ruling colonial peoples "in their best interests". Argentina is thus not a credible defender of the islanders' interests.

The only people qualified to decide on the interests of the Falkland Islanders are of course the Falkland Islanders themselves – according to their wishes. There is no difference between interests and wishes. That rules out any Argentine claim to the islands from the outset.

10.17 The UN International Covenant on Civil and Political Rights (ICCPR), 16 December 1966: all peoples of Non-Self-Governing Territories have the right to self-determination

On 16 December 1966 the UN General Assembly adopted the International Covenant on Civil and Political Rights (ICCPR; in force since 23 March 1976),[2] which made it even clearer that the right of self-determination was possessed by the peoples of all non-self-governing territories without exception. Its Article 1 reads as follows:[3]

1. All peoples have the right of self-determination. By virtue of that right they freely determine their political status and freely pursue their economic, social and cultural development.
2. All peoples may, for their own ends, freely dispose of their natural wealth and resources without prejudice to any obligations arising out of international economic co-operation, based upon the principle of mutual benefit, and international law. In no case may a people be deprived of its own means of subsistence.
3. The States Parties to the present Covenant, including those having responsibility for the administration of Non-Self-Governing and Trust Territories, shall promote the realization of the right of self-determination, and shall respect that right, in conformity with the provisions of the Charter of the United Nations.

Self-determination was thereby confirmed as a right of all peoples including those of non-self-governing territories, and it became an obligation on states responible for such territories to promote "the realization of the right of self-determination" for the peoples living in them. That self-evidently

---
[1] Quoted in Michael Charlton, *The Little Platoon: Diplomacy and the Falklands Dispute*, Oxford 1989, p. 20.
[2] The ICCPR came into force once 35 states had ratified it; that number was reached on 23 March 1976.
[3] Text of ICCPR here from the website of the Office of the United Nations High Commissioner for Human Rights.

means external as well as internal self-determination – without external self-determination (the right to decide their relations with other countries) those peoples would not be able to "freely determine their political status", as paragraph 1 of the ICCPR puts it.

Thus Britain is obliged to promote external self-determination for the Falkland Islanders. To hand the islands to Argentina would be a breach of that obligation; it would mean treating the islanders "like chattels in real estate", as Rosalyn Higgins puts it[1] (e.g. like the contents of a house which are sold with the house). Such a practice was condemned over a century ago in 1917 by US President Woodrow Wilson, who stated that:[2]

… no right anywhere exists to hand peoples about from sovereignty to sovereignty as if they were property.

Britain did exactly that with the Heligolanders in the age of Classic Imperialism in 1890 when there was nothing to stop it (section 8.29), but today it would be a breach of international law for Britain to hand the Falkland Islanders to Argentina.

10.18 UN Resolution 2625 strengthens Resolutions 1514 and 1541; ignored by Argentina

As described above in sections 10.8 and 10.9, United Nations Resolutions 1514 and 1541, both passed by the UN General Assembly in December 1960, stated that the peoples of all non-self-governing territories (the "Chapter XI territories" covered by Chapter XI of the UN Charter) have the right of self-determination. That basic principle was repeated and strengthened by UN Resolution 2625 (XXV), passed on 24 October 1970, which added a further option ("the fourth option") to the ways in which self-determination may be put into effect.[3]

Most of Resolution 2625 consists of an Annex containing a long first operative paragraph, which lays down a number of principles regulating friendly relations between states. The principles are not numbered, and the text runs continuously without numbered sections; the fifth of them is "The principle of equal rights and self-determination of peoples"; it begins by making extensive reference to resolutions 1514 and 1541 (though without explicitly naming them):

By virtue of the principle of equal rights and self-determination of peoples enshrined in the Charter of the United Nations, all peoples have the right freely to determine, without external interference, their political status and to pursue their economic, social and cultural development, and every State has the duty to respect this right in accordance with the provisions of the Charter.

Every State has the duty to promote, through joint and separate action, realization of the principle of equal rights and self-determination of peoples, … in order:
 a. To promote friendly relations and co-operation among States; and
 b. To bring a speedy end to colonialism, having due regard to the freely expressed will of the peoples concerned;
and bearing in mind that subjection of peoples to alien subjugation, domination and exploitation constitutes a violation of the principle, as well as a denial of fundamental human rights, and is contrary to the Charter.

Thus Resolution 2625 confirms once again, as does the ICCPR, that all peoples possess external self-determination ("the right freely to determine… their political status"), and that colonialism is to be ended according to "the freely expressed will of the peoples concerned".

After stating that every State has the duty to promote universal respect for and observance of human rights, Resolution 2625 goes on to establish four options by which self-determination can be realised (the text is one continuous sentence; our numbering here):

1. The establishment of a sovereign and independent State,
2. the free association or
3. integration with an independent State or
4. the emergence into any other political status freely determined by a people
   constitute modes of implementing the right of self-determination by that people.

---

[1] Rosalyn Higgins, "Judge Dillard and the Right to Self-Determination", in *Virginia Journal of International Law*, vol. 23 (1982-3), p. 393, quoted in Trinidad 2018, pp. 178 and 230.
[2] Sarah Wambaugh, *Plebiscites since the World War*, Washington DC 1933, vol. I, p. 5, quoting President Wilson's speech to the US Senate, 22 January 1917, from the US Congressional Record, Vol. 54, Part 2, p. 1742.
[3] UN Resolution 2625 (XXV), 24 October 1970; full text in UN document no. A/RES/25/2625.

Option 4 is new – Resolution 1541 of December 1960 (see section 10.9) had only contained the three options of: (1) Emergence as a sovereign independent State; (2) Free association with an independent State; or (3) Integration with an independent State. Resolution 2625 added option (4), which allows any people to freely choose "any other political status" – therefore including what the Falkland Islanders have now: full self-government in all fields except defence and international relations.

Resolution 2625 extends self-determination to all non-independent territories of all kinds:

The territory of a colony or other Non-Self-Governing Territory has, under the Charter, a status separate and distinct from the territory of the State administering it; and such separate and distinct status under the Charter shall exist until the people of the colony or Non-Self-Governing Territory have exercised their right of self-determination in accordance with the Charter, and particularly its purposes and principles.

The wording "a colony or other Non-Self-Governing Territory" includes the Falklands, and it confirms that the Falkland Islanders are the holders of territorial sovereignty (section 10.6), since it is only when they exercise their right of self-determination that their current status shall cease.

Like Resolution 1514 (see section 10.8), Resolution 2625 also enshrines the protection of territorial integrity:

Nothing in the foregoing paragraphs shall be construed as authorizing or encouraging any action which would dismember or impair, totally or in part, the territorial integrity or political unity of sovereign and independent States conducting themselves in compliance with the principle of equal rights and self-determination of peoples as described above... Every State shall refrain from any action aimed at the partial or total disruption of the national unity and territorial integrity of any other State or country.

Like Resolution 1514, Resolution 2625 makes it quite clear that its reference to territorial integrity refers only to *future* actions (i.e. after 1970) which "would dismember or impair" territorial integrity, and that every State "shall refrain" from such actions (our emphasis). So Resolution 2625 does not apply to past events such as the expulsion of the Argentine garrison from the Falklands in 1833 (for the non-retroactive principle see section 10.8). Bonifacio del Carril's specious theory that it would be a breach of UN resolutions to award the islands to any state except Argentina (section 10.15) was invalidated by the ruling of the International Court of Justice in the *Western Sahara* case in 1975 (section 10.21). In addition, Resolution 2625 protects the territorial integrity only of such states as are "conducting themselves in compliance with the principle of equal rights and self-determination of peoples", which Argentina is not doing. Resolution 2625 thus unambiguously extends external self-determination to the Falkland Islanders and prevents Argentina from asserting that Argentina's territorial integrity is breached by Britain's possession of the islands.

To sum up: United Nations resolutions 1514, 1541, 2625 and the ICCPR all make it abundantly clear that Falkland Islanders have the right to choose the way in which they wish the Falklands to relate to other countries – they may choose independence, integration with a UN member country, free association with a UN member country, or (under Resolution 2625) "any other political status". In other words, they possess the full right to external self-determination.

10.19 The 1960s and 70s; more amateur invasions, 1966 and 1968; Argentina treats UN Resolution 2065 as void, February 1976

Resolution 2065 (see section 10.15) did not constitute any judgement by the United Nations as to the merits of Argentina's or Britain's case for possession of the Falklands,[1] but only an invitation to find a peaceful solution. It was left to the two countries to decide what that solution was to be. It could have been a decision to refer the case to the International Court of Justice; it could have been a decision by Argentina to drop all claim to the islands; it could have been a decision to give the islands independence, or for them to become associated or integrated with Britain under UN

---

[1] Unlike, for example, UN Resolution 3161 (XXVIII) of 14 December 1976, which supported the territorial integrity of the Comoro archipelago (a French overseas territory, which was dismembered when France separated one of its islands, Mayotte, from the rest). With reference to the Falklands, Jamie Trinidad comments "There is no comparable endorsement by the General Assembly, at any stage, of the Argentine territorial claim" (Trinidad 2018, p. 146).

Resolution 1541, or for Britain and Argentina to rule the islands jointly, or (from 1970) any other peaceful solution freely chosen by the Falkland Islanders under UN Resolution 2625.

What actually happened was that there were desultory negotiations between Britain and Argentina at various times from the 1960s to 1982 in pursuance of UN Resolution 2065, aiming to find a "solution" to the Falklands "problem", while Argentina's annual presentations at the C24 continued to repeat the standard, untrue, Argentine version of the case, in speeches that became mere routine after the passing of Resolution 2065. For Argentina the only acceptable "solution" was a handover of the islands, whereas Britain attempted to satisfy the islanders' wishes – Argentina wanted the land, Britain was concerned for the people. The two positions were incompatible, but Britain's heart was not in the job, whereas Argentina was dedicated and tireless.

So for the Falkland Islanders the 1960s and 70s were a depressing time. The islanders were faced with pressures from several directions at once: in the first place, there was a continuing chronic lack of investment by Britain, though the islands were still bringing Britain a profit and there was a constant outflow of capital from the islands to absentee landlords (as revealed in the *Shackleton Report*, see section 10.4), so the islands' economy stagnated; secondly, there was increasing pressure both from Argentina at the United Nations aiming at a takeover of the islands, and from Britain too, which was negotiating with Argentina over the heads of the islanders about their future. All that led many islanders to leave and seek work elsewhere, and the population slowly dwindled to a mere 1800 people by 1980.

And thirdly, yet another form of pressure appeared in the 1960s: the first three Argentine "amateur invasions", in 1964, 1966 and 1968, of which the first (relatively harmless) one, Fitzgerald's flight in 1964, was described above in section 10.13.

The second one was the most sinister and potentially the most dangerous. On 28 September 1966 a group of 18 radical Peronists armed themselves to the teeth with two sub-machine guns, two rifles, three pistols, three revolvers, knives, chisels, screwdrivers and razorblades (there were no luggage-checks in Argentina in those days); they hijacked a 4-engined DC4 of Aerolíneas Argentinas on an internal Argentine flight, with a crew of six and 44 passengers including five women and five children, and forced the pilot, Ernesto Fernández García, at gunpoint to fly to Stanley. Their plan was to seize the Falklands and hold the islands for their hero, the exiled Juan Perón, to use as a base to reconquer Argentina and return to power.

They had, however, neglected to take the elementary precaution of finding out whether there was an airport in the islands – and at that time there was no airport at all. They were crackpots of course – who in their right mind hijacks an aircraft to a place with no airport to land at? They became distinctly edgy on realising there was no airport, and the lives of all on board were saved by the weather (it was clear and there was no typical Falklands storm or low cloud or fog) and by the skill of the pilot, who successfully brought the plane down on Stanley racecourse. If there had been a storm, or fog, or there had been vehicles parked on the racecourse, all on board would have died.

As soon as the plane was down, some Falkland Islanders came to see if they could help, but the hijackers seized them at gunpoint and handed out an idiotically-worded proclamation in bombastic but laughably defective English, which among other absurdities announced that "TO THE NAME CALLED PORT STANLEY WILL BY CHANCED BY "PORT RIVERO" TO MEMORY ARGENTINE MAN" [*sic*]. Changing the name of Stanley to "Port Rivero" was an early manifestation of the "Rivero Myth" (and the same was proposed in 1982, to "Puerto Rivero", section 6.33). By chance Governor Sir Cosmo Haskard and Colonial Secretary Willoughby "Tommy" Thompson were both away in Britain, so the authorities on the spot were all Falkland Islanders: Acting Governor Les Gleadell, born in 1921 at Fox Bay, West Falkland; Acting Colonial Secretary Horace "Nap" Bound, born in Stanley in 1919 (a great-grandson of Jacob Napoleon Goss), and police chief Terry Peck, born in Stanley in 1938. They handled the bizarre crisis in their country cool-headedly and with humour – Les Gleadell burst out laughing when he heard the hijackers' plans, and made it abundantly clear that they were on a fool's errand. The hijackers eventually surrendered and were taken back to Argentina. The affair is still known in the islands as "the DC4 Incident".[1]

Britain attempted to twist the Falkland Islanders' arms into accepting an Argentine takeover of their country, and in November 1968 sent Lord Chalfont (Alun Gwynne Jones, 1919-2020) to sound out their opinions (and to persuade them to accept a compromise agreement with Argentina). Chalfont and his party spent a week in the islands, during which there occurred the third "amateur invasion", on 27 November 1968, while Chalfont was meeting the chairman of the Falklands Labour Federation, Dick Goss (another descendant of Jacob Napoleon Goss), and other trade union representatives. Just as Chalfont was saying that the islanders were wrong to worry about Argentine aircraft flying in, and that it would never happen again, a plane flew past the window.

Dick Goss said "There's one flying past now!"; Chalfont said "You know it's an Argentine one?", to which Dick said "It's not one of our buggers, anyway!"[2] It was Miguel Fitzgerald again, flying a twin-engined aircraft owned by the Buenos Aires tabloid *Crónica*, whose manager Héctor Ricardo García was also editor of the sensationalist magazine *Así*. García himself was aboard again, as he had been in 1966 (he was clearly behind both incidents), but this time Fitzgerald only managed a crash-landing south of Stanley on the Eliza Cove Road. The plane and passengers were quickly bundled off back to Argentina without any opportunities for propaganda.[3]

The first three amateur invasions (of over a dozen so far) took place against a background of negotiations between Britain and Argentina following UN Resolution 2065, partly behind the islanders' backs, though Sir Cosmo Haskard broke the rules and kept them informed of what was going on, earning their lasting gratitude. Small wonder that the islanders felt they were under attack.

And in February 1976 Argentina breached Resolution 2065, having in 1975 unilaterally extended Argentine territorial waters to a 200-mile limit, including the waters around the Falklands. On 4 December 1975 the British naval attaché in Buenos Aires was told by an Argentine vice-admiral that if the Royal Research Ship *Shackleton* entered the "Argentine 200-mile limit" she would be arrested and Britain might lose contracts with the Argentine navy. On 4 February 1976 the Argentine destroyer *Almirante Storni* sighted the *Shackleton* 87 miles from the Falklands approaching Stanley. The captain of the *Almirante Storni* ordered Captain Philip Warne to stop and receive a boarding party and to proceed to Ushuaia, but Warne refused. The *Almirante Storni* then fired three shots across the *Shackleton*'s bows; Warne signalled that he was carrying explosives for scientific purposes, so a hit on his ship might be disastrous, but the Argentine destroyer fired twice more and threatened that the next shot would be aimed to hit. Warne calmly held to his course; the *Almirante Storni* did not fire again and the *Shackleton* continued to Stanley, arriving the same afternoon. For his coolness under fire Warne was awarded the OBE in the 1977 New Year's Honours list.[4] There were no repercussions from the affair; it remained a mere "pinprick".

But to fire five shots at an unarmed research ship, and to threaten to fire to hit it, cannot be said to be part of a "peaceful solution" as required under Resolution 2065 – Argentina was treating Resolution 2065 as void. And of course Argentina's military invasion of the Falklands in 1982 definitively set aside Resolution 2065.

---

[1] See articles on the DC4 Incident in *FIJ* 2016, vol. 10 (5), pp. 42-93, and the eyewitness account by Graham Bound in *Penguin News* 8 January 2016, p. 5 – he says: "From a local political viewpoint, the situation was also significant. In old-style socially-stratified and colonial Stanley... all major decisions were made by the career Colonial Service officers sent from London. But now, just when London would have said they were needed most, both the Governor, Sir Cosmo Haskard, and the Colonial Secretary, Tommy Thompson (whom I recall as kind and good men) were taking leave in the UK. Perhaps for the first time, the administration of the Islands was entirely in the hands of local people" [i.e. Graham's father Nap Bound, Les Gleadell and Terry Peck]. Graham says it "brought the revelation that ordinary Islanders were tough and more than capable of looking after themselves." (Gleadell is pronounced "Gleddle").

[2] John Smith, in an interview by Corina Bishop broadcast on the 40th anniversary of the DC4 Incident, 28 September 2006, by the Falkland Islands Radio Service (FIRS), in which Terry Peck and John Smith recalled the two incidents (we are grateful to the late Jane Cameron for providing us with a recording; transcript by Graham Pascoe in JCNA).

[3] Some details here from entry on Fitzgerald by Edmundo Murray in *DFB*.

[4] Details from entry on Warne in *DFB*.

10.20 Kohen's and Rodríguez's misunderstanding of the Falklands constitution

Resolution 2065 is now over half a century old, and a great deal has changed in that time. In the 1960s the situation in the Falklands was still colonial – the Governor still nominated some members of the Legislative and Executive Councils, and he was still appointed by the Colonial Office in London (the last one appointed by the Colonial Office was Sir Cosmo Haskard, Governor 1964-70, one of the best-loved of all Falklands Governors). Since then the Falklands constitutions of 1985, 1997 and 2009 have steadily reduced the Governor to a mere figurehead with a role comparable to that of the Queen in Britain. The islanders rule their country themselves.

Kohen and Rodríguez misunderstand – or misrepresent – the real constitutional situation by failing to take into account the vital difference between theory and practice in British-style jurisdictions. Thus in Britain the power of the Queen is *in theory* unlimited: she is commander-in-chief of all British armed forces, she appoints the Prime Minister and members of the Cabinet, she can refuse her assent to laws passed by Parliament, she appoints high-ranking military officers and British ambassadors, she can requisition ships (which she did during the Falklands War), and she has many other powers – the list is almost endless. But of course *in practice* her power is severely circumscribed; power is exercised not by her personally but in her name. Thus there are no *theoretical* limits on her appointing powers, but *in practice* she appoints as Prime Minister the person who can command a majority in the House of Commons, and all her other powers are delegated in various ways. It would be ridiculous to describe the Queen as an absolute dictator.

Yet that is exactly what Kohen and Rodríguez do (pp. 273-275) in describing the Falklands constitution. They say "Article 11 reserves the absolute power for the Queen to pass laws for 'the peace, order and good government' of the islands, as well as to amend legislation currently in force" – but they fail to point out that that is the case in Britain too. That is how the unwritten British constitution works; it is the British way of doing things. Other countries whose democracy is less old than Britain's possess written constitutions in which the limits of executive and political power are spelt out; in Britain the limitations have arisen gradually in the course of centuries, and it is now Parliament (of which the Queen is part) that possesses sovereign power.

The same is true in the Falklands. Kohen and Rodríguez say: "The Governor of the islands, elected [*sic*] in London by the Foreign Office, is a British career diplomat who occupies the position for an unlimited duration. He has broad political power in the executive, legislative and judiciary", and proceed to give a long list of his powers, which might give the impression that he is an absolute dictator and can rule the islands as he wishes. But nothing could be further from the truth; the changes of the last half-century have reduced his role to a merely formal one – *in practice* the islanders rule their country themselves.

In short, Kohen and Rodríguez paint a false and outdated picture of the Falklands constitution. The islands are no longer ruled by a colonial power, but democratically by their own people.

10.21 Court cases, III: the *Western Sahara* case at the International Court of Justice, 1975

In an attempt to dilute the validity of the principle of self-determination in reference to the Falklands, Kohen and Rodríguez refer to the *Western Sahara* case, heard before the International Court of Justice (ICJ) in 1975 (see also section 8.12). The two authors say:[1]

... the International Court of Justice, in the *Western Sahara* case, stated that:

The validity of the principle of self-determination, defined as the need to pay regard to the freely expressed will of people, is not affected by the fact that in certain cases the General Assembly has dispensed with the requirement of consulting the inhabitants of a given territory. *Those instances were based either on the consideration that a certain population did not constitute a 'people' entitled to self-determination, or on the* conviction that a consultation was totally unnecessary, in view of special circumstances.

Those were indeed some of the general principles discussed by the ICJ, but Kohen and Rodríguez suppress the Court's actual decision, which is relevant to the Falklands.

---

[1] Kohen and Rodríguez 2015, Spanish ed. p. 278, quoting paragraph 59 of the ICJ's decision in the *Western Sahara* case; italics added by Kohen and Rodríguez in both Spanish and English eds. (not in the text of the original judgement).

The question at issue in the *Western Sahara* case was whether the people of the Western Sahara, who were largely nomadic, had a close enough connection with the territory for them to possess the right of self-determination, which is defined by, among other things, the association of a people with their territory (section 10.10). Three countries (Morocco, Mauretania and Spain) asserted their right to sovereignty over the territory, maintaining that the Saharawis did not possess the right of self-determination since they were not settled but moved around, so they did not have strong enough links with the region.

However, in its decision the Court explicitly upheld the Saharawis' right of self-determination, in paragraphs 70 and 162 of its Advisory Opinion of 16 October 1975:[1]

70. In short, the decolonization process to be accelerated which is envisaged by the General Assembly in this provision is one which will respect the right of the population of Western Sahara to determine their future political status by their own freely expressed will. [... ...]

162. ... the Court has not found legal ties of such a nature as might affect the application of General Assembly resolution 1514 (XV) in the decolonization of Western Sahara and, in particular, of the principle of self-determination through the free and genuine expression of the will of the peoples of the Territory.

In other words, though the ICJ did find evidence of various historical and other links ("legal ties") between the Western Sahara territory and the three countries that claimed it, those links were not sufficient to override the principle of self-determination (see also section 10.15).

The people of the Falklands are permanently resident, so their connection with the territory is clearer than that of the Saharawis. If the Falklands case were taken to the ICJ, the Court might decide along similar lines: that there were certain historical links between Argentina and the Falklands, but they were not sufficient to override the self-determination of the Falkland Islanders.

Jamie Trinidad states that in the *Western Sahara* case the ICJ "focused heavily on the principle of self-determination", and that the Court quoted its own *Namibia* Opinion of 1971:[2]

... the subsequent development of international law in regard to non-self-governing territories, as enshrined in the Charter of the United Nations, made the principle of self-determination applicable to all of them.

Trinidad goes on to say that after citing paragraphs 2, 5 and 6 of the "Declaration on Decolonization" (i.e. UN Resolution 1514), the Court stated:[3]

The above provisions, in particular paragraph 2, thus confirm and emphasize that the application of the right of self-determination requires a free and genuine expression of the will of the peoples concerned.

In short, as Trinidad makes clear, the International Court of Justice emphasised "the centrality of the popular will in the decolonization of Non-Self-Governing Territories", which was to be "proceduralized" with a "self-determination act"; he states in summary that "the ICJ implicitly rejected the notion... that the resolution of irredentist claims based on territorial integrity must necessarily be a prior consideration in the decolonization process" (see sections 10.8, 10.9, 10.18).

Finally, concluding his analysis of the *Western Sahara* case, Trinidad says:[4]

It is clear that the ICJ conceived of the decolonization process as an opportunity for an expression of the popular will of colonial peoples, rather than as a forum for righting colonial wrongs visited by sovereign States on each other in centuries gone by.

Sadly, the UN's decolonisation committee, the "C24", has allowed itself to be subverted by Argentina so as to become just such a forum for "righting" what Argentina sees as "colonial wrongs" (see sections 10.12, 10.14, 10.15, 10.16, 10.18, 10.26).

---

[1] Quotes from the Advisory Opinion of the International Court of Justice on the Western Sahara, 16 October 1975, from the ICJ's website, http://www.icj-cij.org/files/case-related/61/061-19751016-ADV-01-00-EN.pdf.
[2] Trinidad 2018, p. 50, quoting the Advisory Opinion of 21 June 1971, cited in paragraph 54 of the *Western Sahara* Advisory Opinion.
[3] Trinidad 2018, p. 51, quoting the *Western Sahara* Advisory Opinion, paragraph 57.
[4] Trinidad 2018, p. 68.

10.22 Argentina's inconsistency, III: British arbitration over Argentina's territory, II, 1964-6[1]

One of the most bizarre aspects of the developing Falklands dispute in the 1960s was that precisely during the years when Argentina was escalating its activities at the United Nations, with Ruda's speech and the passing of Resolution 2065, Britain was again arbitrating in a border dispute between Argentina and Chile. In other words, Argentina was yet again accepting Britain as a judge entitled to rule on how far Argentine territory extended.

Argentina had accepted British territorial arbitration in a dispute between Argentina and Chile in 1899-1902 (section 9.1); Britain's arbitration was lamented by speakers in the Argentine Congress in 1950 (section 7.17), but nevertheless in 1964 Argentina and Chile retained the British Crown as Permanent Arbitrator, and invited Britain to arbitrate again in another border dispute between them. This time it was over the position of the Argentine-Chilean border in an area around the Río Palena and the Río Encuentro, between 43 and 44 degrees South. Arbitration by the British Crown was requested by Chile on 15 September 1964; the Chilean and Argentine foreign ministers met at Santiago on 6 November and agreed that the dispute should be settled by Britain, and on 25 November the Argentine government accepted the arrangement.[2] Thus at the same time as claiming that the Falklands were Argentine territory, Argentina accepted that Britain was entitled to decide what was Argentine territory and what was not. That required "doublethink" of a high order.

Britain appointed a Court of Arbitration consisting of three British judges: the appeal judge Lord McNair (president), Mr. L. P. Kirwan and Brigadier K. M. Papworth, with Professor D. H. N. Johnson as registrar – as in 1902, no Argentinians or Chileans were involved. The judges appointed a Field Mission in December 1965, which visited the area in January and February 1966, and oral hearings were held between 19 September and 21 October 1966 at which Argentina and Chile put their cases to the Court. The Court delivered its ruling on 24 November 1966, and it was signed by Her Majesty Queen Elizabeth II at the Court of St James's on 9 December 1966.[3]

The Court awarded roughly 70 per cent of the disputed territory to Argentina, 30 per cent to Chile;[4] both governments accepted the ruling, and Britain appointed a Demarcation Mission consisting of four British military officers, who then actually laid out the border between Argentina and Chile in the disputed area, beginning in January 1967.[5] Naturally Kohen and Rodríguez say not a word about any of this, or about the previous British arbitration.

The acceptance of British territorial arbitration is of probative value in assessing Argentina's attitude to the Falklands dispute during the two arbitrations of 1899-1902 and 1964-6. In accepting Britain as a territorial arbitrator, on two occasions over 60 years apart, Argentina accepted Britain's credentials as a judge entitled to decide what was Argentine territory and what was not. That acceptance is incompatible with Argentina's refusal to accept Britain's definition of the Falklands as not being Argentine territory.

10.23 Another Resolution "emptied" by Argentina: UN Resolution 31/49, 1 December 1976

In Argentina there was a military coup on 24 March 1976, the sixth in the 20th century after those of 1930, 1943, 1955, 1962 and 1966. The armed forces seized power and set up a government with sinister Fascist leanings under a three-man military junta. The junta soon began to press the Falklands issue at the United Nations, and Argentina sponsored a resolution which was passed by the UN General Assembly on 1 December 1976 as Resolution 31/49. It runs in part:[6]

---

[1] Full account of this British arbitration, entitled *Reports of International Arbitral Awards / Receuil des Sentences Arbitrales, Argentine-Chile Frontier Case, 9 December 1966*, Volume XVI, 2006, pp. 109-182, available on the United Nations website under http://legal.un.org/riaa/cases/vol_XVI/109-182.pdf (henceforth "*Argentine-Chile Frontier Case*, UN 2006"); shorter account on the US Department of State website, entitled *International Boundary Study No. 101 – May 25, 1970: Argentina-Chile Boundary (Country Codes: AR-CI)...*, under http://www.law.fsu.edu/ library/collection/limitsinseas/ibs101.pdf. (henceforth "US State Department 1970)".
[2] *Argentine-Chile Frontier Case*, UN 2006, pp. 111-112.
[3] *Argentine-Chile Frontier Case*, UN 2006, pp. 112-114.
[4] US State Department 1970, p. 5; Hernekamp 1980, p. 12.
[5] *Argentine-Chile Frontier Case*, UN 2006, p. 113.
[6] Text on the UN website (www.un.org/documents) under A/RES/31/49.

Resolution 31/49 Question of the Falkland Islands (Malvinas) 1 December 1976:
The General Assembly…
2. Expresses its gratitude for the continuous efforts made by the Government of Argentina, in accordance with the relevant decisions of the General Assembly, to facilitate the process of decolonisation and to promote the well-being of the populations of the islands;
3. Requests the Governments of Argentina and the United Kingdom of Great Britain and Northern Ireland to expedite the negotiations concerning the dispute over sovereignty, as requested in General Assembly resolutions 2065 (XX) and 3160 (XXVIII);
4. Calls upon the two parties to refrain from taking decisions that would imply introducing unilateral modifications in the situation while the islands are going through the process recommended in the above-mentioned resolutions;…

Paragraph 2 is absurdly one-sided in thanking only Argentina – it was actually Britain that had been making efforts to "promote the well-being of the populations of the islands" (i.e. the populations of each island in the group), whereas Argentina's efforts had been devoted to taking over the territory against the wishes of those populations.

In 1976, paragraph 4 was quite natural – a process of negotiation over the islands was going on between Britain and Argentina, following resolutions 2065 and 3160 (the latter, of 14 December 1973, merely expressed regret that no "progress" had been made in implementing 2065), and it was logical to ask both sides to refrain from preempting the result by making unilateral changes to promote their own interests. For over five years both sides practised restraint and continued negotiating, until Argentina suddenly invaded the islands on 2 April 1982. That "emptied" Resolution 31/49 since its basic premise had changed – the process of negotiation mentioned in paragraph 4 had ended, so the resolution had become empty; there was nothing it referred to.

There were no diplomatic relations between Britain and Argentina for 7 years till they were formally resumed in 1989, but then Argentina made unilateral moves which again breached Resolution 31/49:

(1) The incorporation (in Argentine law) of the Falklands into the province of Tierra del Fuego, which was passed by law 23,775 in the Argentine Congress in April 1990. President Carlos Menem vetoed part of the first clause of that law so as to exclude the Falklands, to avoid the argument that Argentina would not be able to protect the Islanders' "interests" as called for by Resolution 2065 if it included them in Tierra del Fuego with its population of about 127,000. Nevertheless, the more aggressive Argentine government under President Cristina de Kirchner "incorporated" the Falklands into Tierra del Fuego in 2009.

(2) The inclusion of the claim to the Falklands in the Argentine constitution of 1994 (see section 10.25).

(3) The repudiation of the 1995 "Oil Agreement" with Britain in March 2007.

All those actions were incompatible with any idea that Resolution 31/49 was still operative. Nevertheless, Argentina continues to demand that Britain should respect Resolution 31/49 – an impossible demand since the premise on which it is based (ongoing negotiations) no longer applies. It is also an extraordinary demand given that Argentina breached it unilaterally in 1982 and later performed acts contrary to its provisions, thus continuing to treat it as void. It is not acceptable to demand that one's opponents keep to agreements which one has oneself breached.

10.24 The Third Falklands Crisis – the unmentioned war, 1982; the Falklands at the UN, 1982, 1986, 1987 and later

Kohen and Rodríguez say next to nothing about the Falklands War of 1982 – they refer only to "the Argentine actions of April 2nd, 1982" – though the war is the one thing most people have heard of in connection with the Falkland Islands. We refer to it as the Third Falklands Crisis, since it was of major international importance, like the First and Second Falklands Crises. It is dealt with in detail in *The Falklands Saga*, by Graham Pascoe (forthcoming), but only very briefly here, since Kohen and Rodríguez say little that needs refuting.

The basic facts are that the Argentine military junta (in power since the coup of 24 March 1976) invaded the Falklands on 2 April 1982 without warning,[1] and occupied the islands with some 10,000 troops. The islanders then lived under foreign military occupation, in Stanley for the full 74 days that the War lasted, in other parts of the islands for less. The Argentine secret police were much in evidence, mainly in the person of the sinister Major Patricio Dowling, who is remembered with revulsion by Falkland Islanders. Some islanders were imprisoned by the Argentinians (including 115 people at Goose Green for four weeks, a breach of the 1949 fourth Geneva Convention, see section 10.8), and the locals witnessed many cruel and brutal punishments imposed by Argentine officers on conscripts, especially around Stanley and Fox Bay. Many Stanleyites took pity on the starving Argentine conscripts and gave them food. Some parts of the islands were extensively mined, but only parts of the minefields were properly mapped by the Argentinians; de-mining has been carried on for some years now but is nowhere near complete. Britain sent a task force of ships and soldiers, and in a gruelling campaign involving hand-to-hand fighting at night and the sinking of ships on both sides, the Argentine forces were defeated and surrendered on 14 June 1982. It was not till many years later that Argentina punished some officers for their crimes against their men in the islands; some cases are even now (2022) not concluded, and one wonders if any officers would have been punished at all if Argentina had won the Falklands War.

The Falklands War was a textbook case of the policy of "land before people" that was standard in the age of Classic Imperialism in the 1890s (section 8.29): Argentina fought for the land; the people who lived on it did not count. But Britain reversed the principle that it had applied so successfully a century earlier and fought for the people. Argentina had all the advantages – surprise, easy logistics, massive forces in possession – while Britain had to conquer formidable logistical problems and fight at an immense distance from home. But Britain had a unique asset – the Mark I British soldier – and managed to win in the end. So, as Major General Jeremy Moore announced on 14 June 1982 after the Argentine surrender: "The Falkland Islands are once more under the government desired by their inhabitants."

In suppressing the Falklands War, Kohen and Rodríguez follow other Argentine authors, who write as if the war was irrelevant to the legal situation. That is like arguing that the Second World War is irrelevant and that previous arrangements such as the 1919 Treaty of Versailles and the Munich Agreement of 1938 are still in force – neither has ever been formally abrogated, and the Second World War has never been ended by a peace treaty. The absurdity of such a position shows that the Falklands War changed the legal situation of the Falklands. Argentina fought a war to acquire the Falklands and lost, so Argentina's acquisition of the islands was definitively reversed.

When the Falklands were first discussed at the United Nations in 1964-5 (sections 10.12, 10.14, 10.15), the basic facts about the islands' history were still unknown; some central documents were published by Ernesto Fitte in 1966, others in *Episodio Ocurrido* in 1967. All UN delegations on Argentina's side can therefore be excused for expressing what was then generally believed, though the British delegation did refute Argentina's assertions that the population was "transient" and that "Argentina had never ceased to protest" (section 10.14). But after the publication of the documents, that excuse disappeared; one might have expected that UN debates in the 1980s would take account of the newly revealed facts, but that did not happen. If Argentine diplomats knew of the new publications on Falklands history (which is by no means certain), they kept quiet about them, and British and other diplomats based in Buenos Aires did not take the trouble to find out. It is at least arguable that the Falklands War might not have taken place if the facts had been known. But nothing changed; Argentina continued to present a false version of Falklands history, and UN delegations supporting Argentina discussed it as if it were true.

During the Falklands War the islands were much discussed at the UN, including at meetings of

---

[1] What went on behind the scenes in Argentina before, during and after the Falklands War is described in detail by the former Argentine security chief Juan Bautista Yofre in *1982 – Los Documentos Secretos de la Guerra de Malvinas/ Falklands y el Derrumbe del Proceso* ["1982 – The Secret Documents on the Malvinas/Falklands War and the Collapse of the Proceso" (i.e. the junta's ideology)], Buenos Aires 2011, based on extensive access to secret internal documents (some illustrated in photographs). He demonstrates that the Falklands War was not premeditated by Britain but was planned beforehand by the junta.

the Security Council, in which the Argentine deputy foreign minister Enrique Ros said on 22 May:[1]

278. ... this dispute... was not begun by the Argentine Republic but precisely by this British fleet which, in a full upsurge of British imperialism, came to our coasts, expelled our authorities, imprisoned our inhabitants and expelled them to Montevideo. This was the act of force which gave rise to this problem. It is not a problem of today, it is a problem which goes back a long way. My country never signed a treaty, never accepted any declaration. On the contrary, it constantly protested against this usurpation of its territory, of a piece of our territory on which a colonial regime was imposed, and today it is claimed that we should accept it as if it were a fact which all Argentine generations have constantly rejected.

That passage is full of historical errors, as anyone will know who has read this book this far. In the first place, it was not Britain who "imprisoned our inhabitants and expelled them to Montevideo"; it was of course the United States – Captain Silas Duncan of the USS *Lexington* imprisoned the 7 men who had seized the American sealing ship *Harriet* in 1831, took them and some 40 other inhabitants including 14 black slaves to Montevideo, and took the 7 prisoners to Rio after releasing the others (sections 6.3, 6.12). Britain was not involved.

And it is not true that Argentina "never signed a treaty": Argentina ratified the Convention of Peace with Britain in 1850 and thus definitively accepted that the Falklands were British territory (sections 7.10-7.19). Nor is it true that Argentina "constantly protested against this usurpation of its territory" – Argentine protests ceased entirely for over a third of a century after the ratification of the Convention of Peace and again for many decades after 1888 (sections 7.19, 8.18).

On 24 May 1982 there was a General Assembly debate, in which South American delegations all supported Argentina, but the Kenyan UN ambassador Charles G. Maina said:[2]

Argentina is engaged in a pure territorial claim against the United Kingdom based on history, in total disregard of the people who now live on the Falkland Islands. I am not qualified to state whether or not the claims are valid, but if we accept that they are, they should not be settled at the expense of people who now live in the Falkland Islands. They are paramount, and in our view their interests are paramount... If we bend the principle of decolonization of peoples to look like the redistribution of territories, the United Nations is in real trouble... A lot of play has also been made about colonialism and the decolonization of the Falkland Islands contrary to the letter and spirit of General Assembly resolution 1514 (XV), whose thrust is the granting of independence to colonial countries and peoples, not, as some would have us believe, the settlement of territorial claims... Argentina... cannot claim any right to impose its own form of colonialism on the people of the Falkland Islands.

That is as true now as it was then. Argentina is still trying to "bend the principle of decolonization of peoples to look like the redistribution of territories". Above all, though, in starting the Falklands War Argentina breached all previous UN Resolutions on the Falklands.

Later debates at the UN showed that little had changed, though speakers ("petitioners") from the Falklands were permitted to attend and speak, as well as petitioners from Argentina. The statements by the Falkland Islanders were consistently ignored while the untrue version of Falklands history presented by Argentina was repeated *ad nauseam*. For example, at the C24 on 2 November 1982, the Panamanian representative Ozores Typaldos began by saying he was speaking for 20 national delegations, all South American:[3]

2. Mr. OZORES TYPALDOS (Panama) said that he wished to make a statement on behalf of the delegations of Argentina, Bolivia, Brazil, Colombia, Costa Rica, Chile, Cuba, Dominican Republic, El Salvador, Ecuador, Guatemala, Haiti, Honduras, Mexico, Nicaragua, Panama, Paraguay, Peru, Uruguay and Venezuela.

3. With reference to the Assembly's decision to permit petitioners currently resident in the Malvinas Islands to be heard by the Fourth Committee, the 20 Latin American States wished to place on record that the original population of the Islands were Argentines who had been expelled when the Islands had been

---

[1] UN Security Council 22 May 1982, UN doc. S/PV.2362, accessed under https://documents.un.org/prod/ods.nsf/ home.xsp; much of text also in *MGSS* vol. III, p. 215.
[2] Speech by Kenyan delegate Maina to the UN General Assembly at its 2364th meeting, 24 May 1982, from UN website under Official Document System of the United Nations (ODS), no. S/PV.2364(OR).
[3] All quotes from speeches at this session of the C24 are from UN document A/C.4/37/SR.12.

occupied, illegally and by force, in 1833; since that year, Argentines had not been permitted to become permanent residents of the Territory.

    4. In those circumstances those who currently inhabited the Malvinas Islands did not have the legitimate relationship with the Territory necessary to have the right to self-determination. The Latin American countries... considered that the current residents of the Territory, including the petitioners, did not meet the standards laid down by the United Nations to be entitled to that right.

    5. Such was indeed basically the position of the General Assembly, which, in its three resolutions on the question of the Falkland Islands (Malvinas), had stipulated that the only way in which the Territory could be decolonized was by solving the sovereignty dispute between Argentina and the United Kingdom and that the Governments of those two States were the only parties to that dispute.

That statement was full of errors, including as usual the Expulsion Myth. As we explained in sections 6.24 and 6.25, it was not true that Britain had expelled the "original population"; Britain expelled only the mutinous, murderous Argentine garrison and encouraged the civilian inhabitants to stay. There was no mention at the UN that the removal of the civilian inhabitants had not been carried out by Britain but by Louis Vernet (who on 7 November 1831 removed 29 people, over a quarter of the then population, section 6.9) and by the American warship USS *Lexington*, which on 22 January 1832 removed some 47 people (over half the remaining 80 or so; section 6.12). Britain was not involved in those removals of people, but that remained unknown at the United Nations even though the basic facts had been available for 15 years in books published in Buenos Aires.

The national representatives at the United Nations had an entirely false idea of the "original population"; many must have imagined there had been a long-established population of Argentinians in the islands. The delegations at the UN remained unaware that in January 1833 not a single person had been in the islands for even as much as 5 years, nor that the population had constantly changed, with most people only staying a few months; there were no permanent inhabitants at all but only constantly changing temporary residents. And they were not all Argentinian; there were several other nationalities including from 1828 to 1832 some two dozen black African slaves (sections 5.1, 5.9). Moreover, it was not true that "Argentines had not been permitted to become permanent residents of the Territory" – as we pointed out in sections 7.7 and 10.1, at least 17 Argentinians went to live and work in the islands in 1847, and there are Argentinians living there now (10.4).

Against that, the two Falkland Islander petitioners, John Cheek and Tim Blake (members of the islands' Legislative Council), made statements the same day, 2 November 1982, presenting the islanders' position, and stated no false history at all. John Cheek said:

    15. The roots of the community went back to the first half of the nineteenth century. His own great great grandfather had arrived in the Falkland Islands in the 1850s while the arrival of his wife's family dated back to 1841. What had been created over the past hundred or so years was a society with a culture and a tradition all of its own. Most of the islanders came from British stock and much of the way of life had evolved from the British. There had been influence from other countries, particularly from southern Argentina and Chile, and representatives of other nations and cultures had been welcomed. The society was tolerant and democratic, and its political institutions had developed considerably over the years and provided the islanders with effective control over their own affairs. Institutions were constantly evolving at the pace and in the direction wished by the islanders... in full accordance with Article 73 of the United Nations Charter. [...]

    17. ... The United Kingdom was certainly not a colonial Power nor an imperialist Power. However, the islanders had found earlier in 1982 that there was a colonial or imperialist Power in the region which was quite prepared to trample on their rights and to inflict suffering on the people. It was the United Kingdom which had come to the rescue, and for that the islanders were grateful...

Tim Blake said:

    20. He would not wish the experiences of the Falkland islanders between April and June 1982 on any other people. The effects of the Argentine invasion were still with the islanders and it would be some time before the Territory could recover from the material damage, quite apart from the emotional strain on the inhabitants. The Argentines had frequently said that they had come to protect the interests and rights of the islanders, but the... democratically elected representatives of the islanders had been totally ignored; the right

to free speech was subject to restrictions which, if broken, resulted in long-term prison sentences. [...]

21. The islanders had seen people beaten and tied up for long periods for listening to English-speaking broadcasts. People had been shot at and run down by helicopters in the course of providing food for islanders in isolated areas. Individuals had been interned with no reason given; some had been parted from their families without notice; entire farming communities had been imprisoned in small buildings and their houses and property had been smashed, soiled and looted. [...]

25. The Argentines had always said that they respected the interests of the islanders. Everything they had done during their occupation of the Islands showed that they... had no concern for the interests of the islanders... Still less did they ever ask about the wishes of the islanders. All they had received had been orders from the military commanders. One of the first had been to the effect that the official language had become Spanish and that all would be required to learn that language. News and radio reporting had been heavily censored and later shut off; the schools had had to be shut down because the Argentines had permitted them to be used only for their own propaganda purposes. There had never been any understanding of the culture, traditions or democratic rights of the islanders.

And John Cheek made a final concluding statement:

28. He understood that, at the United Nations, the Argentines were now saying that they wanted to negotiate with the United Kingdom about the Falkland Islands. As usual they were not interested in the wishes of the Falkland islanders and did not accept that the latter should have any say in what happened to them. Yet, in April 1982, it was the Argentines who had decided that negotiations were not the path for them. It was they who had reneged on the joint communique[1] and turned to the use of force in defiance of the United Nations and in total disregard of the wishes of the Falkland islanders... He asked how it was possible to take seriously their request for negotiations after their attitude in the past and the way they had treated the islanders during the summer of 1982... Their claim to respect what they described as the interests of the Falkland islanders were outrageous and hypocritical. The islanders appealed to delegations to respect their wish to decide themselves how they wanted to live and to leave them alone to get on with the task of rehabilitation and reconstruction, which were now foremost in their minds...

Those statements were completely ignored, though they were made by representatives of the people of the territory involved. That shows that Argentina had subverted the C24 from its original purpose and remit. It was founded to *promote* self-determination, but Argentina converted it into a vehicle for the *abolition* of self-determination and the realisation of Argentina's colonialist aims.

Two days later on 4 November 1982 the Falklands were discussed in the 55th plenary session of the United Nations General Assembly. The Madagascan representative Mr Rasolondraibe said:[2]

2. ... might does not make right, and while the Republic of Argentina succumbed twice – in 1833 and 1982 – to superior military force, it none the less has maintained its sovereignty over the Malvinas Islands and is no less justified in calling for restoration of the Islands to it. That is the meaning of its present initiative in the General Assembly. That sovereignty, deriving from the succession to the rights enjoyed by Spain, is clearly established, because the titles of the Spanish sovereign were recognized by the Powers of that time, including France and Great Britain.

3. On the other hand, nothing would justify a statement that... the United Kingdom acquired sovereignty over those Islands. First of all, its illegal occupation was challenged by Argentina, both in London and in Buenos Aires, after the act of force of 1833, and the Argentine authorities have never renounced their rights.

Mr Rasolondraibe stated two standard falsehoods which have frequently been repeated on behalf of Argentina, at the UN and elsewhere. It was untrue that "the titles of the Spanish sovereign were recognized by the Powers of that time, including France and Great Britain" (sections 2.3, 7.2), and it was untrue that "the Argentine authorities have never renounced their rights" (sections 7.11-7.19).

By contrast, the British representative, Sir John Thomson, referred back to the statements by John Cheek and Tim Blake, and pointed out that:

124. ... If the Argentines had genuinely wanted to reassure the Falklanders and to influence Britain, they

---

[1] Negotiators for both sides in the talks in New York on 26 and 27 February 1982 agreed on a joint communiqué on the talks, but the text was much too feeble for the junta, and Argentina took the undiplomatic step of issuing a unilateral communiqué different from the one agreed with Britain. Argentine foreign minister Nicanor Costa Méndez rewrote the text, tightening up the timetable and at the end adding a threat of military force.
[2] UN document A/37/PV.55.

would have referred not to the interests of the people, but rather to their wishes. Who can be a better judge of their interests than the Falklanders themselves? Anyone who listened to the cross-questioning of the petitioners in the Fourth Committee two days ago will have realized what a mockery it is for the Argentines to talk about their respect for the interests of the people. There is no sign in the draft resolution or in the sponsors' speeches of any recognition of the fundamental fact that these people have been for generations, and continue to be, the people of the Islands. It is ludicrous for the Argentines to refer to them as "immigrant communities". They, and only they, are Falklanders and the Falkland Islands are their home.

As pointed out in section 10.16, the difference between interests and wishes is spurious; it is impossible to rule a population according to their interests but against their wishes.

Finally, a draft resolution (A/37/L.3/Rev.1) was presented and voted on; it was passed by the General Assembly by by 90 votes to 12, with 52 abstentions, and duly became UN Resolution 37/9, which merely "Requests the Governments of Argentina and the United Kingdom of Great Britain and Northern Ireland to resume negotiations in order to find as soon as possible a peaceful solution to the sovereignty dispute relating to the question of the Falkland Islands (Malvinas)".[1] In other words, Resolution 2065 was merely repeated, as if the Falklands War had not happened.

For a long time Falkland Islanders urged Britain to declare a fisheries[2] conservation zone around the islands – they saw it as absurd that the surrounding waters teemed with fish, and by 1986 some 600 fishing boats from many countries were exploiting those waters without restriction, but the only fish many islanders ate was in the form of fish fingers imported from Britain. Eventually, on 29 October 1986, Governor Gordon Jewkes signed a proclamation establishing the Interim Falklands Conservation Zone, with a radius of 150 nautical miles (later extended to 200 nautical miles, 370 km), and on 1 February 1987 the Falkland Islands Fisheries (Conservation and Management) Ordinance came into effect. Ever since then, the islands have had their own fishing industry – a third of the "calamares" (squid) eaten in Spain are actually from Falklands waters.

As a result of the establishment of the fishing zone, the Falklands were discussed at the United Nations in November and December 1986. As usual Argentina and Argentine apologists continued to misunderstand (or misrepresent) the basic facts of the islands' history, thus seriously misleading the UN. For example, on 24 November 1986, Marcelo Delpech, Argentina's permanent UN representative, stated before the C24:[3]

> 34. He did agree with the petitioner who had stated that the Malvinas did not have an indigenous population. Until 1833, when the British had illegally occupied the Islands, the sole inhabitants had been 40 or 50 Argentines living there peacefully.

Apart from the statement that the islands did not have an indigenous population, the rest of that is incorrect. Britain did not occupy the islands in 1833 (no British presence was left there), and the British presence, which only began in 1834, was not illegal in international law or in the law of any country except Argentina, and it ceased to be illegal even under Argentine law upon the ratification of the Convention of Peace in May 1850 (chapter 7). And as we demonstrate in sections 6.21, 6.24 and 6.25, and Tables 6.24c and 6.24d, it was untrue that the sole inhabitants had been "40 or 50 Argentines living there peacefully" – the Argentine garrison had behaved abominably, had murdered their commanding officer in cold blood and had terrorised and robbed the civilians, and of the 37 civilian residents not connected with the garrison, only 10 were Argentinians, of whom only 2 were taken away (Ventura Pasos, who left of his own free will, and the prisoner Maximo Warnes, who was taken away by the garrison).

As we said in the Introduction, history is the raw material of justice, and no correct judgement can be based on false history. The false history presented at the United Nations on behalf of Argentina has inevitably led to false judgements on the real legal situation of the Falklands.

As well as at the C24, the Falklands were discussed at the United Nations General Assembly on

---

[1] UN document A/RES/37/9, 4 November 1982, paragraph 1.
[2] By this time "fisheries" meant of course the catching of fish proper, plus also squid and other species such as krill, but not mammals such as seals or whales, which the term had included in the 19th century.
[3] UN document A/C.4/41/SR.19, 24 November 1982.

1 and 2 December 1986, in debates that centred on a draft resolution, A/41/L.19.[1] On 1 December the discussion revolved almost exclusively around the fishing zone. The British UN ambassador Sir John Thomson drew attention to the element of hypocrisy in Argentina's complaint against the zone, and also pointed out the possible legal consequences if Britain had not declared such a zone:[2]

... The Foreign Minister of Argentina did not mention that his country, under the same international law as my Government used, already has a 200-mile zone stretching from the shores of Argentina. Nor did he make it clear that his Government also claims a 200-mile zone centred on the Falkland Islands.

... since there is a dispute, it is hard to see why the United Kingdom can be making it worse by claiming 150 miles, for the time being, around the Falkland Islands. It seems to me that we are only following in the path already taken by Argentina. Indeed, we are forced to follow. If we had not made such a declaration, we might have found Argentina arguing that since its law said the 200-mile centred on the Falkland Islands was Argentine, and we had done nothing corresponding, that we were in effect admitting their sovereignty.

... for us conservation is the reason for the declaration. But as I have just indicated there is some tincture of sovereignty in the problem. I have mentioned the Argentine claims... These claims have existed for some time. But Argentina took a new step this year which brings the whole matter vividly before us.

The next day, 2 December 1986, the General Assembly discussions involved speakers from a number of countries; as always, all the South American delegations supported Argentina, as did several other countries' delegations, and as always, their speeches contained false history. For example, the Bolivian delegate Jorge Gumucio Granier said:[3]

... historical evidence shows that the Argentine population inhabiting the Malvinas Islands up to 1833 was expelled by the invaders. For example, a number of families expelled from the Malvinas sought refuge in Chuquisaca, Bolivia. I need not refer to the historic bond with Bolivia which, until 1825, shared [sic] with the Argentine provinces, including the Malvinas, which were part of the Viceroyalty of La Plata. In our view, the legitimate population of the Malvinas, which could have sought self-determination, was expelled, and therefore we cannot agree that the civil servants or descendants of civil servants of the British colonial administration should now seek, on the pretext of self-determination, to jeopardize the unquestionable rights of Argentina by perpetuating a colonial situation clearly contrary to the course of history and one which wounds the feelings of the peoples of Latin America...

There is in fact no evidence whatever that any of the people who left the Falklands in 1833 went to Bolivia; Granier provided none, and it is impossible to see what "families" he could be referring to. As we pointed out in section 6.24, the legitimate population of the islands was not expelled.

Quite apart from the erroneous Falklands history repeated by most Latin American delegates, some of them said other incorrect things, for example Oscar Oramas Oliva of Cuba:[4]

For some years now the General Assembly has been clearly and firmly stating its view that the Malvinas Islands and the waters adjacent thereto belong to the Argentine Republic.

That was untrue – the General Assembly has never stated any such view; it has never taken any position as regards the respective merits of the British and Argentine claims to the Falklands.

The British representative Sir John Thomson pointed out that the draft resolution was by no means as innocuous or as neutral as it seemed:[5]

Sir John THOMSON (United Kingdom): ... The draft resolution before us is seductive in its simplicity and cosmetic appeal... Some of the sponsors of the draft resolution have claimed that it is purely procedural and that it in no way prejudices the position of either the Argentine or the British Government.

This is not so, sadly. The draft resolution... does actually prejudice the position. As I pointed out yesterday, the draft resolution calls, in operative paragraph 1, for negotiations on all aspects of the future of the Falkland Islands. Unless I have misunderstood the Foreign Minister of Argentina, he insists that "all aspects" must include the question of sovereignty. In his speech yesterday he said:

---

[1] Verbatim records of speeches in UN documents A/41/PV.82 and A/41/PV.84 (paragraphs not numbered).
[2] UN document A/41/PV.82, p. 57-58.
[3] UN document A/41/PV.84, pp. 34-35.
[4] UN document A/41/PV.84, p. 52.
[5] UN document A/41/PV.84, concluding remarks, p. 90-92.

"So long as the core problem" – he meant sovereignty here, of course – "is ignored, we shall not be able to solve the accessory problems." (A/41/PV.82, p. 21)

So the draft resolution supports the Argentine contention that sovereignty must be discussed. It opposes the United Kingdom contention that sovereignty should not be discussed. Therefore, the resolution is not neutral; it is pro-Argentine. [...]

I got no answer to my question yesterday. I suppose that is because Argentina refuses to discuss what it calls the accessory problems, without discussing sovereignty. In other words, Argentina is putting a condition on the opening of any talks.

My Government also has a condition. The Argentine condition is that sovereignty must be discussed; our condition is that it must not be discussed... In these circumstances, I ask the Foreign Minister, or the Permanent Representative of Argentina, once again, whether Argentina would not be willing to enter talks with us designed to improve our relations by dealing with some or all of the questions other than sovereignty, which he has listed in his speech? Surely, this is a reasonable offer. I hope he will accept it. I hope also that he will accept that the principle of self-determination is applicable in this colonial situation, as it is in others.

Many speakers have insisted that the Falklands is a colonial situation. Well then, self-determination applies...

All that was true of course, but the debate had been hijacked by Argentina, and the result was a foregone conclusion – draft resolution A/41/L.19 was adopted by 116 votes to 4 (Belize, Oman, Sri Lanka, UK), with 34 abstentions, and became the very brief UN Resolution 41/40,[1] which in its paragraph 1 calls on Argentina and Britain to "initiate negotiations with a view to finding the means to resolve peacefully and definitively the problems pending between both countries, including all aspects on [*sic*] the future of the Falkland Islands (Malvinas), in accordance with the Charter of the United Nations." The resolution thus repeated the call for negotiations stated in Resolution 2065 (see section 10.15), but with two significant differences: it says "all aspects" of the future of the Falklands (thus including sovereignty, as Sir John Thomson pointed out) – and it does not even mention the interests, let alone the wishes, of the people of the islands.

In passing that resolution, the United Nations General Assembly, and the decolonisation committee, the C24, had abandoned their principles as laid down in the UN Charter, and had become an instrument for the imposition of colonialism, not for its abolition.

A year later on 14 August 1987 one of the petitioners for Argentina was a member of the Vernet family (as on several other occasions). His speech is not recorded in UN documents but only in the Argentine account *MGSS*, which does not give his first name, so we refer to him as "Señor Vernet". However, his surname did not stop him from talking complete nonsense. His speech reflected the standard Argentine view of Louis Vernet's settlement in the islands, and like José María Ruda's speech at the United Nations in 1964 (section 10.14), it would be hard to beat for sheer concentrated inaccuracy. In the course of his speech he said:[2]

At the end of November 1824 the brigantine "Fenwich" sailed and the schooner "Rafaela" with Emilio Vernet, brother of Luis Vernet, significantly increasing the establishment of Argentine citizens in Malvinas. His arrival date was 2 February 1825... [all *sic*!]

To set the record straight: before the expedition's ships arrived there were no Argentinians at all in the Falklands, so their numbers were not "increased"; as we described in section 4.9, the cutter *Rafaela* sailed on 29 December 1823 (not November 1824) but then disappeared; the American brig *Fenwick* (not "Fenwich") sailed on 11 January 1824 with Pablo Areguati's group, who reached Port Louis on 2 February 1824 (not 1825), and the British brig *Antelope* sailed around 1 March 1824 with Schofield's group including Emilio Vernet (who was not aboard the *Rafaela*), and reached Port Louis on 26 March 1824. Every detail of Señor Vernet's account was factually wrong. He also failed to say that the entire expedition left again four months later, so he left the impression that they remained in the islands. He continued:

---

[1] Full text in UN document A/RES/41/40.
[2] Speech by Señor Vernet (first name not recorded) at the C24, 14 August 1987, in *MGSS* vol. VII, Part 1, pp. 257-262; quotes here from pp. 258, 260, 261. *MGSS* gives "A/AC.109/PV.1327" and "A/AC.109/920 and Corr. 1; A/AC.109/L. 1644" as the numbers of the United Nations documents, but those numbers are not registered on the UN website.

> The inhabitants began to prosper in the Malvinas, whose capital was Puerto Luis. The settled population was already some two hundred people, which was the approximate number at the time of the violent usurpation by the United Kingdom.
>
> Communications with Buenos Aires and between the islands required several boats, and Vernet constructed a schooner, christened "Aguila", which was the first Argentine naval construction in the Malvinas… [all *sic*!]

That is nonsense too, and reveals how the Argentine view of the Vernet period in the Falklands is based on the crassly erroneous work by Antonio Gómez Langenheim (see sections 5.1, 5.19).

To set the record straight: the figure of 200 people is a wild exaggeration; the maximum number of people at Port Louis at any one time was briefly 128 in mid-1831; it soon declined (sections 5.1, 6.2, 6.12, 6.23), and on 1 January 1833, the day before the *Clio*'s arrival, there were (apart from ships' crews) exactly 82 people there: 45 connected with the garrison plus 37 civilian residents, of whom only 10 were Argentinians (section 6.24). And the fictitious account of the so-called "Águila" is from Gómez Langenheim: Louis Vernet never saw the ship, which was the shallop *Eagle*, built on Eagle Island by the *Belleville* men. The "Águila myth" was repeated by María Angélica Vernet (another descendant of Louis Vernet) at the UN on 20 June 2013 (section 5.19).

Señor Vernet continued, in his speech of 14 August 1987:

> Thus far it has been amply proved that we Argentine citizens lived peacefully in the Malvinas, and any Malvinas Islander who comes to this Committee can confirm that today, 154 years later, Vernet's house in the Malvinas is standing. My ancestors were deprived of all their possessions by the British. Those ancestors had arrived in the islands legitimately, and were expelled from them by force in 1833, in a barbaric act that did not conform to international law. That usurpation continues to the present. [all *sic*!]

That too is twaddle. To set the record straight: Señor Vernet's ancestors were not expelled by the British – Louis Vernet left the Falklands by his own free decision, with his family, servants and slaves, on 7 November 1831 (section 6.9), over a year before the British arrived in the form of HMS *Clio*. And Vernet's house is not still standing; it is a ruin, parts of which are almost 2 metres high. The house wrongly identified as Vernet's house by many Argentinians, and by Argentine governments, is actually the British barracks built in 1843, twelve years after Vernet left the islands (section 5.4, figures 5.4b, 5.4c, and section 7.2, fig. 7.2a).

Of the people in the Falklands on 1 January 1833, the longest-established whose arrival date is known were the two black African former slaves Carmelita and Gregoria, who had arrived in the islands on 2 September 1828. They had been there for 4 years and 4 months; not a single person is known for certain to have been in the islands longer than that (section 5.9).

Several standard untruths were repeated two months later on 17 November 1987 at the United Nations by Argentine foreign minister Dante Caputo – he said:[1]

> British acquiescence in Argentine sovereignty over the Malvinas Islands was confirmed in 1825, through the bilateral treaty by which London formally recognised Argentine independence. On that occasion England did not make any reservation with respect to any part of Argentine territory. Despite having previously recognised Argentine sovereignty, in 1833 – as is known – the United Kingdom occupied the archipelago by force. That act was accompanied by the expulsion of the original Argentine population and since 1833 Argentines have been prohibited from living in, or possessing property in, the archipelago… The Argentine republic has never consented to the occupation of the Malvinas Islands by the United Kingdom…

That is all nonsense. As we pointed out in section 4.12, the 1825 Treaty of Amity (like any recognition treaty) did not recognise any specific extent of Argentina's territory, and thus did not indicate British acquiescence in Argentine sovereignty over the Falklands. There was no "original Argentine population" – on 1 January 1833 only 10 out of the 37 civilian residents were Argentinians, none of whom had been in the islands even as long as 5 years, and only 2 of those Argentinians were taken away. It is untrue that Argentinians have been prohibited from living in the islands, and it is not true that Argentina has "never consented" to Britain's possession of the

---

[1] Report of the UN Fourth Committee to the General Assembly, 17 November 1987, UN document A/42/PV.70; *MGSS* vol. VII part 1, pp. 297-298.

Falklands – Argentina's consent was definitively given by the ratification of the Convention of Peace in 1850 and confirmed in many ways thereafter (chapters 7, 8).

Those and other historical and legal falsehoods are still presented annually by Argentina at the UN, for example by the then Argentine foreign minister Rafael Bielsa on 18 June 2004 and his successor Jorge Marcelo Faurie on 20 June 2018 (section 8.11). Argentina is invariably supported by the delegations of other South American countries, and a few others, who of course merely repeat what Argentina constantly asserts. Britain's refutations of some of the most central falsehoods are ignored and the falsehoods are restated, again and again and again.

Truth is stranger than fiction, as the saying goes, but when the United Nations considers the Falkland Islands, fiction is stronger than truth.

Small wonder, then, that in 1990 Britain announced to the C24 that it "considered the colonial era as over and therefore saw no further need for the United Nations to devote time and resources to the special study of the affairs of the non-self-governing territories". And two years later in 1992 the United States drew the necessary conclusion and "decided after careful thought to suspend its cooperation with the C-24 until the Committee takes the steps needed to bring its work in line with the current focus and spirit of the United Nations".[1] Those steps have never been taken; even now in the 21st century, year after year the C24 continues to give Argentina a forum to proclaim its colonialist aim of taking over the Falklands against the wishes of the Falkland Islanders, directly breaching UN Resolutions 1514, 1541, 2625, and the ICCPR.

10.25 Transitory disposition – Argentina's claim enshrined (but destroyed), August 1994

Following the Falklands War there was a consensus among political parties in Argentina that the country's constitutional arrangements were unsatisfactory. In theory the constitution in force (that of 1957, an amended version of that of 1853) was admirably democratic, but it had not been respected by the political and military elite and was due for updating. On 22 October 1993 President Carlos Menem signed decree no. 2181/93, providing for a National Constituent Convention to prepare a new constitution. The convention met for three months in the middle of 1994, and on 22 August 1994, by acclamation, accepted the text of the new Argentine constitution.

For the first time the constitution gave expression to social and political rights; it mentioned the environment for the first time, and it made various alterations to the political system, altering the terms of senators from nine to six years, removing the requirement that the president must be a Roman Catholic, and importantly from Menem's point of view shortening the presidential term from six to four years but permitting two consecutive terms.

And for the first time the Falkland Islands were mentioned – they had not been included in any previous Argentine constitution.[2] After the main text, the new constitution contained 17 "transitory dispositions" (statements of official aims, which would cease to be part of the constitution once they had been achieved), the first of which enshrined Argentina's claim to the Falklands:

TRANSITORY DISPOSITIONS
First.– The Argentine Nation ratifies its legitimate and imprescriptible sovereignty over the Malvinas, South Georgias and South Sandwich islands and the corresponding maritime and insular areas, as being an integral part of the national territory. The recovery of those territories and the full exercise of sovereignty, respecting the way of life of their inhabitants, and in conformity with the principles of International Law, constitute a permanent and unrenounceable objective of the Argentine people.

This "transitory disposition" introduced three new elements into the Falklands dispute:

First, it anchored the "recovery" (i.e. the annexation) of the Falklands and "the full exercise of sovereignty" in the Argentine constitution and committed future governments to work towards that end. So Argentina had "painted itself into a corner" – any future negotiations with Britain would be

---

[1] Both quotes here from Huntsman and Kalolo 2007, pp. 151, 152, quoting file 449/13/2, part 4, in Archives New Zealand (the New Zealand national archives, Wellington)– see section 10.8.
[2] Complete text of the 1853 and 1949 constitutions, plus other constitutional documents, in Faustino J. Legón and Samuel W. Medrano, *Las Constituciones de la República Argentina*, Madrid 1953; complete text of 1957 Constitution in *Constitución de la Nación Argentina*, published by the Imprenta del Congreso de la Nación, Buenos Aires 1958.

pointless since Argentina could only accept a complete British surrender. The International Court of Justice stated in its ruling on the *Bolivia/Chile* case in October 2018 that when negotiating, countries "are under an obligation so to conduct themselves that the negotiations are meaningful, which will not be the case when either of them insists upon its own position without contemplating any modification".[1] So in any negotiations with Britain over the Falklands, Argentina would be negotiating in bad faith.

Secondly, the "transitory disposition" fatally undermined Argentina's claim to the Falklands by the statement that it is "imprescriptible", i.e. eternal unless voluntarily relinquished. The "imprescriptibility" of Argentina's claim had been asserted twice by José María Ruda in his speech to the C24 on 9 September 1964 (see section 10.14), and it has been repeatedly asserted by Argentine speakers at the UN and elsewhere. The term "imprescriptible" means "not subject to prescription", i.e. eternal, permanent, not lapsing after a certain time. The term is used in discussing, for example, human rights, which are permanent and do not lapse. Territorial claims, by contrast, are not permanent attributes and may lapse or be abandoned or cancelled in various ways. And of course no claimant is entitled to lay down how long his claims are to subsist. The notion that Argentina's claim to the Falklands is "imprescriptible" is incompatible with international law. It is a version of the medieval principle *nullum tempus occurrit regi* – "to the king, no time passes": the sovereign is immune from the operation of statutes of limitation and his claims are eternal unless he renounces them (section 8.11). It operates in national law within a given country in maintaining the permanent rights of the sovereign (i.e. the government) against the rights of lower-level authorities or private citizens, which are temporary, but it is not applicable to international law – there is no hierarchy between states, no "top state", so no state can maintain that its claims against any other state are eternal. It is obvious that if Argentina can assert an eternal claim despite the passage of over 180 years of British administration in the Falklands plus very extensive evidence of overt Argentine acquiescence in British sovereignty, then Britain can equally well maintain an eternal claim from Captain John Byron's possession-taking ceremony at Port Egmont on 21 January 1765, despite the absence of an official British presence for almost 60 years (1774-1834) and an Argentine settlement at Port Louis from 1826 to 1833. And if Argentina can maintain – as Argentine governments regularly do – that the British "takeover" was "illegal" because the islands were rightfully Argentinian, then Britain can equally well maintain that the Argentine settlement from 1826 to 1833 was "illegal" because the islands were rightfully British. Any assertion of "eternal" or "imprescriptible" claims in international law is therefore pointless and invalid.

And thirdly, the "transitory disposition" begs a vital question: it states that the "way of life" of the islands' inhabitants is to be respected – but who is to lay down which aspects of that way of life are to be respected and which not? Argentina is not offering to respect all aspects, otherwise the islands would remain British – one of the most vital aspects of the islanders' way of life is their right of self-determination, which they have exercised for a long time and would lose if Argentina took their country over. The obvious people to lay down what is important would be the islanders themselves, but Argentina is not prepared to permit them to do so – Argentina's claim to the Falklands can only be maintained in direct opposition to the people of the islands. At most, Argentina is only offering to grant the islanders a limited form of internal self-determination (accepting what Argentina regards as the islanders' way of life, such as driving on the left, etc.), but all the United Nations resolutions described in this chapter (1514, 1541, 2625, and the UN International Covenant on Civil and Political Rights; see sections 10.8, 10.9, 10.18 and 10.17), give Falkland Islanders the right to decide the foreign relations of their country, whether in complete independence, in free association or integration with a UN member state, or in any other status; in short, the right to full external self-determination. They gave expression to that right in the Falklands Referendum of 2013 (section 10.6), and made their views on the matter abundantly clear – they wished to remain an Overseas Territory of the United Kingdom. They chose their "political status freely determined by a people", as UN resolution 2625 puts it. The assertion that Argentina

---

[1] International Court of Justice, ruling in the *Bolivia/Chile* case, 1 October 2018, para. 86, quoting *I.C.J. Reports 1969*, p. 47, para. 85.

will respect Falkland Islanders' way of life, while at the same time demanding to take over their country against their wishes, is contradictory and devoid of credibility. In short, the first "transitory disposition" in Argentina's constitution destroys Argentina's claim to the Falklands.

10.26 Argentina's failed attempt to move the goalposts at the UN, 2008

Since 1964 the United Nations Decolonisation Committee, the "C24", has been regularly misused by Argentina as a forum in which to present its territorial ambition of taking over the Falkland Islands, and the C24, to its shame, has permitted Argentina to subvert the Committee's discussion of the Falklands to that end (sections 10.8, 10.12, 10.14, 10.16). Every year a high-level Argentine delegation attends the Committee's sessions in New York (on 14 June 2012 the then Argentine president, Cristina de Kirchner, attended with a 90-strong Argentine delegation), and Argentine speakers present the standard, untrue, Argentine account of the case and receive loud applause from the Argentinians present, whereas the Falklands petitioners are heard in stony silence, even though they are the people representing the territory concerned. After the Falklands and Argentine speakers, the representatives of several other C24 member countries make speeches supporting Argentina, often declaring support for Argentina's "legitimate rights over the Malvinas, South Georgia, South Sandwich Islands and the surrounding maritime areas" – in 2018 Uruguay, Brazil, Costa Rica and Peru used more or less exactly those words, while Ecuador, Syria, El Salvador, Paraguay and Colombia did so without the word "legitimate". Naturally those countries have no independent policy of their own on the Falklands; they simply regurgitate Argentina's false version of the case. The C24 debates (if they can be called debates) are yet another bizarre aspect of the Argentine claim to the Falklands.

The Committee have never accepted invitations to visit the Falklands,[1] although they have visited other non-self-governing territories and also Argentina. In October 2010 Donatus Keith St. Aimee (1944-2015), UN Permanent Representative of St Lucia, who was then the chairman of the C24, visited Argentina at the invitation of the Argentine government, and on 18 October 2010 he gave a seminar at the University of Belgrano which Peter Pepper attended. Afterwards Peter asked him if he would visit the Falklands if he were invited; St. Aimee said he would, and Peter passed that information to the Falkland Islands Government. They wrote to him inviting him to visit the islands, but he never replied.

In allowing Argentina to make a bid to take over a non-self-governing territory, the Committee is blatantly misusing its remit – instead of promoting the self-determination of the Falkland Islanders as it should be doing, it has become a mouthpiece for Argentina's colonialist aim of taking the islands over. However, nothing comes of it since the C24's mandate is merely to consider cases of colonialism against the background of the relevant United Nations resolutions and to report annually to the UN General Assembly on progress towards "the eradication of colonialism in all its forms". Thus the Committee is not empowered to make any territorial recommendations, and merely submits a report calling for negotiations.

In 2008 an attempt was made by the Argentine C24 delegation to exclude the Falklands from any future consideration of self-determination by changing the wording of the Committee's yearly report. At the C24 meeting on 11 June 2008, a phrase was added to a draft resolution in the 2008 report at the instigation of Argentina (new phrase underlined here):[2]

The General Assembly [... ...]

> 2. *Also reaffirms* that, in the process of decolonization, <u>and where there is no dispute over sovereignty</u>, there is no alternative to the principle of self-determination, which is also a fundamental human right, as recognized under the relevant human rights conventions...

---

[1] Nor to visit Gibraltar, despite repeated requests from Gibraltar (Trinidad 2018, p. 208). That reveals the clear bias of the C24 towards the claimant countries in the cases of both Gibraltar and the Falklands.

[2] [Anon.], *Report of the Special Committee on the Situation with regard to the Implementation of the Declaration on the Granting of Independence to Colonial Countries and Peoples for 2008* (i.e. the report of the "Committee of 24" or "C24"), Official Records, Sixty-third Session, Supplement No. 23 (doc. A/63/23), United Nations, New York 2008, transmitted for consideration to the UN General Assembly on 30 June 2008, p. 67, underlining here by us.

The phrase we have underlined was included in the text of the draft resolution in the 2008 report. If confirmed by the UN General Assembly, it would have "moved the goalposts" and removed territories over which there was a sovereignty dispute (notably the Falklands and Gibraltar) from the universal principle that there is no alternative to self-determination.

Four months later on 20 October 2008 Argentina's attempt to deny self-determination to the Falkland Islanders was defeated by the UN General Assembly. Britain's UN ambassador Sir John Sawers tabled an amendment removing the added phrase; the British amendment was passed by 61 votes to 40, with 47 abstentions,[1] so the phrase added by the Committee at Argentina's behest, limiting self-determination to cases in which there was no sovereignty dispute, was deleted from the resolution passed by the Assembly. So Argentina failed to remove the Falklands from the universal applicability of self-determination.

10.27 Ban Ki-moon affirms the universality of self-determination, 2016

The universality of the right to self-determination for the peoples of all non-self-governing territories, which had been stated in UN Resolutions 1514, 1541, and 2625, and in the UN International Covenant on Civil and Political Rights (ICCPR), was confirmed in May 2016 by Ban Ki-moon, the then Secretary-General of the United Nations, in a message read out at the opening of the Pacific Regional Seminar on Decolonization in Managua, Nicaragua. He said that according to the Charter of the United Nations and relevant General Assembly resolutions, "a full measure of self-government can be achieved through independence, integration or free association with another State. The choice should be the result of the freely expressed will and desire of the peoples of the Non-Self-Governing Territories."[2] He thus confirmed the three methods of achieving self-determination laid down in Resolution 1541 and made no exceptions. Possessing the right to choose between those options means that the peoples of *all* non-self-governing territories have the right to full external self-determination. That was confirmed by the International Court of Justice in its advisory opinion on the Chagos Islands in 2019 (see section 10.28). That rules out any Argentine takeover of the Falkland Islands.

10.28 Self-determination: the Chagos connection[3]

Kohen and Rodríguez entitle the last section of their book "The manipulation of the right of peoples to self-determination by history's principal colonial power" – and here they mention the one thing on which we agree with them: Britain's disgraceful treatment of the people of the Chagos Islands, an archipelago of some 65 scattered islands and atolls in the Indian Ocean, with a total area of 56 square kilometres; the largest island is Diego Garcia, with an area of 33 sq. km.

The history of the Chagos Islands offers some illuminating similarities to that of the Falklands. Like the Falklands they were uninhabited, were apparently discovered by the Portuguese in the 16th century, were first settled in the 18th century by the French and later passed to Britain. The French brought slaves from Africa and Madagascar to work on coconut plantations, and the British brought workers from India. Britain ended slavery in 1840, and by 1900 the islands had over 500 inhabitants, 60% of them of African and Madagascan origin, 40% from India, and there were many children.[4] By 1965 the population was 1,800, like the Falklands at that time. The people were native to the islands, and generations of them lay buried in the cemeteries.

Nevertheless, in the 1960s, at the same time as it was negotiating over the Falklands with Argentina, the British government negotiated with the United States to build a military base on

---

[1] Voting details from UN press release www.un.org/News/Press/docs/2008/gaspd406.doc.htm, 20 October 2008.
[2] Details and quote from the MercoPress website, 1 June 2016.
[3] Details mainly from *Diego Garcia: a contrast to the Falklands,* Minority Rights Group Report no. 54, ed. John Madely (hereafter "Report 54"), London 1982, p. 4; from the documentary *Stealing an Island* (ITV 6 October 2004); and from the book *Freedom Next Time*, London 2006, both the latter by the Australian journalist John Pilger, a tireless campaigner against the manifold injustices perpetrated by the strong upon the weak all over the world. The story of the disgraceful involvement of the US government is told in David Vine, *Island of Shame: The Secret History of the U.S. Military Base on Diego Garcia*, Princeton and Oxford 2009.
[4] Report 54, 1982, pp. 4 and 5.

Diego Garcia. And disgracefully, both countries agreed to expel the inhabitants from all the Chagos Islands. This was done in an underhand manner – from 1965, when they visited Mauritius (whence the islands were administered), they were simply not allowed to return home.[1] In 1965 the British government offered independence to Mauritius on condition that Mauritius sold the Chagos archipelago, for which Britain paid £3 million. Britain then set up a new artificial dependency, the British Indian Ocean Territory (BIOT) by an Order in Council on 8 November 1965.[2]

In so doing, Britain was of course breaching paragraph 6 of UN Resolution 1514 (see section 10.8): Britain dismembered a colonial territory (Mauritius) by detaching the Chagos Islands from it; Resolution 1514 applied because the events took place after the resolution was passed in 1960.

Britain successfully kept its actions secret from world attention, and began the removal of the Chagossians from their country. It was an atrocious example of colonialism at its worst, similar to the Classic Imperialism of the 1890s – in its treatment of both the Falklands and the Chagos Islands, the British government was behaving much like Lord Salisbury in 1890, who handed Heligoland to Germany against the wishes of its people (section 8.29). In the case of the Falklands, Britain had made a clear profit out of exploiting them for 80 years, and now that they were no longer profitable, was negotiating to hand them to a foreign country against the wishes of their people. But the Falkland Islanders had the good fortune to speak English and to succeed in mobilising enough British public opinion to thwart the government's intentions in the nick of time; the tragedy of the Chagossians was that they were not articulate (their language, Ilois, was a French creole; few spoke English) and that at a critical juncture in their history no one in Britain spoke up for them.

British governments in the 1960s and 70s were keen to promote British exports and to shed Britain's commitments abroad, including colonies. One part of that policy was Britain's approach to Argentina over the Falklands, and another was keenness to cooperate with the Americans, leading to Britain's disgraceful treatment of the Chagossians with American connivance. As a US official put it, the United States wanted the Chagos islands "swept" and "sanitised" – of their people.[3]

Accordingly, the Commissioner for the BIOT issued "Immigration Ordinance 1971", effectively expelling all people from the islands. In March 1971 the first American servicemen arrived; the last islanders were taken away in September, and the base on Diego Garcia was constructed; it was used by US aircraft in the Gulf Wars of 1991 and 2003. Many Chagossians ended up in Mauritius, living in despair in the slums; others went to Britain, where there is a notable community of them in the town of Crawley in Sussex. Eventually Britain offered them £4 million in compensation; Mauritius offered land worth £1 million, and the Chagossians accepted. The agreement was initialled on 27 March 1982, six days before Argentina invaded the Falklands.[4]

In 1999 a Chagos islander called Olivier Bancoult (pronounced "Bankwu") sought a judicial review in the High Court in London to decide on the legality of the BIOT Immigration Ordinance 1971. The High Court's judgement in the case ("the Bancoult case"), on 3 November 2000,[5] was that the BIOT Immigration Ordinance was illegal. In his summing-up Lord Justice Laws quoted some revealing documents, such as a British government minute of June 1966, which ran:[6]

They [sc the Colonial Office] wish to avoid using the phrase "permanent inhabitants" in relation to any of the islands in the territory because to recognise that there are permanent inhabitants will imply that there is a population whose democratic rights will have to be safeguarded... It is... of particular importance that the decision taken by the Colonial Office should be that there are no permanent inhabitants in the BIOT...

The anonymous writer of that government minute assumed that the Colonial Office[7] could *decide*

---

[1] Report 54, 1982, p. 5.
[2] Bancoult case 2000, paragraph 2 (see below).
[3] Pilger 2006, pp. 24 and 316, fn. 6.
[4] Report 54 1982, pp. 8, 9, 11; "Deed of Acceptance" on p. 15.
[5] Title of case: Regina (Bancoult) versus Secretary of State for Foreign and Commonwealth Affairs [2001], QB 1067, also known as "Bancoult (1)"; here "Bancoult case 2000"; materials accessible online under "Case No: CO/3775/98".
[6] Bancoult case 2000, para. 13; square brackets in original; sc[ilicet] = "i.e.".
[7] The Colonial Office was merged on 1 August 1966 with the Department of Commonwealth Affairs to form the Commonwealth Office, which in turn disappeared on 1 October 1968 when the Foreign Office and the Commonwealth Office were merged to form the Foreign and Commonwealth Office (FCO).

whether or not there were permanent inhabitants on the islands. Other government documents likewise denied that the islands' inhabitants were indigenous.

But that was the reverse of the truth. The generations of graves in the cemeteries were proof that the inhabitants were native to the islands, and the same is true of the cemeteries in the Falklands. It was a lie to say that the population was not native to the islands, and the same untruth has been stated by Argentina in reference to the Falklands for over 50 years at the United Nations.

The decision of the High Court in the Bancoult case helped to bring about the passing of the British Overseas Territories Act 2002,[1] which applied to all Britain's 13 overseas territories. This act replaced the terms "colony" and "dependent territory" by the term "British Overseas Territory", and granted the 200,000 inhabitants of those territories full British citizenship with right of abode in Britain. But Britain continued to deny the Chagossians the right of abode in their own country – the British government issued two ordinances preventing the islanders from returning home, the first on 3 November 2000 (the day of their victory in the High Court!), the second on 10 June 2004 (election day in Britain!).[2] The cynicism of both those ordinances is obvious.

The British government appealed against the High Court decision in the Bancoult case, and the appeal was heard by the Law Lords, who at that time were still Britain's highest court of appeal (they were soon afterwards replaced by the United Kingdom Supreme Court). On 22 October 2008, by a vote of three to two, the five lords denied the right of the Chagossians to return to their country;[3] subsequent court hearings and a defeat for Britain over the issue at the United Nations have not changed the situation, though the Chagossians have not given up fighting for their right to return, supported by the UK Chagos Support Association (contact@chagossupport.org.uk).

Their position was greatly strengthened by the International Court of Justice (ICJ) in a landmark advisory opinion delivered on 25 February 2019. The background to this highly significant opinion by the ICJ is that on 22 June 2017 the UN General Assembly passed Resolution 71/292 (A/71/L.73), requesting the ICJ to deliver an advisory opinion on the legality of Britain's separation of the Chagos Islands from Mauritius. The Court took "written statements" from 31 interested countries plus from the African Union, followed by "written comments" from 10 states plus the African Union. Some countries, including Argentina and Britain, submitted both a "written statement" and separate "written comments" (below). The texts of all the statements and comments are online on the ICJ website under https://www.icj-cij.org/en/case/169, from which the quotes below are taken.

In September 2018 the Court heard oral statements from 22 countries, plus the African Union; the speakers for Argentina were Mario Oyarzábal, legal adviser to the Argentine foreign ministry, and Professor Marcelo Kohen. The British and United States governments argued that the Court should refrain from issuing an advisory opinion, but the Court did not follow that line, and in the end voted by 13 to 1 (the 1 being the US judge) that Britain's possession of the Chagos archipelago was illegal. With that view we heartily concur.

In press reactions in Argentina, including one in the national newspaper *Clarín* on 3 March 2019 by Marcelo Kohen ("La Corte de La Haya y Malvinas" ["The Hague Court and Malvinas"]) the decision was celebrated as a defeat for Britain and as support for Argentina's claim to the Falklands. It certainly was a defeat for Britain, but it was actually also a firm rejection of Argentina's argumentation in the Falklands dispute, as can easily be demonstrated.

In its written statement, Argentina mentioned not only UN Resolution 1514, which it correctly saw as central to the case, but also Resolutions 1541 and 2625 (see sections 10.9, 10.18), which rule out any claim by Argentina to the Falklands (though Argentina did not treat them in detail). Much of Argentina's argumentation concerned the question of territorial integrity:

34. The obligation to respect the territorial integrity of others is not confined to the idea of exercising State authority over the territory of another State or to avoid trespassing across borders, but to acknowledge and

---

[1] British Overseas Territories Act 2002 (c.8; Royal Assent 26 February 2002).
[2] Pilger 2006, pp. 50-51; 54-55.
[3] Text of the judgement online under http://www.publications.parliament.uk/pa/ld 200708/ldjudgmt/jd081022/banc.pdf; it contains a summary of the dispute up to 2008.

protect the territorial composition of other States. It includes a guarantee against dismemberment. This stems from the use of the noun "integrity": not only territorial sovereignty is protected, but also the integrity of this territorial sovereignty.

35. In its *Kosovo* advisory opinion, the Court stressed the importance of the principle of respect for the territorial integrity in inter-State relations. In international law, States have the obligation to respect the territorial integrity not only of other States, but also that of the countries of the peoples who have not been able to achieve statehood, i.e. who are under colonial rule or foreign occupation.

The Argentine statement here suppresses two important aspects of the ICJ's Kosovo opinion (for which see section 10.30): first, the Court made it clear that respect for territorial integrity is not a "guarantee against dismemberment" (which it demonstrated by dismembering Serbia's territory) and secondly the Court stated that "the principle of territorial integrity is confined to the sphere of relations between States", confirming that it does not provide a guarantee that territory once possessed by a state may always be claimed by that state.

Argentina applied its own special slant on the meaning of paragraph 6 of Resolution 1514:

40. In paragraph 6, the... context demonstrates that what was at the core of Resolution 1514 (XV) was the end of colonialism in all its forms. In some cases, the victim of colonialism through the disruption of territorial integrity can be a State, but yet in many others they are "colonial countries and peoples". Indeed, the entire object and purpose of the resolution was to put an end to all grievances originated by the persistence of colonialism...

That last sentence enshrines Argentina's erroneous view that Britain's possession of the Falklands gives Argentina a "grievance originated by the persistence of colonialism". As we have demonstrated in this book, the islands were never 100% Argentine territory in the first place (chapter 3), and Argentina accepted Britain's possession of the Falklands in 1850 (sections 7.11 – 7.16). The drafting history of paragraph 6 of Resolution 1514 shows that its purpose was not to redress grievances by one state against another dating back to the distant past, and that it did not dilute the applicability of self-determination to all non-self-governing territories (section 10.8).

Argentina is keen to "solve" the Falklands dispute by negotiation (naturally resulting in a handover of the islands against the wishes of their people), which explains the special emphasis on negotiations near the end of Argentina's written statement (referring to earlier ICJ cases):

61. The obligation of States to settle their disputes by peaceful means is a fundamental principle of contemporary international law set out in Article 2 paragraph 3 of the United Nations Charter... The obligation to negotiate, according to the Court, "constitutes a special application of a principle which underlies all international relations..." [...]
63. Finally, the obligation to negotiate must be performed in good faith, as explicitly required in Article 26 of the Vienna Convention on the Law of Treaties and largely referred to by the Court.

Naturally the obligation to negotiate does not in any way lessen the rights of the peoples of non-self-governing territories – it does not give states the power to negotiate over the heads of those peoples and hand them over from one state to another. Such a practice was controversial even in the age of Classic Imperialism, as the case of Heligoland showed in 1890 (section 8.29). And the first "transitory disposition" in Argentina's 1994 constitution, anchoring the "recovery" of the Falklands as a "permanent and unrenounceable objective of the Argentine people", thus making it impossible for Argentina to accept any result of negotiations except a handover of the islands, means that in any negotiations Argentina would not be acting in good faith (section 10.25).

Argentina's written comments on the case are likewise tailor-made to fit Argentina's claim to the Falklands, and similarly present a distorted account of the facts. Thus paragraph 38 has to be read against Argentina's unstated background assumption (which is of course untrue) that the Falklands are Argentine territory in which Britain is unlawfully exercising authority (italics in original):

38. The interpretation to be given to the terms of paragraph 6 is straightforward. "Any attempt" refers to any action or claim, actual or potential, going against territorial integrity. Examples can be a mere exercise of authority on foreign territory or the occupation of and claim of sovereignty over territory of others. The word "attempt" also allows including a *factual* situation such as the latter, which cannot change the *legal* situation:

it is merely an *attempt* to change it.

In its advisory opinion, however, the Court made it clear that Resolution 1514 applies only to non-self-governing territories (below).

Argentina's paragraph 41 suppresses important details from the UN debates in which the wording of Resolution 1514 was decided. Argentina's written comments state (whole paragraph):

41. The preparatory work also confirms this interpretation of paragraph 6. When the Afro-Asian draft was presented (including paragraph 6 as it is), Guatemala wished to add a further paragraph after it, willing to make a particular situation clearer and specified. After the explanation given by one of the States authors of the draft resolution that the situation envisaged by Guatemala was indeed included in paragraph 6, Guatemala withdrew its draft amendment. Both Iran and Afghanistan, equally co-authors of the Afro-Asian draft, also agreed on this interpretation. There was a discussion between two States about a particular situation and whether this was covered by paragraph 6 or not, but no State challenged the content of this paragraph or criticized it for that matter.

As we recounted in our section 10.8, Jamie Trinidad says Guatemala was concerned that the original wording of paragraph 6 did not sufficiently restrict self-determination in disputed territories (such as Belize, the Falklands or Gibraltar), and had suggested an extra paragraph 7. In paragraph 41 of its written comments, Argentina mentions the proposed paragraph, but does not quote it nor the objections which led to its being dropped (since to do so would show that the UN did not accept that territorial integrity trumped the right of self-determination). Guatemala's proposal ran "The principle of the self-determination of peoples may in no case impair the right of territorial integrity of any State or its right to the recovery of territory". That would have strengthened Argentina's case over the Falklands, but the Soviet Union objected that it would limit the fundamental right of all peoples to self-determination (thus being contrary to paragraph 2 of Resolution 1514), and said that "no attempt should be made to raise private claims to the level of a general principle restricting the inalienable right of every people to self-determination". The UN General Assembly agreed with that position, and Guatemala dropped its proposal. That of course weakened Argentina's argument that paragraph 6 placed Argentina's (purported) territorial integrity above the right of the Falkland Islanders to self-determination.

Once all states wishing to do so had delivered their written statements and written comments, the ICJ considered the Chagos case, and on 25 February 2019 delivered its advisory opinion (like all the written statements and written comments it is available on the ICJ website under https://www.icj-cij.org/en/case/169, whence all the quotes below are taken). It was a stinging indictment of Britain's behaviour over the Chagos Islands, but also contained no comfort for Argentina.

The Court first outlined the circumstances of the case, then considered the applicable international law, making it clear that paragraph 6 of Resolution 1514 referred to the territorial integrity of non-self-governing territories, and that self-determination applies to *all* non-self-governing territories (we emphasise those aspects by **bold print** in the extracts below; no bold print in the original texts); the Court did not accept Argentina's argument that it referred to old grievances:

146. The Court will begin by recalling that "respect for the principle of equal rights and self-determination of peoples" is one of the purposes of the United Nations (Article 1, paragraph 2, of the Charter). Such a purpose concerns, in particular, the "Declaration regarding non-self-governing territories" (Chapter XI of the Charter), since the "Members of the United Nations which have or assume responsibilities for the administration of territories whose peoples have not yet attained a full measure of self-government" are obliged to "develop [the] self-government" of those peoples (Article 73 of the Charter).

147. In the Court's view, it follows that the legal régime of non-self-governing territories, as set out in Chapter XI of the Charter, was based on the progressive development of their institutions so as to lead the populations concerned to exercise their right to self-determination. [...]

153. The wording used in resolution 1514 (XV) has a normative character, in so far as it affirms that **"[a]ll peoples have the right to self-determination"**... this resolution further provides that **"[i]mmediate steps shall be taken, in Trust and Non-Self-Governing Territories or all other territories which have not yet attained independence, to transfer all powers to the peoples of those territories, without any conditions**

or reservations, in accordance with their freely expressed will and desire". In order to prevent **any dismemberment of non-self-governing territories**, paragraph 6 of resolution 1514 (XV) provides that:
"Any attempt aimed at the partial or total disruption of the national unity and the territorial integrity of a country is incompatible with the purposes and principles of the Charter of the United Nations."
154. Article 1... reaffirms **the right of all peoples to self-determination**, and provides, *inter alia*, that: "The States Parties to the present Covenant, including those having responsibility for the administration of Non-Self-Governing and Trust Territories, shall promote the realization of the right of self-determination, and shall respect that right, in conformity with the provisions of the Charter of the United Nations." [...]
156. The means of implementing the right to self-determination in a non-self-governing territory, described as "geographically separate and ... distinct ethnically and/or culturally from the country administering it", were set out in Principle VI of General Assembly resolution 1541 (XV), adopted on 15 December 1960:
"A Non-Self-Governing Territory can be said to have reached a full measure of self-government by:
(a) Emergence as a sovereign independent State;
(b) Free association with an independent State; or
(c) Integration with an independent State."
157. The Court recalls that, while the exercise of self-determination may be achieved through one of the options laid down by resolution 1541 (XV), it must be the expression of the free and genuine will of the people concerned. However, "[t]he right of self-determination leaves the General Assembly a measure of discretion with respect to the forms and procedures by which that right is to be realized" (*Western Sahara, Advisory Opinion, I.C.J. Reports 1975*, p. 36, para. 71). [...]
160. ... Both State practice and *opinio juris* at the relevant time confirm the customary law character of **the right to territorial integrity of a non-self-governing territory** as a corollary of the right to self-determination... States have consistently emphasized that **respect for the territorial integrity of a non-self-governing territory is a key element of the exercise of the right to self-determination**...
161. In the Court's view, the law on self-determination constitutes the applicable international law during the period under consideration, namely between 1965 and 1968. The Court noted in its Advisory Opinion on *Namibia* the consolidation of that law: "**the subsequent development of international law in regard to non-self-governing territories, as enshrined in the Charter of the United Nations, made the principle of self-determination applicable to all of them**". [...][1]
168. The General Assembly has consistently called upon administering Powers to **respect the territorial integrity of non-self-governing territories**, especially after the adoption of resolution 1514 (XV) of 14 December 1960... [...]

The International Court of Justice clearly regarded paragraph 6 of UN Resolution 1514 as being part of the international law of decolonisation, and hence as being applicable only to non-self-governing territories, not to established countries such as Argentina, and the Court regarded self-determination as applicable to *all* non-self-governing territories. In the extracts above we have emphasised phrases in bold print that illustrate those two aspects in the Court's advisory opinion (no bold print in the original texts). They show that Argentina's often-repeated assertions that "Argentina's territorial integrity is being violated by Britain's possession of the Falkland Islands," and that "the Falkland Islanders do not possess the right to self-determination", were not supported by the Court.

Another Argentine assertion that was not supported by the Court is that the Falkland Islanders are not a "people" and are thus not covered by UN resolutions on decolonisation. The Court stated in paragraph 147 that "the legal régime of non-self-governing territories... was based on the progressive development of their institutions so as to lead the populations concerned to exercise their right to self-determination". The Court's reference to "the populations concerned" includes all inhabitants of non-self-governing territories without distinction; it does not divide them up into those who are "peoples" and those who are not. Attempts by Argentina to deny self-determination to the Falkland Islanders because they are not a "people" are not supported by the ICJ.

The Court's final conclusions (paragraph 183) were that the decolonisation of Mauritius in 1968

---

[1] As Stephen Potts points out, the ICJ has confirmed in five separate judgements that self-determination is applicable to all non-self-governing territories: Legal Consequences for States of the Continued Presence of South Africa in Namibia 1971, p. 31-32; Western Sahara Advisory Opinion 1975, p. 68, para 162; East Timor Judgment 1995, p. 102, para. 29; Legal Consequences of Wall in Occupied Palestinian Territory 2004, p. 171-172, para. 88; and the Kosovo Advisory Opinion of 2010, p. 37, para. 79 (Stephen Potts, in letter to *Penguin News* 7 June 2019, p. 5).

was not lawfully completed; that "The ... United Kingdom's continued administration of the Chagos Archipelago constitutes a wrongful act"; "the United Kingdom is under an obligation to bring to an end its administration of the Chagos Archipelago as rapidly as possible", and that all UN member states are obliged to cooperate with the UN in completing the decolonisation of Mauritius.

Despite that, there have been reports at the time of writing that Britain is apparently planning to deport British-born grandchildren of Chagossians from Britain to Mauritius.[1] Those children have grown up in Britain and are in Britain as a result of the forced deportation of their grandparents from their country despite being innocent of any crime. In our view, Britain's treatment of the Chagossians can only be described as damnable.

Three months after the ICJ's advisory opinion, the UN General Assembly considered the Chagos question, and by a large majority passed a motion condemning Britain's occupation of the Chagos Islands. The motion was passed by 116 votes to 6 (UK, US, Hungary, Israel, Australia and the Maldives), and set a 6-month deadline for Britain to withdraw from the islands and for them to be reunited with Mauritius. The countries voting for the motion and against Britain included Austria, Greece, Ireland, Spain, Sweden and Switzerland, while the 56 abstentions included France, Germany, the Netherlands, Portugal, Poland and Romania. The ICJ's opinion and the UN General Assembly vote left Britain severely isolated on the world stage, and also revealed how the United States has lost much of its former influence, having campaigned energetically at the UN and in national capitals for countries to support Britain's possession of the Chagos Islands (and hence to support the US base on Diego Garcia too).[2]

Kohen and Rodríguez (p. 276) rightly castigate Britain's denial of self-determination to the Chagossians – that is the one matter on which we are in full agreement with them – but they also say that Britain's policy was "indisputably inconsistent". In fact that was not the case in the 1960s; at that time Britain was denying self-determination to both the Chagossians and the Falkland Islanders, and negotiated with Argentina for a long time in the 1960s and 70s, and right up till March 1982, to find a way to hand over the Falklands against the wishes of the islanders.

Kohen and Rodríguez fail to see the obvious parallel in the Chagos case – Britain denied self-determination to the Chagossians, and Argentina is now attempting to deny self-determination to the Falkland Islanders. Britain was wrong then, and Argentina is wrong now.

10.29 Territorial integrity, I: the Kuwait connection[3]

Argentine governments have since 1960 relied heavily on the fallacious argument that Britain's possession of the Falkland Islands violates Argentina's territorial integrity. They have been forced to base their case on paragraph 6 of UN Resolution 1514, distorting it to fit their argument. In fact that resolution, and other UN resolutions, destroy Argentina's case (see sections 10.8, 10.9, 10.18 and 10.28). Two recent examples of the use of territorial integrity as an argument cast a revealing light on Argentina's behaviour: the Iraqi invasion of Kuwait in 1990 and the Kosovo case heard before the International Court of Justice in 2009 (section 10.30).

The Gulf War of 1990-91 began when the Iraqi dictator Saddam Hussein invaded and occupied Kuwait on 2 August 1990. The arguments he used to justify his invasion were similar to those regularly used by Argentina to justify its claim to the Falklands: he claimed that Kuwait was originally a *velayet* of Basra province under Turkish sovereignty which had been artificially detached from Iraq by Britain in 1899, and that since 1932 Iraq had persistently challenged the legality of that separation. Saddam's justification was actually better founded than the Argentine claim to the Falklands: the alleged separation of Kuwait from Iraq was much more recent than that of the Falklands alleged by Argentina; Kuwait and Iraq were contiguous (i.e. they had a common land border), not separated by hundreds of kilometres of ocean; and the people of Kuwait and Iraq are culturally very similar and speak the same language.

---
[1] Article by Joe Wallen on the *Telegraph* website, 1 March 2019, entitled "Chagos Islanders treatment leads to fears of new Windrush scandal".
[2] Details from the *Guardian* website, www.theguardian.com, 22 May 2019.
[3] Unless otherwise indicated, details in this section are from Lawrence Freedman and Efraim Karsh, *The Gulf Conflict 1990-1991: Diplomacy and War in the New World Order*, London 1993, pp. 42-43.

The Iraqi occupation of Kuwait was defeated by an international military campaign entitled "Desert Storm", involving forces from the United States, Britain and several other countries, which began on 16 January 1991; the last Iraqi soldier left Kuwait on 27 February, and Kuwaiti forces entered Kuwait City on 28 February. The campaign ended with a ceasefire on 3 March 1991.

After the ceasefire Saddam Hussein behaved just like Argentine governments after the Falklands War – he continued to press his claim as if nothing had happened. In a long letter to the UN Secretary-General on 1 June 1992, he repeated "the standard Iraqi version of its historic relations with Kuwait"; in 1992 "the Iraqi media repeated the claim that Kuwait had always been part of historic Iraq", and Saddam Hussein's special adviser, Abd al-Jabir Muhsin, stated "Kuwait had always been an integral part of Iraq, and will return to Iraq".[1] Those statements resemble the innumerable assertions in the Argentine media and by Argentine governments that the Falklands have always been part of Argentina and will return to Argentina one day.

Not even his final defeat in 2003 and capture by the Americans in 2004 induced Saddam Hussein to drop his claim to Kuwait. On 1 July 2004 he appeared for the first time before an Iraqi judge, who read him a list of the crimes he was charged with, including the mass killing of Kurds by chemical weapons, the murder of many religious and political leaders, and the invasion of Kuwait in 1990. He reacted sharply to the mention of Kuwait and said to the judge: "I am surprised you are charging me with this. You are Iraqi and everyone knows Kuwait is part of Iraq."[2]

In Kuwait in 1990, as in the Falklands in 1982, a dictatorship invaded and occupied a territory against the wishes of its inhabitants. Both dictatorships alleged that their invasions were justified because those territories had formerly been part of the country they ruled. But whereas no one now seriously maintains that Kuwait is rightfully Iraqi territory, Argentina continues to assert that the Falklands are rightfully Argentine territory. The justification for that assertion is non-existent.

10.30 Court cases, IV: Territorial integrity, II: the Kosovo case at the International Court of Justice, 2010

Another notable example of the use of arguments based on territorial integrity is provided by the Kosovo case, which is especially significant for two reasons: it was heard before the International Court of Justice (ICJ), and Professor Marcelo Kohen acted as counsel and advocate for Serbia, which lost the case. The case clarifies the principle of territorial integrity, and the Court's decision shows that Kohen's (and Argentina's) view is not supported by international law.[3]

In the Middle Ages Kosovo was a province of Serbia, and was regarded by Serbs as the cradle of Serbian culture, but for centuries it had an overwhelmingly Albanian population, the majority of whom were in favour of independence. On 2 July 1990 the provincial legislature in Prishtinë (Serbian: Priština) declared Kosovo an independent state, whereupon Serbian president Slobodan Milošević invaded Kosovo to enforce Serbian sovereignty. NATO responded by bombing Serbia; Milošević was deposed and put on trial for crimes against humanity, but died on 11 March 2006 before he could be convicted. On 17 February 2008 the Kosovan authorities again declared the country independent; diplomatic recognition was soon given by 69 countries, including 22 EU member states, and the Republic of Kosovo is now (2022) recognised by 97 countries.

Serbia still regarded Kosovo as an integral part of its own territory, and asked the UN General Assembly to request the ICJ to rule on the legality of Kosovo's independence. On 8 October 2008

---

[1] Quotes in this paragraph from Freedman and Karsh 1993, preface to 2nd ed. 1994, pp. xxxvii and xxxviii.

[2] Article by Rory McCarthy in *The Guardian*, 2 July 2004: "I am Saddam Hussein, the president of Iraq".

[3] The text of the ICJ opinion, "International Court of Justice, Year 2010, 22 July, General List No. 141, Accordance with International Law of the Unilateral Declaration of Independence in Respect of Kosovo" (henceforth "ICJ Kosovo judgement 2010"), is online under http://www.icj-cij.org/docket/files/141/15987.pdf (45 pages). The British statement, "Request for an Advisory Opinion of the International Court of Justice on the Question 'Is the Unilateral Declaration of Independence by the Provisional Institutions of Self-Government of Kosovo in Accordance with International Law?': Written Statement of the United Kingdom 17 April 2009" (henceforth "British Kosovo statement 2009"), is available under http://www.icj-cij.org/docket/files/141/15638.pdf (138 pages), and the Argentine statement, "Accordance with International Law of the Unilateral Declaration of Independence by the Provisional Institutions of Self-Government of Kosovo: Written Statement of the Argentine Republic 17 April 2009" ("Argentine Kosovo statement 2009"), is under http://www.icj-cij.org/docket/files/141/15666.pdf (50 pages).

the General Assembly asked the Court to render an advisory opinion as to whether Kosovo's declaration of independence was in accordance with international law. The Court accepted the request and during 2009 took submissions from 36 states and comments by 14 states, and heard 45 oral statements on behalf of 29 states, of which 16 argued for, 13 against, the legitimacy of Kosovo's independence. Britain argued that it was legitimate, while Argentina argued that it was illegitimate and a breach of Serbia's territorial integrity.

About a tenth of Argentina's written submission (at least partly composed by Marcelo Kohen) was devoted to the principle of respect for the territorial integrity of states.[1] By contrast, the much longer British statement (138 pages as against Argentina's 50), treated the principle of territorial integrity more briefly, arguing in favour of the independence of Kosovo and thus against Serbia's territorial integrity. Quoting Article 2 (4) of the UN Charter,[2] Britain stated that "the principle of territorial integrity of States is a principle of international law", and went on:

5.9 The protection of the territorial integrity of States is a protection in "international relations". It is not a guarantee of the permanence of a State as it exists at any given time…

On 22 July 2010 the Court delivered its opinion, which was that the independence of Kosovo was legal and legitimate. The Court's brief treatment of territorial integrity closely followed Britain's view; it likewise quoted Article 2 (4) of the UN Charter, to which it added a reference to UN Resolution 2625 (see section 10.18) and to the Helsinki Final Act, 1975, before concluding:[3]

Thus, the scope of the principle of territorial integrity is confined to the sphere of relations between States.

That closely parallels the argument in the British statement that "The protection of the territorial integrity of States is a protection in 'international relations'. It is not a guarantee of the permanence of a State as it exists at any given time." In other words, the Court's decision showed that the ICJ did not regard the principle of territorial integrity as a guarantee that territories once possessed by a state may always be claimed by that state.

The decision by the ICJ thus invalidated Marcelo Kohen's statement in his 1997 book:[4]

The third idea which underlies the principle of respect for territorial integrity is that of a *guarantee against all dismemberment* of territory.

That was precisely what was denied by the International Court of Justice. In accepting the independence of Kosovo, the ICJ dismembered Serbia's territory, underlining the fact that respect for territorial integrity does not involve a guarantee that the territory of a state as it stood at some specific time in the past will always remain inviolable and immune to dismemberment.

Argentina constantly contends that Britain's possession of the Falklands violates Argentina's territorial integrity – Kohen and Rodríguez assert (pp. 183, 188) that Britain's actions in 1833 were contrary to international law because the United Kingdom was obliged to respect the "territorial integrity" of a state with which it maintained peaceful relations. They say (p. 183) that "The obligation to respect territorial integrity of States in peacetime is inherent to the existence of relations based on international law, regardless of the period of time in question", to which they give as a reference a passage from Kohen's 1997 book,[5] in which, however, he does not consider how it applies when there is no consensus among states on the rightful ownership of a territory.

As is typical of Argentine writers, Kohen and Rodríguez automatically assume that the Falkland Islands were Argentine territory in 1833, and naturally assert that Argentine territorial integrity was

---

[1] Argentine Kosovo statement 2009, paragraphs 69-87, 121-122 (about 5 whole pages).
[2] Article 2 (4) of the UN Charter reads: "All Members shall refrain in their international relations from the threat or use of force against the territorial integrity or political independence of any State, or in any other manner inconsistent with the Purposes of the United Nations."
[3] ICJ Kosovo judgement 2010, para. 80.
[4] Marcelo G. Kohen, *Possession Contestée et Souveraineté Territoriale* ["Adverse Possession and Territorial Sovereignty"], Paris January 1997, p. 375 (Kohen's italics). The first and second idea that he refers to are, first, *plenitude* of a state's control over the whole of its territory, and second, the *inviolability* of a state's territory.
[5] Kohen 1997, p. 369. Kohen and Rodríguez refer to pp. 369-371 of Kohen 1997, but he refers to territorial integrity several more times on pp. 372-378.

at stake. But in the case of the Falklands from the 1820s to the 1840s, there were four countries (Argentina, Britain, Spain and the United States) that were involved in the islands and thus held a view on the matter, and there existed no international tribunal or organisation such as the International Court of Justice or the United Nations that could decide such questions. And as pointed out in sections 4.5, 4.8, 5.21, 6.40 and 7.2, those countries disagreed about whose territory the islands were – to Argentina they were Argentine territory, to Britain they were British territory, and to Spain they were Spanish territory, so those three countries each had an *animus domini* ["mind of a master", i.e. claim of ownership], but the United States held that they were no country's territory and were part of the high seas. It was thus impossible to decide whose territorial integrity was at stake – if anyone's.

To sum up: it is untrue that Britain's possession of the Falklands is illegal in international law. In the first place, in 1833 the islands were a disputed territory, not Argentine territory, and secondly it is not true that international law protects the territorial integrity of a state as it existed at any given time in the past. The principle of territorial integrity gives no support whatever to Argentina's claim to the Falklands. The ICJ's decision in the Kosovo case makes that abundantly clear.

10.31 Conclusion: the Falklands are not Argentine territory

In this book we have presented a wealth of historical and legal evidence to establish the facts and refute the assertions of Marcelo Kohen and Facundo Rodríguez. We have shown that their account of the history of the Falkland Islands is erroneous, and that their presentation of the legal status of the islands is incorrect. We summarise our conclusions in chapter 11.

As Dame Rosalyn Higgins says, addressing practitioners and students of international law:[1]

There is no escaping the duty that each and every one of us has to test the validity of legal claims.

That duty is incumbent on anyone who tries to resolve a question of any kind, whether legal, political, religious, philosophical, or other – it is imperative to test the validity of all claims, beginning with their initial axioms. Some axioms, for example in religion, are not testable, so no final resolution is possible, but axioms involving history can be tested by establishing the historical facts, which in turn establish whether legal claims are valid or fallacious.

That is the duty we have tried to perform in this book. We have tested the validity of Argentina's claim to title over the Falkland Islands by examining the historical documentation to see whether the islands are, or are not, Argentine territory. Argentina's argumentation always proceeds from the axiom that the Falklands are Argentine territory; we have demonstrated that it is a fallacy. There is abundant historical and legal evidence that the Falklands are *not* Argentine territory; they were never 100% Argentine territory at any time, and since 1850 have not been Argentine territory at all; Argentina consented to Britain's sovereignty in 1850 and confirmed its consent by many acts of omission and commission over many years thereafter. Argentina's argumentation thus collapses.

The Falkland Islands are a self-contained territory which is geographically separate from Argentina and has been entirely distinct from Argentina in history, development, population and language for over 180 years. The islands are ruled democratically by the Falkland Islanders themselves, who have now (2022) lived there for nine generations. The Falklands are their country, over which they are the holders of territorial sovereignty with the full right of external self-determination in international law. At the wish of their inhabitants, the Falklands remain at present in partnership with Britain – that is the status they have freely chosen, fulfilling United Nations Resolution 2625.

Argentina has no title whatsoever to the Falklands. Its claim was partial, encumbered and restricted from the outset, and it was dropped by treaty over 170 years ago. After ratifying that treaty in 1850, Argentina repeatedly demonstrated overt acquiescence in British sovereignty.

The Falkland Islands are not part of the territory of Argentina.

---

[1] Higgins 1994, p. 7.

CHAPTER ELEVEN: Summary of conclusions

In this last chapter we summarise the conclusions to be drawn from the documentary evidence we have presented. That evidence disproves every major point made by Kohen and Rodríguez and by many Argentine authors and governments. All those points are discussed in detail in the preceding chapters of this book. Briefly summarised, the truth is as follows:

(1) Neither the papal Bulls of 1493 nor the Treaty of Tordesillas of 1494 had the slightest validity as regards the possession of the Falkland Islands. Neither Spain nor Portugal regarded the papal Bulls as binding, and breached them by signing the Treaty of Tordesillas. The Treaty of Tordesillas applied to no countries except Spain and Portugal – from the point of view of all other countries, it was *res inter alios acta* ["a matter arranged between others"].

(2) The Falkland Islands were not discovered by the expeditions of Amerigo Vespucci (1502) or Ferdinand Magellan (1520) – neither went anywhere near the Falklands. The surviving documentation suggests that they were discovered at the latest around 1518-19 by an otherwise unrecorded Portuguese expedition, who made the original map on which André Thevet's map of 1586 was based, and perhaps also made the original version of Pedro Reinel's map of 1522-4. Magellan's cartographer Andrés de San Martín had nothing to do with the making of the map on which Thevet's map was based.

(3) The account by Sir Richard Hawkins makes it clear beyond doubt that he sailed past the Falklands in 1594.

(4) The 17th- and 18th-century treaties between Britain and Spain did not prohibit British possession of the Falklands; none of them described the extent of Spanish possessions in South America.

(5) Britain's abandonment of a secret plan in 1749-50 to send an expedition to the Falklands did not indicate recognition of Spain's sovereignty in the islands, but the reverse – it was planned in defiance of Spain, and was intended to confront Spain with a *fait accompli* that Spain would be too late to prevent, hence the need for secrecy. The British government did not inform Spain of the plan; Spain found out from leaks in Britain, and was informed by France after French agents in Britain had got wind of it. It is not true that Spain had the right of first occupant (Britain's occupancy preceded that of Spain), nor that the main European maritime powers recognised Spanish sovereignty in the islands – none of them ever recognised it.

(6) It is absurd to maintain that Spain inherited France's title to the islands, since Spain always denied that France had possessed any title at all.

(7) The 1771 Anglo-Spanish agreement preserved the claims of both Spain and Britain in the Falklands, not Spain alone. It is a myth (the "Spanish Rights Myth") that Spain "formulated a reserve of sovereignty". Spain attempted to do so, but Britain refused to permit it, and in the final text of the agreement the "prior right of sovereignty" in the islands was left undefined. Both countries continued to claim exclusive sovereignty; neither recognised the other's sovereignty, but they agreed not to go to war over the issue. There was no secret promise by Britain to evacuate the islands after the restitution of Port Egmont.

(8) The Nootka Sound Convention of 1790 did not exclude Britain from the Falklands but forced Spain for the first time to consent to British commercial activity and settlement in the islands. Britain and Spain had hitherto each maintained their former claim to exclusive sovereignty under the 1771 agreeement, but under the Nootka Sound Convention Spain accepted that in about 80% of the area of the islands she had lost the right to prevent British exploitation, and in about 20% to prevent British settlement. That meant that Britain (and Britain alone) was entitled to treat large areas of the Falklands as *terra nullius*. Thereafter Spain ceased to maintain or assert exclusive sovereignty against Britain in the islands, and specifically stated that British subjects ("English royalists") were permitted to exploit the islands.

(9) Argentina did not inherit a perfect title to the Falklands from Spain, for the following reasons: **(1)** The principle of *uti possidetis* was not formally adopted in South America till the 1840s; it was not a fixed, immutable principle but allowed for fairly free interpretation and the readjustment of borders, and in the Americas it was only operative between the newly independent Spanish-speaking republics, not in cases such as the Falklands where non-South-American countries were involved. So *uti possidetis* never applied to the Falklands in the first place. **(2)** Any Argentine title was <u>incomplete</u> from the outset since the Viceroyalty of the River Plate split into a number of provinces, some of which became the United Provinces of the River Plate; two of those provinces became independent countries (Uruguay,

Paraguay), while some became the Argentine Confederation (with varying membership and for 9 years without the province of Buenos Aires), most of which from 1862 became Argentina, while some areas of the Viceroyalty became parts of Chile or Peru. Thus any Argentine title to the Falklands was subject to agreement between the successor countries (which was never obtained). **(3)** Any Argentine title was <u>encumbered</u> by the pre-existing rights of Spain and Britain, which weakened Argentina's rights yet further; Spain's protests to the United States in 1822 and to Britain in 1825 against those countries' recognition of Argentine independence upheld Spain's rights over all her South American territories for some time. **(4)** Any Argentine title was <u>restricted</u> since Argentina could not inherit more than Spain possessed. Spain's sovereignty in South America was limited in respect of Britain by the Nootka Sound Convention, so any rights inherited by Argentina were limited in the same way. In short, Argentina never possessed 100% sovereignty; the Falklands were always subject to multiple overlapping claims. At no time during Argentina's 8-year presence in the islands did Argentina possess more than <u>part of an encumbered and restricted title</u> to the islands. It is untrue to say "Argentina inherited the Falklands from Spain".

(10) When David Jewett arrived in the Falklands in 1820 in the *Heroína*, he was already a pirate, since he had captured the neutral Portuguese ship *Carlota*. He had therefore ceased to be a legal privateer (it was not possible to be a pirate and a privateer at the same time), and all his acts were illegal – no action by a pirate had any legal validity. His ceremony of "taking possession" of the Falklands on 6 November 1820 therefore had no relevance whatever in international law, so there was no official possession-taking of the Falklands by Argentina. Berkeley Sound was empty when he arrived, and only a few ships were present when he performed his ceremony; he did not attempt to apply fishing regulations, or Argentine laws, or tell any ships to leave. Jewett's commission did not order him to claim the Falklands or to go there at all, and in his first communication from the islands to Argentina (his "Letter 3" of 1 February 1821), he did not mention his "possession ceremony", so the Buenos Aires government knew nothing about it. If he had been ordered to take possession of the Falklands he would scarcely have omitted to mention that he had done so. And even when the Buenos Aires government found out he was in the Falklands, it did not give him or his successor William Mason any official role in the islands (such as governor), nor issue any instructions that implied that they were on Argentine territory, but merely ordered Mason to continue the privateering voyage and hence to leave the islands. So Mason left again in the *Heroína* after only 3 weeks, and continued privateering. Initially Mason was not a pirate himself, but became one on capturing the Portuguese ship *Viscondesa do Rio Seco* on 11 July 1821. In 1822 the *Heroína* was captured by the Portuguese frigate *Perla* and taken to Lisbon to be adjudged for piracy. The Portuguese prize court ruled that the *Heroína*'s captains Jewett and Mason, and the ship and her crew, were all piratical; the ship was confiscated and sold, and Mason and his crew were imprisoned. Jewett escaped imprisonment because he was not present in court – by 1822 he was in Brazil, where he became an enemy of Argentina.

(11) The 1824 expedition to the Falklands, partly financed by Louis Vernet, was not an example of the "exercise of sovereignty" by Argentina. It was not publicised in any way, not even in Argentine newspapers, and there is no record of any demonstration of authority in the islands such as a possession ceremony. It was in the islands only from 2 February to 24 July 1824; it was an utter failure and burdened Louis Vernet with debts for the rest of his association with the Falklands. Its leader Pablo Areguati never held any official rank in the islands, nor did he attempt to enforce Argentine laws or fishing regulations. The presence of his group in the islands was seen as illegal by the captain of the British sealing brig *Adeona*, who threatened to denounce them to the British government. Areguati and his group struggled to survive; he and some of his men were taken away by their ship *Fenwick* on 7 June, and the remaining eight men were rescued by the British ship *Susannah Anne* on 24 July 1824.

(12) On hearing that US President James Monroe was about to recognise the independence of the new republics in South America, Spain made a formal protest to the United States on 9 March 1822, asserting that such recognition would not in any way lessen Spain's rights to those territories. On 21 January 1825, hearing that Britain was about to recognise the independence of Argentina, Spain made a formal protest to Britain, claiming that the whole of South America was still legitimately Spanish territory. Spain was applying the "legitimist" view of sovereignty, regarding sovereignty as an abstract quality that exists independently of practical considerations such as passage of time, active presence or acceptance by other countries. The current Argentine claim to the Falklands today is based on such a view. Spain's protests upheld her claim to the Falklands (as far as it existed), thus "encumbering" any claim by Argentina at least for some years.

(13) In 1824-5, before the signing of the 1825 Treaty of Amity between Britain and Argentina, Britain asked Argentina for information on its territory, natural resources and economy. That information was duly published in a 300-page book in London and Paris in English, Spanish and French (Ignacio Núñez, *An account, historical, political, and statistical, of the United Provinces of Rio de la Plata...*, London 1825). The book describes the extent of the territory of each of the provinces, and mentions places on the Argentine coast, but the Falklands are not mentioned at all and were thus clearly not seen as Argentine territory. The 1825 Treaty of Amity was a recognition treaty and as such did not specify Argentina's territory or boundaries – it did not mention any territory at all, so it is irrelevant that it did not mention the Falklands.

(14) The British vice-consuls in Buenos Aires, Richard Poussett and Charles Griffiths, did not inform the British government that Louis Vernet had presented his Falklands concessions, awarded by the Buenos Aires government, at the British consulate for authentication in 1826 and 1828. Britain remained ignorant of those concessions until Vernet showed them to Consul-General Woodbine Parish in April 1829 and Parish passed the information to London. Britain thereupon protested promptly against the presumption of sovereignty in the Falklands by Buenos Aires. Britain's failure to protest earlier was not because of any doubts as to the validity of Britain's claim to the islands. Vernet wrongly thought he had successfully informed Britain of his activities and had demonstrated that he was not operating behind Britain's back; he clearly regarded the lack of a reaction as a form of British authorisation.

(15) The rescue of Mathew Brisbane's men shipwrecked on South Georgia in the sealer *Hope* in 1829 was not an official act by Louis Vernet as "Comandante Político y Militar de las Malvinas", and he played no active part in it. The rescue was arranged by the British Consul-General in Buenos Aires, Woodbine Parish, three weeks before Vernet was appointed Civil and Military Commandant of the Malvinas; it was financed by the British government, and Vernet's role was merely to transfer part of his charter for the American brig *Betsey* to Brisbane; that part of the fee was then paid by Britain. Woodbine Parish paid Brisbane money for supplies, which was reimbursed by the British government; Brisbane performed the rescue as arranged, and brought his nine surviving men to Port Louis in October 1829.

(16) Louis Vernet's establishment at Port Louis on East Falkland was never financially viable. For most of its existence it had under 100 residents, including some 30 black slaves, and there was a constant turnover of population, which only briefly reached its maximum of about 128 residents in July 1831 and then started to decline, before any American or British involvement. About a dozen people left in the brigantine *Elbe* in September 1831, leaving about 114-115 people, and Vernet himself left in November 1831 after 5½ years (of which he had been absent almost half the time) in the seized American ship *Harriet*, which took 29 people (over a quarter of the remaining residents), leaving about 85, and in January 1832 the USS *Lexington* took about 47 people (over half the remainder), leaving some 38 at the settlement. Britain was not involved in any of those removals of people.

(17) In issuing paper tokens to pay his employees, Louis Vernet was setting up a truck system – a closed economy without real cash – and the tokens were merely his own private "IOUs"; they were promissory notes not backed by negotiable currency, and he did not redeem them in cash for their face value. In other words, he was signing bouncing cheques. That does not constitute "currency issuance", let alone a "demonstration of Argentine sovereignty".

(18) Louis Vernet had nothing to do with the building of the small schooner *Eagle* (which he alone called "Águila"), and never even saw her. She was built by a group of Americans (and one Englishman) on Eagle (now called Speedwell) Island at the south end of Falkland Sound, and was unfinished when Vernet left the islands on 7 November 1831. She was built only to kill seals; she never belonged to Vernet, and she never flew an Argentine flag. She was completed in December 1831 (after Vernet had left), and operated in the Falklands till 1837 under the US flag with her mainly American crew.

(19) The United States Supreme Court ruled in 1839 that Vernet's seizure of the American sealing ships *Harriet*, *Breakwater* and *Superior* in the Falklands in 1831 had been illegal since in US law the Falklands were not part of the "dominions within the sovereignty of Buenos Aires". Vernet had therefore been guilty of piracy.

(20) Britain's actions in 1833 were not in any way "illegal", as has often been asserted by Argentina. They were a perfectly legitimate action, in a disputed territory, to defend British interests after the *Lexington* raid in 1831-2. It is untrue that Britain expelled the Argentine population from the Falklands in 1833, as has been repeatedly asserted by Argentine authors and by the Argentine government at the UN. Britain had protested promptly in September 1832 against the appointment of Commandant Mestivier and the

sending of the Argentine garrison, and Britain did not expel the civilian residents of the islands. There was in 1833 no "original Argentine population": of the 37 civilians remaining on 1 January 1833, only 10 were Argentinians, of whom only 2 were taken away. The longest-established inhabitants whose arrival date is known were the two black African former slaves Carmelita and Gregoria, who had been there for 4 years and 4 months since 2 September 1828. Not a single person is known for certain to have been in the islands longer than that. And it is untrue that Britain expelled "peaceful" Argentine authorities – there were no "authorities" at all in the sense of a proper government with governmental structures. Britain expelled only the mutinous, murderous Argentine garrison, which had no roots in the islands having been there for less than 3 months, and which was about to leave anyway. Adjutant Gomila had decided to evacuate the entire garrison in the British schooner *Rapid*; their weapons and tools were put aboard and he arranged with Captain John Ross for all of them to leave the islands on 31 December 1832. They would have left had not José María Pinedo arrived back and countermanded the order to leave. Almost half the people belonging to the garrison would have been removed by Argentina anyway: 10 soldiers were taken for trial in Buenos Aires and punished (7 shot, 2 flogged, 1 banished); they had with them 5 women and 4 children, so 19 people (42% of the remaining 45 belonging to the garrison) would have been taken away by Argentina irrespective of any actions by Britain. The garrison had brutally murdered Mestivier, and far more than the 10 punished soldiers were involved in the mutiny. They had terrorised, robbed and traumatised the civilian residents of Port Louis, of whom a dozen (a third of the total civilian population of 37 people) sought shelter aboard a British and a French ship that happened to be present. To count the garrison as part of the population is absurd. After the departure of the garrison the civilian settlement continued, and over half its remaining inhabitants were from Argentina or Uruguay (8 and 5 people respectively, out of 22). Britain expelled no civilian residents – but Argentina did: 3 long-serving gauchos (Mariano López, Manuel Ruiz and José Báez) were put aboard the *Sarandí* before the *Clio* arrived and were removed from the islands by Argentina without any British involvement.

(21) The British schooner *Rapid* did not "escort the Argentine schooner *Sarandí* for the British". Before the British arrived she had been chartered by Adjutant Gomila to take the whole Argentine garrison from the islands back to Argentina. The *Rapid* was a commercial whaling schooner with 2 guns, and was not the same ship as the 10-gun British warship HMS *Rapid*, which visited the Falklands in 1834 and 1835, and Buenos Aires in 1835-6.

(22) In August 1833 Antonio Rivero's group did not consist of 8 gauchos (there were only 7 gauchos left in the islands); they comprised 3 gauchos (Rivero himself, José María Luna and Juan Brasido) and 5 Charrúa Indians. Only Rivero was Argentinian; Luna was Chilean, Brasido and the Charrúas were from Uruguay. They did not murder representatives of Britain; they murdered Juan Simon (the official representative of Argentina), the Argentine clerk Ventura Pasos, and 3 other employees of Vernet (who was still running his establishment from Buenos Aires), in a dispute over pay. The reason why there was no trial of Rivero and the other suspects was nothing to do with the status of the territory; Britain held the Falklands to be British without question. The British government and its legal advisers also held the suspects to be British subjects and hence liable to conviction (and execution), but there would have been serious doubts as to the fairness of any trial. The British public would have seen the men as exotic and would have had great sympathy for them; a trial would have been seen as a mockery of justice given the difficulty of communicating with the men, since the three surviving Charrúas spoke only their own language (which was on the point of dying out), little Spanish and no English, and also the fact that all the men would have been without lawyers in court. A trial would have been a major public spectacle; it would have attracted extensive critical press coverage and would have provided the Opposition with welcome material with which to attack the government. It was those essentially party-political considerations that led the legal officers to advise against conducting a trial. There was no trial, so no judge was involved, and the remaining men were sent back to South America.

(23) It is untrue that Britain prevented Argentinians from returning to the Falklands. In the first place, the Argentinians Ventura Pasos and Domingo Valleja returned to the islands in the *Rapid* in March 1833 (together with Mathew Brisbane, the Charrúa "Manuel González" and the Uruguayan Juan Brasido). Secondly, Britain permitted around 150 people to go to the islands from Montevideo in the years 1847-9, including at least 17 Argentinians, probably more. And thirdly, there have almost always been Argentinians in the islands, and there are some there today.

(24) In his reply to Argentine ambassador Manuel Moreno on 8 August 1849, the British Foreign Secretary Lord Palmerston did not imply acceptance of Moreno's view that the Falklands were rightfully Argentinian. In his protest to Palmerston on 31 July, Moreno had repeated two versions, from two different newspapers, of what Palmerston had said in the House of Commons; in saying in his reply "whatever the newspapers may have represented me as having said" Palmerston was merely noting that the newpapers differed as to his exact wording; he was not saying they had reported him untruthfully. By July 1849 Palmerston knew that Argentina was negotiating a peace treaty with Britain and was dropping its claim to the Falklands; it is absurd to imagine that only a week after he stated in the House of Commons that the Falklands dispute had ended by acquiescence, he told Moreno that he had been lying to Parliament. Palmerston could not refer openly to the treaty as it was still secret, so he simply turned Moreno's own statement against him. In his letter Moreno had quoted Palmerston's phrase that the correspondence had ceased by "the acquiescence of one party and the maintenance of the other" or "the acquiescence of both parties", which allowed Palmerston to reply in effect that "you are right in saying in your letter that I referred to acquiescence over the Falkland Islands" – in other words, he *confirmed* his Parliamentary statement by confirming Moreno's account of the situation.

(25) Argentina maintained its claim to the Falklands (with all its limitations) by regular protests to Britain for 17 years from 1833 to 1849 inclusive. Those protests consisted of annual statements in the official Messages to the Buenos Aires provincial legislature (comparable to the US President's State of the Union address) plus three sets of formal diplomatic protests by the Argentine representative in London (1833-4, 1841-2 and 1849). After ratifying the Convention of Peace on 15 May 1850 Argentina completely changed its behaviour and dropped all protests to Britain over the Falklands, and did not even mention the islands to the British government for 34 years – over a third of the 19th century. There was one more protest on 20 January 1888 (over 38 years since the symbolic last protest in December 1849), but since then there have been no more Argentine protests. The Falklands were not mentioned in any official Message to the Argentine Congress for 91 years from 1849 until 1941.

(26) Far from being of "supreme importance", Argentina's protest before the Buenos Aires legislature in 1849 was merely symbolic, since it was made after the Convention of Peace had been signed but before it was ratified. The Convention had thus not yet come into force, so anything said at that time was legally irrelevant and did not contradict or cancel the treaty. The decision to drop the Falklands claim had been made and the Convention of Peace had made it official, but before the Convention was ratified the Argentine leader General Juan Manuel Rosas could "go to town" and give vent to his sense of pique that he had lost that minor point, knowing that whatever he said at that time was without force. That is strongly suggested by the length and repetitiveness of the 1849 protest – its 728 words were 15 times as long as most protests in the Messages in the 1830s and 40s, and almost 40 times as long as the 19 words of the 1846 protest. Three passages are repeated almost *verbatim*, thus hammering home Rosas's frustration at having to give up the Falklands, but without affecting the renunciation he had made.

(27) Argentina dropped its claim to the Falklands in 1850 by ratifying the Convention of Peace with Britain. Failure to mention that this ended any Argentine title to the islands is a gross distortion of history. It is also a distortion to refer to it as "the Arana-Southern treaty"; that name was not used before the 20th century, and in the 19th century both Argentina and Britain called it "the Convention of Peace". It is untrue that Argentina made no attempt to include the Falklands question – on the night of 10-11 December 1849, after the signing of the Convention (on 24 November) but before its ratification, General Rosas attempted to point out to the British negotiator Henry Southern that he had left the question of the Falklands for later discussion, but Southern said "All national differences are terminated by solemn and public Conventions of Peace", making it clear that the Convention had terminated all disputes between Argentina and Britain, thus ending any Argentine claim to the Falklands. Southern included that statement in a written memorandum to Rosas on 11 December 1849, and on 15 December Rosas sent Southern a written reply in which he did not contradict Southern's statement but repeated it. Argentina was not coerced into signing the Convention of Peace; Britain would have preferred a lower-level, *ad hoc* agreement to return captured ships, etc., but Argentina refused to accept such an arrangement and forced Britain to sign a treaty of peace, thus compelling Britain to accept Argentina as having been a belligerent with equal rights to Britain's, i.e. a country of equal rank with Britain, France or Spain, not merely a place where Britain could intervene at will. The object and purpose of the Convention of Peace is stated three times in its text: it was to restore "perfect friendship" between Britain and Argentina, which of itself ended the Falklands dispute. Between signing and ratification, Rosas could have abrogated the Convention or refused to ratify it, but did neither, so it came into force upon ratification by both sides on 15 May 1850. That date, Wednesday 15 May 1850, is therefore the

critical date in the legal status of the Falklands, since it marked the final end of Argentina's title and hence the date at which the dispute "crystallised". Until that date Britain's sovereignty in the Falklands had been *de facto* (since Britain held the islands) but not *de jure* (since Argentina contested the validity of Britain's title), but since that date Britain has held both *de facto* and *de jure* sovereignty over the islands. In short, Argentina has since 1850 held no title whatever to the Falklands.

(28) There is abundant evidence that Argentina regarded the 1850 Convention as a peace treaty, and it is universally agreed by writers on international law that territories not mentioned in a peace treaty are fixed by the treaty in the possession of the state that held them when the treaty was signed. The Falklands were not mentioned in the Convention of Peace, so in ratifying it in 1850, Argentina confirmed that the Falklands were British.

(29) The fact that the Convention of Peace ended the Falklands dispute (and hence any Argentine title to the Falklands) was noted in press reports in Britain and Argentina in the late 1840s and early 1850s; it was also noted by the Mexican historian Carlos Pereyra in a book published in Spain in 1919, republished in Argentina in 1944; the effect of the Convention on Argentina's claim was criticised by the congressman Absalón Rojas both in the Argentine Congress and in a book in 1950, and by the Argentine historians Ernesto Fitte (in books published in Argentina in 1969 and 1975), and Alfredo Burnet-Merlín (in a book published in Argentina in 1974 and 1976), while the absence of a proviso for the restitution of the islands in the Convention was noted with irritation by Argentine historian Juan José Cresto in 2011. Thus it has been known in Argentina for a long time that the Convention of Peace ended any Argentine title to the Falklands.

(30) It is not true that the present population of the Falklands was "implanted" by Britain; Britain never had any population policy for the islands, and virtually all inhabitants arrived under their own steam without any action by Britain. The largest group of people who arrived in the 19th century were some 150 people who arrived from Montevideo in the late 1840s, most of whom were Spanish-speaking including at least 17 Argentinians. It is not true that land concessions were awarded exclusively to British nationals; non-British people ("aliens") held land on exactly the same terms as British nationals, and several non-British people held large areas of land without taking British nationality. "Aliens" had exactly the same rights and obligations as British nationals except for holding public office and serving on a jury. And it is not true that the present population of the islands is "mainly temporary"; the largest group of inhabitants now, as at all times in the past century and more, are those born in the islands.

(31) The Falklands (i.e. Malvinas) were not mentioned in the 1853 constitution of the Argentine Confederation, and they were not mentioned by any speaker during the debates of the special congress in March and April 1854 which drew up the constitution of the independent State of Buenos Aires, nor in the 1854 constitution itself, nor were they mentioned by any speaker in the constitutional convention that met in Buenos Aires from January to May 1860 to make initial preparations for the State of Buenos Aires to rejoin the Argentine Confederation and thus to reunite Argentina. Various territorial questions were discussed in the debates on both those constitutions, and some of the speakers were well informed about the recently-ended Falklands dispute between Britain and Argentina, so the reason for their failure to mention the islands was not ignorance. The complete absence of any reference whatever to the Falklands in both those constitutional conventions shows that Argentina's political leaders did not see the Falklands as Argentine territory.

(32) The Spanish expedition that visited the Falklands in 1863 was not merely scientific but had an official diplomatic function – it opened negotiations for the resumption of diplomatic relations between Spain and the recently-united Argentina. Its visit to Stanley was not forced by bad weather or lack of supplies, and it was not hindered in any way by the Falklands Governor, Captain James George Mackenzie. In fact he had cordial relations with the expedition and allowed its members to land and move around freely in the islands; they collected many specimens, which are now in the Museo de Ciencias Naturales in Madrid. The expedition fired a salute to the British flag, and fully accepted the Falklands as British. The legal significance of their visit is that it formally ended any possibility of a Spanish claim to the Falklands, which had theoretically continued since the Spanish garrison left in 1811, and had been preserved by Spanish protests to the United States in 1822 and to Britain in 1825 against the recognition of the independence of the new republics in South America.

(33) In the 1850s, 1860s, 1870s and well into the 1880s Britain performed innumerable administrative and jurisdictional acts of sovereignty (« effectivités ») in the Falklands, such as the first settlement of several islands including the whole of West Falkland, without any reaction from Argentina, although the

Argentine government was aware of those acts and indeed made arrangements to obtain settlers and sheep from the islands. If a party to a territorial dispute performs acts of sovereignty in a territory without any protest from the claiming party despite the claiming party's being aware of those acts, the claiming party is acquiescing in the sovereign party's possession of that territory.

(34) Argentina gave repeated and abundant evidence of overt acquiescence in Britain's possession of the islands, in various acts of omission or commission between 1849 and 1888, and again during a long period after 1888. The dropping of the Argentine claim in 1850 was repeatedly confirmed in the 1860s in official Messages to Congress by Argentine leaders: Vice-President Paz stated in 1866 that a minor problem regarding private compensation for British citizens was the only dispute between Argentina and Britain (thus confirming that there was no dispute over the Falklands), and other leaders stated in more general terms that Argentina had no dispute with Britain, for example President Domingo Sarmiento stated in his Message to the Argentine Congress on 1 May 1869 that "the state of our foreign relations fulfils the aspirations of the country. Nothing is claimed from us by other nations; we have nothing to ask of them…". Those statements, especially that by Vice-President Paz, parallel the "Ihlen declaration" of 1919: a statement by the Norwegian foreign minister Nils Claus Ihlen (who said Norway would make no difficulties if Denmark claimed Eastern Greenland) was ruled by the Permanent Court of International Justice in 1933 to be binding on Norway and to void Norway's claim to the territory.

(35) On 29 July 1882 the Argentine government declared in the Argentine Congress that Louis Vernet's concession of 5 January 1828 had been null and void from the outset. So in 1882 the Argentine government regarded the basis of Vernet's activities in the Falklands (the decree under which he operated from 1828) as having been illegal.

(36) Argentina published several maps which either omit the Falklands or show them in the same colour as countries outside Argentina. The 1882 Latzina map was financed by the Argentine treasury and states on its cover that it is a "Publicación Oficial"; it marks the Falklands in exactly the same colour as Chile and Uruguay, thus showing them as being outside Argentina. It was printed in 120,000 copies, in separate Spanish, English, French, German and Italian versions, and was distributed to Argentine consulates in Europe and North America. For most of the "Affair of the Map" (1884-8) it was the only map of Argentina that Argentina was distributing.

(37) There was an estoppel that prevented Argentina from raising a claim to the islands in 1884 in the "Affair of the Map". The Falklands had been a loss-making concern for Britain until that time, but from the early 1880s began to make a profit. That "estopped" Argentina from claiming the islands then or later, since Britain had incurred a loss in relying on Argentina's previously manifested abandonment of its title.

(38) Despite the estoppel preventing any claim to the Falklands, Argentina attempted to open the question with Britain in 1884, in the "Affair of the Map". This was a new initiative, not the revival of an existing claim. Argentina's title to the islands (which had always been partial, encumbered and restricted, and had thus never amounted to 100% sovereignty) had been definitively ended by the Convention of Peace in 1850 and the many acts of omission and commission by Argentina that followed it. There was therefore no Argentine title to the Falklands whatsoever, and Argentina's last official protest to Britain, on 20 January 1888, was devoid of validity. Argentina has not made any official protest since then.

(39) Further significant publications by Argentina between 1888 and 1900, including several maps, indicate the Falklands as being outside Argentina and hence that all Argentine title to the islands had been abandoned. Those publications include two editions (1891 and 1899) of the comprehensive *Diccionario Geográfico Argentino* by Francisco Latzina, director of the Argentine national statistical office and hence a high-ranking Argentine government official, which either omitted the Falklands completely (1891) or stated that they "belong today to England" (1899).

(40) Ten countries (Belgium, Chile, Denmark, France, Italy, Germany, Norway, Sweden, the United States and Uruguay) maintained consulates in Stanley for decades at various times from the 1850s to the 1970s, implying recognition of Britain's possession of the Falklands – they accepted that the Britishness of the Falklands was "in conformity with international order". It is untrue that consular recognition is irrelevant to questions of sovereignty, as is revealed by Argentina's sharp protest to Uruguay in 1952 against the Uruguayan consulate in the Falklands – Argentina stated that the presence of the consulate "violated" Argentina's sovereignty in the islands.

(41) Argentina twice accepted arbitration by Britain in territorial disputes with Chile, in 1899-1902 and again in 1964-6. On both occasions the border between Argentina and Chile was drawn by an exclusively

British team of experts without Argentine or Chilean participation. Argentina therefore accepted that Britain was entitled to decide what was Argentine territory and what was not. That is incompatible with maintaining a valid territorial claim against Britain over the Falklands.

(42) Argentina has never had any title to South Georgia, the South Orkneys, the South Sandwich Islands and the South Shetlands. Britain has administered all those islands with various officials since 1909, with Argentina's knowledge and without protest. They were only formally claimed by Argentina after the Second World War, after decades of acquiescence in Britain's sovereignty. In 1906 a lease of land on South Georgia was drawn up in Stanley and signed at the British Legation in Buenos Aires, and in 1909 another such lease was signed at the British Consulate in Buenos Aires, in the presence of Falklands Governor William Allardyce; it reverted to the Falkland Islands Government in 1927. By Letters Patent issued on 21 July 1908 Britain set up the Falkland Islands Dependencies (South Georgia, the South Sandwich Islands, South Orkney Islands, South Shetland Islands, Graham Land, and all land in the South Atlantic south of 50° South and between 20° and 80° West), and new Letters Patent were issued on 28 March 1917, further defining the Dependencies. Both sets of Letters Patent were sent to the Argentine government, who on both occasions acknowledged receipt but showed no other reaction (and nor did Chile, which had received them too). Like other whaling companies active in the Antarctic, the Argentine whaling company "Pesca" recognised British sovereignty on South Georgia. In 1909 Britain appointed a resident magistrate on South Georgia (who from 1914 to 1927 was Edward Binnie, a native-born Falkland Islander), and from 1910 a police officer from the Falklands. Ever since then and right up to the present day, there have been British officials resident on South Georgia, including the magistrate, customs officer and assistant customs officer, scientific staff and many others. For well over a century Britain has performed innumerable administrative and jurisdictional acts of sovereignty (« effectivités ») on South Georgia and the other islands. Throughout that period there have been no Argentine officials present; Argentina exercised no sovereignty whatever. Visiting Argentine ships complied with British customs and immigration procedures without question. Britain took the dispute over the Falklands Dependencies to the International Court of Justice in 1955, but Argentina refused to accept the Court's jurisdiction in the case. Argentina could of course take the Falklands dispute to the ICJ at any time, but has never done so, presumably doubting the strength of its case.

(43) No United Nations resolution supports Argentina's claim to the Falklands. Operative paragraphs (1), (2) and (5) of UN Resolution 1514 of 1960 rule out any Argentine claim – they state: "(1) The subjection of peoples to alien subjugation, domination and exploitation constitutes a denial of fundamental human rights…"; "(2) All peoples have the right to self-determination…", and (5) "Immediate steps shall be taken, in Trust and Non-Self-Governing Territories… to transfer all powers to the peoples of those territories, without any conditions or reservations, in accordance with their freely expressed will and desire…". Paragraph (6) has been misused by Argentina: it condemns "Any attempt aimed at the partial or total disruption of the national unity and the territorial integrity of a country…", and is thus irrelevant to the Falklands since its wording refers only to the future after 1960. UN Resolution 1541 (which Argentina avoids mentioning) clearly applies to the Falklands – for almost 60 years since 1960 Britain has submitted regular reports on the islands to the UN as required under Resolution 1541, without any objection or protest from Argentina or any other country. Those reports have always been accepted by the UN General Assembly, showing that the Falklands are a "Chapter XI Territory" under the UN Charter, so Resolution 1541 applies to them, which Argentina has always accepted. Resolution 1541 states that any change in the status of a non-self-governing territory has to be by a "free and voluntary choice by the peoples of the territory concerned", and refers three times to the "wishes" of those peoples, making it abundantly clear that their wishes are paramount in the decolonisation of their homelands. That of itself rules out any Argentine claim to the Falklands, since it could only be realised against the wishes of the people of the islands. Resolution 2625 of 1970 likewise states that colonialism must be ended in all non-self-governing territories according to the "freely expressed will of the peoples concerned", and as well as listing the three options for the realisation of self-determination given in Resolution 1541 (independence, free association with an independent state, or integration with an independent state), it includes a new fourth option: "the emergence into any other political status freely determined by a people", which covers any arrangement the Falkland Islanders may choose. And like Resolution 1514, it protects the territorial integrity of states only against future actions and does not apply to the results of any events in the past, such as the expulsion of the Argentine garrison from the Falklands in 1833.

(44) Argentina's claim to the Falklands violates the International Covenant on Civil and Political Rights (ICCPR), adopted by the UN General Assembly on 16 December 1966, which states that the right of external self-determination is possessed by the peoples of all non-self-governing territories, and obliges all countries "having responsibility for the administration of Non-Self-Governing and Trust Territories" to promote the realisation of the right of self-determination for the peoples of those territories. For Britain to hand the islands to Argentina would be a breach of that obligation.

(45) The first mention of the Falkland Islands (i.e. "Islas Malvinas") in any Argentine constitution is in that of 1994. That constitution states that Argentina's claim to the Falklands is "imprescriptible", and the same has been stated several times by Argentina before the United Nations. In stating that the Argentine claim is imprescriptible, Argentina is asserting the principle of *nullum tempus occurrit regi* ["to the king, no time passes" or "time does not run against the king"], which is not applicable to international law. However, if territorial claims were imprescriptible under international law, the British claim under *nullum tempus* would annihilate the Argentine claim.

(46) The Argentine argument that Falkland Islanders have no right to self-determination is incorrect. UN Resolutions 1514, 1541 and 2625, and the UN International Covenant on Civil and Political Rights, confirm that the right to self-determination is possessed by all the peoples of non-self-governing territories. That was restated by the International Court of Justice in its advisory opinion on the Chagos case in February 2019; the Court also stated that under Chapter XI of the United Nations Charter "the legal régime of non-self-governing territories... was based on the progressive development of their institutions so as to lead the populations concerned to exercise their right to self-determination." The Court's reference to "the populations concerned" includes all inhabitants of non-self-governing territories without distinction; it does not divide them up into those who are "peoples" and those who are not. Attempts by Argentina to deny self-determination to the Falkland Islanders because they are not a "people" are thus not supported by the ICJ. In 2008 Argentina attempted to get the report of the "C24" (the UN decolonisation committee) altered so as to limit self-determination to territories over which there is no sovereignty dispute (i.e. to exclude Gibraltar and the Falklands from the right to self-determination), but that attempt was rejected by the UN General Assembly on 20 October 2008. That confirmed the universal applicability of self-determination to all non-self-governing territories. UN resolutions 1514, 1541, 2625 and the ICCPR all unambiguously confirm that Falkland Islanders possess not only internal self-determination (the right to govern themselves internally), but also the full right to external self-determination, i.e. the right to choose their international relations, including independence from all other countries, integration with a UN member state, free association with a UN member state, or "any other political status". That means that the Falkland Islanders are the holders of territorial sovereignty over their country, the Falklands. They are thus not in a colonial situation but are themselves sovereign; Britain is no longer the colonial possessor of the Falklands but merely the "administering power". Britain holds rightful and exclusive title to the islands; in addition the Falkland Islanders possess the right of external self-determination and therefore have the right to decide how their country is decolonised. At present they freely choose to remain in partnership with Britain.

All those points are proved in this book with extensive documentary evidence which establishes the facts and refutes the contentions of Marcelo Kohen and Facundo Rodríguez. To quote the words of Margaret MacMillan at the head of our Introduction, we have fulfilled "The proper role for historians... to challenge and even explode national myths"[1] – we have exploded the Argentine national myth that the Falklands are Argentine territory and demonstrated that it is a fallacy.

Argentina has absolutely no title to the Falklands. Successive Argentine governments have asserted a claim to the islands for well over half a century, but that claim is devoid of validity.

Kohen and Rodríguez have failed to refute our online papers *Getting it right* and *False Falklands History*. Their work is based on erroneous versions of the history of the Falkland Islands, and is disproved by this present work. The evidence we have presented demolishes all their arguments except one: the appalling treatment of the Chagos Islanders by the British government in the 1960s and 70s. On that one point, we agree with them.

But on the history and legal status of the Falkland Islands, their book *Las Malvinas entre el Derecho y la Historia / The Malvinas/Falklands Between History and Law* has no value as history or law. It stands completely refuted.

---

[1] Margaret MacMillan, *The Uses and Abuses of History*, Toronto 2008, p. 39.

GLOSSARY OF TERMS (as they are used in this book), and LIST OF ABBREVIATIONS AND CONVENTIONS

[ ]	square brackets enclose translations, additions, clarifications, etc., inserted by us
[*sic*]	"thus" (Lat.): the preceding word or words are exactly thus in the original; "[*sic*]" has been added by us
(sic)	"(sic)" is present in the quoted text, not added by us
…	text passages here omitted by us
[…]	longer omission by us
/	A *solidus* or slash may indicate either **1.** two alternatives, e.g. "Falklands/Malvinas", or **2.** a new line to save space, e.g.: "Dear Louis, / Malvinas 4 April 1824 / We arrived here safely…" = 3 lines
§	section (of a book, treaty, etc.)
p. [95]	page not numbered in the quoted work; page no. added here by counting from the nearest numbered page
AGN	Archivo General de la Nación, Buenos Aires, Argentina. The roman figure is the "Sala" (room); under the new reference system the second number indicates the "legajo" (file, batch), mostly with a document number, e.g. "AGN VII, 130, doc. 62"; under the old system, the first Arabic numeral indicates the "cuerpo" (corpus), the second the "anaquel" (shelf), the third the batch number, e.g. "AGN X, 5-1-3".
AGNM	Archivo General de la Nación, Montevideo, Uruguay
b.	born
BDFA	*British Documents on Foreign Affairs* (reprint of the *Foreign Office Confidential Print*), Bethesda, Maryland
BFSP	*British and Foreign State Papers*, London
BL	British Library, London
Blue Books	Books sent to the Colonial Office in London annually from the 1840s by the governors of all British overseas territories, with annual returns on the territories under their authority, entered by hand on blue pre-printed forms, bound into books. Complete set of the 99 Falklands *Blue Books*, 1846-1944, in PRO, CO 81/1 to CO 81/99; incomplete set in JCNA, Stanley.
BN	Bibliothèque Nationale de France, Paris
BPAN	*British Packet and Argentine News*, Buenos Aires
brig	a two-masted sailing vessel
brigantine	a two-masted sailing vessel, square-rigged on the foremast, fore-and-aft rigged (schooner-rigged) on the mainmast; also referred to as a "hermaphrodite brig" or "brig schooner"
c.	*circa*, "around" (Lat.)
C24	Committee of 24 (the UN decolonisation committee)
Camp, camp	(Falklands usage) the whole of the islands outside Stanley (earlier: the whole of the islands outside Port Louis); used with or without "the"
capataz	head gaucho
captain's log	a fair copy of the ship's log, often neater but usually less detailed
CB	Companion of the Most Honourable Order of the Bath
cf.	*confer* (Lat.): "compare"
civil day	the ordinary day of 24 hours beginning at midnight; cf. nautical day
col.; cols.	column; columns
Colección 1832	*Colección de Documentos Oficiales…* ["Collection of Official Documents …"], Buenos Aires 1832 (full title in Bibliography)
con.	continued
copyist	a person employed merely to copy out documents by hand without any other role
corvette	(see under "sloop")
CPM	Comandante Político y Militar [Political and Military Commandant]
cutter	a single-masted sailing vessel
d.	died
DBE	Dame of the Most Excellent Order of the British Empire
DFB	*Dictionary of Falklands Biography*, ed. David Tatham, Ledbury 2008
DNB	*Dictionary of National Biography*
do, do.	(in documents) ditto
doc.; docs.	document; documents
dollar	**1.** (usually in this book) the "peso fuerte", the universal currency in South America from the 16th to the 19th centuries, first issued as a silver coin by Spain in 1497, known in English as a "Spanish dollar" or "piece of eight", since it was divided into 8 reales; for much of the 19th century a peso was worth about 4s 4d sterling (four shillings and fourpence, i.e. about 4.6 pesos to the pound); **2.** the United States dollar (here usually stated as such, e.g. "United States dollars" or "US$"
Downs, the	a fairly sheltered anchorage off Hythe in Kent, between the Goodwin Sands and the Kent coast
draft	(letter) rough version sketched out as it is being written, with evidence of ongoing composition such as crossings-out, interlineated text, asterisks, arrows, etc.; cf. fair copy, keeping-copy
ed.	edition; editor; edited (by)
effectivités	acts of administration and/or jurisdiction indicating the exercise of sovereignty
e.g.	*exempla gratia*, "for example" (Lat.)
esp.	especially
estancia	a cattle-grazing establishment

et al.	*et alii*, "and others" (Lat.)
exequatur	"let it be executed" (Lat.): in international law, a document issued by a government, formally recognising a consul of a foreign country and guaranteeing the rights and privileges of office to that consul
f; ff	and following page; and following pages
facsimile	also "facsimile reprint": a photographically reproduced ed. exactly preserving the typography of the original ed.
fair copy	(letter etc.) clean text copied without crossings-out, interlineations, etc.; either sent (with original signature) or retained for reference, in which case the signature is often absent or abbreviated, often preceded by "(signed)"; cf. draft, keeping-copy
FCO	Foreign and Commonwealth Office
FIC	Falkland Islands Company (numbers in photo credits indicate FIC album and photo no., e.g. 5.057 = album 5, photo 057)
FIG	Falkland Islands Government
fig.	figure (illustration)
FIJ	*Falkland Islands Journal*
FIM	*Falkland Islands Magazine*; from June 1907: *Falkland Islands Magazine and Church Paper*
FIMR	*Falkland Islands Monthly Review*
fish; fishing	(in early documents) both terms refer to any aquatic creatures, often principally seals, sometimes whales as well, but less often fish proper
fn.; fns.	footnote; footnotes
FOCP	*Foreign Office Confidential Print*
fol.; fols.	folio; folios, i.e. sheet(s) of a bound text that has no page-numbers; folios may or may not bear numbers
foliated	with the folios numbered (numbers consecutive but on right-hand pages only)
FSR	Falklands Shipping Register, in the JCNA, Stanley, now available to consult online under: https://www.nationalarchives.gov.fk/online-collections/shipping/shipping-registers
gaucho	**1.** in the Falklands: a farm employee working as a cowboy (in Spanish usually called "peón", plural "peones", i.e. "farmhand", "farm labourer"); **2.** in Spanish-speaking South America: a free, nomadic cowboy
GCMG	Knight Grand Cross of the Most Distinguished Order of St Michael and St George
henceforth	from this point onwards
HMS	His/Her Majesty's Ship (prefix of Royal Navy ships, not used before about 1789-90)
ICCPR	the UN International Covenant on Civil and Political Rights (1966)
i.e.	*id est* (Lat.): "that is"
ibid.	*ibidem*, "the same place" (Lat.): a reference is to the work mentioned immediately previously
ICJ	International Court of Justice, The Hague, Netherlands
id.	*idem*, "the same (one)" (Lat.): the author of a work is the same as the author of the preceding work
ILR	*International Law Reports*
irredentist	a person or view claiming that certain territories formerly belonging to a country are "unredeemed" and should be "redeemed", i.e. they should once again belong to that country
JCNA	Jane Cameron National Archives, Stanley
keeping-copy	(letter etc.) a copy retained for reference, not a draft but copied from a clean version; not as careful as a fair copy but without crossings-out, interlineations, etc.; cf. draft, fair copy
KG	Knight of the Most Noble Order of the Garter
legajo	file or batch of documents (in Spanish-language archives)
legitimist	a person or view claiming that rights of sovereignty exist eternally unless voluntarily given up, independent of any factual changes in the world; see also *nullum tempus*
loc. cit.	*loco citato*, "in the quoted place" (Lat.): a quotation is from the same place as the preceding one
MBE	Member of the Most Excellent Order of the British Empire
MGSS	*Malvinas, Georgias, y Sandwich del Sur: Diplomacia Argentina en Naciones Unidas*, Buenos Aires
MS; MSS	manuscript; manuscripts
NARA	National Archives and Records Administration, Maryland, USA
nautical day	the 24 hours from noon on one day to noon the next day; the date and day of the week changed at noon, 12 hours ahead of the civil day
NB, N.B.	*nota bene*, "note well" (Lat.)
NMM	National Maritime Museum, Greenwich, London
no doc. no.	no document number (a document has no individual number in a file, folder, etc.)
no.; nos.	number; numbers
NRG	Naval Record Group (in US National Archives, Washington DC)
nullum tempus	in full: *nullum tempus occurrit regi*, "to the king, no time passes", or "time does not run against the king" (Lat.): the sovereign's claims are eternal unless he gives them up voluntarily; see also "legitimist"
OBE	Officer of the Most Excellent Order of the British Empire
OED	*Oxford English Dictionary*; references are to CD-ROM Version 3.1.1 (Oxford 2004)
op. cit.	*opus citatum*, "the quoted work" (Lat.); a quote is from an author's previously mentioned work
p.; pp.	page; pages
paginated	with page numbers, i.e. with odd nos. on right-hand pages and even nos. on left-hand pages
passim	"throughout", "everywhere" (Lat.)
pers. comm.	personal communication (information given direct to the author)
PLSR	Port Louis Shipping Record (1826-32), entitled "Arrivals and Sailings of Vessels touching at the East Falklands Begun the 9th June 1826", in AGN VII, 129, doc. 61

pr, pr, pr	per; via (aboard a stated ship); as per (according to orders)
presidio	(in South America) a frontier garrison, usually partly manned by convicts sentenced to serve on the frontier
PRO	Public Record Office, London (now part of The National Archives, TNA)
QC	Queen's Counsel (a senior barrister)
recte	"correctly" (Lat.)
recto	"on the right"(Lat.): right-hand page; front (of a folio)
ref.; refs.	reference; references
reparagraphed	a quotation that runs to more than one paragraph has here been arranged in fewer paragraphs to save space, without altering the text; only the paragraph divisions have been changed
reprint	a later printing of a work, with text identical to an earlier edition but not a photographic facsimile
res nullius	"no one's thing" (Lat.)
Rio Negro	the standard English name (sometimes used in Spanish too) for Carmen de Patagones on the Patagonian coast
RMS	Royal Mail Ship
Sala	room (at the AGN); "la Sala" was also the Spanish name for the main room in Vernet's house at Port Louis
scribal	(handwriting) of a paid scribe, i.e. a copyist, a person employed merely to copy out documents by hand without any other role
secretarial	(handwriting) of a secretary, i.e. a person employed to perform writing and other tasks for a specific person
shallop	a small vessel of some 20-50 tons, often used as a tender to transport cargo such as sealskins to a larger vessel, often either: **1.** a completely or partly prefabricated vessel carried dismantled in the hold of a ship and assembled where it is to be used; or: **2.** a vessel built out of the wreckage of another vessel. Also spelt "chaloupe" as in French.
ship's log	the logbook written as events occurred (later called the "deck log"); pronounced "<u>ship's</u> log", e.g. "the *Clio*'s <u>ship's</u> log" (cf. captain's log)
sloop	**1.** in this book almost always a "sloop-of-war", a small warship, ship-rigged (i.e. with square sails on each mast), with about 12-20 guns, also often called a corvette; a brig-sloop had two masts, a ship-sloop three; **2.** a shallop (rarely in this book)
SPRI	Scott Polar Research Institute, University of Cambridge
Statenland	the Isla de los Estados, off the eastern tip of Tierra del Fuego; in the 1820s and 30s it was often called Statenland in Spanish-language documents as well as English ones
station	(Falklands usage) a (large) sheep farm
tender	a small ship that ferried sealskins, supplies and people between the shore and a larger ship
terra nullius	"no one's land" (Lat.)
TNA	The National Archives, Kew, London (in this book usually referred to as PRO)
ton	(in descriptions of ships): in this book all figures for the tonnage of sailing vessels do not give displacement (= the actual weight of a vessel), but the "Builder's Measurement", under which tonnage had been calculated since the early 18th century, using the formula k x b x ½b ÷ 94 (k = keel length; b = breadth); the tons are Imperial tons of 2240 pounds (20 hundredweight each of 112 pounds)
UKHO	United Kingdom Hydrographic Office, Taunton, Somerset
UPU	Universal Postal Union, Berne, Switzerland
USNA	US National Archives, Washington DC
usufruct	the right to exploit another's property without owning it and without destroying it
verbatim	"word for word", in exactly the same words (Lat.)
Vernet's "Memoirs"	a 90-page MS in English by Louis Vernet, entitled "Memoirs on the Falkland Islands", in AGN VII, 141 (no doc. no.)
verso	"back" (of a folio); left-hand page (Lat.)

SELECT BIBLIOGRAPHY

[**Anon.**, but by **Johnson, Samuel**], *Thoughts on the Late Transactions Respecting Falkland's Islands*, London 1771; Spanish translation, *Pensamientos acerca de las últimas negociaciones relativas a las Islas Malvinas y otros escritos*, Buenos Aires 2003.

[**Anon.**, but by **Lundin, Richard**], "Narrative of a Voyage from New South Wales in 1812-1813", in *Lowe's Edinburgh Journal*, October 1846.

[**Anon.**, published by the Argentine army], *Conflicto Malvinas*, Buenos Aires 1983.

[**Anon.**], *Argentina – Reino Unido; Acuerdos Bilaterales y Otros Documentos 1823-2002* ["Argentina-United Kingdom; Bilateral Agreements and Other Documents 1823-2002"], Buenos Aires 2004.

[**Anon.**], Argentine pamphlets: (1) [Observatorio Malvinas], *Islas Malvinas*, March 2007 (English: *Islas Malvinas, Georgias del Sur y Sandwich del Sur / Malvinas, South Georgia and South Sandwich Islands*, December 2007); (2) [foreign ministry], *Argentine Republic / The Question of the Malvinas Islands / A story of colonialism. A United Nations cause*, September 2012; (3) [foreign ministry], *Islas Malvinas. Argentina, sus derechos, y el diálogo necesario / Malvinas Islands. Argentina, its rights and the need for dialogue*, February 2013; (4) [education ministry], *Malvinas para todos: Memoria, soberanía y democracía, Un material para compartir en la escuela, en la familia, en el barrio, en las redes sociales* ["Malvinas for all: Memory, sovereignty and democracy, Material to be shared in school, in the family, in the neighbourhood, on social networks"], April 2014; (5) [Malvinas secretariat], *Soberanía Argentina en Malvinas a 50 años del "Alegato Ruda" / Argentine Sovereignty over Malvinas 50 years after the Ruda Statement*, September 2014; (6) [foreign ministry], *La Cuestión Malvinas: A 50 años de la resolución 2065 (XX) de las Naciones Unidas* ["The Malvinas Question: 50 years after United Nations Resolution 2065 (XX)"], June 2015.

[**Anon.**], *British and Foreign State Papers* (*BFSP*) *1833-1834* (London 1847); *1848-1849* (London 1862); *1865-1866* (London 1870); *1866-1867* (London 1871); *1870-1871* (London 1877).

[**Anon.**], *Colección de Documentos Oficiales con que el Gobierno Instruye al Cuerpo Legislativo de la Provincia del Origen y Estado de las Cuestiones Pendientes con la República de los E[stados] U[nidos] de Norte América sobre las Islas Malvinas* ["Collection of Official Documents with which the Government Instructs the Legislature of the Province on the Origin and State of the Issues Pending with the Republic of the United States of North America on the Malvinas Islands"], Buenos Aires 1832 ("*Colección 1832*").

[**Anon.**], *El Episodio Ocurrido en Puerto de la Soledad de Malvinas el 26 de Agosto de 1833...* ["The Episode that Occurred at Puerto de la Soledad in Malvinas, 26 August 1833..."], Buenos Aires 1967.

[**Anon.**], *Hansard's Parliamentary Debates*, London 1848 and 1849.

[**Anon.**], *International Law Reports* (*ILR*) vol. 52, Cambridge 1979.

[**Anon.**], *Laws and Ordinances of the Falkland Islands from the Settlement of the Colony to the year 1884*, Stanley 1884.

[**Anon.**], *Malvinas en la historia: Una perspectiva suramericana*, ["Malvinas in history: A South American Perspective"], Lanús (Buenos Aires) 2011.

[**Anon.**], *Revised Falklands Ordinances 1915*, Stanley 1915.

[**Anon.**], *Revised Statutes of the United States, passed at the First Session of the Forty-Third Congress, 1873-'74, Washington DC, 1878*.

[**Anon.**], *US Consular Regulations*, Washington DC 1881.

[**Anon.**],"A Visit to the Falkland Islands", in *The United Service Journal and Naval and Military Magazine*, London 1832.

Acosta y Lara, Eduardo F., *La Guerra de Los Charrúas*, ["The War of the Charrúas"], Montevideo 1969-70.

Arnaud, Vicente Guillermo, *Las Islas Malvinas: Descubrimiento, primeros mapas y ocupación, Siglo XVI* ["The Malvinas Islands: Discovery, first maps and occupation, 16th Century"], Buenos Aires 2000.

Barnard, Charles, *A Narrative of the Sufferings and Adventures of Capt. Charles H. Barnard...*, New York 1829; new ed. by **Dodge, Bertha S.**, *MAROONED: Being a Narrative of the Sufferings and Adventures...*, Middletown, Connecticut, 1979.

Basílico, Ernesto, *La Armada del Obispo de Plasencia y el Descubrimiento de las Malvinas* ["The Fleet of the Bishop of Plasencia and the Discovery of the Malvinas"], Buenos Aires 1967.

Baudry, Jean, *Documents inédits sur André Thevet...*, ["Unpüublished documents on André Thevet"], Paris 1982.

Becerra, Alfredo, *Protestas por Malvinas (1833-1946)*, Buenos Aires 1998.

Beccaceci, Marcelo, *Gauchos de Malvinas*, Buenos Aires 2017.

Berasategui, Vicente E., *Malvinas, Diplomacía y Conflicto Armado: Comentarios a la Historia Oficial Británica*, ["Malvinas, Diplomacy and Armed Conflict: Commentaries on the Official British History"], Buenos Aires June 2011.

Bernhardson, Wayne, *Land and Life in the Falkland Islands* (doctoral thesis, Berkeley, California, 1989, unpublished).

Bertrand, Kenneth J., *Americans in Antarctica*, New York 1971.

Black, William George, *Heligoland and the Islands of the North Sea*, Edinburgh 1888.

Blake, Sally, Cameron, Jane and **Spruce, Joan**, *Diddle Dee to Wire Gates: A Dictionary of Falklands Vocabulary*, Stanley 2011.

Bologna, Alfredo Bruno, *Los derechos de la república Argentina sobre las islas Malvinas...* ["The rights of the Argentine republic to the Malvinas islands..."], Buenos Aires 1988.

Bound, Graham, *Falkland Islanders at War*, Barnsley 2002; 2nd expanded and updated ed., *Invasion 1982: The Falkland Islanders' Story*, Barnsley 2007.

Bourne, Kenneth and **Watt, D. Cameron**, general eds., *British Documents on Foreign Affairs: Reports and Papers from the Foreign Office Confidential Print* (*BDFA*), Bethesda, Maryland, USA 1991.

Boyson, V[iolet] F[enton], *The Falkland Islands*, Oxford 1924.

Bravo, Enrique, *La guerra de las i* ["The war of the i's"], Buenos Aires 1999.

Britain, David, and **Sudbury, Andrea**,"Falkland Islands English", in Daniel Schreier, Peter Trudgill, Edgar W. Schneider and Jeffrey P. Williams (eds.), *The Lesser-Known Varieties of English: An Introduction*, Cambridge 2010.

Burnet-Merlín, Alfredo R., *Cuando Rosas quiso ser inglés: historia de una anglofilia* ["When Rosas wanted to be British: history of a case of Anglophilia"], Buenos Aires, April 1974, June 1974 and October 1976.

Cady, John F., *Foreign Intervention in the Rio de la Plata 1838-50*, Philadelphia 1929.

Caillet-Bois, Ricardo (ed.), *Colección de Documentos relativos a la Historia de las Islas Malvinas*, ["Collection of Documents relative to the History of the Malvinas Islands"], Buenos Aires 1957.

Caillet-Bois, Ricardo R., *Una Tierra Argentina: Las Islas Malvinas* ["An Argentine Land: The Malvinas Islands"], 1st ed. Buenos Aires 1948; 2nd ed., 1952; 3rd ed. Buenos Aires 1982.

Campbell, R. J., *The Discovery of the South Shetland Islands, 1819-1820: the Journal of Midshipman C.W. Poynter*, London 2000.

Canclini, Arnoldo, (1) *Malvinas: Su historia en historias* [The Malvinas: their history in stories], Buenos Aires 2000; (2) *Malvinas 1833: antes y después de la agresión inglesa* ["Malvinas 1833: before and after the English aggression"], Buenos Aires March 2007.

Carranza, Ánjel Justiniano, *Campañas Navales de la República Argentina* ["Naval Campaigns of the Argentine Republic"], 1st ed. Buenos Aires 1916; 2nd ed. 1962.

Cawkell, Mary, *The History of the Falkland Islands*, Oswestry 2001.

Charlton, Michael, *The Little Platoon: Diplomacy and the Falklands Dispute*, Oxford 1989.

Cisneros, Andrés and Escudé, Carlos (eds.), *Historia General de las Relaciones Exteriores de la República Argentina* ["General History of the Foreign Relations of the Republic of Argentina"], Buenos Aires 1998, 11 vols. and online.

Connolly, T. W. J., *The History of the Corps of Royal Sappers and Miners...*, vol. I, London 1855.

Cordasco, Francesco, *Junius: A Bibliography of the Letters of Junius with a Checklist of Junian Scholarship and Related Studies*, Fairview (New Jersey) and London 1986.

Cresto, Juan José, *Historia de las Islas Malvinas...* ["History of the Malvinas Islands..."], Buenos Aires 2011, 2 vols.

Da Fonseca Figueira, José Antonio, *David Jewett; una biografia para la historia de las Malvinas*, ["David Jewett; a biography for the history of the Malvinas"], Buenos Aires 1985.

Dahlgren, M. E. W., « Voyages Français à Destination de la Mer du Sud Avant Bougainville (1695-1749) » ["French Voyages to the South Sea Before Bougainville (1695-1749)"], in *Nouvelles Archives des Missions Scientifiques et Littéraires...*, vol. XIV, Paris 1907.

David, Andrew, (1) "Anthony Hunt and his encounters with Spanish vessels when stationed in the Falklands, in HMS *Tamar*, 1768-70", in *FIJ* vol. 8 (4), 2005; (2) "The Massacre of Matthew Brisbane and his Companions at Port Louis in 1833 and the Fate of their Murderers", in *FIJ* vol. 9 (1), 2007.

David, Andrew, et al., eds., *The Malaspina Expedition 1789-1794*, vol. I, London 2001.

Davis, William Columbus, *The Last Conquistadores: the Spanish Intervention in Peru and Chile 1863-1866*, Athens (Georgia, USA) 1950.

Day, Vice-Admiral Sir Archibald, *The Admiralty Hydrographic Service 1795-1919*, London 1967.

De Angelis, Pedro (ed.), *Archivo Americano y Espíritu de la Prensa del Mundo* ["American Archive and Spirit of the World Press"], Buenos Aires 1850.

De Bernhardt, Gaston, "Memorandum respecting the Falkland Islands", 7 December 1910, doc. 9755 in the *Foreign Office Confidential Print* (*FOCP*), London 1910; reprinted as doc. 259 in *British Documents on Foreign Affairs* (*BDFA*), ed. George Philip, Part I, vol. 1, Bethesda (Maryland, USA) 1991; Spanish translation in **Ferrer Vieyra** 1993.

De Gandía, Enrique, "Claudio Alejandro Ptolomeo, Colón y la exploración de la India Americana", in *Investigaciones y Ensayas*, no. 13, Buenos Aires, July-December 1972.

De Marco, Miguel Ángel, *La Armada Española en el Plata (1845-1900)* ["The Spanish Navy in the River Plate (1845-1900)"], Buenos Aires 1981.

De Vattel, Emer, *The Law of Nations or the Principle of Natural Law* [translation 1797], Philadelphia 1829.

De Visscher, Charles, *Théories et Réalités en Droit International Public*, Paris 1953; English translation by **Corbett, P. E.**, *Theory and Reality in Public International Law*, Princeton 1957.

Deas, Malcolm, "Notes on the issue of Falkland Islands sovereignty for House of Commons, Committee on Foreign Affairs", in House of Commons, Foreign Affairs Committee, Minutes of Evidence, 17/1/83; Spanish translation in **Ferrer Vieyra** 1993.

Destéfani, Rear Admiral Laurio H., *Las Malvinas en la época hispana (1600-1811)* ["The Malvinas in the Spanish period (1600-1811)"], Buenos Aires 1981.

Destombes, Marcel, (1) « L'Hémisphère austral en 1524: une carte de Pedro Reinel à Istanbul » ["The southern Hemisphere in 1524: a map by Pedro Reinel in Istanbul"], in *Comptes rendus du Congrès International de Géographie*, Amsterdam 1938, vol. II ; (2) "The Chart of Magellan", in *Imago Mundi* vol. XII, 1955; (4) « André Thevet (1504-1592) et sa contribution à la cartographie et à l'océanographie » ["André Thevet (1504-1592) and his contribution to cartography and oceanography"], in *Proceedings of the Royal Society of Edinburgh 1972*; facsimile Utrecht and Paris 1987.

Díaz Cisneros, César, "La soberanía de la República Argentina en las Malvinas ante el Derecho Internacional" ["The sovereignty of the Argentine Republic in the Malvinas in International Law"], in *Soberanía argentina en el Archipiélago de las Malvinas y en la Antártida*, La Plata 1951.

Dodds, Klaus, *Pink Ice: Britain and the South Atlantic Empire*, London 2002.

Dolzer, Rudolf, *The Territorial Status of the Falkland Islands (Malvinas): Past and Present*, New York/ London/ Rome 1993; German version: *Der völkerrechtliche Status der Falkland-Inseln (Malvinas) im Wandel der Zeit* ["The international-law status of the Falkland Islands (Malvinas) through the ages"], Heidelberg 1986.

Drower, George, *Heligoland: the True Story of German Bight and the Island that Britain Betrayed*, Stroud 2002.

Dunmore, John, *Visions & Realities: France in the Pacific 1695-1995*, Waikanae, New Zealand, 1997.

Duperrey, Louis-Isidore, *Voyage Autour du Monde...*, 11 vols., Paris 1826-30.

Escudé, Carlos, "Contenido nacionalista de la enseñanza de la geografía en la República Argentina 1879-1986" ["Nationalist content in the teaching of geography in the Republic of Argentina 1879-1986"], in *Malvinas hoy: herencia de un conflicto*

["Malvinas today: legacy of a conflict"], Buenos Aires 1989.

Fabry, Mikulas, *Recognizing States: International Society & the Establishment of New States Since 1776*, Oxford 2010.

Fanning, Edmund, *Voyages round the World...*, 1st ed. New York 1833; 2nd ed. New York 1838; new ed. Salem, Massachusetts, 1924.

Fernández-Armesto, Felipe, *Amerigo: The Man Who Gave his Name to America*, New York and London 2006.

Ferns, H. S., *Britain and Argentina in the Nineteenth Century*, Oxford 1960.

Ferrer Vieyra, Enrique, (1) *Las Islas Malvinas y el Derecho Internacional* ["The Malvinas Islands and International Law"], Buenos Aires 1984; (2) *An Annotated Legal Chronology of the Malvinas (Falkland) Islands Controversy*, Córdoba 1985; (3) *Segunda Cronología Legal Anotada Sobre las Islas Malvinas (Falkland Islands)* ["Second Annotated Legal Chronology on the Malvinas Islands (Falkland Islands)"], Buenos Aires, 2nd ed. April 1993.

Fery y Torres, Alejandro, *Viaje de regreso de la Resolución* ["The return voyage of the *Resolución*"], Madrid 1882, reprint Madrid 1940.

Field, John W., *Memorandum respecting the Falkland Islands and Dependencies*, 29 February, 1928, in PRO FO 371-12735, fol. 157ff; Spanish translation in **Ferrer Vieyra** 1993.

Fisch, Jörg, "The Falkland Islands in the European Treaty System 1493-1833", in *German Yearbook of International Law / Jahrbuch für Internationales Recht*, Berlin, vol. 26, 1983.

Fitte, Ernesto J., (1) *La Agresión Norteamericana a las Islas Malvinas* ["American Aggression against the Malvinas Islands"], Buenos Aires 1966; (2) *La disputa con Gran Bretaña por las islas del Atlántico Sur* ["The dispute with Great Britain over the South Atlantic islands"], Buenos Aires 1968; (3) "Cronología Marítima de las Islas Malvinas" ["Maritime Chronology of the Malvinas Islands"], in *Investigaciones y Ensayos* vol. 4, Buenos Aires January-June 1968; (4) *Crónicas del Atlántico Sur: Patagonia, Malvinas y Antártida* ["Chronicles of the South Atlantic: Patagonia, Malvinas and Antarctica"], Buenos Aires 1974; (5) *Crónicas de Rosas* ["Chronicles of Rosas"], Buenos Aires 1975.

FitzRoy, Robert, *Narrative of the Surveying Voyages of His Majesty's Ships Adventure and Beagle...*, London 1839.

Freedman, Lawrence and **Karsh, Efraim**, *The Gulf Conflict 1990-1991: Diplomacy and War in the New World Order*, London 1993.

Freedman, Sir Lawrence, (1) *Britain & the Falklands War*, Oxford 1988; (2) *The Official History of the Falklands Campaign*, Abingdon 2005; 2nd ed. 2007.

Gamba, Virginia, *El Peón de la Reina* ["The Queen's Pawn"], Buenos Aires 1984.

Gerding, Eduardo C[esar], *La Saga de David Jewett*, Buenos Aires 2006.

Goebel, Julius, (1) *The Recognition Policy of the United States*, New York 1915; (2) *The Struggle for the Falkland Islands: A study in legal and diplomatic history*, New Haven (Connecticut) 1927; 2nd ed. Port Washington (N.Y.) 1971; 3rd ed., New Haven and London 1982; Spanish translation, *La Pugna por las Islas Malvinas*, Buenos Aires 1983.

Gómez Langenheim, Antonio, (1) *La tercera invasión inglesa* ["The third British invasion"], Buenos Aires 1934; (2) *Elementos para la Historia de nuestras Islas Malvinas*, ["Materials for the History of our Malvinas Islands"], Buenos Aires 1939, 2 vols.

González Bollo, Hernan, "Una Tradición Cartográfica Física y Política de la Argentina, 1838-1882", ["A Physical and Political Cartographic Tradition in Argentina, 1838-1882"] in *Ciencia Hoy*, vol. 8, no. 46, Buenos Aires, May/June 1998.

González, Martín Abel, *The Genesis of the Falklands (Malvinas) Conflict...*, Basingstoke 2013.

Gough, Barry, *The Falkland Islands/Malvinas: The Contest for Empire in the South Atlantic*, London 1992.

Gower, Sir Erasmus, *An account of the loss of His Majesty's sloop Swift: In Port Desire, on the coast of Patagonia, on the 13th of March, 1770, and of other events which succeeded, in a letter to a friend*, London 1803.

Grotius, Hugo [Huig van Groot], *De Iure Belli ac Pacis Libri tres...* ["Three books on the Law of War and Peace"], Amsterdam 1646.

Groussac, Paul, *Les Iles Malouines: nouvel exposé d'un vieux litige* ["The Malouine Islands: a new account of an old legal dispute"], Buenos Aires 1910; Spanish translation, *Las Islas Malvinas por Paul Groussac. Edición castellana ordenada por el Congreso de la Nación Argentina (LEY 11904)* ["The Malvinas Islands by Paul Groussac: Spanish edition ordered by the Congress of the Argentine Nation (Law 11904)], Buenos Aires 1936.

Guillemard, F.H.H., *The Life of Ferdinand Magellan...*, London 1890.

Gurney, Alan, *Below the Convergence: Voyages towards Antarctica 1699-1839*, London 1997.

Gustafson, Lowell S., *The Sovereignty Dispute over the Falkland (Malvinas) Islands*, New York 1988.

Hakluyt, Richard, *Principal Navigations...*, London 1600, vol. III.

Hart, Ian B., *Pesca: A History of the Pioneer Modern Whaling Company in the Antarctic*, Salcombe 2001.

Hawkesworth, John, *Account of the Voyages...*, London 1773, vol. I.

Hawkins, Sir Richard, *The Observations of Sir Richard Havvkins K^{nt}, in his Voiage into the South Sea. Anno Domini, 1593*, London 1622, reprint ed. by **Bethune, C.R. Drinkwater**, London 1847.

Headland, Robert, *The Island of South Georgia*, Cambridge 1984.

Herms, Michael, *Flaggenwechsel auf Helgoland: Der Kampf um einen militärischen Vorposten in der Nordsee* ["Changing flags on Heligoland: the struggle for a military outpost in the North Sea"], Berlin 2002.

Hernekamp, Karl, *Der argentinisch-chilenische Grenzstreit am Beagle-Kanal* ["The Argentine-Chilean border dispute on the Beagle Channel"], Hamburg 1980.

Hervé, Roger. *Découverte Fortuite de l'Australie et de la Nouvelle-Zélande par des Navigateurs Portugais et Espagnols entre 1521 et 1528*, Paris 1982; English translation: **Dunmore, John**, *Chance Discovery of Australia and New Zealand by Portuguese and Spanish Navigators between 1521 and 1528* (Palmerston North, New Zealand, 1983).

Hidalgo Nieto, Manuel, *La Cuestión de las Malvinas* ["The Malvinas Question"], Madrid 1947.

Higgins, Rosalyn, *Problems & Process: International Law and How We Use it*, Oxford 1994.

Hoffmann, Fritz L., and **Olga Mingo**, *Sovereignty in Dispute: The Falklands/Malvinas, 1493-1982*, Boulder (Colorado) and London 1984.

Holdich, Col. Sir Thomas Hungerford, *The Countries of the King's Award*, London 1904.
Hope, Adrián F. J., "Sovereignty and Decolonization of the Malvinas (Falkland) Islands", in *Boston College International and Comparative Law Review*, vol. VI no. 2, Spring 1983.
Hunter Christie, E. W. [Bill], *The Antarctic Problem*, London 1951.
Huntsman, Judith and **Kalolo, Kelihiano**, *The Future of Tokelau: Decolonising Agendas, 1975-2006*, Auckland and Honolulu 2007.
Ireland, Gordon, *Boundaries, Possessions, and Conflicts in South America*, Cambridge (Massachusetts), 1938.
Jenkinson, Charles [1st Earl of Liverpool], *A Collection of all the Treaties…*, London 1785, vol. iii.
Jennings, Sir Robert and **Watts, Sir Arthur** (eds.), *Oppenheim's International Law, vol. I, Peace, Introduction and Part I*, 9th ed. Harlow 1992.
Jewett, Frederic Clarke, *History and Genealogy of the Jewetts of America…*, New York 1908.
Jones, A. G. E., (1) "Captain Matthew Brisbane", in *Notes & Queries* 1971, reprinted (without footnotes) in *FIJ* 1975; (2) *Ships employed in the South Seas Trade, 1775-1861*, Canberra (Australia), vol. I, 1986; (3) *Polar Portraits: Collected Papers*, Whitby 1992.
Karrow, Robert W. Jr., *Mapmakers of the Sixteenth Century and their Maps*, Chicago 1993.
Keynes, Richard Darwin (ed.), *Charles Darwin's Beagle Diary*, Cambridge 1988.
Kinney, Douglas, *National Interest/National Honor…*, New York 1989.
Kobylanski, Juan K., *El Conflicto del Beagle y la Mediación Papal* ["The Beagle Channel Conflict and the Papal Mediation"], Montevideo, September 1987.
Kohen, Marcelo G. and **Dumberry, Patrick**, *The Institute of International Law's Resolution on State Succession and State Responsibility: Introduction, Text and Commentaries*, Cambridge 2019
Kohen, Marcelo G. and **Hébié, Mamadou**, eds., *Research Handbook on Territorial Disputes in International Law*, Cheltenham (UK) and Northampton (USA), 2018.
Kohen, Marcelo G. and **Rodríguez, Facundo**, *Las Malvinas entre el derecho y la historia: Refutación del folleto británico "Más allá de la historia oficial. La verdadera historia de las Falklands/Malvinas"* ["The Malvinas between law and history: Refutation of the British pamphlet 'Beyond the official history. The True History of the Falklands/Malvinas' "], Buenos Aires November 2015; English translation *The Malvinas/Falklands between History and Law: Refutation of the British Pamphlet "Getting it Right: The Real History of the Falklands Malvinas*, July 2017 and online.
Kohen, Marcelo G., *Possession Contestée et Souveraineté Territoriale* ["Adverse Possession and Territorial Sovereignty"], Paris January 1997.
Kohl, Johann Georg, *Die beiden ältesten General-Karten von Amerika…* ["The two oldest general maps of America…"], Weimar 1860.
Kretschmer, Konrad, *Die historischen Karten zur Entdeckung Amerikas* ["The historical maps on the discovery of America"], Frankfurt am Main 1892; new ed. by Günter Braun and Albrecht von Gleich, Hamburg 1991).
Laguarda Trías, Rolando A., *Nave Española descubre las Islas Malvinas en 1520* ["Spanish ship discovers the Malvinas Islands in 1520"], Montevideo, Uruguay, 1983.
Lastra, Antonio Montarcé, *Redención de la Soberanía…* ["Redemption of Sovereignty…"], Buenos Aires 1946.
Latzina, F[rancisco], (1) *Geografía de la República Argentina*, Buenos Aires 1888; (2) (adapted French translation): *Géographie de la République Argentine*, Buenos Aires 1890; (3) *Diccionario Geográfico Argentino*, 1st ed. Buenos Aires 1891; 3rd ed. Buenos Aires 1899.
Laudy, Mark, "The Vatican Mediation of the Beagle Channel Dispute: Crisis Intervention and Forum Building", in *Words over War: Mediation and Arbitration to Prevent Deadly Conflict*, New York 2000.
Lawrence, T[homas] J[oseph], *The Principles of International Law*, 4th revised ed., Boston (Massachusetts) 1910.
Legón, Faustino J. and **Medrano, Samuel W.**, *Las Constituciones de la República Argentina*, Madrid 1953.
Leguizamón Pondal, Martiniano, *Toponimía Criolla en las Malvinas* ["Native South American toponymy in the Malvinas"], Buenos Aires 1956.
Lesson, René Primevère, *Voyage autour du monde…*, Paris 1838.
Lestringant, Frank, *André Thevet: Cosmographe des derniers Valois* ["André Thevet: Cosmographer of the last Valois kings"], Geneva 1991.
Lombardi, Cathryn L. and John V., and **Stoner, K. Lynn**, *Latin American History: a Teaching Atlas*, Madison (Wisconsin) 1983.
Lynch, John, (1) *Argentine Dictator: Juan Manuel de Rosas 1829-1852*, Oxford 1981; (2) *Argentine Caudillo: Juan Manuel de Rosas*, Wilmington (Delaware) 2001.
Mabragaña, H[eraclio], ed., *Los Mensajes 1810-1910*, Buenos Aires 1910.
Madely, John, *Diego Garcia: a contrast to the Falklands*, Minority Rights Group Report no. 54, ed. (hereafter "Report 54"), London 1982.
Magnaghi, Alberto, *Amerigo Vespucci; studio critico*, Rome 1926.
Manning, William Ray, (1) "The Nootka Sound Controversy", in *Annual Report of the American Historical Association for the Year 1904*, Washington DC 1905; (2) *Diplomatic Correspondence of the United States Concerning the Independence of the Latin-American Nations*, Washington DC 1925, vol. I; (3) *Diplomatic Correspondence of the United States: Inter-American Affairs 1831-1860*, vol. I: *Argentina, Documents 1-387*, Washington DC 1932.
Martin-Allanic, Jean-Étienne, *Bougainville navigateur et les découvertes de son temps* ["Bougainville as navigator and the discoveries of his time"], 2 vols., Paris 1964.
Martinic, Mateo, (1) "Falkland Islands Immigration to the Magellanic Region", in *FIJ* vol. 6 (5), 1996; (2) *Cartografía Magallánica 1523-1945*, Punta Arenas (Chile) 1999.
McIntosh, Gregory C., *The Piri Reis Map of 1513*, Athens (Georgia, USA) and London 2000.
Miller, David, *The Wreck of the Isabella*, Barnsley (Yorkshire), 1995.

Miller, Robert Ryal, *For Science and Glory: the Spanish Scientific Expedition to America, 1862-1866*, Oklahoma 1968; Spanish translation by **Regueiro, Antonio M.**, *Por la Ciencia y la Gloria Nacional: la expedición científica española a América (1862-1866)*, Barcelona 1983.

Molinari, Diego Luis, *La Primera Unión del Sur...*, Buenos Aires, 1961.

Moore, John Bassett, (1) *Digest of International Law*, 7 vols., Washington DC 1906; (2) *Costa Rica-Panama Arbitration: Memorandum on Uti Possidetis*, Rosslyn, Virginia (USA) 1913.

Muñoz Azpiri, José Luis, *Historia Completa de las Malvinas*, 3 vols., Buenos Aires 1966.

Mustapich, José Maria, *Código Civil de la República Argentina...*, Madrid 1960.

Myhre, Jeffrey D., "Title to the Falklands-Malvinas Under International Law", in *Millennium Journal of International Studies*, Oxford 1983.

Napp, Richard [ed.], *Die Argentinische Republik. Im Auftrag des Argentin. Central Comité's für die Philadelphia-Ausstellung...* ["The Argentine Republic. Commissioned by the Argentine Central Committee for the Philadelphia Exhibition..."], Buenos Aires 1876.

Norden, Deborah L., *Military rebellion in Argentina*, Nebraska 1996.

Northup, George Tyler, *Amerigo Vespucci: Letter to Piero Soderini, Gonfaloniere* (*Vespucci Reprints, Texts and Studies: The Soderini Letter in Translation*), 2 vols., Princeton 1916.

Núñez, Ignacio, *Noticias históricas, politicas, y estadísticas de las Provincias Unidas del Río de la Plata...*, London 1825; English translation: *An account, historical, political, and statistical, of the United Provinces of Rio de la Plata...*, London 1825; French translation: *Esquisses, historiques, politiques et statistiques de Buenos-Ayres, des autres Provinces Unies du Rio de la Plata...*, Paris 1826.

O'Brien, John, *International Law*, London 2001.

Oppenheim, L[assa], *International Law: A Treatise*, 7th ed. by **Lauterpacht, H[ersch]**, London 1952, vol. II, *Disputes, War and Neutrality*.

Palacios, Alfredo L., *Las Islas Malvinas, Archipiélago Argentino* ["The Malvinas Islands, an Argentine Archipelago"], Buenos Aires 1934.

Parkes, Oscar, *British Battleships: A History of Design, Construction and Armament...*, London 1957.

Penrose, Bernard, *An Account of the Last Expedition to Port Egmont, in Falkland's Islands, In the Year 1772...*, London 1775.

Peña, Manuel Pedro, (1) *Malvinas: Mito & Realidad: Desde los primeros avistamientos, hasta la consolidación de los derechos* ["Malvinas: Myth & Reality; From the first sightings to the consolidation of rights"], Buenos Aires April 2016; (2) **Peña, Manuel Pedro**, and **Peña, Juan Angél**, *Falklands or Malvinas: Myths & Facts*, Sevilla (Spain) 2018 (partly extended and adapted English version of 1).

Pepys, Samuel, ed. **Latham, Robert** and **Matthews, William**, *The Diary of Samuel Pepys*, 11 vols., London 1970-83.

Pereyra, Carlos, *Rosas y Thiers: La diplomacia europea en el Río de la Plata (1838-1850)* ["Rosas and Thiers: European diplomacy in the River Plate (1838-1850)"], 1st ed. Madrid 1919, 2nd ed. Buenos Aires 1944.

Perl, Raphael, *The Falkland Islands Dispute in International Law and Politics*, London / Rome / New York 1983.

Pernetty, Antoine-Joseph, *Histoire d'un Voyage aux Isles Malouines...* ["History of a Voyage to the Malouine Islands..."], Paris 1770.

Peters, Richard (ed.), *Reports of Cases Argued and Adjudged in the Supreme Court of the United States. January term, 1839...*, vol. 38 ("Peters 13"), Washington DC 1839.

Philpott, Robert A., (1) *The Early Falkland Islands Company Settlements: An Archaeological Survey*, Stanley and Liverpool 2007; (2) *Keppel: The South American Missionary Society Settlement 1855-1911, An Archaeological and Historical Survey*, Stanley and Liverpool 2009; (3) *Port Louis. The first capital of the Falkland Islands...*, Stanley and Liverpool (forthcoming).

Pilger, John, *Freedom Next Time*, London 2006.

Pine, Lynda and Nicholas, *William Henry Goss: the story of the Staffordshire family of Potters who invented Heraldic Porcelain*, Portsmouth 1987.

Pohl, Frederick J., *Amerigo Vespucci: Pilot Major*, New York 1944.

Puig-Samper, Miguel, *Crónica de una Expedición Romántica al Nuevo Mundo* ["Chronicle of a Romantic Expedition to the New World"], Madrid 1988.

Richardson, James D., *Messages and Papers of the Presidents* (ed.), e-book version.

Robben, Antonius C. G. M., *Death, mourning and burial: a cross-cultural reader*, Oxford 2004.

Rodger, N. A. M., *The Command of the Ocean: A Naval History of Britain, 1649-1815*, London 2004.

Rogers, Woodes, *A Cruising Voyage round the World...*, London 1712.

Rojas, Absalón, *Rosas y las Malvinas* ["Rosas and the Malvinas"], Buenos Aires 1950.

Rubin, Alfred C., "Historical and Legal Background of the Falkland/Malvinas Dispute", in **Coll, Alberto R.**, and **Arend, Anthony C.**, (eds.), *The Falklands War: Lessons for Strategy, Diplomacy and International Law*, Boston 1985.

Rüger, Jan, *Heligoland: Britain, Germany and the Struggle for the North Sea*, Oxford 2017.

Ruiz Guiñazú, Enrique, *Proas de España en el Mar Magellánico* ["Spanish prows in the Magellanic Sea"], Buenos Aires 1945.

Samwer, Charles (ed.), *Nouveau Recueil Général de Traités...* ["New General Collection of Treaties..."], vol. XV, Gottingue [= Göttingen] 1857.

San Martino de Dromi, María Laura, *Gobierno y administración de las Islas Malvinas (1776-1833)* ["Government and administration of the Malvinas Islands (1776-1833)"]. Buenos Aires 1996.

Schilder, Günter et al., *Marcel Destombes (1905-1983)*, Utrecht and Paris 1987.

Schlesinger, Roger, ed., *Selections from André Thevet's "Les vrais pourtraits..."*, Urbana 1993.

Shackleton, Lord, *et al.*, *Economic Survey of the Falkland Islands, presented to the Secretary of State for Foreign and Commonwealth Affairs*, 2 vols., London May 1976 ("the *Shackleton Report*").

Shucksmith-Wesley, Marc Jonathan, *The Falklands (Malvinas) Dispute: a critique of international law and the pacific settlement of disputes*, Nottingham May 2018 (doctoral thesis, unpublished but available online).

Shumway, Nicolas, *The Invention of Argentina*, Berkeley 1991.

Sielemann, Jürgen, „Louis Vernet: ein Hamburger kolonisiert die Falkland-Inseln" ["Louis Vernet: a Hamburger colonises the Falkland Islands"], in *Hamburgische Geschichts- und Heimatblätter* ["*Hamburg Historical and Local Studies*"], vol. 11, 1987.

Sinclair, Sir Ian, "Estoppel and acquiescence", in *Fifty Years of the International Court of Justice: Essays in Honour of Sir Robert Jennings*, Cambridge 1996.

Smith, Herbert Arthur (ed.), *Great Britain and the Law of Nations*, London 1932.

Smith, John, *An Historical Scrapbook of Stanley*, Stanley 2013.

Smith, Thomas W., *A Narrative of the Life, Travels and Sufferings of Thomas W. Smith...*, Boston (Massachusetts), 1844.

Spears, John R., *Captain Nathaniel Brown Palmer: An Old-Time Sailor of the Sea*, New York 1922.

Spruce, Joan and **Smith, Natalie**, *Falkland Rural Heritage: Sites, Structures and Snippets of Historical Interest*, Fox Bay (West Falkland) and Stockholm (Sweden), 2018.

Stackpole, Edouard A., (1) *The Sea-Hunters*, New York 1953; (2) *The Voyage of* The Huron *and* The Huntress: *The American Sealers and the Discovery of the Continent of Antarctica*, Mystic (Connecticut), November 1955.

Sudbury, Andrea, *Dialect Contact and Koineisation in the Falkland Islands: Development of a Southern Hemisphere English?* Unpublished doctoral thesis, University of Essex, July 2000.

Tatham, David (ed.), *The Dictionary of Falklands Biography...*, Ledbury 2008 (and online).

Terragno, Rodolfo H., *Historia y Futuro de las Malvinas* ["History and Future of the Malvinas"], Buenos Aires 2006.

Tesler, Mario D., (1) *Expedición de David Jewett a las Islas Malvinas 1820-1821* ["David Jewett's Expedition to the Malvinas Islands (1820-1821)"], Santa Fe 1968; (2) *El Gaucho Antonio Rivero...* ["The Gaucho Antonio Rivero..."], Buenos Aires 1971; (3) *Malvinas: Como EE. UU. provocó la usurpación inglesa* ["Malvinas: How the US provoked the English usurpation"], Buenos Aires 1979.

Thevet, André, (1) *Le Grand Insulaire et Pilotage d'André Theuet, Angoumoisin, Cosmographe du Roy. Dans lequel sont contenus plusieurs plants* [sic] *d'isles habitées, et deshabitées, et description d'icelles* ["The Great Insulary and Pilotage of André Thevet of Angoulême, Cosmographer to the King. In which are contained several plans of inhabited, and uninhabited, islands, and descriptions of the same"] (1586-7), Bibliothèque Nationale de France, Paris (BN), Ms. fr. 15 452 (vol. I) and 15 453 (vol. II), unpublished MS; (2) *La Cosmographie universelle d'André Thevet, cosmographe du roy* ["The universal Cosmography of André Thevet, cosmographer to the king"], Paris 1575; (3) *Les vrais pourtraits et vies des hommes illustres* ["The true portraits and lives of illustrious men"], Paris 1584.

Trinidad, Jamie, *Self-Determination in Disputed Colonial Territories*, Cambridge 2018.

Velázquez, Carlos María, "Some Legal Aspects of the Colonial Problem in Latin America", in *The Annals of the American Academy of Political and Social Science*, Philadelphia July 1965.

Vernet, Louis, "Informe del Comandante Político y Militar de Malvinas", 10 August 1832 ["Report of the Political and Military Commandant of Malvinas"; "(Vernet's) 'Report'"] in *Colección de Documentos Oficiales con que el Gobierno Instruye al Cuerpo Legislativo de la Provincia del Origen y Estado de las Cuestiones Pendientes con la República de los E[stados] U[nidos] de Norte América sobre las Islas Malvinas* ["Collection of Official Documents with which the Government Instructs the Legislature of the Province on the Origin and State of the Issues Pending with the Republic of the United States of North America on the Malvinas Islands"], Buenos Aires 1832 ("*Colección* 1832"), also in *BFSP 1832-1833*, vol. XX, London 1836.

Vine, David, *Island of Shame: The Secret History of the U.S. Military Base on Diego Garcia*, Princeton and Oxford 2009.

Von Martens, Georg Friedrich (Georges Frédéric de Martens), *Recueil de Traités...* ["Collection of Treaties..."], 2nd ed. Gottingue [Göttingen, Germany], vol. II, 1817.

Von Wieser, Franz, *Die Karten von Amerika in dem Islario General des Alonso de Santa Cruz, Cosmógrafo des Kaisers Karl V.* ["The Maps of America in the Islario General of Alonso de Santa Cruz, Cosmographer to Emperor Karl V"], Innsbruck 1908.

Walter, Richard / Anson, George, *A Voyage round the World in the Years MDCCXL, I, II, III, IV...*, 5th ed., London 1749.

Wambaugh, Sarah, (1) *A Monograph on Plebiscites*, New York 1920; (2) *Plebiscites since the World War*, 2 vols., Washington DC 1933.

Watts, Patrick J., MBE, *The Christmas Sports: a History of the Stanley Sports Association 1908-2012*, Stanley 2012.

Weddell, James, *A Voyage towards the South Pole...*, London 1825; 2nd extended ed. London 1827; facsimile reprint of 1827 ed. Newton Abbot 1970.

Wheaton, Henry, *Elements of International Law: with a Sketch of the History of the Science*, London 1836; 2nd ed. ("*Lawrence's Wheaton*"), ed. by **Lawrence, William Beach**, London 1863; 8th ed. by **Dana, Richard Henry**, London 1866.

Yofre, Juan Bautista, *1982 – Los Documentos Secretos de la Guerra de Malvinas/ Falklands y el Derrumbe del Proceso* ["1982 – The Secret Documents on the Malvinas/Falklands War and the Collapse of the Proceso" (i.e. the junta's ideology)], Buenos Aires 2011.

Yrigoyen, Hipólito Solari, *Malvinas: lo que no cuentan los ingleses (1833-1982)* ["Malvinas: what the English don't say (1833-1982)"], Buenos Aires 1998.

Zorraquín Becú, Ricardo, *Inglaterra prometió abandonar las Malvinas* ["England promised to abandon the Malvinas"], Buenos Aires June 1982.

www.ingramcontent.com/pod-product-compliance
Lightning Source LLC
Chambersburg PA
CBHW042301010526
44113CB00047B/2767